MW01196454

# Enemy Views

## The American Revolutionary War
### As recorded by
### the Hessian Participants

Compiled, Edited, and with an Introduction
by
Bruce E. Burgoyne

and
with a Foreword by John Gardner

Heritage Books, Inc.
Bowie, MD, 1996

Other Heritage Books from Bruce Burgoyne

*Waldeck Soldiers of the American Revolutionary War*
*A Hessian Officer's Diary of the American Revolutionary War*
*Eighteenth Century America*
*Georg Pausch's Journal and Reports of the Campaign in America*

Published 1996 by

HERITAGE BOOKS, INC.
1540E Pointer Ridge Place
Bowie, Maryland 20716
1-800-398-7709

ISBN 0-7884-0563-2

A Complete Catalog Listing Hundreds of Titles
On History, Genealogy, and Americana
Available Free Upon Request

# Contents

## Enemy Views (Contents)

Clinton's Attack on the Hudson River Forts; Disaster at Sea; Lieutenant Feilitzsch's Return to Europe; The Evacuation of Rhode Island; Clinton's Expedition Against Charleston; December 1779

The Winter Voyage to Charleston; The Siege of Charleston; The Occupation of Charleston; Clinton's Departure from Charleston; The Battle of Camden; Activity in West Florida; A Cold Winter in New York; General Knyphausen's Move into New Jersey; Arnold's Treason; The 1780 Transfer of Troops to Canada; Comments of Convention Prisoners; Canada 1780; Continuation of Feilitzsch's Return to Europe

Mutiny in the American Army; The Siege and Surrender of Pensacola; Garrison Duty in Charleston; the War in the South; The Battle of Cowpens; The Battle of Guilford Courthouse; A Naval Engagement; Activities in Virginia; The Summer of 1781; The Siege and Surrender of Yorktown; Clinton's Indecision; Captivity; Other Activities in 1781

Activity in the Southern Colonies; Correspondence of Hesse-Hanau Officers; Reports from Canada; Events in New York

The Return to Hesse-Cassel; More Hesse-Cassel Returnees; Departure from Canada; The Return of the Hesse-Hanau Troops; The Return of the Ansbach-Bayreuth Troops

The Late Returnees

Hessian Church Books; The Anhalt-Zerbst Church Book; The Ansbach-Bayreuth Church Book; Autograph Books

# Foreword

Bruce Burgoyne has spent the greater part of the years since his retirement from the military translating the diaries and letters of "Hessian" officers and men who fought for the British in the American Revolution. *Enemy Views; The American Revolutionary War As Recorded by the Hessian Participants* is the latest in a series of at least six books of his translations from the German. It differs from his earlier works, which have been translations of single diaries, or, in one case, the short diaries of a chaplain and his assistant. In *Enemy Views; The American Revolutionary War As Recorded by the Hessian Participants*, Mr. Burgoyne publishes parts of the whole diaries, letters, and regimental records from thirty-four individual sources from five of the six German states which rented their armies to Great Britain. Only Brunswick is unrepresented in *Enemy Views; The American Revolutionary War As Recorded by the Hessian Participants*. Since all of the translations are by Mr. Burgoyne, and the majority are previously unpublished, the sheer quantity of his work in translation, editing, and interpretation makes the book impressive and daunting.

The arrangement essentially is chronological; Mr. Burgoyne publishes the description of an event or sequence of events in each of his sources on each subject. Thus, to give one example, three Hesse-Cassel sources: The Jaeger Corps Journal, the diaries of Lt. Carl Rueffer of the Mirbach Regiment, and J.R. of the Leib Regiment give some indication of the Hessian and Scottish occupation of Wilmington, Delaware, from September 14 to October 17, 1777, following the Battle of Brandywine. Nearly all of the information on the occupation appears in a few pages, in which each source is quoted in full on the subject of the Battle of Brandywine. The withdrawal of the Hessians is noted in the Rueffer diary a few pages later in another section on the clearing of the Delaware.

Mr. Burgoyne makes little commentary, either in the text or in the notes at the end. Rather, he lets the Hessians tell what they thought and experienced in their own words, not his. This works well. Literacy was higher in the smaller German states than in England or America, outside of New England. Crossing the Atlantic, visiting America, and fighting a war were fearful and exotic experiences to these largely young and untravelled soldiers. Because what they saw and heard was entirely different from anything they had seen or heard before, some wrote down everything they encountered. Their diaries tell of the common and uncommon. Often the common is the most valuable, since it was frequently overlooked by American And British writers of letters, journals, and diaries. The J.R. diary, for example, is the only source that indicates that about 325 American soldiers captured at Brandywine and some local patriots were imprisoned in Wilmington at the "gymnasium," apparently the Delaware Academy on Market Street. This is new information on a war and era we thought we knew all about!

That is what makes Mr. Burgoyne's translations so very interesting. Little Hessian material had been published in English before he started. The few German sources previously translated have been valuable; Mr. Burgoyne has actually translated as many sources as ever had been translated and published before. His earlier translations have yielded many varied contributions, ranging from detailed, vivid descriptions of New York City, Kingston, Jamaica, and Pensacola during the war to descriptions of cotton fields near Yorktown, Virginia to descriptions of military punishments.

Mr. Burgoyne is a modest man who does not fully realize how important his translations are. His work represents a vast increase in the data available on the Revolutionary War and on America during the war. A student who had taken a course with Mr. Burgoyne recently asked me, "How soon will his work be appearing in books on the Revolution?" The answer is very soon; the books will be incomplete without it.

John Gardner
Delaware State University
Dover, Delaware
January 5, 1996

Men of the Hesse-Cassel Von Donop Regiment Re-enactment Group

Men of the Von Donop Regiment Re-enactment Group

# Wilmington in the Revolution

A   Old Swedes Church
B   Presbyterian Church, used as a hospital by Brits & Hessians, Sept. 14-Oct. 17, 1777
C   Friends M. H., John Dickinson grave
D   Academy, about 325 American POW's imprisoned here, Sept. 14-Oct. 17,1777
E   Town Hall, built 1796. Old one was over the 2nd St. Market House
F   Baptist M. H.
G   Capt. Henry Gedes, U.S.N.
H   Market houses
I   Brandywine bridge and mills. Hessian fort with 2 officers, 100 men
J   French encampment, Sept. 6 1781
K   Pres. John McKinly's house. McKinly was captured by British
L   Patrick O'Flynn's Sign of the Ship. Washington stayed here. Gen. William Smallwood's headquarters, Dec. 21, 1777-June 7, 1778. Later Happy Retreat, then Lafayette Inn
M   Washington's headquarters, Sept. 1777
N   Gunning Bedford Jr.'s house. French HQ in 1781
O   Christina ferry house. Washington often ate here
P   Hessian and Scottish encampment, Sept. 14-Oct. 17, 1777
Q   Hessian earthwork, 1 officer, 20 jaegers
R   Hessian earthwork, 2 officers, 100 men
S   2 Hessian earthworks, checkpoint
T   Hessian strongpoint, 1 officer, 15 men
U   Hessian log palisade and central fort. 1 officer, 30 men
V   Maj. John Patten
W   Academy Woods, scene of many meetings and picnics
X   John Dickinson House, cabin of Lydia Hall, an African American woman whose two sons fought in the Revolution. One was executed by the British.
Y   Hanson house, scene of Tilton and Bellach's escape
Z   Joel Zane house. Mrs. Zane supplied free vegetables and flowers to the French

Courtesy of Dr. John Gardner, Delaware State University

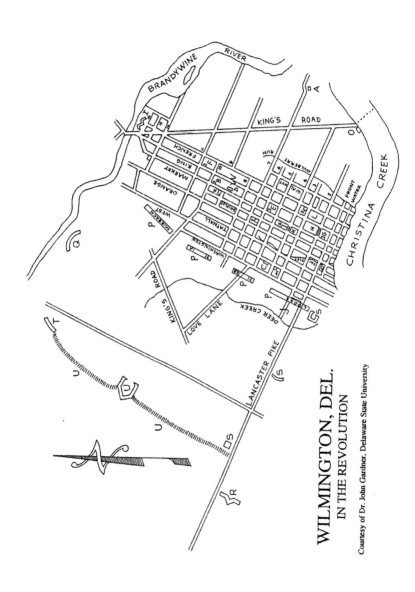

WILMINGTON, DEL.
IN THE REVOLUTION

Courtesy of Dr. John Gardner, Delaware State University

Re-enactor of the Brunswick Specht Regiment

Re-enactors of the Hesse-Cassel Jaeger Corps

# Preface

After almost twenty years of translating the diaries and journals of Hessian soldiers who fought against the colonists during the American Revolutionary War, I have amassed sufficient material to provide an account of the Hessian participation which shows those 'enemy' soldiers to be very human and not at all the monsters of the propaganda reports of that time.

In the accounts which follow I have extracted the diary entries of privates, non-commissioned officers, and officers from the infantry, artillery, jaegers, and grenadiers, from five of the six petty German states which furnished the so-called 'Hessians', in order to depict the life of those eighteenth century soldiers, from the time of their departure from Germany to their return home. I have also used information from their unit order books, unit journals, church books, letters, and even autograph books, all of which were translated by me.

A large part of the volume concerns life aboard ship as the diarists had more time and opportunity to write during the ocean voyages, and for some of the men, life at sea filled more of their time than life on land in America. The diaries do not provide true information in all cases. Many of the entries appear to be the recording of rumors and often information was added at a later date when the memories may not have been as good as we would desire.

All events of the war, some very important and the campaigns in the Illinois Country in particular, were not even mentioned by the Hessians because no Hessian units were employed there, or in other cases, possibly because of a reluctance to record embarrassing defeats. Some Hessians, however, Waldeckers who deserted from Spanish prisoner of war status, did join George Rogers Clark in the Illinois country and fought for American independence. To the best of my knowledge, they did not record their activity.

Similar books have been published before, but never on such a large collection of 'Hessian' first person accounts, nor from material translated by a single individual, nor so completely covering the men, their activities, and their observations of events and places during the war. I have tried to provide new information which will cause the reader to have a better understanding of the men, from both sides, who fought the war leading to our nation's independence.

## Editorial Procedures

In taking excerpts from the various Hessian accounts, I have tried not only to present the Revolution as the Hessians saw and participated in it, but have sought to include some of the more interesting comments and anecdotes. In some cases I have included duplicate, confirming information from several diarists, but usually only when more detailed information is provided by the second or third account. I have not tried to resolve errors or inconsistencies in their accounts. I have tried to present dates in a consistent manner, and frequently changed the spelling of names for the sake of consistency. Umlauted letters have also been transcribed by placing an 'e' after those vowels. Also, parentheses are as used by the authors and my comments are in brackets. To reduce the number of footnotes, I have used some bracketed information within the text.

## Acknowledgments

The persons and repositories from which I have obtained materials are noted below in the section on Authors and Acquisitions. They have provided me with years of pleasure and led to travel adventures and many new friendships. Special thanks must be given to Eckhart G. Franz, Inge Auerbach, and Otto Froehlich for *Hessische Truppen Im Amerikanischen Unabhaengigkeitskrieg (Hetrina)*, 5 vols., Der Archivschule Marburg, Institut fuer Archivwissenschaft, 1972-1976. It has since been expanded to include the Hesse-Hanau troops. One individual deserves special mention - my wife Marie. She has been a source of not only constant encouragement, but also accompanied me on my travels and read and reread everything which I have written so as to insure the best and most readable translations. Nevertheless, any and all errors remain mine alone, and I hope they are few in number.

Bruce E. Burgoyne
Dover, DE
1996

# Introduction

As the antagonism between England and the American Colonies increased during the mid-eighteenth century, a series of confrontations developed. Clashes of will and arms led to the Boston Massacre, Lexington and Concord, and eventually to the Battle of Bunker Hill. Faced with the ever-present threat of an invasion from France, England could not raise an army in the British Isles which was large enough to defend the home islands and also control the American colonists on the other side of the Atlantic Ocean. Therefore the government sent a minister plenipotentiary to a number of small German states with the mission of hiring organized and trained units of German soldiers who could be used immediately. Those units, plus such English units as could be spared, were then sent to America.

Eventually treaties were signed with six German states - Hesse-Cassel, Hesse-Hanau, Ansbach-Bayreuth, Anhalt-Zerbst, Brunswick, and Waldeck. Because the largest contingent of troops were from Hesse-Cassel and because Hesse-Cassel had provided troops to England in 1745 to suppress a revolt in Scotland, all the foreign troops were referred to as 'Hessians'.

Some 30,000 Hessians made the trip from their homelands in the interior parts of Germany, across the often wild and frightening ocean, to America. In America they encountered blacks, mostly slaves, and red Indians for the first time, and found people living in a vast area where land was available almost for the taking, with very little taxation. The Germans could not understand why anyone would rebel against the ruler God had placed over them and engage in a war so destructive of their personal property and pleasant living conditions.

In the pages which follow, extracts from diaries written by the German soldiers provide an account of their experiences, including their comments on their daily activities, the war, America, and life in this strange new world.

In an effort to present the material in a proper sequence, I have traced the participants' roles from the training and departure from Germany, through their activities in America, and to their return to Europe. In that manner the comments can most easily be associated with the readers' knowledge of the progress of the war and the eventual acknowledgment of American independence.

## The 'Hessian' Forces

Probably one-third of all the men who fought against the Americans during the Revolution were German auxiliaries hired by England. It is hoped that this summary of the composition of those 'Hessian' forces will assist the reader in fitting the individual accounts into the larger framework of the war.

### Anhalt-Zerbst

On 28 September 1778 an Anhalt-Zerbst regiment of 626 men embarked for Canada, and in 1781 the strength was increased to 933 men, apparently by the addition of two companies. Only limited information is available on these men, who served primarily in Canada.

### Ansbach-Bayreuth

Initially Ansbach-Bayreuth placed two infantry regiments of 570 men each, a jaeger company of 101 men, and an artillery unit of 44 men, in English service. Eventually the jaeger company was expanded to become a jaeger regiment, making the total treaty strength 1,559 men. Available manuscripts, many of which are in the New York Public Library (NYPL), provide a rather complete account of the Ansbach-Bayreuth role in the Revolution.

### Brunswick

The Duke of Brunswick placed 4,300 men into English service. This contingent of a general staff, four infantry regiments, a light infantry battalion, a grenadier battalion, and a dragoon regiment, was sent to Canada. As part of General John Burgoyne's army trying to split the colonies in 1777, the Brunswickers were captured and held in captivity in New England and later in Virginia, prior to being exchanged. While considerable information is available on their activities, primarily in the state archives in Wolfenbuettel and the Library of Congress, I have never completed the translation of any such documents.

## Hesse-Cassel

Hesse-Cassel furnished an eventual treaty strength of 13,472 men and the designation of 'Hessian' for all the German auxiliaries taken into English service during the Revolution. In 1776 Hesse-Cassel provided nineteen battalions of foot soldiers (fifteen infantry regiments and four grenadier battalions - the terms regiment and battalion are often used interchangeably), one jaeger company, and five artillery companies. These units were augmented later by the addition of more jaeger companies. That German state also provided a large medical contingent. Numerous documents concerning the soldiers of Hesse-Cassel are available; the state archives at Marburg being the largest repository, but with considerable holdings in the Library of Congress, the Clements Library of the University of Michigan, the Morristown National Historical Park (MNHP), and the New York Public Library.

## Hesse-Hanau

Hesse-Hanau furnished a 668-man infantry regiment and a 128-man artillery company in 1776 and a 412-man jaeger corps in 1777. Another 111-man jaeger company was furnished in 1779 to offset losses. All of these men were initially sent to Canada and many were captured at Saratoga in 1777. In 1782 the Hesse-Hanau treaty strength was increased by 884 men when a 'free corps' was sent to New York, and the eventual treaty strength reached 2,257 men in 1783. Many documents pertaining to the Hesse-Hanauers are available in the archives at Marburg and a number are also available in the MNHP archives at Morristown, New Jersey.

## Waldeck

The tiny principality of Waldeck furnished a 670-man infantry regiment and a 14-man artillery unit for service in America. The only two known diaries written by men of this contingent are in the NYPL and an autograph book is in the Waldeck Historical Society archives in Arolsen.

# Authors and Acquisitions

The following brief description of the authors and documents used in the preparation of this book will give the reader background for understanding the role of the authors and bibliographic information on the manuscripts.

## Anhalt-Zerbst

Johann Gottlieb Siegismund Braunsdorf, born 31 March 1752 in Zerbst, son of a ticking and damask weaver, was a chaplain with the Anhalt-Zerbst contingent of Hessians sent to Canada in 1778. He kept the regimental church books, recording marriages, births, baptisms, and deaths among the men of the unit and their families. My translation was made in part from a copy of the original in the Evangelical-Lutheran Church archives in Jever, and in part from an article by Brigitte Heinicke and Georg Jahn, published in the *Norddeutsche Familienkunde for* January-March 1896, which was sent to me by Michael P. Palmer of the German Genealogical Society of America.

## Ansbach-Bayreuth

Christian Friedrich Bartholomai, lieutenant in the Ansbach-Bayreuth Jaeger Corps, kept a diary of his participation in the Revolution. My translation, from a document in the Bancroft Collection in the NYPL, is from an extract covering the expedition to the southern colonies, and in particular the siege and capture of Charleston, South Carolina, by Sir Henry Clinton. The German manuscript is very detailed and contains many of Bartholomai's personal observations and comments on the war. There are several other diaries, or extracts of his diaries, and letters written by Bartholomai in the collection.

Johann Conrad Doehla, born 6 September 1750 in Oberhaid, near Zell in the Fichtel Mountains of Bavaria, was the son of a brickmaker and had been a private in the Bayreuth Regiment of the Ansbach-Bayreuth military since 1768. His diary covers the period from February 1777, when the Bayreuth Regiment marched out of Bayreuth, until his return to Germany and his discharge, still as a private, in December 1783. He then became a brickmaker and possibly a school teacher. He died 14 January 1820, a widower, at Zell. His diary, covering the Bayreuth Regiment's service in New York, Rhode Island areas, also contains a detailed account of the siege of Yorktown and the period of captivity following General Charles, Earl Cornwallis' surrender. My translation was made from a book published in Germany in 1913 which was edited by General W. Baron von Waldenfels. I have limited my quotes from this document as the University of Oklahoma Press currently holds the copyright. Nevertheless, Doehla's diary is extremely interesting, sometimes as much for his misinformation as for his record of events.

Heinrich Carl Philipp von Feilitzsch, a lieutenant in the Ansbach-Bayreuth Jaeger Corps, departed from Ansbach on 7 March 1777 and returned to Germany in June 1780. During that time he kept a diary of his service in the New York area and during General Sir William Howe's Philadelphia campaign in 1777. He recorded his return to Europe in 1780, during the war, also, and this is the only such account with which I am familiar. My translation was made from a copy of the diary obtained from the Bavarian State Archives in Munich, the original of which is in the archives of the University of Bayreuth. I am hoping to publish this diary, combined with the Bartholomai diary, in full, in the coming months.

Christian Theodor Sigismund von Molitor was a captain and company commander in the Bayreuth Regiment when the regiment sailed to America. His interesting, but short, diary in the Bancroft Collection of the NYPL covers the regiment's activity up to its arrival in New York in June 1777. After the war Molitor took his family and a number of other 'Hessian' soldiers to settle in Nova Scotia. My translation was published in the Johannes Schwalm Historical Association, Inc. (JSHA) *Journal*, Vol. 4, Nr. 4, 1992.

Johann Ernst Prechtel went to America in 1777 as sergeant major of a company of the Bayreuth Regiment and was later promoted to 2nd and then 1st lieutenant in the Ansbach Regiment. He served in the New York, Rhode Island, and Philadelphia area, and was taken captive at Yorktown. He then accompanied the troops into captivity in Virginia and Maryland. He may have served in the Jaeger Corps after his return to Germany in 1783. As with the Doehla, Feilitzsch, and Bartholomai diaries, Prechtel wrote a very detailed diary containing considerable information on deaths, promotions, desertions, and troops activity. My initial translation was of a copy of the Prechtel diary in the Bavarian State Archives. However, Dr. Mary Robertson, curator of manuscripts at the Huntington Library, San Marino, California, shortly thereafter asked if I were interested in translating an anonymous Old German script manuscript in the Huntington archives. It became apparent at once that the Huntington manuscript was a portion of the original Prechtel diary. Another coincidence followed. The first page of the Huntington manuscript was missing, but when I obtained a copy of an anonymous diary from the Nuernberg State Archives in Germany, that diary turned out to be a beautifully handwritten copy of the Huntington version of the Prechtel diary - with the first page intact. However, that version of the diary covers only the years through the surrender at Yorktown. A very short translated portion of the manuscript from the Bavarian State Archives, covering the period of captivity at Frederick, Maryland, was published by Professor Harold Clem in the *Maryland Bulletin*, Vol. LXVII, Nr. 5, in February 1947.

Georg Adam Stang sailed to America as a hautboist with the Bayreuth Regiment in 1777 and served as such throughout the war. His "March Routes" contains very little information except dates and places along routes taken by the regiment. The original German manuscript is in the Nuernberg State Archives and a copy is in the archives of the University of Bayreuth.

Georgius Michael Stroelein, Ansbach chaplain, wrote the church book entries, from Chaplain Georg Erb's notes and by collecting information from the Ansbach Infantry Regiment company sergeants, for the Ansbach-Bayreuth troops during their service in America. The church book, covering only births and baptisms, is in the Landeskirchliches Archiv, Zentrale Kirchenbuchstelle, Am Oelberg 2, 8400 Regensburg, and my translation was made from a Xerox copy of the original.

### Hesse-Cassel

Valentin Asteroth, born 12 October 1758 in Treysa, was a conscript private in the Hesse-Cassel von Huyn Regiment when the unit left Germany for service in America. Asteroth, a stocking knitter by trade, because of his singing voice became the song leader (chaplain's assistant) to Heinrich Kuemmell, chaplain of the von Huyn and von Buenau Regiments. His very brief but most interesting diary covers the entire period of the war. The regiment saw duty in New York and Rhode Island areas and accompanied General Clinton's southern expedition in late 1779. Among other duties, Asteroth was the school teacher for the children of the regiment while in Charleston, South Carolina. After his return to Germany, he married in 1785 and died on 18 October 1804. The original of the diary used for my translation, published as a part of *Diaries of a Hessian Chaplain and the Chaplain's Assistant*, by JSHA in 1990, is in the Murhard Library in Kassel. I also received permission from Dr. K. Freytag, president of the Society for Hessen History and Culture, Treysa/Zeigenhain Branch, to use a version of the diary in the society's publication. The Pfaltzgraff Company of York, Pennsylvania paid for the printing of this book, proceeds of which go to the JSHA Endowment Fund.

Johann Heinrich von Bardeleben, lieutenant in the von Donop Regiment, was the apparent author of an anonymous diary found in the New York Historical Society archives, a copy of which was given to me by Donald Londahl-Smidt of Montvale, New Jersey. The diary, which contains entries in two different codes, one of which was very easy to decipher, covers the period 29 February 1776 to 22 June 1777, and provides an insight into the lifestyle of an obviously young Hessian officer.

Georg Christoph Coester, baptized 15 December 1751 in Ersen, son of the pastor in Ersen and Hofgeismar, served as the chaplain of the Hesse-Cassel von Donop Regiment in America from 1776 to 1784. After the war he served as the pastor in Malsfeld until his death in 1790. Coester kept the regimental church book, recording marriages, births, deaths, confirmations, and penance situations. This church book was translated from "The Diary of Chaplain G.C. Coester, 1776-1784", in *Geschichtliche Nachrichten aus Treysa*, reproduced by A. Giebel, A. Helwig, and H. Krause in 1969. The article also contains an excellent summary of the chaplains who served the Hesse-Cassel units in America, as well as the journal of the von Donop Regiment kept by Regimental Quartermaster Johann Georg Zinn. (See below.)

Johann Heinrich Henkelmann (or Henckelmann) sailed to America in 1776, in the 2nd Division of soldiers from Hesse-Cassel, as a 2nd lieutenant in the Leib or Body Regiment. He was promoted to 1st lieutenant in 1779 and sometime during the war married the daughter of a German born resident, possibly of Nova Scotia, where he settled after taking his release from the Hesse-Cassel military. He then joined the Nova Scotia Volunteers. His letter, translated from a published copy in the periodical *Hessenland*, (Marburg, 1906), to a friend in Germany in late 1783, and the editor's comments, contain information on the post-war life of a Hessian who 'stayed behind' in America and about several of his friends.

J.R. (not further identified), of the Hesse-Cassel Leib Regiment kept a short diary covering the years 1776 to 1784. However, the entries were not made on a daily basis and many important events are not even mentioned. The author of the diary gives considerable space to the sea voyage to America, and to the return to Europe by way of Ireland, so that the reader gets a detailed picture of the dangers of sea travel at that time. My translation, made from a copy which is in the Clements Library at the University of Michigan, was published in the JSHA *Journal*, Vol. 4, Nr. 4, 1992.

Berthold Koch, born 8 July 1742 in Grebenstein, son of the local pastor, was a career soldier who had fought in the Seven Years' War. He sailed to America in early 1776 as a sergeant in the von Truembach Regiment. While there are large gaps when no entries are made, he does report the 1780 move into New Jersey by Lieutenant General Wilhelm von Knyphausen, the Battle of Guilford Courthouse, the siege of Yorktown, and the subsequent captivity at Frederick, Maryland. My translation was made from an article in *Zeitschrift fuer Heereskunde*, (Berlin, 1932), provided by my friend Klaus Scholz of Korbach, Germany.

Heinrich Kuemmell was born 6 December 1753 in the Hessen city of Vacha, son of the city's assistant pastor. After the war Kuemmell served as a pastor and church official in the district of Schmalkalden, married in 1785, and died on 17 December 1830. He had studied at Rinteln and Marburg. He was named chaplain of the Hesse-Cassel von Huyn and von Buenau Regiments in 1776 and ordained to that service on 7 February 1776. His diary covers his activities in the regiment only from March 1776 to August 1777, with a few notes for church book entries thereafter. Dr. K. Freytag of Schwalmstadt, Germany provided me with an article by Otto Gerlach, published in *Hessenland*,

Vols. 6 and 7, (Kassel, 1894), from which I made my translation. (See Asteroth above.)

Johannes Maurer, regimental surgeon of the Hesse-Cassel von Truembach Regiment, wrote a letter from shipboard prior to sailing to America in March 1776, in which he mentions his duties, personnel going to America, and concern for his family's welfare. He died in America in 1777. My translation is from an article written by Maurer's great-great grandson, Fritz Maurer, and published in *Hessenland*, (Marburg, 1906) and sent to me by Klaus Scholz.

Jacob Piel (or Biel) was a 2nd lieutenant and the adjutant of the Hesse-Cassel von Lossberg Regiment when he marched out of Rinteln on 10 March 1776. His diary records activity during the Battle of Long Island, White Plains, the capture of Fort Washington, and General Washington's attack on Trenton which led to Piel's capture. He then recounts his march into Virginia as a prisoner of war and his ultimate exchange. He marched from Philadelphia when the city was evacuated by the British in 1778 and participated in the Battle of Monmouth. When his unit sailed to Canada in 1779, the fleet encountered a severe storm. Men of two companies and several ships were lost and the remnants of the fleet returned to New York. The following year Piel accompanied the greatly reduced regiment which sailed to Canada, where it performed routine duties until returning to Europe in 1783. The Piel diary, translated from a manuscript in the Bancroft Collection of the NYPL, was published in the JSHA *Journal*, Vol. 4, Nrs. 1 and 2, 1989 and 1990.

Caspar Recknagel, an as yet unidentified 'Hessian' participant in the Revolution, was the author of a diary in the University of Pennsylvania archives covering activity in Rhode Island in 1778 and the return to Europe in 1783. Recknagel did not identify his unit, and the only Caspar Recknagel listed in the HETRINA was a member of the von Seitz Regiment which sailed to America in 1776 but transferred to Nova Scotia in October 1778. While there is a possibility that the diary is a forgery, it is also possible that he may have been some sort of batman, servant, or driver and not listed by name on any military roster. The contents of the diary indicate that he may have been attached to the Landgraf Regiment.

Johannes Reuber, born 25 February 1759 in Niedervellmar, was a private in the Rall Grenadier Regiment. His diary covers the period from 1 January 1776 to 29 November 1783. He described the sea voyage, fighting on Long Island, White Plains, Fort Washington, and the fall of Trenton. That is followed by his account of his captivity and exchange, the 1778 movement to Georgia and South Carolina, the evacuation of Charleston in 1782, and his return to Europe. My translation was made from a typed script of the diary received from Kenneth Jones of Worcester, Massachusetts. One version of the diary, translated by Herbert H. Freund from a manuscript in the NYPL, was previously published in the JSHA *Journal*, Vol. 1, Nrs. 2 and 3, 1978 and 1979.

Carl Friedrich Rueffer was an ensign and later a lieutenant in the Hesse-Cassel von Mirbach Regiment. His diary covers the period from March 1776 to December 1777. Although he reported some details of the battles in and around New York, his account of the Philadelphia campaign and the attack on Fort Mercer at Red Bank are of the greatest interest. My translation was made from a copy of the diary in the Bancroft Collection of the NYPL.

Andreas Wiederhold, lieutenant in the Hesse-Cassel von Knyphausen Regiment, wrote a very interesting diary of his adventures during the American Revolutionary War. The translation used in the following pages was made from a copy in the Bancroft Collection, NYPL, covering the period 7 October 1776 to 7 December 1780. I also had access to a German language version published by M.D. Learned and C. Grosse in *America Germania*, vol. iv, (New York, 1901), which is similar. Previously published portions of the Wiederhold diary , to which I also had access, are "The Capture of Fort Washington, New York, Described by Captain Andreas Wiederhold, of the Hessian 'Regiment Knyphausen'," *The Pennsylvania Magazine of History and Biography* (PMHB), vol. xxxiii (1899), pp. 95-97; "Colonel Rall at Trenton", *PMHB*, vol. xxxii, pp. 462-467; and William Frederic Wormer's "Captain Wiederholdt in Lancaster", *Historical Papers and Address of the Lancaster County Historical Society*, vol. xxxiii (Lancaster, 1929) pp. 65-73. Wiederhold recorded the events at Trenton in 1776, including his disgust with Colonel Rall's behavior, his period of captivity in Virginia, and the 1778 disaster which struck the fleet carrying reinforcements to Canada. After the war Wiederhold eventually rose to general officer rank in the Portuguese army.

# Enemy Views (Introduction)

Christian Friedrich von Urff, captain and later major in the Hesse-Cassel Leib Regiment, maintained an autograph book throughout his service in America between 1776 and 1783. He died 8 September 1793 during a campaign against France, at Hondschotten in Flanders, as it is told, by the last shot fired by the enemy during that battle. Extracts of his autograph book were published in an article in *Hessenland* (Kassel, 1899), which was sent to me by Klaus Scholz.

The "Order Book of the von Mirbach Regiment" is a translation of a manuscript from the Lidgerwood Collection in the MNHP archives. It covers the period 10 March to 31 December 1778, although the title page indicates a period ending 28 June 1780. The order book is an excellent document for order of battle information and as an indicator of the activities of both the unit and individuals within the unit while performing routine garrison duty.

The "Platte Grenadier Battalion Journal", covering the period from 1776 to 1784, was translated from a manuscript in the Lidgerwood Collection and was probably written originally by the Regimental Quartermaster Carl Bauer, as unit journals were normally maintained by the regimental quartermasters. The manuscript had been translated earlier by a Miss Raahage, to whose translation I had access, but the curator, James L. Kochan, requested that I do a new translation. In addition to detailed accounts of the sea voyage and spending the winter of 1783-1784 in England, the journal contains significant information on the southern campaign and capture of Charleston.

Johann Georg Zinn, auditor and regimental quartermaster of the Hesse-Cassel von Donop Regiment, maintained the regimental journal from 29 February 1776, the day of marching out of Hesse, to 17 May 1784, the day of marching back into the garrison at Kassel. The journal is brief and concise and primarily of value for identification of regimental officers and a quick overview of regimental activities. My translation was made from an article in *Geschichtliche Nachrichten aus Treysa*. (See Coester above.)

Since originally compiling the manuscript for this book, I have translated the diary of Captain Andreas Wiederhold of the Hesse-Cassel von Knyphausen Regiment, which I obtained from Donald Londahl-Smidt. He obtained it from the Clements Library at the University of Michigan. I have added only a few of Wiederhold's comments to the present volume, but hope to have it published in the near future. Portions of the diary have been published previously as it provides an excellent account of the capture of Fort Washington, the Battle of Trenton, and the disaster at sea when the regiment was being transferred to Canada.

## Hesse-Hanau

Wilhelm Rudolph von Gall, colonel of the Hesse-Hanau Infantry Regiment, maintained an order book, part of which is a manuscript, Tom IX, in the Lidgerwood Collection in the MNHP archives. My translation of the manuscript covering the period 28 October 1776 to 19 June 1777 was made under a grant from the Eastern National Park & Monument Association.

Georg Pausch, captain and later major of the Hesse-Hanau Artillery Company, maintained a journal on orders from his prince, which covers the period from 1776 through the surrender at Saratoga in October 1777. The manuscript, Tom VII, from the Lidgerwood Collection in the MNHP archives, also contains letters to his prince from 1776 until his return to Hanau in 1783. My translation was made under a grant from the Washington Association of New Jersey. The Pausch diary was previously translated by William L. Stone and published as *Journal of Captain Pausch* by Joel Munsell's Sons, (Albany, 1886) and republished by The New York Times and Arno Press (n.p., 1971).

Paul Wilhelm Schaeffer, auditor of the Hesse-Hanau Infantry Regiment, was possibly the author of an anonymous diary covering the period 15 March to 4 June 1776. The diary contains information on the voyage from Hanau to Quebec and a brief recital of the American siege and assault on Quebec during the previous winter. My translation was made from an article by Dr. Heiler published in the *Hanauisches Magazin Monatsblaetter fuer Heimatkinde*, Nr. 9/10 (Wiesbaden, 1935) sent to me by John Merz of Hamilton, Ontario, Canada.

"Journals and Reports of the Campaign in America, 1778-83", Tom VI, of the Lidgerwood Collection, is, as the name suggests, a collection of documents from Hesse-Hanau soldiers to the prince. My translation was made under a grant from the Eastern National Park & Monument Association.

"Letters and Reports from Hesse-Hanau Officers", Tom VIII, of the Lidgerwood Collection, contains letters to the prince during the period 1776 to 1780. It was translated under a grant from the Eastern National Park & Monument Association.

"Order Book of the Hesse-Hanau Regiment, April-Sept 1777" is also a manuscript from the Lidgerwood Collection of the MNHP archives which I translated under a grant from the Eastern National Park & Monument Association. The manuscript at Morristown is an incomplete copy of an order book covering the period ending on 31 December 1781, I can give no explanation of why the copy was not completed.

## Waldeck

Philipp Marc, born 1739 in Arolsen, son of the court agent, was the auditor for the 3rd Waldeck Regiment throughout the Revolution. While in America he carried an autograph book, the original of which is in the Waldeck Historical Society archives in Arolsen. My translation was made from a copy of the original. The book is of value as it shows the friendship between elements of the British forces, the language fluency of those individuals, and something of their thoughts and attitudes. After the war, Marc took his discharge in America and later became the American consul at Bamberg, Germany, where he died on 5 May 1801.

Carl Philipp Steuernagel, born 15 November 1754 in Helsen, the son of a cantor, was a corporal in the 3rd Waldeck Regiment which left Waldeck for service in America on 20 May 1776. Later he was promoted to quartermaster sergeant. He served throughout the war, although his diary ends with the surrender of the garrison at Pensacola. He noted that the remainder of the diary had been lost when a ship sank. He wrote a very graphic description of the capture of Fort Washington, and his description of the great size of an American alligator may be an indication that Max von Eelking was referring to Steuernagel when he wrote that Johann Gottfried Seume, another Hessian diarist, received his information from a Waldecker who was a great story-teller. My translation was made from a copy of a manuscript in the NYPL.

Johann Philipp Franz Elisaus Waldeck, born 9 March 1750 in Hemfurth, the son of a clergyman, assumed the position of chaplain of the newly raised 3rd Waldeck Regiment in 1776 and served in that capacity throughout the period of the war. His diary, covering the period from the departure from Waldeck to New Year's Eve 1780, is by far the most valuable document concerning the American society of that period that I have ever seen. He described every imaginable facet of American life, as well as the Waldeck Regiment's military involvement at Fort Washington and in the seldom mentioned activity in West Florida and present day Louisiana. After the war he returned to Waldeck and died on 20 March 1784 of a fever. The manuscript of the diary which I translated is in the NYPL, and my translation was published as *Eighteenth Century America; As Noted in the Diary of Chaplain Philipp Waldeck, (1776-1780)*, Heritage Books, Inc., (Bowie, Maryland, 1995). A German language version of the diary was published by Professor Marion Dexter Learned in *Americana Germanica*, (New York, 1907) and an English language translation of that version was published by William E. Dornemann in the JSHA *Journal*, Vol. 2, Nrs. 3 and 4, 1983 and 1984, and Vol. 3, Nr. 1, 1985. A small portion of my translation was then published in the *Journal*, Vol. 3, Nr. 2, 1986, to cover the remaining portion of the Waldeck diary.

## Future Translations

Although I have not previously translated any diaries of Brunswick soldiers, I am currently translating the journal of Friedrich Julius von Papet, Jr., 1st lieutenant of the Brunswick von Rhetz Regiment and brigade major of the German troops left in Canada when Burgoyne marched to his defeat at Saratoga in 1777. I have not used any of his diary entries in the pages which follow.

## A Hessian Appraisal of How England
## had to Conduct Military Operations in America

Lieutenant Bartholomai, of the Ansbach-Bayreuth Jaeger Corps, in an explanation of the Charleston campaign in 1779 and early 1780, considered it necessary to inform his European readers of the 'peculiarities of the American War and to point out the differences between it and the European ones.' His explanation, in part, reads as follows.

"It is my belief that the following three propositions are applicable:

"I. The war in America must be conducted primarily from the sea because for the most part the operations of the army are dependent upon the activity of the fleet.

"II. The army can accomplish nothing of importance without the support of the fleet, and may,

"III. above all, not venture very far inland without risking a great danger.

"As we know, America is a large and extensive part of the world and, in order to successfully conduct the war there, it is necessary to have 200,000 to 300,000 men. However, neither the great size of the rebel army, nor the special bravery of the Americans, whom we have learned to respect, would be able to stand in the way of an army of 16,000 to 20,000 English and Germans, if they decided to march through all of America, except for the reason that the land is such a great expanse. But England can not send such a large army here.

"If, however, it is assumed that this march could take place, the coast is so long and harbors for small craft so plentiful, that it would be impossible, despite all precautions, to close all the entrances which the inhabitants use for smuggling and obtaining war materials from the French and Spanish. Because of this, an enemy sea power can not be prevented from landing somewhere and thus placing our army between two forces.

"From these circumstances it is easy to understand that it is necessary, first of all, that England must control the local waters before the war can be conducted on land, and if the English fleet suffers a reverse, the army can accomplish nothing, which proves my first proposition. [Therefore, Cornwallis was defeated at Yorktown.]

"If this point, the supremacy of the English fleet on the water, is accomplished, two important advantages accrue to the army. First, under its protection the recruits and, more importantly, the provisions for the entire army can be brought here safely from Europe. Secondly, it protects the coast from an enemy landing and thus covers the rear of the army. Then the operations on land can begin, but always under the fleet's protection, because, as I said at the start, the land is extensive and the commanding general is forced to act first in the northern and then in the southern provinces. Therefore it is not only necessary for the fleet to serve by escorting the troops swiftly from one place to another, and to cover the troop landings with gun fire, but to carry weapons, munitions, and provisions, because the troops are widely dispersed and separated by great rivers in the trackless areas, and where the storage of forage exists, the army is prevented from attacking under advantageous conditions. This supports my second proposition.

"What I said in my third proposition, that the army dare not move far inland without the greatest danger, results in part from the previously noted consideration of the great risk and because of the shortage of forage. All the oats must be brought here from England and the campaign can never begin, because of the shortage of hay, until the grass is high enough to be used as fodder. On the other hand, however, because of the necessity in which we find ourselves, provisions for the army must follow, because enough for subsistence can not be found deep in the countryside.

"This circumstance must be more fully explained.

"There are very few cities or villages in America, and these lie widely separated. The residences of the inhabitants on their estates are so scattered that it is impossible, in a radius of twenty or thirty miles, because each estate cultivates only a small area, to obtain subsistence even for a corps of several thousand men.

"However, these few inhabitants have enough produce to support a corps. Therefore at the first reports of the army's approach, on orders of Congress, all supplies are sent away so that we must always live on our own provisions, transported by the army.

"Even though I concede that enough provisions are available and that it would be possible therefore for magazines to be established, which could support the army, as is customary in Europe, it is not possible in America.

"For example, I will assume the enemy were defeated in New York province and we must follow it to Pennsylvania. Therefore the army must move 100 miles from its magazines. First, just to occupy the conquered countryside and the magazines which would be set up, a large occupying force would be necessary. Next, more troops would be necessary to escort provisions deep into the land than would be required for the expedition itself. The reason is this - the inhabitants of the land, all of whom are rebels in their hearts and constitute the local militia, can not be trusted for this reason. At the moment all hide themselves under the mask of being king's people, but as soon as our army withdraws the least distance, they secretly assemble and attack our army in the rear and on the flanks. However, the primary concern is that they make the transportation of provisions unsafe and dangerous and there can never be certainty that such provisions will arrive. The rugged terrain is partially responsible for this. However, when the provisions are actually delivered by a large escort, we still lose much throughout the year due to the many skirmishes with the militia and the weakened army, which each year receives only a few recruits. This can not be tolerated. As a result of these circumstances, and examples, I hope to have made clear that the conduct of the American War is unusual and that there is a difference between this and European wars.

"How many opportunities a commanding general-in-chief must consider here before he can undertake something, and how many advantageous projects must be allowed to pass because he can not undertake them without the fleet, without mentioning the disappointing delays which must be considered for an expedition because of having to cross a body of water due to storms, tides, and other inconveniences. All these circumstances are unknown to a European commander and despite all these various hindrances, a general in America is compelled to conduct the undertakings, which, from reports of the present war, must seem completely illogical, and of which our expedition will be an example.

"To these large and apparent differences of the war, I must also note two necessary elements are unavailable to the local general in conducting the war, namely spies and local guides. I am not saying that these two things can not be had, but rather that they are insufficient. Concerning the spies, it is difficult here because such a man, in a country where everyone is the enemy, can learn little of what is desired and at times, nothing at all. On the other hand, nothing can be attempted nor can the parties trust one another.

"Concerning the local guides, they are very much, almost entirely, controlled by the general-in-chief and as the war must be conducted in so many various regions, the commanding general often has no available guides. How can they provide help then for a staff officer who must conduct a small expedition? And when help is provided by a guide, the cost of providing the same for a junior officer is too expensive, as they cost fourteen or more Spanish dollars. Efforts have been made by the use of special signs to offset this shortage, but in part they have been inadequate, in part they do not indicate all the short cuts, and can not always be trusted, as I myself have learned.

"Opposed thereto is the enemy general who is well supplied with these two items. First, every inhabitant is his spy, and second, he or his troops are absolutely familiar with the land and he is given timely notice of every moment by his enemy, which is provided by the many listeners. Yes, the most unpleasant and most dangerous factor for the local general consists of the situation that because we need vegetables and other foodstuffs, we are compelled to allow every spy, dressed as a farmer, free entry and exit from our camps, and they know well how to take advantage of this situation.

"When such a farmer learns something about us, he immediately mounts a horse, which year in and year out he has had grazing in a fenced off piece of land not far from his house. He hastens over hill and dale by a back road to another estate. The neighbor, in the same manner, takes the report to a third person, and so forth until it is delivered to headquarters.

"Even the ordinary soldier must be able to understand the difference between a European war and one in America because he must frequently go aboard ship, tolerate a sea voyage, going in a short time from a cold climate to a warm one or from a warm climate to a cold one.

"In short, just the thought that an army of 16,000 to 20,000 men would detach a corps of 6,000 to 7,000 men and send it 800 miles away, would rightly be considered a great folly, which in America, however, is a reality and often employed."

The validity of Bartholomai's diagnosis is demonstrated in the Hessian accounts of battles and campaigns which follow, and by the eventual American victory and independence.

—

# Enemy Views
## The American Revolutionary War
## As Recorded by the Hessian Participants
Translated and Compiled by
Bruce E. Burgoyne

- - - - - - -

## Travel to America

- - - - - - -

### Departure from Home

He [King George III] is at this time transporting large armies of foreigner mercenaries to compleat the works of death, desolation, and tyranny." [The Declaration of Independence.]

After various German princes had signed treaties to provide troops to help England suppress the revolt in the American colonies, it became necessary for them to prepare their troops for movement to America. Vacancies in the ranks had to be filled in some cases, in others, new units had to be organized, still others however were almost immediately ready to march. The later situation appears to have been the case for the Bayreuth Regiment of the Ansbach-Bayreuth contingent.

Although the first troops from Ansbach-Bayreuth did not leave for America until 1777, the diary of Private Johann Conrad Doehla of the Bayreuth Regiment provides a clear indication of how many men felt about their mission, and partially refutes the often made statement that the Hessians were forced to serve in America against their will; some were, but obviously not all.

"In the year 1777 A.D., on 28 February, on the gracious order of Our Most Serene Prince and Lord, Christian Friedrich Carl Alexander, Margrave of Brandenburg, we began our march to America and entered the service of His Royal Majesty, George III, King of England and Great Britain, as auxiliary or relief troops.

### To Wit

"At seven o'clock in the morning, our illustrious Bayreuth Infantry Regiment of Colonel [August Valentin] von Voit, 600 men strong, marched out of the barracks. We entered upon our march and employment, in another part of the world, in God's holy name, and were accompanied, amidst moaning and prayers, with much sobbing, sorrowing, and lamenting, followed by wishes for a speedy and joyful return, by a large gathering of people and relatives."[1]

Not all of the troops were as well-trained as the Ansbach-Bayreuth soldiers, however. Sergeant Berthold Koch of the Hesse-Cassel von Truembach Regiment noted: "The recruits were drilled throughout the winter. It was a cruel, cold winter, during which the troops froze their noses and ears. Uniforms and all necessary company equipment were put in the best order."

Private Johannes Reuber received orders on 1 January 1776, "To report to Major [Johann Justus] Matthaeus' Company at Immenhausen. Further, it was ordered that the grenadier companies of all the field regiments were to assemble together and four companies formed a detached grenadier battalion. Each battalion was quartered in a small country city, issued equipment, and commenced training.

"On 2 January, early in the morning, we marched out of Immenhausen and into permanent quarters at Grebenstein, and remained there until all the companies were brought up to strength equal with the field regiments. We were equipped and drilled twice a day until the regiment was in condition. We received Colonel [Johann] Rall as a regimental commander and were called the Rall Grenadier Regiment. We had to drill twice every day, even in the deep snow and great cold, all through February, until we were in as satisfactory condition as the other field regiments. Then we heard that the 1st Division of Hessians, a jaeger corps, three detached grenadier battalions, and ten regiments, were to go to America. The first march began under General [Leopold] von Heister on 20 February. The Rall Grenadier Regiment remained in Grebenstein until 3 March, when we received live ammunition, sixty rounds per man, flints, kettles, flasks, axes and broadaxes, hoes and shovels, knapsacks and linen breadsacks, and everything needed for war. We looked around in bewilderment and then each one saw that this was serious. Each one realized there was nothing else to do but remain patient. In the evening the order came to march to Kassel the next morning, to be mustered before Landgrave Friedrich."

Training for the Platte Grenadier Battalion was recorded in the battalion journal, as follows: "On the 14th, 15th, and 16th of February [1776], in accordance with orders, the four flank companies of the

Rall, Stein, Wissenbach, and Buenau Regiments marched out of their respective quarters and into cantonment quarters at Wolfhagen. There they were formed into a grenadier battalion, the command of which was entrusted to Lieutenant Colonel [Johann Jacob] Koehler and received his name....

"The non-commissioned officers were mostly taken from other field regiments and the privates were nearly all raw recruits called up for the first time.

"From the sixteenth to the end of the month, the troops were issued uniforms and weapons. They were drilled twice a day. As it was still very cold, this was done in small groups in houses and barns, and, weather permitting, outdoors.

"When the weather began to improve, during the first days of March, the battalion conducted training in the fields outside the city....

"Otherwise, nothing occurred during the month except for a continuation of training. Everyone prepared for the anticipated departure. Constant turn-overs were made of the untrainable for men who could be trained. This situation made the work of the officers even more difficult because the new replacements were nothing but raw farmboys, which greatly hindered the completion of training.

All the various uniforms and weapons, which the companies had brought from their previous regiments, were delivered to the local commissary at Spangenberg and as of now the battalion has been outfitted with the same new equipment.

"On 19 and 20 March the battalion fired live ammunition for the first time.

"We remained peacefully in our cantonment quarters throughout the month of April. Training continued as in the previous month, as the weather was very pleasant."

Although Doehla indicated that some Hessians accepted the role of auxiliaries almost as a religious duty, the more traditional view of the recruiting methods was mentioned by Corporal Philipp Steuernagel, another career soldier, of the 3rd Waldeck Regiment. Commenting on how the regiment had been raised by supplementing soldiers from the 1st and 2nd Waldeck Regiments, he wrote: "The greater part were forced into service, persuaded by speeches, and so procured. Yes, even preached to from the pulpit, and this last place should not be unaware of the 13th verse of the 44th Psalm. [The 12th verse in the King James version of the Bible.] 'Thou sellest thy people for nought, and dost not increase thy wealth by their price.' I, myself, frequently remember the words of the old and honorable master-of-the-hunt, von Liliva, who during our evening march through Arolsen, on the 20th of May [1776], said, 'Those who return will all be riding in coaches.'

"At that time I believed all the promises made by important officials." However, Steuernagel recognized that all the men were not susceptible to religious or official words, as can be seen by this comment recorded separately in his memoir. "On the great day of prayer held on 3 May 1776 under the direction of Army Chaplain Philipp Fraz. Elias Les Waldeck and Sig. Schumacher. They preached to the Infantry Regiment entering English pay. (I think they wasted their time and effort preaching to these soldiers.)"

J.R., an anonymous diarist of the Hesse-Cassel Leib Regiment, began his account by noting that in February 1776, "We marched out of Kassel toward Bremerlehe, as ordered. At Varlossenour, our first night's quarters, however, we received countermanding orders to return. No one knew why. [It was because there were no transport ships at the port to take them on board.] On the sixteenth and seventeenth we rested and on the eighteenth marched back to Bettenhausen, where the staff and two companies remained. On Sunday, the 25th, we received orders and on the 27th moved out and resumed our march."

Sergeant Berthold Koch noted on 13 February 1776, "Finally the dreadful day of departure arrived ... when the Truembach Regiment had to march out of its peaceful resting place. The regiment marched out of Hofgeismar at three o'clock in the morning, when men were forcibly torn from their wives and children and sons from fathers and mothers. It was a terrible parting as each one said the final farewell. The sobbing of mothers and children, parents and families, was so great that we had to be driven out.

"I left my wife and two sons behind. I allotted two guilders each month to my wife, which she received in Hofgeismar."

Lieutenant Johann Heinrich von Bardeleben, of the Hesse-Cassel von Donop Regiment, wrote on 29 February 1776, "The von Donop Regiment marched, leaving Homberg at ten o'clock in the morning. Most of the city residents gave us the fondest farewell. Everyone at

4

this moment seemed to show more than the usual emotion. The deepest feelings of pain spread over everyone and their melancholy glances followed us. Inconsolable mothers, weeping wives, and whining children in great numbers followed the regiment and made with this sad scene the most heart-rending impressions. Personally, I could not remain indifferent to the situation and less so as I, possibly more than any other, wished to express my distinct views and ideas. However, I decided to hold my unspoken sorrow as much as possible within my heart and tried not to notice the mixture of pleasure and pain that I felt. Anyone who knows how to relieve the sorrow which I felt has my permission to tell me."

Chaplain Heinrich Kuemmell and Private Valentin Asteroth, soon to become the chaplain's assistant, used nearly identical words to report their departure on 7 May 1776. The von Huyn Regiment "moved out on this day with beautiful weather, to the sad lament of many people and marched via Wabern to Gudensberg."

Reuber recorded the departure of the Rall Grenadier Battalion without any reference to the reaction of the soldiers or the citizenry. "When we arrived at the Holland Gate, the command was given and we swung onto the racetrack. When His Serene Highness arrived, we were inspected by him and had to march in review past him. We then exited through the Leipzig Gate, passed through the forest and entered quarters at Krumbach and Ochsenhausen, where we had a day of rest. We were well-received in Kassel in quarters and the companies were issued all necessities so that nothing more was lacking."

Auditor Wilhelm Paul Schaeffer wrote of his unit's departure in equally unemotional terms on 15 March 1776. "The Hesse-Hanau Hereditary Prince Regiment received orders, after having been sold into English service on 1 January 1776, to assemble on the usual parade ground. And, after being reviewed by the gracious rulers, the mentioned regiment marched to the Main River above Kesselstadt, where seven transport ships and two yachts were already standing, waiting to be boarded."

Captain Georg Pausch, commander of the Hesse-Hanau Artillery Company, recorded the same circumstances on 15 May 1776, but more fully. "In accordance with your most gracious orders, general march was beaten at three-thirty in the afternoon, the company was brought out of the mill fortification onto the parade ground, and assembled with all its equipment. One-quarter hour later, assembly was beaten, [the troops] were aligned by height in ranks and marched through the old town and out the Hospital Gate, not far from the wood magazine. There the company was at once embarked on ships assigned for our transportation in the most gracious presence of our most gracious officials. Farther along the right bank of the Main [River] it pleased the most gracious and best Prince of our Land to accompany us with the most fatherly favor and love, which caused the most tender, truest stimulation of the spirits among all the men so graciously entrusted to me. Amidst a great many good wishes and tearful farewells, we began our journey here. Here we saw our most dearly beloved, best Prince and benefactor for a long while, for the last time. He then left us and our journey continued on until opposite Offenbach, where we anchored in the middle of the Main River and remained overnight."

Although the diarists generally noted the sad emotions of those left behind, or reported only the event of their own departure, Chaplain Philipp Waldeck of the Waldeck Regiment, reported in a more elated manner, on 20 and 21 May 1776. "The 3rd [Waldeck] Regiment marched from Korbach. The weather was very pleasant. The throng of people along the road all the way to Arolsen was unbelievable. The first night's bivouac was at Cuelte.

"At four o'clock [the next morning] march was sounded. The crowd of people who stood to the right and left was as great as yesterday. I wished the Herr Fector Stoecker of Herbsen and my many good friends good morning."

One of the good friends of the Waldeck Auditor Philipp Marc was the artist C.W. Tischbein, who was not attached to the military and who remained behind in Waldeck. He drew a pen sketch in Marc's autograph book and wrote, "My friend, with this sketch remember your true friend and servant."

## The March to the Port

The Hesse-Cassel, Brunswick, and Anhalt-Zerbst units marched overland from their home area to the embarkation ports at the mouth of the Elbe and Weser Rivers. The men were billeted and fed along the way as best possible and it was necessary to cross the territory of other states, Hannover, Prussia, Saxony, etc., to reach the ports. Those states generally provided a military escort, to protect their own citizens and to prevent desertion from the ranks of the marching units. Along the route there were new sights and experiences for the men, many of whom had never before been far from their own villages.

Some of Reuber's comments on the march follow. "We continued to move out early in the morning and to march steadily on the great heath. [On 24 March] there was no rest until we arrived at the place where the 1st Division, to which we belonged and which had marched ahead of us, was. Therefore we had to make forced marches so that we would also arrive at the designated place.

"We continued our march [on 30 March] and during the evening of the 31st were still about twenty miles from Bremen. The Weser had overflowed its banks and flooded the entire region this side of Bremen. Everything had to be carried back and forth in wagons.

"We marched again during the morning [of 2 April after a day of rest] until noon, when we suddenly came to water which had broken out of the Weser and flooded a large region. We could see nothing but villages, houses, and trees. All fields were covered with water and we traveled through to the village quarters in wagons. We had a day of rest so that we could put our equipment in order.

"The farmers had to load us into wagons [on 4 April] and we rode as far as Bremen. At the Bremen bridge we halted and climbed out of the wagons. We marched through the Imperial City of Bremen with dressed ranks.

"On 7 April [after] arriving at Gestendorf ... we saw the large ocean-going ships, swaying at anchor when the wind blew."

Asteroth, marching with the Hesse-Cassel 2nd Division, noted in mid-May, "We continued our march to Frenke, but at all times were accompanied by mounted patrols of Hannoverian heavy dragoons.

"We marched through the Naumberg [Gate] of the city of Rodenberg in Hesse [on 19 May], which as a city pleased us. The people with sympathy and sorrow did everything possible good for us.

"I saw my first windmill [at Altenhagen on the twentieth. Next day we went to Strecken, where] it was clear we would receive pancakes, of which one was enough for ten men, for our evening meal.

"When the drums beat [at Verden on 25 May] all of us had to hurriedly continue our march. However, the good people felt sorry for us, and young and old accompanied us to the edge of the city and bade us farewell with tear-filled-eyes.

"They burned rosin, as we would call it, [that night at Ottersberg] and the houses are not built in a pleasing style. It is as a barn at home; a great door and on one side of the door stand the animals and on the other side the fireplace where we live. They wear wooden shoes and their dress is not pleasing."

As a staff officer, conditions on the march were somewhat better for Chaplain Kuemmell than for the ordinary soldiers. "The march continued to Uslar, a small Hannoverian city [on 11 May 1776]. I was quartered alone at the home of Pastor Koehler, and during the afternoon visited magistrate Brunsing, who fed nearly all the officers and gave a dance. [Next day] the assistant pastor Schmidt, at that place [Dassel], preached a sermon on Psalms 18, verses 53 and 54, on our day of rest, at the request of our general. The text read, 'And He led them on safely, so that they feared not: but the sea overwhelmed their enemies. And He brought them to the border of His sanctuary, even to this mountain, which His right hand had purchased.'

"We marched a short distance [on the 26th] to Willstadt, a small village, where there were no houses where officers could be quartered, and I and the auditor were quartered in the mill where we were well treated. All the officers ate their noon meal at Pastor Pelius' house and we were served primarily on porcelain.

"The high bailiff, Herr von Grote, on the 28th and 29th served the staff officers, captains, the auditor, regimental quartermaster, and me a splendid meal which was eaten on oilcloth, without a tablecloth. The whole table was covered with flowers and decorated with porcelain, pewter, and other ornamental objects. The high bailiff was very merry and his five daughters, who were of great beauty and charm, were very cordial to all the officers present."

The Platte Grenadier Battalion journal provides a more business-like account of the march to the port. "We received orders [on 12 May 1776] from General [Wilhelm] von Knyphausen that the best discipline be maintained and that the troops should demand nothing while in quarters except that which their hosts voluntarily provided.

"A better order was to be maintained with the baggage wagons. As of today the provisioning of the non-commissioned officers and privates by the hosts was to be without charge. The quarters and rations were terrible and many individuals complained that they were not provided with the least bit.

"The quarters and rations [on the fourteenth] were as on the twelfth. In most of the houses not even straw was provided [to sleep on].

"The battalion continued [on the 27th] to march through a dreary region where nothing but heath and sand were to be seen.... The quarters were so-so. Selsingen is a rather pleasant place. Here for the first time the officials put us under the regulations of the Hannoverian government regarding rations and the saddle and wagon horses. The natives were paid for these items. Also here, we first learned that each man's rations were to be paid at the rate of two groschen per day. The officials and their assistants had never previously made the least mention of this part of their instructions, intentionally, in so far as possible no doubt, as disputes might otherwise arise regarding receipt for rations issued but not delivered to the men.

"Today, [28 May], we passed Bremervoerde, a rather pretty, well-laid out, little city, lying to the east [of Bremen]. Here it was already possible to see the Elbe River and to notice the tide.... Most of yesterday's march was made in sand and heath. The region of both of the above villages [Koehler and Ringstaedt] was wretched, which could also be said of the quarters. Here we received orders so that we could be prepared for the muster which is about to take place and the embarkation which is to follow. Six hundred dollars are to be paid in advance for the necessary provisions for the officers for the month of June. At the same time we were notified that upon entering cantonment quarters the rations, which the non-commissioned officers and privates had received at no cost to this time, would cease.

"The region around Dorum was pleasant and fertile. The inhabitants are friendlier that those we met in other places on our march, despite having to give credit to the Hannoverians for having shown every consideration in their power. Nevertheless, we must praise our present cantonment quarters even more. They took a pleasure in serving us, which was especially welcome in view of our pending embarkation and the need for adequate provisions

"We moved out of our cantonment quarters at six o'clock this morning [3 June] and entered Ritzebuettel toward ten o'clock. The many people who accompanied us, part on horseback, part on foot, were innumerable. As it was very warm and the road from Dorum to Ritzebuettel is very sandy, our escort made the march quite unpleasant for us. Because of the great amount of dust it nearly impossible to see one step ahead. Many of them expressed their sympathy but could not understand the sweat on our overheated brows."

Lieutenant Bardeleben's diary indicates that for the officers, life on the march had it enjoyable moments, and the soldiers and citizenry also found time to relax. "We had adequate quarters [in Electoral Hannover]. Every farmer was so busy between trying to provide everything for the comfort and feeding of his billeted soldiers that there was no shortage of food and drink, such as beer, brandy, and coffee, but even the greatest surplus. And truly, the kind-hearted people did everything possible for the soldiers. Above all, in the conduct they showed true sympathy for 'Sold individuals.'[2]

"My quarters [on 3 March 1776] were in Benterode by a farmer, whose entire house seemed in a condition of deterioration. At the same time they allowed nothing to interfere, and their cautious and modest situation made me very attentive. Coffee and food were very tasty. I found upon my entering the house that everything was arranged as would be according to the ways of a polished townsman. These good people required nothing more and refused to accept any payment. However, I left something behind for them. The other farmers also took absolutely nothing from the soldiers, but each one had requested, out of kindness, that his guests even take bread and ham for on the march.

"We remained for a day of rest [at Edesheim, Hollenstedt, and Stoeckheim on 6 March]. Soldiers and peasants considered this to be an exceptionally fortunate day. Everyone got drunk and nothing disturbed them in their pleasure.

"We marched into Brunswick, to Dillegen and Kayser [on the seventh]. These quarters were certainly not as good as those in Hannover. At the same time nothing was missing of the necessary foodstuffs, and nothing was had without being paid for. Nevertheless, every official or administrator of the villages was given receipts for the provisions, which we supposed would be made good by the King....

[At Gresdorf next day the dinner] "was especially good and consisted of a delicious veal soup, mashed peas with sugar, and sausage, roast veal, butter and cheese, also wine and beer. We sat together at the table and ate with good appetites. This fine reception pleased me all the more as we had made a long and difficult march today. Upon our departure I asked him what I owed, but his answer convinced me that his almost slavish hospitality gave the appearance but not the intention of being to my advantage. Therefore I lay the amount on the table so that everything was paid for in full.

"At about nine o'clock in the morning [of 9 March] the captain, Lieutenant [Wilhelm Carl] von Donop, and I took leave until the following day. [I obtained a horse and driver from the postmaster and] I made it my business to put the driver beside me in order to give him a feeling of importance and understandably to make that exceptional feeling, an exceptional reward.... We stopped at an inn [because the driver wanted a drink] and drank, maybe more than we should have, because we were alone and it was cold.... The full-of love behavior of my brother mislead me into drinking more with him and as a result I became really drunk. I pleaded great tiredness and hurried off to bed.

"After we drank coffee I rode in company with my brother, at eight o'clock [next morning] to Oberkirchen.... My brother and I dismounted there, paid our respects to Fraeulein von Gilsa, and went into the city with her to watch the von Lossberg Regiment march through.

"I joined Lieutenant Colonel [Carl Philipp] Heymel, who with his company had to take quarters in Dedendorf [on 12 March]. A captain of the Prussian service provided quarters for the lieutenant colonel [and me].... The good man could perhaps have had more money than influence. I can say nothing more definite about him because I was responsible today for the wagons and engaged with the ordnance horses.

"The lieutenant colonel obtained quarters with a noble official [at Sudweyhel on the fourteenth].  The individual was not obligated to provide quarters, but because of politeness and a shortage of good quarters, he agreed to forego his rights.... The lieutenant colonel was kind enough once again and took me with him.  I then received the best of quarters and hospitality also.... In short, I ate, drank, and slept like a prince.  I have forgotten the noble's name.

"We crossed the Weser [next day], passed through Bremen ....  Throughout this entire area the Weser had done much damage.  In many places it had flooded and especially a few miles outside of Bremen, near the village of Brinkum, which we had to pass, it burst its dams so that the water poured over a paved section about two miles long.  There the regiment had to be carried across, in part in small boats, and in part in wagons....

"The food was exceptionally good at Vegesack [on 16 March] and I can not remember having had any better.  The politeness of these people went so far that because it was still rather cold, they even warmed my bed.... I slept but little and only because the bed was too good and seemed different to me.  The private soldiers measure their life in the same way.  They minimize the greatest good fortune of their whole life, which they have here for the first time.  How can they think otherwise?  Strong brandywine and beer would serve as their wine.  This good life continued until the seventeenth, since we were fortunate enough to have a day of rest here.  The overdone kindness of the apothecary [on whom I was quartered] told me because of his obvious embarrassment and many kindnesses, that I should not pay for fear that I would thus embarrass a man of consequence and believed nothing should be forced on him.  Instead I sought to buy something of equal value as he had supplied everything for my entire provisioning on the ship's voyage.  I also brought many of our officers to him so that they could buy their necessities from the man, and I had the best results in filling my intent.  With the greatest joy he hugged me upon our departure, and during those days he had more joy than in all his years.  I took the liberty to offer something, but this was his emotional answer, "Pay me for your indebtedness by giving an occasional thought to me."

"The pleasant must always be followed by the unpleasant, and in this manner first the true value must be determined.  I even learned this

12

here [on 18 March] with full conviction. Misery and pain, thirst and hunger, are found everywhere. I had my quarters in Driftsethe. My host was an old man, whose only room seemed, by all indications, to be furnished comfortably. Pigs, geese, chickens, dogs, and cats were his companions and all slept together in this room. And, furthermore, at night it became a smoky room, perhaps out of custom or necessity, even during my stay. The smoke had its effect to upset me, or at least during the day, to cause some smoked effect. Even though I opened the windows and doors, it was all in vain. The room was a sort of sleeping compartment, which was never meant to serve as an open area, but was a hole which my host and I had to share. The night was full of smoke and foul odors, and despite all that, I had to sleep therein. I acquired lots of fleas when I crawled in bed and they advanced against me, so that all my defensive measures were not enough to drive them away. I killed herds of them but their numbers were unending. Later I slept quite well and gladly paid for my nights lodgings.

"To Stotel, Nesse, and Gackstadt [on 19 March]. These were our cantonment quarters and from this time on our rations from Electoral Hannover subjects ceased. Every soldier had to pay for everything he consumed, and at a high price. The local farmers had been forced into such terrible circumstances for some years by an animal disease; they have barely enough for their own needs. Some of the landed people have lost more than twenty cattle in a year, and this also made food, especially meat, very scarce. Each noon meal cost the officers eight [groschen], and still it did not taste good."

Travel for the Waldeck Regiment on the Weser River, as recorded by Corporal Steuernagel, was much easier. "I must mention here that we were accompanied/guarded to the borders of our fatherland, or more accurately, to Beverungen, by a corps of Waldeck green-clad palace guards.

"This display of mistrust gave, especially to the good soldiers of the regiment, mostly a feeling of resentment, and certainly was a factor in several desertions during the march to Beverungen.

"We continued during the following [May] days, on our own ships, without a need for wind or sail from Beverungen,... [and] arrived at Vegesack where we halted at noon on the 29th. I must note here that from Beverungen, we were accompanied by an outrigger ship called *Krueger*, from which we received our rations of soup, meat, and bread. In addition, everyone received -- and a very necessary ration -- a deduction from our pay.

"Nevertheless, the rations were considered not too bad by members of the regiment, and the days which we spent on the Weser were without care or worry."

Chaplain Waldeck reported on the travel as follows, "We arrived at Beverungen in good time. The regiment immediately boarded the boats which were waiting there for us. We [officers and staff] ate in a group in the city, took our farewell from friends who had accompanied us to this point, and departed at seven o'clock.....

[On the 23rd at Holzmuenden] "we grounded hard, and the sailors from the other boats had to help us to get free. This region, especially near the Weser, is somewhat hilly, and many cliffs rise near the river. We passed very close to one of these cliffs, which was steeper than the others. From the midst of the cliff a spring ran, which powered a mill built close to the cliff, and which was named the Devil's Mill.[3]

"At eleven o'clock [on 25 May] we arrived at Hameln.... The streets were in part deserted, because everyone had gone to see the regiment, which, here also, received everyone's approbation.

"26 May - ... A man fell into the water, but was saved by a sailor's quick reaction.....

"Because we were in such a hurry, and could not stop along the way, the Whitsuntide service was celebrated with only a singing of hymns. The boatman himself fell into the water today, and was saved by some timely help.

"27 May - Two soldiers fell into the water, and one swam over three hundred yards before being noticed, but no one drowned."

The Hesse-Hanau Infantry Regiment and Captain Pausch's Artillery Company sailed down the Main and Rhine Rivers to Holland. In the anonymous diary, possibly written by Auditor Schaeffer, there is an account of being stopped along the river whenever another sovereign area was encountered, and it was apparently necessary to use Dutch boats in Holland. "We arrived near Emmerich [on 21 March 1776] at two o'clock and at once anchored. The soldiers received both pay and bread here. Also, it was necessary to pay two English bank notes of 200 pounds sterling for the exorbitant Prussian customs ... before receiving a Prussian permit to continue our voyage.....

14

"On 23 March we left our ships [at Nijmegen] and the entire regiment, by companies, took the oath of allegiance to the King of England. Afterward we embarked on the twelve Dutch ships and three yachts."

Captain Pausch had even more trouble crossing borders, especially the Dutch border. "We were not inspected by anyone there [Frankfurt on 16 May 1776], but about eleven-thirty, when we reached Mainz, we had to tie up and two customs officers searched both ships, even though I had sent Lieutenant [Carl Ditmar] Spangenberg ahead with the most gracious free pass.

"During the then convenient high water on the Rhine River, our journey went so quickly that toward six o'clock we already reached Bingen.... I considered the so-called Pfalz, on that island, [opposite Caub], to be the most secure place to spend the night, and at once found the most peaceful place, where the troops could move about for a few hours, outside the ships.... In Caub I had it announced that the residents could bring over wine and other requisites for my troops, for which they would be paid in cash.

"The seventeenth just happened to be a weekly market day in Caub. Therefore I did not allow the departure until seven-thirty so that the troops profited therefrom.... To this end, excluding the wives, eighteen men, under two officers and six non-commissioned officers, brought it in so that the buying could take place correctly and without any difficulty.... Reveille is held every morning at daybreak and in the evening, after anchoring, retreat is held at about eight-thirty.... [The troops] never forget, after retreat and reveille, to present, as a required offering, an hour of morning and evening songs to the Omnipotent Protector.

[On 18 May] "I sent two officers,... the first sergeant, nine non-commissioned officers, and from each squadron several men, with six loaded and an equal number of unloaded weapons, into Cologne, in order to obtain local currency in exchange for the convention money, Erfurt currency, which they had with them.

"Prior to six o'clock [on the 21st] we arrived at Schenken Schanz.... This was the first Dutch customs, where it was forbidden for the ships to pass, as they had not the least knowledge that we were arriving and were to be granted free passage.... No matter where I turned, I heard nothing but that the court agent, the court director, must give the order first. It had been eleven o'clock in the morning when I first arrived at Arnheim from Schenken Schanz, and until after two o'clock, I grappled with the situation. Shortly thereafter I resolved to take a coach to the Hague" where the problem was resolved.

On 23 March 1776 Captain Friedrich von Germann of the Hesse-Hanau Regiment wrote to his Prince, concerning conditions on the river passage, from Bommel in Holland. "At the muster held yesterday the company was complete. This morning we exchanged ships for ones from Holland, and each company was assigned two. The situation on board these is much better than on those, but warm food, tea or coffee, is just not to be had. On the first ship I arranged at once so that the men could have warm meals and did everything in my power to insure tea and such for the sick."

A mutiny, which according to Doehla, had been started by the Ansbach Regiment, was reported a bit differently by Sergeant-major Johann Ernst Prechtel of the Ansbach Regiment. "10 March - During the morning both regiments rebelled. They wanted to leave the ships and did so. During the afternoon they were to return aboard ship, which the Eyb [Ansbach] Regiment did, but the Voit [Bayreuth] Regiment refused to do so, and instead fled from the spot. As the Field Jaegers were sent after them, an attack occurred during which one man of the Voit Regiment was killed and two wounded. Following this, orders were received for the regiments to march back to Uffenheim, but the men allowed themselves to be talked into returning aboard the ships."

However, another version of the Prechtel diary, one which may have been meant for publication, or at least to be read by individuals not connected with the military, reports the situation at Ochsenfurt with no reference to such conduct. "9 March - The march continued to Ochsenfurt and the regiments were loaded aboard ships during the evening.

"10 March - Because the ships were rather crowded and therefore more had to be brought from the ships' [supplier] at Wuerzburg, they remained lying at anchor on the Main River.

"11 March - The Prince arrived at his regiments at Ochsenfurt this morning, and himself made the journey to Dordrecht in the staff ship.

"We departed from Ochsenfurt this morning at nine o'clock."

Lieutenant Heinrich Carl Philipp von Feilitzsch of the Jaeger Corps provides another version of the mutiny. "9 March - ... This body of troops entered Ochsenfurt in the afternoon and went aboard ships. We had to remain lying there at anchor overnight, however, because there was not enough room in the ships and we had to wait for more.

"10 March - was a memorable day as the regiments went on land, early and without permission, where they were allowed to cook. They were then to embark; the Jaegers first and then the Eyb Regiment. When it was the turn for the Bayreuth Regiment, its grenadiers began a serious rebellion, which the others joined. They fled and our corps was ordered to stop them. We were ordered to fire at them and this was done, killing some and wounding others. I encountered those being pursued at the Cloister Tueckelhausen, into which some deserters had fled, and remained there until I received orders during the evening to return to Uffenheim to allow the musketeers' hatred to cool off. During the night, the Prince met me on his way to Ochsenfurt and I arrived at Uffenheim at two o'clock in the morning with a detachment of twenty men. We remained there until we received orders to move."

Captain Christian Theodor Sigismund von Molitor also reported on the movement of the Bayreuth Regiment to the Dutch port, with the following incidents being of interest. "1 March 1777 - The regiment marched to Bayersdorf which was also closely guarded to prevent desertion.... Ridingmaster von Gravenreuth [a Bamberg hussar] reported that he had orders from his commander to employ his hussars so as to prevent all desertion in Bamberg....

"5 March - was a day of rest. During the day tents and other necessary items were packed at the barracks [in Ansbach] and the heavy baggage was sent to Ochsenfurt under guard by a Jaeger detachment. At noon the Prince gave a large dinner with fifty covers. Some officers joined the guests and had the pleasure before the meal of kissing the Margrave's hand. The dessert was a presentation, during which the Jaeger Corps and both regiments paraded in uniform....

"9 March - ... The corps marched to Ochsenfurt at seven o'clock in the morning and went aboard twelve ships there. We could not proceed farther on this day because the troops were too crowded and more ships had to be requisitioned.

"10 March - At seven o'clock in the morning the ships were still not ready and therefore the troops were allowed to prepare a meal [on land ?], which by one o'clock in the afternoon developed into a revolt that lasted until five o'clock in the evening. The troops finally allowed themselves, after strong requests and pleading by their officers, to be reembarked, and after several men had been wounded by the Field Jaegers. During the night, at twelve o'clock, His Serene Highness arrived at the staff yacht, visited the companies of both regiments on 11 March, and in return received their assurances of fidelity. When everything was again peaceful we were embarked on nineteen ships and at evening anchored at Gross Geminden. The Prince of Wuerzburg extended his compliments to our Prince, who was on board the staff yacht and who decided to accompany us to Dordrecht, and sent a large amount of stone wine, red and black venison, and rabbit to the officers....

"14 March - Our corps was transferred to Hanau ships and toward noon, raised anchor. The Hereditary Prince and our Serene Highness had previously inspected the officers' cabins. Because of violent weather we could not sail and therefore our Serene Highness remained in the castle [of the Hereditary Prince]....

25 March - At eight o'clock in the morning, first the von Eyb and then our regiment was set out, companywise, on the bank at Nijmegen, and then marched to the parade ground. There the regiments were mustered and in the presence of the English colonel,[4] sworn in. At noon the staff officers and adjutants ate with the Prince at the Swan in Nijmegen. During the afternoon our leaders were cheered with cannons, especially the staff of the von Eyb and von Voit Regiments. During the departure Colonel [Charles] Rainsford, who sailed in his own yacht, began a cannon fire. The other yachts answered and the fleet sailed this evening to Tiel. This morning the Hessian recruits also arrived at Nijmegen from Coblenz,[5] and then sailed with us....

"27 March - Our Prince gave us some livestock such as sheep, geese, chickens, raisins, pigs, and lemons, and for every ship eight barrels of sauerkraut, some bags of potatoes, peas, lintels, flour, plums, and barley. I was sent to Dordrecht and bought two hundred pounds worth of wine and various supplies for our ship. Dordrecht is a beautiful and large city, provided with a good harbor, where there are always many ships. I made some good friends in the city, especially a rich merchant by the name of van der Loon. I ate in company with about twenty officers from our regiments, at a coffee house near the fort. This evening our Prince went aboard each boat and said his farewell to the officers."

Finally, Hautboist Georg Adam Stang's terse entry in his 'March Routes', taken alone, would leave most readers with some questions about the mutiny on 10 March 1777. "The rebellion." Nothing more.

### Going aboard Ship

Having arrived at the coast, been mustered, and sworn into English service, the troops were now ready to go aboard the ocean-going ships. J.R. noted on 23 March 1776, "Our regiment was taken in small boats to four large ships in the Weser River. The hautboists played, but the mood seemed more like a tragedy than a triumph. I did not feel well either, about leaving solid ground, which a person accepts because it is familiar, for the elements where the mighty waves offer a resting place for the dead. Our destination was falsely stated to reduce [our fear]. At seven o'clock we boarded the ship. The ship was 112 feet long, not counting the bowsprit; forty feet high, not including the masts; and thirty feet wide, with sixteen sails. It could be loaded with 200 tons of cargo. The weight was 400 tons. Two hundred men, not counting women, were on board the *Fame*.....

"We remained there [in Bremerlehe] until the seventeenth [of April], when the 44 transport ships sailed with a good wind. It was very beautiful weather and we sailed with cannons firing and music playing."

While on board, Regimental Surgeon Johannes Maurer, of the Truembach Regiment, wrote a last letter home before sailing; a letter expressing a father's concern for his son's welfare with overtones of those written by soldiers of every land, yet today. "Our cabin is nice, but not very large. Colonel [Carl Ernst] von Bischhausen has a separate cabin where he sleeps. The rest however, sleep in the cabin in regular beds, except for the regimental quartermaster and me, who sleep in hammocks, where we sleep very well. Lieutenant [Christoph Georg] Hoepfner, beside whose bed I hang, often rocks me to pass the time. All together there are 191 men on board [the *Charming Sally*]....

# Enemy Views (Travel to America)

"I greet you and my dear Fritz a thousand times.... Be sure Fritz behaves and take care to insure that he is raised with a fear of God. Do not let him spend too much time in the streets, and always keep an eye on him."

The activity of 23 March and the following days in April were elaborated upon by Lieutenant Bardeleben. "By eleven o'clock in the morning we were on board our ships. What wonders, what amazement, and what thoughts I had as I went aboard ship. I, who had never imagined such a large ship, still less actually seen one, clearly experienced something that I was in no condition to evaluate. A silent wondering, a boundless astonishment overtook me and dark images crossed my mind. In short, my ideas were too wild and too imperfect. I was understandably preoccupied trying to bring all my thoughts into a clear comprehension.

"This is the place for a brief description of our cabin.

"This cabin is not exceptionally large, about four paces long and equally as wide. It has four small windows and is otherwise equipped with equal decoration and comfort. So for example, there are four bedsteads therein, which quite fortunately are made according to the rules of need, and on the side, nailed fast, is a square table, which nearly fills the entire cabin, four wooden chairs, a stove, a large medicine chest, which is firmly tied to a bedstead, and in case of need, has to serve as a chamber pot, and several portmanteaux, which when necessary serve the same purpose. This especially chosen furniture was meant therefore for our comfort and outside the room had very necessary decorations, five frightfully large hams hung outside the window in a row and nevertheless gave off a smell. In addition to these, twenty weapons lay above the hams, also a drum, and finally the wig of the pastor hung with other unending expensive things, according to the rank of each, and made the contrast complete....

"From the tenth to the sixteenth of April all ships lay peacefully at anchor on the Weser near Bremerlehe. Nothing of significance occurred for us during this time. On the eleventh of the month I wrote to Kassel to L. von G. [Gilsa ?] and sent other letters with it. Just during these days we were visited by seven people. These were Captain [Julius Friedrich] Venator, Lieutenant [Heinrich Ludwig] Nagel, Sr., two Freyenhagens [Lieutenant Carl August and Ensign Wilhelm Johann Ernst], Ensign [Jeremias] von Lossberg, and two ship's captains, making with us, fifteen people -- a real party. At the same time we were all in the cabin and had to take turns sitting on one another's laps, and patiently wait to see what we would get for food and drink. It is easily understood from the above comedy, that everything tasted good to us and we toasted one another.

"16 April - Because a favorable wind arose, all the small boats were taken up and the anchor raised during the evening. The sails were unfurled so that on the following day we could depart for Portsmouth. His Excellence, Lieutenant General von Heister therefore came aboard ship this afternoon and from most of the ships his departure was signaled with cannonfire."

Von Heister's going on board was also reported by Rueffer on 16 April. "Von Heister, with his staff, embarked aboard the ship *Elizabeth*, which occurred to a continuous cannonade. On the seventeenth the first fleet sailed to a constant cannonfire.... The fleet carried the regiments: Leib, Hereditary Prince, Prince Charles, Ditfurth, Donop, Lossberg, Truembach, and four companies of Knyphausen, and the grenadier battalions Linsingen, von Block, and Minnigerode, plus one company of jaegers, and consisted of 42 [sic] ships."

Bardeleben's account continues on 17 April, "At eight o'clock in the morning, all the ships set sail from Bremerlehe with a very good wind and exceptionally beautiful weather. The view of so many ships, about forty in number, was impressive. About eleven-thirty in the morning the land had almost completely disappeared and by three o'clock in the afternoon we left the Weser with the very best wind and entered the North Sea, from which land could no longer be seen. From Bremerlehe to the North Sea the distance is seven German miles [forty-two English miles]. We covered this distance in a period of seven hours. From three o'clock this afternoon until six o'clock this evening, on almost all the ships during such bright weather, the music of a continuous cannonfire. The splendor and pleasantness of this event can not be described. It is a situation which must be experienced to fully grasp. It was therefore a theater whose presentation caused the most wonderful reception of awe."

Piel, who was also with the 1st Division of Hesse-Cassel troops, also reported on the 17 April departure. "This morning at eight-thirty the entire fleet, which consisted of 48 [sic] ships, went under sail....

Toward four o'clock we reached the sea. The ship *Union* sailed so close to the side of the general's ship for two hours that it was possible to speak to people on the other ship. During this time the hautboists of the Lossberg Regiment played a continuous concert. Cheers and the thunder of cannons reverberated from all the ships.

"18 April - At eleven o'clock several Holland fishing ships came alongside, from whom we bought some fish which are called kungen.... The sea became rough and the people, especially the wives, became seasick. In the cabins one noticed the movement of the ship most. Therefore, the officers had more cases of seasickness than the privates. Because the night was very dark, from time to time, aboard the ships, drums were beaten and bells rung."

Private Reuber, also part of the 1st Division, could not sail with the main group of that division due to a shortage of ships. His entry for 12 April was written after he was already aboard ship, however. "First we looked back on the land, then again at the water, noticing how the sweet water mixed with the salt water.... This was interesting to watch. The one [ship] on which I found myself was the *Success Increase* Supposedly it had been built three years ago at a cost of 2,300 pounds sterling. The owner of the ship was paid 150 pounds a month, from which he had to provide the crew, which normally consisted of twelve men. On a royal transport ship however, there are twenty sailors. The ship was a knee [?], 92 feet long and 92 feet wide [sic], of 320 tons.... In addition [to the captain] aboard ship there are a mate and his assistant, a carpenter, a purser or steward, a cook for the sailors, and cabin boys who are in training and also wait upon the captain. The ship has a spacious and pleasant cabin for the officers, which is sixteen feet wide and eleven feet long, and eight feet high. Beds for the officers are placed along the sides.... In this room [for the soldiers] there are three rows of beds, between which are passages. There are two-tiered beds, one above the other. Each soldier received a mattress, a colored and a white blanket, and a small cushion or pillow, all of which were new. There were more than 250 men on board, not counting the officers and servants.... The usual ship's provisions, which are also served to the officers when they so desire, and for which three pence is withheld from the pay, are as follows:

Every morning six men receive four pounds of ship's zwieback or bread, one and one-half as salted biscuits. On Sunday six men, as a group receive peas and four pounds of pork. Monday a gruel is cooked from oats, butter, and cheese. Tuesday six men receive four pounds of beef, three pounds of flour, one-half pound of raisins, and an equal amount of beef fat, from which a pudding is made. Six men receive a numbered pouch in which the pudding is served. Wednesday again a cooked gruel, plus butter and cheese. Thursday six men receive four pounds of cooked pork and peas. Friday again oatmeal gruel, plus butter and cheese. On Saturday again a pudding as on Tuesday. Every day six men receive four measures of small beer to drink and every morning a can of rum. These are served at eight o'clock. The officers have their own victuals cooked by our cook in the German manner and eat together.

"19 April - At eleven o'clock the anchor was raised and we sailed from Gestendorf, with great pleasure, down the Weser toward Helgoland. Now it was possible to see the strong waves from the sea which beat against the shore and created a great spray; also, a few sea gulls and other birds.... How happy we were when we were assured that we would be in England in three days and could anchor at Portsmouth.... We were cheerful and confident, but how quickly our pleasant hopes disappeared. The wind changed suddenly and again blew from the west. Our commodore at once turned around and at four o'clock in the afternoon we again dropped anchor near Helgoland, on the Danish side, by a village on the coast. Here we could see the Bremen bouy near Helgoland, which stands as a sign of the entrance to the Weser, which all seamen depend upon. We lay once again quietly at anchor and again waited for the good south wind. Meantime the wives were set on land, on the Danish side, from the ships, in order to wash the soldiers' shirts, and even the husbands of the women were landed to help with the laundry....

"Sunday [21 April] - The anchor was raised and we quickly sailed into the sea. Our wives and their husbands remained in the Danish village until the last fleet came to America, and brought them again to us in New York.

"29 May - Here I shall note our housekeeping. In the morning at eight o'clock, bread, meat, butter and cheese are issued by a sailor who is called the steward, in the presence of an officer from the soldiers. Each man receives a small can of rum and vinegar. When it is cooked and is done, every six men have a wooden bowl with a number thereon representing the berthing spaces, from number one to the end. The cook calls the first and fills it, and so until the last. And what we receive each day, I have previously noted. The soldiers must stir the pudding themselves, and for every six men, a bag is provided on which is the number of their berthing place, also. When it is ready, the cook calls the number and the six men divide the pudding. The same procedure is used with the meat -- one piece for six men, which is then divided into six pieces. The one who divides it points with his fork and asks who should have it. Another [of his men], who has turned away, gives the answer. It would be a great pleasure to watch this activity if the portions of meat were not so small. Often a piece of meat is served which consists of more bone than meat. While we remained on the deck of the ship, it was cleaned below. The berthing places were sprayed with vinegar and made clean. They had a device like a sack, but made of four strips of cloth about a meter in width and sewn together. One end is open and at regular intervals a round hoop holds the device open so that it resembles a barrel. On the end where it was sewn together, a hole has been cut resembling a sentry-box. This sack is tied to the mast and hangs down into the ship. The hole faces the wind and leads the wind into the sack and under to the lower deck of the ship and all the bad air from the ship goes out. Then it was as fresh below in the ship as it was on deck. It was called a *windsack*."

On 9 June Reuber also noted the interaction between the ship's crew and the Hessian soldiers. "The sailors are becoming more trustful of us soldiers because many of us drink no rum, which can be traded to the sailors for bread. However, the captain and mate must not see this. It must be done secretly."

On 12 June 1776 Asteroth recorded that, "No one lives on this land [Helgoland], except sailors. When ships arrive there, these sailors get into their boats and travel out to the ships, where they then beg for alms. I have seen this to be true. The people do nothing but beg from the ships."

The Platte Grenadier Battalion Journal entry for 6 June contains information on the crowded conditions aboard ship. "Although our ship [*De Riviere Divina*] was the largest ship in the fleet, there were too many men on board and all of them could not find a berthing space. The heat between decks is exceedingly great. If, as promised by Colonel [William] Faucitt, some of the men are not transferred to another ship when we reach Portsmouth, it is to be feared that a contagious illness will strike us.... The provisions are not nearly as good as on [the *Vrou Classina*].... The cleanliness aboard our ship can not be compared with that on the *Vrou Classina* and therefore it is obvious that our ship's captain is not a Hollander.

"The captain has nothing to say about the provisions, as that, as on all non-English ships of the fleet, is under the direction of an Englishman called the superintendent, who is supposedly a midshipman from a warship.

"The provisioning is done in Hamburg and it is the agent's fault that it is so bad, because, according to rumor, he has made a profit on it. Zwieback, made of coarse rye grain, has been delivered instead of wheat flour, as on the other ships. The water already stinks. This is the result of buying old wine barrels in which red wine has been, rather than new, or even old water kegs. The ship, counting the captain and mates, of which there are three, has a crew of 45 sailors. It is already rather old and was built on the Divina River in Russia, hence the name. It is 140 feet long and 33 feet wide. Now many are sadder and wiser.... All the things which we have learned are necessary for our pending voyage are simple articles, the purchase of which no one gave any thought. It was clear that few ships departed from this harbor supplied with these same articles. Another reason we were so ill-prepared was that no one of us knew what to take on such a voyage. Those of us who had previously been to sea did not know.... We had to wait patiently until we reached England.

"9 June 1776 - The entire fleet sailed out [at about five o'clock].... It consisted of nineteen large transport ships."

Sergeant Berthold Koch of the Hesse-Cassel von Truembach Regiment noted that, "Each man was given a pound and one-half of snuff which was to be taken aboard ship, because smoking was not permitted on board and the English do not smoke tobacco."

Captain Pausch recorded going aboard his transport ship on 26 March 1776, with Lieutenant Wilhelm Dufais and the English Commissary, Colonel Rainsford. "We boarded with the colonel in order to check everything and to make arrangements with the ship's captain, especially concerning berthing and feeding. For this the presence of the colonel and Lieutenant Dufais was most necessary in order to reach agreement with the captain, and to be able to understand him, as he spoke nothing but English and even less French than I.

"Our ship named *Juno* has three masts and is commanded by Captain Eduard Schmitt. N.B. - He is a very proper and pleasant native Englander, about 36 to 39 years old. This is no ordinary transport ship, but noticeably smaller. Previously it was used in the slave trade. [There are some who would say on this voyage it was still being used in the slave trade.]

"On the main deck it was designed for eighteen short, iron ship's canons, but has only seven 4- and 6-pounders on board at this time. Those missing are to be requested at Portsmouth by the captain. In the event of an emergency, the colonel told me that I must unhesitatingly have my troops handle and serve those ship's pieces, and work with such, so as to provide help in defending the ship in every possible manner, if it should be attacked. This request and the English order, I have kept secret until now, except from Lieutenant Dufais and the other officers, until such time when it becomes necessary, to prevent the troops becoming frightened before time, and possibly without cause.

"The berths and small mattresses, without padding, are of such mediocre good or bad, as you wish, quality, that I have allowed the company blankets to be issued. The company will be very confined in this ship. The berths, constructed so that two, one over the other, are each meant for six persons. The six men and six men receive their sustenance together, as each section, one [non]-commissioned officer and eleven men, are berthed together. The men and wives, however, lie three couples together in each berth, in order, in so far as possible, to prevent any disorder. I and my three officers have a rather spacious cabin....

"The chosen ship was much too small, because all the next two days were spent in arranging and stowing. The cannons and the gun carriages and limbers were taken down below, put on the ballast and barrels so that during the unloading, because of the tight quarters, many repairs will be necessary to everything. N.B. - The large pine cases, in which the harnesses were, could not be taken below, but had to be unpacked, tied together, and the harnesses, including lines, sacks, cribs, and feed bags, etc., were taken below in the ship. Nevertheless, however, the captain must and wishes to attach a small vessel behind his ship at Portsmouth or Spithead, so that the main deck will be completely empty, free, and open."

Sergeant Prechtel described the ships, their crews, and the crew pay in his diary on 27 March 1777. "The transport ships [for the Ansbach-Bayreuth and Hesse-Hanau troops] were mostly three-masters and the ship companies thereon consisted of:: one ship's captain, who, however, is not a naval officer, one helmsman or mate, one assistant helmsman, one steward, who issues the provisions and keeps the ship's accountants, one ship's carpenter, one ship's cook, and twenty sailors, a total of 26 men.

Monthly pay, in pounds sterling, of the ship's crew, in addition to the ship's food twice a day and a berth: ship's captain - 10 pounds; helmsman - 5; assistant helmsman - 3.5; steward - 3.5; ship's carpenter - 4; ship's cook - 3.5; and sailors - 3....

"Each provision is paid for at five coppers or 6 and 1/4 groschen.

"Note - On land four men daily receive as many provisions as six receive daily aboard ship.

"The wives receive a half portion and children a quarter portion, without receiving any rum."

In a letter to his prince on 25 June 1776, Captain Pausch noted the overcrowding aboard the ships carrying the Brunswick troops, also. "On one of the Brunswick ships, on which I visited Colonel [Friedrich] von Specht -- a large Dutch ship called *Friesland* -- there were 450 men, not counting women and children. In three shifts it is impossible for all of them to enjoy fresh air on deck. The colonel himself, with sixteen officers and the ship's captain, all live in one cabin, which is no larger than ours.... Colonel von Specht therefore has sent a captain to London, to ask the King himself if a change can not be made."

Steuernagel recorded the Waldeckers going on board on 31 May 1776. "Orders were given for everyone to be prepared to leave our little ships and to board three large Holland transport ships lying not far from us on the North Sea, in order to complete the dangerous voyage across the unknown ocean to America. "Heaven help us! What thoughts came to mind as we gazed on the most frightful, raging North Sea. Country, parents, family, all our friends, yes, even the world seemed to have deserted us and delivered us up to the unknown ocean and its powerful waves. Here friends opened their hearts to one another. Filled with sorrow and grief as to our future fate and the dreadful appearance of the raging sea, we even forgot to look back for one last glimpse of our beloved Germany, and surrendered ourselves to the rushing waters of the wild ocean.

"Truly a sad situation! Within -- a heart torn by grief; without -- nothing but fear, need, and danger....

"The number of crew which were on each of the three ships is not necessary for me to list, except to say, that each ship had 250 men of the regiment in addition to the ship's crew, and each was loaded with the officers and their equipment, the food provisions, coal, wood, water, weapons, and ammunitions, without taking into account what the crews required in the way of equipment and wares and the many materials and utensils which were provided in the event of an emergency during such a long trip. Everyone can readily understand why such extraordinary costs were involved.

"To return to our story, we departed from here on the 3 June 1776, completely lost the German coast, and consoled one another to have patience on this dangerous journey, and to leave to fate whatever might be in store for us. We went to bed that evening as usual, full of fear and concern, only half sleeping.

"Our bunks were so tightly arranged that we had to lay pressed against one another and no one could move, let alone turn over. Six by six. In general there was space for a board which was five feet long and six feet wide. When we were tired of lying on one side in this narrow holder, the senior, or one in command, gave a signal so that all could turn onto the other side at the same time, and without this, since we were so closely packed, we often ended up with our heads where our feet had been, or because of the violent movement of the ship, fell upon one another, or as often happened, fell out of bed....

"Six men received four pounds of ship's bread daily, or the so-called biscuits, which were made without salt and baked so hard that it was necessary to beat them against a stone with a stick, or to soak them for a prolonged period in water, before eating. This bread was made from a bad wheat meal, hard, without salt, baked a half finger thick and round, about the size of the bottom of a coffee cup, in order that it would not mold....

"Also, during the week we were given, alternately, peas and oatmeal, and each week we received on two days boiled pork and twice salted beef. Of the first, six men received four pounds and of the other, eight pounds. These were placed daily, when not stormy, in a very large copper kettle like a pot with a secure top, then fully cooked over a coal fire and rationed to us.

"In lieu of meat, three times a week, butter and cheese were issued, but not enough of the last to worry about, which provided a man, when I may make the comparison, the support of a fluid, at first adequate, but later somewhat insufficient for a young person. Something now of the brandy -- wine bond, which was such a small portion as not to suffice during a twenty-four hour period, so some traded their bread, which was barely a half pound per day, with the young people who were not accustomed to brandy, but who had more appetite for the first, and in this manner each made his own way through the unpleasant and difficult journey....

"To say something of the ever-prevalent vermin. I can assure you in truth, that whoever had the most white shirts, also caught the most lice. Although a daily delousing parade was held, because of the length of the voyage, the vermin were so prevalent among us, that even the officer needed to feel no shame to pluck a louse from his sleeve and throw it overboard. The cause of these unpleasant companions on our ship resulted from most of the soldiers being people brought together from many regions by slick recruiters. The drafts were without a shirt to their name, but were given two issue shirts which were not enough to prevent a strong visit of lice."

In the anonymous diary attributed to Prechtel the following information was recorded under an entry of 7 June 1777, off Staten Island. "The ship *Myrtle*, on which were half of the Major's Company and half of Captain Stains' Company, 150 men, had three masts and was two stories high. The magazines were below and the soldiers and sailors, who were separated, however, were above. The officers and the ship's captain, named William Walker, were in the cabins in the stern. Above on the deck were nine cannons....

"Four men were assigned two beds, one above the other, and each berth had a small mattress, a small pillow, and two English blankets."

After having gone aboard ship, but before sailing from Gestendorf, Lieutenant Carl Friedrich Rueffer, of the Mirbach Regiment, recorded the following series of events affecting the ship *Henry*, beginning on 26 April 1776. "About one o'clock during the night a powerful storm sprang up. At daybreak our captain lowered all the masts, but the wind still rolled the ship so violently that we were in the greatest danger of losing our lives. Toward three o'clock in the afternoon the storm became so strong that we broke our anchor line. The captain put out a second anchor, and as this one also broke, he tried a third one. All was in vain; the last one broke, just as the first one had and we had to put our trust in the Lord. At four o'clock in the afternoon we were driven, by frightful pounding, so firmly into the sand that I can not describe it.

"27 April - This morning at ebb tide our ship stood high and dry on land and we could see clearly how we had been watched over during yesterday's storm. Three strides distance lay a stone of tremendous size, and the captain assured us that we would have foundered without hope of rescue had we run against it yesterday.

"28 April - All the seamen of the entire fleet were engaged in an effort to refloat our ship, but to no avail. Lieutenant [Friedrich Andreas] Schotten was sent by the general to find out how we were doing. He was able to walk to our ship with dry feet, as the tide was out.

"30 April - The occupants of our ship, plus provisions and baggage, were put aboard other ships as the weight prevented our ship being refloated.

"2 May - To our great joy, our ship *Henry* was refloated and this afternoon General [Werner] von Mirbach again came aboard.

"6 May - Once again we were all loaded aboard our ship and received orders at the same time not to allow anyone to leave the ship as we were to remain ready to sail at anytime."

### Crossing the Ocean

As the *Henry* and the remainder of the 1st Division were getting underway from Germany, the main part of the division was also encountering stormy weather, as indicated by Lieutenant Bardeleben's diary. "7 May 1776 - During the past night a strong wind again arose and the movement of the ship was unpleasant, although I slept well. At seven o'clock in the morning the wind was still strong and again contrary so that we had to sail back to St. Helens and await the coming of day. With this strong wind all the ships tacked with the greatest care so that they would not ground in the Channel. This special maneuvering by the ships caused all the troops such a feeling of sickness that they could not prevent vomiting and everything connected therewith. At six o'clock in the evening the waves rose much higher. No one could stand or even sit. We lay down therefore, part in bed, part on the bare floor, but we were still not secure. Soon the tables and chairs flew together, although they had been tied, which helped but little, and we were in the midst of them. We had our noon meal in great discomfort. One took his plate in bed, the next one sat down under the bed, and still another sat in the middle of the cabin and wrapped his arms around the table. In this manner we ate our meal. I sat on the deck beside my bed, holding onto it, ate some from a wooden bowl and accepted an incomparable taste. Now we understood how necessary it was to tie everything as tight as possible....

"9 May - Beautiful weather. The wind again soft and also favorable. At eleven o'clock in the morning we left the Channel, praise God, safely. As long as we were still in the Channel, our ship's crew had to sail no less carefully, because the dangerous sandbanks can make this region of the coast difficult to travel. Throughout the day we sailed four, five, and even six English miles in an hour.....

"Although the wind was not strong [on 16 May] the sea was rough and our ship plunged first forward and then sideways and today we also lurched about in the cabin like a bunch of drunks. We were thrown from one corner to the other. We tied our coffeepot on a line this morning and fastened it on a nail where everyone put it to use and held his cup to be filled with unsteady hands and feet. It was no better with our noon meal. We had to put things together around the table and sat on the cabin floor while the servants, with the help of the table, held silverware and dishes. Under these conditions each helped the other as best he could. All this unpleasantness shook us a great deal. At least for my part I continued to eat and drink just as much as before....

"17 May - During the past night ... all the chairs, books, valises, and even Captain [Johann Matthias] Gissot, flew about in the cabin, and of all the things in the cabin, not much was spared. I myself nearly had the same fate when I was caught in the first tumult. I held as tightly as possible and heard thereby the various events which occurred. Suddenly one of the other officers awoke, 'Well!', he shouted. Then another, 'Well, what's happening?' The puzzle soon solved itself. One severe rocking of the ship followed another and suddenly such a jolt struck that it nearly threw Captain Gissot out of bed. At the same time, and just at that moment, everything was a cause of alarm. I lay absolutely quiet, said nothing, and acted as if asleep, but I thought to myself, Heavens! There is no storm but still such a violent rocking. A secret shudder seized me as I have never heard of such a rolling, still less, felt the same. I believed nothing more than that the ship would sink. I remained in this anticipation until daybreak, when it abated....

"18 May - ... A young lad from our ship's crew, of about eleven years of age, fell from the lowest part of the mast into the sea this morning at six o'clock. The ship's captain had the small boat lowered immediately, went after him, and found him after he had been swimming around for twenty minutes. He was still alive and had all the life signs.

"19 May - ... The young boy was already on deck again today and almost completely recovered."

Private Reuber reported a similar incident on 24 June aboard the *Success Increase*. but with a less fortunate outcome. "Toward noon the sea grew restless and some waves beat against the ship. One of these grabbed a brave little cabin boy who was forward by the bowsprit, where there is no railing, and at once carried him overboard into the ocean. We watched in sorrow, but could do nothing to help him."

On 14 August 1776, Private Asteroth also reported the loss of a crew member during a storm. "We had a half storm at five o'clock in the afternoon. The crew had to climb the rigging to shorten sails. We saw a sailor fall into the water. He remained on the surface a long time. He cried and shouted for help but it was not possible to save him because of the raging sea. The ship sailed so swiftly that after four minutes we could no longer see him."

Lieutenant Bardeleben's account of storms continued on 21 May 1776. "The night was very restless. The back and forth rocking of our ship was very violent so that when we awoke in the morning, books, hams, chairs, and everything similar was scattered about the cabin.... The constant restlessness of the ocean alone caused the rocking. At twelve o'clock noon, around the horizon, it was overcast and a strong north wind arose so quickly that we believed the strongest storm was upon us. The waves rose so high at this time that they beat over the ship with the greatest force. The wind was also terrible and this weather continued the whole day. Our ship's crew did not consider it a storm, but for us it was one of the strongest because at noon today we could only eat and drink less serenely than usual. Our meal was very scant, only a pudding, but it could not be eaten peacefully. When it was placed on the table, it fell out of the wooden serving dish, rolled about on the table, and nearly fell on the floor. However, because all of us, as we were accustomed to doing, had previously situated ourselves advantageously, we were quick enough to catch it again. This pudding stayed on the table, completely clean, but it was in numerous small pieces. This could not be prevented because one hastily grabbed it with a fork to keep it from falling on the floor, another used two or three knives, the third with a spoon, and the fourth with only his ten fingers. We were happy, however, that we had been able to save it. The small pieces tasted just as good to us and nothing remained afterward."

On the same day, Regimental Quartermaster Zinn, of the Donop Regiment, on board the *Hope*, noted that, "Toward twelve o'clock the wind became very strong so that our after mizzenmast broke."

Bardeleben continued his account next day on 22 May. "Once again sleep was very restless. The stormy weather continued throughout the night without letup and also just as severe today. The ocean raged frightfully and the crashing was fierce and frightening. Monstrous waves beat against the ship and with such force that we believed the constant creaking of the masts must soon lead to our sinking. At eleven o'clock noon the strength of the storm increased. Almost no one then remained on deck. All the food flew off the stove and lay scattered about. It was peas and ham. Therefore this afternoon we had nothing to eat but cheese and bread. We lay down in bed with this and ate our little bit with pleasure. We had tied a small cask with beer to the stove and this beneficial drink satisfied us very well. Toward evening the wind abated, but only a little.

"23 May - The past night was a bit more peaceful. The violent rolling, however, began again this morning, even stronger than on the previous day. It was very dark during the whole morning. The howling of the wind and waves mixed together, threatening us with a sad day. Our dinner again consisted of bread and cheese. At two o'clock in the afternoon the stormy weather abated and the weather improved. How this pleasant change pleased us and how eagerly we hurried to cook. Each one on this evening wanted that which for the past several days was denied his stomach. During the past night the wife of one of our soldiers went into labor and fortunately delivered a fine son. The child was healthy, but the mother was weak.

"24 May - ... At three o'clock in the afternoon the child was baptized. Lieutenant Colonel Heymel, our ship's captain, and Mr. Ego were the godfathers. The lieutenant colonel held for the christening. He was named Carl for the lieutenant colonel, Hamilton for the ship's captain, and Henrich, my name. The mother was already much better today."

Chaplain Georg Christoph Coester reported the event in his church book and concluded, "He was the first child that I baptized and possibly the first Hessian to be baptized aboard a transport ship on the Atlantic Ocean. N.B. - The child and his mother died in the autumn of 1777."

Coester was to baptize two more children on the crossing, and there are numerous reports of children being born and baptized aboard ships making the journey from Germany to America.

On 27 May 1776 J.R. reported activity aboard his ship during a storm. "Because we could not stand against the waves, the rudder was tied fast and the ship was given over to God and the waves. Toward ten o'clock the wind tore the lone sail in use from top to bottom."

Bardeleben continued his account on 30 May 1776. "This is the first time in five days that I can take up my pen and I am glad that I am able to do so. A storm, a real storm, which struck at twelve o'clock noon on the 25th, did not allow me the least opportunity to write. Those days were exceptionally frightful from the 25th to the 29th. We had to tolerate the most violent sea storm of varying degrees during this time, and none of the other various storms could compare with this storm. The west wind blew constantly, so that we had the ever-present fear of losing our masts, or even losing the ship. My pen is too weak, the language too poor, to fully describe all the danger. Here the waves could hardly be called hills any longer, but seemed to be monstrous, even incalculably high mountains. Wave after wave rolled and raged against one another in the dreadful crashing. The waves often covered our entire ship so that the water was two or three feet deep on the deck. Therefore no one dared to go on deck without risking his life if hit by a wave. Even our ship's crew had difficulty just to stand. When they stood by the helm, they had to be tied to the mast. From five to six o'clock on the 28th our danger was greatest. The waves surrounded us on all sides. Our ship seemed to lie at the bottom of the deepest pit. The water beat against the hatches and flowed from the deck into our cabin like a stream. The lieutenant colonel, who had stood up so that his bed could be made and only held firmly onto the door of the cabin while this was done, was struck by a wave which beat over this place with its full fury during this hour and so drenched him that he came into our cabin thoroughly soaked.

This same wave also hit me. Hunger had driven me from my bed, which I crawled out of with great effort. I sat on the deck near a cabinet in order to get a bit of bread and cheese. However, I had barely opened the cabinet when the water came in through the stove pipe and struck my leg. At this moment the lieutenant colonel, and shortly thereafter the ship's captain, entered the cabin no less dejected and ill at ease. At this moment everything was in disarray. We were a sad sight to one another and fearfully awaited that moment when we would become the victims of this wild flood. We could not shut our eyes during this entire period and if we rested a little, it was a fitful sleep that weakened more than refreshed us. Despite all of this, the new mother and her child, without anxiety or fear, spent these terrible days in the best of health. May the Lord be eternally praised for our rescue and the most fortunate survival of all the dangers which we had to face. During this entire day pleasant weather. What a chance for us to quickly recover, as we had barely seen the light of day for five days. Each one crawled feebly out, weakly looked about to ascertain if the frightful theater of nature, of fear and grief, had really passed. Everyone then breathed with eager gasps the soft air and everyone was gradually stimulated from his almost completely exhausted spirit to display a bit more liveliness. The commodore aboard the *Preston* made a signal early this morning that all the ships' captains were to come to him in order to learn if any misfortune had occurred. However, the fleet was so scattered that he could get these reports from only a few ships. The ships gradually drew together and almost all had been lucky. A few had lost masts."

Reuber reported one of the most bizarre incidents on 23 July 1776. "In the middle of the night a row of berths collapsed and the soldiers and their beds flew about, and all of that in the dark. Anyone can understand what a person must think when more dead than alive. During this [episode] the kitchen was crushed and fell into the water due to the frightful storm. The captain had three pigs on the ship in a stall made of boards. One of them broke out of the stall and fell through a hole among the soldiers. It could not free itself, but squealed from fright in a berthing area among the soldiers. Then the sailors came with a lantern and a rope, which they tied around the sow, raised it in the air, and again put it in the stall, where it was secured."

Captain Pausch, en route to Canada, reported on 17 July 1776 that even the captain and crew of his ship lost courage during a storm. "Beginning at four o'clock in the morning it once again became most frightening. Soon it was so bad that the ship's captain, who is a very competent and courageous seaman, and all his sailors lost courage. All the sails which were still spread were torn to shreds in short order, and the middle mast, namely the strongest mast, was broken. One wave came after the other, beat against and over the ship, and so much water came in that the people lying below deck, in the lowest position, together with their equipment, were nearly swamped, despite all entrances and air vents being securely covered."

Another of the many storms encountered was reported by Asteroth on 5 August 1776. "A strong storm arose and the sailors had to quickly take in all the sails. Then they let the ship go wherever it wished; they tied the rudder fast. The wind moved the ship so violently that three berths collapsed and as three were arranged one above the other, and six persons occupied each one, eighteen men fell out."

Finally, on 11 July 1776, Lieutenant Bardeleben, making the crossing with the contingent from Hesse-Cassel, reported an electrical storm. "At nine o'clock in the evening we had a nature scene which we had not had before. A strong and frightful electrical storm struck. The crash of thunder was accompanied by the most terrible lightning so that it often seemed that fire, water, and ship were a single object. The rain fell like a torrential rain. This weather continued without letup and in the strongest manner until one o'clock at night. One ship lost a mast. Our ship's crew assured us that they could not remember ever experiencing such weather before."

The diarists of the other contingents also recorded the violence of storms at sea. Chaplain Philipp Waldeck, of the Waldeck Regiment, even found humor in one situation on 25 September 1776. "Strong winds, very foggy, rain. About noon the winds became so strong that the grenadier ship *John Abraham* lost its middle mast.... For our evening meal we had a burnt soup, over which we had a hearty laugh as the oats settled to the bottom leaving only water above. The surgeon, Herr [Carl Friedrich] Pfister, sat beside me, and as the ship rolled a great deal, everyone had to hold onto his plate. Like a flash of lightning a wave struck the ship, the soup flew out of my bowl onto Herr Pfister, from top to bottom, and I was left with only the soup bowl in my hand."

## Collisions while Sailing

Storms were not the only dangers faced by the Hessians while aboard ship. Ramming was a threat for sailing vessels in all kinds of weather. Lieutenant Piel noted several incidents in which ramming or avoiding collisions were of importance. "24 May 1776 - Weak southwest wind and pleasant weather. This evening at six o'clock a large ship, on which was a part of the English Guards, rammed the middle of our ship with its bow. Its bowsprit struck the stays of our foremast, snapping the thickest stay, and damaged some of our sails. Meanwhile, the other ships altered their course and we escaped without suffering serious damage. It was a frightful moment, as the ship came toward us. The women on both ships screamed loudly and the faces of the men became deathly pale. Meanwhile, the damage, which our ship had suffered, was repaired within an hour.....

"28 May - The storm continued. We could only use one sail and the helm was tied most of the time. During the afternoon a ship sailed directly toward us. We called out from our ship, but no one was to be seen on the other ship. Apparently no one could remain on the deck because the sea constantly ran over it. Finally, our people had to come on deck and call out in unison until we saw people on the other ship, which changed its course and so the danger, fortunately, passed by.....

"2 June - Calm, with warm weather. We lowered a boat and towed the ship a short distance so that it would not collide with others....

"6 June - The past night was very dark and foggy. Therefore, aboard ship the drums were beaten regularly and the commodore fired several cannon shots."

On 18 June 1776, Lieutenant Reuffer referred to cannon fire which had been heard previously. "Today we learned the significance of the cannon fire on the night of the thirteenth. The ship *Gobarth*, which had provisions on board, rammed the *Albion*, not only knocking down the jack mast, but doing such great damage that the ship took on much water and because it was believed on the ship that it would founder, they had fired the signal for help."

Lieutenant Bardeleben reported a ramming accident near the North American coast on 9 July 1776. "Pleasant weather all day with the light wind, almost calm. The fireship *Strombolo* collided with a transport ship during the afternoon so that those two ships hung together more than half an hour and caused a great excitement. *Strombolo* lost its bowsprit but otherwise had no damage."

He also recorded another near collision on 9 July. "Late in the evening a great disturbance occurred on our ship. A transport ship came so close to ours that on both sides every effort was made so at least not to come together too hard. Only by a small degree was our cabin spared from damage because just behind it the other ship had approached and the bowsprit extended nearly to our rigging. These collisions, when one ship rams another, are not rare during calm and fog and occur almost daily. Major [Erasmus Ernst] Hinte's ship, among others, suffered much damage and nearly sank. This happened in Portsmouth as we lay at anchor, when a fireship tore loose from its anchor and crashed into his ship so hard that all the lines from the forward part of the ship tore loose. The ship also suffered large holes in several places."

A collision was also recorded in the Platte Grenadier Battalion Journal on 15 August 1776. "At nine o'clock this morning, during a wind calm, a horse ship of the 17th English Dragoon Regiment collided with our ship. It was a Dutch ship, the *Rogge Bom*, and much larger than ours. It hit in the middle of our ship and the bowsprit caught in our sails and rigging, tearing away not only some sails and rigging, but also the bowsprit. The alarm on board ship was general as each faced the danger which created the alarm but could not think of a means of saving himself. If it were stormy or windy it is possible that the ship could have sunk before anyone thought of averting the danger. However, the damage suffered was only to the sails and rigging and the loss of some ropes and the bowsprit. We were at $37^0$ 22' north latitude and had sailed five miles [that day]."

In the anonymous Hesse-Hanau diary, under the date of 16 May 1776, a collision near Newfoundland was entered. "We had no wind and it was very foggy, which resulted in a special situation arising, which fortunately did not cause serious damage. About nine o'clock, one of the transport ships collided with one of ours and their bow crashed into the window just behind the right side of our cabin, where Lieutenant [Carl August] Sartorius had his bed, which was not disturbed. At once in both ships efforts were employed to separate the ships. On the other ship more than twenty people, part from the English Artillery on board, part sailors with bare feet and only a shirt, worked at this. Our loss was a window and the glass therein; and so we were separated."

Captain Molitor wrote about several collisions, on the Rhine River on 21 March 1777 and at sea on 12 April of the same year. "The journey continued into the night, the staff yacht came too near a Dutch ship which sat on a sandbank and all possible effort was needed to avoid it. The staff yacht lost a small piece of the rudder and another boat from the von Eyb Regiment was also slightly damaged.....

"12 April - During the night it rained heavily and in the darkness two ships, *Stag* and *Lively*, ran into one another, which damaged them somewhat, but not seriously.....

"17 April - We had good weather but a complete wind calm. One would believe that this day would be very peaceful, only the swaying of the ship increased as it sailed with a half wind and rolled all the more because the ship did not move forward, but right and left. The ship *Symetry* rocked against us (on the *Durand*). The wind calm prevented the necessary maneuvering and caused a rather scary outcry and work among the sailors. They could not get the ships separated quickly enough, because without the wind the steering rudder took no effect. Both bowsprits barely touched, but the *Symetry*'s broke off like a splinter and ours cracked so that it was necessary for the crew to cut three feet off the length. They had to work all day to restore everything to a proper condition and we finally and fortunately were separated."

First Sergeant Prechtel also recorded an incident on the Waal River in Holland on 25 March 1777. "Underway at Nijmegen at one o'clock in the afternoon. During the departure a Dutch single-masted, wooden ship ran against our number four, which was punctured, but at once repaired."

## Other Dangers

There were still other dangers during an ocean crossing as indicated by J.R. in an entry dated 14 June 1776, and comments by Reuber and Pausch. "On orders from the King the fleet was to sail far to the north on the crossing," and Reuber, who was sailing with the second section of the 1st Division, seems to confirm that in his entry of 21 June, which must have been written at a later date. "The first fleet, with the Hessians, had been driven northward by a strong storm on the second Whitsunday and surely must have been frightfully frozen. When we came together again [near Sandy Hook on 12 August], they told us of the storm they had encountered. On the second Whitsunday we could not move from the place where we were, because we had absolutely no wind, although we were on the ocean the same as they were."

On 22 June J.R. wrote, "Today was the longest day in Europe and therefore bright summer. Here, however, we must dress as in October or November and we sail past large icebergs, which are said to come from the North Pole.... We were also in the region called Newfoundland."

Finally, Captain Pausch, on 29 July 1776, reported the possible consequences of those icebergs. "During the morning, at ten o'clock, a cannoneer who was on watch discovered land. However, after we had drawn nearer and the very thick fog had raised a bit, it was a driven together and floating iceberg from Greenland, which, with a length of three-fourths of a mile and a width of one-half mile, was at least 240 feet high, despite fifty or sixty feet being below the water.[6] Because we now had more than a three-quarters contrary wind, this came right into the course which we would have had to sail during tacking. As throughout the night it was not only rather dark, but there was a thick fog, therefore, if this almost unbelievably large, floating body of ice had not appeared during the daytime, but rather during the night when no man on the ship would be concerned about the ship, an unfortunate collision could not have been prevented and would have led to our complete destruction."

Fire, however, is probably the most dreaded disaster at sea and was feared by everyone on board the sailing ships, as reported by Steuernagel in 1776, after passing the Azores. "Shortly thereafter we had a great misfortune in that a fire broke out aboard our ship *Benjamin*. The provisions commissary caused the misfortune because, in serving provisions, which was done far below deck, he brought the light too near the rum cask and thereby, as the cask, which held more than 600 gallons, ignited and burst with a threatening, fearful crash, the rum flowed throughout the ship setting it afire. Now our Hollander [ship's captain] was in the greatest need and the earlier fear and danger [of sinking due to a storm] was again present, only now much greater than that experienced on the North Sea.

"Where now -- we apologetic-mouthed martyred sons of Waldeck? Where now? Where can we, in this fearful and dangerous situation find refuge and safety? Everyone saw death staring him in the face, either from fire or by drowning, if the Divine Providence did not come with some special training or method of help. Each of our soldiers in this great danger took his most cherished possessions up on deck and gave himself over to God's will.

"I must not allow myself to exaggerate how excited we were, but everyone in this time of great need was completely out of his head.

"It is true that among the crew there were many evil and disreputable people. However, I myself saw that even the most beastly and inhuman showed their desire to live.

"It was a great misfortune [Steuernagel or the copier must have erred, as it was most fortunate] that just at this time the sea and the wind were still and calm, such as we had not seen on our entire journey. Therefore, the warships, which halted near us, quickly sent their small boats in order to ease our misfortune, or, as much as possible, to save our crew from drowning, and others fired cannon shots and made other signals of the distress aboard our ship, which brought the remaining ships, where possible, to help.

"But this could not have happened unless, as already mentioned, the sea and wind had not been exceptionally calm. Many of our people, though not in danger, tried to save themselves by jumping, senselessly or fearfully, into the sea, toward the nearby small boats, in such a manner as to make a person believe they would never again be seen. However, the English sailors in the small boats showed their compassion for our unfortunate comrades and spared no effort to save those who sought refuge in the boats.

"Meantime the other ships had hastened to us and the officers and men came aboard and worked diligently to extinguish the fire and fearlessly showed, here also, their true, inborn courage to the highest degree, because they came to our burning ship and, without a second thought, plunged into the interior of our ship to try to extinguish the fire, and thus, in a short time the fire was put out.... If this fire had broken out by night and with a strong wind, everything would have gone wrong and all hope of saving our lives would have been lost."

Two other accounts mention the fire aboard *Benjamin*. The first from the Platte Grenadier Battalion Journal on 10 September 1776 notes, "Fire broke out on a transport ship loaded with Waldeckers. Because of the wind calm, however, boats from [other] ships could go to help and in a few minutes sixty boats were on hand, and with their help the fire was extinguished. It had started in a storeroom when a keg of rum caught fire, but fortunately was put out."

Chaplain Waldeck wrote, in part, concerning the accident, "A ladder on the ship [*Benjamin*] became overloaded by too many people, broke, and two soldiers and the ladder landed in the sea. Both held fast to the ladder, however, until help from a boat was hurried to them."

Less dangerous to the welfare of the ship than storms, collisions, and fire, accidents to individuals were common and often deadly. A few examples of individuals falling overboard have already been given. The Platte Grenadier Battalion Journal recorded another such accident on 11 September 1776. "While raising a sail, a rope broke so that one of the sailors, who was 76 years old and who from his youth had spent his entire life aboard ship, had the misfortune to fall into the ocean and drown before our eyes."

Captain Molitor reported two accidents in his diary entry of 31 May 1777. "Today the anchor ropes were fastened on [the anchors] and the anchors secured on the sides of the ship. The 1st mate Briggs, in so doing, had the misfortune that an anchor of sixteen hundredweight, which slipped, fell on him. It hit him in the groin above the right hip and knocked him, seriously injured, under it. The mast, which it fell against at the same time, absorbed part of the heavy weight and saved his life. Today we received the report that during the last storm a sailor from the ship *Symetry* fell from the mast and was never seen again."

A less spectacular accident was recorded by Chaplain Waldeck about an incident which occurred while making the rounds of the other ships for the purpose of conducting religious services in Plymouth harbor on 7 July 1776. "This morning the sea was so rough that it was nearly impossible to travel in the boat. [Private Philipp Henrich] Volcke, who sat in the boat with us, fell in the water when attempting to leave the boat. A sailor quickly grabbed him and threw him back in the boat."

Prechtel reported on the death, or suicide, of the servant Peter on 18 May 1777. "Officer's servant Peter, servant to Lieutenant [Justus] von Diemar, Sr., lowered himself into the sea from the ship *Myrtle* on a rope at five o'clock in the evening. He was seen swimming in the water, because the waves did not immediately pull him under. A quarter hour later he was brought back to the ship dead, in a boat which had been sent after him. He was buried in the ocean with a bag of sand hung on him."

Feilitzsch also recorded this death. "During the afternoon Lieutenant Diemar's servant fell overboard from the ship *Myrtle*. Because it was not far from us we were able to see how they pulled him out of the water, but it was to no avail. They threw him back overboard at once."

Reuber recorded what he thought was a sad event on 21 July 1776. "There was a sad event today. A soldier named [Hermann] Dietz, of the Lieutenant Colonel's Company, has been missing since two o'clock this morning. We believed he had hidden himself in the hold of the ship for fear of punishment he was to have received this morning, having committed a theft, but to our greatest wonder, after thoroughly searching everywhere, he was not to be found, so that no other thought remained except that through intent or carelessness, he had fallen overboard."

Then on 5 August the disappearance was clarified. "We were sure the missing soldier Dietz had drowned on 21 July, so that it was unexpected when at ten o'clock our Quartermaster Canade found him when Dietz asked for some water. He was immediately brought on deck and admitted stealing things since our voyage began. He had also nourished himself during his desertion by theft and had been in the ship's supplies as well as on deck every night in order to get something to drink. The lieutenant colonel feared he would now do what we thought he had done. Therefore, he was locked up and watched with a guard. He had grown so weak and miserable under the casks in the ship, where he had hidden, that a person could not approach him without his fainting."

One of the more unpleasant events during the ocean crossing was the burial of those who died aboard ship. Most diarists had occasion to comment on this custom. One such report was written on 16 July 1776 in the Platte Grenadier Battalion Journal. "A grenadier named Lohmann of Captain [Friedrich Wilhelm] Bode's Company died early this morning of a high fever. He was left lying until this evening. I asked the reason and the ship's captain told me that he did not like to throw a body overboard during the day. During the evening the body was sewn in a hammock and blanket, in which stones and sand had been placed. It was the full cost of the burial, if I do not include a bottle of cognac which Captain Bode gave the sailors for their efforts."

Scurvy was one of the more common causes of death during the crossing, and as the voyage progressed, so did the number of cases of scurvy. The Platte Grenadier Battalion Journal indicates the spread of the disease. "27 September 1776 - Scurvy is very prevalent among the sailors, and also among the soldiers.

"28 September - A third sailor died of scurvy.

"6 October - Scurvy among the men is so rampant that few of them can perform their duty.

"18 October - Due to the wide-spread scurvy among the sailors we were only able to get under sail this morning with the greatest effort.... After we finally, with great effort, got the ship underway with the help of the soldiers, we steered to the north, toward Long Island."

Chaplain Waldeck also reported a death due to scurvy and the resulting burial at sea on 5 October 1776. "This morning the soldier [Friedrich] Teigtmeyer from Goettingen died of scurvy. I had served him communion yesterday, and one could hardly stay by him an hour, due to the terrible smell in the stuffy ship. He was sewn in a hammock, a song was sung, and the words of the twentieth chapter of the Apostles, thirteenth verse, struck me, 'And the sea surrendered her dead'. I do not believe a funeral service has ever before been based on this text, in my country. The body was lowered into the sea from the right side of the ship."

Finally, Asteroth noted the spread of the disease and the transfer of sick personnel to the hospital upon the arrival of the fleet in New York. "20 August 1776 - For sixteen weeks we were all healthy, but suddenly many were sick with scurvy. Five men on our ship died.....

"21 October 1776 - The sick were landed at the large hospital on Long Island. On our ship more than 100 were sick. They were lowered into a boat in a chair and within two hours were in the hospital where the sick from the first fleet were also taken."

Not all deaths were accidental or due to illness. J.R. reported on one duel aboard the *Unanimity* on 4 June 1776. "At twelve o'clock we received an order that Lieutenant [Carl August] Kleinschmidt had fatally wounded Captain [Simon Ludwig] Count von der Lippe....

"The 5th - At six o'clock in the evening Captain Count von der Lippe died.

"The 6th - At twelve o'clock he was laid on a board in his dress uniform and wrapped in a blanket. A prayer, Our Father, was said, and the board was lowered into the water."

Lieutenant von Bardeleben recorded the duel upon learning of the incident on 14 June and on 28 June provided further details. "We learned the bad news today that Captain Count von der Lippe and Lieutenant Kleinschmidt, both of the Leib Regiment, fought a duel aboard ship on the sixth of this month. The Count was mortally wounded and died soon thereafter of his wound. [Marginal note - after two days] Lieutenant Kleinschmidt was taken on board Colonel [Friedrich Wilhelm] von Wurmb's ship as a prisoner.

"28 June - At two o'clock in the afternoon the ship's captain and I went to the ship *Unanimity* on which the dispute had arisen between Count von der Lippe and Lieutenant Kleinschmidt. Lieutenant [Christoph] Bode, Lieutenant [Justus Heinrich] Ernst, and Ensign [Johann Anton] Germer, all of the Leib Regiment, were on board that ship. Those officers told me that the cause of the dispute was only over the treatment of a dog which Lieutenant Kleinschmidt owned. As he went about on the deck, he misstepped and this caused the dog to begin to howl.

"The Count heard this in his cabin and immediately ran out on deck and asked what had happened to the dog and who had mistreated it. Lieutenant Kleinschmidt explained with diffidence that he had accidently bumped the dog and that nothing else had occurred. However, the Count immediately went to his cabin, secretly took out his pistols, and so abused Kleinschmidt that Kleinschmidt had no choice but to shoot him. The officers in the cabin, however, knew nothing of all that until the Count entered and told them he was wounded.

He lived another 27 hours and prior to dying wrote for the officers that no one else was responsible and especially that the other officers in the cabin knew nothing of the affair. The interrogation of the Count had been considered very open and serious and, because until the last hour of his death, he was still rational, he was questioned about the whole incident by the chief auditor, [Justin Heinrich] Motz."

All was not routine aboard ship during the crossing. One transport carrying men of Hesse-Cassel had become separated from the fleet, and on 7 July 1776 Bardeleben recorded that, "*Malaga* had caught a small American ship."

Asteroth reported on 12 September 1776 that, "Our warship captured a rebel ship with ninety sailors, twelve cannons, and munitions." Possibly the same capture was recorded by Chaplain Waldeck in his entry of 29 September. "The *Unicorn* brought an American ship of ten cannons and a ninety-man crew [back to the fleet]."

As the Hessians approached the American coast, defensive measures were reported by Rueffer on 23 July 1776. "Each transport ship should furnish a guard force of one officer and twenty privates under orders of General von Mirbach."

The Platte Grenadier Battalion Journal noted defensive measures to be taken on 28 September 1776. "At eleven o'clock tonight the ship's captain came into the cabin and gave us the surprising news that enemy ships were nearby.... As the ship's captain had no cannons, he requested Lieutenant Colonel Koehler to load our regimental cannons, which were then secured on the foredeck. This was done. As our artillerists were unfamiliar with this method of handling the guns, it required nearly a quarter hour to accomplish this."

There are numerous references to officers visiting back and forth among the ships of the fleet, frequently for the purpose of buying supplies, and for religious services. Heavy drinking at those times also caused problems. On 4 June 1776 Lieutenant Bardeleben recorded, "At ten o'clock this morning Lieutenant General von Heister visited the commodore on board the *Preston* to help celebrate the birthday of the King of England."

Two days later, "During the afternoon, Captain Venator and Lieutenant Nagel, Sr., visited us in order to buy sugar and other foodstuffs from our ship's captain, because for a long time already they have had nothing but ship's provisions."

Again, on 17 June, "During the afternoon we had a visit. Major Hinte, Captain [Adam Christoph] Steding of the von Lossberg Regiment, Chaplain [Georg Friedrich] Heller, and two ship's captains. A pleasant day. We enjoyed the time drinking punch, a bit too much, and a very innocent gaiety prevailed."

On 16 July, "Chaplain Coester, our ship's captain, and I went aboard the ship *Hope* this morning to visit the major.... After dinner a child was baptized."

On 27 July, "At noon our ship's captain went to another ship. While he was gone the mate and several sailors became very drunk. One of the sailors was so drunk that he jumped into the ocean several times and each time was again pulled out with the help of a rope."

Also, on 1 August, "At two o'clock in the afternoon, Captain [Donop] and Lieutenant [Wilhelm Carl von] Donop, Lieutenant Colonel Heymel, Mr. Sahe, with Ensign [Ludwig Ferdinand] von Geyso of the von Knyphausen Regiment, and four ship's captains came aboard our ship. One of the ship's captains was most welcome. He delivered 48 bottles of porter beer, each bottle for one groschen, also twelve pounds of sugar at fourteen groschen a pound. Once again we lived well. It was no longer necessary to drink water."

Rueffer recorded a shopping visit on 30 July 1776. "Lieutenant [Carl Friedrich] von Wurmb went to the *Eagle* and purchased not only sugar and tobacco, but also two flagons of red wine and a pound of coffee."

Chaplain Waldeck noted a visit on 1 September 1776. "Our captain put a boat over the side and sent the ship's quartermaster to the ship *Unicorn* to get some [tobacco]. He returned with twenty pounds.... Once again all was well because the soldiers could smoke a pipe of tobacco. They had helped themselves to this point, and the least quantity that one or the other still had hidden, when it became known, would then be smoked, and then the ashes would be given to those accustomed to the use of snuff, for that purpose."

Recreation was limited but Rueffer reported dancing and a crossing indoctrination ceremony, and took to knitting from boredom. "12 July 1776 - Toward evening our soldiers entertained with dancing on the deck, and we were moved to do the same, but unfortunately without the company of women.....

"16 July - The sailors held a christening today for those who had not previously been to America. They put blindfolds on them, used fat and lampblack to blacken their faces, and then those black faces were shaved so closely with a wood rasp that afterward the blood flowed. Next they were dunked in barrels of water as if being baptized."

"From boredom [already on 15 May] I began to knit an apron from netting.... Because of a shortage of coffee, today, [27 May], we began the sorry practice of only drinking it once a day. I knit diligently on the netting to somewhat reduce my brooding over coffee."

On 12 August Rueffer commented, "It was the first fleet which had an unfortunately long voyage. There are regiments in it which have been on board since 23 March."

Captain Pausch noted however, on 20 June 1776, while still at Portsmouth, that, "A large number of recruits, raised by Scheiter [in Germany for the English army][7] are still lying here in the roadstead, ready to sail.... These men have already been divided troop-wise among the British regiments in America, and already, according to their numbers. It is said they are to go under sail at the same time we do. A part of these ships have lain here in the roadstead for eighteen to twenty weeks."

On 4 August 1776 Reuber gave an indication of some of the other shipboard activities. "A heavy rain forced us to remain in the ship and we had to have lectures until the weather improved. From our sailors we learned how to speak better English. Therefore our time is passed pleasantly. We read, write, and perform our housekeeping chores and such other things."

The rain was a blessing in another respect, according to Chaplain Waldeck's entry of 22 August 1776. "We had a heavy rain and gathered all the empty casks to fill with rain water. This water was a special refreshment; everyone drank his fill and felt much better."

Somewhat surprisingly, the anonymous Hesse-Hanau diary even recorded a mutiny by the crew of a transport ship during the crossing on 9 May 1776. "The sailors rose up in anger against the captain and his officers and fought them so that most had bloody faces.

"10 May - A long smoldering hatred broke out among the sailors against the captain, who was more than an infamous ruffian, so that they called him all possible bad names to his face and really would have thrown him overboard if he had not been protected by the colonel and all the other officers, who forbid them laying hands on him anymore. Therefore he called to the man-of-war for help. The warship at once lowered a boat and a marine officer came to our ship and settled the matter at once. He took two of our best sailors back to the frigate with him, which meant the most severe punishment for them."

### Arrival in America

Having arrived at New York, Koch reported on 15 August that, "Our von Truembach Regiment as well as many other Hessian and English regiments debarked and entered camp on Staten Island.

"We remained there the next three days. There some of the troops received sauerkraut for cooking and the regiments had to cook sassafras wood for tea, which cured scurvy and purified the blood."

J.R. reported landing on the 15th of the month and that camp was set up about four miles from the water. Then, on 24 August, "A corps from our troops proceeded against Long Island. However, our regiment, Prince Charles Regiment, and Ditfurth Regiment remained in camp on Staten Island. Our regiment entered camp opposite the city of Amboy, which is across the border in New Jersey and which the rebels still occupy."

On 13 August 1776, Lieutenant von Bardeleben notes as the fleets sailed into New York harbor, "From this point we could see the

English who were in camp on Staten Island. We also learned here that the rebels occupied everywhere. Only this small island was free. The ship *Surprise*, with Captain Venator and which we had thought lost, had lain here at anchor already for eight days."

He continued his account of the arrival and on 15 August wrote, "We landed at nine o'clock in the morning. The entire army of about 25,000 men was here on Staten Island. Our camp site was excellent. The smell of cedar, sassafras, and other local woods made it very pleasant. There was a scarcity of fresh food. Every effort was made to obtain it but in part because the English, and before them the rebels, had used it, even on land we had only ship's rations to eat. Almost no vegetables were to be seen. Now and then potatoes were available....

"16 August - Last night was the first in camp. I slept exceptionally well. However, upon awakening it did not clearly register that I was on solid ground and further, suddenly everywhere, everything looked war-like to me. I looked around, even walked around, and did this time and again. I could not believe that I was in America....

"17 August - Nothing new. I went hunting but saw nothing but some ducks, a few of which I shot. Most of our officers must cut the rank insignia from their uniforms, supposedly because the rebel so-called riflemen had their greatest interest in officers, and so that these will not be distinguishable from the privates, gold and silver insignia will not be worn and now in many regiments all uniforms are similar. Our regiment continued without change. Terribly hot.

"18 August - Rain during the entire past night, which continued until twelve o'clock noon. Although the rain beat through my tent, I slept well. At five o'clock in the morning there was a heavy cannonade between some frigates and the rebels in the batteries of New York City. Those frigates had taken a position on the North River in order to bombard the city. Today, however, they had to return to the fleet. In the process of passing the forts lying at the point of the city, they drew a heavy fire against themselves. One ship lost the middle mast. The firing continued intermittently until nine o'clock in the morning."

On 15 August Reuber, sailing in the second section of the first division of Hessians, also recorded the arrival of the Hesse-Cassel fleet at New York. "About ten o'clock we saw a great many ships, warships and transport ships, all standing in the harbor and also saw the Englanders on land, in the defensive positions on a high hill. We saw all this but could not go to them [because an unidentified fleet was seen bearing down on the Hessians].... Suddenly our command ship lay to, fired another cannon shot, and raised another English flag on the middlemost mast. Then the strange fleet, which approached us with their three-decked ships, which had sixty, seventy, and eighty cannons, gave a signal and raised an English flag.

"Because the command ship now saw that it was the first fleet, which had sailed twelve days ahead of us, we had joy upon joy, as did our comrades who had sailed earlier. Our command ship fired a *feu de joie* with 32 cannon shots. When that was finished, the ships in the harbor also fired a *feu de joie*. The English, who were in the defenses on the heights on Staten Island also took part in the *feu de joie*, because of the Hessians' safe arrival in America. As we, the second fleet [of the Hessian 1st Division] swayed outside New York Harbor, and could not enter, there had suddenly been an alarm. The French were approaching with a great fleet [supposedly]. This caused anxiety and fright among us outside the harbor, because we could not enter; the war fleet could not come out because of the flood tide, and our fear continued until ten o'clock. Suddenly we sailed, both fleets mixed together, into the harbor near Staten Island, about twelve o'clock, and thereby our voyage ended happily, under God's protection. Praise the name of the Lord, that the All Gracious God had protected and sheltered us from all harm and misfortune up to this time. God will continue to shelter and protect us on the solid ground, when we march against our enemies, so that we might be happy and remain happy until eternity....

"And with this, I close my sea voyage journal and with God, begin a new one on the solid ground."

When the 2nd Division from Hesse-Cassel arrived near New York, the Platte Grenadier Battalion Journal entry of 16 October 1776 gives an indication of the feelings on seeing land once again. "At nine o'clock, to our great joy, the commodore and several transport ships raised flags to indicate land had been sighted. Toward one o'clock in the afternoon we saw some low hills to the north. It is doubtful that [Christopher] Columbus could have had greater joy upon catching his first glimpse of the New World, than we had. At once everyone seemed to come alive. The sick allowed themselves to be brought up on deck so as to be convinced of this discovery. Still, another sailor died."

After lying off the city for several days due to contrary winds, the account continued on 19 October. "We weighed anchor at six o'clock this morning and entered the channel between Long and Staten Islands. On both islands pleasant estates were to be seen. We dropped anchor toward seven o'clock, in the dark of night, in the North River, near New York. As the wind was not the best for entering today, most of the fleet remained lying at Sandy Hook, which is thirty miles from New York.

"20 October - ... At noon today the rest of our fleet joined us with the incoming tide. Despite our long journey, we had to consider ourselves lucky that we had not had a prolonged storm, and the entire fleet of 63 ships arrived here without a single loss. In this harbor we encountered more than 400 large and numerous small ships.....

"21 October - Finally today the deeply wished for moment arrived, whereby we left our residence of 142 days, in which we had put up with so much fear, distress, and many sad hours."

Chaplain Kuemmell arrived at New York with the Huyn Regiment of the 2nd Division of Hesse-Cassel troops. On 20 October, he wrote, "The 1st Division had already arrived in August and had taken the city from the enemy. Most of the local residents favored the rebel cause and very many, about half, of the houses stood empty. Gradually they returned to their dwellings after forming another opinion of the Hessians. They had been told that the Hessians ate children and were all very hostile.... The island of Manhattan was still not clear of the enemy. Two English miles from the city a position called Fort Washington was still occupied by a large number of rebels."

Steuernagel, of the Waldeck Regiment which arrived at New York with the Hesse-Cassel 2nd Division, wrote in his account, "After prolonged and numerous spectacular dangers and hardships, the coast of North America came into view.

"The joy, which each of us experienced, I can not adequately describe. We forgot at this time all the previous dangers we had faced, even forgot to eat and drink, until the land came nearer and we could recognize it, as we were still doubtful and thought it to be only a brief consolation for what we had been through. With the joy and assurance that for the first time since 3 June the land would free us from the miserable ship, still we persisted in our yearnings, not wanting to be disappointed, until early the next morning when we saw the large, solid land lying before us.

"It is not possible to describe the joy among the soldiers.

"All that I can say is, we all swam in a sea of joy.

"On 13 [October] we entered New York Harbor and lay at anchor.

"Already from a distance we could perceive the radiance of freedom which the inhabitants of this new world had previously enjoyed and of which they were now to be robbed by the oppression of war, against these German slaves. Every plantation, every farm, seemed a shelter in a fool's paradise; the good harmony between neighbors, where a beggar was never seen on the street and certainly never encountered. All this made us think it to be a blessed land when compared to Germany.

"The Americans [he wrote in a note to his diary entry] look us Germans over carefully, with distaste, because we have come to help steal their freedom, and, because of our fine issue uniform shirts and the appearance of our other clothing, say -- Your country must be poor!"

Continuing his diary entry, "The land, which so many poor and needy Europeans had made worthwhile -- and shortly, where among those inhabitants, love, truth, faith, and freedom of speech were to be found, were now, through war, to have their customs and well-being completely destroyed."

Chaplain Waldeck, who was the most diligent 'Hessian' recorder of people, places, and events, wrote many pages about his sojourn in America, beginning on 16 October 1776. "Soon land could be seen from the mast, and about noon it could be seen from the deck. I will write nothing of our joy. This the pen can not describe, but the heart beat faster. God be praised and thanked; that was the expression used by every soldier, even those who seldom had used such language.....

"21 October - The sick were landed and sent to the hospital on Long Island, and the order was given that we should be prepared to land....

"22 October - I went into the city to buy some things because it was apparent that we must spend the night in the boats. I returned, and my good Captain [Johann Christoph] Alberti had departed. I remained the rest of the day in the city, and was quite at ease as I felt the regiment would go no farther than Long Island, where I could go the next day with ease. I was so fortunate as to find a German inn. I ate my evening meal with a large clientele, among whom was the German Lutheran preacher of the parish. This man asked about my background, and told of having studied at Goettingen with a person of similar name, and that was my brother. He brought me a book in which stood my brother's name. His name, [the preacher], was Prell. The inn was so full, that I and also two Hessian doctors, had to sleep on the billiard table.

"Now for the first time, I realized my embarrassment. No one could tell me where the troops, which landed yesterday, had gone. I asked at General Robinson's headquarters, at the Hessian port company, in short, everywhere. At evening I could not find my inn, and had forgotten to ask the name of the street or of my host, as I had expected to join my regiment.

"An old woman approached me in the street and spoke to me in German. Who was happier than I, when she offered me her home as a place to spend the night. Her friendliness and her excessive concern awoke my distrust. There are no witches in America,[8] otherwise I am sure she would have been one. I patiently followed her, although I thought she would deliver me to the rebels. Finally, we came to her house, situated in an out-of-the-way alley, which only increased my fear. She busied herself preparing an evening meal. She asked what I wished and I said boiled eggs. She gave me her own bed on which she placed a lace spread, and slept on the floor with her husband. This politeness awoke another feeling in me, could it be there were kidnappers here?

"To this point my hostess did not know who I was. I pulled off my overcoat, and my dress caused her to ask my title. I was the field chaplain of the Waldeck Regiment. 'Oh, a holy man,' she said. She would have kissed my feet, believing her house thus blessed. How unjustly I had treated this good woman. She was a woman full of loving kindness. That night I slept well.

"24 October - My honorable country-woman bought oysters for my breakfast, fried them in butter and pepper, and felt bad that there was nothing more she could do for me. I could not adequately appreciate her kindness. She accompanied me over the East River to Long Island.

"25 October - Even here at the ferry, no one could tell me further news of the regiment, except that all the troops had gone down the river. I decided it best to follow the river as long as people could tell me they had seen the boats. Need teaches prayer, but it also teaches one to use English. I could express myself to the extent that I could ask if a boat with soldiers had been seen, what their uniforms were like, etc. Mainly our guard caps served as a distinguishing characteristic, as these had caught everyone's eye. Night overtook me, and I turned in at the house where a true Hollander lived....

"26 October - I continued my journey. I passed through some abandoned rebel defenses. Twice I had to cross over water inlets, where I nearly drowned, as the boat was so full of holes. A black boatman. I arrived at Flushing just when a single-masted ship was preparing to sail to the army. The commanding officer could speak some Latin, and had the kindness to offer to take me with him. My companions were 24 oxen and a Hessian regimental quartermaster, Herr [Johann Andreas] Ungar [of the Minnigerode Grenadier Battalion]. The space was very crowded and we both had to sleep on a sailcloth. He had a bottle of wine and I had a loaf of bread. One shared with the other, and thus we had an evening meal."

[Waldeck retained none of these embarrassing details in the polished version of his diary which was published in the America Germania by Professor Learned.]

Although the Ansbach-Bayreuth troops did not arrive in New York until the following year, their joy must have been equally great. Captain Molitor recorded the entry into New York on 3 June 1777 in the following words. "At four o'clock in the afternoon we dropped anchor a rifle shot from the city. We were informed this evening by some English officers that General [William] Howe and his brother, the Admiral Lord Richard Howe, were in New York but the army was at Amboy and the campaign had not yet begun.

"4 June - The staff officers were sent to New York to receive orders from General Howe. They were told that the troops were to go to Staten Island the next day, to debark there, set up camp, and to recover [from the sea voyage]. In the city there were some English regiments and not far away stand various Hessian regiments, camped separately.... Here and there the colonists have laid out defensive positions but they have all been abandoned....

"5 June - The fleet sailed at eight o'clock and dropped anchor at Staten Island. At two o'clock we landed. The von Voit Regiment occupied the height on the shore to the right and had the Jaegers on another height in front of them. The von Eyb Regiment took the camp a mile farther to the left in the valley and posted pickets in the defenses on the height. In addition two English regiments are in the middle of the island and one on the point on the right side. Because of the approach of nightfall, all the necessities to set up camp could not be unloaded. Therefore, the regiment had to help during the night.

"6 June - The camp was set up and the provisions for the troops were brought from the ships."

Prechtel also recorded his thoughts on 2 June 1777 and on the following days concerning the arrival of the Ansbach-Bayreuth troops. "This morning, after finding bottom at forty fathoms, toward nine o'clock land could be seen. Thank God!...

"The fleet had to halt this evening because it was only thirty miles from Sandy Hook and could no longer enter the harbor at New York.

"3 June - At four o'clock this morning we sailed past Sandy Hook and Staten Island, in the Jerseys, on our left, and Long Island on our right.

'"At five o'clock in the evening we anchored in the seaport of New York close to Fort George....

"What our arrival in America seems to mean, is this: That we went aboard ship in Germany shortly after wintertime and came to America during the most beautiful summertime, when everything was in the most prosperous condition; came to this land and here have seen a true paradise....

"5 June - Our troops received orders that they were to debark at Staten Island. The transport ships therefore traveled three hours back [down the bay]. Also we were landed during the afternoon on this island near Cole's Ferry and entered our first camp close to the ferry.

"Anyone who has been on a ship for a long time, and comes on land, can believe nothing other than that the land quivers."

# 1776

## The Campaign from Canada

While the Hessians arriving at New York were greeted by the sight of a city and a developed rural landscape on Staten and Long Islands, the men from Brunswick and Hesse-Hanau sailed through a still wild, under-developed portion of Canada, along the St. Lawrence River. After leaving their ships, the 1776 contingents were immediately employed pursuing a retreating American army which had failed to capture Quebec during the past winter.

The anonymous diary probably written by Auditor Schaeffer of the Hesse-Hanau Regiment recorded the voyage up the St. Lawrence River as follows. "Toward evening [on 28 May] a small ship, with one mast, which had sailed from Quebec with 41 pilots meant for us on board, approached from the north side. Each transport ship was assigned one as a sure guide because of the dangerous voyage. The pilot had hardly come on board the ship before everyone's curiosity to see and speak with this first Canadian arose, not only to hear the news of the recapture of Quebec from rebel hands, but also to learn the situation inland, all of which he reported completely and truthfully.....

"30 May - A boatload of Brunswickers went on land to buy food.....

"1 June - To our joy and great astonishment, [at Quebec, we] met our long lost transport ship *Margaritha Mathias*, on board which were our colonel, his company, and half of the Grenadier Company, as well as many other war and transport ships. They had arrived two days previous and told us that ... already ships with troops had been sent to the second most important city, Montreal, as well as men on land, and an equal number to Trois Rivieres."

The diary then continues an account of the siege by the Americans under Generals Richard Montgomery and Benedict Arnold during the winter of 1775-76. General Guy Carleton was in command in the city. The diary continues, "I have not meant to neglect the cloister, which lies a half hour outside Quebec, in which the rebels had their hospital, and among the nuns were two sisters of General Carleton, who, as I will explain, had an important influence on the restoration of freedom to Quebec. They promised their brother, Governor and General

Carleton, above all, to give news of what the rebels were preparing to undertake and by means of a certain sign, ringing of a bell which was in the tower of the cloister and whose peal was very familiar to the inhabitants of the city. They actually did this, and on the day when the Americans planned their attack it was very dark and unfriendly weather. The inhabitants also anticipated an attack so that everyone felt that if this warning were not received, the city would surely be taken by the Americans. Therefore the two sisters gave the general the appropriate sign at the right time, so that the inhabitants took up their weapons and were placed in a defensive condition. About two o'clock in the afternoon General Montgomery attacked on one side and Brigadier Arnold, a former horse handler, on the other side of the city. They were at once beaten back and Montgomery remained, as he was about to climb a wall, on the spot, while Brigadier Arnold barely had time to retreat with his command....

General Arnold changed the siege into a blockade, remaining in place until 6 May 1776, when to the great joy of all the inhabitants of Quebec, the frigate *Surprise* entered the harbor at Quebec from England. This joy was doubled on 8 May when Commander Douglas also entered here with the warship *Thio*, of 54 guns, bringing some fresh troops who were immediately put ashore....

"On 3 June we again went into the city not only to eat, but also to visit the captured [American] officers.... Now the Brunswick Dragoons and the Prince Friedrich Regiment from Brunswick have received orders to land and will be garrisoned in Quebec."

That same day Captain Germann of the Hesse-Hanau Regiment wrote to his prince. "I arrived here in Quebec, with the company entrusted to me, on 1 June at six o'clock in the evening. All the non-commissioned officers and privates are well which is surprising considering the exceptionally long and very unpleasant voyage and the poor rations."

Captain Pausch had sailed from Europe with his artillery company at a later date and his letter written to the Prince from Chambly is dated 8 September 1776. "Since the fifth of this month I have once again , for the first time, been on dry land with my troops, and we have finally reached the place of our final destination. Possibly, however, even here our stop is for not more than a few days. Therefore it is possible that quite soon we may find ourselves in another province, but which one? If it is to be Pennsylvania, New York, or New England, will depend on the fortunes of war and the determination of our enemies. An expedition across Lake Champlain is to be undertaken in the next few days, according to all indications, with small boats and floating batteries, under the escort of several frigates and other armed ships being built on this lake, on which the Bostonians also have similar ships. If this day goes well and if we become masters of the enemy forts and defenses lying in the local mountains, then the situation will have a better outlook than that which exists here at present. Be the result as it may, it will be a difficult campaign for the officers at all times, especially because of the [shortage of] horses and the poor situation regarding their baggage transportation."

His arrival in Canada on 4 August 1776 and participation in the above mentioned expedition, which included a naval battle on Lake Champlain, were recorded in his journal. "4 August - Saw Cape Ray at nine o'clock in the morning on our right side, and opposite, on the left side, the North Cape, which together with this island creates the entrance to the channel, or the Gulf of St. Lawrence. Here, according to the reading from the quadrant and the statement by our ship's captain, we had to figure to have sailed 2,103 English miles from Portsmouth, and were now actually in the mentioned gulf.....

"12 August - Early in the morning, [we were] truly in the St. Lawrence River, south of Anticosti Island. Here a two-masted ship was encountered, which had rum and the wives of English soldiers on board. It was coming from Halifax and was delivering these wares to Quebec. There was a pilot from the island of Orleans, this side of Quebec, on board, with whom our captain reached an agreement to take us there.....

"19 August - We reached Quebec initially about five o'clock in the evening.... At Quebec we received the order to continue onward, under sail, with this favorable wind, to Montreal....

"Near Point Neuf we met a frigate, from which we were given a new order, to continue sailing.....

"28 August - ... The frigate *Blonde* lay at anchor [at Champlain] with orders for us to continue on to Trois Rivieres.... Last evening and this morning our ship scraped over two rocks so hard and with such a bump that it barely came off without any damage. The mate as well as the ship's captain and, from them, all of us, were not a little frightened because a short time previously we had passed an unfortunate ship, which two months earlier, in just such a manner, had been left on its side after having the rigging taken off. A few hours later, another order arrived [at Trois Rivieres] that we should depart with this transport ship toward Sorel, lying across Lake Pierre to the southward at the mouth of the Richelieu River. The mate and the captain refused to do this because of the many dangers and the shallow water.... Nevertheless, despite all those protests, it was absolutely to be done, with the expression, no matter how great the mentioned dangers might be. This order was delivered by a rather young gentleman from the navy. Here, the company having been so fortunate as to get this far, and in order to go another forty miles with this ship, to be placed in danger at once by being finally sacrificed in water, I also refused to sail farther, with the argument that my most gracious prince had transferred this artillery company to His Royal Majesty's service, but not to be drowned in the St. Lawrence River. Therefore I immediately went very quickly in a coach, overland, with Lieutenant Dufais -- because of his French language, I had to take him with me -- [to Montreal].

"But the general had taken his headquarters with the army to Chambly, a little more than nine English miles from Lake Champlain, where the [Hesse-Hanau] regiment and detachments were located, here and there, in camps and cantonments as far as Sorel."

Pausch was successful in preventing a continued forward movement in the transport ship, as noted in the journal entry for 1 September. "I had received orders in Chambly to canton in Trois Rivieres with my troops until the arrival of our cannons and all the equipment in the other ship, which were with the fleet. However, after my arrival, I found another order already there, namely to depart quickly for Chambly, in small boats, of which a great many have been made here of pine wood....

"2 September - ... At one o'clock in the afternoon I began debarkation [from the *Juno* and] at once ... sailed up the river with God's grace. In each boat there were two Canadian subjects as guides. There were eight boats and my men had to row, whether they could or not. As poorly as this began, it went just as well by the end."

Pausch's account continues, after further details about the forward movement, on 7 September. "The regiments continue to draw closer together and today some of them must march somewhat closer to St. Jean. The finished boats, which had lain here on the river, have for the most part been taken to Lake Champlain, which is still at this time occupied by both sides. Our side has two frigates on the lake, and according to indications, will make an expedition and attack thereon without waiting for the rest of the 2,000 Brunswick troops which have departed for that area. Supposedly the rebels have strongly fortified themselves in the mountains on the other side. Reportedly about 600 Indians are to make the attack over the mountains on the right wing. Everyone here must walk. I must walk with them, and to obtain a two-wheeled coach, for which every officer's batman must pay one shilling an hour, is not possible."

On 28 September Captain Pausch with part of his command was ordered on board the radeau, a large floating barge-like gun platform. "I complied with this order on the same day, embarked in small batteaux, departed, and arrived the same evening on board the radeau. It was already so well-filled with men that not all of them could be accommodated. We were all English because the space was too tight for an unpleasantness....

"29 September - We had no wind today and the radeau had to be pulled ahead by the troops. This was done by taking a heavy anchor ahead in a sloop and dropping the anchor in the lake. A strong line had been run through the anchor ring and tied to a pulley. By pulling the loose end of the line on the radeau, this heavy, flat piece was moved ahead. When there is a good wind, this heavy vessel moves very easily and well."

Pausch was ordered off the radeau on 1 October and recorded this order in his journal with the following comment. "I had wished for this order, which I received, since the first hour of going on board, as there was already all sorts of difficulties among the soldiers of both nations and in order to suppress this in their attitude and to maintain a good harmony, I no longer dared to leave the deck, because as soon as I did, first a sailor, then a soldier, then another, and then one of my men would start a quarrel.

"2 October - I camped on the Isle aux Noix where several days earlier the division of German troops, including the Hanau Regiment, had arrived.... His Excellency, [Lieutenant General John] Burgoyne commanded this entire corps."

As the English and German troops advanced on Lake Champlain, Pausch and his men were ordered to overtake and join them, traveling in batteaux. "10 October - Prior to daybreak I left from here and reached the radeau that evening, far beyond Point au Fer in Lake Champlain."

## The Battle of Valcour Island

"11 October - We had very good winds and early in the morning we raised anchor and set sail. At five o'clock in the morning we received the order, from batteau to batteau, to be prepared for an attack. Already at about ten-thirty a cannonfire was heard and shortly thereafter, with very good winds, all the batteaux came upon the enemy ships in a bay lying behind an island. One enemy frigate, named *Royal Savage*, with sixteen cannons, run aground on a small stone outcropping or island, which the enemy had already abandoned upon the arrival of the advance guard, was the first one we saw, and shortly thereafter two frigates engaged in a full and steady cannonade. In addition, they had several of the so-called gondolas, which came frequently, one after the other, from behind a bay of the island, fired lively and well, and then to regroup, retreated again, and then came out again. Our attack with the small, about 27, batteaux armed with 24 x 12- and 6-pound cannons and several howitzers, was furious and after all had come together, very lively. Finally, however, our frigates drew near and one, *Maria*, on board which was His Excellence, General Carleton, moved ahead and vigorously cannonaded the enemy with much accuracy. This one then moved to the side and somewhat to the rear and was then relieved by the *Carleton*. This was followed in turn by the third one, called *Inflexible*.

"One of the enemy frigates, of which two lay in a bow and quarter line or rather in staggered [echelon] formation behind one another, began making a move to one side. Nevertheless, despite this, it continued firing. The rebels directed their cannons none too badly, because our frigates, as I later saw, were patched with boards and caulking. During the affair, it could have been a bit after one o'clock, the naval battle became very serious. Lieutenant Dufais had the misfortune to run aground with all of his troops because his ammunition exploded when hit by an enemy cannonball. He stopped a great distance off to the right, and the sergeant major, whom I had with me in my batteau, first became aware of the fire. He called this to my attention as I was just in the process of directing my cannon. I could not immediately recognize the men, until shortly thereafter a case flew into the air and, after the smoke had cleared, I then recognized my troops by cords on their caps. This batteau came back burning furiously and I hurried in order to save the lieutenant and his crew, if possible, as by now his batteau was completely filled with water.

"Those who could, jumped into another batteau, which was also about to sink from being over-crowded. Finally a lieutenant of artillery by the name of Schmidt, came and took the lieutenant, Bombardier [Jacob] Engelhard, and one cannoneer into his batteau. I had taken the other nine cannoneers and nine sailors into my boat, together with my ten cannoneers, one drummer, one sergeant, and ten sailors, altogether 42 people in this small batteau, so that I was now overloaded and no longer in condition to move away from the spot where I had embarked these half-lost individuals, and taken them on board. Here I had each moment to fear suddenly drowning both myself and all those with me. As it would soon be evening, the batteaux pulled back.

"The radeau now arrived, but not until dusk. Because of weak, although favorable winds, this vessel could not move swiftly. Nevertheless, it tested its 24-pound cannons against the enemy frigates, but the distance was too great so that no cannonball could have effect, and furthermore, nightfall prevented the radeau moving farther forward. A chain was made with all the batteaux during the night, and everyone had to be awake and alert. In the dark the frigate, which had run aground and been captured, was set on fire on orders of His Excellence and the munitions thereon exploded. This provided a very brilliant fire as the ship burned throughout the night.

"Until now nothing more occurred, because the enemy frigates remained lying at the same place, where they had defended themselves. Toward morning it became apparent that they had escaped. We hurried after them, and several of the enemy vessels were overtaken. Five large and small ones had entered a bay on the left bank. All of them were set on fire and burned. During the following night, I, together with several armed English batteaux, separated from the fleet. Therefore during the entire night I had to row with certainty and then uncertainty, in order not to be left behind. Toward morning however,

I was lucky enough, at daybreak, to meet several English, who had the same fate as I had. Still others came behind me so that both timely, and with the others, on

"13 October - I arrived at nine o'clock in the morning at Crown Point. From this time until

"23 October - all the batteaux, 21 in number, the others were detached, formed a chain on the river every night. During the mornings, from ten to eleven o'clock, the batteaux sailed to each bank. The troops cooked and ate, and when the sun set, lay themselves again at anchor in the river.... There was no shortage of the necessary provisions. Everyone received enough salted meat, zwieback, and rum. They are respected by our Indians, trading and buying fresh mutton and beef from them, so that during the entire time the privates and non-commissioned officers have not missed the least thing. However, on the officers' part, they are short of tea, coffee, wine, and other cold drinks. During this affair, Lieutenant Dufais lost Cannoneer [Johann] Rossmer, who was killed; Drummer [Jacob] Billand [or Billiu] and the helmsman were burned to death; and a sailor, when the cannoneer was killed, had his leg shot off by the cannonball, which had bored through the bow under the cannon support, three inches above the water."

Captain Pausch continued on to St. John and Longueuil, where he received orders to enter winter quarters at Montreal, and then at Pointe aux Trembles, in the brigade of Brigadier Wilhelm Rudolph von Gall.

"Here in the barracks my company received six large rooms with fireplaces, and my junior officers two of the same. All the artillery captains, including me, are quartered in the city.

"In each common room are ten bedsteads with two men per bed. Every Saturday wood and coal are received from the supply magazine, also candles. Every week good provisions are issued in a sufficient amount. Throughout almost the entire winter the men have received fresh meat and a very good bread. Now however, except for the sick, they receive salted beef or pork, and a very good butter issued one pound per man per week. Almost every time they also receive peas and oatmeal, whenever salted meat is issued. For this uniquely good care, the company has General [William] Phillips to thank, who is as concerned that the portions are as good for them as for his own and the other Royal Artillery companies. Upon entering winter quarters, upon orders of the general,... winter clothing was supplied."

According to the von Gall Order Book, General Sir Guy Carleton made the following brigade assignments for German officers on 28 October 1776, while the troops were in winter quarters. "Colonel von Specht is announced as brigadier general with the army. He commands the 1st Brigade of German troops, consisting of the [Brunswick] von Rhetz and Specht Regiments; Brigadier von Gall commands the 2nd Brigade, consisting of the [Brunswick] Prince Friedrich and the Hesse-Hanau Regiments. As the von Riedesel Regiment lies in general quarters, it will stand alone this winter, but is to come under the orders of Brigadier Specht eventually. The [Brunswick] Dragoons, Grenadiers, and Light Infantry also remain unassigned and at the disposition of His Excellency, General Carleton....

"It is worth mentioning that all French noblemen, priests, and the captains of militia are free of the obligation of providing winter quarters, and one or two quarters must be left unoccupied in each parish in order to provide convenient quarters to officers traveling in the King's service, whether English or German. Otherwise the regiments are to be spread as evenly as possible, and it is wished the men can be assigned one or two together."

Thereafter directives were also issued on quarters, wood-cutting, price-fixing, treatment of venereal disease, practice on snowshoes, and even on the proper way to store batteaux during the winter. Finally, orders were published authorizing cash awards for wounds or deaths and a thanksgiving celebration for the liberation of Canada.

"General Orders in Headquarters, Quebec, 16 December 1776

"Negotiations in London have provided a sum of money for those soldiers wounded or killed in the service of the King in America, specifically, ten thalers for a wounded individual and for the widow of one killed, five pounds, which they will receive upon presentation of an attestation by an officer under whom her husband served, and the wounded are to be paid by the Receiver-General of the Province, Mr. Dunn. -- [Julius Ludwig August] von Pollnitz, Brigade Major

"Trois Rivieres, 22 December 1776

"On orders of His Excellency, General Carleton, a thanksgiving celebration is to be held on the 31st of this month in honor of the liberation of Canada. Those regiments which have chaplains are to conduct church services on that day and the chaplains are to preach on this subject. -- von Pollnitz, Brigade major"

## The Campaign in the New York Area

The Hessians on Staten Island had hardly gotten their land legs back when preparations to attack the Americans on Long Island began. Rueffer wrote on 17 August 1776, "As the cartridges which we brought from Hesse are mostly spoiled, we have turned in our cartridges and each man has received sixty new ones, but the younger recruits waste powder."

Next day he recorded, "There was a strong exchange of cannon-fire this morning in the harbor at New York between three English and four American frigates. The first wished to reconnoiter the harbor and apparently they did very little harm. The Hessian Grenadiers and Jaegers and four English regiments received orders today to be transferred over to Long Island. About eight o'clock however, because of incessant rain, they were ordered back.

"19 August - Today nine English battalions were embarked. The brigade of General [Johann Daniel] Stirn occupied their camp, as it was feared the rebels in New Jersey would make a descent against us because the water near this place was very shallow.....

"21 August - All the Hessian Grenadiers and one company of Jaegers were embarked today in order to approach the shore of Long Island tonight, thus making the attack that much easier tomorrow morning. General [Charles, Earl] Cornwallis commands the entire operation.... We had a much stronger storm today that no one can remember ever having experienced a stronger one."

Reuber's report of 20 August 1776 begins correctly but then contains events of a later date. "All the English and Hessian Jaegers, the detached Grenadiers, and all the light troops received the order to be transferred to Long Island, where the rebels were in defenses and camps. All the English warships which lay at anchor in the harbor made a chain, one behind the other, on the enemy side toward Long Island. Then all the soldiers were put in small ships and had to hang on behind the large warships so the enemy could not see them. When everything was ready, all the warships suddenly began firing their cannons at the rebels on Long Island. The Americans retreated, abandoning everything. As soon as they had left their positions, the boats with all the soldiers pulled up and set them on shore on the enemy side and the soldiers at once moved forward toward Flatbush."

Lieutenant von Bardeleben recorded the heavy rain and the English frigates firing on New York on 18 August. Then on 20 August wrote in his diary that, "Our Grenadiers and the English Light Infantry were ordered to be ready to march."

But bad weather returned on 21 August. "From seven o'clock yesterday evening until one o'clock at night we had the most terrible weather. No one could remember ever having had such a storm. Lightning, thunder claps, storms, and driving rain, all in extremes. My tent, surrounded by a constant fire, seemed to tremble with the ground at every thunder peal. At ten o'clock in the evening three English brigades and our Grenadiers and Jaegers embarked on some transport ships and lay at anchor at a certain distance from Long Island....

"22 August - At six o'clock in the morning the embarked brigades, a few hundred light cavalry, as well as the English Light Infantry, Grenadiers, and Scots, were landed on Long Island from small boats. The warships had lain for some time as close to the shore as possible in order to provide support against any resistance. Although the rebels had a strength of more than 5,000 men and, if needed, could have been reinforced quickly from New York, they allowed our troops to land unopposed and made not the least resistance. Our corps immediately advanced, occupied the level fields and the nearby lying city of Flatbush, without being bothered by the rebels.....

"25 August - The Hereditary Prince, von Donop, von Mirbach, von Knyphausen, von Lossberg, and Rall Regiments were transferred across to Long Island. We joined the others and camped in the region of Flatbush."

During the following days several minor incidents occurred in which the Hessians and Americans exchanged fire. Rueffer recorded some of this activity. "23 August - We still remained quietly here [on Staten Island]. On the other hand, our Grenadiers and Jaegers on Long Island have small skirmishes daily. Still the enemy every time gets the worst of it.

"24 August - We changed our camp today and are again in battalion formation. In another skirmish on Long Island today the worthy Colonel [Carl Emil Ulrich von] Donop was in danger of being shot by an enemy sharpshooter, or as they are called, rifleman. By the greatest good fortune when the rebel met him, the rebel's rifle misfired, so the colonel took his weapon and shot him through the head. [It is not clear whose weapon was used by the colonel.] Major [Georg Henrich] Pauli of the Artillery and Lieutenant von Donop, adjutant to Colonel von Donop, were both slightly wounded. One jaeger was killed and five wounded, and ten grenadiers were wounded.

"25 August - At twelve o'clock tonight the Stirn and Mirbach Brigades ... received orders to be ready by the water at eleven o'clock to be transferred across to Long Island. As soon as we landed on that side and assembled, we began to march. Toward evening we joined Cornwallis' corps and moved into camp at Gravesend, where the Hessian headquarters was set up. We found this corps had very little concealment. About one hundred yards from our front was a thick forest in which many rebels were lurking. We had been allowed to bring nothing but tents and the most necessary items from our baggage.... The Lossberg Brigade ... remained on Staten Island. We passed through a pleasant region, now and again country homes which had been completely destroyed. This island is about 160 miles long and in many places 25 miles wide, very fertile and pleasant.

"26 August - We moved a few miles farther to the settlement of Flatbush. Lieutenant [Johann Conrad] Schraidt and I were ordered to cover the riflemen and a short distance ahead could vaguely see the rebels. A picket of the 71st Scottish Regiment was constantly engaged with the enemy close by my post."

Although Reuber's date of 21 August is obviously incorrect, he provided an account of an incident which, if true, must have endeared Colonel Rall to all of his men. "All the remaining regiments were carried across the harbor to Long Island and landed behind the detached grenadiers. They all marched toward New York and the warships also moved before the city and anchored. Colonel Rall with his grenadier regiment entered the line in the brigade commanded by General von Mirbach. The Old Lossberg Regiment was on the right.[9] The Knyphausen Regiment was on the left wing, and the Rall Grenadier Regiment in the middle of the brigade. 'It had the duty of protecting the flag.' We now stood in the line before Flatbush and the entire army moved forward toward a woods in which the rebels were hiding. The Rall Regiment had to turn to the right and pass through a narrow opening through which we could see a rebel corps of fifty men with flags flying, coming toward the Rall Regiment. Colonel Rall ordered the regiment to fire at the Americans. When they saw what was in store they surrendered and dropped their weapons, calling out, 'Pardon!', and laid down all of their equipment before the Rall Regiment. A non-commissioned officer of our regiment seized the rebel flag and wanted to present it to Colonel Rall at the head of the regiment. Before this could be accomplished, Brigadier General von Mirbach came riding from the left flank and tried to take the American flag captured by our regiment from the hands of the non-commissioned officer and claim the prize for himself as brigade general. However, the colonel said, 'Nothing doing, general. My grenadiers captured the flag and they shall keep it and no one will take it from them.' Therefore they separated in anger and both intended to enter a complaint at headquarters. But what happened? Colonel Rall was named inspector general of his brigade."

Lieutenant Piel, of the Lossberg Regiment, also noted the movement of his regiment to Long Island on 25 August and briefly described the island. "We were transferred across to Long Island in flat boats after our Grenadiers and several English regiments had already made this landing several days previously....

"Today [26 August] we changed our camp and set it up near Flatbush. The enemy had occupied every height and thicket ahead of us. Colonel [Henrich Anton] von Heeringen was commanded to occupy an advance post with 300 men. The rebels fired heavily with small arms against this command; cannonshots from our side silenced them."

Bardeleben provides further details on Heeringen's command of 26 August and also recorded a description of Long Island. "As the enemy had a detachment in the woods on our front [according to a marginal note], they attacked single outposts now and then, from that place. To prevent this, Colonel Heeringen ordered the pickets of Stein and Mirbach Brigades, which amounted to 250 men, to occupy a mill, lying to our left, on the water. The two brigades, Stein and Mirbach, changed camp and marched one mile farther inland. On this march signs of the enemy's mood were found everywhere. During their flight from our initial landing on this island, they left behind burned-out houses, grain standing in the fields, some of it in ashes, and the road lined with dead cattle. Now and again old people, with sad glances, looked back at their homes, which the flames had destroyed and which appeared previously to have been a paradise standing in blooming abundance. Our regiment was camped amidst orchards of apple and pear trees. Here, too, the picture of destruction was to be seen on all sides. Almost everywhere there were chests of drawers, chairs, mirrors with gold-gilded frames, porcelain, and all sorts of items of the best and most expensive manufacture. It was sad to see how all this and also our things, misused and destroyed, were lying about. At seven o'clock in the evening the Scots and English marched off and took positions far beyond our right wing, in order to try to attack the enemy's rear. Quite good weather."

Regimental Quartermaster Zinn, of the von Donop Regiment, also recorded the regiment's move to Long Island on 26 August. "Our regiment broke camp on Staten Island and sailed in flat boats to Long Island, where we entered camp not far from Flatbush."

### The Battle of Long Island

Zinn then summarized the role of the regiment in the Battle of Long Island on 27 August 1776. "The enemy was attacked by the English at daybreak. The von Donop Regiment was in camp just below the hill which the Grenadiers marched up in order to attack the enemy. The regiment had to move out at about ten o'clock in the morning and occupy the woods behind the Grenadiers. The regiment made no direct contact with the enemy, but several patrols sent out captured 83 rebels, including eight officers. We remained under arms, near these woods, during the night and until the morning of 28 August.

However, Lieutenant Bardeleben, also of the von Donop Regiment, provides a much more detailed account in his 27 August entry. "Early, before daybreak, a heavy firing was heard beyond our right wing. It was soon learned that the English and Scots, who had marched yesterday evening, had fallen on the enemy flank and attacked. -- *The commanding general-in-chief had not informed Lieutenant [General] von Heister of this plan.*[10]

"At seven o'clock in the morning we broke camp, also. Our Grenadiers closed to the English on the right and formed the middle [of the line]. The other Hessian regiments occupied all the heights and valleys around the woods. Shortly after taking these positions, the English had already overrun the enemy flank and the enemy retreated to the heights in the center, where our Grenadiers had planned to take post. However, even here, it was necessary for the enemy to withdraw farther without being able to make any resistance.

"Because of the landscape and the terrible hills, they could not be attacked *en masse* but only by groups. All the regiments at once sent strong patrols, as strong as possible, in general, to attack the enemy. Only then did a general engagement begin. The enemy, who was surrounded on all sides by small arms fire, suddenly fell into the greatest confusion, scattered, and therefore soon fell into our hands, first to this patrol and then to the next, completely cut up, without having offered any great resistance. I was sent with some volunteers into a woods lying in front of us to seek out that which could not be found."

Following a brief coded entry which I could not decipher, he continues, "I saw nothing. One of our soldiers found a silver mounted knife. Another patrol from our regiment brought in many prisoners, however. [Code - Many high ranking individuals at this time shed their ideas of being heroes. The prisoners who knelt and sought to surrender were beaten.] This skirmishing lasted four or five hours. According to all estimates, the rebels suffered 1,200 dead and wounded and 1,097 prisoners.... The Hessians suffered two privates killed and 25 privates wounded. All the other rebels fled, part into the defenses which they had at Brooklyn Ferry, directly opposite New York, and part hid in the woods. The rebels who were in complete confusion could have been pursued on this day and attacked in their defenses with great success, and their entire strength of 10,000 men, which had occupied this island, would have been ours, if the commander-in-chief had not called a 'halt'.

"All the regiments had to remain in their camps, under arms the entire night, because the woods had not been cleared [of rebels]. The clothing of the enemy is bad. A few wear black, white, or violet linen, short blouses with fringes, and of a Spanish style. They also have a linen sack in which they carry their rations, and a powder horn. Others, on the other hand, have nothing but a wretched farmer's costume and a weapon. Most of their officers are no better dressed and until recently were only ordinary manual laborers.

"Lieutenant General von Heister, who had remained with our regiment during this affair, had all the prisoners captured by the Hessians brought to him and then held them under a detachment behind our regiment. A number of wounded were treated and others were gradually sent from here to where they could more safely be guarded. His Excellence engaged in conversation with several rebel officers and gave them wine with which to drink the health of the King of England. One of these officers, however, who was a well-situated schoolmaster, refused to accept the glass because he did not want to drink the King's health. He was told and threatened with being shot dead on the spot if he continued to act like a rebel here. Nevertheless, all the threats were to no avail. He answered in each instance that he was a school teacher and because he felt it a duty to his position and had tried with all his effort to instruct his students never to declare themselves for the King, he would gladly sacrifice his life and lose everything before he would change his sentiment."

Lieutenant Rueffer recorded the events of the day from his position with the von Mirbach Regiment. "Our commands and pickets were engaged with the enemy the entire night. As day broke the Grenadiers moved out of their camp to make the first serious assault. It was not long before the firing increased. Toward eight o'clock General von Heister came and ordered the Stirn and Mirbach Brigades to break camp at once, which was done. Adjutant Lieutenant [Carl Levin] Marquard withdrew the Hereditary Prince Regiment in order to advance it toward the Grenadier Battalion von Minnigerode. Donop [Regiment] won a height in its front without meeting resistance. The Mirbach Brigade ... for the most part covered our left flank. Our regiment advanced on the height with Donop on our left. As soon as we reached this point, the enemy opened fire on us with small arms from the woods. As nothing was to be accomplished however, because of the great protection afforded the entire [enemy] battalion, Lieutenant Schraidt and I were sent into the thicket with some eighty flankers, which resulted in each of us taking some captives in a distance of only about fifteen yards. The enemy were hidden in the thickest bushes and no one could have known where they were if they had not made their presence known by firing on their opponents. They were all so fearful and would almost rather be shot dead than surrender, because their generals and other officers had told them they would be hanged. Because our drive had such success, we continued the push until after dark and the command led by Lieutenant Schraidt and me captured 61 prisoners, including eleven officers. I was fortunate enough to capture a horse with a saddle and bridle, which according to our captives had belonged to a Colonel Miglain of the sharpshooters, who had been shot dead. They could not have been taken for soldiers as they had no uniforms, but only torn blouses of all colors; no similar weapons, but one had a musket while another was armed with a rifle. Our entire corps bivouacked this night."

Then continuing in an entry of 26 August, which probably should be dated 28 August, he reported the next day's activity. "This morning at daybreak we were again sent into the woods with our flankers of yesterday to seek out those rebels still in hiding. We only found 23 men. Toward nine o'clock we returned to camp, received orders to make a change, and marched about two miles farther, where we again had the rebels very close to our front and were only separated from them by a swamp. During yesterday's affair the rebels lost two generals, [John] Sullivan and [William Alexander, Lord] Stirling, 35 other officers, and 485 men, all of whom were captured alive."

Finally, the Lossberg Regiment's participation in the battle was recorded by Lieutenant Piel on 27 August, as follows. "Today the enemy was attacked on all sides. The Lossberg Regiment advanced up to a woods, which was full of rebels, and was ordered to halt there. Meanwhile, Lieutenant [Hermann Henrich Georg] Zoll with fifty volunteers was sent into the woods and exchanged shots with the rebels, killing and wounding several and brought out 64 prisoners, among whom were six officers. Our regiment had no one wounded. After the enemy had everywhere been driven back, we spent the night lying under the open sky."

Following the Battle of Long Island, Lieutenant Bardeleben's diary contains frequent references to interesting incidents. "28 August - From two o'clock in the afternoon until seven o'clock in the evening, even as we moved into camp, it rained without let up and very heavily. Our tents were so wet that they were barely able to keep out the water. In such a rain I was sent out with a detail of thirty men to help cover our regiment, or so I was told, at least. It appears to be the general's intention in this war to be very deliberate in his efforts. Two English soldiers came with the order for our colonel that the pickets were to hurry with the two soldiers to the support of an English detachment which had been pinned down under fire for some time. I marched with my troops to the desired location. Instead, however, of covering the regiment, I was sent about two miles away from it. I arrived at my designated position and, according to my orders, reported to an English major under whose command several pickets served. This major ordered me to take my post immediately. Because I did not know where I was, had no knowledge of where the rebels were, nor what forces were to my left or rear, I asked for the information first. However, the major gave me this answer. I could place the posts at my discretion. The rebels had their many posts about 200 yards away, to the left and behind us. Then I sent out patrols. By so doing I learned that our rear was secure, but far to the left we had no one. If the rebels had only a little courage and determination all of our pickets could have been captured. Because I did not have enough men to occupy this pass, I detached a non-commissioned officer with a few soldiers to go there and also sent out frequent patrols.

"29 August - The night was quiet and no rebels were seen. Some of my troops fired, but it was too dark to be able to recognize anyone. In the morning before daybreak, my command was reinforced by six jaegers and one officer and twenty men moved up on my left. As soon as it was light the rebels began moving about a great deal and began working diligently on their defenses. Many also risked sneaking up on us. The jaegers fired at them, wounding several. Their audacity disappeared and they sought revenge. They had barely regained their redoubt when they opened fire with cannons and cannonaded us. Their aim was excellent. As soon as two or three men were seen, a cannonball was on its way and often hit near the sentries. At seven o'clock in the morning they ceased this activity and everything was quiet. I was relieved at seven o'clock in the evening by Captain Venator with two officers and 100 men, who were then fully capable of occupying my posts. Marching back into camp I lost the way and had to go a long way before I found the camp. I had almost feared falling into the rebels' hands, as it was impossible to see your hand before your face. I marched from one [camp] to the next until I finally entered a Hessian camp, where I received the necessary directions. All day long rebels had been brought in who had hidden in the woods on the 27th and sought thus to escape to return to their troops.

"30 August - In the morning no rebels were to be seen. They had evacuated all their defenses and taken flight during the past night. Lieutenant Colonel [Ernst Rudolph] von Schieck, who commanded all the pickets and detachments, discovered their flight at daybreak. He immediately advanced, sent a captain with ninety grenadiers into the enemy lines, and 24 of these men then occupied their largest position. General [James] Grant, who commanded the left wing, had the brigade of Colonel von Donop follow at once. At three o'clock in the afternoon the von Lossberg and von Donop Regiments occupied the enemy defenses opposite New York as well as those houses lying along the shore. The enemy had in part crossed to New York at Brooklyn Ferry, and in part gone to Red Hook, a small, nearby island.

"The rebel defenses of the so-called Brooklyn Line were of the type that determined troops could have held against a far stronger enemy than we were. They had star fortifications on the wings. The line itself also had the same. The right wing was also protected by a marsh and woods, and was also strengthened by small outworks and an abatis. Also on this wing there was a large battery on Red Hook Island to cover the channel from New York and the woods. The left wing was protected by a strong abatis. The front had double palisades the entire length of the trenches, half trenches, and all surrounded by an abatis. Behind these defenses, on all the hills, were redoubts, some well-started, some finished, including one 'snail' redoubt with a casement for 300 men provided with rations, and the so-called Stirling Redoubt, which was occupied by five companies, both lying opposite New York and being the most significant. At every position we found a great amount of provisions and ammunition, and many cannons, although most were spiked. Our regiment occupied three positions lying along the shore. In one of these, where I was, there were 250 men and three staff officers. Toward five o'clock in the evening the English Artillery joined us with four 24-pound cannons, in order to fire upon a detachment of about 200 rebels who were directly ahead of us on a small island called Governor's Island, and who were being transferred to New York in small boats. Firing against these had barely commenced when the order arrived to cease fire. As it did not cease immediately, two boats occupied by about twenty men were sunk by the English.

"31 August - At six o'clock in the evening the von Knyphausen Regiment relieved us. We returned to our camp. Governor's Island was occupied this evening by a captain, two officers, and 100 men, who were taken there in sloops. Otherwise everything was peaceful. Good weather.

"Four 18-pound cannons and six 32-pound cannons were found on Governor's Island.....

"14 September - At six o'clock in the evening we were notified to break camp tomorrow at daybreak. Good weather."

A marginal note on 15 September notes that, "Lieutenant General von Heister with six English regiments and the von Mirbach Brigade remained in camp on Long Island. The von Mirbach Brigade -- von Lossberg, von Knyphausen, and Rall Regiments."

The account for that date then continues.

## Kip's Bay

"At three o'clock in the morning we broke camp and marched along the South River to the place where the troops were to be embarked. The baggage was left behind. At nine o'clock in the morning we arrived at our designated place and found the small boats waiting, which came from the warships that had arrived during the night. At ten o'clock in the morning the English Light Infantry, the Scots, our Grenadiers and Jaegers, and a part of the English with a little artillery were embarked. Each small boat could carry sixty to seventy men. Five warships, which were in the East River to protect the crossing, took these boats between them and sailed briefly on the water.

"The rebels, who had only a few batteries and guns in their lines on the shore, seemed confused by these various maneuvers by the ships and could not determine where we would land. Soon the frigates drew together, formed a line as near as possible to the shore, and fired a terrible cannonade against the enemy batteries and guns. The enemy evacuated his lines under this cannonade and pulled back into the woods. Our troops landed without the least resistance being made. They immediately formed with the English on the right, the Grenadiers on the left, and marched off against the enemy, who had quickly sought shelter a few hundred yards ahead of them in a woods. Our forces attacked by companies. The Block Grenadier Battalion, which constituted the left wing, encountered a rebel regiment of 500 men, which indicated it wished to surrender. However, when the battalion approached, the regiment fled, firing a general volley backwards from weapons lying over their shoulders. This killed two men and wounded thirteen. A colonel, two captains, a brigade major, five lieutenants, and 47 privates, of the 500 rebels, were captured. At four o'clock in the afternoon the rest of the English and General Stirn's Brigade were transferred across the river. Stirn's Brigade followed the others, without, however, making contact with the enemy. After a march of three or four English miles, the troops halted at a good position.

"The garrison at New York abandoned the city as soon as they heard of our landing, marching alongside the North River and then occupied the forts in the area."

Quartermaster Zinn of the von Donop Regiment recorded the activity of his regiment, beginning on 15 and 16 September in far fewer words. "15 September - At two-thirty in the morning the regiment broke camp, leaving knapsacks and tents, as well as the regimental artillery, behind, and marched farther up the East River, where it then was carried across the river at four o'clock in the afternoon with the Hereditary Prince and Mirbach Regiments, as the three regiments now constituted the brigade of Major General von [sic] Stirn, landing in the region called Turtle Bay, and occupied a height not far from the bay, where it bivouacked this night until

"16 September - when we entered the camp site designated for the regiment near Bayard's house on the North River."

Rueffer recorded the activity of the von Mirbach Regiment beginning on 14 September as follows. "This evening we received orders to march tomorrow morning at two-thirty....

"15 September - Yesterday's orders were put into effect today. At three o'clock everyone was under arms and we marched off from the left. About six o'clock General Grant's Division, to which our brigade belongs, halted. A short time later a strong firing of both cannons and small arms was to be heard, which was our warships firing at the enemy shore. General Clinton then moved his first division,... into the flatboats which were ready on the shore and made his attack, whereupon the second division immediately followed and landed at Purtee Bay on New York Island, fortunately without the least resistance. The enemy had fled from all his positions and this prevented our making many captives. Because of a language misunderstanding the Grenadier Company of the Wutginau Regiment suffered one man killed and eleven wounded, when Captain [Friedrich] von Eschwege attacked a troop which wished to lay down its arms. Because he did not understand and continued to advance, the enemy kept their weapons and kept firing during their retreat. Because we had left our baggage behind, we spent the night behind the Grenadiers, without our tents.

## The Battle of Harlem Heights

"Monday, 16 September - Our situation during the past night was not pleasant. It was so terribly cold all night that despite our many and large fires, there was no protection from the cold. We lay in bushes and the area seemed to have more rocks than dirt. The rural homes in this region suffered some, even much, damage. All their livestock was seized; also all other useful items were not left lying about. And never before have so many geese, chickens, ducks, sheep, cattle, and pigs been slaughtered, as were killed during the night from yesterday evening to this morning. Very early this morning a strong enemy troop moved into position ahead of the English outposts and immediately attacked the Light Infantry. -- The troops drove the English into their outer defenses. When the enemy discovered the weakness of the English, his forces were reinforced by a new corps of 2,000 or 3,000 men, which attacked these three regiments. The English reserve, the Linsing Grenadier Battalion and the Jaegers, with two field pieces, hurried forward to assist while the Minnigerode and Block Grenadier Battalions occupied the defile along both sides of the road to New York, to cover the rear. As a result the enemy was driven back into his outer defenses with heavy losses. The Scots and Light Infantry suffered seventy dead and 150 wounded during this affair. Our Jaegers had one officer, Lieutenant [Johannes] Heinrich, and seven men wounded. Good weather."

Rueffer recorded the following significant events, including the burning of New York and the capture of Nathan Hale, during the dates indicated. "21 September - There was a great fire behind our front at twelve o'clock at night, which we assumed to come from New York, and which we found to be the case as soon as it was light. About 100 rebels, who had remained hidden in the empty houses and cellars, set the fire and even though the English garrison, which consisted of three battalions, turned out at once, two churches and 400 houses to windward were laid in ashes. One of these criminals was thrown into the fire, another hung by the legs and burned....

"22 September - Today an enemy spy was captured near the English artillery park. [This was probably Nathan Hale.]....

"11 October - Tonight at eleven o'clock nearly all the English, as well as the Hessian Grenadiers and Jaegers, marched, even the Leib Regiment and the Prince Charles and Ditfurth Regiments, which until now have remained on Staten Island, and even the Lossberg, Knyphausen, and Rall Regiments, which were on Long Island. The English and Donop Brigades were landed on the East River and all the listed regiments landed at Rockpoint in Connecticut, a peninsula considered part of New York [?]. General von Heister went with this corps. Here at Blumenthal four English regiments and the Stirn Brigade remain under the command of [Hugh], Lord Percy.....

"18 October - Today our third fleet dropped anchor between Staten and Long Islands.[11] It contained the Wutginau Regiment, Grenadier Battalion Koehler, the four garrison regiments of von Stein, von Wissenbach, von Huyn, and von Buenau, as well as one company of Jaegers, one company of Artillery, and a Waldeck regiment. General von Knyphausen and Major General [Martin] von Schmidt are with this fleet.....

"25 October - It was reported that on the 23rd, the third fleet passed up the East River in flatboats and landed at Frog Neck and encamped near New Rochelle."

Bardeleben made similar observations and notations during the same period. "Saturday, 21 September - During the past night the rebels set fire to a number of places in New York. At midnight flames broke out everywhere in the northern part of the city. A strong wind helped their plan. More than 500 houses, including the best in the city, and the English and Lutheran churches were victims of the flames. Those individuals, who could save almost nothing from this disaster and who were taken by surprise during their sleep by this midnight fire, were fortunate enough to save their lives. The English Grenadier Brigade, which was in camp just outside the city, hurried there along with the sailors and by nine o'clock in the morning had prevented the entire city from being laid in ashes. Everything was in confusion and the garrison had difficulty restoring order. Several persons were arrested, who were running about with incendiary materials with which to set additional fires. The evil intentions of this nation can not be described. One, disturbed at his intended activity and who had to flee, called back during his flight that if he could not carry out his intent, he would still find opportunity later to set fire in the city. Another, who planned to set his own house on fire, but who was prevented from doing so by his wife who hugged him and tearfully asked him not to do so, was so cruel that when his wife would not let go of him, he nearly cut her hand off with his knife. The soldiers, who came to her rescue, grabbed this malcontent and hanged him without ceremony on his own house. Several other suspicious persons were now and again thrown into the flames.....

"Monday, 23 September - I rode to New York. The fire still burned in several places near the North River. [Even] the worst houses were occupied and there was almost nothing unoccupied. The shortage of money is noticeable everywhere and only paper money was in use. It already has no value, except that which has the royal seal has the same value as gold and silver. Good weather.

"24 September - An English regiment landed on Paulus Hook under the cover of a warship. This peninsula had to be occupied according to the plan so that the enemy could not fire on the city. Until today the rebels still had one which fired intermittently on the city, but upon the approach of the warship, it had been withdrawn. Good weather. At ten o'clock in the morning our brigade was mustered.

"25 September - Dysentery is rampant in the Hessian corps and a great many lay dangerously ill from its effects. In our regiment I was almost the only one free of the disease. Good weather.

"Thursday, 26 September - Lieutenant General Howe began raising provincial regiments. General [Oliver] DeLancey was in charge of the recruiting and made Hamster on Long Island the assembly point. Although that island is under the control of the King's weapons, there are still a great many secret traitors thereon. They seek only a slight advantage before showing their rebel inclinations. One of the officers of the mentioned [provincial] corps is proof of this. He was secretly shot by a resident when on his way from Petforth to Flatbush. Today Colonel Heeringen of the Lossberg Regiment was buried. He died of dysentery from which we have lost many, and still a large number of men lie dangerously ill. Good weather.....

"11 October - Nothing new during my duty. The night was very cold. At ten o'clock in the evening our Grenadiers and Light Infantry marched to the East River in order to go aboard ship.... I bathed this afternoon in the North River. At one o'clock last night the Grenadiers and English Light Infantry embarked near Hellgate in eighty sloops. One of these boats, occupied by 25 English artillerymen with three cannons, ran aground there. The cannons and thirteen men were lost and the others saved themselves. At nine o'clock in the morning the troops landed in Connecticut, fifteen English miles from their place of embarkation and marched inland without meeting any great resistance. During the afternoon Lieutenant General von Heister, with his corps of six English regiments and the von Mirbach Brigade, crossed from Long Island to Connecticut and joined the other troops. Good weather. I bathed. The water was very cold but felt good.....

"14 October - Twenty provision ships with 600 recruits arrived. These men, who had been recruited in Germany for the Schreiber Corps[12], were immediately distributed among the English regiments.....

"Friday, 18 October - The English Lieutenant General Howe transferred with his corps to another side of Connecticut named New Rochelle. Colonel [Friedrich Wilhelm] von Lossberg's Regiment, which previously had been on Staten Island, and the Ditfurth, Leib, and Prince Charles Regiments joined the army, leaving only the Truembach Regiment on Staten Island.....

"27 October - At six o'clock in the morning we received orders to be ready to march immediately. At eight o'clock our brigade, less the von Mirbach Regiment which had to remain in camp, and the English moved in front of the enemy lines not far from Fort Washington. Near, about 2,000 yards, in front of the first abatis we halted, brought up our cannons, and fired most of the day against their trenches. The enemy appeared to think our attack was a sham and not meant in earnest. They remained quietly in their trenches and laughed at us for firing such a heavy cannonade. Although we were a few thousand yards from them, they fired their rifles so effectively at our outposts that two guys from the Hereditary Prince Regiment were wounded. In marching through the woods, which lay just before our camp, I commanded the leading element and when our regiment halted, I was sent with a detachment to establish outposts a few hundred yards ahead of the regiment. The von Donop Regiment was on the left wing, and occupied the side from the North River to the command post. The Hereditary Prince Regiment was beside us and in front of a woods with their command post therein. English were on the right wing and extended close to the Harlem River, where the enemy lines ended. The rebels fired on all these units sporadically so that no one dared raise his head, and when they saw our posts were to be relieved, ten or fifteen men would fire at the same time. Toward evening everything quieted down. At seven o'clock in the evening I relieved Lieutenant [Emanuel Rosinus] Hausmann and the regiment remained in bivouac at the place where we had initially had our outposts. Good weather."

Although Reuber's dates are in error during this period, his account of passing through Hellgate on 5 September is of interest. "All the English and Hessian troops which lay in New York broke camp and marched to Hellgate, a place in the harbor near Long Island, where a whirlpool exists which draws in ships when they sail by without a favorable wind. There is such a rushing of water there as when it pours over a dam spillway and there is nothing but water to be seen. When it first takes hold of a ship, it draws it in and spins it around until it grounds and the raging never ceases."

Although the troops of the Hessian 1st Division at New Rochelle were soon to march against General George Washington at White Plains, the newly arrived 2nd Division and the Waldeckers were to move against Fort Independence. Shortly after the Waldeckers had sailed up the East River to West Chester, the then Corporal Steuernagel recorded casualties in the Waldeck Regiment. "27 October - Some of our regiment, who had wandered too far in order to buy some things at a plantation, were attacked by a part of Americans. Some were wounded and taken prisoner. Among these were Corporal [Johann Christian Friedrich] Nelle and a number of privates. Several of the wounded ransomed themselves and returned a few days later. Two privates, [Johann Friedrich] Zoellner and [Johann

Friedrich Philipp] Steinmeyer, who were rather seriously wounded"
were left on the field."

Chaplain Waldeck's account of the next few days contains the
following description of activities. "29 October - We marched from
West Chester to New Rochelle.....

"1 - 4 November 1776 - We lay in camp at New Rochelle.
Occasional alarms at night which had no significance. It required only
that we dress, and then lie down again on the hay. The nights were
getting rather cold, so that a bottle of water in my tent froze. I find
the present life in the company very pleasing. Currently we go for a
week at a time without spending money. We wrote our first letters
home. My good Captain Alberti and I wrote at a house situated near
our company. In this house was an old family, consisting of a great-
grandmother, a grandmother, her daughter, and the daughter's many
grown children. The location here is on the coast, and the ground is
fertile. We encountered many barns full of wheat, corn, etc., which
the owners had deserted, as well as several fine houses and gardens,
and especially orchards. Next to our camp is a field of fine flax, which
was carried to our tents to use in making fires.

"5 November - We broke camp and marched nine miles farther.
The weather was very pleasant, such as on a beautiful fall day at home.
Along the route one could get apple cider and milk. At two o'clock
we arrived at our designated camp, called the Sun Redoubt. All the
tents had not been put up before we received orders from General
Knyphausen's headquarters to continue our march to another strong
point, which was called Fort Independence. We arrived after dark....
We lay down to sleep in a stall which still had some hay. We slept
well, but from this lodging we collected so many lice that it took all of
the next day to pick them off.

"6 November - Two companies were posted inside the fort and
the others outside. The view was as good as that from the castle at
Waldeck, although the fort is not so elevated. In the fort lay many
cannons, cannonballs, and chainshot, which the enemy had left
behind.... Captain Alberti, I, and others put our noon lunch and bottle
in our packs, went to a fresh spring on the other side of the hills, and
drank, with pleasure, all kinds of toasts, as if we were enjoying the
best wine, because we tasted the heavenly pleasure of health and

contentment. We had tasted just such a glass of water during our 22 week long crossing.....

"9 November - The regiment sent out strong patrols in the region of Fort Washington, where our outposts were always under fire.

"10 November - Twenty-four of our men returned to the regiment from the hospital."

Steuernagel gives a brief, but in some respects more meaningful account of the period. "The 2nd of November we marched from here [New Rochelle] toward a great defensive position called Independence, near Kingsbridge.

"This fort was very strong and well-constructed by the rebels, with one side on a very steep rise, but we forced the rebels to retreat into the main defenses at Fort Washington, which lay nearby.

"Between us and Fort Washington was a stream which was the division between this land and that land, with two bridges over this stream."

The Platte Grenadier Battalion Journal traces the movement of the battalion after arriving at New York. "22 October - We were loaded onto a sloop and for a time everyone seemed melancholy as if mutually recalling all the dangers from which we had been released. We sailed in the East River between Long and York Islands until we came to a whirlpool, where there are large rocks. The passage between these rocks is very narrow and dangerous and it is called Hellgate. Here many old remnants of wrecked ships are to be seen. The channel is so narrow that objects can be thrown on land on either side of the ship. However, with favorable wind transport ships and frigates can sail through with ease. The master of our sloop told us that when the troops landed here, a boat with British grenadiers and artillery had gone under.

"Note - Sir James Wallace, in the year 1758, sailed through Hellgate with the warship *Experiment*, fifty cannons.

"We weighed anchor this morning at daybreak and were landed on solid ground at New Rochelle at ten o'clock. General Howe was in camp about three miles from here. Here we met the other troops of the 2nd Division which had come from Europe with us. They had come in flatboats and landed before we did. We had to leave our baggage behind on the ships and were permitted to take nothing with us but our tents.... We began our march to New Rochelle, actually in the direction of the church.... Although we only marched three English miles, many troops dropped out from fatigue. Near the church at New Rochelle we entered camp in the army line.... The Jaeger Company which landed with us today, had an engagement with the rebels already this evening, and Lieutenant [Carl] von Rau was severely wounded in the leg. Most of the surrounding region has been laid waste by the rebels.....

"28 October - The corps commanded by Lieutenant General von Knyphausen, consisting of the Koehler Grenadier Battalion, and the Wutginau, Stein, Wissenbach, Huyn, and Buenau Regiments, and the Waldeck Regiment, marched from New Rochelle to Mile Square. The march was about six English miles. The road was bad and stony. The houses which we passed were all empty and in disrepair.....

"30 October - At nine o'clock yesterday evening 1st Lieutenant von Romrodt, of the Wutginau Regiment, was ordered on a command with 300 men of that regiment. They marched out of camp at midnight. About three o'clock in the morning the entire corps commanded by Lieutenant General von Knyphausen moved out and an hour after daybreak arrived at a height on the east side of Kingsbridge. En route many burned-out huts were seen which had been built in the form of barracks. The remnants of destroyed magazines were also found. On the previously mentioned height 1st Lieutenant von Romrodt and his command had occupied a fort named Independence, which the enemy had vacated tonight. It was rather large, at least 900 to 1,000 men would be needed to defend it. The enemy had left cannons and ammunition behind. The fort had other additional small redoubts which we marched past on the right and left this morning. Fort Independence covers the entire region and is especially laid out to cover the crossing from Kingsbridge on the land side to this side. A creek runs through the hills and cliffs about three-quarters of a mile from here, which joins the North or Hudson River and the East River. Both rivers and this creek create an island, called York Island, on which New York City lies. A small wooden bridge, called Kingsbridge, connects the mainland and this island and gives the region its name. The enemy is now engaged in tearing down this bridge to hinder our crossing to York Island. They are also taking the magazines from both sides of the bridge to their camp at Fort Washington. That fort lies about two and one-half miles in direct line from us to the highest point, one could say cliff, on York Island. The area surrounding is covered with thick woods, marshes, and stony cliffs. Nature has provided far more defense than the art of fortification. The enemy say it is unconquerable but it appears as if our present situation is for the purpose of capturing the fort, so it remains to be seen how long this saying holds true.....

"31 October - The Kingsbridge destroyed by the rebels was repaired during the night and Captain [Johannes] Neumann, of our battalion, crossed the Harlem Creek over the Kingsbridge this morning with 100 men and drove the enemy outposts back to the woods near Fort Washington. He then established himself securely on a height on the other side of the bridge.

"The command which crossed the Harlem Creek today sent some of their lightly wounded back.

"2 November - This morning our battalion marched over Kingsbridge and entered camp on a height. Fort Washington now lies a bit more than a mile from us.

"3 November - The Koehler Grenadier Battalion outposts were engaged throughout the day with enemy patrols and suffered three men wounded.

"4 November - Three more men of the Koehler Grenadier Battalion were wounded at the outposts....

"5 November - ... Today several men were again severely wounded."

On 2 November Lieutenant Rueffer also commented on the action in which Lieutenant Rau had been wounded. "Captain [Johann] Ewald's Jaeger Company, which had just gotten on land, made an attack near Mile Square, which was not successful. The enemy stood fast and Ewald had two men killed, Lieutenant von Rau and two jaegers wounded, and two men missing. However, on the 26th [of October] when General [William] Erskine, with Ewald's Jaegers, the Rall Regiment, and a squadron of light dragoons was on recon-naissance beyond Mile Square, Ewald got his two captured jaegers back, captured nineteen men, and destroyed a magazine for rum and flour."

As members of the von Huyn Regiment, Chaplain Kuemmell and Private Asteroth were also in General von Knyphausen's command which moved to Kingsbridge. Asteroth's diary entry for 22 October gives the following account of traveling to New Rochelle. "The [soldiers from the] entire fleet were loaded into small boats in three and one-half hours. I joined the chaplain with his most necessary baggage, four servants, and two commanders in a boat. The regiment was already at its destination. Our boatman did not know the exact course to take with our boat and so set us on land. There for the first time in 22 weeks I touched land again. We satisfied our hunger with apples and then entered a small house. There we found three Negroes. They were reserved. We obtained wholesome potatoes from them, but they could not understand us, nor we them. We remained there three hours until sunset. When they went to bed we returned to our boat. Our sailors rowed us farther and sought to deliver us to the right place. Then night overtook us. At nine o'clock we finally reached a man-of-war. They challenged us. When they heard that we were from the troops, we had to pull-up beside the ship as there was danger from the rebels. We went aboard the ship. At ten o'clock another boat approached and halted beside the ship. The ship challenged it; that is what the watch did. It was a captain with twenty men of our troops. They had remained behind. The ship's sailors accepted us among them and gave us food and drink. At two o'clock the order arrived that we were to reenter our boats at once and we traveled all night until arriving at New Rochelle at seven o'clock in the morning, where we met all the other transports. There were some who had slept all night.

"23 October - The order came from General von Heister that we were to set up camp in this same region. The chaplain and I took our lodgings in an empty house which stood near the camp. I discovered that I also had scurvy and was indisposed for a month."

Chaplain Kuemmell wrote about the American pastors in an entry of 22 October. "During the morning we were taken by boat in the canal [East River] and put ashore at New Rochelle. We remained under the open sky during the night and next day marched into camp at New Rochelle, not far from the main army. There we had the enemy all about us and the regiment had to be constantly on alert. There were few occupied houses in this region; families had left their belongings behind, and among others, many dwellings contained the most beautiful furnishings. In this camp we were lodged with the colonel in a house where a pastor, who had joined the rebels, had lived. There was a beautiful library in the house, mostly English and

Latin, plus a few Greek books. Behind the house in the garden was a cemetery in which a chest full of magnificent silver utensils had been buried, and which some English soldiers dug up during the night. A small church stood not far from the house. It was built on a square plan. In the middle of one wall there was a pulpit and before this the lectern. On the pulpit, as I have found in many churches, lay some large folio volumes of books of martyrdom, Greek and Latin accounts of martyrdom, especially the apostles and avid religious followers, from which I concluded, and accounts I received confirmed. that the pastors sought to influence their congregations, by explaining and illustrating every tale of murder, to rise up and fight for their freedom and complete independence. Indeed, pastors have even raised troops and led those so influenced. In this camp we were frequently, but not seriously, disturbed.

"28 October - We moved ... to the neighborhood of West Chester, (and for the first time religious services were held in the field)."

On 28 October Lieutenant Rueffer recorded that, "General von Knyphausen supposedly has suffered greater losses at Kingsbridge than the rebels."

Nevertheless, they could not have been very heavy for either the Hessians of the Americans, and Bardeleben wrote in his diary on 2 November that, "Lieutenant General von Knyphausen crossed to York Island at Kingsbridge with the Koehler Grenadier Battalion and the Wutginau, Stein, and Wissenbach Regiments. Upon his arrival the enemy pulled back to the defenses before Fort Washington....

"3 November - Rather cold. It froze again during the past night. The nights are very cold now and nearly unbearable. Almost all officers and many privates, too, have built huts. They have dug deep holes in the ground and covered the roofs with cases to make surviving the cold easier. I disliked the huts. Our entire camp was constructed of earthen-work huts and looked quite disorderly....

"4 November - Rather cold. Our troops are sick and continue to die. Lieutenant Colonel Heymel, Major Hinte, and Captain von Donop have lain dangerously ill with dysentery for some weeks."

Enemy Views (1776)

<u>The Battle of White Plains</u>

Information on the Battle of White Plains on 28 October 1776 is rather incomplete considering the number of documents used in preparing this account of the role of the Hessians in the Revolutionary War. J.R.'s account dated 26 October is very brief. "We engaged the rebels in the area called White Plains. We captured the site but sustained considerable losses. The rebels moved back two miles and we followed them. During the night we remained under the open sky and awaited orders at any moment to again attack the enemy. However, the enemy left his camp and we set up our camp there, near Connecticut."

Although the Reuber diary entries indicate the Battle of White Plains was fought in September, this may be due to a copyist error. However, he also recorded the battle as having taken place on the 26th of the month, as did J.R. Despite such errors, it seems at least possible that Reuber's account contains elements of what actually happened at that time. "All the English and Hessian troops broke camp and marched against the Americans in a line on a hill or height at White Plains. Then both sides commenced firing at one another with cannons. The Old Lossberg Regiment had to advance toward a stream, the Bronx Creek, which lay in a valley. However, it suffered great losses of wounded and had to pull back. The Rall Grenadier Regiment had the left wing from which Colonel Rall saw the situation which now existed. Therefore, as the Americans were before us, Colonel Rall ordered his regiment to turn, to immediately ascend the hill through the water, through the Bronx Creek, and again up the hill where the Old Lossberg Regiment stood and united with the other English and Hessians. We could see above on the hill that the rebels were advancing and also meant to occupy this hill. We were able to move behind the Americans and our army obtained an advantage. We captured a powder wagon. If we had two cannons with us we would have been able to capture more. This we would have done, but night was upon us. It was so dark that no one could see. The order was given that each man should make a fire and should run back and forth, making noise, so that the enemy would believe that we were being reinforced on the hill. Colonel von Donop, who commanded the Jaegers and detached Grenadiers, also made plans to influence the

Americans during the night by driving the artillery horses back and forth and with the rattling of chains and the commands of the drivers to make them think that additional heavy artillery had arrived. At daybreak the American army had withdrawn and we marched all in a line and set up camp at that place all together, for some time."

Bardeleben, in an account obviously written at a later date, made a diary entry on 26 October of the casualties suffered by the English and Hessians during the Battle of White Plains. "On this day His Excellence Lieutenant General Howe attacked the enemy at White Plains.... The rebels had excellent positions at White Plains. They had made their defenses better than usual and maintained their posts with extraordinary tenacity. During the battle the von Lossberg Regiment lost [according to a scratched out entry] - 3 dead and 47 wounded; Rall 1 dead and 2 wounded; the English 195 men dead and wounded."

In place thereof is a marginal note, "English dead - 1 staff officer, 4 subalterns, 58 privates; wounded - 1 staff officer, 8 subalterns, 137 privates; Hessian dead - 42; wounded - 2 officers, Lieutenants [Johann Christoph] Muehlhausen and Rau, and 96 privates."

Surprisingly, Rueffer's diary provides some of the most interesting highlights of 28 October, in an entry of 2 November. "The following announcement was received today from White Plains.

'Announcement from the Adjutant General:

'His Excellency Lieutenant General von Heister, Captain Baurmeister, dated 31 October 1776.

'On the 24th of this month we marched from York's Continent to Chester, where Philipp's men live, and on the 28th to this place, where we encountered the enemy at the start of the Whiteplain, and battled against them from one height to the next for an hour and a half until he crawled back into his fortified camp and darkness settled over the clash.'

"The Lossberg Regiment performed miracles. My general, Lieutenant Werner, and I were caught in such a hail of bullets that the dragoon orderly was wounded and Lieutenant Werner's horse was shot in the flank. This fire lasted only eight minutes until the Rall Regiment helped the Lossberg Regiment out of the tight situation with a general discharge, formed in line in the best order, and captured the height. Lossberg, whose left wing had to wade water up to the waist and then had to move through a burned-out woods, suffered thirteen men wounded. Captain [Friedrich Wilhelm] von Benning and a standard bearer [Free Corporal Georg Henrich] Kress were nearly drowned. Free Corporal [Gottlieb] Waldeck had the colors shot out of his hands and the flag flew in such a manner that it was a joy to see. The field pieces of the Lossberg, Knyphausen, and Rall Regiments began such a racket that it became impossible to hear or see, but the enemy withdrew so quickly that there was little effect to be noted from the cannonade. A discharge from the Knyphausen Regiment struck a rebel regiment so solidly that it wounded 92 men. The English 49th Regiment which followed Lossberg also suffered a great many casualties."

Lieutenant Andreas Wiederhold, of the von Knyphausen Regiment, also wrote a detailed account of the Battle of White Plains on 28 October. "We again moved forward, causing the enemy to fall back three miles to a position on a steep height, behind a thick woods, before which flowed a rather deep stream. It was necessary to capture this height. Therefore, our brigade and an English regiment, the 32nd, were ordered to seize it. Lossberg and the English regiment made a frontal attack. However, we and the Rall attacked on the right flank. As they had not properly covered it, our attack on this flank took place at just the right moment, otherwise the Lossberg Regiment, which attacked through the woods, which had been set on fire by the enemy, would have suffered heavy losses in as much as there were already 45 dead and wounded. However, we had only one wounded and Rall one dead and two wounded. It was necessary to wade through the water which in some places was so deep that it reached to the soldiers' cartridge boxes. Lieutenant [Johann Friedrich Wilhelm] Briede and I were the first to enter the water in order to give the soldiers a good example and to motivate them to hurry through and up the height before the enemy saw their mistake and could cover their flank, or at least, if not with cannons, could position a party of riflemen so as to make our attack more difficult. The next day our brigade received special commendation from General [William] Howe, in orders, concerning the above. The success of this affair was not completely inconsiderable in that the enemy had been posted immediately to the rear, and on a nearly unconquerable rocky height, and occupied with entrenchments which could not have been captured without a great loss. It would surely have resulted in many attempts which would have been fruitless and with many casualties. Still, it served such a purpose that the enemy, by our maneuvering, made mistakes so that they quickly left their favorable positions and heights on their left wing. This region was named White Plains."

In a marginal note to the diary entry of 13 November, Bardeleben noted that, "The Commanding General Lord [sic] Howe moved from White Plains with the army today and settled on the heights at Kingsbridge"

The attack on Fort Washington was about to begin.

### The Capture of Fort Washington

Having driven Washington's army back from White Plains, Howe next turned his attention to capturing Fort Washington. By far the most informative, and most graphic description of what it was like to be engaged in battle, is to be found in the account recorded by Steuernagel. "Finally, 16 November was set as the time for the attack and conquest, from all sides, on Fort Washington, as the entire British army had been gathered in the area for this purpose for a number of days.

"The following orders were issued by headquarters to the various regimental commanders:

'Order of 15 November 1776
'Headquarters, Kingsbridge
'Tomorrow morning early, an hour before daybreak, the regiments will fall out in front and form in ranks. Each regiment will leave one officer and thirty men in camp as a baggage guard. The six regiments on this side of the island and the Waldeck, Knyphausen, and Huyn Regiments will cross the bridge and take post behind Wutginau and Stein Regiments. The remaining regiments, Buenau, Rall, and Lossberg, will cross the other bridges where the ship lies and fall in behind Wutginau and Stein Regiments, also.

'The order for battalions follows:
'The Jaegers together with one officer and forty grenadiers, under the command of Captain Borrin, will follow the 160 men in the woods under Colonel von Borbe as the advance guard, followed by the Grenadier Battalion Koehler, then Wutginau, Lossberg, Rall, Knyphausen, Huyn, Buenau, and Waldeck. The flank patrols will be deployed on the left side.

## Enemy Views (1776)

'Tomorrow, one hour before daybreak, 200 men of the Grenadier Battalion Koehler will assemble without weapons, in order to carry fascines, shovels, and axes. The Stein and Wissenbach Regiments remain here. The Stein Regiment is assigned the left wing and will detach 180 men. The Wissenbach Regiment will occupy the place now held by Wutginau, and will detach one officer and forty men to Fort Independence, as well as one non-commissioned officer and fifteen men to each bridge, to depart before the general movement tomorrow morning. Further, one captain, two non-commissioned officers, and seventy men will be dispatched at once to form in front of the Wutginau Regiment. The following from the eight marching battalions in the woods on the right will be commanded by Lieutenant Colonel von Borbeck [Friedrich von Porbeck ?]: one captain from Huyn, four officers, one each from Huyn, Buenau, Waldeck, and the Koehler Grenadier Battalion, ten non-commissioned officers from the battalions, and one man from Huyn and two men from Buenau, and 150 privates from the battalions, nineteen grenadiers and eighteen men from Wutginau are to assemble at the same time in front of the Grenadier Battalion. The 200 men, each of whom is to take a fascine and an axe with him, are to be commanded by one officer from Wutginau and two non-commissioned officers from the Waldeck Regiment and the Grenadier Battalion. Stein and Wissenbach will provide 25 men each for the 200-man command, and they are to be sent early tomorrow to the gathering place.'

"Meanwhile the following night quickly became 16 November, as young soldiers, mostly the regiment consisted of a bunch of kids, nervously awaited the dreadful and bloody event.

"Few, almost none, of the regiment had participated in such a pay-day formation [battle].

"All the troops were out an hour before daybreak, ready to go against the enemy and his defenses, according to the previous orders. Everyone, including ourselves, proceeded to our breakfast [initiation to battle] through a terrible cannonade, and advanced ever nearer against the enemy fortifications, as scheduled, through a continual and dreadful fire from the terrible guns, in regular order, although many of our unfortunate comrades had carried their booty away [been killed].

"About eight o'clock both sides ceased their terrible cannonading, whereupon a trumpeter from our side was sent over to the enemy.

The cause for this might have been to discuss the enemy's surrender of the fortifications. However, as these words were seen to be of no avail by both sides, in about three-quarters of an hour the heavy cannonade resumed and all troops were commanded, 'Forward march!' and to take the enemy position by storm. This happened at nine o'clock.

"If we had not had a pitiful situation before, we had it now. Before us, beside, and behind us, we saw our unfortunate comrades lying beside and upon one another. They lay battered and in part shattered; dead on the earth in their own blood; some whimpering, looked at us, pleading that in one way or another we would ease their suffering and unbearable pain. But in the circumstances, no one could help them. -- Among other things, one heard the most gruesome reproaches and pleadings. Our unfortunate ones even pleaded to that generally impartial great court of last resort, of which however, I will forego further mention.

"Everyone pressed on with a courage beyond expectation, through the rain of bullets, against the enemy and his defenses, through trenches and palisades, with shooting and flashing bayonets, in order to conquer the near invincible enemy and his fortifications.

"The continual thunder of cannons, the drum beat of small arms fire, the screaming of men, and the whinnying of horses completely deafened the participants. One was robbed of all sense and reason and lost all feeling. Shortly, even the air seemed filled with fear and the impact of the attack. The sensations and impressions of every kind and in such situations, are above all others, impossible to describe.

"One thinks of all the rest, and then from the place of a young person, one thinks of a particular from which much can be inferred, because most of the regiment was, so to speak, recruits of tender years. Still, I must say, that I have noticed in particular, that a regiment composed of young men advances more readily into combat than those which consist primarily of older men.

"As we now stormed the heights of the hills, which were surrounded with steep cliffs on our right flank, we saw that the enemy had been forced from his outer works, setting fire as a result to his powder magazines, and in so far as time allowed, spiking the about-to-be-captured guns, and retreated to the nearby, gigantic main fortification, Fort Washington.

## Enemy Views (1776)

"But as the enemy could not hold out long against our overpowering assault, even here, in a short time, he had to raise the white flag, and must surrender with all munitions and war materials, as dictated by us, and must then march between two rows of our troops and lay down his weapons. The number of Americans made prisoner at this place, I have not been able to determine exactly. More Americans could have been made prisoners, if the advice of both Hessian commanders, Generals von Heister and Knyphausen, had been heeded. They wanted to cut off all possible paths along which the enemy could retreat, and thereby would have captured the greatest part of the enemy army, and provided the greatest future success for England. However, the English commander-in-chief, Howe, did not approve of such a course of action as he preferred to consider the land and the troops as English subjects. Many had retreated to Fort Lee, by crossing to the opposite side of the river, which shortly after this affair, also had to surrender to us, and their troops continued their retreat.

"To return to our story, first we had to locate our dead and wounded. Fort Washington was surrounded by woods and the dead had to be buried and the wounded taken to a hospital. A few regiments remained to man the conquered fort. The others marched back to their previous camp sites, where we arrived late at night, tired, hungry, and thirsty, in our camp once again.

"From this time on, Fort Washington lost its name, and for the future was known as Fort Knyphausen....

"Following this action, I was commanded with a few of our soldiers and Surgeon's Mate [Johann Henrich Daniel] Beck to transport our wounded to a hospital in the village of Harlem, in the region of Morrisania.

"But how difficult was the journey. The most hard-hearted would have had to show compassion for the pain and whimpering which our wounded were suffering because of the journey in the back and forth shaking wagons, which caused ever greater pain. But who here could help these unfortunate ones or lessen their suffering? Certainly, here both sick and well must have patience together, until finally, after a long journey, we arrived at our destination, toward evening. Here we also found a great number of Hessian wounded.

"I went directly to the Hessian commanding, a Captain von Griesheim, while Surgeon's Mate Beck went to the hospital doctors and surgeons to report the wounded Waldeckers. The latter were so compassionate as to immediately visit our wounded, diagnose and treat them with the greatest attention, and assure their future attention to the wounded, some of whom died of their wounds.

"Meantime the commanding general, on 19 November, ordered the regiment to an encampment about one-half mile from Fort Independence, and on 28 November, to Delaney's Mill, not far from the village of Harlem.

"The weather was so bad during this time, that the tents were useless. Therefore, the regiment was quartered by companies at various plantations. A short while later, I lost my advantageous position. I fell ill with a fever, from which I lay sick for fourteen weeks, and nearly an equal time was needed to restore my health.

"My illness quickly got the best of me and within fourteen days I looked more like a statue than a living person.

"Combined therewith was a dizziness and loss of reason wherein I lay for some weeks suffering fantasies day and night, which sapped my little remaining strength.

"Everyone in the regiment received reports of my death during this time. During my illness this hospital was moved to a suburb of New York. Possibly my illness was contracted from those persons arriving by sea, many of whom carried a contagious scurvy."

Chaplain Waldeck, also of the Waldeck Regiment, also provided a vivid account of the capture of Fort Washington. "15 November - Orders were received to assemble the regiment as quietly as possible at three o'clock tomorrow morning.

"16 November - The regimental surgeon and I took our places with the regiment. We passed Kingsbridge while still not daybreak and arrived at our assigned positions. We marched through a ground where the cannonballs screamed terribly overhead. Fortunately, they were aimed too high. A Hessian, Lieutenant [Georg Wilhelm] von Loewenfels, that I had met in Bremerlehe, shook my hand as we passed near a woods, and we expressed our pleasure at having arrived in America in good health. Half an hour later his body was brought back. Of fate of mankind! He had to make such a long journey in order to find his grave at Fort Washington. The English batteries had found the range so exactly that shot after shot burst among the advanced enemy, and they were finally forced to retreat.

## Enemy Views (1776)

"Our flankers, commanded by Lieutenant [Johann Wilhelm] Leonhardi with such honor, and the Hessian Jaegers, suffered heavy losses. The rebels posted themselves behind trees and boulders, and always took careful aim at their targets. The flankers kept pushing forward under the covering fire of the cannons and the firing could be heard steadily nearing the fort.

"The abatis was amazing to see and one would have thought such a thing could not be surmounted. But then it happened, but not without difficulty and the loss of many good Germans. It was nearly impossible for one man after the other to get over the interlaced trees. One held out his hand to help the next man, and in this way, the passage was forced. About twelve o'clock the hill had been climbed, all the rebels had pulled back into the fort, and they capitulated. A frigate received a heavy cannonade from Fort Lee when it sailed up the North River.

"As I went forward, I saw many dead and wounded; among others, a Hessian jaeger who had just been shot through the head. His brother stood over the body, complaining that he could not be buried. Another jaeger had both eyes shot out. He still lived. Farther along, the rebels lay packed together like herring. The capitulation was completed toward evening. The prisoners, who numbered about 2,000, were led through the regiments, and had to stack their weapons. For a dollar one could buy a beautiful box. Despite the strictest orders, the prisoners received a number of blows. Especially comical, I watched the treatment handed out by a Hessian grenadier. One of the rebels being led through looked around proudly to the left and right. The grenadier grabbed him on the ears with both hands, and said, 'Wait a bit, and I'll show you the big city.'[13] Another tied him with his scarf. Two others hit him on the sides of his head. A third gave him a kick in the rump, so that he flew through three ranks. All of this took place in half a minute. The poor guy never knew what hit him, nor why he had been hit. About nine o'clock we marched back to our camp, hungry and still thirsty, arriving at eleven o'clock. Our regiment had six killed and seventeen wounded.

"19 November - The Hessian Grenadiers marched past our camp in order to be carried across the Hudson River to attack Fort Lee.

"20 November - We began to dig in as it began to get really cold. We had hardly gotten well started, when we had to break camp and march to General Howe's headquarters, near Delaney's Mill. On the march we met General Howe. The regiment came to present arms and the officers led with drawn swords, until he had passed.

"21 November - Foggy and rainy weather. No one was dry day or night, and our boots nearly rotted on our feet. Another thirty men, who had regained their health, returned from the hospital. We received the news that Fort Lee had been taken without the loss of a single man. The rebels fled at the approach of our army, after having lost their greatest hope, Forts Washington and Lee. General Howe had a beautiful concert, which we could hear in our camp. We all long to go into winter quarters."

Lieutenant Wiederhold, a young company officer, was also an active participant in the capture of Fort Washington, as noted in his diary entry of 16 November. "This day brought us Hessians glory which could be shared by every good man with honor. At five-thirty in the morning we crossed over Kingsbridge to York Island with the following regiments: Knyphausen, Huyn, Buenau, Rall, Lossberg, and Waldeck, joined by Wutginau and the Koehler Grenadier Battalion, and formed in two columns. The column on the right, led by Colonel Rall, contained Lossberg, Rall, Koehler, and Waldeck, and took post in a woods until the appointed time. The column on the left, led by Major General [Martin] Schmidt, contained the regiments Wutginau, Knyphausen, Huyn, and Buenau. His Excellency, Lieutenant General von Knyphausen, commanded the entire attack and he was at all times where the resistance on the attack was the most fierce. He seized some of the fences with his own hands in order to tear them down and to motivate the soldiers. He was exposed to the cannon and musket fire as well as the rifle fire, like a common soldier. It was surprising that he came away without being killed or wounded.

"The advance guard for the column on the right consisted of a troop of Jaegers and 100 men according to the plan [mit prima plana], commanded by Major [Karl Friedrich] von Dechow; the advance guard for the column on the left consisted of 100 men commanded by Captain [Friedrich Moritz] Medern of Wutginau, and included Lieutenant [Georg Wilhelm] von Loewenfeld and me. Both the captain and the lieutenant are dead. The first one died the next day; the latter, however, on the field. However, God be praised! I am still alive and came off unharmed, except for a small scratch in my face, caused by a small branch shot off a tree, even though I led the vanguard of thirty men from this advance guard and was foremost among them. Here I recall the old saying, weeds never die.

"A heavy cannonade began at seven o'clock to draw the enemy's attention so that they would not know where the actual attack was to be made. If we had continued the attack we had already begun, we would not have had one-third as many casualties as resulted in the end, as I had already advanced far up the hill with my advance guard, when General von Knyphausen received orders to pull back because General Howe informed him that all preparations for the feint had not been completed and he should therefore delay the attack. At seven-thirty the English General [Hugh], Lord Percy with two English and a Hessian brigade, consisting of the regiments Hereditary Prince, Donop, and Mirbach, attacked the lines between the fort and New York, and captured them without a great loss, having only two wounded, while the enemy left those defenses. At eleven o'clock the boats with two brigades of Englanders came down the Harlem Creek to take post in a woods on our left and formed to make a feint.

"Now we began the real attack and we discovered the enemy's main force with rifle and musket men all on a nearly insurmountable height directly before us and surrounded by a morass and with three abatis, one above another. Nevertheless, all these hindrances were removed, the abatis broken through, the morass waded through, and the riflemen, who directed a heavy fire at us from their fortified positions, driven out. We reached the formidable height and hill, chased the retreating enemy behind their lines and batteries, drove them from those positions also, captured the batteries of which one sat high up on the height, and followed the fleeing enemy until they entered the fort, where we sheltered on the side of the fort, in the defile of a hill, in order to be protected from the cannonade from the fort. But at this time we were only our regiment and the Rall Regiment. The fort was called upon to surrender and in about half an hour, 2,600 men marched out, laid their weapons down at our feet, and surrendered to His Excellence, Lieutenant General von Knyphausen, who was present and had signed the capitulation. As prisoners of war, they delivered over all munitions, provisions, and similar items. The Koehler Grenadier Battalion occupied the fort this evening and we returned to our camp where those in good health could not adequately thank God for their preservation. The loss to the Hessians amounted to more than 300 men dead and wounded. Among the dead officers were Captain [Johann Friedrich] Walter of Rall Regiment and Lieutenant Loewenfeld of Wutginau Regiment. Those who died of wounds were Captain [Wilhelm August] Barkhausen of Knyphausen Regiment and Colonel [Henrich] von Borck of the same regiment,[14] Captain Medern of Wutginau, Lieutenant Briede of Knyphausen, and Lieutenant [Franz Hartmann von] Ende of Wutginau. Colonel von Borck and Lieutenant Briede died the same day, and all the others on the second or third day afterward. Major von Dechow of Knyphausen and Lieutenant of Rall were slightly wounded."

Lieutenant Rueffer was on the opposite side of Fort Washington and his description of events during the battle on 16 November is from that viewpoint. "Today the glorious event was undertaken which earned Lieutenant General von Knyphausen such great honor, that is, the capture of Fort Washington. The Stirn Brigade marched out of camp at seven o'clock. The Donop Regiment remained behind to protect the camp. The attack from this side was supported by some English regiments and our entire force was commanded by Lord Percy. Lieutenant General von Knyphausen led the attack from the other side with the Lossberg, Wutginau, Knyphausen, Rall, and Huyn Regiments. Here the enemy had strong abatis which were nevertheless poorly defended. In four hours they were driven from all these positions and we advanced so near the fort that they could not bring their cannons to bear. Lieutenant General von Knyphausen encountered far more resistance. Nevertheless our troops, under the severest cannon and small arms fire, overcame the steepest rock formations and abatis. The enemy, on his side also, was forced to withdraw into the fort, whereby General Knyphausen had the advantage for entering the fort, and made preparations for taking it by storm. But first the general offered them the opportunity to surrender. The occupants requested half an hour to consider the offer, which was granted. As soon as this time expired, they considered it advisable to raise a white flag rather than face an assault, whereupon the entire garrison of 3,800 men stacked arms and surrendered as prisoners of war. Colonel [Johann August] von Loos ordered me to take 45 flankers and we captured 21 prisoners. The loss on our side, including officers, was 351 dead and wounded. About six o'clock our regiment took all the prisoners to Harlem, put them in houses and barns, and guarded them. The number of cannons which the rebels had in the fort amounted to 94. All the regiments returned to their camps, except for the 10th which reinforced us at Harlem.....

"18 November - Today we brought all of the prisoners to the road leading to New York, where we delivered them to the 1st English Brigade, which escorted them to New York."

The Platte Grenadier Battalion Journal entries provide another account of the assault on 16 November and of events shortly thereafter. "From the sixth until today nothing more occurred, except that daily we suffered wounded and killed at the outposts. The entire army commanded by General Howe came from White Plains and entered camp the other side of Kingsbridge, on the height behind Fort Independence. A battery of heavy cannons was established on the height opposite Fort Washington. Early this morning, at daybreak, a detachment of Jaegers under the command of Captain [Friedrich Henrich] Lorey and [nine regiments] ... under the command of Lieutenant General von Knyphausen, marched into the woods which lay to the right of our camp and on the North River. The Stein Regiment occupied a redoubt to the left on a plain. The nine regiments, battalions, and corps ... formed for the mass attack at the edge of these woods at about seven o'clock. The many and strong abatis and swamps made it necessary for them to remain in place until about ten o'clock before they could clear space enough to get through. At ten o'clock the main attack began against a stony cliff covered with trees, which they had to occupy before they could go against the fort. By eleven o'clock they were masters of this cliff, where nature had formed a defensive point, or more nearly a breastwork, between the cliff and Fort Washington. This had been occupied by the rebels with cannons, without revetments. This breastwork was quickly overrun but not without great loss on our side, especially by the Wutginau Regiment, because the greatest part of the left flank of this corps was outflanked by cannons on the cliff, firing grapeshot. As soon as this strong point, called the Stone Redoubt was in our hands, we halted.

"In addition to the corps commanded by Lieutenant General von Knyphausen, the fort was fired upon by several frigates lying in the North River and attacked from the side toward New York by a division of Englanders brought over the Harlem Creek in flatboats and who made a descent below Laurel Hill. The fire from all sides was very heavy until the Stone Redoubt was taken, and then suddenly ceased. The troops halted here and began to surrender. During the afternoon the fort capitulated and the occupants were made prisoners of war. The number of those captured amounted to more than 3,000 and the loss on our side, from the time of crossing over Kingsbridge to the surrender of the fort, in dead and wounded, amounted to nearly 400 men. The Koehler Grenadier Battalion had 38 men dead and wounded of that number....

"The prisoners were sent to Harlem, where a Hessian hospital was established."

The entry in J.R.'s diary for 16 November is covered in four sentences, despite the casualties mentioned. "We attacked Fort Washington. The defenses were all taken by storm and in so doing the Hessians had 400 men killed and wounded. They captured 2,600 men. Lieutenant General Knyphausen commanded the troops and thereafter the fort was named for him."

The Donop Regiment played only a minor role in the conquest of Fort Washington, as recorded by Zinn in the regimental journal on 16 November. "The von Donop Regiment had to move forward another two miles, but did not come under fire, but Lieutenant von Nagel, Sr., with thirty men, and Lieutenant [Wilhelm] von Lepel, with fifty men, were detached. The first drove the enemy from his defenses which contained a cannon; the second had two men wounded."

Bardeleben, as was his practice, gives a much more detailed account of the battle and of the von Donop Regiment's role in capturing the fort. "15 November - We received the order at five o'clock in the evening to be prepared to attack the enemy lines outside Fort Washington....

"16 November - At five o'clock in the morning we took up our weapons but only began our march against the enemy line at seven o'clock. After a half hour march we arrived before it. Several regiments formed at once on the small heights lying directly opposite the enemy defenses. After all the regimental pieces and several English 12-pound cannons were moved up, from the English on the right and us on the left, a prolonged bombardment was fired upon the enemy trenches. During this cannonade the advance guard moved up through a valley lying ahead of us, and the supporting regiments immediately followed. The von Donop Regiment took a position close to the North River and, with five accompanying cannons, covered the left flank. The rebels, who had no heavy cannons in their line, fired only a few rifle shots against the advance guard from the trenches and then took flight. On the opposite side of Fort Washington, near Kingsbridge, Lieutenant General von Knyphausen attacked.... The corps on the opposite side of Kingsbridge served as a support force as well as to prevent the enemy forces left behind at White Plains from being able to disrupt our forces during the attack.... [The regiments under General von Knyphausen] had to make a more difficult and dangerous attack than we had on this side. Natural and artificial defenses on that entire side were the best and well-constructed. All the enemy batteries surrounding Fort Washington were on cliffs, whose impossibly steep sides were so rocky and whose abatis of interlocking and nearly insurmountable trees, had to be overcome. However, despite all these hindrances, the two columns, with a most praise-worthy effort, climbed the cliffs and attacked the enemy with such rare energy and such ardor that the enemy had to flee into the main fort in complete confusion, and shortly thereafter was forced to surrender.

"By four o'clock in the afternoon all fighting had ceased and terms had been agreed upon. Initially the enemy had requested being allowed to march out free, but this was not allowed. They next asked to be allowed to take out their weapons. With this understanding, and with no further conditions, 3,000 men surrendered.

"During the battle the Hessian deaths were 2 captains, 3 subalterns, and 172 privates; wounded were 2 staff officers, 2 captains, 6 subalterns, and 274 privates.

"English deaths were 1 captain and 19 privates; 4 officers and 90 privates were wounded.

"Enemy deaths were 3 officers and 60 privates; and 10 officers and 100 privates wounded.

"Captured artillery amounted to: four 32-pound cannons, two 18-pound cannons, seven 12-pound cannons, five 9-pound cannons, fifteen 6-pound cannons, eight 3-pound cannons, and two howitzers, beside considerable munitions.

"Our troops earned great honor today, and even more so because this victory in many respects was very deceptive and especially because the plan had excellent preparations as the city of New York was completely protected. Our brigade moved back into camp at nine o'clock in the evening, except for the von Mirbach Regiment which had remained behind to escort the prisoners to Harlem and guard them at that place."

The entry of 16 November made by Chaplain's Assistant Asteroth, reads in part, as follows. "As there was a high cliff which had been fortified so well and advantageously, and as it was impossible for us to attack with artillery, our cannons stood opposite and useless while our regiment stood below in a valley. About nine o'clock in the morning there was a heavy cannonfire which wounded many of us, but we advanced and God was with us. By one o'clock we had captured it [Fort Washington] and it was renamed Fort Knyphausen. We captured 2,300 men. These were lead off to New York under a strong detachment of Englanders and put in prison there. Huyn had 48 men wounded and Lieutenant [Henrich Friedrich] Justi and two privates of our regiment were killed."

As is to be expected, because Colonel Rall and his regiment played such an important part in capturing Fort Washington, Reuber covered the battle in some detail. "15 November - The order arrived from the headquarters of the English Field Marshal, General [Henry] Clinton [sic], that the attack against Fort Washington should be four-pronged, three English and one Hessian.... On the North Harbor a warship lay at anchor to cover our flank. A warship lay off the South Harbor to cover the English flank when the action began.

"17 November - During the morning of the sixteenth all the regiments and corps assembled before daybreak; the Hessians on the right wing on the North Harbor; the English on the left wing on the South Harbor. At daybreak the Americans became aware of us, but it was too late. Suddenly the two warships on either side opened fire against Fort Washington. At the same time the land attack began with cannon fire and ship fire, all the regiments and corps marched forward in order to clamber up the hills and stone cliffs. One fell down, still alive, the next one was shot dead. We had to pull ourselves up by grasping the wild boxtree bushes and could not stand upright until we finally arrived on top of the height. As the trees and large rocks were encountered close upon one another and [the terrain] did not become more even, Colonel Rall commanded, 'All who are my grenadiers, forward march!' All the drums beat a march. The musicians played a march. Suddenly everyone still alive shouted, 'Hurrah!' Then everyone was at once mixed together, Americans and Hessians were as one. No more shots were fired but everyone ran toward the defenses. As we approached the height where the Americans had a trench around the defenses, we had to halt. Then the Americans pressed on at a run to the defenses, but we stopped them. 'You are prisoners of war!' General von Knyphausen called on the fort to surrender and two hours later the rebels surrendered Fort Washington, and all munitions and provisions in and outside the fort were turned over to General von Knyphausen. Everyone had to lay down his weapons and after this transpired, the Rall and Old Lossberg Regiments formed two lines, between which [the rebels] had to march. Then the English came and led them off to captivity in New York. After the first contingent had departed, the second, which was as strong as the first, marched out of the citadel. They also lay down their weapons and the English took and marched them into captivity in New York. While this transpired night set in so the Hessians occupied Fort Washington. The others marched back to Kingsbridge during the night and entered their former quarters where we had lain so long before, prior to the attack."

## The Capture of Rhode Island

Following the capture of Fort Washington, plans were immediately initiated for the conquest of Rhode Island. Bardeleben wrote on 18 November 1776, "Two Hessian brigades, those of Colonels von Lossberg and von Huyn marched today from Kingsbridge to near New York, in order to go to Rhode Island, and entered camp near the city until they could embark."

Chaplain Kuemmell began his account of the move of the Huyn Regiment to Rhode Island on 25 November. "At nine o'clock in the morning the regiments marched with dressed ranks through the city of New York and, together with six English regiments, embarked, with each regiment boarding three ships. I, the auditor, and Captain [Melchior] Martini boarded a Scottish ship called *Clinevern* [possibly *Glencairn*].

"25 November to 8 December - We remained on the water and then debarked at Rhode Island. All the preparations had been made before our departure from New York so that this island could be taken by assault, but the rebels gave way before us without causing any problems. The regiments lay in camp for several days and then entered cantonment quarters with each company entering at most five houses.

"26 December - All the regiments entered their winter quarters with the Lossberg Brigade in the city [Newport], together with two English brigades.... The second Hessian brigade and especially the Huyn Regiment lay close to the water opposite the enemy, who gave us many sleepless nights. Many nights the regiment had to take up arms. During this winter pause, on 2 January 1778 [sic], the regiment received a visit from some 'very high-born ladies'."

Even more details of the voyage to Rhode Island and the ever threatening dangers at sea are provided by Asteroth's diary commencing on 20 November, "We received the order to be prepared to march and to go aboard ship on the 25th. That morning we marched through New York with flags flying, all six regiments, or two brigades. The Leib Regiment, Prince Charles Regiment, and Ditfurth Regiment constituted Colonel Lossberg's Brigade. [Colonel Christoph] von Huyn had the Landgraf, Huyn, and Buenau Regiments in his command. Eight English regiments were also embarked and sailed with our fleet. The commander of this corps was Lieutenant General Clinton....

"26 November - We departed in the morning and sailed through a very dangerous channel. We sailed twelve hours but then had to drop anchor primarily because of the ebb and flood tides. Our transport fleet numbered about sixty ships escorted by fourteen men-of-war, with three gun decks and 70 to 74 cannons.

1 December - We left the channel and entered the ocean. The ships then turned east and were on the proper course. As the wind was rather contrary, a ship under full sail came toward us and our ship had no wind. The other ship had a full wind so that these two ships came together in such a way that it broke off our bowsprit and a sixty pound fluke from an iron anchor. The raging wind coupled the masts of each ship with the others rigging so that it took considerable time before the two ships could be separated. On the other ship the sails were torn to shreds but it did not suffer as much because it was a good deal larger and hit with the most force. A drummer, who already had

his knapsack on his back, sought to save himself by jumping onto the other ship. However, his effort failed.

"7 December - At five o'clock in the evening we dropped anchor at Rhode Island, where there were many rebels. They had taken the precaution of fortifying the city and the harbor with three forts, in the first of which there were thirty cannons, in the second fifteen, and in the third eight. It seemed impossible for us to capture the city. However, our admiral led us in so that we fortunately were able to anchor in the middle of [the bay at] Rhode Island. He took us into an impassable harbor which the rebels thought could not be entered. When they saw us and saw our fleet enter, there was a great outcry and they fled to Providence with bag and baggage. But something terrible happened. They ran about in the streets telling one another their opinion, because they had heard such tales about us, that we were not human, we plundered everyone, and burned and killed everything and everyone in our path. Therefore, these rebels were happy to run from us even in their great fear. Commander Clinton during the evening gave the order that on the eighth, the following morning, at six o'clock, we were to debark. According to the order also, each regiment was to assign 35 privates, one non-commissioned officer, and one officer to the Jaeger Corps.

"8 December - We landed but they [the American military] had all left. We set up our camp, in the snow, in the same region.

"13 December - Huyn's Brigade and an English brigade were landed and the Lossberg Brigade and the other English regiments and the general staff entered empty houses in the city of Newport. A bridge led from the land which we occupied to Providence. Therefore, the brigade furnished a detachment of 160 men and every evening a picket of sixty men from the detachment was sent out near Howland Ferry. And, as these three regiments were quartered five hours from one another, each company had to provide a watch with a captain for the posts on the water's edge. Near Fogland Ferry there was a defensive position in which were cannons and a twenty-man detachment. The detachment was relieved every 48 hours. Indeed, we were constantly disturbed. We held religious services in a Quaker church during which the soldiers had to have their weapons and cartridge pouches with them. When we marched to church the weapons were stacked together and a watch posted over them. The soldiers kept their cartridge pouches with them."

J.R.'s entries for 28 November and thereafter provide a few more details, as he was a member of the Leib Regiment. "We marched from there into camp in New York. Six Hessian and ten English regiments were embarked. We did not know where we were bound, but sailed past Hellgate with a good wind.

"4 December - After the fleet had passed Hellgate it consisted of six men-of-war and about fifty transport ships. We sailed with Long Island on our right and New London and Connecticut on our left. This province is part of New England. We then anchored.

"7 December - The troops landed. The rebels had occupied the city of Newport, but they abandoned it at once and our troops occupied it without firing a shot.

### The Capture of Fort Lee

Back at New York, Lieutenant Bardeleben recorded a rather lengthy account of the attack on Fort Lee. "Wednesday, 20 November - Our Grenadiers and Jaegers, the English Grenadiers, light troops, and Scots marched from Kingsbridge under the command of General Milord Cornwallis and were then carried across the North River to New Jersey.

"The opposite shore, where these troops landed, was surrounded with cliffs of a fearful height. The entire corps had to climb the high cliffs on a small footpath only a few paces wide. The height from the shore to the woods above, which were also surrounded by cliffs, was a bit more than a mile, and several hundred courageous men, posted on these heights could have held off our entire corps and could have killed the greatest part. [Marginal note - The enemy left his guard at Fort Lee and our troops captured them, taking one lieutenant, one quartermaster, three surgeon's mates, and 99 privates prisoner.] The rebels still shaken by the capture of Fort Washington and surprised by the landing of our troops, fled, abandoning another strong fort. This fort lay just opposite Fort Washington and had the name Lee. Our troops found 26 cannons and much ammunition and more than 2,000 tons of the best flour" [or possibly powder as the last word is too faded to read.]

## Winter Quarters

Thereafter the English and Hessian forces drove the Americans out of New Jersey and entered winter quarters.

Steuernagel described the Waldeck Regiment's quarters area and conditions encountered in his entry of 9 December. "We marched from there [Perth Amboy ] to the village of Woodbridge and from here to the little city of Elizabethtown....

"Even though it was near mid-winter and extremely cold with deep snow, our men were without permanent quarters, and the duty was monotonous and difficult as can be imagined. The regiment was entirely on its own in this place and the surrounding area.

"The regiment was constantly harassed, day and night, by the Americans and frequently attacked. If a man came off guard duty, he was immediately called upon for picket duty to repel an American attack, which came often, necessitating a continuous alert so that all of the few men not on duty had to be ready for immediate response. Therefore, a large building had been designated as the alarm house and in this house everyone held himself ready for an immediate response to an attack. No non-commissioned officer, during this period, which lasted until 9 January, dared to remove his shoes and socks, let alone his shirt. This contributed to our people being strongly infested with bugs. It was pitiful to see the men wandering about barefoot in the snow, during the coldest weather."

Chaplain Waldeck also provided a description of the officers' quarters of some of his comrades as of 9 December and life in winter quarters in the following days. "About one o'clock we entered Elizabeth, a village that right from the start was a source of special activity for us. We met the Lossberg Regiment here. Captain Alberti, Herr [Ensign Johann Henrich Friedrich] Noelting, and the regimental surgeon took quarters for the night in the home of a lawyer, as no quarters had been assigned as yet... Herr Noelting prepared a good evening meal which tasted delicious, as we had lived on bread and schnaps for the last six days.

"The owner of the house, like many other residents, had fled with his entire household, but had been so friendly as to leave behind a cellar full of potatoes, squash, beets, and an ample supply of cider. We knew how to use all of these things. I did not begrudge the private soldiers all these things, as they needed beef, potatoes, and cider in order to recover from a long sea voyage, and an autumn campaign. Besides, the rascal was reportedly an arch rebel.

"10 December - The Lossberg Regiment departed for Brunswick and we immediately moved into their former quarters....

"11 December - I had no quarters and Captain Alberti was so kind as to put me up for the night. The captain had quarters with a coppersmith, and the room was furnished and papered in a manner not to be expected from a man of his class. The man supported the King; his wife supported the rebels. But she was a good cook and, in her way, very good. Toward midnight there was an alarm when the rebels attacked our pickets, and three men were wounded. The remainder of the night there was no rest.

"12 December - The regimental surgeon and I obtained quarters with good landlords. It snowed for the first time....

"The large English church was swept out after the troops which arrived yesterday departed, but a company of light dragoons arrived, causing such a disturbance that no church service could be held. Many rumors circulate. [General Charles] Lee is captured; Washington has quit his command. But one allows himself the freedom still to doubt such tales.

"The spoiled Sunday was recovered and I preached in the large English church. Our officers were very gallant and escorted the ladies from their quarters to the church. We brought the year to a close in fine quarters with many pleasures. The many inhabitants, who had fled from fear, now returned again because of the reports of the good conduct of the regiment. We celebrated Christmas in peace and quiet. On both the first and second holiday,[15] communion was served as there had been no time to do so during the autumn campaign, and many now took part. On the second holiday a very heavy snow fell."

Lieutenant Bardeleben recorded in a marginal note on 8 December that, "The [von Donop] corps in Jersey arrived at Trenton. The night before our troops arrived, the enemy crossed the Delaware River, completely evacuating Jersey."

In another marginal note prior to Christmas, he reported on sickness among the officers of his regiment. "Major Hinte, Lieutenants [Friedrich Ferdinand] Murhard, von Nagel, Sr., and [Carl

Friedrich] von Nagel, Jr., and Ensigns [Eitel Wilhelm] von Trott and [Carl] von Knoblauch are sick."

Also, while moving into winter quarters, the Platte [Koehler] Grenadier Battalion Journal recorded another danger of traveling by ship - starvation - in journal entries beginning on 20 December 1776. "This evening we received orders to be prepared to embark tomorrow.

"21 December - The previously mentioned [Koehler] Grenadier battalion embarked, the staff on the transport ship *Acolus*, Captain Bode's and Captain [Henrich Christian] Hessenmueller's Companies on the ship *Symmetry*, and Captain Neumann's and Captain [Georg] Hohenstein's Companies on the ship *Royal Exchange*.

"22 December - At eight o'clock this morning our ships departed and we set a course for Perth Amboy, but anchored at Prince's Bay on Staten Island.

"27 December - We remained lying at anchor at Prince's Bay until today. We have had to put up with a great deal during these days. The weather was so very cold and continuously stormy so that it was necessary to put out three anchors to prevent the ship from breaking loose. The Second Christmas Day[15] was the worst for us as we expected the storm to tear us loose at any moment. Our sorrow was made all the worse because we had no food with us. We had been told at New York that we would debark on the 23rd or 24th and that it was not necessary to take provisions with us, as these would have to be left behind when we landed. Relying on this, we had taken nothing more with us than was necessary for needs until the 23rd. Unfortunately, the ship had taken no provisions, either, and we had to tolerate these miserable conditions until today, when the wind eased and we received fresh provisions from Perth Amboy. Here in Amboy we received the news that Colonel Rall's Regiment had been captured on the 26th of this month at Trenton."

The embarkation of the Koehler [Platte] Grenadier Battalion was noted by Rueffer in his diary entry of 21 December, together with the Hessian troop dispositions in winter quarters. "The winter quarters are therefore divided, thus:

"New York - English and Hessian headquarters; English generals - 1) General-in-Chief Howe, 2) [Samuel] Cleaveland of the Artillery, 3) Governor [William] Tryon, 4) Commandant [James] Robertson, 5) Johnson, 6) Quartermaster General Erskine. Hessian generals - 1)

Lieutenant General von Heister, 2) Lieutenant General von Knyphausen, 3) Major Generals Stirn, 4) Mirbach, 5) Schmidt. The last two are sick. Regiments - 17th Light Cavalry, the 4th, 15th, 27th, and 45th Infantry, and Stirn's Brigade consisting of the Hereditary Prince, Donop, and Mirbach Regiments.

"In the harbor there are six warships and the admiral commanding all the ships in America, Lord [Richard] Howe, has his quarters in the city, also.

"Fort Knyphausen - 1) Schmidt's Brigade consisting of the Truembach, Stein, and Wissenbach Regiments and the 1st English Brigade.

"Kingsbridge - The 4th English Brigade. These three brigades [at Fort Knyphausen and Kingsbridge] are commanded by His Excellency, Lieutenant General von Knyphausen, and because the barracks have not yet been completed, the Schmidt Brigade is still camping.

"New Jersey - Two English brigades, Hessian Jaegers, Donop Grenadier Brigade, Rall Brigade, and the Waldeck Regiment, all under General Grant's command.

"Rhode Island - Nine English regiments, Lossberg Brigade consisting of the Leib, Prince Charles, and Ditfurth Regiments, and the Huyn Brigade consisting of the Wutginau, Huyn, and Buenau Regiments, all of which are commanded by Lord Percy and Lieutenant General Clinton."

## The Battle of Trenton

Suddenly, the good reputation of the Hessian soldiers, won at such a high cost at Fort Washington and in the fighting in and around New York, was to be lost in a single day. Although his dates are still in error, Private Reuber recorded the following account of the Hessian defeat at Trenton, commencing with his date of 16 December 1776. "We marched out of Old Brunswick early this morning toward Trenton and this continued until late at night, when we arrived in quarters at Kingston. Because during the darkness of night, when everything was peaceful and still, all the drums suddenly beat an alarm, we had to move out at once. The Rall Brigade marched on into the dark night, until near daybreak, we passed through the small city of Princeton. As dawn approached on

## Enemy Views (1776)

"17 December - we entered Maidenhead. We received no night quarters but rested there for two hours. Due to the tiredness everyone fell asleep and when we awoke, it was day. We were all covered with snow and could not see one another. When we had crawled out from under the snow we saw that we lay in a churchyard and there was only a church, a parsonage, a schoolhouse, and an inn. Colonel Rall looked about and gave the order that those of his grenadiers who had something to cook should do so because our march would continue in two hours. When that was done we moved out and resumed our march toward Trenton on the Delaware. At noon we were already outside Trenton, entered the city, and relieved the Hessian Jaegers, detached Grenadiers, and the English Light Infantry. The Rall Brigade remained in Trenton and those we had relieved marched down the Delaware against Philadelphia. It was quiet for us at Trenton and we posted our watches, commands, and pickets as usual. It also began to freeze which was also our desire as we then would be able to cross [the river] on foot and capture Philadelphia.

"20 December - The ice on the Delaware froze quite solid but not enough for us to cross on foot. We had to have patience with the difficult task which we had in Trenton and the inhabitants of the city told us the American army planned to attack us Hessians. However, we gave no thought that the rebels would do that.

"21 December - Early in the morning Colonel Rall took a large detachment, formed in two divisions, from his brigade, and a cannon, and marched to the Delaware in order to determine if the Americans were making preparations to come across the Delaware and secretly to attack us. Nothing was to be seen or noticed during this movement and march which went as far as a point opposite New Frankford, which lay on the other side of the river and where the Americans could be seen. Colonel Rall halted there and the two divisions joined together and marched back into the quarters at Trenton from which we had marched out. Everything was quiet and peaceful. Nevertheless, it was ordered that every evening a company was to remain in the alert house with the weapons provided for that post stacked three to a stack before the house door. The soldiers were to remain dressed as if on watch or on a command and the officers and non-commissioned officers were to enforce strict compliance. Therefore it remained quiet and peaceful.

"22 December - 'During the night the black Negroes and yellow dogs planned to attack us at reveille', but nothing came of it. A detachment at the Delaware was attacked by Americans who crossed the Delaware to our side, set some houses on fire, and then retreated back across the Delaware to their side. Again, everything was quiet, but at night the companies had to enter the alert house as usual and stack their weapons before the night posts.

"23 December - A 100-man detachment from our three regiments was ordered to a bridge across the Delaware not far from Philadelphia and this prompted the inhabitants to intensify their alarm of a rebel attack. 'However, who could have imagined that it could have come to such a point.'

"24 December - On the afternoon of the Christmas Saturday three English regiments came to Trenton from Princeton in order to reinforce us. When they paraded before Colonel Rall's quarters in the city and reported to him, they were required to turn about and march back to Princeton. During the evening a 100-man picket was stationed outside the city. In the dark of the night there were suddenly alarm shots at our outposts. An American patrol, or advance guard, had approached too close to our outposts. As they then fired upon our outposts, all three regiments had to move out. Colonel Rall took two companies and one cannon and marched through the woods in order to reconnoiter around the outposts, but nothing happened and he returned. After his return with the two companies, everyone had to enter the alert houses and occupy our positions.

"25 December - On the first blessed Christmas morning,[16] at daybreak, the Americans marched against our 100-man picket and at the same time the Americans fired on our outposts. At the first salvo, we turned out from our alert houses and went to the alert areas to form and prepare our battle formations. Now the rebels pressed in on us. At Colonel Rall's quarters there was a wall of boards before which our two cannons stood in the street, opposite the seven American cannons, and they destroyed one of the American gun carriages. Now the Americans charged Colonel Rall's quarters, overran it, and took the cannons from the regiment. Then Colonel Rall charged with his grenadiers. Although we went against enemy cannons, we took our cannons and retired from the city into the fields. Now Colonel Rall commanded, 'All those who are my grenadiers, charge!' and they stormed against the city as the Americans retreated before us. However, after we had entered the city, the rebels, in three lines, marched around us and as we again tried to retreat, they again brought seven cannons into the main street. We had to go past them but things went badly for us before we could accomplish this purpose. If the colonel had not been so seriously wounded, they would not have taken us alive, even though they were 15,000 men and our brigade was only 1,700 men strong. We were too weak, the headquarters had been lost, and in the end all was lost. With his last breath he thought about his grenadiers and asked General Washington to take nothing from them except that which was considered as weapons, but it was taken and kept. It had now reached the point where as quickly as possible they rounded us up, escorted us to the Delaware, carried us across to the Philadelphia side near New Frankford, and we were confined in a rotten prison. So the period of fighting the war ended on 25 December 1776. The Knyphausen Regiment and the Rall Grenadier Regiment on

"26 December - began their first march to New Frankford and into a large prison with a surrounding wall. Ship's bread was shaken down out of a basket from above into the bare courtyard and onto the snow, among us. This was not a very pleasant sight. It can well be imagined how angry this made us and especially during such a cold spell, as it was then. Then we heard we were to enter barracks at Philadelphia where we could finally come to rest. Then things could happen as they might. We were 900 Hessians and the three English regiments, which had been sent as a reinforcement on 24 December and which Colonel Rall had sent back, were captured during the excursion. Those 900 English prisoners of war were also with us. We remained there quietly in our miserable and depressing circumstances until 1777."

The Piel diary, which has a gap beginning on 1 September, resumes on 26 December, with an account of the attack on the Rall Brigade at Trenton on that date, and gives Piel's appraisal of Rall's abilities. "The Rall Brigade, since the fourteenth of the month, had occupied the small city of Trenton on the Delaware. The enemy stood on the opposite side of the river, and because they had boats and we had none, they could cross at any point and harass us. Yesterday evening, at twilight, they attacked our outposts, but pulled back almost at once after wounding six men.

115

# Enemy Views (1776)

"Between six and seven o'clock this morning we were formally attacked by a corps of 6,000 to 7,000 men under General Washington. Our outposts soon found it necessary to retreat and we barely had time to take up our weapons before we lost many of our people in the city, due to the small arms and cannon fire of the enemy. We were surrounded on all sides but defended ourselves for two full hours, until the Knyphausen Regiment was cut off from us; our weapons, because of the rain and snow, could no longer be fired; and the rebels fired on us from all the houses. There remained no other choice for us but to surrender. The Lossberg Regiment lost about seventy men, dead and wounded, in this engagement. Among the first were Captains [Johann Caspar] Riess and von Benning and Lieutenant [Georg Christoph] Kimm. Captain [Ernst Eberhard] von [Alten-] Bockum and Lieutenants [Ernst Christian] Schwabe and Zoll were wounded. We had only Colonel Rall to thank for our complete misfortune. It never struck him that the rebels might attack us, and therefore he had made no preparations against an attack. I must concede that on the whole we had a poor opinion of the rebels, who previously had never successfully opposed us. Our brigadier was too proud to retreat one step from such an enemy, as from the start, there was no other choice for us but to retreat.

"Colonel Rall was mortally wounded and died the same evening, satisfied that it was not necessary for him to outlive his honor.

"General Howe judged the man from an incorrect historical point. Otherwise he would hardly have entrusted to him such an important post as Trenton.

"Colonel Rall was truly born to be a soldier, but not a general. This man, who by capturing Fort Washington earned the greatest honor because he was under the leadership of a great general, lost his entire reputation at Trenton where he was himself a general. He had courage enough to undertake the most audacious task. However, he lacked the presence of mind which it is necessary to have in such an engagement as the attack on Trenton was. His love of life was too great. A thought came to him, then another, so that he could not settle on a firm decision. Considered as a private individual, he merited the highest respect. He was generous, magnanimous, hospitable, and polite to everyone; never groveling before his superiors but indulgent with his subordinates. To his servants he was more a friend than master. He was an exceptional friend of music and a pleasant companion."

Wiederhold's account of the battle provides additional details of the battle and expresses a far less favorable opinion of Colonel Rall. His entries, beginning on 14 December, clearly indicate that much of the diary was written after the events described. "We marched to the famous place Trenton, which I shall never forget in my life, and where our all too easy-going brigadier took us because of his conduct, as it is said. How much better off he would have been if he had not sought, and would not have received the undeserved praise that had been directed at him. He might have kept his reputation. However, here in truth everyone lay in pleasant quarters. Our army's exhausted and destitute of small clothes soldiers could recover even less here than in the field. The duties were exceptional, guard duty, special detachments, picket duty without end, even though they were unnecessary and served no purpose, but only senseless employment throughout the day in the vicinity of the brigadier's quarters. Whether the guards and detachments were relieved, whether the soldiers were wearing pants, shoes, shirts, etc., or nothing, whether or not ammunition was wasted; these things were immaterial, and he never inquired about them.

"But the hautboists! They were his thing, and as the main watch was six or eight houses from his quarters, they could not play long enough. The officer had first to march with music around the neighborhood church, which stood near his quarters and into which a small doorway led. This looked like a Catholic procession. Nothing was missing except the flag with a cross and a number of small boys and girls, singing at the head. He always followed the parade as far as the guard post, so as to hear the music during the change over. Another commander, like him, during this time would have met with the staff officers and others coming from duty to discuss the well-being and security of the garrison and other matters.

"Toward two o'clock the detachments were relieved and about four o'clock the pickets. All officers and non-commissioned officers had to be present then at his quarters so that it looked like an important headquarters. The cannons, which should have been on the street or at places where they were ready for instant use, had to be brought to stand before the quarters and every morning two of them had to be taken to the upper part of town so that there was a constant uproar and commotion.

"Personally, he enjoyed himself until late at night, then peacefully went to bed, slept until nine o'clock, then paraded between ten and eleven o'clock and then entered his quarters. He sat reclining in his usual bath and therefore the watch often had to wait half an hour to be formed.

"Not the least precaution was taken, no assembly point nor alert system was prepared in case of attack. Even less thought was given that an attack was even possible. Major von Dechow made the excellent suggestion that some defensive positions be thrown up and the cannons placed therein so that everything would be ready in case of an attack and the best defense could be made.

"' Unnecessary nonsense' [in a much more vulgar expression], was the colonel's reply. 'Let them come! Why defenses? We will go at them with the bayonet'."

"Major Dechow sought to persist and said, 'Colonel, it does not cost anything. If it does not help, it also does no harm,' and suggested that I undertake this project. I gladly accepted this task and asked him where and how he wished it done. He repeated his first words, laughed at both of us, and walked away.

"He believed the name Rall was so frightening and stronger than the works of Vauban and Coehorn, against which no rebel would attack. A clever man to defend a position which stood so close to the enemy, where he had more than 100 advantages. He did everything without consideration and forethought. Proof of this is that once he wished to send a letter, possibly of no great significance, with two dragoons to General Leslie at Princeton. They were fired upon in a woods by a running party or possibly only farmers, which resulted in one dead. The other returned and reported this. N.B. - This occurred about three miles from Trenton on the road to Maidenhead.

"He immediately ordered a captain, three officers, and 100 men with a cannon and the necessary artillerymen, including me, to deliver this letter. The weather was exceptionally bad. We delivered our letter, slept on God's earth during the night, and returned home early the next morning without seeing or hearing anything. The Englanders made great fun of us, and it was truly laughable, because a non-commissioned officer and fifteen men were adequate to execute this because it was to our rear and the whole distance between both garrisons was only about eleven miles.

"When we marched from Kingston to Maidenhead, Major von Dechow reported to him that as many troops had fallen behind, he would like to make a brief halt so that they could rejoin us. He [the colonel] answered that they would catch up; he had to and would proceed, even if he were only able to take half of the troops with him. So it was, and during the following days some from his regiment caught up.

"Where the enemy always caused us false alarms, he sent more than enough troops, and where the actual attacks were to be expected, and actually did occur, he gave little consideration. A non-commissioned officer with twenty men stood in the road where the attack took place, and as this post on the previous evening had been attacked by an enemy patrol, on orders of General Washington, under the command of a captain who was to have made only a reconnaissance, but with the specific order not to engage, but in case he was discovered to pull back as quietly as possible. However, this captain believed he would demonstrate his bravery if he made an attack and wounded four or five men of the non-commissioned officer's post. The entire garrison was alerted, placed under arms, and a division of the Rall Regiment was sent to see what was happening. That was all that he did, except for sending me and another nine men and a non-commissioned officer to reinforce the post.

"As soon as I arrived at my post, I set out seven posts, as well as I could during the night and sent out one patrol after another to prevent being surprised.... The night passed quietly. About an hour after sunrise, after my morning patrols had been back for some time and had reported everything quiet, and the Jaegers under my command had pulled back from their night post, I was attacked out of the woods, along the road from Johns Ferry. If I had not stepped out of the picket hut and seen the enemy, they would possibly have been upon me before I could take up arms because my guards were not alert enough because it was a holiday.

"Furthermore, the advance guard did not expect the enemy, but a patrol from Captain [Johann Henrich] Bruebach's picket, which had not yet returned. I had taken up arms in time and awaited the enemy,

119

but I too assumed it to be a raiding party. They fired three salvos at me and the seventeen men that I had under arms. After the third round, I gave the order to fire and engaged them until I was nearly surrounded by several battalions. I then pulled back, under a steady fire, to the Alten-Bockum Company, which had assembled during my engagement and had formed at an angle across the street before the captain's quarters.

"I placed myself on the right wing and continued to fire individually. However, at the mentioned place, it was necessary, in order not to be cut off from the garrison, to retreat toward the garrison as no one came to see what was happening nor to reinforce and assist us, even though the Rall Regiment was the duty watch on this night. I positioned myself in the city at the first houses and fired at the enemy which was forming for battle on the city's heights.

"At this time the brigadier made his appearance and did not know which way to turn. I considered it to be my responsibility, as he did not know what had happened outside the city, to report what I had seen and knew, and said the enemy was strong, that they were not only above the city but were already around it on both the left and right sides so that he should not consider this to be only a minor thing. He asked me how strong the enemy was. I replied that I could not say with certainty as I had to give my attention to my men, but that I had seen four or five battalions moving out of the woods and had received fire from three of them before I had to retire from my post.

"He called to his regiment then, before mounting his horse. 'Forward march! Advance! Advance!' and staggered back and forth without knowing what he was doing. Thereby losing the time and the still available moment to move to another location, honorably and without injury. He moved out with his regiment to the right of the city, under the apple trees, first wanting to attack from the Princeton Road. When the loss of the baggage, which had been left in the city, was mentioned to him (I do not know by whom), he changed his mind and attacked toward the voluntarily surrendered city with his and the Lossberg Regiments. What nonsense this was! To try to retake, with 600 to 700 men, a city which was of no value and which had been left ten or fifteen minutes previously, which was now filled with 3,000 or 4,000 enemy, in the houses, and behind the walls and fences. An only slightly more clever and less talented but knowledgeable person could see the weakness here.

"He can not be forgiven for the following four mistakes. 1) That he did not know the enemy was in the vicinity with such a strength and able to attack his garrison across such a wide river covered with ice, with so much difficulty that it took sixteen hours, after having been warned and having gotten wind of it. 2) That after the pickets had been attacked the night before and had indications enough, not to have sent strong patrols instantly to reconnoiter the ferries and woods, to seek out the enemy and to pack and send off all baggage during this time so as not to be burdened by excessive baggage and equipment. 3) To have had the garrison under arms during the night and to march across the bridge to the heights of the upper city in a position to await the enemy and his undertakings. 4) That after all this neglect and at the time of the surprise, not to have crossed the bridge, and in case this was prevented, to use every effort and means, first to form a solid corps and force a path to a place, which was still possible, from which the garrison could still be saved.

"It is a fact, and if we have learned anything from the experience, that when a person is surprised and initially tries as much as possible to keep the private soldiers from panicking, and then when that happens and they have partially recovered and seen that the danger is not as great as it appeared initially, it is then possible for an individual to once again set himself straight. But he had neither the disposition nor the necessary resolution, and there was more stupidity than courage in his conduct. If there is not much courage in a commanding officer, but only stupidity, he most often reacts in confusion with few indications of bravery and [considerable] weakness. This is the true reason that the three battalions were captured. He was twice fatally wounded because of making the ill-considered attack, died the same evening, and lies buried at the Presbyterian Church in this place which he made so famous.

"Sleep well, dear commander! The Americans reportedly erected a marker on his grave later and wrote the following words, 'Here lies Colonel Rall. His life is over.' During the battle a certain character came forth. I do not know what brought it on. I believe a heavy heart. Therefore, he went home and lay down in bed. That was sensible. In this mentioned attack the Lossberg and Rall Regiments became so confused and mixed together that it was impossible to reestablish order. Thereafter as they were nearly surrounded, they had to surrender. Our regiment did not participate with them during the attack, as I heard later when I returned to the regiment with my picket, but had been ordered to cover the flank. After the above two regiments had been repulsed and captured, our regiment sought to secure the bridge, but this was already strongly occupied on both sides so that it was impossible to move over it. We sought to wade through the water but it was not practical at that point and two enemy battalions, with four cannons, marched up close in front of us and seized the only possible place of rescue. We had to follow the two other regiments and surrender as prisoners of war. In so doing, we were able to arrange a sort of capitulation whereby we retained our swords and baggage and the troops their knapsacks. General [William Alexander], Lord Stirling promised this on his word of honor. However, already in the city the baggage was plundered, and our swords were taken from us on the march, but returned on orders from General Washington. However, General [John] Sullivan had taken one of our swords and gave his in exchange. Major von Dechow was seriously wounded in his left hip and Ensign [Ludwig Ferdinand] von Geyso was lightly wounded. The first died of his wound in Trenton. Captains [Friedrich Wilhelm] von Benning and [Johann Caspar] Riess of the Lossberg Regiment, as well as Lieutenant [Georg Christoph] Kimm, were killed. Captain [Ernst Eberhard] von Alten-Bockum, Lieutenants [Hermann Henrich Georg] Zoll and [Ernst Christian] Schwabe of Lossberg and Lieutenant Harnickel of Rall Regiment were seriously wounded.

"General Stirling assured us that he had not more than 6,000 men and fourteen cannons and two howitzers with him. This was enough to surround 1,000 men as they were not in the best disposition and were under the orders of a careless commander. Our fame and honor, earned at White Plains and Fort Knyphausen, suffered a severe blow here. After being made captive we were immediately transferred across the Delaware in boats, the river being full of ice, so that we had to resign ourselves to the possibility of death. The wind was so strong against us, and the ice prevented the boat I was in from reaching the shore, so that we were driven almost two miles down the Delaware. I therefore resolved, in order not to spend the night on this river, in such dreadful weather, and gradually to die, to jump into the river and either die quickly or to get on land. I did that and Lieutenant [Wilhelm] von Drach followed me, as did the troops in the boat. Fortunately we reached land, but had to wade through water up to our chest for seventy yards, breaking through ice in many places. It would have been no surprise if this destroyed our health and instead of a promotion and a good nest egg, returned home to an unhappy prince with a wasted body.

"Still, I must say I have no reason to reproach myself. With the seventeen men whom I had with me, I did all that was possible and all than an honorable man could be responsible for doing. Even the enemy, and especially General Lord Stirling, who commanded the advance guard and as a result was engaged with me, added his praise and acknowledgment, which is of special worth [as can be attested] by Lieutenant Piel and Lieutenant [Christian] Sobbe, who also dined with him at a midday meal. When I dined with General Washington, he made the pleasant compliment, and expressly asked to meet me in order, as he said, to get to know such an excellent officer in person. He had asked about my name and character and noted such on his blackboard, and authorized and offered free access to himself at all times, wherever he might be. What good did this do me? None! I am and probably will remain the lieutenant from Capernaum.

"But woe to him who is responsible for misfortune of many honorable men. The loss of all fortune, the unnecessary and unmeaningful blood that was spilled, is on his hands and charged to him. Enough about all that. I wish to Heaven it had not been necessary for me to enter such sad news in my journal. My own loss, although I saved some things, was nevertheless considerable. The honor, gained and previously enjoyed, had made an honorable man grievous and painfully ill.

"Trenton is a small place, lying on the left bank of the Delaware River, which separates the Jerseys from Pennsylvania and in which, quite near the city, there is a sort of waterfall, making navigation above and past the city impractical. The city is divided into two parts, the upper and lower city, by a creek which parts are joined together however, by a stone bridge. It has about 100 houses, which had been abandoned by most of the residents.....

"As stated, I and several officers dined with General Washington. He did me the honor of conversing extensively with me concerning the unfortunate affair. As I frankly spoke my opinion, that our dispositions had been bad and otherwise we would not have fallen into his hands, he asked me how I would have made them. So I replied, mentioning the mistakes to him, showed what I would have done, and how I would have escaped this situation with honor. He not only applauded these but addressed his praise to me about them and for my alertness and defenses with the few men of my picket on the morning of the attack.

"General Washington is a polite and refined man, seldom speaks, and has a cunning physiognomy. He is not especially tall, but also not short, but rather of middle height with a good body. His face bears a resemblance to that of Captain [Georg Wilhelm] von Biesenrodt of the Knyphausen Regiment. I received permission from him to return to Trenton on parole in order to look wherever possible for my writings.....

"31 December - ... N.B. - The following American generals were at the attack on Trenton: 1) General Washington 2) General Lord Stirling 3) General Sullivan 4) General [Hugh] Mercer 5) General [Nathanael] Greene 6) General [Adam] Stephan 7) General Guin and 8) a French general that I did not know and whose name I have forgotten. The first evening in Philadelphia we were entertained at the Indian Queen on the orders of Congress, with a splendid dinner, at which there was plenty of wine and punch. Afterward each found quarters as best he could."

Lieutenant Piel's diary also describes events following the capture of the Hessians at Trenton. "Immediately after our capture, we were brought over the Delaware, by Johnson's Ferry to Pennsylvania. The privates were brought to Newtown on the same day and we officers, 25 in number, remained in a house not far from the Delaware, in a small room, altogether, where we spent this night very miserably.

"27 December - This morning the captured officers were brought to Newtown under escort of the rebel Colonel [George] Weedon. To say a little about this man - His lowly origins spoke to his advantage, and thus he won all of our hearts through his friendly treatment toward us. The officers were quartered in Newtown in several inns and private houses and the privates in the church and jail. Our staff officers ate at noon with General Washington.

"28 December - This morning we visited General Lord Stirling, who conducted himself in a very friendly manner toward us. He received us with these words, 'Your General von Heister treated me like a brother when I was a prisoner, and so gentlemen, you shall be treated by me in the same manner.'....

"Lord Stirling ... asked if it would be our pleasure to accompany him to see General Washington. That one received us very politely, but we understood very little of what he said because he spoke nothing but English - a language which at that time none of us handled well. In the face of this man nothing of the great man showed for which he would be noted. His eyes have no fire, but a slight smile in his expression when he spoke inspired love and respect. He kept four of our officers for the noon meal and the rest of us ate with Lord Stirling."

Lieutenant Bardeleben, who seems to indicate in his diary that he was only eighteen years old at this time, commented on the Hessian defeat in an entry dated 25 - 26 December, "This Christmas holiday - Rall's Brigade was attacked and almost immediately captured. Washington crossed the Delaware with his corps a few miles above Trenton, where this brigade of the von Knyphausen, von Lossberg, and Rall Regiments were quartered. The brigade had to cover the right wing of the corps which had winter quarters in the cities of Princeton, Brunswick, Amboy, Elizabethtown, and Newark. The brigade of Colonel von Donop lay at Bordentown and Burlington in order, together with Rall's Brigade, to occupy the banks of the Delaware as much as possible. Washington, who during the night, disregarding a really terrible storm with snow and strong hail mixed together, had remained hidden in a woods in order to attack the city before dawn with his full force and to break into it with all his strength. The enemy was so suddenly in the city and posted so quickly before the houses that almost no one was able to take any countermeasures. The rebels, with this advantage, at the same time seized the brigade's six cannons and at once put them to their own use, firing heavily against everyone who tried to gather or tried to escape. Colonel Rall was wounded at the start and by his own host, as he came out of the house. Because he continued to live and refused [to surrender, or die ?], he was stabbed several times with bayonets and quickly died therefrom.

"Concerning this unfortunate experience, much has been discussed and criticized. In part it is not, as is now said, proper to have eighteen year old individuals as the subalterns of regiments. Still I prove the advantage which I am to the general officers, staff officers, and captains. Also, I am seen in a favorable way by all my comrades and loved from the heart by the non-commissioned officers and privates.

"Due to my fortunate situation, I find more opportunities to experience things than would otherwise have been possible. However, only the wisest of the wisest Germans can fully understand the peculiar attitude of the English toward the Americans. And therefore, the average uninitiated person of my age and experience understands even less."

Lieutenant Rueffer added a few details concerning the disaster in his diary entry of 28 December. "We received the sad news that at eight o'clock on the morning of the 26th, the Rall Brigade at Trenton in Jersey was attacked by 30,000 rebels and nearly everyone was made captive. Lieutenant [Jacob] Baum, who with Lieutenant [Johann Nicolaus] Vaupel and Ensign von Geyso of the Knyphausen Regiment escaped, and who arrived here first, confirmed the brigade's misfortune. Captain [Henrich Ludwig] Boecking and Lieutenant [Johannes] Stoebel [of the Rall Regiment], Ensign [Henrich Reinhard] Hille [of Lossberg Regiment], and Ensign [Henrich Christoph] Zimmermann [of Knyphausen Regiment], who were on command, have also escaped. Fortunately about 500 men got away. All flags and cannons were captured. Colonel Rall, who commanded, would not accept a parole and according to reports, has died. Major Dechow [of Knyphausen Regiment] has died of his wounds, and most of the officers were either killed or wounded."

Waldeck seems to have made the earliest diary comment concerning the capture of General Lee, as noted above. Rueffer's information of 17 December is a bit more concrete. "We received confirmed reports that Lieutenant Colonel [William] Harcourt of Burgoyne's Regiment of Light Cavalry had captured the famous General Lee outside his lines. A French colonel was captured with him."

# Enemy Views (1776)

Bardeleben, as usual, seems to have been able to gather all the rumors and sort out the facts. His account of General Lee's capture was recorded as an addendum at the end of the year 1776. "Lieutenant Colonel Harcourt of the King's Dragoons made a patrol into Jersey with thirty of his troops in order to learn the enemy's dispositions. After traveling several English miles he captured an enemy captain from whom he extracted various reports, among others, that General Lee was staying in a house about seven miles farther away and had only a guard with him.

"Lieutenant Colonel Harcourt marched with his detachment, unmolested, to that house, to which the captured captain had to show the way. As soon as the lieutenant colonel was near the house, he divided his troops into several small groups and rushed the house from all sides. General Lee's adjutant tried to alert the guard but the lieutenant colonel's determination soon caused the guard to flee and General Lee and his adjutant were fortunately taken to Brunswick" [on 14 December].

# 1777

## Captivity after Trenton

For the men captured at Trenton 1777 was a year in captivity. Lieutenant Piel of the Lossberg Regiment wrote the following account beginning on 1 January. "We visited General [Israel] Putnam. He shook hands with each one of us and we had a glass of Madeira. This gray-haired, old fellow might well be an honorable man, but hardly anyone but the rebels would have made him a general. We were quartered in private homes, for which we had to pay a high price.....

"5 January - Our non-commissioned officers and privates were sent to Lancaster. As much as we would have liked to remain with our troops, Congress would not allow it, but considered it best to send us to Baltimore, where Congress also sits at this time.

"6 January - Today we begin our journey to Baltimore under the escort of Captain Farmer, a German. We crossed the Schuylkill with a ferry and remained overnight in Chester, a small place where we were quartered in three inns.

"7 January - At noon today we arrived in Wilmington.... We remained overnight in Newport, a small town.

"8 January - We ate our noon meal in the small city of Christiana, and were quartered for the night at Head of Elk.

"9 January - 'Charlestown in Maryland, where we took our noon meal today, is a terrible place.... We arrived toward evening on the Susquehanna, which at this point is very wide, and we all entered the ferry house, where, because the river was frozen over, the next morning we saw that it would be necessary to spend two miserable nights. The rumor quickly spread that the captured Hessian officers were in the ferry house. This drew a lot of unpleasant visitors to us. There was no gentleman in the entire region who did not come riding to see the Hessians, about whom he had heard so many stories. They had come to see strange animals and found to their disgust that we looked like human beings.

"It seemed comical, but it is true, that they had formed such an idea of the Hessians, but in the beginning they would not believe our words that we were really Hessians.

## Enemy Views (1777)

"11 January - After we had sent our wagons ten miles up the river to have them taken across at that place, we crossed the Susquehanna in boats and went to Bushtown.

"13 January - Yesterday our wagons rejoined us and today we resumed our journey. We remained overnight in a single inn. The farther we travel in America, the less pleasing it is to us. We see more woods and fewer houses, and these should sooner be called huts than houses. But, nevertheless, the inhabitants are so enthused that they can not believe that there is any other in the world that can replace theirs. If I go into the most miserable one, the first question that the master asks me, 'How do you like this country?' I answer simply, 'Good.' He shrugs and can not understand why it does not please me above all others.

"14 January - We arrived in Baltimore. Here we had the good fortune to meet some French officers who showed us every possible kindness.... We would have liked to have spent the time of our captivity here but it was Congress' pleasure to send us to Dumfries in Virginia.

"18 January - This afternoon we began our journey to Virginia and Lieutenant Lindenberger, the worthy joiner guild master, will accompany us as our leader. We remained overnight in Elkridge Landing, a wretched town.

"19 January - We spent the night in two single houses whose owners were brothers and who were Quakers, and who jointly owned an ironworks.

"20 January - We arrived at Bladensburg....

"21 January - To Georgetown ... on the Potomac....

"22 January - Today this river was frozen so solid that we could cross with our wagons. We remained overnight in Alexandria....

"23 January - We had rain and bad roads all day and took a wrong road in the woods so that we arrived at dusk in Colchester.... Here we had a very poor evening meal. The only bread was made from Indian corn.

"24 January - The crossing of the Occoquan was very difficult. The ice was no longer solid. Therefore, after much effort, we got our wagons on the other side. This evening at six o'clock we arrived at Dumfries, our final destination, where several inns were offered for our stay.... We go about here freely on our word of honor, but are not allowed to go farther than six miles. The most genteel inhabitants of this district are very hospitable and they appreciate our visits to them.

"25 August - Because the English General [Richard] Prescott was taken prisoner on Rhode Island and the rebels therefore had a man of comparable rank to General Lee in their hands, the sentries guarding our staff officers -- since March -- were removed today and they were allowed the same freedom as the other captured officers.[17]

"4 September - Since the English fleet has shown itself in Chesapeake Bay, the captured officers are no longer considered secure enough in Dumfries. Therefore, it was decided to send us to Winchester, which lies eighty miles farther inland. Therefore, this morning we began our journey.

"6 September - Today we passed the mountains known as the Blue Ridge and spent the night in a small inn on the Shenandoah.

"7 September - At noon we arrived at Winchester and were quartered in several inns.... Congress ordered Winchester to be the place for detention for 300 of our captured privates, who until now had been in Pennsylvania; and Staunton, which lies 100 miles south of Winchester, was considered for the captured officers. But because this is considered to be such a wretched place, we were allowed to write a petition to the governor of Virginia to suggest that we be held in Fredericksburg. Meanwhile we had to evacuate Winchester, and Millerstown was the place where we had to await the governor's answer. Today we began our journey there and remained overnight in Stoverstown, or Strassburg, eighteen miles from Winchester.....

"1 October - Today we arrived in Millerstown.....

"30 October - Millerstown [also called Woodstock] was too small and too miserable to provide 28 officers with adequate quarters and therefore it was allowed that half of us might move to Stoverstown.

"8 December - Congress ordered the captured Hessian officers to be sent to Fredericksburg. Today we began our journey there. The Americans have now put such a trust in our honor that they allowed each of us to travel according to his fantasy and to choose the route which suited him best. Therefore, some took the way over Dumfries, where we were taken in very politely by our acquaintances and given three days of the best treatment.

"13 December - Today all of us entered Fredericksburg. As we did not wish to be quartered in inns, and it would have been difficult to stay in private houses, each one was permitted to rent quarters in Falmouth, which permission was utilized by most of us."

Private Reuber of the Rall Grenadier Regiment recorded captivity from the enlisted man's view, including the move from Pennsylvania to Winchester in Virginia, beginning on 1 January 1777. "We prisoners of war moved out from New Frankford and marched to the great capital city of Philadelphia ... where we were to have entered the large barracks. As we neared the city, all the people left the giant city, big and small, old and young, and assembled to see what kind of men we were. When we came face to face so that they could see us, they looked directly at us. The old women who were present screamed and scolded at us in a terrible manner and wanted to strangle us because we had come to America to steal their freedom. Others, despite all the scolding, brought cognac and bread and wanted to give it to us. But the most violent were the old women who still wanted to strangle us. The American guard which escorted us had orders from General Washington to lead us through the entire city so that we could be seen by everyone in the city. However, because the people were so angry and so threatening toward us and nearly over-powered the guard, and we were just then at the barracks, our commander said to us, 'Dear Hessians, we will march into the barracks.' They were built with three wings, and for our safety we Hessians had to march into the barracks at once and the entire American escort had to control the angry people. Then General Washington had a broadside posted in the city and surrounding countryside that we were innocent people in this war and were not volunteers, but forced into this war. They should not treat us as enemies but accept and treat the Germans as friends. 'And because General Washington had given his word of honor' conditions improved for us. Old, young, rich and poor, and all treated us in a friendly manner and each day we received one pound of bread and meat, and we lay quiet.

"8 January - We moved out of Philadelphia, were carried across the Schuylkill, and escorted to Lancaster in the province of Pennsylvania, where we again entered night quarters in a church.

"9 January - We moved out early in the morning, marched all day, and again were quartered for the night in a church. Next morning we marched on under the escort of an American detachment. Toward noon we came to a river called the Big Brandywine, which we were carried across on rafts and at night, for security, again entered a church. Every evening wherever we had arrived, our food was delivered to us.

"11 January - We marched farther and came to the Little Brandywine which we had to wade through. We again entered a church for the night quarters and had to dry our clothing in and around the church.

"12 January - We again moved out early and arrived at Lancaster at noon and entered the barracks. We Hessians were in the middle wing; the English were in the side wings, for security, and were watched by an American guard force, and everything was peaceful and calm for us. Daily we received one pound of bread and as much meat, and such wood as necessary for cooking and heating, and everything which we needed for conducting our households was delivered to us. As summer drew closer, the American officials came to us in a friendly manner and said, 'Dear Hessians, those who wish to work on the land for the farmers shall be allowed to do so. Their pound of bread and meat shall be paid in cash by the city commandant each month. The Hessian non-commissioned officers shall remain in the barracks to receive and take care of the money. When an American farmer comes and wishes to take a Hessian, he must first register with the city commandant as one who wishes to obtain a Hessian to work on his land. Next, he must present a signed declaration that he will honestly and truly return him. In case he can not deliver him, or if he has taken the Hessian to the English army or allowed him to desert, he must pay a fine of 200 pounds to the city commandant. Also, the farmer shall provide food and drink and pay a wage of fifteen stivers daily, which is equal to about six of our pfennigs.'

"So far so good. As it is now the middle of summer, it was the King of England's birthday. The English prisoners of war, who were here in the barracks at Lancaster got together and made a bonfire in the barracks' courtyard from their wood supply. This displeased the American guards. Because they [the English] were so drunk and created such a disturbance, fifteen men of those who were on guard wanted to stop this stupid action. However, the English prisoners refused to desist and attacked the fifteen men of the American guard, took their weapons, broke them into pieces, and threw them into the fire. The guard withdrew without further action. But what followed next? It was not long until an entire regiment with two cannons marched into the barracks' courtyard, swung toward the first wing and delivered a fire against the English. Some were initially killed and some wounded, and the others crept behind the brick walls. We Hessians were not involved and we did nothing to get mixed up with this affair. Therefore, the English were our enemies and bore a grudge because we Hessians thereafter received better treatment than the English. Now, as we were prospering in the land, the English fleet suddenly approached, forced its way into the harbor, and landed at the Elk River on

"25 August - in the province of Maryland and with forced marches came unexpectedly among the Hessian prisoners of war. Those who were in the neighborhood of Philadelphia were recaptured and returned to the English army. The Americans could not round up the Hessian prisoners fast enough. Those whom they could catch were transported fifteen miles farther to Newtown where a church belonging to the Herrnhuters was used as an assembly place for the Hessian prisoners of war.

"20 September - We were moved there and lay in the church until

"26 September - when the general commandant at Newtown ordered 300 Hessian prisoners and 300 of the English to march to the wild borders of Virginia. We were put under escort and marched the same day out of Newtown. The remaining Hessians and English stayed in Newtown but we continued to march, and on

"4 October - were in the province of Maryland and passed the capital city of Baltimore. We were suppose to have been quartered in the city and had actually moved into the city hall. However, the citizens of Baltimore were so bad that they wished to strangle us and our guards. The captain of the guard became infuriated, and his drummers beat an alarm at once to assemble his guard, and had them load their weapons with fresh charges. Then he said to the Hessians and English, 'Let's get out of here. We will march onward another hour.' Then the captain ordered the city council to furnish axes and broad axes, and to send pots to the next woods. When we arrived there we halted. There we could stay and rest. There we could take care of ourselves. The people of Baltimore had to send everything that we needed to us. We hurriedly made huts in the woods and lived peacefully. The captain who had to escort us 300 Hessians and 300

English prisoners of war to Virginia said, 'Dear Hessians and Englanders, it is better to have come this extra hour's distance than to have remained in the city hall where your lives were in danger.' The Congress of Maryland sits in this city which is why the residents are proud and so bitter against us, but it did not help them.

"6 October - We soon arrived in the Blue Mountains and then at the 'Sweet John and Johannes Stock' were three rivers come together and make such a frightful noise that one must think it is the dreadful raging of the ocean. On the east side were the Blue Mountains and cliffs so high one believes they will fall over. The road is hardly a wagon track wide between the water and the cliffs as it is hacked through [the cliff]. The water makes such a frightful roar because it rushes over the stony cliffs. We had to march beside this water nearly the entire day before we came to a crossing point. One stream is called Johannes Stock; the other is called Sweet John. These two streams divide Maryland and Virginia. Just now we were by the first one, marching on the Virginia side.

"But what now? Our old guard or detachment, which we had from Pennsylvania had orders to go no farther than this point on the Johannes Stock. There we were to be met by a new guard from Winchester, Virginia, but it had not yet arrived. The old guard fired their weapons [in the air ?] and marched back to Lancaster. Now we 600 men had no guard and no longer any guard with us except for our old captain, who had escorted us. We must continue our march without a guard or escort, for which we would be well-cared for when we arrived at our destination. He could not remain with us because he had to continue on to Winchester in order to get a new guard to take over our escort. He would be waiting for us in three days and then rejoin us. Now we Hessians and English prisoners of war marched on alone as far as we could. When we tired, we cooked for ourselves, and then continued marching until we finally reached a place where we could halt and where we would be provided with food and wood. The second day we continued marching, but the English did something completely different and many of them turned around and started back, swam through the water, and planned to desert to the English army. But it was to no avail. They were captured by the American residents. At noon on the third day our old captain returned from Winchester with a new guard from Virginia and the city of Winchester.

## Enemy Views (1777)

"We had just arrived at an inn where we halted and waited until all who were still present assembled. We were delivered over to the new detachment. All 300 Hessian prisoners of war were present. Not one Hessian was absent and we received a gratuity of a half can of cognac from our old captain, who had led us. However, when it came to the English, many were missing who had fled. After our new guard had taken over we continued our march toward Winchester. Our old captain went with us until he personally delivered us at the proper place to the city commandant of Winchester, and could insure that we 300 Hessians were taken care of and received the proper liberties, which also were received. The English prisoners received harder treatment, however, and were guarded in a prison while the Hessians were not guarded and were allowed freedom to go about the city.

"8 October - We arrived in Winchester in Virginia and each company of Hessians received a room in a citizen's house in the city for its use and daily everyone received a pound of bread and a pound of meat as our pay, but had to buy our vegetables. The English were put in a prison and guarded and if one wished to go into the city, he was escorted by a guard and all were treated much harder [than the Hessians]. We Hessians were allowed to go ten to fifteen miles and even farther and no citizen stopped us as an enemy, but as friends of America, because the inhabitants of the land believed that the Hessian prisoners of war would not return to the English army, but would rather remain in America. Many did this and remained in America and some of the Rall Regiment married. The other Hessian and English prisoners were still in Pennsylvania while we in Virginia were 500 miles farther inland on the wild border.

"During the spring the farmers again came from the countryside and took Hessian soldiers to work on the land and as a rule we received our bread and meat on the last day of the month. This continued until into the summer of 1778."

## Winter Quarters and Garrison Life

In the days following the American attack on Trenton the English and Hessians in New Jersey were frequently harassed by the rebels. Steuernagel recorded Waldeck losses in his diary, beginning on 5 January. "Captain [Georg Ludwig Ferdinand] von Haacke, Lieutenant [Gerhard Henrich] Heldring, and Corporals [Carl Friedrich] Bruehne, [Philipp] Reismann, and [Henrich] Bruckhaeuser, plus two drummers, [Jacob Conrad] Heinemann and [Christian] Huthmann, and fifty privates, who were on a patrol, were surrounded and captured by the enemy.

"Again on the ninth, a small command, consisting of Captain-at-arms [Caspar] von Nehm and thirty men, was captured.

"This same day, the order quickly followed, that the regiment should leave Elizabethtown and pull back to Amboy, because the enemy were much stronger than our forces, which had lost so many taken prisoner and because we could no longer defend the area. The main reason however, was that the Americans, a few days before, had attacked Colonel Rall and his entire brigade, consisting of three Hessian grenadier battalions, at Trenton, a town not far from us. The most part, which could not escape, were captured, which resulted in the Americans become bolder, braver, and more audacious."

Chaplain Waldeck's diary clearly reflects the attitude which developed among some of the Hessians after the defeat at Trenton, but which improved as the weather improved. "2 January - With the new year, new disturbances for us. Our outposts were attacked and several men wounded.

"3 January - The bad news from Trenton spread more and more and could hardly be doubted any longer. Our pleasure in Elizabethtown has passed. One can no longer lie down to sleep without thinking this is the last night, the last night of freedom. Instead of, as usual, undressing in the evening, one becomes accustomed to dress completely, and to go to bed in this manner. Here, except for rest, we have everything. Only none of this.

"4 January - The light dragoons ride out, and suddenly one is wounded, the other shot dead. These are victims of the war, who are shot dead in a dastardly fashion by the rebels that had hidden behind bushes and houses. This evening our regiment sent out a strong patrol. It captured a few prisoners, but on the return took a heavy fire from the enemy, who had taken a position in the nearby woods.

"5 January - Captain von Haacke and Lieutenant Heldring went out with a fifty-man patrol and several light dragoons. A few hours later, the dragoons returned at a full gallop. Their horses were in part wounded, and all had been ridden so hard they could hardly go farther. They brought the sad news that the patrol, after suffering a visible loss in dead and wounded from an enemy which outnumbered them four to one,[18] had been captured. Today we did not feel secure enough to hold church service, and the entire regiment had to be on the alert. Everyone had a feeling of loss concerning the fate of both men, not knowing if they were dead, wounded, or still alive. Man is inclined by such misfortune, always to fear the worst; such was the case here. As we were not safe from an enemy attack at any moment, three regiments of Scots were sent to our assistance.

"6 January - We were ordered to pull back to Amboy, as quietly as possible, in order to have the shelter of Fort Washington, which again held 20,000 men from New Jersey. But then received counter orders, and the regiment occupied all the entrances to the city. Everyone moved to the neighboring places at the same time.

"7 January - We broke camp early, but marched only at eleven o'clock. It was a very cold day and we arrived at Amboy at dusk. There were no quarters, no shelter. The barracks, which was the English hospital, were quickly evacuated. The rooms were so filled, that the troops could hardly lie down. The officers were all assigned in two rooms. How unbearable this was compared with our Elizabethtown quarters, which were so comfortable, so pleasant. Here was neither bed nor space, also no fire, also no wood with which to make one. I went with some others to the best restaurant in the city. And in this establishment, there was not even a piece of bread and butter to be had. Finally, after a hungry four hour wait, we got a bone from which all the meat had been scraped four days earlier. We returned to our barracks and fully clothed, laid down on the cold, dirty floor.

"8 January - Nothing was available here. Everything had to come from New York. In addition, we had the tension which results from never getting a full night's rest. As soon as one would lie down, he would be turned out by shots fired near the outposts. And this happened repeatedly.

"February 1777 - The winter was quite severe throughout the month. Our rations were nothing but the royal issue which was fed to the ordinary soldiers. Toward the end of the month, much sickness spread, especially high fever. Eventually, one became so accustomed to the firing near the outposts, that he would not even bother to get out of bed.

"March 1777 - The weather became more pleasant day by day. Our main diversion was riding, which we did every day.

"April 1777 - The bushes and woods began to turn green. Walking, especially in the morning and evening, was made even more pleasant by the singing of the birds. Most of our time was spent bowling, as the place was very close to our barracks. Many foodstuffs were now brought here from Staten Island.

"21 May 1777 - The garrison moved again to a site without quarters and the Waldeck Regiment was assigned on the right wing, half an hour from the city of Amboy. This was the assigned site, developed later into a very pleasant camp in a pleasant grove of trees. I continued, while the camp was so near, to live in the barracks. Captain [Christian Friedrich] Pentzel, because of a leg injury, Lieutenant [Carl Theodor] Wiegand, and the regimental surgeon did likewise. And this time, I can honestly say, was the most pleasant period that I spent in America. Captain Pentzel, who was always the life of the party,[19] would entertain us with his stories, often until after midnight. We were ready to move at a moment's notice from this location. The rooms were no longer straightened out, no longer swept, and everything began to pile up in a heap. At this time, the colonel traded me a fine brown horse for the one I owned, which was nice also, but for a rider who was a member of the clergy, too wild; and when riding, had several times put me in danger of breaking my neck. Mine was a spirited steed of four years, which I had purchased during the winter for one guinea. After the affair at Trenton, the servants of the Hessian officers fled on their masters' horses. Their masters were in part captured, in part killed, in the battle. They had no fodder for the horses and could not take them into New York. And this was the basis by which a horse could often be purchased for next to nothing. Mine was too spirited, and for me too wild. Therefore, the colonel traded with me."

Steuernagel's account also provides an indication of life in winter quarters in New Jersey in early 1777. "The regiment returned to Amboy where we were quartered in a barracks on the outer edge of town, and spent the remainder of the winter, although the enemy followed and frequently disturbed us. Here we were attached to the brigade of the English General [John] Vaughan. The other regiments near us were English, Scottish, Irish, and a combined battalion of the remaining Hessian grenadiers not captured at Trenton.

"22 May - We returned for the first time this spring to the area near Elizabethtown and reestablished our camp.

"On 18 June, Lieutenant Becker, with recruits from Waldeck arrived at our location. This was the first [Waldeck] recruit transport."[20]

The Platte Grenadier Battalion, also in New Jersey during the early days of 1777, has journal entries about the Battle of Princeton, but then notes the English pull-back to Brunswick and an uneventful winter. "1 January - Instead of entering the new cantonment quarters as expected, we received orders tonight to move out at once. At two o'clock at night the three English regiments and our grenadier battalion marched to Princeton. The baggage remained in Hillsborough. The three English regiments remained under the command of Colonel [Charles] Mawhood in Princeton. The Koehler Grenadier Battalion joined Colonel Donop's Brigade in Trenton....

"3 January - General Washington marched to Princeton and attacked Colonel Mawhood, who lost many men from the three regiments which he had with him. Today a grenadier of the Koehler Grenadier Battalion was shot dead and another man wounded.

"4 January - The corps commanded by Lord Cornwallis marched back from Trenton today to New Brunswick on the Raritan. The corps consisted of sixteen battalions and regiments and two companies of Jaegers. All of these troops entered winter quarters in a line about four miles long on both sides of the Raritan at Brunswick, which, taking the many troops into consideration, must be terrible. All the officers of the Koehler Grenadier Battalion were in two rooms. Small redoubts were constructed in the Brunswick area....

## Enemy Views (1777)

"The rebel army had drawn in around us and taken cantonment quarters which could instantly harass our outposts from all sides, and often did so. General Washington had his headquarters at Morristown. They were in the hills and were covered by strong defenses on all sides. We had no other posts in Jersey except Perth Amboy, which lies at the point where the Raritan River exits. It is about sixteen or eighteen miles from Brunswick. However, we had no communications with the corps there, except that provided by strong detachments which had to be taken from troops outside our area, when the opportunity arose. The only communications between New York and Amboy are carried on by water, but even this is uncertain because the enemy patrols on land often attack the ships.

"If I exclude two unprofitable expeditions, or more accurately, sallies, to Bound Brook, the entire winter was spent on the defensive, except to acquire forage. For this purpose it was often necessary to send out five or six regiments in order to dislodge the enemy. Duty for the troops was extremely difficult and very hard. Everyone who went on duty had to sleep under the open sky. Snow fell often and was deep and it seemed colder to us here than in Europe. Except for the delivered provisions there was nothing for the troops to buy. When the miserable and wretched quarters are considered with this, it is easy to understand why sickness could not be kept down. These evils hit the Koehler Grenadier Battalion especially hard. This unit consisted of young people only, who still suffered from scurvy from the ship. Because of the cold the scurvy returned and became an illness. Because the number of sick increased every day, and because of the circumstances that those convalescing in the hospital in New York often had to remain there for a month before they had an opportunity to return to the battalion, the duty for those still healthy naturally became ever more frequent. This caused them to become sick, until finally it reached a point where the battalion was no longer able to perform duty like the other grenadier battalions.

"10 May - To the present nothing has changed, except that nearly every day we were alarmed and disturbed, especially the Hessian Jaeger Companies which had the outposts toward Bound Brook and Quibbletown. At about five o'clock today a heavy cannon and small arms fire was heard toward Piscataway on the road to Perth Amboy. Not only was it very heavy, but it continued for a long time. The 42nd

Regiment (Scots) had planned to attack the enemy in his quarters but was beaten back with a loss of fifty men killed and wounded. This regiment had previously lost 36 men dead, wounded, and captured, including the major who was wounded.

"11 May - The garrison from Bound Brook and surrounding places made an attack on the Jaeger Company and the English Guards, but also found it necessary to fall back with losses. We now hear from the prisoners and deserters that during yesterday's attack a misunderstanding arose. According to one account, the enemy had decided to make a general attack on Bound Brook this morning at four o'clock. Because the side toward Princeton was most strongly occupied by us, a false attack was to be made there, and to accomplish the main objective, they meant to send their main force against Amboy, on the other side, where we were weaker. They hoped to defeat our troops completely, or at least to force our side to retreat, which would naturally cause us considerable loss and drive us into a corner."

On 6 June the battalion went aboard ship. "We were given the names of the transports to which each battalion was assigned. The Koehler Grenadier Battalion received one called *Bird* [and one called] the *Twiet....* Today a rebel captain who had lived in Brunswick for some time as a spy, and during that time passed himself off as a merchant, was hanged on a tree close to our camp. A letter, which he wrote to General Washington, and in which he promised to set fire to all the magazines in Brunswick on the King's birthday, 4 June, had been given for delivery to an English grenadier who had offered to desert for a promised amount of guineas. The grenadier, however, delivered it to Lord Cornwallis. The plan was exposed that General Washington was ready that same day, as soon as the fires were set, to attack us. The enthusiasm of this spy was so great that as he came to the ladder and was about to climb it, he pulled the white hood over his eyes and said, 'I die for liberty'."

However, the journal fails to indicate whether the unit sailed away or if the men were debarked.

Bardeleben also noted the execution of the spy in a diary entry of 12 June. "I received a letter ... from Brunswick that on the sixth of this month a spy was hanged who had exchanged letters with a rebel general, and who sought to get an English grenadier to desert. This spy tried by so many means to get an English grenadier to come over to him, that finally he believed the grenadier to be his friend and confidant. The spy gave him a letter to take to a rebel general which contained information that at present Brunswick was so weakly occupied that it would not take much effort to capture it. And, to make even more certain that it would be captured, the spy, as soon as he heard of the pending attack, would set fire to the city.... The grenadier was so conscientious however, that as soon as he discovered the intent, he reported it.

"The spy supposedly died in the most noble manner and his death has been celebrated as a sacrifice for freedom, that is, at the gallows he said, 'I die for liberty, and do it gladly, because my cause is just'."

Lieutenant Bardeleben recorded the following comments, among others, during early 1777, while in garrison in New York. "18 January - Early this morning the rebels advanced with a large corps up to the lines at Kingsbridge and called upon one of the main defenses to surrender with the threat of no mercy if this were not done. Shortly after giving the challenge, the enemy brought up his cannons and a heavy exchange followed. The heavy cannonade from our side, including a few lucky shots, resulted in the loss of one of their cannons and several men, drove them away so that they abandoned their appeal for the time being, and sought a complete withdrawal. We lost an artilleryman in the defenses when he was hit by a cannonball.

"It appeared the rebels had made their intended effort today because the Queen of England's birthday was to be celebrated with great pomp and ceremony, and already early in the morning many of the soldiers were in an unusually drunken condition.

"As a result His Excellence, Lieutenant General Lord [sic] Howe, on this day had made all possible festive preparations to celebrate the event. At eight o'clock this evening, before the house of Lord Howe, a rather large fireworks was displayed. Afterward a ball was held and a grand dinner. All the junior officers were also invited to attend these activities. However, as most of them were on duty, few could attend. To insure the security of the city, the usual guard on picket duty was strengthened by an additional captain, two subalterns, and fifty privates, who had to move out during the evening and were posted both in and outside the city by Lieutenant Colonel von Schieck, staff officer of the day, in order to keep watch over the entire city.

Although I was free of all duty, I settled for drinking a glass of wine in peace and quiet.....

"21 January - At nine o'clock in the evening a fire broke out not far from my quarters. During this alarm it was my fate to lose my sash and some money, about thirty thalers, in a most innocent fashion. Soon after the fire broke out I sought to bring together the men on picket duty from my quarters as well as those from other areas, so that when officers to assume command arrived, they would find the troops ready and could march off at once. After this activity I ran to the fire. As I looked about and because I noticed no picket had moved out and help was very much needed, I returned to see if an officer had arrived. However, the troops were still standing as I had left them. For fear that my commander would be held responsible for their being detained so long, I took the picket, marched to the fire, and directed the necessary action. Still none of the other officers appeared. When the fire was out I first noticed that I had lost my sash and my efforts to find it again were in vain. Most of the sailors from all the ships had been sent to help. This happened whenever there was a fire alarm.....

"6 February - Toward evening I went to the East River to shoot ducks. On this venture I nearly lost my life. A bullet flew past my ear, about the width of my hand away, without my being able to determine where it came from. The local inhabitants are still staunch rebels and go out to them [the rebels] almost daily.....

"8 February - The Combined Battalion of 500 to 600 men, from Rall's Brigade,[21] marched from here to New Jersey today, under the command of Lieutenant Colonel Schieck of the von Mirbach Regiment.....

"15 February - Again toward evening there was a fire in the city. As determined as this evil nation is to lay the city in ashes, it does not appear that they will be able to accomplish their goal. The firefighting preparations are the very best and at most, only one house can be affected by the flames.....

"21 February - His Excellency Lieutenant General von Heister was informed from Kingsbridge that Ensign [Christian Friedrich August] Cleve of the Truembach Regiment had been stabbed to death by an officer during a social evening; not in a duel, but in an unknown manner.....

"24 February - At nine o'clock in the evening our sentry was fired upon. It was a Negro, who was arrested.....

"11 March - At parade today several officers of our regiment mentioned that reports had been received that my mother was not dead, but lay dangerously ill, without hope of recovery. Lieutenant Nagel, Jr., soon found out for me that Captain Venator had received the report from a friend a few days earlier when a packet boat arrived here and his correspondent had assured him the report was well-founded -- a situation which made me uncommonly sick and whose sad images made me mad because Captain Venator did not want to tell me this secret. There was nothing more definite that I could discover in this situation; I distrusted all the rumors.

"12 March - During the past night again, Captain [Johann Friedrich Zacharias] Wagner of the Huyn Regiment, who lay sick here in New York, committed suicide by making two cuts in his neck. The reason for this terrible death is unknown.....

"15 March - Because the weather tends to get steadily warmer, we started drilling today. At two o'clock in the afternoon the regiment marched outside the city to some open fields. An ordinary drill by files was held.....

"23 March - [Code -- Captain Gall received a letter.] [Marginal Note - containing the information that my mother had died], that my brother had married Carolina von Gilsa from the establishment at Obernkirch and whose sister Charlotha had taken over the establishment again. Therefore the death of my beloved mother was sufficiently disseminated. Sad in consideration of all the circumstances. So what help is all the worry and to what purpose all the gloomy pictures which thoughts of the future increase? In the future, what I can neither see before time nor change, I will leave to God.

"24 March - On our return on most of the roads we found cattle lying, and that only because of a shortage of fodder. Above all, at the present time the maintenance for cattle is so scarce that many farmers either ship their cattle away or slaughter them. Even food for people is becoming scarce and costs more each day.....

"31 March - An English corps of 500 men under the command of Colonel [John] Bird embarked here on the North River and departed in the evening. It landed at Peekskill, thirty English miles from New York, where the rebels had established several magazines. The rebels, completely surprised by the unexpected arrival of our troops, took flight after setting some storehouses on fire. This did not prevent the destruction and burning of -- large quantities of provisions -- ... The value of all this was estimated at about 70,000 pounds sterling. Our troops could take very little of this with them because not far away, the enemy had a strong corps. They could not delay, but as soon as their goal was accomplished, they had to return to New York.

"Not one of our men was lost on this expedition.....

"5 April - At twelve o'clock noon, two men were sentenced to death. A soldier who deserted during a skirmish with a troop of rebels but was immediately recaptured; the other was a sailor who stole. Both of them had taken this well and faced death with considerable courage.....

"19 April - There was no drill. At nine o'clock in the morning the companies were measured.[22] A rather great number of rebel deserters arrived here today. According to a written proclamation today [Marginal note - from General Howe], namely that all those who prior to 1 May of this year voluntarily come in, shall, if they bring their weapons, receive not only 24 florins for each weapon, but also shall have duty [with the English], or their previous freedom.....

"21 April - At one o'clock in the afternoon the English regiments lying here in the city and nearby were embarked on the North River close to new York. No one yet knows where these troops are bound. The three Hessian regiments alone must now provide the services here.....

"26 April - Fate often takes strange twists. A butcher from Germany travels, based on his skills, and fate leads him here to America. Tiring of his profession he becomes a preacher, and finally, with the rebels, a soldier. He demonstrates some ability and presently is a general"

This last remark is apparently a reference to Peter Muhlenberg, an American general. Bardeleben's comments on garrison life continue. "1 May - The corps consisting of 1,600 men, with six cannons, under the command of Generals Tryon and Erskine, which left here on 21 April, returned to their quarters at six o'clock this morning. This detachment, as already mentioned, embarked on 21 April, went up the East River, and landed about six o'clock on the evening of 25 April, near Norwalk. The landing was completed by ten o'clock. The troops marched inland 25 English miles and arrived at Danbury at three o'clock in the afternoon, without having met any resistance. The following day and a part of the next morning was used to destroy the enemy's preparations at that place. At nine o'clock on the morning of 27 April the troops returned from there, boarded ship, and departed from there to continue on to Ridgefield, where they initially encountered a corps of rebels who had constructed defenses at the pass leading to the mentioned city. The rebels had to abandon the defenses after a minimal attack and did nothing to save their established magazines. After taking all necessary protective measures against the enemy, our troops marched again at four o'clock on the morning of 28 April, in order to return to new York. The rebels harassed them on their march and fired heavily against our troops on the flanks and on the rear guard. As the corps halted about a half mile from the ships, a rebel party of about 4,000 men, who everywhere lay behind the stone fences (which surround the fields in that region), delivered a heavy fire. Columns of our troops made a sham attack against them and while this was being carried out, General Erskine with another part charged them with fixed bayonets, scattering and massacring them. The troops then rode to the ships and were embarked at once. The losses on this expedition for the English troops consisted of ten privates dead and ten officers and eighty men wounded....

"Fortunately for this corps, nothing hindered their return route as there would have been no way to rescue them. Immediately after their departure for New York, the rebels received a reinforcement of 4,000 men......

"26 May - I finally received a letter from Sippenhausen. It had been brought by the packet boat which arrived here yesterday and was from my second sister. She informed me of my mother's death. I only learned that my old father had died shortly thereafter from Schultz, our wagonmaster, who brought the report to me later."

As noted earlier, David Grimm was one of the few men doing business in New York at this time and Bardeleben's comments contain frequent references to Grimm and his establishment. "15 February - Mr. Lepner was my guest and we ate at Grimm's house."

` "16 February - We had dinner at Grimm's house."

"25 February - During the evening several officers from our regiment and the Hereditary Prince Regiment had a picnic at Grimm's house."

"3 April - My good friend Lieutenant Bardot [Leopold Friedrich Bertaud ?] of the Landgraf Regiment arrived here yesterday and took lodgings in the Grimm house."

"7 April - Berdot was my guest and we ate at Grimm's house."

"18 April - At seven o'clock in the evening there was a small party at Grimm's house. Mr. Grimm had been so good as to have a life-size likeness of our Landgrave made and displayed it as a shield on his house. Today was set aside for this celebration. The portrait was hung. We drank a toast to our prince in silence in the house. Soon the party became noisier. Chaperons and ladies entered and we had a picnic. I was present in this group, and as usual the odd person. I danced, at first alone and then a Scottish quadrille with two young ladies (nymphs). With them I ended my presence, and it was eight o'clock in the evening when I again returned home."

Continuing his diary as summer approached, Bardeleben noted on 28 May that, "The Leib and Prince Charles Regiments and the English 63rd Regiment arrived here from Rhode Island. During the afternoon Lieutenant General von Heister received information from Kingsbridge that Captain [Georg] Stoebel of the Wissenbach Regiment had committed suicide by cutting his throat, but that the reason was unknown.

"The money for every officer from the Crown of England was received today namely, each colonel [blank] pounds sterling, each lieutenant colonel and major [blank] pounds sterling, each captain twenty shillings, each subaltern eight to twelve shillings.....

"3 June - At three o'clock in the afternoon a fleet of sixteen sails entered here. There were some Hessian and English recruits, also two regiments, or 1,200 men, of Ansbach on board. [Marginal note - The Ansbach regiments included a company of jaegers, who are to be mixed in with ours.]

"4 June - It was the King of England's birthday. Therefore at twelve o'clock noon, Fort George fired some twelve cannon shots and afterward, at one o'clock, all the warships and several transports fired [their cannons]. At nine o'clock in the evening the entire city was illuminated as proof that all the inhabitants at least gave the appearance of being good subjects of the King.....

"17 June - Late this evening a Hessian jaeger transport arrived, but one ship with sixty jaegers has fallen into enemy hands."

Lieutenant Rueffer of the Mirbach Regiment also recorded his activities in garrison in New York in 1777, confirming many of Bardeleben's comments. "14 January - The troops of the Rall Brigade not captured at Trenton arrived today from Jersey. Lieutenant Colonel [Johann Friedrich] von Cochenhausen is in command for the time being. A battalion will be formed from these men and as soon as they can be supplied with the necessary supplies and personal equipment, they will be returned to the Donop Brigade.....

"18 January - This morning at eight o'clock the rebels attacked Fort Independence on the other side of Kingsbridge. However, they were driven off with the loss of one cannon. Today was the Queen's birthday. His Excellency, General Howe, was awarded the Order of the Bath. In turn, he presented a very beautiful fireworks display this evening at seven o'clock. There was also a ball and a grand supper. All the officers were invited. All the reserve pickets were on duty to prevent any disturbances in the streets....

"19 January - This morning the rebels again attacked Fort Independence but were again forced to pull back. Captain [Alexander] von Wilmowsky of the Truembach Regiment, who was commanding there, earned much honor for his preparedness and good conduct.....

"25 February - According to Regimental Quartermaster Mueller of the Knyphausen Regiment, who visited our prisoners of war in New Castle, they are being well-cared for and he also said that after the rebels were victorious at Trenton their courage has improved and they have received an astonishing number of new recruits.....

"9 March - Captain Wagner of the Huyn Garrison Regiment cut his throat with a razor tonight due to melancholy brought on by a prolonged illness.....

"5 April - Today the admiral's ship, which previously had remained in the East River, moved, with many other warships and transports, into the North River and we anticipate an expedition is about to be undertaken.....

"13 April - Today a colonel, six officers, one adjutant general, and 88 privates of the rebel army were brought from Brunswick as prisoners. About 200 had been killed and these captured, as well as three metal cannons."

## Enemy Views (1777)

On 5 June 1777 Quartermaster Zinn of the von Donop Regiment noted that, "At five o'clock in the morning [the regiment] was embarked on three transport ships in the North River....

"In addition to our regiment, the Leib and Mirbach Regiments, which three regiments made the brigade of Major General von Stirn, and several English regiments, were also embarked, so that our corps consisted of 4,000.....

"8 June - At eight o'clock we raised anchor and sailed to Port Amboy,... landed, and entered camp."

Lieutenant von Bardeleben had been left behind in New York to watch over the regiment's baggage.

### Howe's Invasion of New Jersey

It appears that General Howe's plan for campaign for 1777 had been developed during the winter to include a move into Jersey to try to draw Washington into a major engagement and/or to proceed against Philadelphia.. Failing that, his incursion might at least draw the Americans away from Philadelphia allowing him to move by sea to a point in the Delaware or Chesapeake Bay from which he could move over a relatively level route against the city. With the return of a number of regiments from Rhode Island to New York, the arrival of the Ansbach-Bayreuth contingent from Europe, and additional Hessian recruits and jaegers from Hesse-Cassel, Howe was ready to begin the campaign.

Bardeleben wrote on 27 May 1777, "All the preparations for the new and second campaign were finished. The two English regiments which had been in winter quarters in the area just outside the city went aboard ship on the North River. The Hessian regiments, including Stirn's Brigade, were to be prepared to embark, also, to collect the heavy baggage, and to assign an officer from the von Donop Regiment to be responsible for it. This morning Colonel [David Ephriam] von Gose called me to him and gave me the assignment."

Rueffer's diary contains the following entry on 4 June. "Today we received ... the order to be standing by ready on the common place at six o'clock in the morning in order to be embarked at the King's Wharf on the North River."

Bardeleben's diary continues on 5 June. "Immediately after day-break the regiments of the Stirn Brigade sent all their heavy baggage to the baggage house where I then had to take care of it. At five o'clock in the morning the above regiments, plus the Leib, von Donop, and von Mirbach Regiments, marched to their embarkation, close to the city on the North River. The departure of the von Donop Regiment was very grievous and disturbing to me, as I was left behind, alone.

"8 June - The above mentioned troops arrived at Amboy and set up camp a few English [miles] from the city, near the corps which was already there.

"The united troops now at Amboy consisted of the 42nd and 71st Regiments of Scots, the later contains three battalions, 4th, 10th, 15th, 17th, 23rd, 27th, 35th, 38th, 40th, 44th, 46th, 55th, and 64th English Infantry Regiments. Also, the 17th Dragoon Regiment, Stirn's Brigade, the Combined Battalion under Colonel Loos, and the Waldeck Regiment.

"The listed troops are camped on the heights near the Sound to the banks of the Raritan River.

"The corps of General Cornwallis consists of the two Hessian Jaeger Companies, two battalions of English Light Infantry, two battalions of English Grenadiers, four battalions of Hessian Grenadiers, including the Koehler Grenadier Battalion, two battalions of Guards from the 5th, 7th, 26th, 33rd, 37th, 49th, and 52nd English Infantry Regiments. In part this corps was camped from the far side of Brunswick to the Raritan and the jaegers are on this side of the Raritan and the two battalions of guards are on the heights behind them, which allows the road to Bonhamtown to be kept open.

"General Washington now has taken positions from Elizabethtown to Bound Brook and his army consists of about 12,000 to 14,000 men, who are in the so-called Blue Mountains near Bound Brook."

Rueffer's account then resumes on 5 June. "Yesterday's orders were carried out this morning when ... our regiment was sent aboard the assigned ships ... *Jenny* ... *New Blessing* ... *Mermaid* ... *Lord Howe* ... and we sailed from New York on [7 June].

"9 June - At ten o'clock we could see Port Amboy, the capital city of Jersey. At one o'clock we dropped anchor and prepared at once to debark, which happened."

# Enemy Views (1777)

The Platte Grenadier Battalion Journal fills in some of the details of the army's movements beginning on 12 June. "The Commanding General-in-Chief Sir William Howe and Lieutenant General von Heister with many English regiments and Major General von Stirn's Brigade, consisting of the Leib Regiment, the Donop and Mirbach Regiments, and the Combined Battalion, arrived at Brunswick. As soon as the regiments entered camp, many defensive positions were thrown up on both sides of the Raritan River.

"13 June - Many flatboats came up the Raritan River from New York. In each flatboat was a wagon which could be put in the water easily and the boat was then loaded on it. In a short time the boats which arrived by water were seen moving on the land. At nightfall the army began the march to Princeton but then halted at the Mills River in the region of Hillsborough and Middlebush. The rebels had entered the hills on the other side of the Mills River and fortified the area. Several English regiments, the Koehler Grenadier Battalion, and the Combined Battalion remained in Brunswick under the command of General [Edward] Mathew."

After the Leib Regiment's transfer from Rhode Island to Howe's army in New Jersey, J.R. provides details of the army's movements beginning on 12 June. "We continued our march toward Philadelphia. During the afternoon we marched toward Bonhamtown and set up camp about half a mile from Brunswick.

"14 June - During the evening the entire army received orders to move out. The heavy baggage and the wives were shipped to Brunswick and remained there.....

"22 June - The entire army marched back to Amboy. All the houses along the road were set on fire. We entered camp on Staten Island. It rained all night, so hard that no one had dry clothing on his body.

"24 June - The army received orders to go aboard ship. Our ship was the *Badger*. Toward noon the fleet received orders to sail to Amboy. We were landed again at midnight. The army had an engagement in which we captured 100 men and five cannons. Our losses were about twenty men."

The Platte Grenadier Battalion Journal continues on 24 June. "His Excellence, Lieutenant General von Heister, left the army today to return to New York and it was made known to the army that he was returning to Hesse and that His Excellence, Lieutenant General von Knyphausen, had been given the command. At eight o'clock this morning, completely unexpected, the Stirn Brigade received orders to embark....

"25 June - Captain [Friedrich Ernst von] Muenchhausen, adjutant to the general-in-chief, came and brought every ship's commander the order to disembark.

"26 June - Our march was to Woodbridge and Westfield, where English headquarters was established and which is eighteen miles from Amboy, with Brunswick on our right. Meanwhile Koehler Grenadier Battalion, an English battalion, two Ansbach regiments, and the Waldeck Regiment remained at Amboy. The Combined Battalion, Donop Regiment, and two English regiments commanded by Colonel von Loos occupied the route to Brunswick. In the extreme heat the march was very tiring. The Jaegers and the English Light Infantry were engaged with the enemy from morn until night. The Minnigerode Grenadier Battalion ... suffered seven men wounded and according to reports made by two deserters, the rebels lost nearly 600 men. Our regiment lost two non-commissioned officers and two privates who remained behind too long and we assume they were captured.

"27 June - At ten-thirty the entire army marched away from the left. The march was very strenuous again and the day unbearably hot, to which was added a shortage of beverages. Our regiment lost a man who was so worn out by the heat and the march that he dropped dead....

"28 June - We continued our march toward Amboy and upon our arrival, our regiment and the Leib Regiment were immediately embarked on the previously utilized ships....

"29 June - Part of the army was transferred over to Staten Island.

"30 June - The rest of the army, numbering about 8,000 men followed. Now all of Old and New Jersey has been evacuated.

"1 July - At daybreak we raised anchor.... By evening at seven o'clock we lay at King's Ferry on Staten Island where we dropped anchor.....

"5 July - The Grenadiers and the Combined battalion and all the English regiments, as well as the Light Cavalry and for the most part, all the rest of the army embarked....

"13 July - The order came that tomorrow everyone was to be aboard ship and we hope to sail soon. The Koehler Grenadier Battalion, four English regiments, both Ansbach battalions, and the Waldeck Regiment were transferred to New York....

"17 July - We again received permission to go to New York and our hopes of an early departure were for nought, but were again raised because the admiral's ship and other warships came from New York and anchored with our fleet. Therefore no use was made of the permission.

"18 July - We received orders upon our debarkation -- wherever that might be -- to carry two days' rum, and four days' bread, and at the same time we were ordered to be on our best behavior because the general had reason to believe [the area] which the army was about to occupy had been forced to take part in the rebellion and the indiscriminate seizure of horses and other livestock was strictly forbidden....

"23 July - About eight o'clock in the morning the warships which had remained behind came out to our fleet but stayed under sail and the fleet followed after them with a northeast wind. It was a lovely day."

Bardeleben, as usual, provides more details of the movement into New Jersey than the diarists who were actually present. "14 June - During the past night the army at Brunswick had to strike their tents and form two columns with the intent of drawing nearer to the enemy, who was in camp at Bound Brook.

"Lord Cornwallis' column marched in the following order: the Hessian and Ansbach Jaegers, two battalions of English Light Infantry, of which however, four companies under Major Gray had to be transferred to Lieutenant Colonel Twisleton, the English Grenadiers, Lieutenant Colonel [Thomas] Stirling's Brigade, Lieutenant Colonel Calder's Brigade, the Hessian Grenadiers, the 16th Dragoon Regiment, of which one officer and sixteen men remained in Brunswick, and two light 12-pound cannons and four 6-pound cannons.

"General von Heister's column, with Generals Stirn, Vaughan, [Charles] Grey, and Brigadier Generals [James] Agnew and [Alexander] Leslie, followed the other column with four companies of Light Infantry under Major Gray, the Light Infantry Company of the Guards with the English Jaeger Company, all under the command of Lieutenant Colonel Twisleton, a corps of pioneers Lieutenant Colonel Trelawney's Brigade, Stirn's Brigade, the 2nd, 4th, and 3rd Brigades which have two light 12-pound cannons and eight 6-pound cannons with them, and the 17th Dragoon Regiment, mounted and on foot.

"General Leslie's Brigade had the lead and followed immediately behind General Cornwallis.

"The regiments left their tents and baggage behind and were allowed to take only two wagons per battalion for the provisions and to carry the officers who were at the head of each brigade.

"In addition to these wagons, the army had 300 others loaded with salted meat and rum, which traveled between the columns.

"General Mathew's Brigade remained behind with the 7th English Regiment, the Combined Battalion, and the Koehler Grenadier Battalion to cover Brunswick.

"At eleven o'clock yesterday evening the army set out in the previously described order and marched along the road to Princeton. After two hours it had to halt before everyone had begun to march. Because the enemy had destroyed the bridge near Kingston and the bridge near Rocky Hills over the Millstone River, the first column had to move farther to the right and take the road over Middlebush to Hillsborough, where they arrived, unhindered, after a two hour march and camped there. [Marginal note - at ten o'clock this morning] The right wing stretched along the Millstone River and above Hillsborough formed an angle.

"Captain [Carl August von] Wrede with the 1st Jaeger Company and a part of the Ansbach Jaegers was posted forward where the abatis began, and Captain Ewald and the remaining jaegers on the left to cover that flank.

"The pickets of this column formed the chain between both Jaeger companies and extended as far as the bank of the Millstone River.

"The enemy had strong detachments in the woods, which lay before this column. They moved these detachments toward the main picket on the left, from which an officer and thirty men were detached to both the left and right. The enemy moved forward to attack these two posts with about 200 men and because the mentioned detachments were in danger, they were pulled back a short way and at the same time the captain of the main picket moved forward to support them, driving the enemy back again. Two grenadiers of the Minnigerode Battalion were wounded during this action.

"The second column moved along the road to Hillsborough to Middlebush in Somerset county and took the left road through this place which the Guard Battalion with the Light Infantry and also the English Jaeger Company followed on the road to Brunswick. The von Donop and the von Mirbach Regiments had formed a straight line. The Leib Regiment formed a blunt angle to this road, which from there on made the flank with the English regiments to the 64th Regiment. The second line connected with the first and had a front toward Princeton which ran over Middlebush through the 71st Regiment of Scots, behind which stood the 17th Dragoon Regiment, the Artillery, the Engineers, and the Pioneer Corps, and joined the first line, and with this column formed a five-sided angle. In addition the 4th Regiment was so posted on the road to Bound Brook that the left wing had its pickets joined with those of the Leib Regiment on the right wing and also an abatis.

"The English Jaegers with the Light Infantry covered the left flank and that of the 4th Regiment between which they were joined with the pickets of the other regiments of the first line and covered the right flank.

"The pickets of the 64th Regiment and those of the other lines, according to the way they were camped, were placed a half mile ahead of their front.

"18 June - At daybreak an enemy corps moved against the left flank of Cornwallis' Corps. The farthest forward pickets of the Hessian Grenadiers immediately sent out a patrol to reconnoiter the enemy. This patrol had hardly neared the woods on our front when the rebels came out of the same. The rebels would have surrounded our picket if a jaeger company, with an amusette, had not come to their help, fortunately, and driven the enemy back with their fire. The rebels fled back into the woods. We had two subalterns and one private killed, three grenadiers and two jaegers wounded, the latter being captured by the enemy. Otherwise the army remained quiet.

"19 June - Because the enemy would not leave the so-called Blue Mountains near Bound Brook, which were fortified, and would not let us enter them under any conditions, and as nothing could be undertaken against the enemy in his present position, our army left its position to attempt a different approach. Therefore, at daybreak, the army had to move out and formed in two columns. Lieutenant General von Heister's column took the lead and began the march an hour before the other [column]. Previously however, the 23rd and 40th Regiments had to march half way to Brunswick to secure posts there.

"The Light Infantry with the English Jaegers, under the command of Lieutenant Colonel Twisleton, covered the right flank and the 71st Regiment the left flank. The column itself marched in the following order: The Grenadier Company of the Guards, the Guard Battalion, the 3rd Brigade, the 4th Brigade, the 2nd Brigade, whose two regiments, that is, the 23rd and 40th Regiments, then closed with the column.

"The Stirn's Brigade with the Cavalry and all the pickets.

"The baggage wagons went in front of the light corps under Lieutenant Colonel Twisleton. After a half hour march the column halted long enough for the second column to close up, while Lieutenant Colonel Stirling's Brigade covered both flanks.

"Lieutenant Colonel Calder's Brigade was in the lead, followed by the Hessian Grenadiers, then the English Grenadiers. The English Light Infantry and the Hessian Jaegers formed the rear guard. The wagons were as divided by the other columns.

"During the withdrawal of these two columns, small detachments of the enemy were occasionally seen, which also fired, but from a great distance, on the rear guard. However, they did nothing more and the army arrived unhindered at Brunswick.

"Lord Cornwallis' column camped, part on this side, part on the other side, of Brunswick, and the Jaegers took post beside the Minnigerode Brigade on the road to Bound Brook and in such a manner that they had the Raritan on the left flank.

"20 June - The munitions wagons with the pontoons and flat boats went to Amboy under the escort of the 31st, 38th, and 52nd Regiments, and the 17th Dragoon Regiment. All the sick were escorted to Brunswick in order to sail to Amboy on the ships lying there.

"22 June - Because the enemy's positions were too advantageous and the operations in Jersey could not be continued, the Commanding General Lord [sic] Howe decided to leave the area. Therefore, at four o'clock this morning the army left the region of Brunswick and moved to Amboy with the intention of withdrawing the troops as soon as possible to Staten Island, where they are then to embark aboard ship for another destination."

The Platte Grenadier Battalion Journal records the closing days of June 1777, in part, as follows. "20 June - According to orders received yesterday, this morning our battalion moved out with Major General Vaughan and escorted the flatboats on wagons to Perth Amboy. We met two jaeger companies newly arrived from Hesse and two Ansbach [-Bayreuth] regiments and the Waldeck Regiment.

"22 June - The entire army arrived from New Brunswick, also, and entered camp on a height near us. The English Light Infantry suffered forty dead and wounded today in the rear guard. The region between Brunswick and Amboy is a solid woods and ideal for the rebel manner of fighting. Between the two places lies the small, pleasant village of Bonhamtown. Six English regiments and Major General von Stirn's Brigade embarked today and went to Staten Island where they will board transport ships.....

"25 June - The six embarked English regiments and Stirn's Brigade came to Amboy on their transport ships and were landed this evening.

"26 June - The army moved out again and marched in several columns to Brunswick to attack the rebels who had moved out of their defensive camp. After the loss of sixty prisoners, many dead, and the loss of three cannons, they pulled back into the hills. Many of us died from the heat. When the advantage of this last expedition is considered, being able to cross the North River, the loss on both sides seem to balance one another. Several of the regiments which returned from the expedition were embarked yet today.

"30 June - At three o'clock this afternoon the Light Infantry and the Hessian Jaegers, which constituted the rear guard, also came here across the North River. With this we completely evacuated the province of New Jersey, which was of little use to us and had cost many lives. Perhaps it would have been better if we had not gone there, or if we had stayed. The enemy's light cavalry was already in Perth Amboy before the last boat left.....

"2 and 3 July - The army on Staten Island began a march. This proceeded very slowly as there is only one road on Staten Island, which runs from the southwest to the northeast, along which we had to march. This road is seventeen miles long, which is the length of Staten Island. Near Cole's Ferry, opposite New York, we entered camp. This place is also called the Watering Place because the ships take on water here."

Regimental Quartermaster Zinn's account of the activities of the von Donop Regiment in late June is as follows. "24 June - At nine o'clock in the morning we again received orders to take down the tents and to embark on board the ... ships, which were lying in the bay not far from the camp.... This embarkation took place with the intention of returning to Amboy to drive back the ever-continuing pressure from the enemy.

"26 June - We again received orders to debark. We were to have sailed to Amboy with the troops on the transport ships, but the light winds and the ebb tide, which just at that time ran against the ships, prevented it, and the embarkation could not take place until

"27 June - at two o'clock in the morning, and even then the troops on the *Charming Nancy*, which had run aground on a sandbank, had to travel nearly three English miles, or one [German] hour,[23] in flatboats to the landing place at Amboy. At that place the brigade of General von Stirn was formed, and because the cannons of the von Donop Regiment could not be brought up so quickly, it was necessary to take the artillery of the Koehler Battalion until, after several hours, their own regimental guns arrived. The von Donop Regiment and the Combined Battalion and an English regiment remained near Bonhamtown, in order to cover the army's left flank, where it also, because the other regiments were with the main corps and had already returned, embarked alone. The heat was so exceptionally great on this day that several soldiers collapsed and died on the march."

Although the Waldeck Regiment fought well in the assault on Fort Washington, the regimental losses in New Jersey weakened the regiment and may have caused Howe to doubt the regiment's capability as a combat unit. Whether or not that was the reason, they were assigned holding positions at Amboy during Howe's incursion into Jersey. The untested Ansbach-Bayreuth troops, which had mutinied while still in Germany, may have been assigned the same role due to Howe's lack of confidence in their fighting spirit, or merely to give them time to regain their health after the long sea voyage. The

Ansbach Jaegers, however, were integrated with the Hesse-Cassel Jaegers and Lieutenant Feilitzsch's diary provides information on the Jaegers' activity as a screening force for the main army during June 1777, "12 June - I was carried across [to Amboy] with a detachment. At seven o'clock in the evening I marched to Brunswick, under the cover of an infantry detachment.

"13 June - I arrived at daybreak, but as the company was already several miles ahead at a landing, I moved out at once and joined it at eight o'clock.

"This entire province is called New Jersey. Because I had not slept for five nights, I was very tired and slept until nine o'clock at night, when the entire army moved out. We marched throughout the night.

"14 June - At noon we arrived at Hillsborough. A detachment of English engaged the enemy. During the evening Captain Ewald of the Hessian Jaegers and I were sent to Millstone, an outpost commanded by Colonel Donop.

"18 June - Our picket was attacked by the enemy. However, as usual, they were driven back with light casualties on our side.

"19 June - The entire army marched back to Brunswick. We halted not far from the landing.

"22 June - We moved out. I was in a flanking patrol which the enemy attacked with a heavy fire, but which failed to wound any of our men. The enemy, on the other hand, had to pull back with a number of dead and wounded, and we arrived fortunately not far from Amboy.

"25 June - I went on picket duty. Toward evening about 2,000 enemy, infantry and cavalry, attacked. The entire [Jaeger] Corps at once came to my support. It was a sharp engagement. We lost no one, however, and the enemy again had to retreat with losses.

"26 June - The entire army moved forward in two columns. The enemy had occupied every height. The two columns charged against them. Our losses were not large, while the enemy lost four cannons and had many dead and wounded. This occurred near West Litt.

"28 June - We arrived at our former place at Amboy."

The journal of the Hesse-Cassel Jaeger Corps begins with the following entry, dated 23 June 1777, and then indicates that the corps was immediately involved in field operations. "Lieutenant Colonel

[Ludwig Johann Adolf] von Wurmb of the distinguished Leib Regiment assumed command of the distinguished Field Jaeger Corps today, which consisted of the squadron, dismounted, and the Company of Major [Ernst Carl] von Prueschenck, both of which have just arrived from Europe, and the companies of Ewald and Wrede, which have already participated in the last campaign, as well as the 105-man company of Ansbach-Bayreuth Jaegers, commanded by Captain [Christoph August] von Cramon -- making in all a force of 600 men -- to which a detachment of one officer and thirty Hessian grenadiers have been assigned to protect the two 3-pound cannons attached to the corps. The army had returned from Brunswick and lay encamped three-quarters of an hour from Amboy. The enemy lay at Morristown.....

"25 June - About six o'clock in the evening the outposts of the Jaeger Corps, which had about 400 men on duty, were attacked by 400 dismounted and 200 mounted enemy, but beat the enemy back without loss except for one man who shot himself. The enemy suffered several killed and we took a number of prisoners.

"26 June - The enemy army advanced as far as Basketreach, in order to attack the rear of our force during the crossing to Staten Island. The royal army marched therefore at daybreak, in two columns, and Lieutenant Colonel von Wurmb, with the companies of von Prueschenck and Wrede, formed the advance guard. Several skirmishes occurred involving the right column -- the Jaegers and Light Infantry driving the enemy from some heights, without significant loss in that the Light Infantry had only a few killed and wounded.... General Howe reconnoitered the enemy positions at Basketreach and found them too strong, so on 27 June he marched back to Rahway.... The march was very tiring and the heat exceptionally great; we lost several men who died of the heat, in particular, four men of the squadron who had marched on foot."

Lieutenant von Molitor, described the limited activity of the Ansbach-Bayreuth regiments during the summer of 1777 in a letter to a female friend in Germany, and expressed his desire to be home in Germany. "This is the third letter that I have written to you since I have been in America. I do not know if you have received them. I wish nothing more than to know how you and your children are doing, and if you are still my gracious and good friend, and that you have not forgotten me. We are all well and it seems as if the strenuous duty makes your husband and me healthier and stronger.

"We are now in camp outside Amboy, about seven and one-half miles from New York. Today five English and Hessian regiments came from Brunswick, which is about fifteen miles from here, and joined us in camp. How long we are to remain here and where we are then to march, I am unable to write. General Howe and the main army moved forward a few days ago to attack General Washington, who is not far from Brunswick. The rebels were so well entrenched that it was impossible [to attack them], even if our army were twice as strong. Our pickets were attacked twice by the rebels. Captain [Friedrich Ernst] von Beust and I were ordered to the reserve. We had to move forward and drive the enemy, consisting of about 300 men, out of the woods. We had to withstand many bullets, before we forced them into the open, where we attacked them with bayonets and drove them into flight. Only a grenadier of ours was wounded, and we killed three rebels.....

"We still receive salted pork and peas and rice, just as we did aboard ship. We also receive a portion of rum to drink. For these, from both officers and men, six coppers are withheld daily. We have received no pack horses and had to send all of our baggage and saddles into storage at New York. Each officer has only a few shirts and stockings and that which is most essential with him, because each company has been given only one wagon on which the tents, blankets, and officers' baggage must be loaded. The officers must be satisfied walking, regardless of how long the march might be. And anyone who does not wish to die of thirst, must carry his own canteen. No staff officer has a horse. They must walk like all the rest. Therefore we have taken off our boots and wear long white linen breeches and shoes, with the sword on a belt over the shoulder and the canteen on the right side. Our hair has been cut short. You would laugh and be sorry for us if you were to see us. We have received no forage money yet, and in many other areas the gracious intentions of our most gracious prince have not been fulfilled. I wrote you in my last letter that I had been recommended for captain, but I have not yet been promoted. Colonel von Eyb will wait until 1 July, because he believes Captain [Andreas Friedrich] Rheyer should return.[24] Your husband, considering his duties, is very fortunate. He cooks for himself and his officers, from the company, and they can rely upon him in every situation.... I have already written to you that Lieutenant [Carl Alexander] von Weitershausen had the misfortune to lose his mind. A Captain [Friedrich Carl] von Weitershausen was also killed in America.....

"When we march, it may well be against Boston. When we again return to Ansbach, I will bring you a black slave."

Prechtel's diary also provides details of the Ansbach Regiment's activities during this period. "13 June - Because of our eventual retreat and transfer back across the Kills River, two English frigates are lying at anchor on the water side of the city [of Amboy]. On the land side two large redoubts have been thrown up. Between the redoubts, which were provided with some iron cannons, the Ansbach regiments were posted.....

"28 June - Because the main army, under the command of General Howe, near Princeton, could not accomplish its purpose, it marched back today and was carried over to Staten Island.

"29 June - The two defensive positions between which the Ansbachers were posted, were destroyed and the troops remaining here, at the same time, were carried over to Staten Island and entered camp about two and one-half miles from the Kills River.....

"13 July - The first Ansbach Regiment received the order to be shipped to New York and is to enter camp at Harlem on York Island....

Second Lieutenant Kublan died of a high fever at New York and was buried at the Schwan Church.....

"15 July - More than 300 men of the 2nd Regiment have gradually been struck down with high fever and almost one-half of them have died from it."

## Howe's Philadelphia Campaign

General Howe's plan of campaign now called for an attack on Philadelphia from a sea-borne force. J.R. noted the preliminary steps taken for sailing to Philadelphia. "28 June - We returned aboard ship.

"1 July - We sailed out of Amboy harbor and anchored near Cole's Ferry, ten miles from New York, where the troops from Staten Island were embarked.

"18 July - The fleet, which consisted of 156 transports as well as men-of-war, frigates, sloops, and hospital and provision ships, all told nearly 300 ships, sailed from here. Toward evening it anchored near Sandy Hook."

The Platte Grenadier Battalion Journal entry for 7, 8, and 9 July 1777 noted that, "The fleet, counting the warships and all the other ships, contained 300 to 400 ships. It is the largest fleet the inhabitants of this region have ever seen."

On 23 July J.R. noted that, "The signal was given to get underway and the anchor was raised. We had a weak but good wind.....

"26 July - The wind increased and became similar to a small storm. Many ships were damaged, losing sails and masts.....

"3 August - The heat was exceptionally great and toward evening there was a storm of such force that all sails had to be lowered. We tacked from the twelfth to the fifteenth. We saw the tip of land called Cape Henry. It is the first land belonging to Virginia which is met. A river flows here between Maryland and Virginia, which is called the Northeast. Today makes one year since we first landed in America and a year and one-half since we marched out of Hesse; nine months have been spent on water and nine months on land.....

"16 August - The lightning hit one of our ships carrying English cavalry, breaking the middle-most mast in two and killing two horses.....

"24 August - We learned for the first time that we had made a voyage of 700 miles to attack Philadelphia from the rear. Therefore we were landed not far from the city of Elkton which the rebels still occupied."

Feilitzsch recorded the voyage in more detail, part of which is as follows. "23 July - We set sail at nine o'clock with a west wind. Our course was toward the east and this day on the ship *Martha*, Captain Wrede was in command and under his command were Lieutenant [Friedrich A.J.] von Wangenheim, Lieutenant Schaeffer, and I

"25 July - We sailed south to Pennsylvania. We thought we were going to Philadelphia.

"26 July - The wind was contrary and very strong from early in the morning until the next morning. Once again I realized what an unfortunate life it is at sea.

"28 July - Heavy fog and at ten o'clock thunder storms and rain, and then a strong wind from the east. At six o'clock in the evening the thunder resumed and at seven o'clock we had a frightful storm. Here I will add something. Storms here in America are much stronger and last longer than in Europe. A storm is therefore much more dangerous because our fleet consists of about 300 ships, more or less, and when there is such weather it is usually accompanied by strong winds, making it difficult for the ships to sail in company. Up to this point we had remained fortunate. God will continue to help.

"29 July - The wind was from the northwest, very strong and good. However, I did not feel well and I considered my fate again and sincerely wished I were back in Germany. Who knows where we are bound? This day we passed Delaware. We changed our course toward Pennsylvania and believed we were going to Virginia. How much heat will we have to tolerate there? The experience will certainly calm our curiosity.....

"1 August - There was a west wind and we were already far out to sea by morning. We still sailed southward toward Virginia. No one any longer knew where we were bound. Everyone said something different and everyone had to leave the decision to General Howe. We still had the strong south wind and were on a westerly course. Throughout this period the weather was beautiful and we believed we were heading for Baltimore. Captain von Cramon and his company were on the ship *Two Brothers*.....

"5 August - Although we are hardly thirty miles from the Delaware. I still believe that we are going to Philadelphia and that this maneuvering is only a subterfuge in order to get the rebels away from the Delaware and, upon news of that, we will at once enter. During the evening at eight o'clock there was frightful lightning, such as is never seen in Germany....

"6 August - Dull weather and almost no wind. I will very briefly record my thoughts on this day concerning life at sea. Anyone who has a desire to experience misery and misfortune should go aboard ship. Everyone can believe me that when I am again in Europe, should the opportunity arise for another such trip, I would certainly not go. 1) There is no bread except for zwieback which is spoiled or full of worms. 2) Stinking water with all possible impurities mixed in, because on this trip, from the beginning until now, we have not had one good drop. 3) The meat is miserable and frightfully salted so that it can hardly be eaten and then one nearly dies of thirst. 4) The entire ship is full of lice, and when it storms no one can think of anything else. Anyone who has never been to sea can not understand how miserable that can be. It is nearly impossible to take a step without risk of breaking your neck or a leg. Everything has to be securely fastened and still everything breaks and busts to pieces. If there is no wind the water is generally restless, which causes the ship to sway back and forth in one place in a dreadful manner. There is seldom a day when a person is satisfied, but how can I describe all of it as it is? God will surely help to return me to my fatherland.....

"8 August - Beautiful weather, very warm, good wind, and we sailed rapidly. The mate was very sick with a high putrid fever, very contagious, and lying not far from my bed. One can imagine how pleasant all of that is in the year 1777. Let me note here also, that the days are much shorter than in Europe, because now it is daylight about three o'clock and about, or just after, seven o'clock again night.....

"10 August - At about one-thirty in the afternoon the mate died. I must admit that I was glad because he could not have recovered and was no longer able to resist death. At five o'clock in the afternoon he was buried at sea. This took place in the following manner. He was laid on a board to which twelve cannonballs had been tied. The second mate gave a short speech in English and finally asked some sailors if this death occurred naturally and not in a violent manner. They answered this with a yes and then the body was thrown overboard.

"11 August - Beautiful weather with contrary wind and we had to tack. About six o'clock in the evening, today became memorable to me. A year earlier this incident would have affected my mind. However, since my first sea voyage on the ocean, when everything seemed miserable and unusual, I have accepted that as long as I am in America, everything will be different and consider this as something to be expected. Therefore, for this reason, this incident did not affect me as much as otherwise.

"A large East Indiaman ship of about 800 tons, which had 1,000 English troops on board and was three times larger than our ship, which had only 200 men on board, sailed directly at us with a strong wind and full sails. Everyone called for the ship's captain and mate, even while it was some distance from us. It did not turn and it appeared it would run us down. This ship, fortunately, only wiped out the after part of our ship. Two large sails with all their rigging and a small boat were smashed and broken into many pieces. The so-called bowsprit or nose of the other ship penetrated about two yards into our cabin. The force can be imagined of a piece of wood going through a solid wall. On the other ship our anchor tore out a large piece of the cabin. Other than that, we know of nothing. All the jaegers and grenadiers responded to the call and terrible frightful cracking on the deck. Everyone threw up his hands and shouted for help. Everyone can imagine how such an event seemed without my describing it further. The medic from the Hessian Jaegers jumped from our ship onto the other ship. God, however, helped us out of this great danger, The ship's captain assured us that if it had hit at the middle of the ship instead of the after part, we would all have been lost. I was prepared for anything, even this, but God helped us once again.....

"15 August - At six o'clock in the morning we raised anchor and at ten-thirty, with great pleasure and quite clearly, we finally saw Cape Henry. However, at this time the fleet also anchored because the ebb tide was running against us. At one-thirty we again set sail and despite a heavy cannonade entered the Chesapeake Bay. We also saw smoke and some ships. We assumed it to be frigates from our fleet engaged with the enemy but could not tell if the enemy were on water or on land.....

"19 August - I also heard today that a few days ago lightning had struck an English ship killing four dragoons and six horses.....

"23 August - We lay still. Some ships set sail but we did not know where. At five o'clock a frigate fired a cannon shot toward land and chased the people, who had ridden up to the water's edge, away. At once we saw cannon fire, on land in the distance, against our ships, which then replied. The point of land where we lie is called Turkey Point, Kent Island. Today a jaeger from the Major's Company died and was immediately thrown in the water....

"24 August - We still lay at anchor here. During the afternoon we received an order to disembark tomorrow morning at three o'clock, that is, the English Grenadiers and Light Infantry, and the Hessian Jaegers and us. These are the First Brigade and are to be the first ashore.

# Enemy Views (1777)

"25 August - We entered the flatboats at two o'clock in the morning. The First Brigade formed and sailed eight miles into the Elk River. The entire fleet sailed behind us and at ten o'clock we arrived at Elk Point where we landed. We occupied the heights at once without seeing a single rebel. Later we marched three miles. The heat was terrible. A Hessian jaeger dropped dead and I myself was sick."

Lieutenant Rueffer, among other comments on the voyage, noted another collision at sea in his diary entry of 26 July. "About ten o'clock the wind picked up and during the afternoon developed into a violent storm. At about three o'clock we experienced a dangerous moment. Just as our ship was turning, the *Lord Howe* bore down under full sail on our ship and caused a jarring crash that can not be described. *Lord Howe* completely broke off the cutwater, or the so-called sock-mast. No less damaging, one of our anchors, which had a circumference of eighteen inches and was fastened on the side, broke through and ruined the entire outboard side of our cabin. The *Lord Howe* had at the same time suffered even greater damage. Most of its sails were torn and a large part of his cabins were left on our ship, and furthermore, as our sailors say, our anchor did great damage and gouged a great hole in his side. Our sailors inspected our ship as soon as the two ships, with the greatest effort, had been separated, and found to our dismay that we had taken much water and we were thereafter compelled to assign six men daily to pumping every second hour. Each hour the water rose one foot....."

"3 August - This day we, and all who are on our ship, hold in memory because as the result of a thunder storm our lives were placed in an incomparably frightful fear of death. Toward six o'clock we saw thunder and lightning in the distance. At this time the admiral gave a signal to change course toward the southeast. Our ship had hardly turned when the storm hit with indescribably frightful thunder and lightning and so suddenly that the crew, because of the terrible storm and hurricane winds which it carried, nearly were robbed of their sense to lower the sails, which resulted in the ship being rolled far over on the left side and nearly covered by waves so that we were sure that we would be drowned in the inevitable sinking of the ship. The wind, coming from the right side, tore all the upper sails to shreds and then, as the wind slackened after a while, the ship rolled slowly from the left side to the right side and our fear of entering eternity, at this time, generally began to abate. Everyone involved turned his first thought to giving thanks to Heaven for having saved him from this danger.....

"15 August - As we would have had to pass the dangerous sandbanks between Cape Charles and Cape Henry at dusk, a signal ordered us once again to anchor.....

"21 August - At nine o'clock this morning to our left we saw the capital of Maryland, named Mundeltown or Annapolis, numbering about 160 houses. It lies close on Chesapeake Bay on a peninsula of land on the Severn River. This and two other small streams form the peninsula. Two flags, which were to be seen just outside the city, showed that the commander-in-chief's warning of 18 July did not apply, but that the city's inhabitants, like most of the Americans, were rebels. Through the telescope it could be seen that there were thirteen red and white stripes in these flags, which represented the thirteen provinces....

"22 August - At eleven o'clock we anchored again and in Elk River. The flatboats, in compliance with yesterday's orders, were immediately lowered into the water. We had to go through a narrow passage which small ships had marked by putting out white flags. Toward five-thirty a boat carrying a sea officer notified the fleet to anchor as close as possible between the admiral and the battery ship *Vigilant*. Therefore, this was done at six o'clock. On our voyage we have not been as close to land as we are now....

"24 August - On a given order all the flatboats were called to the admiral's ship and there is no longer any doubt that this is the place where we shall once again stand on solid ground. At eight o'clock this morning a signal from the admiral's ship reaffirmed the 18 July order to go on land with provisions, and these were immediately issued. We hope to debark this afternoon. Toward two o'clock this afternoon His Excellence, Lieutenant General von Knyphausen, had himself transferred aboard the *Elizabeth* because the *Nonsuch*, due to shallow water, could no longer sail farther....

"25 August - This morning we raised the anchor and sailed a few miles farther on Elk River and anchored at two o'clock. From that place we could see, only a short distance away, that the English and Hessian Grenadiers had already landed. Toward evening our brigade also began to land. Major [Emanuel Anselm] Wilmowsky with fifty men was also fortunate enough to land by Elk's Ferry. But as evening came on too quickly and the admiral was traveling around in the fleet, and further, as a strong storm struck, the admiral ordered that no further landings be made this evening. And we therefore had to spend another night aboard ship. According to the orders issued, the debarkation was to be made in the following order:

"1st Debarkation: under General Earl Cornwallis, and under him, Colonel von Donop. The 1st and 2nd Battalions of Light Infantry, the 1st and 2nd Battalions of Grenadiers, and the Hessian and Ansbach Jaegers.

"2nd Debarkation: Hessian Grenadiers, Queen's Rangers, Guards, 4th and 23rd Regiments.

"3rd Debarkation: 38th, 49th, 5th, 10th, 27th, 40th, 55th, 15th, and 42nd Regiments.

"4th Debarkation: 44th, 17th, 33rd, 37th, 46th, 64th, and 71st Regiments.

5th Debarkation: Stirn's Brigade, consisting of the Leib, Donop, and Mirbach Regiments, and the Combined Battalion.

## The Move Inland

"26 August - This morning at daybreak the flatboats for our debarkation arrived and we went on land at Elk's Ferry. We stood around in confusion, without tents because they had been left aboard ship."

According to the Hesse-Cassel Jaeger Corps Journal the situation by 28 August had not improved. "The army departed Turkey Point and marched to Elkton which had been deserted by all the inhabitants. We had no reports about the enemy, and no maps of the interior of this land, and no one in the army was familiar with this area. After we had passed the city no one knew which way we were to go. Therefore, men were sent out in all directions until finally a Negro was found, and the army had to march according to his directions. This Negro knew nothing about the enemy army himself, but said that a corps of the same was reported to be in the area, and some of their scouting parties were seen by the Jaeger Corps, which constituted the advance guard. We remained lying here [in camp] until 3 September and meantime took several prisoners from the frequently observed scouting parties.....

"3 September - The Jaegers, consisting of the companies of Prueschenck, Wrede, Ewald, and Ansbach, in all about 400 men, were the advance guard [for a column under Cornwallis] and learned during the march that enemy pickets had been there [Cecil Courthouse].... After half an hour our flankers saw the enemy's rear. The mounted jaegers engaged them at once, and Captain Ewald, who led the corps' advance guard, soon came under fire. Then we saw the enemy, consisting of about 1,000 men, as they marched into a thin woods. The Jaeger Corps deployed from the middle, to the right and left, and formed so that the Ansbachers were in the middle, the point which the enemy at once attacked. They were driven back into another woods with considerable effort. Here they defended themselves obstinately, which brought our right wing, under Captain Wrede, with the hanger [saber] to the attack. We also drove the enemy from this place, and they took a third position behind Cutger's Bridge.... We buried between thirty and forty of the enemy dead, not counting those concealed by the bushes. Our loss was one dead and fifteen wounded Hessians, and four wounded Ansbachers."

Lieutenant Feilitzsch's diary entries for the period, in part, are as follows. "28 August - At three o'clock we marched. I had the advance guard and soon ran into the rebels. After a few shots they retreated. We took a few prisoners. Not far from Elkton an officer of our corps took fourteen small ships on which there was sugar, coffee, tobacco, and other provisions and also a great amount of silver products from Philadelphia.[25] The value was estimated at one million guilders. This day we marched about eight miles.....

"31 August - Here I must say that this region of Maryland does not appeal to me. Compared with other provinces where we have been, this region is not well-developed. A bare woods, here and there a small place with a house and field, but where not a soul is to be seen....

"1 September - It was exceptionally hot. During the night there was a false alarm when a jaeger deserted his post and ran back into camp claiming that the rebels were coming and were only 300 yards from us. This was all untrue.....

"3 September - We marched out of camp at four o'clock in the morning. At a distance of about two and one-half miles we entered Pennsylvania and shortly thereafter encountered an enemy corps of

3,000 men in the region of Wellstreg, or the Fort Euren Kill or Kat-scher"s Mill. The enemy stood firm. The fire was extremely heavy and lasted about two hours. Only our corps was engaged and a few English. The enemy attacked three times. We lost one dead and ten wounded, while the rebels suffered nearly fifty dead and according to the deserters, very many wounded. We made few prisoners. Our jaegers conducted themselves well and after the enemy was driven back, we entered camp during the afternoon not far from this place. The affair began at eight o'clock and lasted until ten. The company had two wounded, a corporal and a jaeger.....

"8 September - We moved out at five o'clock in the morning. We marched about seven miles along a route not suspected by the enemy, although he had obstructed the obvious route with chopped-down trees and entrenchments.....

"10 September - I must note here in Pennsylvania, that the inhabitants are encountered everywhere. This province is more loyal to the King than all the others. Therefore nothing is taken from the inhabitants. It is not more heavily populated than the others."

Ensign Carl Friedrich Rueffer, of the Hesse-Cassel von Mirbach Regiment, entered comments about the progress of the army in his diary also. "29 August - In this stretch of land we have not seen any females because they were told by the rebels that the Hessians would have misused them in an unpleasant manner, so they have all fled....

"30 August - At noon today we received orders to march tomorrow and those among the sick needing special care were sent aboard the hospital ship....

"31 August - At every house we passed a pardon letter was nailed, and a watch was posted to prevent looting.....

"3 September - Today for the first time, the Jaegers and Light Infantry were engaged sharply with the enemy. Our losses were about twenty men. The loss to the other side is still unknown.....

"5 September - According to the statement of a dragoon deserter, the enemy has withdrawn across the so-called Christiana Bridge, which they reportedly had strongly occupied, and their corps, which was commanded by two generals, [Charles] Armand and Holzendorf, of the French service, on the third lost 300 men, including those carried as missing.....

"8 September - At two o'clock we passed Newark, a very pleasantly built city of about sixty houses, but completely uninhabited. Also, now and again, very pleasing country homes which previous to this time we had seldom encountered in this area because it is rather thinly settled....

"9 September - From this date we encountered many owners of houses, most of whom were Quakers and who appeared to be loyal to the crown.... Toward ten o'clock this night our patrols encountered parties of the enemy. However, it was an adjutant from the commander-in-chief with an escort of dragoons, bringing an order to General von Knyphausen to change his march route because information concerning a change in the enemy's dispositions had been received during the march. Unfortunately the adjutant was fatally wounded."

## The Battle of Brandywine

Feilitzsch wrote the following account of the events of 11 September. "We marched at four o'clock in the morning. At eleven o'clock we halted in a woods in order to first reconnoiter the enemy. An hour later we resumed our march until two o'clock, when we again halted because no one knew where or how the enemy was located. During this time we heard a heavy cannonade from near where we had been in the morning. This was General von Knyphausen, who had gone a different way with the first column and attacked the enemy's left wing. That was only a feint, however, to draw the enemy attention to himself until both columns could attack at the same time. At three-thirty our advance guard encountered the enemy. At once the army marched into battalion order. Our corps entered the line on the end of the left wing. At exactly four o'clock the battle began. The small arms fire was terrible, the counter-fire from the enemy, especially against us, was the most concentrated. All the battalions made the attack. The enemy had made a good disposition with one height after the other to his rear. He stood fast and was certainly four times as strong as we were. However, all the English and Hessians conducted themselves as they are well-known to do. They attacked with great strength and with the bayonet. The enemy was defeated and had to retreat. [The battle] lasted until seven o'clock and during their flight Knyphausen strongly cannonaded them. Our company suffered four wounded and five dead, including one officer who will surely die later. The loss for the entire army amounts to about 500 men. The enemy loss can not be determined because, in so far as possible, they took their wounded with them. Still their losses are much greater than ours according to the statements of the many deserters. They also lost fourteen cannons, one howitzer, and one field culverin. The battalions took post on Brandywine Hill not far from Brandywine Town, or Delanot. At eight o'clock in the evening we entered camp not far from that place. Once again God had helped us."

The Hesse-Cassel Jaeger Corps Journal provides a far more detailed account of the battle. "At daybreak the army moved forward in two columns. The right under Lieutenant General von Knyphausen, including Major General Grant, took the road to Chadds Ford, seven miles from Kennett Square, and arrived at ten o'clock in front of the enemy. The advance guard of that column, consisting of the Queen's Rangers, skirmished with the enemy outposts as the column moved into position, and as General von Knyphausen was not to attack before the left column under Sir William Howe and Lord Cornwallis attacked the enemy's right wing, he engaged the enemy only with artillery fire, as if he intended to force the ford. Meantime Sir William Howe marched to the first arm of the Brandywine Creek, a distance of twelve miles. The Jaegers were the advance guard for that column and were supported by the 1st and 2nd Battalions of Light Infantry commanded by Lieutenant Colonel [Robert] Abercromby. These were followed by the Grenadiers. Captain Ewald with fifty jaegers, supported by Captain [William] Scott with his company of light infantry, had the most advanced position before the Jaeger Corps. About two miles this side of the Brandywine we met an enemy patrol of 100 men, which retreated into the woods, leaving a few prisoners behind. That force was the one which notified General Washington of our approach and convinced him to change his belief, which up till now, was that our army really intended to cross at Chadds Ford, and to detach the largest part of his army to oppose us.

"Meanwhile we crossed the first arm of the Brandywine Creek at Tinckloss Ford, and the second at Jeffreys Ford. Here was such a high hill that 500 men with two cannons could have made passage impossible, or at least extremely difficult, and since this was not occupied, the general was reinforced in his belief that Washington wanted to retreat and did not wish a battle. Further, that it was not his wish to engage, but that Congress had given him positive orders to attack. It was extremely difficult to move the artillery over the height, and therefore the column halted on the opposite side of the height until two o'clock. After the artillery had been brought over and we could resume our march in columns, in this rather open area, Captain Ewald, about three o'clock, reported the enemy army was marching toward us. Thereupon we received orders to form in line. The advance guard deployed from the middle to the right and left. The Jaeger Corps had the honor to man the extreme left wing and consisted, after the departure of the detachments under Captain Ewald and the cavalry, which because of the difficult terrain could not follow us, to something over 300 men with two English 3-pounders, which were covered by the Hessian Jaeger Lieutenant Balthasar Mertz with thirty grenadiers, but during the advance had to be left behind with the Grenadiers. The Hessian Grenadiers supported the right wing and the 3rd Brigade of Englanders likewise was to support the Jaegers and Light Infantry in the second encounter. But, because of the uneven terrain and the movement toward the left by the column, we saw nothing of it during the battle. About three-thirty the Jaeger Corps found itself close to an enemy advance post with two 6-pounders and 600 men, which stood on a height, with woods in front of it. Our two 3-pounders opened fire first, the Jaegers attacked the enemy, drove them into a bush, and dislodged them three different times before they retreated back to the main body of the army. The main army was advantageously posted on a not especially steep height in front of the woods, with the right wing resting on a steep and deep ravine. That wing was directly opposite the Jaegers, and in the same bushes from which the Jaegers had driven the enemy corps; and the Jaegers were engaged for over half an hour, with grapeshot and small arms, with a battalion of light infantry. We could not see the 2nd Battalion of Light Infantry because of the terrain, and because we received only a few orders, each commander had to act according to his own best judgment.

"Meanwhile the firing became more general and stronger, and Lieutenant Colonel von Wurmb heard that the right wing was advancing. Therefore, he had the call to attack sounded on the half moon [hunting horn], and the Jaegers and the battalion of Light Infantry stormed up the height. The enemy retreated in confusion, abandoning two cannons and an ammunition caisson, which the Light Infantry, because they had attacked on the less steep slope of the height, took possession of. We had no cavalry, our people were very fatigued, and in only a moment, the enemy were out of sight. Therefore, we made no prisoners. The Jaegers lost Lieutenant [Carl von] Forstner of Ansbach and six men killed, as well as Hessian Jaeger Captain [Johann Friedrich] Trautvetter, three sergeants, and 35 men severely wounded. Of these, the first and most of the latter died. The losses by the Light Infantry were not as great, and of the enemy we saw many dead and wounded. Thereafter, as the 2nd Battalion of Light Infantry had attacked so far to the right, we stood at a great distance from the army and not until about seven o'clock in the evening, on order, were we rejoined to the army at Dilworth, where they had encamped on the battlefield rather than continuing in pursuit of the enemy. Lieutenant General von Knyphausen, according to the agreed upon plan, had advanced over Chadds Ford as soon as he heard firing on our front, taking three cannons and a howitzer in a small redoubt, which was overrun, and also forced the enemy into flight. The total losses to the royal army are about 400 dead and wounded. The enemy, on the other hand, is figured to have had 300 killed, 600 wounded, and 400 taken prisoner.....

"14 September - Today the sick and wounded of the army were sent to Wilmington, escorted by Colonel von Loos with the Combined Battalion.....

"16 September - The Mirbach Regiment marched to Wilmington to provide protection for the hospital."

Rueffer also gives a rather detailed account of the battle in his diary. "10 September - According to statements of two spies who encountered a picket, a forward detachment of the enemy, consisting of about 1,000 men, mostly cavalry, is only a quarter of an hour away from us and the army is on Brandywine Hill, three or four miles from here -- a half hour beyond Kings Square.

"11 September - This day has earned the right to special recognition because it has given us the greatest glory. At daybreak the entire army marched in two divisions, by half companies, from the right. General Cornwallis' division, which the commanding general accompanied, was on our left. General von Knyphausen's division, consisting of the following troops assembled on the road to Welsh

# Enemy Views (1777)

Tavern: one officer and fifteen dragoons, the English Jaegers, the 1st and 2nd English Brigades, baggage and livestock, and the rear guard consisting of three battalions of the 71st Regiment, of which the 2nd Battalion covered the rear of the baggage, the 3rd Battalion was on the right flank, and the 1st Battalion was on the left flank. Hardly one and one-half miles had been marched when the most advanced regiments were in a sharp engagement with the enemy, in which they suffered a great loss. Toward nine o'clock, after the most advanced troops captured one height after another with great difficulty and heavy losses, we received the order not to advance farther and we lay on the heights at Chadds Ford opposite Brandywine Hill, which according to statements by deserters and prisoners was occupied by 24,000 men, who except for a continuous cannonade remained unengaged. Also, the Queen's Rangers and English Jaegers were in continuous hand-to-hand combat with the most advanced enemy parties. At four o'clock in the afternoon we heard, on our left wing, the heavy fire by General Cornwallis' corps, at which instant we moved out and advanced on the enemy's left wing, by Brauntown, or Schatzes Ferry, through the Brandywine Hills, and seized them, whereupon the enemy retired in great fear, and in a battery from which he had done us much harm and which the 4th English Regiment had stormed, he left a Hessian cannon which had been captured at Trenton, two French cannons, and a howitzer. The approaching dusk prevented our pursuit of the enemy. Therefore we camped on the Brandywine Hills. The enemy losses are still not known, but certainly so many that their army was scattered during their flight and is near complete collapse. The bravery displayed by all the English troops today, those under the command of General Cornwallis as well as General von Knyphausen, can not be described with too much enthusiasm. Our loss is still not known. Everyone thinks however that is very large. The corps commanded by General Cornwallis was also very fortunate, having captured a Hessian cannon lost at Trenton, eleven French cannons, and one howitzer. Stirn Brigade lost seven men, of whom two of those killed and one man wounded were from our regiment. The Congress had eaten at a house which we passed today, Welsh's Tavern, and they had strongly recommended that their troops hold Brandywine Hill....

"12 September - The English headquarters was at Dilworth, the Hessian's at Brauntown, and the field hospital set up at Talbot.

"13 September - We remained in the same camp as yesterday. Our losses consist of 58 English and four German officers killed or wounded, including Captain Trautvetter from the Hessian and Lieutenant von Forstner of the Ansbach Jaegers, Lieutenant von Baumbach of the Guards, and Lieutenant [Conrad] Du Puy of the Linsing Grenadier Battalion, as well as thirty jaegers, of the total loss of 400 men, and on the enemy side, about 800 men....

"14 September - We remained quiet and are occupied with the search for wounded. The Combined Battalion marched toward Wilmington today, escorting a part of the prisoners and the wounded."

J.R. noted the Battle of Brandywine in a few brief sentences, commencing on 10 September. "We marched until the tenth, when we were ten miles from Brandywine Hill, where the rebel army stood in full strength awaiting us.

"11 September - We attacked the rebels from three sides. The battle lasted from ten in the morning until six in the evening, when the rebels vacated their defenses. The entire first line had to wade through the Brandywine River which was a half mile in front of the trenches. The rebels were fortunate that they surprised us [by retreating suddenly], otherwise they could have been easily pursued. The loss on our side consisted of 500 dead and wounded. The rebels losses were ten times as great. We captured eleven cannons and one howitzer, including three cannons which had been lost by the Rall Brigade at Trenton.

"14 September - Our troops took Wilmington [Delaware], where the hospital was established until we could capture Philadelphia."

## Events Leading to the Capture of Philadelphia

We learned today that General Washington has withdrawn to Germantown.... Unfortunately our destination, based on a report from Colonel Loos, was to march to Wilmington, as he felt his force too weak to combat the rebels there, who were commanded by Generals Rotley [Caesar Rodney ?] and [William] Smallwood.

"At five o'clock this morning the entire army had marched from the right. Our regiment crossed the Brandywine Creek, through which we had to wade on the day of the battle at Brandywine, and ... joined the Combined Battalion and two battalions of the 71st Regiment of

Scots.... The prisoners, except for the wounded, who were initially held at the so-called Gymnasium, number about 325 men.....

"17 September - Our regiment changed camp and moved from the road leading to the Christiana ridge to the right wing, resting on the road to Philadelphia, which is some 27 miles from here.....

"19 September - From a captured letter written by an outwardly loyalist-inclined Quaker to a friend in the rebel army, the Quaker expressed his desire to be with his friend in order to avoid the Hessian tyranny. Although the best order and conduct are maintained here, many who secretly support the rebels live here. The author at the moment sits with his comrades in the Gymnasium.

"20 September - News from a resident of Philadelphia is to the effect that the enemy army, as well as most of the inhabitants, has fled the city. As the prisoners and the wounded are to be put aboard ship as soon as the fleet arrives here, we hope to leave this place soon and to return to the army.....

"23 September - An enemy deserter brought the news today that an enemy corps had been attacked by General Erskine and had suffered 200 dead and wounded.

"25 September - This morning at about nine o'clock, quite unexpectedly, we heard a heavy cannonade from ships' cannons on the Delaware, mixed with small arms fire. The rebels, who still occupy New Jersey with a part of their army, had engaged our fleet, which consisted of eight armed vessels, with a strong battery. Therefore ten flatboats with marines were sent to demolish it. We could clearly see how they landed during the bombardment and disregarding the small arms fire of the enemy, not only carried our their orders but pursued the enemy several miles.

"26 September - ... Colonel von Loos however, has learned from an inhabitant from Philadelphia that General Washington had still strongly occupied the bank of the Schuylkill River, because General Howe made him believe he would cross near the enemy's front from that place where he then stood. Therefore General Washington had lined the complete bank with artillery. However, General Howe, during the night, had marched twelve miles farther up the river, crossed with the greatest expedition, and stood more nearly in the enemy's rear than in his front.

"27 September - The news of yesterday was confirmed. This entire morning we heard a nearly uninterrupted cannonade, whose cause however, is not yet known.

"28 September - Through an expedition which came in during the night to Colonel von Loos, the news of the twentieth that all the inhabitants of Philadelphia had fled, was contradicted, The cannonade of yesterday had been fired by inhabitants of Philadelphia, which had been captured yesterday noon, when General Cornwallis entered the town at eleven o'clock with some English and two battalions of Hessian Grenadiers. The only resistance which was found was a 36-gun frigate by the name of *Delaware* and two gondolas of eight and ten cannons, which fired continuously. As soon as Earl Cornwallis neared the city, a battery of heavy cannons opened fire and sank a gondola, at which the frigate, whose wing was being covered, ran fast aground on a sandbank and so fell into our hands and was also immediately occupied by the King's troops.... A patrol sent out today which went as far as Newtown, brought back the news that 800 or 900 rebels reportedly had passed Christiana Bridge six miles from here.

"1 October - We learned from two people who arrived here from Philadelphia that ... General Washington should make a movement ... to take his army into Jersey and to this end he moves ever nearer the Delaware. General Howe reportedly is near him and actually at Germantown, An English grenadier who had been made a prisoner of war came in today as a deserter and brought the news that as soon as General Howe turns more toward the south, all the prisoners are to be sent to South Carolina....

"2 October - Reportedly the enemy militia have withdrawn from Christiana Bridge and only small detachments have been posted along the road to prevent our side from bringing in foodstuffs."

During this same period Feilitzsch, with Howe's main army, recorded the following activity on 16 September. "At five o'clock in the morning we marched. At twelve o'clock there was a heavy rain and at two o'clock we encountered the enemy. There was heavy firing on all sides. We drove them back and they lost four dead, two wounded, and twenty men taken captive. We moved into camp at that place. It rained extremely hard during the night."

When General Grey attacked an American force commanded by General Anthony Wayne at Paoli, Feilitzsch recorded the event in his diary entry of 20 September. "We were to march but were informed of a large enemy supply depot and so remained in place. At one o'clock during the night the English attacked a large enemy corps which was to have attacked our flank during the march. Five hundred men were killed and wounded on the spot and 200 were captured. The remainder escaped to the enemy camp without weapons."

He then describes Howe's maneuvering toward Philadelphia and the local area. "21 September - We marched after the enemy at three o'clock in the morning but as we did not know exactly where they were, we halted....

"22 September - We went on patrol with the entire army but saw nothing of the enemy. However, shortly thereafter they often approached and were observed. During the afternoon a strong detachment of jaegers and grenadiers crossed the water toward the enemy. First there was a heavy cannonade and throughout the night the outposts exchanged fire. We also began building bridges in order to make the enemy believe we would attack this place. At ten o'clock at night, at my picket but not under my responsibility, a great alarm occurred in the corps and nearly in the whole army because a woman attempted to flee [to the enemy]....

"23 September - We had to cross the Schuylkill near Watts Ford. The troops had to wade across with the water up to their body. About two o'clock we entered camp on the road to Philadelphia. Attractive and splendid houses were to be seen here, but few inhabitants.....

"25 September - At eight o'clock in the morning we marched from our camp to Murring Town. We passed this day very peacefully and without seeing a single rebel.... It rained heavily all afternoon and into the night. At five o'clock we entered camp near the Falls of the Schuylkill. From here it was five English miles to Philadelphia.

"26 September - We had a day of rest. Today two English and two Hessian grenadier battalions were placed in a brigade under the command of General Lord Cornwallis so they could march to Philadelphia and take possession of the city.....

"29 September - I went on picket duty. The next morning at three o'clock, while it was still very dark, a young person of about twenty years of age approached the outer sentry very hastily. The sentry challenged him three times, but he gave no answer and continued to come nearer. The sentry fired and shot him dead on the spot.

Enemy Views (1777)

"30 September - At nine o'clock in the morning I had this unfortunate individual buried.

"1 October - Everything remained quiet. It appeared as if we would remain here for a long time. I wish to Heaven the campaign were finished and that we would have the very much wished-for peace, and that in the coming spring we will be able to return to our fatherland in Europe."

Again, the Hesse-Cassel Jaeger Corps Journal gives a more detailed account of events beginning on 16 September and leading to the capture of Philadelphia. "The army marched to the left, to attack General Washington, who was marching on the road toward Lancaster, according to reports received. The Jaegers and Light Infantry actually fell in with these forces and had sharp skirmishes. One captain, one officer, and twenty men of the enemy force were captured and many left on the battlefield. On our side, one man was killed and several wounded.....

"18 September - The army joined together today on the Lancaster Road near White Horse. We learned that the enemy had crossed the Schuylkill and was encamped on both sides of the Perkgomy River.....

"21 September - The past night General Grey, with the Light Infantry and the 42nd and 44th Regiments, was detached in order to surprise an enemy corps of 1,500 men under General Wayne, which stood alone in a woods. He reached the enemy at one o'clock in the night, broke in the left flank, with unloaded weapons, killed and wounded 300 men, took eighty prisoners and the greatest part of the baggage, as well as many weapons, but the enemy had taken their cannons away. The English loss was one captain and three men killed and four wounded.... The army continued up to the bank of the Schuylkill, and the camp extended from Falland Ford to the French Creek. Therefore the enemy left his location and marched to Pottsgrove. The Jaegers and Light Infantry, as usual during the march, skirmished with the enemy at every defile and woods.

"22 September - Sixty jaegers and 100 grenadiers, under the command of Captain von Wrede, crossed the Schuylkill over Falland Ford this afternoon and seized several outposts in order to mask the main river crossing. The army during the night resumed its march. Lord Cornwallis commanded the advance guard -- the Jaegers at the head of the same -- and crossed the river at Chadds Ford, where the

181

entire army crossed without meeting any resistance. Captain von Wrede then recrossed the river and rejoined the army, which by morning was already encamped with the left wing resting on the Schuylkill. The 2nd Battalion of Light Infantry was detached to Swedes Ford, where the enemy had left six spiked, iron cannons....

"24 September - All quiet. General Washington had pulled back to Schibbach Creek....

"25 September - The army marched to Germantown in two columns and entered camp.

"26 September - Lord Cornwallis marched at eight o'clock this morning with the English and Hessian Grenadiers toward Philadelphia, which has already been evacuated by the enemy and the Congress for some time. Cornwallis occupied the city during the afternoon, in order to protect it from the enemy ships lying in the Delaware River, and to throw up three batteries for six 12-pounders. These were still not completed when on

27 September - two frigates and several other ships came from Mud Island and attacked the lower battery of two cannons. The largest frigate of 30-guns, called the *Delaware*, anchored 500 rods from the battery and the others somewhat farther away. At ten o'clock they began to bombard the city as well as the batteries, with a heavy fire, but as the ebb set in, the *Delaware* ran aground. The four cannons of the Grenadier Battalions were then turned on the ship, and so well directed that it struck and was occupied by a company of Englanders. The remaining craft, after the frigate was lost, returned to their former station at Mud Island.

"28 September - Nearly all the residents have left Philadelphia. The enemy have very strongly fortified Mud Island, which is an island in the Delaware River some miles below Philadelphia, and this disrupts the communications by water, which because of provisions, is absolutely necessary for us. In addition to this island and the works on the Jersey shore, the enemy has many ships to aid their defenses. Also the river is barricaded by *chevaux de frise* against the entry of our ships, so that it will be necessary for us to formally besiege the place in order to open communications, to which end, necessary preparations are already under way."

## The Battle of Germantown

"The many detachments which General Howe had sent to Philadelphia and into the Jerseys to besiege and occupy the city caused General Washington to consider a movement, especially since being strengthened from Virginia, to attack the royal army. With this in mind, [as recorded in the Hesse-Cassel Jaeger Corps Journal on 4 October 1777] he broke camp at Schibbach Creek, and about two o'clock in the morning we received reports of his approach. Lieutenant Colonel von Wurmb immediately moved out with the Jaeger Corps, reported the attack to General von Knyphausen, and occupied the bridge over the Wissahickon near Vandernen's house. Shortly thereafter one heard firing on the right wing, and about three-thirty the Jaeger Corps was attacked by a corps of 4,000 men with four 6-pounders. Our corps had to give up the bridge, but took position on a height opposite and defended it with rifle fire against the enemy's repeated attempts to force a crossing. The four enemy cannons fired continuously upon the Jaegers, while our 3-pounders could not reach the enemy. The firing meantime became general and very heavy on the right wing, until about nine o'clock, when Lieutenant General von Knyphausen reported the enemy's left wing turned back. At this, Lieutenant Colonel von Wurmb attacked the bridge again and drove the enemy away, and also away from the opposite heights, with a withering fire. As the attack had to be continued through a long defile, the enemy had time to retire. Therefore we found only twenty dead and, as the jaegers were much fatigued, without support, and were only 300 men, there was no further pursuit.

"In the center of the army the enemy had attacked the Light Infantry and driven it back. Lieutenant Colonel [Thomas] Musgrove threw himself and the 40th Regiment into a stone house, which the enemy then attacked. As a result, the enemy was held up, instead of being able to press his main attack before our entire army took up arms. Then the army counter-attacked the enemy and drove them out of the city, and into flight. They retreated to their previous camp on the Schibbach Creek, leaving behind 300 dead, 600 wounded, and 400 prisoners. Our losses were near 400 dead and wounded, among the first, General Agnew.

"Lord Cornwallis had heard the firing in Philadelphia and at once ordered three grenadier battalions to march from that place. He alone arrived soon enough to take part in the action, but the battalions were too late."

Feilitzsch's account of the battle is quite brief, starting on 3 October. "We heard the enemy was very near us.

"4 October - At daybreak we heard our pickets fire. We moved out at once and then heard a heavy cannonade on the army's right wing toward Germantown. The enemy drove our pickets back; we moved forward. The enemy fire against us from both cannons and small arms was heavy. We answered ineffectually with our rifles because we were too far from them. However, after three hours we heard that our good English allies had repulsed the enemy. We then advanced causing the enemy to take flight. Our corps lost eleven wounded, but the company did not lose a single man. Thank God! However, the army lost about 250 men, dead and wounded. The enemy had 13,000 men, but our army was very weak. No one will believe when I say what our strength was, because of the many necessary posts we had to occupy. The enemy losses in dead, wounded, and captured amounted to about 2,000 men. Fifty-one officers were captured. I went on picket duty.

"5 October - It was reported that the enemy was 24 English miles from here and had a desire to attack us once again with his whole army. Surely God will protect us.....

"9 October - At two o'clock in the morning the picket alerted us and at three o'clock I marched to relieve the picket. This day we learned that the enemy had marched to Parringtown and still desired to attack us again. At twelve o'clock at night I had another fatality when a private in the relief force approached a guard and was accidently shot. This seriously bothered me because he was a very good man."

On 4 October Rueffer noted reports by residents of Wilmington, which may have been planted by Washington to hold those crown forces away from Philadelphia, and on the next day gives a report on the Germantown battle. "4 October - Many residents from this place, who have traveled inland fifteen to twenty miles, have brought dependable information. There are 8,000 to 10,000 rebel militia about ten miles from here, who are on the march from Lancaster to attack us. As a precaution all our pickets have been extended outward and all planks on the Brandywine Bridge have been loosened so that they can be taken up at first alarm. Toward evening we could already see large groups and complete regiments working steadily on defensive positions on the heights which are across from our camp. The approach of darkness prevented more exact observations.

"5 October - As sure as I felt that my outposts would be visited by the enemy during the night, nevertheless, we were undisturbed. Above all, all the reports appear to have been false, as a patrol made by Major [Johann Friedrich Georg] von Stein encountered absolutely nothing, and no one.[26] At noon today a rumor, which is certainly our wish, was spread by a man from Philadelphia, that the main rebel army attacked General Howe at Germantown yesterday morning. The rebels won an initial advantage, not only driving our outposts back, but forcing the army, while still not daylight, to retreat and taking many cannons from the British Light Infantry. However, a colonel of this Light Infantry seized a house in Germantown with his people and prevented the enemy from advancing farther over the bridge at Germantown, on which he could fire from this house, so that General Howe gained the time necessary to regroup and thereby seize the advantage, not only to counter-attack and to retake the captured cannons, but to pursue the enemy for eight miles. The Queen's Rangers and all light troops reportedly have suffered a great deal and it is even said that the Queen's Rangers, who survived Brandywine Hill, have been completely destroyed. More exact news concerning the losses to both sides is still not available. General Agnew is reportedly killed and General Stirn was slightly wounded in the arm.

## The 1777 Campaign from Canada

During the spring of 1777 Captain Pausch noted in his journal that the campaign from Canada was about to get underway. "For three weeks we have been under orders to be prepared to march. St. Jean is the weapons and assembly point and the principal magazine for munitions as well as provisions. Our fleet also lies there, all the large and small vessels at anchor. Everything there is to be transported to Isle aux Noix in batteaux when the army moves out of winter quarters. At that time we will occupy our post at Crown Point, which was captured last year, and from there undertake our expedition against Carillon, or Ticonderoga. The enemy fleet reportedly is still in a poor condition there. On the other hand the fort and its surrounding area is rather well-fortified and equipped with cannons."

However, in the entry of 15 May, Pausch noted signs of animosity developing between the English and German allies, such as "Already for more than three weeks I drill constantly every morning from six to eight o'clock according to our formerly established method, with my company alone. During the afternoon the English use two of my cannons and my company uses two of the same, and drill with cartridges. Personally, for my part, I never participate, but only send an officer, because each time an English captain is assigned thereto, and only an English officer commands at that time. The national pride and haughtiness of these people allows them in their conceit to command my troops, but I can not command them.

"Finally, for my own drill, I requested powder from General Philipps. He also granted it to me. It was during the staff meeting at about one o'clock. By three o'clock the entire idea had been countermanded by the major or whomever, and so due to their jealousy, so contrived that I was not to drill alone, but only with them during the afternoon at four o'clock, according to their commands and drum [beaten commands], which my men do not understand, and which for me, if I were to be allowed to drill them alone, this would soon be learned, and as they now see that my troops are already much quicker and work smoother, they and all the observers of the correctness of this openly give us credit for that. So now the devil with his jealousy has been turned loose. Instead of the previous friendship, only enmity is to be seen....

"Major Williamson got the idea to order me to no longer allow the soldiers to go out in the evening with their sabers. I told him however, that I did not expect this order from anyone else and would permit it to be complied with only if received from my illustrious prince, and, if one of my troops, during the day or before retreat at nine o'clock, were to be seen without his saber, he would receive corporal punishment the next morning. That was also the situation for us in garrison in Germany, where four or five battalions lay, and a standing order required that no soldier was permitted to cross the street unless dressed and wearing his sidearm. I have heard nothing more since, because it would be unfortunate for my troops if fist fights broke out, and one would return home with a black eye, another blind. There is still the greatest friendship and unity between the non-commissioned officers and men of the Royal Artillery and my company, which on my part I have sought to maintain with the greatest attention and concern."

Lieutenant Dufais also noted the friction in a letter to the Hereditary Prince on 1 May 1777. "Your Highness, herewith I lay myself most humbly at Your Highness' feet to present the following problem. Since we have been in this country, we have been in the brigade of Major General Philipps, the chief and commander of the English Artillery. How unpleasant it is for us to have a chief to whom one can not speak nor explain things, and who does not even have an adjutant who can speak to him [for us]. All orders which we receive from him are written, part in French, part in English, and we must guess or run around for a long time until we find someone who will be kind enough to clarify them. How dangerous that is for us, and how easily our honor could be lost, by the failure to understand such an order.... The duty, which we are required to perform with the English Artillery, since our assignment, is that we are forced by our chief, according to their system, to learn a new drill with the understanding that in all things we will be held to the same standard according to the promise of Major General Philipps, and considering the service, that appears to be the situation. However, we have the greatest reason to complain to Your Highness about the pay for the battalion equipment and forage money, as the most junior English artillery lieutenant received 72 pounds sterling during the past year. Even an overseer, who has a grade comparable to our servant supervisor, receives 25 pounds sterling. On the other hand, while we have performed the identical service from the beginning, and during the last campaign did not serve an hour with our German troops, even during that time, we were paid only 12 pounds, 17 shillings. When I asked our chief, General Philipps the reason why in this case we were not considered on an equal footing with his officers, and I told him that we had reason to complain about that, he tried to make all sorts of excuses. Although I tried my best to make him understand that it gave us a reason to be dissatisfied, when he could find no other excuse, he said the money which had been paid to his artillery officers was an extraordinary allowance from His Royal Majesty. As the [treaty] articles were known to me, I pointed out the article in which it is stated that all allowances which it pleased His Majesty to grant, such as in this case, where we had to serve with them, were to be paid to the [German] troops in the same proportion. Although I mentioned this in all the arguments, nevertheless we have received nothing more. I can come to no other conclusion than that he means to do us wrong."

Pausch's entry for 18 May contains the following information. "Major General Philipps received the following order on 10 May 1777 from His Excellency, Lieutenant General and Commander-in-Chief Carleton, from the headquarters at Quebec. "It has pleased His Royal Highness most graciously to order a detachment of the army from my command to go on an expedition under the command of Lieutenant General Burgoyne, which is to consist of: Grenadiers, Light Infantry, the 24th, 9th, 20th, 21st, 47th, 53rd, and 62nd Regiments. A detachment of fifty men from each mentioned regiment is to remain behind. A detachment totaling 650 men from the German troops is likewise to remain behind."

On 19 May Pausch closed a section of his journal with this reference to the 1777 campaign. "P.N. - The start still appears, and possibly will begin, by the end of this month."

Pausch resumed his journal on 21 May, and on the thirtieth of the month wrote, "Everything in the local garrison remains peaceful. The Grenadiers and Light Infantry which have lain here since leaving winter quarters however, began their march toward the Sorel River and are reportedly to continue on to Chambly, St. Jean, and Isle aux

Noix, where, as the advance guard, they are to wait for the army and then march forward."

Then backtracking to the 28th, entered the following notation, "Last Wednesday, the 28th of this month, the English artillery company of Captain Wacker marched from here along the Sorel River to join the advance guard, and from there along the same river. As it is nearly impractical to transport the baggage overland the entire distance, most and possibly all [the rivers] must serve our forward movement.

"30 June [sic - May ?] - I received this order; On orders of His Excellency, General Burgoyne, all officers, without exception, are to take no more equipment with them than that which is absolutely essential. Therefore, they must find a means of storing [the excess] in a safe manner. The officers of the English Artillery have offered to store the equipment of the officers of the Hanau Artillery with their own. On the direct order of General Burgoyne the companies are to take no more than three wives with them. The above order applies to the infantry and not to the others."

Captain Friedrich von Germann, of the Hesse-Hanau Infantry Regiment, mentioned the start of the campaign in a letter to the Hereditary Prince, dated 2 June 1777. "Your Highness, I most humbly report herewith that after we received the order yesterday afternoon to break camp, the company moved out of its previous quarters this morning, the second of June, and rejoined the regiment at Berthier. We are to remain here until the fourth, when the march is to be resumed over Sorel and Chambly to Cumberland Head, the main assembly point for the army. Lieutenant [Maurice] von Buttlar is to take the heavy equipment to Trois Rivieres tomorrow. There is not a single soldier in the company who does not sincerely wish to meet the enemy, and all those detached to remain in Canada show considerable disappointment about that. This attitude will earn the regiment more honors if we have the good fortune to engage the enemy this year."

The following general order concerning the start of the forward movement of the army is contained in the Order Book of the Hesse-Hanau Regiment, having been published at Cumberland Head on 18 June. "After the initial movement, the army is to camp in the following order of battle and until ordered otherwise, the same order is to be maintained.

# Enemy Views (1777)

## Left Wing

| 1st Brigade | | | 2nd Brigade | |
|---|---|---|---|---|
| Regt | Regt | Regt | Regt | Regt |
| Rhetz | Specht | Riedesel | Pr. Fried. | Hesse-Hanau |

Brigadier Specht                                    Brigadier von Gall

The next day's order read in part, "Tomorrow the army is to begin its movement and instead of reveille, general march is to be beaten. At the same time the quartermaster sergeants and guards and the carpenters from the Grenadiers are to embark and depart. They are to assemble in their batteaux on the right wing of the 9th Regiment, where the vice-quartermaster general is to meet them and lead them onward. At the same time, tents are to be struck and the baggage loaded in the swiftest batteaux. An hour after general march is sounded, assembly is to be beaten and each regiment is to embark where the batteaux are standing. As soon as General Burgoyne believes that the regiments can be ready to depart, a cannon shot is to be fired from the ship *Maria* and the sail on the forward mast unfurled. Then the batteaux of all the regiments are to be arranged in the following order and remain so: first the Jaegers, the von Barner Battalion and the Grenadiers, under the command of Lieutenant Colonel [Heinrich] Breymann, are to form the advance guard. They are to be followed by the Dragoon Regiment. The 1st English Brigade is to lead the line, 200 yards behind the Dragoons. The German Brigades are then to follow in order. Each corps is to be formed in columns with a four batteaux front. Each battalion, which is on the flanks, must try to maintain an even distance from the center line. As soon as everyone is in line, two shots are to be fired from the *Maria* and a flag raised on the forward mast. Then everyone is to begin the march and the batteaux are to use sails and oars as necessary to maintain proper distances."

The capture of Fort Ticonderoga and the engagement at Hubbardton with a portion of the retreating Americans, as well as the fighting at Fort Anne, was noted under orders issued at Skenesboro on 10 July. "6 July - The rebels abandoned Fort Ticonderoga. They were driven out merely by the presence of the army. On one side they ran beyond Skenesborough, and on the other side to Hubbardton. They abandoned all their ships, a great amount of ammunition, provisions, and all sorts of baggage.

"7 July - Brigadier [Simon] Fraser with half of his brigade, but without artillery, encountered 2,000 fortified rebels. He attacked and chased them away. The rebels lost many officers, 200 dead, even more wounded, and 200 taken captive. Major General [Friedrich] von Riedesel with the advance guard, consisting of the Jaeger Company and the Light Infantry, arrived in time to support Brigadier Fraser, and with well-directed orders and the brave conduct with which they were carried out, gained a share of the honor of the victory for his troops.

"8 July - Lieutenant Colonel [John] Hill at the head of the 9th Regiment was attacked near Fort Anne by the rebels, who were six times stronger, and after withstanding three hours of continuous fire, he drove them off with heavy losses. After this incident, the rebels abandoned Fort Anne, after setting it on fire. A detachment of our army now occupies the area beyond Fort Anne.

"This rapid progress, for which God can not be adequately thanked, gave our troops much honor, the greatest praise is due the Riedesel and Fraser forces, which by their bravery, demonstrated by both officers and men, have done the greatest service for the King, as they have withstood much fatigue and bad weather, and although they have been without bread, they have not shown the least unwillingness" [to perform their duty]

The animosity between the English and German allies finally resulted in the outbreak of violence on 16 July as noted in the Hesse-Hanau Order Book at Castleton on 18 July, which also called for the assignment of soldiers' wives to hospital duty. "The disturbance between the Germans and the English troops on the sixteenth was caused by the sale of cognac, and some English soldiers forgot themselves to the extent that they violated one of the strictest articles concerning conduct, and attacked a guard. When, in the future, either an English or a German soldier conducts himself so that the good relations between the two nations, which until now have been so praiseworthy and which between good troops must always be maintained, should be damaged, those individuals causing such to happen are to be severely punished. As the inspector for the hospital finds it necessary that two wives from each regiment of the army must be provided to care for the sick and wounded, the regimental chiefs are to give the necessary orders."

The defeat of a primarily German detachment at Bennington on 16 August was noted in the Hesse-Hanau Order Book on the following day. "An effort has been made from the left wing of this expedition to obtain such a supply of cattle and provisions so that the line would be in a condition to continue the march. As this effort has failed because of the fortunes of war, therefore the troops must halt for a few days to allow the movement of foodstuffs. The various regiments are to use this opportunity to collect their sick and convalescents. The 47th Regiment is to march to [Fort] Edward tomorrow, where it is to receive orders from General Philipps. The regiment is to assume responsibility for the prisoners taken by Lieutenant Colonel Breymann, and such others as are here. The flour taken from the enemy must be delivered to the commissariat.

"The vehicles and wagons taken from the enemy are to be delivered to the Breymann Corps and the 47th Regiment tomorrow, and then turned in to the wagonmaster general....

"The corps of Lieutenant Colonel Breymann is to send its wounded with the wagons which brought the flour to Doctor Hess at the hospital, where they are to be taken into the houses and every measure taken for their care. Both regiments are to send their surgeons also, in order to provide the best care for officers as well as privates. General von Riedesel extents his highest praise to both battalions for their bravery and declares that it was not their fault that they could not completely defeat the enemy, but that the time lapse was the cause that both corps could not unite. Honor is always present for troops which conduct themselves well, and the general herewith thanks Lieutenant Colonel Breymann as much for his demonstrated fortitude as for his good dispositions, which allowed him to withdraw from the battle. The same applies to Major von Barner for the bravery which he demonstrated during this opportunity. And, as the general does not which to neglect everyone but the senior officers who distinguished themselves, he is sending a report to His Highness and will himself, at all times, acknowledge the merit that the officers displayed during this opportunity. Although this expedition was not as successful as was anticipated, there is no reason to be downcast, but we must wait for another opportunity to again recapture that which was lost. When the coming day has passed and possibly other troops have been found, who have returned, Lieutenant Colonel Breymann is to submit a casualty list of both battalions."

Although Captain Pausch made no mention in his journal of the artillery roll at Bennington, Lieutenant [Michael] Bach of the Hesse-Hanau Artillery noted his capture and subsequent difficulties in a letter to the Prince on 3 October 1782. "On 16 August 1777 I was captured on the field of battle during the unfortunate affair at Bennington, badly mistreated and completely plundered. I tried to borrow money from some Brunswick officers -- because, as I was the only Hesse-Hanau officer, I had to seek relief and help from strangers. With the money I again bought the most essential items and thereafter I was embarrassed and had to do my own laundry in the river. No sooner did I have this least little bit, than the rebels again stole everything, and once again I was in the same position that I had been after the plundering on the field of battle. Following that we were all brought together on a prison ship, treated very badly thereon, and especially, as I am a Hessian against whom the rebels are very bitter, I would have been lost without the protection of the other Brunswick officers. From the prison ship we were taken to Westminster in Massachusetts Bay, receiving quarters initially, but fed Negro food, and still badly treated. Eventually we received some money through a flag of truce from Winter Hill, from our respective regiments and corps. Thereafter no one could receive lodging or entertainment without paying. We had to pay dearly for everything, even to the point of extravagance, and the most necessary small clothes and uniform items were at such a price that they could hardly be afforded.

"In October 1778 we went with a flag of truce to New York, at our own expense, in the hope of being exchanged, but after many hopeful promises of a speedy exchange by His Excellence, Sir Henry Clinton, we had to undertake our return voyage to our enemies, who then believed that we had brought much money with us, and in consideration the quarters and other necessities became much more barbaric than before. Then we were led through various provinces and through all of Pennsylvania, again at our own expense, as it pleased the farmers and administrators there to charge so much for the quarters and necessities, as well as for the wagons, as to be cruel. This did not cease until the fortunate time of our exchange, when all the inhabitants, with and without character, gave us the final blow and sought to profit therefrom in a revengeful manner, so that when I embarked at Elizabethtown to cross to New York, they also took all my silver, but for the return of my still very few belongings I gave a hearty thanks to most Holy Providence. Now here I was once again, in order to be able to present myself without blushing, at the disdain of strangers for my uniform items, which were not only of the most graciously diverse colors, but still more by their wretchedness and for an appearance unlike that of an officer, unwillingly asking, with an oppressed heart, for another advanced payment, only sufficient so that visibly I would be able to perform duty in the most gracious character of a 2nd lieutenant, because my captain had not yet been exchanged, but was in Virginia."

Lieutenant Spangenberg, also of the Hesse-Hanau Artillery, suffered even more as the result of the engagement at Bennington and eventually his wound permanently crippled his right arm, as he wrote in an undated latter to his Prince. "Your Highness will already most graciously know from the reports submitted that I was severely wounded during the affair at Bennington on 16 August of last year. I originally hoped that my wound would be of a nature which would not prevent my remaining in Your Highness' service in the future, so that I could make myself more fortunate and more worthy of Your Highness' special favor. Unfortunately due to the poorly organized English open field hospital, with the negligent care by the English doctors therein, whose services I had to have initially, and which were of the most intermittent sort, I often went three days without being bandaged, and added thereto was the miserable retreat for the wounded, and finally, as a result of the entire army being captured, the lack of transportation made it necessary, as I could not remain in the hospital, to follow the company. I was always in hope however, that I would have a quick recovery and quickly be able to resume my duty, but my wound grew so much worse from these fatal conditions, despite our Regimental Surgeon [Jeremias] Heidelbach having done everything possible and providing excellent care, while I was under his care, and which I definitely desired, I now no longer have more than a hope of recovery of this shattered member, and throughout my life will have a lame and useless right arm, to which Regimental Surgeon Heidelbach also attests to Your Highness with the proof, which he will present to Your Highness."

Regimental Surgeon Heidelbach confirmed the details of Spangenberg's disability in an attestation dated 24 March 1778. "That Lieutenant Carl Dittmar Spangenberg of His Serene Highness and Hereditary Prince of Hesse-Cassel's illustrious Artillery Corps was wounded by a small ball in the affair at Bennington on 16 August of last year. The ball entered at the lower angle of the shoulder blade, splitting, during its passage, not only the joint of the shoulder bones, but also the upper arm bone near the end of the joint, which was cut out by a surgeon and he then lay seven weeks under the care and dressing of an English doctor in the flying camp hospital. Then, due to disturbances and poor transportation, the damaged bones developed an infection from a lack of proper care and thus made the healing more difficult until now, despite the best care by me. Now however, there appears hope of healing, after which the mentioned lieutenant will remain lame in the upper arm and unfit for further military service. This is attested by me, as requested, in line of duty."

After Bennington drastic measures were introduced to curtail attempts to desert, as noted in orders on 23 August. "There is reason to believe that such individuals have been sent into our camp by the enemy and sought to get the men to desert by promises and with a fluency in the German language. In order to insure that those sent-in individuals receive their just punishment, a reward of 100 thalers is to be awarded to individuals who can expose them, having seen that one of that type of person spoke with the soldiers. In order to prevent such conversations, sentries are to be attentive that no person who is not a soldier or an officer's servant is allowed in camp. The provost, all patrols and guards must inquire, in case they see strangers in the camp, what they are doing there. It is herewith made known that in case a sentry, patrol, Provincial, or Indian captures a deserter, a twenty thaler reward is to be paid. Should the deserter run away however, and then be shot dead, the Indians are to bring in his scalp."

## Enemy Views (1777)

### Freeman's Farm, 19 September 1777

Burgoyne's march from Canada was stopped at Freeman's Farm, near Saratoga, after two battles there on 19 September and 7 October. Captain Pausch's journal contains detailed accounts of his activities in those battles. "On 19 September 1778 [sic] the entire army was set in motion during the morning. However, the Hesse-Hanau Regiment was held back to serve as the rear guard to protect the artillery train, the baggage, and other vehicles, and also the batteaux coming down the Hudson with provisions. Our march dispositions were the same as on the seventeenth, in two columns. The right column consisting of the royal troops, penetrated through the very tiring roads and passages of the mountains and forests, and the left along the plains beside the Hudson. Here we quite soon found another bridge across a swampy ditch demolished. A short halt was made here. This passage was made passable as quickly as possible and the march continued, but not very far, because in a short distance we soon found a similarly destroyed bridge, which had to be reconstructed and made usable. While thus employed, firing could be heard, a bit after one o'clock in the afternoon, on our right wing. It began with small arms fire, but finally was intermingled with cannon fire. This firing, which quickly became very heavy, doubled our attention. General Philipps, who had stopped by our column in order to hasten our march, hurried off toward the right wing. After a short time General Riedesel detached two companies of the Rhetz Regiment, under Captain von Fredensdorf, onto a hill lying to our right and slightly forward, and went there himself at the same time to reconnoiter the terrain. The pickets of our right wing had come in contact with the enemy outposts, before which ours however, as they were outnumbered, halted and again withdrew under the protection of the approaching column of our right wing. Then together with this support a major battle commenced which in a rather short time became a determined action by both sides. General von Riedesel sent one of is adjutants back to us with the order that his regiment was to march at once, and as quickly as possible, up the hill, where he himself would show it where to take position. The regiment had only begun its march when another adjutant came from the general with the order for me to detach two cannons forward. As here at the front of our column, on the left wing on the plain, everything was very peaceful and quiet, I personally joined the two cannons, their ammunition, and carts with trenching tools on the forward march. And, leaving Lieutenant Dufais with two cannons as well as all the baggage and his necessary orders, hurried up the hill, where I found the previously mentioned regiment. I placed my cannons as well as the situation permitted in order, if necessary, to be able to make use of them. The two companies of the Rhetz Regiment previously mentioned had been drawn close to the general, prior to my arrival, in order to cover the right wing of his regiment with the aid of an abatis, which he had them make ahead of the ravine, in thick woods and undergrowth. However, he detached Lieutenant Reineckien of his regiment to a hill ahead of us which was thickly overgrown, with a small detachment to observe, in case the enemy during this situation would attempt a movement, and to provide a timely report thereof. For this purpose he was to send out sufficient patrols, and in case of being attacked by a superior force, he was to fall back on his regiment. Meanwhile we remained quietly in our first position.

"The general at once sent out a patrol of a non-commissioned officer with several troops in an effort to establish communications between us and those heavily engaged in action, so that if it became necessary, he could march to their aid. The patrol remained out. He at once sent off the second and third [patrols], one after the other, because he feared the first had lost its way or perhaps been captured. The firing seemed to draw nearer to us from which it could be assumed that our right wing was retreating. Without having received additional information from the [patrols] sent out, and having no other patrols to expect, we left this, our first position, and marched not more than a quarter hour toward the firing, formed in order of battle, and I occupied the road which led out of the woods with both of my cannons. As at that place damaged fences were to my left, I hurriedly had them torn down so that the enemy could not take cover behind them during his approach. That was our second position.

"Brigade Major [Friedrich] von Geismar, who was now in General von Riedesel's suite, was meanwhile sent by the general to see where it might be possible to pass through to meet General Burgoyne and to report to him how he, [Riedesel], was situated in support with his regiment, two companies of the Rhetz Regiment, and two 6-pound cannons. He only awaited the order if he should advance and thereby reinforce him. During this time the patrols returned, one after the other. The second patrol sent out had found communications between us and the part engaged in the action to be wide open. Therefore the general marched at once. He marched to the right and chose this route so as to make a diversion against the enemy's right flank. He gave the order to beat the march and during the advance 'hurrah' was called out repeatedly. Now having descended the hill, von Geismar returned from General Burgoyne with the order for General von Riedesel to continue on to the attack on the enemy's right flank, and if possible to pursue. However, the woods and intervening marsh, behind which the enemy stood, prevented the last, and I had to hurriedly lend support with my two cannons toward the right wing of the English 21st Regiment. My wagonmaster, who had obtained a good mount, had to go ahead and seek out a good path through a large field of corn in order to find the swampy drainage ditches which had been made therein, so that we did not become bogged down. Fortunately I arrived at the height, under a heavy small arms fire, just as the 21st and the 9th Regiments were being repositioned and were about to abandon the height which I and my cannons were still striving to climb, and worked so hard to do, and had almost accomplished. Upon my arrival General Philipps animated the English regiments and all the English officers and men, also Brunswick chasseurs who were assigned there, grasped and pulled on the lines to maneuver the guns. The entire line of these regiments once again formed a front. My cannons, by means of their faithful assistance, were suddenly on the height. The cartridges were carried up in the men's arms and placed beside the guns, and as soon as I had mounted the terrain, I quickly fired twelve or fourteen shots, one after the other, at the enemy standing under a full fire at about a good pistol-shot distance from me. The small arms fire of our line increased noticeably again, especially the platoon firing on our left, or Riedesel's wing. The enemy fire, as strong as it had been previously, faded in the distance as if cut off.

"I moved forward about another sixty yards, pursued the now scattered and fleeing enemy with a few more rounds, and chased them into a woods with another twelve or fifteen cannonballs. In the space of a quarter-hour after this affair, night set in. From the munition for the English cannons and cassions, which were at the base of the hill, I quickly replaced the ammunition I had fired today.

"The Royal Artillery suffered an astonishing loss in today's action. One captain is dead. Captain Johns [Thomas Jones ?] was fatally wounded and died therefrom the next morning. Brigade Major Captain Bloomfield was shot through the cheek, under the tongue. General Philipps' other adjutants were almost all wounded, as were some of those of General Burgoyne. Somewhat more than thirty non-commissioned officers and cannoneers of the Royal Artillery were killed or wounded, of whom not a single man was less than five feet ten inches tall, all handsome individuals, of whom many died on the field of battle and were laid out in their true five feet eleven inches to six feet. Some lay still with, and some already without, consciousness. With this detachment, separated from my other comrades, I was so fortunate as to suffer not a dead nor a wounded horse, let alone anyone who had been engaged, and my troops suffered only the loss of a few knapsacks with small clothes. The loss on our side is considerable, and all because during the entire action the enemy committed new brigades every half-hour, which relieved the previously committed ones, and in this manner, maintained a fresh force at all times on their side and must have had a strength of 800 to 900 men [sic].

"It is impossible to determine the enemy losses on the field of battle, as each time, the relieved brigades took their dead and wounded back with them, right up to the end when no relief occurred, and the dead and wounded to our right and before our right wing had to be left in the woods, where, the next morning, our small band of Indians made fun with them, plundering the bodies, and in their usual manner cut off their hair [scalped them]. As nightfall came we received orders to pull back and to take position ahead of the road in a woods lying behind us, which extended from the Hudson River to Freeman's house and beyond where today's action occurred. I am to take post in the space between the 9th and 21st Regiments. The entire army bivouacked.

"I passed General Philipp's stopping place. Because it was night he checked to see which artillery brigade was passing, but could not recognize it. I answered that it was a detachment of mine, whereupon I at once received the compliment of his personal satisfaction with our conduct today. The Adjutant General Captain [Friedrich] Clerke expressed the same sentiments of His Excellency, General Burgoyne, the same evening, and the following morning General Burgoyne's satisfaction with me and my men was conveyed by General von Riedesel, as well as making his own known because of yesterday's action, which I also imparted faithfully to my detachment and have made known, on the spot, to the most senior and least important [individuals]. I can not forget to mention the excellent and intrepid courage, the best behavior and alacrity in carrying out their duties by both Bombardier [Carl Ludwig] Hausmann and [Johann] Mueller, and the same praise for Wagonmaster [Johann Georg] Zicklamm during this action. The latter, as it was really not his duty to be at that place where I was under fire, did not leave the spot and he helped insure that there was no shortage of ammunition by unloading the carts which were fifteen yards behind me. Under a shower of small balls he reconnoitered the path for my march right up to the height, as the cannons were already being pulled by the men, so as to see where we were going in case it were necessary to bring up the horses.

"Only one, the well-known surgeon's mate and possibly prior thereto, the quack and charlatan, [Eberhard] Unger -- I assume that is what he was before, because he constantly addressed me and everyone daily as excellence and your grace, until he beat it to death, made himself unbearable and ridiculous, kept us in convulsions, and drank too much -- a perfect example of a complete no-account, the likes of which will not be found again soon in all God's domain. He sought a safe place for himself and remained behind with his small bundle of bandages and wrappings. He grabbed a fellow carrying rum, and drank like a wild man and riff-raff in company with the English drummers.

"The terrain and this height which were held at such a huge cost were occupied today by a detachment and otherwise everyone in the entire army remained under arms throughout the night. However, without hearing a single shot. Everything was quiet.

"During the morning, very early, all the wounded were taken from the battle field on our provisions and infantry ammunition carts, past us, and to a hospital set up in tents and a few sheds on the plain below the hills on the Hudson. I would have wished that they had taken a different route as this is an unpleasant sight for the soldiers, as this awakens a certain reflection, pity, and eventually a fear of what can happen. The establishment for these, from which twenty or more had to be buried each day, was set up on the left wing of the army.

"The dead were buried on the battlefields and meanwhile defenses were thrown up for the detachments on the height we had seized.

"Our very good and capable Regimental Surgeon Heidelbach, for whom we can not adequately thank Councilor Schultze for having brought him into the service of our gracious prince, came to me early this morning with the good intention, if I had been wounded, to provide help. Thank God, however, I had not a single man who had the slightest problem. He then went to the battlefield where the last massacre of the enemy had occurred. Upon his return he told me that just there by the fences, to my right, he had seen more than seventy dead. He had been unable to proceed farther because he had seen a fellow within shooting distance take aim with his weapon from behind a tree and therefore considered it wise to retreat. Shortly thereafter several English, and several Germans also, came in, who had been out looking for booty, and said that they had encountered somewhat more than 250 dead and seriously wounded but still living enemy, and seen even more, that could not be reached however, because they had been fired upon several times.

"This afternoon the army drew together in a line. I sought out the left wing of the German division according to orders received, where I found Lieutenant Dufais already camping with my two other cannons. They had been completely at ease during yesterday's action and until today. I placed my brigade as I thought best on this height and camped with the whole company and command in a line close behind my cannons. My brigade then consisted of four 6-pound cannons under my orders on the left wing of the army and I still have two 6-pound cannons detached, under the command of Bombardier [Conrad] Wall, with the Brunswick von Breymann Grenadier Battalion, which with the Chasseur Battalion and the Jaeger Company, which is still detached therefrom, under the orders of Lieutenant Colonel von Breymann, covers the flank of the army and is again called the Breymann Corps.

"At present we have entered the camp which is called the camp at Freeman's Farm, near Stillwater. The enemy army is at Stillwater, reportedly 12,000 men strong, in an entrenched camp with an abatis, in a very advantageous and nearly impregnable situation. Their right wing standing on the height has the Hudson as a support and is covered thereby. The great plain lying thereunder has been occupied by them with strong troops and detachments, as has the area between the road to Albany, found there, and the river. In the thickest bushes and overgrown therewith gorges of the ravines, lying at the foot of these heights, lie strong detachments, which are their pickets and field watches, from which they set out their posts like a chain in an orderly fashion and from which they patrol. Nothing of their camp and defenses can be discovered, as this is prevented by the thick woods. The enemy left wing moved, according to reports, far beyond our right, outflanking it, and is entrenched in and behind a very thick woods and an impenetrable abatis. Daily and hourly they draw more and more troops from the militia of the surrounding provinces and according to several deserters, already have more than 12,000 men. The left wing of our army, under the orders of General Riedesel, is on a height opposite the enemy right, also in a woods with my four 6-pound cannons on the extreme left. Ahead of these however, on the slope of the hill as a covering force, is Captain von Schachten with the Grenadier Company of the Hesse-Hanau Regiment, behind a small entrenched line. Almost in alinement with the left wing of the army are an officer and fifty men of the Hesse-Hanau Regiment behind a small bridgehead close to the Hudson on the plain ahead of the bridge on the road to Albany. This force has detached a non-commissioned officer with ten men, 500 to 550 yards ahead before a board house. These posts with those of the pickets lying ahead of our field watches make a chain extending to the Hudson. The posts set out by the officer almost make the chain, staggered behind the alinement of our field watches.

"The heavy artillery, ammunition, provisions, baggage train, hospital, and batteaux, all of which are protected by the Hesse-Hanau Regiment, are behind our left wing, below in the plain. Part of the force in trenches, part in the open between our left wing and the enemy's right, drew together in a swampy and thickly overgrown with bushes and trees, very steep ravine, beginning at my posts, stretching to the von Rhetz, Specht, and Riedesel Regiments where the ravine is no longer so steep, but stretches completely around this height and beyond several English regiments to the right. In relation to the natural terrain situation, our army camped more extended, with our right side across a small valley or ravine which separated our line a bit. The English camp at the end turned more toward the right from a woods through a large corn field as far as Freeman's house. On the height captured on 19 September, the brigade of General Fraser, which formed the right wing with the English Grenadiers and his Light Infantry, was camped. At a rather great distance from Fraser, Lieutenant Colonel Breymann was posted with his grenadier battalion, the rest of the von Barner Chasseur Battalion, and the Jaeger Company, before which are the Indians, Canadians, and the whole Albany Volunteer troops, manning their own posts. Taking everyone together, English and Germans, our army then had a fighting strength of 5,000 men, including the still small number of Indians, most of whom have been lost and have returned to their huts. All the Canadians and local volunteers, excluding the forces at Carillon, St. Jean, Chambly, Montreal, etc., on duty in all of Canada, at most amount to 4,000 men.

"This morning our workers, part actual English laborers, but primarily men ordered out of the regiments, who were chopping down trees in the woods to provide more clearing ahead of our front and to open communications between the line of field watches and the pickets, were harassed without any losses.

"That we are very near the enemy camp is proven by their drums, which we can clearly hear and distinguish. Also today, they fired a *feu de joie* with twelve to fourteen cannon shots and thereafter, intermingled with their heavy drumming, we clearly heard the often repeated, joyous shot, 'Hurrah, hurrah.' The reason however for their celebration is as of today still unknown. Today the positions on our left wing were assigned and the tents set up in an orderly fashion; an actual indication that from now on our march would be somewhat slower and possibly also a very warm day [a battle] might be necessary in order to continue.

"A bridge of our batteaux [floating bridge] was built across the Hudson River during the night, and on each bank of the river, construction of bridgeheads were begun. Also this morning a picket from the von Riedesel Regiment brought in a prisoner, who said that yesterday's *feu de joie* and celebration in their camp and army was occasioned because they had surprised and captured Carillon. N.B. -

This can be nothing but an obvious lie. - A man also arrived here this morning who claimed to be a messenger sent with news from General Carleton to General Burgoyne. Initially he was brought to General von Riedesel, who at once sent him to General Burgoyne at the head-quarters which is camped beyond the space of the Riedesel Regiment and an English regiment.

"Between three and four o'clock this morning several cannon shots were fired by our army. However, it is not known with certainty why, if it were a signal of the arrival of a corps of troops from General Howe under General Clinton, or the now awaited arrival over Lakes Champlain and George of Colonel [Barry] St. Leger with his corps. Today the bridgehead on the opposite bank was completed. Other-wise it remained completely quiet today between both parties.

"Before the whole line of the army a trench line was made with laid-together, fallen and recently-cut-down trees. The batteries for the cannons and howitzers were set up on the most suitable heights and the guns moved in. The space between the trees was filled with dirt and dirt was also thrown on the outer side.

"The unpleasant, and in our situation, disadvantageous reports were confirmed, how Colonel St. Leger with his light expeditionary corps withdrew to Oswego, from the Mohawk River and its rough terrain, because of the enemy's superior strength and a shortage of provisions. From there, with difficulty, he will have to repass Lake Ontario and the St. Lawrence River in the region of Montreal. Now we eagerly anticipate the arrival of his relief via the Sorel River, or as it is also called, the Richelieu, across Lakes Champlain and George, and then overland. This is an astonishing detour. I wish the armies of both sides remain patient and with calm dispositions until his arrival, because this represents a time in which one army can defeat, capture, season, roast, and peacefully eat the other. Concerning this report there are also murmurs and nothing definite is said. It is also assumed that this unfortunately failed expedition by St. Leger's corps must have been known here for some time because a trusted, secret, and small detachment from our army has quietly been sent back in order to hide a small number of batteaux in the earth for his use and to fill them [to look] like graves in which dead soldiers have been buried and thus not found by the enemy, nor used, or burned by them. All communications here have been cut between us and Forts George and Carillon and our front is now more secure than our rear, which they cover.

"24 September - This morning the advanced non-commissioned officer post of the Hanau Regiment, on the Albany Road below on the Hudson, was attacked by an enemy patrol, without the least loss to either side however. Otherwise everything was quiet today for both armies.

"25 September - Early this morning, a little after five o'clock, the already previously mentioned non-commissioned officer post was again attacked by a strong enemy patrol, which was at least three times stronger, and driven back to the officer post. Two men from our side were wounded and one taken prisoner. We learned later from the four prisoners which the pickets of our post captured at that time, that their side also had seven men wounded during this small affair. This attack made all of us on the heights rather alert. However, it was not long until the enemy withdrew and it became quiet.

"Toward eleven o'clock at midday, two enemy drummers approached with a small white flag and called to our outpost. Brigade Major von Geismar was sent to meet them and they delivered a letter to Lieutenant General Burgoyne from the enemy commander of the army facing us, by the name of [Horatio] Gates, as well as another packet to the officers, supposedly from our prisoners, and then departed. The Brunswick quartermaster general, Engineer Captain Gerlach, was sent out on the other side of the bridge with a covering force of fifteen to twenty volunteers from the local region and province. They sneaked through the hills and ravines and then lay along the Hudson in a chain, in the hope of learning something of the enemy camp, defenses, and positions. This was impossible however, because the woods in that area prevented seeing through the trees and across the Hudson. Therefore they returned without having seen or learned anything.

"26 September - Everything quiet and peaceful. During the evening some of our Indians returned from their hunt, bringing a living, but half-dead from fright and anxiety, captive, as well as two scalps, which they had taken in the presence of the still living, of the two unfortunate individuals, in their dainty manner.

"27 September - Everything was quiet throughout the entire day. Toward evening three captured enemy officers, as they claimed to be, were brought in from our right wing, but they did not look like such.

"The report, spread about here several days ago of how Washington's army had been totally defeated by General Howe, was confirmed today with much certainty in our army, but still not believed."

## Freeman's Farm, 7 October 1777

Pausch's account of the campaign continued on 7 October. "During the morning I received the order to hold two 6-pound cannons with their ammunition from the brigade under my command in a condition ready to march so that they could move out at a moment's notice. At about ten o'clock there assembled before the camp and on the place d'armes of the left wing of the German troops a detachment of German troops, a detachment of about 300 men selected from all the German regiments present. This detachment was under the command of Lieutenant Colonel von Speth, commander of the von Riedesel Infantry Regiment. The Hesse-Hanau Regiment provided one officer, six non-commissioned officers, one drummer, and 75 men under the command of Captain [Carl August] Scheel. It was marched off from the right and past the front of our army, to the right wing of the same, until it came to the brigade of Brigadier General Fraser. There the detachment of the English grenadier battalions, the Light Infantry, and the other regiments, as well as the Canadians, the Albany Volunteers, and the few remaining Indians had already assembled and were ready to march. The English provided two howitzers, two 12-pound cannons, and four 6-pound cannons to this detachment. I left two behind on the left wing, in our battery, under Lieutenant Dufais, and as it was quiet and peaceful there, I myself went on this expedition with the two mentioned cannons of my brigade. Behind Fraser's defenses and camp, where we then halted and had to await further orders, the general staff assembled in Fraser's tent, before which the Indians had assembled, where they were apparently informed of today's objectives, the march, etc., after their usual ceremonies which are completely unknown and not understood by me. The rendezvous there lasted about two hours, until our march resumed. Finally this assembled corps began its march before whose head the German detachment set the remainder of the Brunswick Jaeger Company, about 100 men of the Brunswick Chasseurs, and an equal number of the Breymann Grenadier Battalion.

"The entire strength of this small corps, taking everyone into account, consisted of about 1,500 men. We left the Breymann Redoubt lying to our right and then to our rear, followed a road which we found there, not far from a house situated there, and also to the right, and passed a new breastwork of wood and bushes, to the left of the road, in which we found and passed a non-commissioned officer outpost of the Breymann Grenadier Battalion. We continued along this road for about another mile and one-quarter. At various times we halted for rather long periods in order to let the Volunteers and Indians make reconnaissance ahead of us and to make the various small pole-bridges along the way passable for the artillery, and, as each time the reports came from the advance guard that everything was in good order ahead of us, we then continued our advance until we had covered the mentioned distance and were on the left flank of the entrenched enemy army, but could still not see nor discover them due to the thick forest in the still considerable distance. Here we found a small cultivated, open field, surrounded by woods, on the end of which stood the small abandoned home of the owner. Its roof was now the observation position and all the adjutants, engineers, and quartermaster generals made their reconnaissance with telescopes and spy-glasses, but nothing could be discovered in the immediate vicinity. We marched together therefore by platoons, wheeling to the left; the mentioned German detachment, behind a fence along the road on the left wing; the English troops to the right, and both of our flanks were covered by Englanders. Our few jaegers and the detachment of the Chasseur Battalion and Grenadiers, were placed ahead and to the sides, in small groups, to cover our line. I placed my two 6-pound cannons on a rather advantageous and open spot somewhat more elevated than the surrounding terrain, about 24 to 26 yards from one another and fifty yards ahead of the front, where 100 men of the detachment from the Hanau Regiment and the Brunswick von Rhetz Regiment joined together. Continuous improvements were made on the defenses on both of our flanks and therefore it required about three-quarters of an hour to march from one wing to the other without seeing anything of, nor being annoyed by the enemy.

"Meanwhile two 12-pound cannons, of the English Artillery, under the command of Major [Griffith] Williams, were driven before the previously mentioned house, unlimbered, and loaded. Nevertheless, no one could learn, even by inquiry, the final meaning of these arrangements. First, I learned from the quartermaster general, Captain Gerlach, that this was a reconnaissance which was being made here and the corps was a covering force for the general staff. Second, we were sent to the Breymann and Fraser Redoubts to serve as foragers to gather the corn which stood behind them so that we were then designated a foraging party. An English officer approached in a hurry because there were no cannons on the left wing on the flank. I was to send one of mine there at once, to which I protested, as I had only two cannons and, as I could only be with one of them. If it were a general order, I would either march there at once with both [cannons], or I would send none. A single cannon would never be commanded by a junior officer, let alone a captain. They certainly had four 6-pound cannons of their own artillery here, one of which even then was passing behind the line toward the left wing. I was rid of that individual. He fluttered away and brought no further orders. I remained at the post, which I had chosen and occupied, for the present. After the passage of at least a half hour, in the woods on the height lying to our right, several patrols were seen. The two mentioned 12-pound cannons fired upon them. After these annoyances had disturbed us for a short time, there were many enemy skirmishers in the bushes, who engaged our forward jaegers, chasseurs, and volunteer at once. The fighting along the entire front became very furious.

"During this lively firing by each side against the other, in which I also became engaged with my cannons, two strong columns hurriedly marched out of the enemy defenses on their left wing, in a disorderly manner, one against our right, the others against our left wing, and a vast number of men in a body approached as reinforcements to those who were already engaged against us. They pressed blindly and frantically forward into our furious firing. On the left wing the attack also began with an enormous small arms firing and in a few minutes the enemy drove back the left wing. The cannons placed there by the

## Enemy Views (1777)

English Artillery were taken as booty by them, without the cannons having been able to fire a single shot. Then it began to get lively on our right wing, with large and small arms weapons, Our left wing retiring in complete disorder caused a similar rout among the Germans of the detachment behind the fences according to the order of battle. All of these men retired, or more correctly said, ran from their positions, into the bushes, without informing me although I stood only fifty yards from them. Now, I and my cannons, without my knowing, held the respect of the enemy, which was before me, with cartridges for some time. How long the infantry left me here alone, I can not say with certainty. But I saw a large number of people off to my now exposed left side, at a distance of about 200 yards, whom I, without deceiving myself, no longer believed to be our men.

"I looked back toward our German infantry, with whose protection I hoped to make my retreat, but not a single man could now be seen. All had crossed the road and run to positions in the fields and bushes, beyond the trees, so that the right wing was close to the house already mentioned several times, but everyone was mixed together and confused by the approaching [enemy]. During this time, on our right wing, both sides were heavily engaged, and our rear was covered by the now parallel force in a thick woods upon a height, after having previously covered our right flank, and the road, by which we had to make our withdrawal to the army from our position, ran through a woods already occupied by the enemy, who were approaching us.

"As I now found myself alone, abandoned, and nearly surrounded in my first mentioned position, and no longer saw an opening before me, except along the road to the house, where the two 12-pound cannons stood, already dismounted and abandoned, I wished to move there with my two cannons, with much difficult effort. I had not only to pull to prevent being stuck, just like my best cannoneers, because I also had to proceed over a damned difficult pathway. When I fortunately arrived at that house, still under the protection of our small arms fire, which coming from the bushes was as dangerous to me as to the enemy, I found a small emplacement protected by wood with the gaps filled with some dirt, about eighteen feet long and five feet high. I put this to my use, placed one on the right, the other on the left, and began firing alternately with canister and balls, whatever the piece would take, without being able to see which of our men were still in

209

the bushes, because the enemy did not fire at them but pushed forward vigorously toward my cannons, in the hope of also dismounting and silencing them. This effort failed twice and was prevented by the canister firing. The two previously mentioned 12-pound cannons, at which Major Williams, Lieutenant [John H.] York, and part of the non-commissioned officers and cannoneers had already been captured and several non-commissioned officers and cannoneers killed, lay like dead and abandoned upon my arrival in this second position. Still a very good English artillery lieutenant named Schmidt [William P. Smith], with a sergeant, were the only ones who still had the determination to put the cannons to use. He came and asked me to provide ten cannoneers and a non-commissioned officer of my detachment to move these pieces.

"I could not grant that request however, as much as I might have wished to do so, as I already had two dead, three or four wounded, and many who had gotten lost, also all those attached from the infantry were useless and had run away. For each cannon I had no more than four or five cannoneers and a non-commissioned officer. Also, considering the rapidity of fire, my 6-pound cannons were more effective here than those 12-pound cannons, from which only one-third the number of shots can be fired effectively as from the others. Also, I did not wish to silence nor lose the cannons, which I actually had and which were still in action with good success, nor to increase his honor by replacing already lost cannons with others, nor placing myself in the opposite situation, in which he had been already for some time, and for which I was in no way responsible.

"Two cart-loads of ammunition were fired by my cannons, and I had started on the third. My cannons were so hot that no one could place a hand thereon. With my cannons, and to their right and left, I and those still in this area, fought a rather tolerable fort. However, this could not continue for long. The firing behind us drew nearer, and finally our right wing, in our rear, was repulsed. Its infantry fortunately retired in a somewhat better order than the left wing had done. I saw, as far as it was clear and visible, my previously used route was still open in this second position, so that I could return. I, Sergeant Hausmann, and two cannoneers pulled the one cannon, in the hope of saving it, along this route. However, the bumpy wood lying thereon made the work too difficult and impossible for four men.

Finally the sergeant-major, followed me with the other cannon, had it limbered, and brought the limber for this one with him. I quickly put the cannon thereon and soon marched on down the road in the hope of joining with a troop of our infantry, so as to be able to rally with it. This hope was fruitless. They were all completely dispersed, one ran here, the other there, and as I came within shooting distance of the woods, the road was already occupied by the enemy. They came toward me, from all the bushes and from behind the trees, and many small balls flew at us therefrom. After I saw that everything would undoubtedly be lost, and also that it was no longer possible to save anything, I called my remaining men together. Whoever could, should save himself. I myself fled, with the last ammunition cart, through a fence, into a thick young growth of trees standing to the right of the road, which I brought away with the help of a cannoneer, with the horses. Herein I encountered all possible nations intermingled, as well as Captain Scheel, who no longer had a single man with him to show from his command from the Hesse-Hanau Regiment. During this confused retreat everyone headed back to our camp and our lines. Breymann's Redoubt was under heavy attack, surprised by the enemy. The camp, situated therein, was set on fire and burned. All the officers' pack horses together with the baggage were captured by the enemy, plus two 6-pound cannons of my artillery brigade. Sergeant Wochler and Cannoneer [Philipp] Fintzell were killed, Bombardier Wall, under whose command the cannons were, and several cannoneers were lightly wounded. The enemy took post in this captured redoubt and remained there this night. Dusk prevented the enemy from taking further action.

"Behind our defenses everyone in our army was active and alert. I thought I had lost my servant and horses at this time. Fortunately, however, this was not the case, as when he saw the battle was taking a turn for the worse, he rode back to the camp to my remaining baggage and the detachment of Lieutenant Dufais, where I found all this with considerable pleasure and approved my servant's settled-upon, fortunate decision. I again found many of my cannoneers, who had disappeared, in the camp, together with all the men assigned to me from the infantry who had run away very early during the battle. -- That those men had left very early during the action was clearly demonstrated by not one being wounded, alone killed or taken prisoner.

"Today I again suffered severe losses from the company, including the crews of the two cannons in Lieutenant Breymann's Redoubt, which was overrun, resulting in the loss of four cannons, Bombardier Wochler, three cannoneers, Fintzell, [Adam] Hanselmann, and [Thomas] Weil being killed; four cannoneers, Heinmueller [Heinrich Mueller ?], [Michael] Paul, [Paul] Hartmann, and [Peter] Scheffer Sr., being wounded and captured; and three cannoneers, [Georg] Zischler, [Johann] Pflug, and Johannes Mueller, Sr., as well as my two artillery servants, Vogt [Johann Peter Focht ?] and [Johann Thomas] Roth captured. Also, two bombardiers, Hausmann and Wall, three cannoneers, Lochmann, Sr., [Johann Georg] Becker, and Zorbach, Sr., were lightly wounded but not captured. Four 6-pound cannons of my artillery brigade were lost and four munitions carts, together with horses and harnesses and British [artillery] servants. -- N.B. All of this artillery equipment belonged to the King and included nothing of ours, except some company items and a few other things entered on the lost and damaged table, along with the listed items.

"All the rest of the equipment from the brigade under my command now consists of only two 6-pound cannons, four munitions and three entrenching tool carts, and four carts for baggage and equipment required in the field.

"During today's action Brigadier General Fraser and Lieutenant Colonel Breymann were severely and fatally wounded. Also captured at the same time were two Brunswick captains, who are unknown, and Ensign [Wilhelm] von Geyling of the Hesse-Hanau Regiment was wounded. Additional, and the total losses, are still unknown to me at this time, except that Lieutenant Colonel von Speth was also captured, together with other officers, during the last moments. This much is certain, however, both sides lost many men today.

"Today it was very quiet on our left wing, except that the patrols and outposts fired occasionally at one another without anyone being wounded on either side.

"I can not adequately praise the especially good and valuable conduct of Sergeant-major [Johann] Moerschell and Bombardier Hausmann during this heated action. It is also my duty to specifically recommend Moerschell, because of his constant and good conduct, ambition, moral uprighteousness, and attention to duty most respectfully and with most sincere submission."

These minimal accounts of Burgoyne's 1777 campaign from Canada, and the brief mention of Colonel St. Leger's attack along the Mohawk Valley, may be partially attributable to a reluctance to write any detailed accounts of an unsuccessful campaign.

However, Captain Germann wrote a brief summary of events following the capitulation at Saratoga to his Prince on 7 December 1777. "Your Highness will have seen in my last most humble report from John's house, our then unpleasant situation. This has since then worsened daily until finally we have reached the epitome of misery. From John's house we marched over Fort Edward, Fort Miller, and Batten Kill, and Saratoga to Freeman's Farm, where General Gates awaited us at the head of an army four times stronger than ours in a well-entrenched camp. Our position was so advantageous that the enemy dared not attack, and certainly we could now be in Albany, or even farther, especially if the recent unfortunate affair of 7 October had not taken place. During that affair, Musketeer [Ludwig] Hoene was shot through the body and lay dead on the spot. Corporal Ewald was twice wounded, once in the chest and the other in the hip. Musketeer [Georg Carl] Ungar received a grazing shot to the neck and [Johann] Sickenberger a ball in the right foot. All three have now completely recovered. Your Highness, please allow me to briefly mention the conduct of Corporal Ewald. To the present he has always sought to out-perform all others in devotion to duty and his behavior at other times is equally faultless. Musketeer [Georg] Tempell, who was sick and with the supplies, was left behind during our retreat from Freeman's Farm and until now I have received no information about him. Our tents and a large amount of gear was lost, so that during the following time, when we were between Batten Kill and Fish Kill, we had to lie out under the open sky. Here the enemy surrounded us and harassed us daily with cannon and small arms fire, until finally General Burgoyne surrendered the entire corps as prisoners of war on 17 October. The same day we were moved to Freeman's Farm and the bad, often even more than vile, meeting of our enemy, whom during the whole march we had to endure, already began by tearing from the bodies the cartridge straps and pouches belonging to the troops on duty with the equipment. Despite the raw weather and the often unbearable bad roads, the inhabitants were very seldom sympathetic as to grant us use of their barns as night quarters. On the other hand, they exerted every effort, by advantageous promises, to entice our troops into deserting. True, many soldiers remained behind during the march, but only because of exhaustion and a scarcity of small clothing. Still, after only a short time, they rejoined the company. [Johann] Rosenberger remained behind during the march from Nobletown to Barrington. [Michael] Herber deserted at the latter place on the morning of 26 October, after company roll call, shortly before marching away.

"Free Corporal [Franz] von Pape, who had been sick for some time, remained behind on 5 November during the march from Marlborough. Spengler, who deserted from the barracks on 11 November, reportedly, as I later heard, prevented the free corporal from returning by the bad description of our quarters. We arrived here at Winter Hill, a half hour from Boston, on 7 November. The barracks in which we lie have been put together with planks and are exceptionally bad. The officers, in this respect, do not have the least advantage. Very narrow confines have been established for us as to how far we can go and everywhere we are watched by a large number of guards. However, they can not, or will not, bother us. Some of us have had their horses stolen, as I have had the misfortune to lose my best horse at this place."

Although Private Tempell had been wounded during the fighting at Freeman's Farm, he was able eventually to return to duty as noted in a letter from Lieutenant Carl von Lindau to his Prince on 15 June 1783. "Your Highness, I must most humbly report that Musketeer Georg Tempell, born at Altheim, 5'11 1/4" tall, returned here to the Leib Company on 28 May, The mentioned Musketeer Tempell was left behind because of illness when the Burgoyne army retreated on 8 October 1777, and he fell into enemy hands. Thereafter he sat for a long time in the jail at Albany, but was finally released. From there he made his way to the Indians and fortunately arrived at Niagara, where he had to take service with Butler's Rangers, a royal provincial corps. After surviving two years, he finally received his discharge and permission to return to the 1st Battalion."

# Enemy Views (1777)

## Activity in the New York Area

While General Howe was moving against Philadelphia and Burgoyne was moving south from Canada, Steuernagel summarized the existing defenses on Staten Island. "In the month of June, two regiments, specifically, Ansbach-Bayreuth, arrived in camp near us from Germany. These two regiments made an exceptionally fine appearance as the men were tall.[27] Toward the end of the month, General von Heister returned to Europe.....

"At the same time, we had to leave Jersey and on 28 June were shipped over to Staten Island, where we were placed under the command of General Campbell, along with the English 52nd Regiment, the Bayreuth Regiment, and 100 provincial troops, as the defense force on the island.....

"We had been ordered by General Campbell to pass in review on 22 August, and were in our assigned places to carry out this order, but instead of a pleasant review, we had a fighting review. The rebels had been transported over from the Jersey shore that morning and quickly drove the provincial troops from their defenses. The Waldeckers and the 52nd Regiment marched in the greatest haste, while the Bayreuth Regiment took defensive posts to protect our camp.

"The oppressive heat during these days debilitated most of our people, some even dying from the heat.

"As the rebels realized that a rather large number of troops were marching against them, they sought to retreat by taking their boats back across the water. Our two regimental cannons made this difficult by firing several salvos among them so that those who were not killed or drowned, had to surrender. Two boats with their crews were forced to ground with many men being wounded. Next day we returned to our camp."

Chaplain Waldeck also recorded the events of 22 August. "The general ordered the regiment to be under arms. At the set time, it was ready at the gate. Suddenly there was an alarm that the rebels were at hand and the regiment had to move out. During the previous night the rebels had crossed over to plunder and quickly storm the defenses. They began to cross by boat at midnight, and by three o'clock in the morning already had 2,000 men and three generals, Sullivan,

Smallwood, and [Prudhomme] DeBorre, on our side. A battalion of provincials, who were first attacked, suffered heavy losses. Two alarm guns were fired by the defenses, and two by the warship *Centurion*. The 52nd Regiment and ours marched down to the water side, and fortunately were able to cut-off the rebels' crossing point. Our cannons and the English cannons were brought into play, and ours in particular, earned high praise. I rode along the way some hours later and met a group of prisoners. The number of prisoners amounted to more than 260 and 21 officers. In dead, the rebels suffered a noticeable loss, as many drowned while attempting to swim to safety. The rebels, who were now completely disorganized, ceased firing and were taken prisoner from behind every bush.

"We suffered no one killed and no one wounded in the action, although three men were struck down by the heat. I would never have believed that this heat, and the strenuous marching, could have such a result. Youths, as strong as trees, crashed to earth and showed no signs of life, but nevertheless, soon recovered. Still, in this manner, four men of the 52nd Regiment died, including one who discovered a pail of cool water, drank, and fell dead. To this was added that the men were hungry, and had marched off without taking anything with them. I had considered this and sent my messmates some cold snacks and wine. The servant did not reach the regiment until midnight, however. The Ansbach Regiment had the duty of maintaining the defensive posts at our camp.

"23 August -This afternoon prisoners were still being brought in from scattered locations. Our regiment and the 52nd returned in the evening, exhausted, in that no one had eaten in 36 hours nor even been off his feet.

"24 August - Because of the unrest, neither communion nor church services were held. The prisoners were loaded aboard ship and sent to New York. They were, as is to be expected, treated with kindness. Not one was deprived of his possessions. A lieutenant colonel of theirs still had his watch on a silver chain. This lieutenant colonel had two brothers who served as good officers with the provincials, and today they conducted themselves very well, fighting against the rebels. Even the close ties of brotherly love can not drive away the spirit of the rebels."

## Enemy Views (1777)

Prechtel, of the Ansbach Regiment, noted activities in the New York area during the fall of 1777. "12 October - Grenadier Captain von Erckert, of the von Eyb Regiment, who was wounded at the storming of Fort Montgomery, and who died of his wounds at New York, was buried today at the Schwan Church. The funeral command was provided by the Hessian Hereditary Prince Regiment which lies in garrison here in New York.

"Grenadier [Johann Michael] Kriegbaum was also killed in the attack on Fort Montgomery....

"13 October - The 2nd Ansbach Regiment today was ordered to Albany to relieve the English General Burgoyne. The von Eyb Regiment was also ordered aboard two transport ships, near John's house on the North River and the von Voit Regiment was embarked at Staten Island.[28] The ships immediately went under sail and by evening anchored in the vicinity of Fort Knyphausen.

"Grenadier Captain von Ellrodt commanded the von Eyb Regiment.

"14 October - At two o'clock in the afternoon they sailed and then anchored during the evening in the North River."

However, the regiment returned to 'Planx Point' on 16 October. "News was received that the entire army of General Burgoyne, consisting of 4,000 men, including most of the Brunswickers under the command of General Riedesel, was captured by the rebels.....

"19 October - The troops were again embarked on the above mentioned transport ships. The defenses built on York Island were demolished and at one o'clock in the afternoon the ships sailed down the stream and anchored at evening in the North River."

Steuernagel's account of the movement up the North River is quite brief. "14 October - Orders were received for the Waldeck and Bayreuth Regiments to be prepared to go aboard ship. We were to go to the aid of General Burgoyne, who had been surrounded and besieged in the area of Albany, at Fort Montgomery, in the province of Connecticut. Here we received countermanding orders. It was within this time that Burgoyne was so heavily attacked by the Americans that he found it necessary to discuss terms with the enemy and to capitulate. He and his army were made prisoners. We sailed from here once again, and on the nineteenth were landed near Fort Knyphausen, and went into camp near Kingsbridge until the twentieth. At noon that day we struck our tents again, went on our former ships, and sailed the old route back to Staten Island, arriving on the 21st, in time to pitch camp at our former site once more. In the absence of General Campbell, Colonel [Johann Ludwig Wilhelm] von Hanxleden was given command over all troops and the island until 2 November. During this period an extremely heavy rain tore our tents to pieces and we were quartered at a nearby plantation."

Chaplain Waldeck noted a visit with the captured American General Lee during this period, recorded some of his many adventures and misadventures, and then the move up the North River. "26 September - An officer from the warship *Centurion* ate with us. He told us that General Lee, who is a prisoner aboard his ship, is very unhappy with the present state of the rebellion, and has openly stated during his captivity that Washington need only move from one province to another until the English are exhausted. The land is so extensive that England can not outlast the colonies. Since Washington has abandoned Philadelphia, he begins to develop a different tune. Washington is clever, who knows why he has done that!....

"30 September - The 52nd Regiment received orders to be prepared to travel.....

"3 October - The 52nd Regiment embarked, reportedly to go up the North River for an attack against Fort Montgomery.

"4 October - There are already fifteen ships in the mouth of the North River this morning, and we have the strongest hopes that we too will soon leave this island. It appears that something of consequence will happen this fall. Among others, I was invited to dine aboard the warship *Centurion*. At twelve o'clock a sloop came to pick us up. We were given a tour of the ship. We made our compliments to General Lee, a man of medium height, very thin; his nose is so large that its shadow darkens the other half of his face. One reads sincerity, thoughtfulness, understanding, and a complete reflectiveness in his appearance. He is very clever and spoke only of inconsequential things. No one, who has not seen it for himself, can picture the order and cleanliness aboard a warship. Every weapon, every line, of which there are many hundreds, has its proper place; every hand knows what it must do, every sailor and soldier knows his station, every cannon has its crew, and when battle sounds, everyone, in an instant, is where he belongs. At two o'clock we sat down to eat, and many flags were

displayed on deck. On our table everything was to be found that anyone could expect in the best restaurant in a great city. On such a ship,
and by such a well-laid table, one can forget that he is on the water,
and instead, without effort, think he is in a beautiful house rather than
aboard ship. After dinner we were served punch, and remained at the
business of drinking until our departure. At six o'clock we entered a
beautiful boat and sailed away.....

"8 October - News was received that General Clinton had taken
Fort Montgomery by storm, during which we lost 300 men. The
enemy had 500 taken prisoner and the rest were massacred.

"9 October - Now one piece of good news follows another. We
have opened the Hudson River as far as Albany. General Burgoyne
has again beaten the rebels in a major battle and made 1,777 prisoners.
Philadelphia has been greatly strengthened.....

"12 October - At nine o'clock church. As we were still standing
together after church, the long awaited order came to prepare to move
up the North River.

"13 October - At daybreak we struck our tents and the regiment
marched toward Jersey, in order to embark at that place. It was a
most beautiful day and instead of being aboard ship by evening, as we
had hoped, at three o'clock the brigade major arrived in all haste with
orders that everyone and everything was to be off-loaded and the regiment was to return to camp. It was impossible to unload all of the
baggage and tents from the ship this evening. Therefore, everyone had
to seek out his own lodgings as best he could. The two grenadier
companies of Waldeck and Ansbach had to take their canteens filled
with water, and we really thought that they were chosen for some
special task. We arrived back at our camp late at night. Old [Claude]
Prieur, the regimental surgeon's servant, offered me a piece of cheese,
but instead of cheese, he gave me hair wax, which he had in the same
bag, and which, because it was dark, I did not realize until I had bitten
into it. That caused me to lose my appetite for cheese, but not for
something else. And Herr Beck did me the greatest favor which I
could expect this evening, considering my day. He provided me with a
good piece of roast. Next we discussed where to sleep. There were
several small huts, previously built, which we took over. However,
these were not the best of lodgings, and because they were damp, I
saw the need for some other quarters, and found truly the best that I

could hope to find. The servants had brought a wagon filled with hay, and tied all the horses to it. I did not hesitate very long, but climbed in and crawled under the hay. I had hardly gotten warm, when I felt the wagon start to move, which was caused by the horses tied to it. The wagon stood on a slight elevation and did not dare to start to roll or it would have rolled into the ocean. What could I do? I climbed out and laid large stones around all four wheels. Then I climbed back into my bed with much effort and slept more comfortably than I had during the entire summer.

"14 October - We made preparations to bring the tents and other belongings from the ship back to camp. I had my tent set up at once and we thought we would remain here in peace. The regimental surgeon sent old Prieur out to get something to cook for our noon meal. He brought back beef and potatoes, and as we had nothing adequate to eat for several days, we prepared to cook our meal immediately. At twelve o'clock our meal was ready and as we were about to sit down to the table, we received orders to strike the tents quickly and march. We just could not bring ourselves to leave our potatoes, but quickly wolfed them down. Here there was no one who would buy our horses and we could not take them aboard ship. We found it necessary to turn them over to the care of the general quartermaster. The embarkation went rather quickly and by ten o'clock in the evening we were all on board. The major and the Grenadier Company, Captain Alberti, Lieutenants [Friedrich Carl Henrich] Strubberg, [Andreas Florentius Georg] Brumhard, and [Carl Theodor] Wiegand, the Regimental Surgeon [Christian] Mattern, and the Field Chaplain Waldeck found themselves aboard the ship *Klenehorn*. That evening aboard ship we drank to a good voyage and sailed at twelve o'clock.

"15 October - In the early morning light we passed New York and entered the North, or Hudson, River. A very beautiful, bright day, just as I like when traveling on water. The ship makes a minimum of movement, but goes steadily onward so that one barely notices the progress. It is beautiful to see such a large ship under sail on a river. We drank our coffee in the cabin early, then took seats on deck, watching the bank to right and left, which gradually held our attention. At nine o'clock we were between Forts Lee and Knyphausen, the most dangerous passage on the river. The rebels have made such a row of submerged hazards across the width of the river here, that only the most careful pilot can conduct a ship through. Two of our ships became stranded and had to await flood tide to be floated free. One other ship, with Ansbachers, passed so close to land by Fort Washington that a person could have jumped ashore. The submersible hazard has been made in this manner: Thick beams with sharpened iron points mounted thereon are fastened on a boat. The boat is loaded with stones and sunk, so that when a ship runs against the hazard, the ship is caught or sunk.

"Toward noon we arrived in the region near Kingsbridge where we saw our camp of last year's campaign, and which reminded us of many things of the first campaign. Now we came to Connecticut, where we saw the finest gentlemen's houses from the ship. The most magnificent of all, laid out so tastefully and with large gardens surrounding it, was Philipsburgh, which belonged to Colonel [Frederick] Philipse, and lies close to the bank of the North River. Not far from there, is an especially beautiful church with a leaf tower, in which all the Germans of the region worship. To our left lay Jersey, which the high walls of the river bank prevented our seeing beyond. At ten o'clock in the evening we came to West Point and anchored after a 54-mile trip up the river. It was in this region where the rebels strung a terribly thick chain across the river in order to hinder the ships. We still had seventeen fathoms of water here. There was beautiful moonlight and Lieutenant Strubberg and I sat on deck gazing on the area as we smoked our pipes until midnight.

"16 October - We hoped at any moment to debark. We suggested to ourselves that we would now march to Albany to join with Burgoyne's army. Our suggestions and dreams of the broad and pleasant expanse of land through which we would wander were interrupted by an order from General Clinton, which commanded our immediate return down river. We did not yet know the reason for this order. We ate our noon meal in disgust, because of the retreat. The rebels fired at our ship from the shore with small arms, but to no effect. We sailed down the Hudson River at about four o'clock. Some, in disgust, lay down, while others discussed the present situation of the war.

"17 October - Before noon we dropped anchor near Fort Knyphausen, previously Fort Washington.

"18 October - We remained aboard ship, not knowing where we should go. Our ship's captain returned aboard ship from New York in the evening with the good news from our army in Philadelphia, and also that General Vaughan's army had pressed on as far as Aesopus. This evening over a glass of wine we made our plans of what would be most favorable to us. But to this came the order that tomorrow at daybreak we were to disembark, leaving all baggage aboard ship. Now new plans had to be made and Major von Horn was in high spirits. We believe we are being landed in order to proceed to a union with the army from Canada. Under this supposition, to which each added his opinion, we spent half the night in discussion.

"19 October - In the early morning light we began to debark and as all the baggage remained aboard ship, we were quickly finished. We marched to Kingsbridge and by two o'clock had a new camp standing. The Hessians, who were next to us, had just beat church parade, and as we were unable to conduct services, I attended with them. Our old Prieur, who cooked for his master, Lieutenant Wiegand, Adjutant [Johann Henrich] Stierlein, and me, prepared a rather good meal. It was necessary here to carry water a half hour's distance, and even then it tasted like manure drainings. Otherwise, it was possible to get everything here that a soldier needed. But there was no further similarity with solid ground. It is a sorry place for the army to have been during the entire year.

"20 October - For me at least, this has been a restful day. Commissary Marc had brought us letters, which until now, because of the continual unrest, could not be answered. I had already written several letters and had just unpacked everything that I had with me, when the order came to strike our tents and return to the ships, which were still waiting for us on the North River. I was rather annoyed with this order. Everything was in complete confusion and it was evening before we arrived near Fort Washington, where the ships lay.

"This was as disadvantageous a point for embarkation as could be found on the entire river. The small boats could only approach the shore under a steep cliff, which it was necessary to descend in order to enter the boats. To further complicate things, it started to rain and the wind blew continuously. The night was so dark that the ships were indistinguishable, and the water became so rough that the sailors were able to row the boats between the ships and the shore only with the most strenuous effort. I still find it difficult to understand why several hundred men were not drowned. Already on a number of occasions the twentieth of the month has had special meaning for us. We arrived aboard our ship late, had nothing to eat or drink, nor even a blanket to lie down upon because our servants were still on land, and the wind was so strong that the small boats could no longer travel back and forth. We sailed at ten o'clock in a strong, driving snowstorm. At three o'clock we were opposite Greenwich, which consists only of garden and summer houses. Opposite, in Jersey, on a very high cliff, stood a summer house. I have never in my life seen a more pleasant place. The gentleman who owns it looks out of his window over the river to the city of New York and the entire surrounding area. He sees the ocean and all the ships coming and going. The eye can never have a larger and more pleasant panorama. Toward evening we dropped anchor at Staten Island.....

"23 October - Reportedly, Burgoyne and his entire army have been captured. We do not believe this in the light of his recent great victories."

After Howe sailed for Philadelphia, the Platte Grenadier Battalion Journal recorded the following events concerning the New York area. "14 July - The Koehler Grenadier Battalion and two English regiments broke camp at Cole's Ferry and were transferred to New York. From Cole's Ferry to New York is ten miles. Two miles beyond New York we entered camp on Greenwich Road.

"16 July - We moved out from Greenwich, passed Fort Knyphausen about noon, crossed Kingsbridge and arrived at camp on the height where Fort Independence lies on the road to Marosing. We noted many newly-built redoubts on these heights. General Schmidt commanded the Hessian regiments here, namely, the Truembach, Prince Charles, Stein, and Wissenbach Regiments, and the Koehler Grenadier Battalion. All the troops in this region and on Long and Staten Island are commanded by General Clinton. Previously Lieutenant General von Knyphausen commanded these posts. Later, however, he sailed with the embarked corps [of Howe's men heading for Philadelphia].....

"19 July - The Koehler Grenadier Battalion marched over Kingsbridge, which it had to repair at the same time, and entered camp on the hill at Spitting Devil on the North River, near the Truembach Regiment.....

"11 September - Until today we have remained in this region completely undisturbed. However, there has been constant activity erecting new redoubts on the surrounding heights of the region and repairing the existing ones. Today General Clinton took most of the troops camped on this island and crossed the North River at three different places, into Jersey. Of the Hessians, only Prince Charles Regiment went with him.

"13 and 14 September - The troops which had gone into Jersey returned, having accomplished nothing, but they brought some live-stock back. Supposedly it was a diversion to give General Burgoyne relief so that he can push on to Albany.

"4 October - Since the fourteenth of the previous month we have remained undisturbed. At the start of this month a fleet arrived from Europe. In addition to the recruit transports, two Hessian Jaeger Companies, uniforms, and other campaign necessities arrived. Colonel [Wolfgang Friedrich] von Woellwarth commanded the transport. General Clinton went up the North River with a corps of troops on transport ships. Major General Schmidt marched at daybreak today to Mile Square with the following corps: the Emmerich Chasseurs, the Stewart Grenadier Battalion, the Koehler Grenadier Battalion, the 35th Regiment, the Truembach Regiment, the York Volunteers, and the newly arrived Hessian Jaegers.

"5 October - The above corps, minus the Hessian Jaegers, the Emmerich Chasseurs, and the Truembach Regiment, returned and entered the camp which had been left standing. Those units which did not return were embarked on the North River and sailed up to Fort Montgomery where thy joined Lieutenant General Clinton's corps.

"12 October - The Koehler Grenadier Battalion embarked below Spitting Devil on the transport ship *Union* and followed the corps of Lieutenant General Clinton. The baggage was left behind as were the tents. At Verplanck's Point, or King's Ferry, the transport ship *Union*, which had been joined by several others with the two regiments from Ansbach and the Waldeck Regiment, joined the fleet under the command of Commodore [William] Hotham, who was on board the *Preston*, 50 cannons. Fort Montgomery and several others, whose defense against capture or conquest depended upon the first, were already in our hands, having been taken by storm. About 300 men, including 23 officers, had been made prisoners by us during the capture of this fort. Also, the enemy had set fire to all of their armed ships which had been lying in the North River, including several small frigates and row galleys, to prevent them from falling into our hands.

"Because the North River gets narrower here and has very high, steep cliffs on both banks, it is the key to the region farther up the Hudson River. For this reason the enemy had strongly fortified it on both sides. A very strong iron chain had been stretched across the river. This fell into our hands and was taken to New York.

"14 October - The troops still aboard ship landed on the east side of the North River and entered the camp from which the troops under the command of General Clinton had marched out. However, they only bivouacked because the baggage was not brought from the ship. We assumed we would proceed toward Albany either to join General Burgoyne coming from Canada, or at least to give him some relief, because the corps under his command was in difficulty and had been surrounded by General Gates. It seemed our forward movement depended on reports from General Vaughan who had gone farther up the North River with four English regiments. General Tryon had already burned down all the enemy magazines, houses, armories, and barracks at Peekskill.

"20 October - A sloop of war came from Philadelphia with dispatches from Sir William Howe for Sir Henry Clinton. Immediately after the sloop arrived, orders were received for everyone to be prepared to embark again. The start was begun today.

"22 October - After everyone was on board again, except for the corps under General Vaughan and some who were on the west bank in New Jersey, near Fort Montgomery and busy demolishing it, part of the fleet again got under sail and returned to New York and Staten Island, including the Koehler Grenadier Battalion. Each regiment entered its former camp. The sudden change was necessitated by a relief force which General Howe had requested for Philadelphia....

"Another year's campaigning is finished and all that we have accomplished, with the loss of a great many men, is the taking of Philadelphia, as according to all reports we have taken nothing else. In balance the conquest of this single city without considering the many people lost during the expedition and with those lost at Saratoga and made prisoners by the truce, makes the scale tip in favor of the enemy. Only future developments will determine whether Philadelphia is of any value to us. It is much to be wished, and it would have been better to capture New Jersey. Everyone here attributes the capture of the Northern Army to General Howe. Some even go so far as to claim it was in direct contradiction to the ministry's plan that General Howe went to Philadelphia by such a round-about route, as he received orders to do nothing which would interrfere with his uniting with the Northern Army. If this were true, which is much to be doubted, he utterly disregarded the orders and instead of going north, he went south, and to such a great distance that it may have been General Howe's intention to draw the enemy away from the main point and into a side issue. This would not only give him an advantage and facilitate General Burgoyne's march, but tire the enemy and lead to his destruction."

### Clearing the Delaware River

Meanwhile, Rueffer's diary, beginning on 8 October 1777, contains the following information concerning the initial measures to clear the American defenses from the Delaware River. "Admiral Howe has sent a flag of truce to Mud Island, lying in the Delaware between Philadelphia and Chester, which the enemy has occupied with a strong force and considers unconquerable. He proposed that if those batteries, which have been supplied with thirteen months provisions and are said to have forty cannons, would surrender, the troops would be allowed to withdraw without opposition. Otherwise they face certain capture as only a few *chevaux de frise* remain in place and Philadelphia is in our hands. The commander reportedly sent back the answer however, that it would not happen until the guns had cooled their freedom's blood.....

"9 October - From just before midnight until nine o'clock this morning we have heard a continuous, heavy cannon fire and we assume it is either from or against Mud Island.....

"11 October - Today we heard a continuous cannonade as strong as the one on 9 October, but do not know the cause and can only assume that our fleet is engaged with the batteries on Mud Island.....

"14 October - The rebels are reported to be only thirteen miles from here [Wilmington], with the intent of paying us a visit. However, as the embarkation lists have been published with orders to march tomorrow, it follows that we do not need to concern ourselves with them.

"16 October - This morning at six o'clock our march began, in the following order: The Jaegers commanded by Lieutenant von Wangenheim, the English convalescents commanded by Major M. Larat, the Scottish Brigade, Mirbach Regiment, and the Combined Battalion.... At ten o'clock this morning the flatboats came to take us to the previously assigned ships....

"17 October - At eight o'clock we raised anchor and sought to reach the fleet at Chester by tacking. Almost at once we sailed too near the land and although in no danger, grounded on the sand, from which we were soon able to work loose by towing with a flatboat.....

"19 October - Dependable reports have come in that General Howe has moved with the army from Germantown to the region of Philadelphia. Today a pontoon bridge was built at the ferry across the Schuylkill....

"20 October - We heard a heavy cannonade throughout the day today, in the neighborhood of our fleet, Mud Island, and Red Bank, which is a fort in New Jersey....

## The Attack on Red Bank

"21 October - Late yesterday we received orders to march and at two o'clock this morning our regiment marched over the Schuylkill and at Philadelphia joined the Grenadier Battalions Linsing, Minnigerode, and Lengercke, and two companies of Jaegers, and under the command of Colonel von Donop, were transferred at daybreak across the Delaware in flatboats to New Jersey. Here we learned for the first time that our destination was to capture Fort Red Bank. As soon as everyone had crossed, we marched and arrived late this evening at Haddonfield, where we camped. Our advance and rear guard were engaged several times with some running troops of the enemy, which resulted in two jaegers being wounded.

"22 October - This morning at four o'clock we broke camp and marched on Fort Red Bank, which for most of the corps under the command of Colonel von Donop will certainly remain in our thoughts forever. Toward eleven o'clock we arrived in the neighborhood of the fort. One hundred fascines were made at once by each regiment.

After Colonel von Donop appraised the situation at three-thirty in the afternoon, he permitted the fort, through the English Major Stewart and his adjutant, Captain [Johann Emanuel] Wagner, the opportunity to surrender. While this transpired, a command of one captain, two officers, and 100 men was commanded to take a position in front of the regiment to carry the fascines, and the Battalion von Minnigerode on the right, Linsing on the left, and our regiment in the middle, were set in a line ready to storm the fort. The Grenadier Battalion Lengercke and the Jaegers covered our rear. Therefore, when Major Stewart brought back a spiteful refusal from the commandant Colonel [Christoph] Greene, the attack was undertaken at once. We took the outer defenses with little effort. This had hardly occurred when, because of the excessive losses and the indescribable cannonade and the small arms fire from the fort, and from the enemy ships lying on the water side, which fired on our right wing, and the almost impassable abatis before the main fort, plus the fascines being of little value at the eighteen-foot high parapet, necessitated a withdrawal without accomplishing our purpose. Our losses on dead and wounded totaled 397 men, and seven dead and fifteen wounded officers, among the last, I am included, having a wound on my left heel, and a bruise on my right thigh. Colonel von Donop, who was wounded in the right thigh also, Captain Wagner, and Lieutenant [Philipp Wilhelm] Heymel were captured. Of these losses, 112 men were from our regiment. As soon as we had again assembled, we marched in the already settling dusk, about eight miles, where we halted at midnight in order to bandage the seriously wounded. Many of these remained lying on the road because we had no wagons to transport them, and so they fell into enemy hands.

"23 October - At two o'clock this morning we resumed our march again past Haddonfield and about two o'clock in the afternoon arrived at the water. Here we met a corps of English light infantry which was to serve as scouts. Since however, the commander of these troops had learned the bad news, that we had failed, from Lieutenant Pertot [Leopold Friedrich Bertraud ?] of Wutginau Regiment, who had been sent ahead to carry the report to the commanding general, therefore they stopped us. The wounded however, were immediately transferred across to Philadelphia and quartered there. At three o'clock the 64-gun ship *Augusta*, which was engaged with the battery on Mud Island, blew up. In the house where the wounded had been bandaged at twelve o'clock on this night, many had been left lying. Lieutenant Pertot, with some jaegers, risked returning to them, pressed some wagons, and fortunately brought them back to us.

"24 October - Yesterday evening all the regiments from New Jersey returned here and the Battalions Linsing, Minnigerode, and our regiment moved into the barracks. Colonel von Bock [Heinrich Borck of the Knyphausen Regiment ?] has been temporarily named commander of our regiment because our commander, Lieutenant Colonel von Schieck was killed. Today Lieutenant von Heister was sent to Red Bank with a flag of truce in order to ask about Colonel von Donop, also for his parole, which was refused out of hand, but granted the request that Colonel Haller request the same of General Washington. Today we received a commendation because of the unfortunate failure of the attack that witnessed the good courage....

"25 October - Because Lieutenant von Heister brought the news back from Red Bank that Colonel von Donop was in danger of dying, also that the rebels had no surgeons for bandaging the wounded, Regimental Surgeons Pausch and [Johann Conrad] Gechter were sent to Red Bank.....

"30 October - Captain Wagner, Lieutenant Heymel, and Regimental Surgeon Pausch arrived from Red Bank and brought the news that Colonel Donop died yesterday and was buried with military honors. Two hundred men marched out for his burial, of whom half fired three times. Also, three cannons were fired. The first two had to swear not to take up arms again until such time as they were exchanged. They gave high praise for the care and treatment provided by the enemy, not alone to Colonel von Donop, but to all the prisoners and wounded."

The Hesse-Cassel Jaeger Corps Journal provides further details concerning the unsuccessful attack on Red Bank. "19 October - The army broke camp at Germantown today and marched to Philadelphia, entering a camp on the heights before the town, near Morris House, in order to be nearer to, and to support the operations against Mud Island.

"21 October - Colonel von Donop with the Jaeger Corps, the Grenadier Brigade, and the Mirbach Regiment crossed the Delaware today near Philadelphia, and landed at Cooper's Ferry in order to capture Fort Red Bank. He marched to Haddonfield and established posts there toward evening.

"22 October - About four o'clock this morning, these troops broke camp and marched over Strawberry Bank against Fort Red Bank, and about midday they arrived within a quarter mile of the fort. The enemy had received reports of the approach of the troops and had set to work to improve his defenses. The fort was at once called upon to surrender, and as the officer commanding therein, Colonel Greene, would not give up, preparations were begun to storm the fort. The attack began at four o'clock in the afternoon and continued until dusk, but to no avail. The Jaeger Corps covered both flanks to the water to prevent a landing from the ships, which nevertheless did the force considerable damage with their cannons. Colonel von Donop was fatally wounded at the edge of the moat and therefore did not desire being brought back. He fell into enemy hands.

"The troops, after having advanced as far as the moat under heavy fire, found the defenses impossible to surmount and retreated. The Jaeger Corps formed the rear guard for some distance, then half formed the advance guard in order to capture the bridge over Timber Creek in case it should be occupied by the enemy. The enemy remained quietly in the fort and our entire force camped on the far side of Timber Creek, returning

"23 October - over Haddonfield and recrossed the Delaware the same day and again returned to camp with the army. Several warships were to have supported the attack on the fort, but because of contrary winds, could not approach near enough. The following day, namely the 23rd, the 64-gun ship *Augusta* and two frigates ran onto the *chevaux de frise* and stuck fast."

Lieutenant Feilitzsch, an Ansbach-Bayreuth Jaeger officer, serving with the combined Hesse-Cassel/Ansbach-Bayreuth Jaeger detachment, recorded his account of the attack, also. "20 October - At ten o'clock at night the order came to be ready to march at three o'clock in the morning.

"21 October - We marched early and passed through Philadelphia before daylight. Close to the city we were loaded in flatboats and at daybreak landed on the other side, in Jersey near Cooper's Ferry, where we saw about thirty enemy. They retreated after a few shots. We remained there until about three o'clock when we marched toward

Haddonfield. Underway we received a few shots. At seven o'clock in the evening we arrived. Our commander was Colonel von Donop and our entire corps consisted of three grenadier battalions and one musket battalion. My captain, [von Cramon], who had not been well for some time, remained in Philadelphia, to my very great sorrow; in part for his person and also because of the company opportunities [which he would miss by not being in the coming battle].

"22 October - At four o'clock in the morning we marched, and at about ten o'clock arrived at our assigned place near Fort Red Bank. Immediately preparations were begun for storming the fort and when everything was ready, at about four o'clock, it began. However, the commandant would not surrender so the attack was launched. The cannonade was severe and the small arms fire very heavy. In addition, several rebel ships joined in, which fired against us on both sides and did great damage. The attack continued a long time until finally our good Hessian Grenadiers had to retreat. (We had only field pieces with us and I do not know what else we were lacking.) This time we jaegers had no part except to cover the rear. Our losses consisted of Colonel von Donop, who remained lying wounded at the fort, another 26 officers who were dead and wounded, and about 350 privates. The exact number was not immediately known. During the night we marched back six miles, arriving at one o'clock.

"23 October - We continued our march at three o'clock, arriving at Cooper's Ferry. I was very sick and miserable. The march was made very quickly and we had nothing to eat. It was my fate to be very indisposed, and I wished to Heaven to be away from there and back home. On this day we also received the sad news that a warship, which had exchanged fire with the second fort, had blown up and that a frigate that was there grounded on a sandbank and had to be set afire. We remained lying there until nine o'clock at night, when we fortunately were shipped across. While still dark, we marched through the city and at one o'clock entered our former camp.....

"30 October - There is a shortage of provisions and food which can be bought. The inhabitants bring us nothing and the rations are the worst imaginable. On their faces their malice and hatred toward us can be seen. We are not allowed to take the least thing here in the province nor to do anything to them. This only increases their evil the more, and therefore we have to be more careful of the farmers than of the enemy soldiers....

"31 October - Beautiful weather. I was told today that Colonel von Donop had died in the enemy's hands. However, his adjutant, Captain Wagner, was brought to Philadelphia very dangerously wounded. The total loss before the fort was 377 men, including 23 officers, dead and wounded."

The fighting at Brandywine and Germantown and the anticipated losses in attempting to capture Red Bank and Mud Island may have prompted General Howe to request reinforcements from Clinton's command in New York. The Prechtel diary contains information of interest on the October 1777 move to Philadelphia. "25 October - The regiments received the order to proceed to the main army at Philadelphia and therefore, during the afternoon, changed ships.

"The von Eyb Regiment went aboard the transport ships:

"1) *John* - the staff ship, on which was Major [Christoph Ludwig von] Reitzenstein

"2) *Hopewell*, and

"3) *Hanyriette*....

"Because of illness, Colonel von Eyb did not go aboard ship, but had to remain in New York and, in the meantime, Major von Reitzenstein commanded the regiment....

"5 November - The troops, which are in the fleet consisting of forty sail, departed from Staten Island, commanded by the English General [Thomas] Wilson, and consisted of the two Ansbach regiments in Colonel von Voit's Brigade....

"6 November - At four o'clock at night a storm with contrary winds struck, and an English transport ship collided with the ship *John*, carrying [elements of] the von Eyb Regiment. The bowsprit broke, which caused much damage and need for repair.....

"12 November - The English warships heavily cannonaded Fort Billingsport, which lay before us, on the Delaware River, in Jersey.....

"15 November - The terrible bombardment by the English warships continued without let-up.

"16 November - The enemy evacuated both Fort Billingsport and Mud Island on the left bank of the Delaware River in Pennsylvania, setting fire to the latter and retreated to Fort Red Bank in Jersey."

## Enemy Views (1777)

J.R. recorded the American abandonment of Mud Island in a diary entry beginning on 12 November 1777. "The rebels had a fort situated on the Delaware which was called Mud Island.... The fort was strongly occupied. Provisions had to be brought past the fort during the night. Twelve to fourteen warships were nearby also, which lay in the harbor not far from the fort and could give it support. They made a beautiful fire after the fort was captured. We lost a warship of 64 cannons which blew up after being hit in the powder magazine by a shot from the fort. This was so loud that it could be heard thirty to forty miles away. There were also *chevaux de frise* in the river which prevented our ships coming here [Philadelphia]. They had left only a narrow passage through which a ship could sail. We knew where the opening was, having been informed by deserters. This fort surrendered in November."

The Hesse-Cassel Jaeger Corps Journal entry is also rather brief. "After this unfortunate affair [at Red Bank], batteries were thrown up with great difficulty in the bogs of Province Island, and initially on

"10 November - began firing, but basically with little effect.

"15 November - The wind was favorable today and especially as there was a spring tide, when the water is a foot or more higher, and this only occurs by every changing phase of the moon, it was possible to employ the ships against Mud Island. The *Vigilant*, a 24 gun ship, with sixteen 24-pounders, sailed with a sloop with three 24-pounders under Lieutenant Hotham through the channel between Providence and Hog Islands, against the fort. There was a heavy cannonade which did great damage to the enemy and forced him on

"16 November - to abandon the fort and the island during the night. The enemy set fire to his ships and retreated to Jersey. If this had not occurred, the English Guards had already been ordered to storm the fort. The English Grenadiers occupied the fort. Reportedly the enemy loss during the siege amounted to about 400 dead and wounded. The King's losses were seven dead and five wounded."

Feilitzsch gives additional details in his diary. "1 November - Beautiful weather but very cold. The captain and nearly half the company unfortunately are sick. We still have no provisions. If the Delaware River were open everything would be different. Also, we learned from deserters that the rebels were also in very poor condition.....

"3 November - The very sad news was received that General Burgoyne, commanding in Canada, had been captured with 4,000 men, mostly Brunswick troops. Good night peace! Without God's help we will not be able to enjoy the sweet hope this year.....

"6 November - Rotten weather. It rained throughout the past night. I had a board hut made for me instead of a tent. After having been disturbed during the night by some random shots which I had to investigate, I wanted to peacefully rest in my warm house. However, after being awake for some hours, it rained through the roof onto my bed and then on my whole body. My bed was completely wet. -- N.B. - This was made with hay and straw underneath and a wool blanket. - My chimney or fireplace smoked terribly. I almost wished again to sleep in a tent where I would have only been wet from below and cold from above. We are never content. It seems, however, we have reason [to be discontented] in America, and I still believe we have earned this right. However, I realized this too late and only wish that every young German who takes the time to read these scrawls, - which anyone can see at the start that this journal was only written as a reminder for me so nothing will be forgotten, - can apply the moral to himself. Then in the future he can think what an unhappy fate we must accept, without knowing what changes to expect in life. Everyone thinks, 'I want my peace [and quiet].' A local farmer assured me that the present weather will continue; usually three days and sometimes three weeks. That would be all right if it were only like a European rain, but everyone dreads the present rain and wind. Today we received our baggage. Since landing from the ship I have had only three shirts, three pairs of stockings and handkerchiefs; otherwise not even an overcoat. Would to God I were in my fatherland and no longer had to worry about it.....

"10 November - The cannonade on the Delaware was very heavy and continued all day. It was from floating batteries which had been made by our side and which were attacked by the enemy ships lying nearby. About one o'clock it began to rain softly. Toward evening it was reported that the fire from the cannons of our batteries was being directed against the enemy fort.

"11 November - Wind and rain, and the cannonade continued without letup.....

# Enemy Views (1777)

"15 November - Today the cannonade was the strongest. It was difficult to distinguish the shots, but there was a constant rumble in the air. During the night a great fire could be seen in the distance.

"16 November - A very dull and cold day. At noon it began to snow. We no longer heard the cannonade. Therefore we waited for good news and heard that the warship *Vigilant* had passed over the *chevaux de frise*, two of which still lie in the river, and on the previous day had heavily damaged the fort so that the garrison therein had to set it afire and then to abandon it. They retreated to the nearby Fort Red Bank, which, however, is surrounded by 4,000 of our men."

Rueffer also recorded the events leading up to the abandonment of Mud Island by the Americans. "3 November - Two floating batteries have been constructed to assist the warships and the batteries on Province Island to attack the forts on Mud Island and Red Bank.....

"12 November - As all the bomb and cannon batteries on Province Island, as well as the floating batteries, are now complete, ten privates from each company of the Light Infantry, as well as the Grenadier Company and the English Guards, commanded by Colonel Osborn, marched to Province Island in order to attack the batteries on Mud Island, with the help of the warships, by the most favorable wind. The 27th and 29th Regiments also marched there at the same time in order to assist Colonel Osborn, should the need arise.

"13 November - Direct bomb hits on the Mud Island fort had started several fires, which were extinguished each time however. Since yesterday evening and throughout the entire day, the fort has been exceedingly heavily bombarded, but the enemy has not answered in a like manner.....

"15 November - Today six warships, including the battery ship *Vigilant* and the so-called *Jorker* sloop, approached Mud Island with the help of the batteries from Province Island, cannonaded and bombarded it so strongly that the noise was comparable to a thunder storm. The fort returned a few shots, therefore the ships, which lay in the neighborhood of Red Bank, fired all the more and despite the indescribable cannonade, still an enemy row galley risked traveling back and forth to Mud Island. In case the ships can not compel the fort to surrender today, the above mentioned troops already on Province Island are to storm the fort tomorrow at four o'clock.

"16 November - This morning, about two o'clock, the rebels evacuated Mud Island after having set the barracks on fire. The damage which the fort received from the ships and the bombardment from Province Island, according to the people who have seen it, is indescribable. There is no place a foot in length where one can walk, which has not been hit by a cannonball. The eighteen-foot parapet is so shot up that entrance ways have been cut through it. The house of the commandant has so many holes that more than 1,000 can be counted and the floors are as blown up as when a herd of swine had been there. Above all, it was evacuated by the rebels in such a deplorable condition that it is as difficult to describe by word of mouth as it is in writing. The garrison, which consisted of 350 men, was evacuated about one o'clock at night to Red Bank. It had been commanded by Baron Arnd, who had previously been in Prussian service. The fort was built by the English during the previous war, but had been made nearly unconquerable by the rebels in this one. About the island they had stretched two strong chains, twisted about one another in the water so as to make it nearly impossible for boats to land. In addition, this chain was connected with the first row of the *chevaux de frise*. Now the fort is occupied by an English regiment and will be repaired by our side. The rebels had thrown all their dead in the water, and of these they had twenty on the fourteenth, and 41 on the fifteenth, and on these two days, 110 seriously wounded. The admiral of their fleet is a slovenly debtor, but has been an experienced English naval officer, and is named Hazelwood. Noteworthy is the fact that one year ago today, Fort Knyphausen fell into our hands."

The Hesse-Cassel Jaeger Corps Journal also contains information on the arrival of the reinforcements from New York and General Cornwallis' operations in New Jersey. "18 November - Lord Cornwallis marched out of camp at Philadelphia tonight with fifty jaegers -- Captain von Wrede -- a battalion of light infantry, an English [grenadier] battalion, and the [Hessian] Lengercke Grenadier Battalion, as well as the 33rd Regiment, and on the nineteenth crossed the Delaware near Chester. There he joined with those forces at Billingsport and with the troops already landed from New York, which were under Major General Wilson.

"21 November - Lord Cornwallis' force, consisting of the above corps, marched to conquer Red Bank, which after the loss of Mud

Island, was still in enemy hands and under [the protection of] whose cannons several enemy ships had retreated. Cornwallis marched over Mende Bridge and camped near Woodbury, where he received news that the enemy had vacated the fort and set fire to all his ships. Thereafter, the general detached the English Grenadiers to occupy the fort.....

"25 November - The march resumed today at Gloucester, at which place the corps recrossed the Delaware and rejoined the army. While the necessary precautions were being made for the crossing, the detachment of jaegers under Captain von Wrede were posted to cover the crossing. About four o'clock in the afternoon, an enemy corps under General Greene came from Mount Holly and attacked, but was repulsed after a hot engagement in which both parties alternately retreated, until at dusk, the enemy pulled back. The loss for the Jaegers was one officer and four men dead, one officer and thirteen men wounded, and ten missing. The enemy loss could not be determined as he took off the dead and wounded, except for one dead officer.

"26 November - The entire corps crossed the Delaware, with only a few enemy causing interference, and rejoined the army in camp at Philadelphia, having finally opened the communications on the Delaware, which had cost considerable time, effort, and men. The enemy losses were estimated at one 32-pounder, one 24-pounder, seven 18-pounders, and one 12-pounder at Mud Island; six 18-pounders, three 12-pounders, two 6-pounders, and five 4-pounders at Red Bank; and between 300 and 400 dead and wounded.

"While all these operations on the Delaware were transpiring, General Washington remained quietly at White Marsh, not far from Germantown, while he fortified it with an abatis and several redoubts, and called in reinforcements from the northern army."

Rueffer noted the destruction of the American fleet on the Delaware River in an entry of 21 November. "This morning at four o'clock we were disturbed by some cannon shots on the Delaware and we noticed that the rebels had set their entire fleet on fire. Some row galleys sought to travel past the frigate *Delaware*. Upon this being noticed, a heavy fire was laid down from both sides, causing the galleys to move away from here. It was a beautiful view to see so many ships drifting and swimming about on fire, under a dark sky, and hearing the sound as still-loaded cannons exploded. Under a flag of truce, our regimental surgeon returned again this afternoon from the rebels and confirmed that the rebels had evacuated Red Bank. He gave high praise to the rebels for their care of our prisoners, of whom only twenty of 63 still survive. Also we learned that the force at Red Bank had been strengthened daily; that it finally reached a strength of 1,500 men who were commanded by General Slocum, and which this day marched to Haddonfield after leaving Red Bank."

Prechtel, also one of the members of the reinforcement sent to Howe from New York, recorded his comments on operations in New Jersey under General Cornwallis, but with a minimum of detail. "18 November - The troops were landed near Billingsport and entered camp, without tents, close to this fort.

"Billingsport, one of America's best designed forts, on the Delaware River, in Jersey, has accommodations for 10,000 men....

"19 November - Today the troops were placed under the command of the English General Cornwallis, who came here from the main army at Philadelphia....

"20 November - During the night the enemy evacuated Fort Red Bank, leaving a great many provisions behind, which were divided among the troops.....

"25 November - This evening the Hessian Jaegers attached to our camp, who occupied the outer posts on the land side, in a woods, were attacked by the enemy.

"The Hessian Staff Riding-master [Georg Hermann] Heppe, of the Mounted Jaegers, was fatally wounded and died the next day.

"During this attack, several jaeger privates were likewise killed.

"26 November - After the chain across the Delaware River between Fort Red Bank and Mud Island, as well as the *chevaux de frise* (*) had been cleared, today the English fleet, which had been lying at anchor at Billingsport, sailed into the harbor at Philadelphia.

"(*) *Chevaux de frise* are large casings filled with stone, which are placed in the water, close to one another, in which large spikes are set. When a ship runs against such, it is seriously damaged and quickly sinks.

"27 November - The army at Gloucester was set across the Delaware from Jersey to Pennsylvania. The last regiments were attacked by the enemy and were carried across under a steady fire from four frigates lying at anchor. The march was immediately made to Philadelphia. The troops joined the main army in camp near Spring Gardens. The two Ansbach regiments paraded through the entire city, along Seventh Street, and entered the barracks there, in which 10,000 men can be quartered....

"Twelve defensive positions, numbered one through twelve, have been built on the land side of Philadelphia."

## Activities During the Closing Days of 1777

Activity in the Philadelphia area during the closing months of 1777 was noted by the diarists as follows. Prechtel noted the move into winter quarters on 13 December. "The main army entered winter quarters in Philadelphia.

"The Ansbach regiments were quartered with the von Eyb Regiment in Water Street; the von Voit Regiment in Front Street."

Feilitzsch recorded the army movements and activities, commencing on 3 December with an entry that, "Toward midday the order to march was received.

"4 December - Suddenly we moved out from our camp at ten o'clock at night. The army, which I estimated at 9,000 to 10,000 men, was commanded by General Cornwallis. We marched throughout the night by way of Germantown.

"5 December - At six o'clock in the morning we arrived at Chestnut Hill. It was astonishingly cold. The English Light Infantry had the advance guard and constantly exchanged fire with the enemy outposts and pickets in the area. After daybreak and after we had put out our usual outposts, the enemy established a picket quite near us. We could see their camp place [in English - called White Marsh]. At two o'clock in the afternoon a large enemy patrol approached and strongly attacked our picket, which was then supported by two companies of our corps. The firing was heavy but did not last long. The enemy had to retreat with losses of five dead and wounded. Our losses were three men wounded, including one man slightly wounded from our company. Shortly thereafter the Light Infantry was attacked. They were more successful. They counter-attacked with bayonets and forced the rebels back, with the loss of fifty men dead, wounded, and captured, including General Arnim.

"6 December - We remained where we were but nothing happened. The enemy camp was very secure and well-entrenched. We marched at twelve o'clock at night. We marched back by our previous route by way of Germantown. At this point, however, we turned left and arrived at twelve o'clock on

"7 December - at Edgehill. After resting an hour under the command of General Grey, we counter-marched and, according to the statements of prisoners, encountered 2,500 rebels who were behind a height. We came within twenty yards of them. The firing was heavy but they had to retreat head over heels. Our losses amounted to one dead and nine wounded. The company, God be praised, lost no one. The enemy left 42 dead behind and ten prisoners. We chased them a short distance and then halted when the Light Infantry beside us engaged them, as usual, with a bayonet attack. Reportedly they suffered 300 killed with bayonets and 200 made prisoners. We moved back into a camp in Abington Township. At six o'clock in the evening I went on picket duty. This was a very restless night for us. The enemy was close to us and fired constantly at us from fear.

"8 December - I was relieved at eight o'clock in the morning. During the afternoon we heard that we would march back because the enemy was too strongly entrenched. When they became aware of this, they approached and fired heavily at our pickets. We drove them off, however, with our amusettes. We moved out at three o'clock. It remained quiet until shortly before night, when they attacked the rear guard. The bullets came thickly toward our company. Later, however, we were undisturbed and arrived at our former camp at Philadelphia at nine o'clock. It was very cold, we had little sleep, and therefore I was very tired and happy to be there and satisfied with my fate.....

"12 December - Fate is catching up with me, and I have the very common ailment of scurvy in the legs. I have great pain and the swelling is pronounced. I had almost decided to request a discharge and, with God's help, to return to my fatherland, when I received a letter from my relatives.....

"20 December - A very cold and windy day. We have hopes of entering winter quarters as it is snowing and the campaign has ended. I am especially happy because now some of the unpleasantness must end. Despite the strict orders many of the inhabitants' houses were burned down over their heads and others were plundered and everything taken. Even if these unfortunate persons at the same time have earned this treatment, through their previous life style or by their present conduct, I still do not wish to be considered an instrument in punishing them, nor even to be witness thereto. If there are those who take pleasure in such cruelties, they may take satisfaction to their fullest, as there are ample opportunities to do so.

"21 December - I was ordered to take the men of the company, who so desired, to church in the city. This was a pleasant duty for me because, since I left Germany, I have seen few churches and those few are mostly in ruins, because most of the preachers have joined the rebels and led their parishioners into their evil beliefs.... During the evening we received the unwished-for order to be prepared to march.

"22 December - Very cold. At eight o'clock in the morning we marched out. The entire army marched, leaving only 1,000 men in Philadelphia. Of our men, however, only Captain von Wrede and our company. We crossed the floating bridge over the Schuylkill and stopped close to it. The left wing of the army extended to the Delaware with the object of collecting all of the forage there.....

"27 December - Once again it began to rain and during the night changed to snow. It can well be imagined what the army had to tolerate without tents and without huts.

"28 December - I went on picket duty at six o'clock in the morning but initially had to take an advance post until it as fully daylight. We had reports that the enemy planned to attack; however they did not do so. At eight o'clock I pulled back to the picket and at ten o'clock received orders to march. We then moved forward a ways in order to cover the army's flank while it moved back across the floating bridge and into the former camp. I formed the rear guard with the picket. Suddenly the enemy came and attacked our cavalry posts but were driven back. At four-thirty we returned to our former camp. It snowed and rained today without stopping.

"29 December - It was so cold and the wind was so strong that it can never be this cold in Europe. We suffer, therefore, very much in camp.

"30 December - We received orders to move into our quarters. At twelve o'clock we marched away. They are about two miles from the city in the region called The Neck. We were all quartered in four houses, so that the company of 74 men was in a house with two small rooms. Lieutenant [Friedrich] Ebenauer and I were together. Our room is very large and cold so that during the night, because it was so cold and we had no bed covers, we froze. Our host is a native born German named Lutz.

"31 December - Still colder. During the night, on our straw we had our previous fate. Today the rebels burned two of our transport ships because they were too close to land along the Delaware River and were frozen in. The English put two howitzers opposite and they were fully occupied just to save ours. I wish with all my heart that with the end of the year, all hostilities will cease and that in the new year I will have only memories, in Germany, although my fate has not been so hard as that of many others. If my system does not improve, however, I can only hope that my strength will hold out as well in the next campaign as in this one. How long will God test us in such a difficult situation, even if we have earned His anger?"

Events of the closing days of 1777 were recorded in the Hesse-Cassel Jaeger Corps Journal as follows, commencing on 4 December. "The army marched at eleven o'clock in two columns, toward Germantown and, because it was night and dark, the Light Infantry served as the advance guard, followed by the Jaegers. The enemy outposts skirmished continuously during the advance, and at daybreak the army reached Chestnut Hill and marched to the front of the enemy's right wing. The Jaeger Corps took its post on the left wing opposite the enemy's right. The Light Infantry was posted about the middle of the army, also in an advanced position. About nine o'clock a corps of about 300 men from the enemy's right wing moved to a position on a height lying opposite the Jaeger Corps, so that the two groups began firing at one another. Toward eleven o'clock the enemy detached another corps of 1,000 men, which attacked the Light Infantry posted in front of the center of the line, but pulled back after a brief exchange of fire. The enemy lost many people in this section and many, including the commander of the corps, were captured.

"6 December - The corps, which had been posted opposite the Jaeger Corps, pulled back during the night without having taken any action, except sending out a few patrols, which wounded three of our men. The two armies stood face to face, the enemy on a height protected by an abatis and a redoubt. Washington appeared to be awaiting an attack and stood his ground. General Howe believed the enemy position here to be too strong, and wanted to test the left wing, so the army left the area and marched on

"7 December - off to the right to Abington Township, toward the enemy's left flank, where it arrived during the afternoon and placed itself before the enemy. It was necessary to dislodge an enemy advance corps before our army could make camp. Therefore the Jaeger Corps was ordered to do this. We found the enemy on a steep height, very advantageously posted. The corps marched against this position in a frontal attack and drove the enemy back, nearly into the abatis. It was a corps of the so-called riflemen, recently arrived from Canada, which had united with General Washington's army, and consisted of about 500 men. As our Cavalry had to content with the enemy, we only took thirty prisoners, and we had three killed and nine wounded, while the enemy lost about twenty killed. Following this action the army encamped. The Jaeger Corps being posted very near the enemy, the pickets fired continuously upon one another.

"8 December - Completely against all expectations, today the army marched back to Philadelphia, because the general found the enemy positions too strong to attack. The return march was uneventful. The Jaegers formed the rear guard which was kept under observation by several cavalrymen.

"10 December - Lord Cornwallis crossed the Schuylkill with 3,600 men in order to gather forage. The advance guard of this corps consisted of a detachment of Jaegers, Captain Cramon, both mounted and dismounted, and Light Infantry. They encountered an enemy party, capturing part and completely dispersing the rest. Cornwallis advanced as far as Swedes Ford, where he met the enemy marching on the other side of the Schuylkill, toward a camp at Valley Forge. The enemy, believing the King's army planned to attack, drew up in line of battle. Cornwallis amused himself at the enemy's expense all day, but on

"11 December - returned to Philadelphia.....

"13 December - Reports are current that General Washington has actually made his camp at Valley Forge and is having huts constructed for use during the winter.....

"30 December - The army went into winter quarters in the city of Philadelphia. The Jaegers were quartered in the so-called Philadelphia

Neck, which is the peninsula between the Delaware and Schuylkill Rivers.

"The winter quarters, although the armies were not far apart, and especially because everyone believed that the enemy camp was much too exposed against everything that was to be expected, and no less to our amazement, remained very quiet. The King's army had very pleasant winter quarters, and was protected by eleven [twelve] redoubts which formed a chain from the Delaware over Morris Heights to the Schuylkill. Each of these redoubts was occupied by a captain with fifty men, who were relieved every 24 hours. Pickets of provincials were posted on the banks of the Schuylkill, and the Jaegers had two pickets on the Delaware at the so-called Howlands Ferry and at Greenwich Point. The enemy was at Valley Forge where he built huts in which to spend the winter. The enemy deserters who came in to us and all the reports which we received, indicated the enemy army was in dire straits, and in particular, equipment, salt, and alcoholic beverages were lacking, and that the shortages in these necessities resulted in dreadful illnesses."

Lieutenant Rueffer also recorded the events of interest during the closing days of 1777. "4 December - This morning at seven o'clock the army is to advance in two columns and only the 2nd Brigade, the Woellworth Brigade, and the 2nd Battalion of the 71st Regiment, the two Ansbach battalions, and the Mirbach Regiment are to occupy the line.

"4 December [sic] - This morning at seven o'clock the army's order to march was countermanded because three English soldiers had deserted. Our Jaegers made a patrol six miles ahead and discovered that the enemy no longer occupied his previous outposts and made contact with them initially at two o'clock in the afternoon, when a brief engagement occurred.

"5 December - The army marched this past night at ten o'clock. The troops listed above, which were designated to occupy the line, remained here under the command of General Leslie. All heavy baggage has remained here. It is reported that during this expedition, Germantown and New Frankford are to be burned in order to drive the rebel army away from our winter quarters.

"6 December - At two o'clock this morning we learned that the army had engaged with the enemy and as the firing did not last very long, it is to be imagined that it was with their outposts.

"7 December - Today a rebel general by the name of Ensign, a hat-maker by profession, born in Philadelphia, as well as some officers and a number of privates, were brought in as prisoners. It is reported that the rebels made an attack on the pickets of our army. Still confirmation is required as to whether heavy and small arms fire was heard at about one o'clock.

"8 December - There were many reports that a large corps of enemy was between here and Germantown and therefore, the entire line moved out, from this morning until this afternoon. They had advanced as far as Chestnut Hill and Poesysound but encountered the enemy in a situation so well-fortified by nature and design, that the commanding general decided that an attack would not succeed.

"9 December - Since the army has moved back into the line, the Ansbach battalions again occupy the barracks. The entire Jaeger Corps received a commendation for its conduct during the last expedition and especially on the seventh. They suffered nine killed and nine wounded and the English Light Infantry lost about 100 altogether."

Rueffer also noted the von Mirbach Regiment's return to New York prior to the end of the year. "15 December - At one o'clock this afternoon, our regiment, as well as the 2nd Battalion of the 71st Regiment, commenced embarking at Bruce's Wharf. Everyone was put on flatboats and sailed to Chester. The sick and wounded were put on a small, two-masted sloop with the name *Fanny*. The cabin was so small and miserable that our group, which consisted of seven people, could hardly turn around. At one-thirty we sailed with the ebb tide from Philadelphia. In the evening, at sunset, we passed the first row of *chevaux de frise* and Mud Island, but as it soon became too dark to see, we anchored at dusk.....

"25 December - Toward evening we arrived at New York. Lieutenant Schotten, Ensign [Hieronymus] Berner, Ship Surgeon [Regimental Surgeon ?] Gechter, Auditor [Johannes] Heinemann, and I at once debarked and took lodgings at Grimm's Tavern.

"26 December - The regiment still spent this day aboard ship."

## Activity in Rhode Island in 1777

Chaplain Kuemmell provides a brief, concise account of garrison duty in Rhode Island during 1777 in a diary entry of 20 February. "I, the auditor, and the regimental quartermaster moved into the city [of Newport] where we had to take quarters in a house where a large amount of regimental equipment was stored. As we could now only visit the regiment with difficulty and after a long trip, we could seldom conduct religious services. Therefore I helped Pastor Schrecker in the city, where we held our services in a very well-built Presbyterian church. The occupying troops had every advantage over the other regiments and Commanding General Lord [sic] Clinton, and later Lord Percy, were especially attentive that the spit and polish in the garrison was maintained. The main watch was led and supervised by a captain and two officers. Two other officers were detailed, one at Southends and one on the Long Way. Each day one officer had duty as orderly for the commanding general. Provisions were made also for entertainment. Twice weekly concerts were presented at the Crown Coffee House. For the officers life was pleasant and comfortable, but the common soldiers had few enjoyments because all the soldiers had their quarters in the rebels' empty houses and because of the high cost of living and scarcity of fresh meat, of which there was none in the end. In April Lord Percy, as a member of Parliament, returned to England. For several days prior to that the officers of the Lossberg Regiment had entertained him with a serenade. With his departure the garrison lost most of its gaiety, and the residents of the city a dear compassionate governor. They presented him with a letter of thanks in which they extended and made known his honorable character as they had suffered little or almost no calamities due to the war while under his rule. He gave numerous presents to the poor and to the English Church; enough so that he proved himself to be an exceptionally compassionate individual. His departure was painful for everyone who knew him, if only by name. He was followed in command by General Richard Prescott. He did not treat the locally born inhabitants well because he had been a prisoner of the rebels previously and had experienced much hardship. As soon as he had the least opportunity to blame someone for something, he placed them immediately in jail.

Therefore, the people of the island had the greatest hatred for him, which they also displayed at every opportunity.

"18 December - The Leib Regiment and the Prince Charles Regiment, as well as the English 54th Regiment, were embarked and went to join the main army at New York. Ditfurth Regiment and the 22nd English Regiment remained in the city.....

"10 and 11 July - During the night we suffered a misfortune when the Commanding General Prescott and his adjutant were cleverly taken away by the rebels. The carelessness of the guard was clearly responsible, although obviously the residents of the island played a role in this coup, out of revenge against his hard, but justified conduct. He took lodging in an insecure house in the country, too distant from the camp. The event awoke a special alertness and caution. In July the new Commanding General [Robert] Pigot entered the harbor in a frigate. He was welcomed by a detachment of one officer and 24 men and the hautboists of the Huyn Regiment."

Kuemmell's diary ends shortly after this entry, but Private Asteroth's diary continues the account of events. "10 July - During the night, due to the carelessness of the English, our commanding general, Prescott, was kidnapped from Rhode Island. He had his quarters in the city where he always remained. He also had quarters on the island where he sometimes slept and which was provided with a guard from the English camp. He rowed over to this quarters on the island, with his adjutant, on 10 July. This place lay two hours from the camp at an insecure place. Because he was rather strict, he was not well liked in the city where there were rebels, in Newport just as in Providence. Here's one! He has a son, another has a daughter, and friends, as is common throughout the world. Therefore, it can be assumed that on this island, one of the inhabitants betrayed him.

"On the night of the tenth, about two o'clock, a boat with a major and seventeen men landed on the island. The major went ashore, took a small flask of rum, and approached the guard. Posing as a deserter from the rebels, he gave the guard some cognac to drink until that one was drunk. Then they, the Americans, entered the house, tied the general, and carried him, his adjutant, and the guard back to the boat. They had successfully captured him. I remember a similar incident involving the English. On 24 March as we entered camp after being relieved by the English at Bristol Ferry, at four o'clock in the afternoon, thirty rebels crossed over and approached the outpost. As he [the guard] had not loaded his weapon, they marched on to the command house. No sentry was posted and the weapons were stacked before the house. A rebel knocked on the window and said to the officer that he should keep a better watch when he was in command. Then the rebels opened fire, killing two in the house and taking the outpost guard with them.....

"19 October - At eleven o'clock at night an alarm was sounded as the rebels were planning to attack us. The regiment was at once under arms. A detachment of our troops was in camp at Fogland Ferry, when suddenly more than sixty boats were seen. The 140-man detachment entered the defenses at once and opened fire with cannons. Captain [Wilhelm von der] Malsburg of Ditfurth Regiment commanded them. They were detached troops of one officer, one non-commissioned officer, and 35 privates from each regiment. The rebels wanted to attack Triporns with 9,000 men, but as they saw that we were prepared, they remained away. It was a special night. The richest merchants and citizens, 82 in all, came running to the main watch and said they wished to help us fight. The captain reported this to General Pigot. They were present but did not know the password, although they were loyal to the King. The colonel from the city commanded them. Therefore, they were permitted to have and were given the password. They may have to fight against their fathers, brothers, and friends. The reason for this is that the rebels have said that if they capture us, they will take all the men who previously served with them and execute them. Therefore, every evening they gather at the headquarters with their weapons and then go on patrol in the city and on the island. They are called 'King's people'. They also report other citizens who were rebels to the commanding general, Pigot. The general then orders the King's people to arrest the others and those who would not swear allegiance to the King were to be thrown in jail as rebels. In general, not many were found who would not take the oath. Therefore, about sixty were put in jail and about eighty on a prison ship, on bread and water. Later many died on the warship. When they saw that nothing would help them, they gradually took the oath to the King."

# 1778

## Prisoner Exchange

The year 1778 began with the Hessians captured at Trenton still in captivity. However, this was to change as noted by Lieutenant Piel. "26 February 1778 - All captured officers, English as well as German, received orders to assemble at Lancaster in Pennsylvania. From there we will go, on our honor, to Philadelphia, and General Howe is to send an equal number of rebel officers back. To make it more agreeable for us, we were allowed to travel in several troops, of which the first left Falmouth today.

"3 March - The last troop departed. We traveled over Leesburg, taking Nolers [Knowles] Ferry over the Potomac and arrived at Friederickstown [Frederick].....

"14 March - Today we arrived at Hanover, or Maccallestertown, in Pennsylvania. Here, to our dismay, we received an order from Congress to stop and not to continue our journey until we received further orders. A secretary from the Commissary of Prisoners gave us this order and in so doing, made such an impression that we considered him to be a person of importance. We had to sign a document wherein we had to pledge that we would not leave the city, and that in the evening, after sunset, we would not leave our quarters. He also had an article added on, namely that we would not speak with any Anabaptists because these were all considered as loyal to the King. -- However, because we told him that we did not have the artistic ability to determine people's religion by their physical appearance, and therefore when we first speak with each individual our first question would have to be if they were Anabaptists, he finally struck out this article.

"8 April - We finally received permission to continue our journey to Philadelphia today and departed from Hanover. The most direct route to Lancaster goes through Yorktown, but because Congress was sitting there at the time, we were not allowed to take that road. We had to make a wide detour over untrodden roads. We spent the night in various individual houses.

"9 April - We crossed the Susquehanna at Lowe's Ferry and spent the night in Maytown....

"10 April - We arrived in Lancaster where, to our great dismay, we found the order from Congress not to continue our trip until we received further reports.... Here we met a large part of our privates, of whom some sat in prison. Most however, had permission to work in the city and on the land.

"17 April - After we had written our pledge not to fight until after we had been exchanged, we finally received permission to continue our journey to Philadelphia. We left Lancaster today, traveled sixteen miles, and spent the night at a single inn.

"18 April - We arrived at White Horn [Horse ?], an inn 26 miles from Philadelphia, and six miles from Valley Forge, where Washington then had his quarters.

"19 April - We were not allowed to depart today until the commissary general had seen the prisoners. He finally arrived from the headquarters about noon. He asked us in a very polite manner if we had any letters addressed to Philadelphia, to let him see them. After this happened, we were allowed to continue on our way. We had traveled thirteen miles when a rebel dragoon met us with an order not to continue on the direct road, but to remain in a private house one mile to the right of the main road, where night quarters had already been made for us.

"20 April - We arrived in Philadelphia about noon today, pleased to be out of the hands of the rebels and by our friends. The army of General Howe lay peacefully in quarters here, although nearly everyday light troops were sent out, which most of the time brought captured rebels back with them. Here we met the remainder of our three captured regiments, from which two battalions were formed, commanded by Colonel von Woellwarth.....

"13 May - Today the Hessian officers who had been prisoners of the rebels received their parole pledges back and were assigned duty with the two battalions which formed the Woellwarth Brigade."

Piel also noted other events concerning Hessian prisoners of war in 1778. "19 July - Today 400 men from the brigade returned [to Philadelphia] from captivity and joined our regiment.

"25 July - The Loos Brigade, which until this time had served as two battalions -- namely Lossberg and half of Woellwarth made the 1st Battalion, and Knyphausen and half of the Woellwarth made the 2nd

Battalion -- was once again divided into three regiments and each served separately.

"6 August - Another four non-commissioned officers and eight privates of the Lossberg, having been exchanged, came from captivity to the regiment.

"16 August - Again, one drummer and five privates came to the regiment from captivity.

"27 October - Today five non-commissioned officers, one drummer, and 87 privates came to the regiment from captivity."

Private Reuber also recorded the events concerning the exchanges during 1778. "Suddenly there was discussion among the Americans concerning a prisoner exchange and this continued quite a while until the August moon arose. Then the order circulated that the Hessians must assemble. Those who so wished, came together. Those not returned had to be paid for. Some [of the farmers] returned their soldiers, who then deserted from us and returned to their masters on the land and remained in America and married.

"26 August - We departed from Winchester in the Blue Mountains of Virginia and marched back the same way that we had come.

"30 August - We arrived at the ferry at Johannes Stock, were carried across, and arrived once again in the province of Maryland and made our night quarters in a woods.

"6 September - We entered Baltimore, the capital of Maryland, and spent the night in the city hall.

"7 September - We marched farther back and in three days were already in the province of Pennsylvania and continued to retrace our march back to the English army.

"10 September - We arrived in Lancaster in Pennsylvania, where we had been from 12 January to 20 September 1777 and reentered the same barracks.

"11 September - We continued on toward Philadelphia, spent the night under the open sky in a woods, and arrived at the Little Brandywine on

"[12 September] - which we had to wade through. After two hours we came to the Big Brandywine and were carried across. On the other side we again made night camp in the woods under the open sky.....

"24 September - We Hessian and English prisoners of war finally reentered Philadelphia and entered the large new jail and were well-guarded.[29] We lay there eight days. We then went aboard ships on the Delaware and sailed to Trenton, where we arrived on 23 October and remained one night.

"24 October - We resumed our march.....

"28 October -To Elizabethtown near Staten Island, across the harbor to Elizabethtown [Point], where we 300 Hessians and 300 English prisoners of war were delivered to the English commissary. After all that had taken place we were carried across the harbor to Staten Island and entered camp by our fellow Hessians. What joy and pleasure that was, when we returned from our slavery as we 300 men had to remain captive longer, because of the long trip of 500 English miles, than the 600 Hessians in Pennsylvania who were considerably closer to the English army than we in the Blue [Ridge] Mountains in Winchester, Virginia.....

"31 October - An English warship arrived here and took us off Staten Island and returned us prisoners of war to land at New York. We disembarked at once and entered quarters for one night by the Bose Regiment.

"1 November - We moved out early in the morning and marched onward to Fort Knyphausen and the former Rall Grenadier Regiment.

"4 November -The former Rall Grenadier Regiment moved out of Fort Knyphausen early and then back into camp at New York. We Hessian prisoners of war again received guns and weapons at the regiment and were again equipped. When we were again organized we received as our regimental commander, since Colonel Rall was dead, Colonel [Johann Christoph] Koehler and Lieutenant Colonel [Johann Wilhelm] Endemann of the Hereditary Prince Regiment and from that time on were called the Truembach Grenadier Regiment."

During the summer of 1778 Chaplain Waldeck noted the return of men of the Waldeck Regiment who had been prisoners of war. "4 July - Today we had the pleasure once again to have Lieutenant Heldring back in camp after having been a prisoner of war, and Captain von Haacke and the remaining prisoners are expected any day.....

"18 July - Finally, a general exchange of prisoners has occurred. We received 39 men back to the regiment from captivity.....

"2 August - I had the honor, together with Lieutenant Heldring, to dine with the colonel. The lieutenant entertained us with interesting tales of captivity.....

"6 August - Seven of our prisoners of war returned to the regiment today."

Steuernagel, by this time a quartermaster sergeant, also noted the return of some of the former prisoners of war. "On 9 July Captain von Haacke and Lieutenant Heldring returned to the regiment from their captivity, and on the sixteenth" other prisoners returned.

Lieutenant Bach, who had been captured at Bennington, noted events of his captivity and release in a letter to the Hesse-Cassel [?] Court Marshal, dated 7 December 1778. "As I am the only officer in this part of the world who has been released from captivity, now on parole, and I know that in the present situation you could have received no news about the Convention troops, I take the liberty, most humbly, to notify you of my exchange....

"On 24 September all the captive officers received orders to assemble in Rutland. Some of them were commanded by General von Riedesel to remain by the captive German regiments of the Northern Army. The rest however, were to go to their designated places. On 2 October we arrived at Providence [Rhode Island], near the rebel General Sullivan. After he gave the order to the commissary, we went to Warwick, where we rented a ship for 100 paper Reichsthalers of our own money, and were taken to Newport on it. We arrived there on 4 October.... On 7 October an officer ... arrived at Newport from Canada with the equipment and uniform items [for the prisoners].... As the entire Convention [army] was now on the march to Virginia, it was said the equipment should sail there. Late on the eighteenth we received orders to sail to New York with a rather large fleet of 54 transport ships, a frigate, and a privateer. We arrived at Hellgate on the seventeenth [sic] and went to New York in small boats.... Each day numerous men of the Convention, which is marching to Virginia, report in, more than 150 in five days."

Captain Pausch noted his captivity in a letter to his prince on 16 July 1778. "Still actually in our Convention's captivity, which only with considerable confusion is the primary reason to call it captivity ... and from all appearances this will remain unchanged until the end of the war."

In a summary of the Artillery Company strength, he listed the following: "Prisoners of war and missing in action -- 1 2nd lieutenant, 1 bombardier, 21 cannoneers, 2 artillery servants, a total of 25 persons" and "Convention prisoners -- 1 captain, 1 1st lieutenant, 1 2nd lieutenant, 1 sergeant-major, 7 bombardiers, 3 drummers, 37 cannoneers, 1 wagonmaster, 1 journeyman smith, 1 journeyman cartwright, 1 saddlemaker, 4 artillery servants, a total of 59 persons."

There were a few pleasant events, even while in captivity, as noted by Captain von Buttlar of the Hesse-Hanau Infantry Regiment in a letter to the prince on 15 October 1778 from Winter Hill, Massachusetts. "Your Highness has granted me the greatest pleasure and been pleased most graciously to promote me to staff captain by a directive of 20 July 1777. I received this on 7 October 1778 while in captivity at Winter Hill near Boston."

Men even re-enlisted while prisoners, as noted in a letter from Captain von Germann to his prince on 9 May 1778 from Winter Hill. "Musketeer [Christoph] Wiskemann, whose discharge year had already passed on 10 December 1777, sought his most honorable discharge, declaring that if Your Highness would do the favor of paying him a new bonus, he was ready to enter a new enlistment and left it to Your Highness' pleasure how much you would allow."

A reference on 29 May 1778 by Regimental Quartermaster Zinn in the regimental journal of the von Donop Regiment may have resulted from a rumor of a move by the Convention prisoners. Under that date he wrote, "When the news arrived that the enemy was moving the captives of General Burgoyne's army to Virginia, and that they were already underway in the near vicinity, the entire garrison, including our regiment, received march orders. We marched to Germantown and occupied that region in the hope of attacking the enemy. However, on the same day we marched back to Philadelphia."

Actually the prisoners began their march from the Boston area on 9 November, and the Hesse-Cassel Jaeger Corps Journal notes the Convention prisoners crossing the North River on 29 November. "Upon receipt of news that the prisoners from Burgoyne's army were to be transported from New England to Virginia, and would cross the North River at King's Ferry, the British Grenadiers, Light Infantry, and the Mirbach Regiment marched to Tarrytown, but arrived too late; the men being transferred having crossed the North River ten hours previously. The reason these troops are being sent to Virginia is supposedly because the New Englanders refused to continue giving them provisions."

Lieutenant Piel, also of the von Donop Regiment, correctly noted the events of 20 May 1778. "Because we had news that the rebel General [Marie Joseph] Marquis de Lafayette had crossed the Schuylkill with 5,000 men and wished to establish himself near White Marsh, the English and Hessian Grenadiers, as well as the Light Infantry, marched out at about nine o'clock in the morning to approach the enemy corps from the rear. This morning at six o'clock, another corps of English, Hessians, and Ansbachers took the road through Germantown in order to make a frontal attack against the enemy. However, the Marquis received timely reports of these movements and hurriedly pulled back over the Schuylkill. The Woellwarth Brigade did not participate in these movements, but remained in Philadelphia under arms throughout the period."

The diarists also recorded information in 1778 concerning Americans who were prisoners of war. The von Mirbach regimental order book entry for 11 April 1778 contains the following information. "A large number of rebels escaped from the sugar house prison [in New York] during the night, two of whom were captured by Major von Wilmowsky's Company, which meets with General Robertson's approval and he has ordered that a reward be paid to the troops who made the arrest. All the pickets and guards will be alert to watch for suspicious persons in order to perhaps catch some more of these deserters."

## Garrison Duty in Philadelphia

Prechtel's diary contains comments on garrison duty in Philadelphia in 1778, including the Mischianza, the entertainment for General Howe prior to his return to England. "18 May - Today the English staff officers held an entertainment for the general-in-chief, Sir William Howe. The entire retinue came together at Redoubt Number One at three o'clock in the afternoon. They embarked in flatboats and passed down the Delaware River with musical accompaniment.

## Enemy Views (1778)

"When the retinue passed the fleet of warships and transports lying at anchor in the harbor, all of which had flags flying, a strong salute was fired from all the cannons. In a garden outside Philadelphia a banquet and ball was held, and at night a magnificent fireworks display was presented."

Feilitzsch made numerous diary entries during 1778 reflecting on his discontent with service in America. "1 January 1778 - Just as cold as previously but then somewhat better in the afternoon. I have never had such a day before at this place. I could not attend church services. In short, we are fated to live as heathens.....

"4 to 6 January - The weather was the same. It froze every night and thawed every day. There was a maid in my quarters, who was not very pretty but had lovers enough because it is like this -- when the sailors come ashore, I amuse myself by watching them. This often annoys them.

"7 January - It snowed and was a dull day. We received orders to visit the captain's host because he had reportedly hidden ammunition for the Americans. However, we found nothing.

"12 January - It froze very hard. There is much talk of peace again, which I wish from the bottom of my heart. I do not believe it, because if it is not my unhappy fate to remain here, nevertheless, I dread the thought of the return voyage. However, I would tolerate all sorts of difficulties to see my relatives and my fatherland once again.

"23 January - There was changeable weather, extremely cold at night and then, within half an hour, the most beautiful spring weather. In general, an unhealthy weather and climate for us Germans. However, everything remained quiet and we lived here peacefully in our solitude and had everything we needed.....

"30 January - Nothing occurred. Today was the most beautiful summer day, but no one could move from one house to another because the mud was so deep and nothing here is firm.

"3 February - I went on picket duty. We received reports that the enemy would attack during the night in order to capture the picket. Therefore I was more alert tonight than usual and at eleven o'clock we actually heard the rebel boats being put into the Delaware on the other side. They set sail but did not attack us, so everything remained quiet.....

## Enemy Views (1778)

"5 February - Currently the rebels are using strong measures to press men into the service of the militia and making all necessary preparations for the coming campaign. Hopes of peace are fading and we must also be prepared and not shy away from any barbarity, regardless of how it might be considered by a European. It is necessary here and done without any thought because that is not considered a vice here.....

"14 February - The wind was still so strong and also as cold as before. The enemy who are only in huts in the field must feel it, as I could not sleep well because of the cold, even when in my bed during the past night, completely wrapped up in a wool blanket. Also, General Washington, if reports are true, has pulled back to Lancaster with his regular troops because he has determined that the impressed soldiers are not trustworthy. However, I do not believe this because so many of the reports are slanted in our favor, all of which anticipate an early peace. We can believe no less than this if we have religion. However, the inhabitants among them have not been punished enough for their wicked conduct.....

"23 February - When I went on watch it was raining very heavily. During the night it was very cold and suddenly it began to snow hard. In a short time the English have captured a great number of rebel officers, who have been betrayed by the farmers, because the officers have been living in the neighborhood. I can not determine the number, but to tell the truth, I would put the number at about sixty. Many of their privates also desert as does an officer, occasionally. From our newly raised provincial troops many also desert. It seems as if the rebels only wish to get uniforms from us because those in the area are poorly equipped.....

"27 February - I went on picket duty. During the afternoon a fleet of 120 ships with provisions came up the Delaware. I saw 37 of them anchor near the ferry at my picket. Our Colonel von Eyb as well as other officers and soldiers came with them, having remained behind in New York sick - and our baggage. Next day the ships raised their anchors and sailed up to the city.

"28 February - As usual, I was relieved. When I got home I heard that a detachment of 200 of our Jaegers had left during the previous night to open the road for people bringing in produce, because the rebels had threatened to hang anyone bringing food into the city.

However, no enemy were encountered and they returned at ten o'clock. It was a very warm summer day.....

"15 April - I heard that Colonel von Eyb and Lieutenant [Johann Friedrich] von Sichart[30] of our regiments had received their discharges, at their request. The rebels were offered peace with very favorable terms. Therefore commissioners were sent from England to carry out the negotiations. Reportedly they are not pleased with this offer, but want their independence. Who knows, however, what they will do, since they have not stated their position. The soldiers desert in large numbers. This happens with every patrol.

"9 May - Thoughts of peace have disappeared. Everyone speaks of war and great changes. France and Spain have joined together and declared war on England. How great the longing is to see our fatherland again this year, but ++++[31] I wish, but very much doubt, that things will change for us.....

"14 May - We received orders that all the baggage which we did not wish to take to the field was to be packed ready to be taken aboard ship.

"15 May - It was a very warm day. Various ideas were held as to what was happening. Some thought we would go to Boston; others, the West Indies; some even Europe, but no one knows. I will not even state my thoughts. I hope for the best but will remain cautious. During the night I was included in a command which marched to the ferry boat at twelve o'clock. I was detached to a point two miles beyond to pick up a family.....

"19 May - During the evening a detachment of Jaegers marched to Germantown.

"20 May - The rest of the Jaegers [marched] early in the morning and also many of the army. A corps of about 5,000 rebels under the command of the Marquis de Lafayette had approached. Our troops marched as far as Chestnut Hill to meet him. As soon as he heard this, he retreated in great haste back across the Schuylkill. The English Dragoons captured some French volunteers and cut down their major. Reportedly seventy prisoners were taken, but I did not see them. Four Indians were reported among them and 150 with the command. I was not relieved from picket duty because the detachment did not return until evening."

## Enemy Views (1778)

The Hesse-Cassel Jaeger Corps Journal contains several interesting entries during the corps' stay in Philadelphia in 1778. "12 March - Several scouting parties were sent out from Philadelphia, consisting of raw, newly-enrolled provincials who use their military role for plundering. However, they never made serious contact with the enemy unless rich booty was to be expected.....

"27 March - A transport ship, *Brilliant*, coming from New York with convalescents and baggage on board, had the misfortune of grounding near Philadelphia during a strong wind storm. All the personnel were saved but the baggage was lost.

"Now we hear of the peace overtures from the Parliament. Everyone was so completely convinced that peace would result and so certain had this belief taken hold, that we were astounded and amazed by Congress' scornful refusal of everything which in the least curtailed independence.

"1 April - Because the enemy prevented, for the most part, all the people who wished, from bringing their produce to market, not only taking their produce but also greatly mistreating the people, Lieutenant Colonel von Wurmb ordered the Jaeger Corps to march out three times a week to prevent this, and to give the people protection. This accomplished the wished-for effect, although these expeditions were very dangerous, and had to be undertaken with the greatest care because the region was densely occupied, and for the most part, covered with woods. But even more so because the enemy always knew before hand the time when we would march out, and that we could not be supported by the line units at any great distance.....

"7 May - Some armed brigantines and schooners went up the Delaware and burned the enemy frigates *Washington* and *Effingham*, as well as a 24-gun ship and several smaller vessels which lay at Burlington. Some houses and a magazine with all sorts of war materials were also burned, which ended this expedition.....

"13 May - A frigate entered Philadelphia bringing the unexpected rumor that France has recognized the Americans' independence and signed a treaty with them.....

"19 May - An enemy command of 6,000 men under Marquis de Lafayette approached the lines before Philadelphia, advancing as far as White Marsh and Chestnut Hill. Therefore a large corps was detached from the army this evening to march to the Schuylkill and wherever possible to engage the enemy. A Jaeger detachment commanded by Captain Ewald constituted the advance guard.

"20 May - The army under Lieutenant General von Knyphausen marched out this morning toward Chestnut Hill. The Marquis had received word of our movement, and pulled back across the Schuylkill as quickly as possible. The English Light Dragoons, who had marched with the first corps, fell on the enemy rear and took some prisoners. The entire army marched out because the commanding general wanted to cut Lafayette off from the main army, and attack General Washington in his camp. As this did not succeed, toward evening the army marched back to Philadelphia.....

"25 May - The army's heavy baggage was taken on board ship.

"26 May - All wives, sick, invalids, etc., also went aboard ship today, and the ships and the army are to be ready to move out at a moment's notice.

"29-31 May - The ships sailed from Philadelphia, and only a few vessels remain for use when the army moves out.

"5 June - The English commissioners arrived in Philadelphia to arrange a peace. All their efforts were in vain however, because the Americans are relying strongly on the French, and will accept no suggestions to the contrary."

### The Evacuation of Philadelphia and the Battle of Monmouth

When the English prepared to evacuate Philadelphia, Prechtel recorded the Ansbach-Bayreuth move to New York beginning on 9 June. "At two o'clock in the morning both Ansbach regiments were embarked on horse ships. The fleet went under sail at daybreak....

"As the tide arrived at nine o'clock in the morning, we anchored near Billingsport.

"Underway at two o'clock in the afternoon and we passed Chester and Willmington on the right. During the evening we anchored here, where the warships lay at anchor.

"10 June - Underway at two o'clock in the morning. At twelve o'clock noon a calm settled in and because the ships could not anchor, they were driven against one another in a surprising manner, which often can cause damage.

"At two o'clock the calm ended and although the wind was contrary, we entered the ocean and the land was lost from view.

"Most of our troops became seasick.....

"20 June - This morning two sailors were hanged for espionage aboard a frigate lying at anchor in this harbor [New York].

"The warship on which the execution was to take place raised a yellow flag first thing in the morning.

"From every warship lying at anchor in the harbor, a boat with a sea officer and about thirty sailors was sent to the ship which had raised the yellow flag. This flag continues to fly until the execution has been carried out.

"Further, a signal is given with a cannon shot, whereupon the criminals are suddenly hanged on the mainyard of the forward mast.

"We went under sail at twelve o'clock noon and passed Martin's Wharf and Turtle Bay on the left, on the East River, and on the right, Brooklyn, a small city lying on Long Island, where there are always many seamen living.

"The transports lay at anchor at Blackwell's Ferry and the regiments were landed on Long Island and entered their camp near Blackwell's house. At that time, the command was held by the English General Tryon."

Feilitzsch also commented on preparations to leave Philadelphia and on the departure of the Ansbach and Bayreuth Regiments on board ship. "25 May - It is said that we will soon leave Philadelphia for fear that the French fleet will blockade us here. It is certain that the ships with our baggage will sail today for New York and we will follow on land. Experience is the best teacher. We continue to work diligently on the defenses and if this report is true it will give comfort to the enemy that our army must continue to exert itself. I hope for the best......

"1 June - It was a cold day with a heavy rain. Great preparations were made for our departure from Philadelphia. In two or three days we will surely depart.

7 June - This morning the five [peace] commissioners, who are to negotiate with Congress, arrived from England. Generally speaking, the peace talks are not progressing as we would wish. God grant His blessing. I wish them to succeed....

"8 June - During the night both of our regiments were embarked and we do not know where they are bound. The separation makes me very sad. If we have to make a campaign it will be all the more unpleasant to be alone."

Stang's comments on the transfer back to New York are very brief. "9 June - at two o'clock in the morning we marched out of Philadelphia again, embarked on a small ship named *Betsy* and set sail.

"14 June - We transferred to a large ship named *Houston* and again sailed into the sea for New York with a fleet of 60 ships.

"20 June - Two sailors were hanged on board a frigate and we disembarked this day where the river is called Hell. As we disembarked, a soldier named Teufel fell into the Hell River and drowned. After we had all landed we set up camp in this province of Long Island."

Zinn's comments on the English evacuation of Philadelphia, the march to New York, and the Battle of Monmouth en route, are also quite brief.

"6 June - A few days after having sent all the heavy baggage, as well as the tents, sick, and wives, aboard ship, the brigade of Major General von Stirn marched to the wharf not far from the upper coal magazine, from which place we were set across the Delaware in flatboats, and went on land near the ferry. We then marched six English miles and entered camp near Newtown.....

"26 June - The Cornwallis corps had a battle with the enemy at Monmouth.....

"5 July - We were taken to the waiting transport ships in flatboats and sailed to New York, where at

"6 July - in the evening, we arrived and the next day,

"7 July - debarked at the Hay Wharf on the North River and entered camp near 6-mile stone, on the Kingsbridge Road, not far from Marsten's wharf."

Piel elaborated a bit more on those events, commencing on 15 June 1778. "After the heavy baggage and the army's tents were sent aboard ship and several English regiments had crossed the Delaware to Jersey ahead of us, the Stirn and Woellwarth, now Loos, Brigades today received orders to march. At six o'clock this evening we were taken across the Delaware in flatboats, marched inland three miles, and camped in Newtown Township.....

"23 June - The army marched out this morning in two columns. General Knyphausen commanded the column on the right and the second body of the Loos Brigade was the rear guard today. During the last three days the Hessian corps has lost many men who deserted. Two non-commissioned officers and two privates deserted from the Lossberg Regiment.....

"25 June - We marched to Freedom Township. It was a very fatiguing march. Almost half of our troops fell along the way due to the heat.....

"28 June - At daybreak this morning the entire army moved out. The Knyphausen Division, which contained all the provisions for the army and the artillery train, constituted the advance guard. The enemy harassed our rear guard, killed several horses from the train, and wounded a few soldiers. At the same time the corps under General Clinton fell on the rebels in hand-to-hand fighting and drove them back. In this combat our army lost about 150 men, dead and wounded, and nearly as many dropped dead on the spot, during the fighting, from the heat.....

"5 July - The entire army marched this morning in several columns from Navesink to Sandy Hook. A part of the army entered flatboats here and were taken to the transport ships. The remaining part, including the Loos Brigade, marched over the floating bridge which stretched from the mainland to Sandy Hook, and bivouacked overnight on this sandy wasteland.

"6 July - The 1st Battalion of the Loos Brigade went aboard the *Bird* and the 2nd aboard the *Diana*.... We sailed and arrived at New York at six in the evening."

The Hesse-Cassel Jaeger Corps Journal comments include the following. "16 June - The army left Philadelphia, and crossed the Delaware to Jersey at Coopers Ferry.

"18 June - Today the rest of the troops left the city and were transported across to Gloucester Point. The enemy army gave not the least indication of harassing our crossing, but remained completely quiet in camp. They were however, ready to march on the shortest notice.

"17 June [sic] - Lieutenant General von Knyphausen set out marching toward Haddonfield with the following troops: Hessian Jaegers in the van, the Queen's Rangers, Hessian Grenadiers, 2nd Battalion of Jersey Volunteers, Maryland Loyalists, Volunteers of Ireland and Caledonia. The rest of the army remained at the river to load the train and baggage of the army and to get reorganized. Near Haddonfield the Jaegers encountered the first enemy posts, which fired and then pulled back.

"18 June [sic] - Major General Leslie was given command of a light corps which is to be the army's advance guard, and which consists of the following troops: Jaegers, Queen's Rangers, a detachment of Jersey Volunteers, and the 7th, 23rd, and 63rd Regiments. The main army is to march in two columns. The Jaegers skirmished constantly with an enemy scouting party, which slowly fell back, giving resistance at every defile, woods, or bridge, and tore up every bridge, and caused whatever other harassment they could.....

"20 June - The march continued today to Mount Holly where the army is to be reunited, and where we made camp. The enemy Major General [William] Maxwell and his brigade had lain in this place and retreated to Trenton. It was a secure post which could have been very easily and well defended, but their retreat was made so hurriedly that they did not even break up the bridge....

"24 June - There were confirmed reports that the enemy army had already crossed the Delaware near Trenton. During the afternoon the Jaegers saw men from previously unseen units, and these troops harassed us greatly.....

"26 June - Today the army marched to Monmouth where it camped on a very beautiful plain. Due to the unbearable heat we lost three men. The march was very tiring, and as we were the last troops and constantly engaged with the enemy, and because of the exhausted and ruined wells, suffered severely from the shortage of water; many of the Jaegers fell on the road and were put on the officers' horses in order to be carried along with us, as we were not allowed any wagons. This happened frequently on the retreat across the Jerseys.

"27 June - Today the enemy launched two very vigorous attacks on our rear in an effort to cut it off, but these were beaten back with losses. We laid an ambush into which a troop of cavalry fell, and several were shot....

"28 June - The army was ordered to march in a column a certain distance to a place where Lieutenant General von Knyphausen was marching with the army's train and baggage. At this point, the Jaegers would become the rear guard, and to this end, joined the column at two o'clock in the morning at Monmouth near the general's quarters, to which the 40th Regiment, under Lieutenant Colonel Musgrove, and the Jersey Volunteers also came. These preparations started the army in motion, and as it took a long time to get the numerous wagons moving, it was already six o'clock in the morning before all were underway. At this time General Washington with his army marched up, and General Clinton awaited contact with only the left column under Lord Cornwallis. The enemy, as soon as he had advanced a pre-determined distance, formed in two lines, and General Clinton advanced against the enemy and drove the first line completely back, and would have pursued it farther if the second line had not been posted most advantageously on a height behind a swamp, which prevented him from doing so. Nevertheless, the English Grenadiers did make an effort to cross the morass but got their cannons stuck, and were only able to retrieve them with the most strenuous effort. During this time various attempts were made to capture the baggage, but these failed, and as a strong corps was reported marching against our train, which was stretched over a very long distance, the Jaeger Corps and the 40th Regiment were detached to provide cover. However, as the enemy had been beaten, that corps of his force was ordered back, and no engagement occurred here. General Clinton harassed the enemy throughout the day with artillery fire, and as his men were extremely fatigued, he did not desire to attack the enemy a second time while they held such an advantageous position. However, he ordered a brigade from General von Knyphausen's column to join with his force in case the enemy should launch an attack.... The losses on the English side in this action amounted to 320 dead and wounded, and on the enemy side, to 600.....

"1 July - We awaited in this position [at Navesink], an attack from the enemy, but no one appeared before our posts except [Daniel] Morgan's Corps.

"General Lee had a falling out with General Washington concerning the action on the 28th, in which Lee was criticized for unnecessarily retreating, and for not maintaining discipline in the first line.....

"5 July - As the enemy army moved to Braunschweig [Brunswick] and from there toward the North River, in order to protect the Highlands, we did not expect further attack from it."

Feilitzsch also recorded the army's march through Jersey beginning on 16 June. "At present there are not more than 6,000 men in the city [Philadelphia]. The army is already on the other side of the Delaware.

"17 June - At three o'clock this morning we were also carried across to Jersey. The heat was terrible. We marched to Haddonfield, seven English miles. On the way not more than eight rebels were seen who were fired upon.....

"26 June - At five o'clock we marched; as usual, the rear guard. The enemy had disturbed us during the night up until we marched. We went about twelve miles. The enemy harassed us the entire day. I led a patrol off to one side. The heat was terrible. It was an extremely tiring day. Would to God it is the last one. The place where we halted is called Upper Freehold. During a marauding expedition the corps lost twenty men, but not one from the company.....

"28 June - At two o'clock in the morning we marched. We were the rear guard for General Knyphausen's column. As this was the first and had nothing to fear, we were thus spared from fatigue.

"The second under the command of General Cornwallis followed us with the Light Infantry as its rear guard and the Queen's Rangers covering the flank. They were attacked at once and the major wounded. Between nine and ten o'clock the enemy came in large numbers. Cornwallis had already passed Freehold. The Light Infantry formed a front, but as they were too weak for this, they were reinforced immediately by the entire column. This consisted of the 1st and 2nd Brigades, English and Hessian Grenadiers, the Guards, the Rangers, and the 16th Dragoon Regiment. We did not think the enemy was strong, but finally discovered that this was Washington with his army. The cannonade was heavy by both sides and continued until four o'clock. However, our Britons again proved their bravery, suffering a loss of 400 to 500 men killed and wounded. The enemy was defeated and pursued as far as a swamp, unknown to us, where we took the greatest losses, which may have been the enemy's plan. However, it failed. Reportedly the rebel losses were more than 800 men. They retreated and our army followed slowly during the night. The heat was terrible and our greatest losses were the deaths due to the heat. Our column marched all night.....

## Enemy Views (1778)

"2 and 3 July - It rained hard, without letup. I was fortunate enough to have a tent, but the troops had to remain outside like dogs.....

"6 July - At seven o'clock we embarked and at twelve o'clock sailed with a favorable wind. We arrived in York at five o'clock. The ship was called *Fortitude*, In addition to our company, Captain Lorey's Company is also on board.

"7 July - We landed at eleven o'clock and marched eight miles to Harlem, in extreme heat."

## New York Garrison Life in 1778

Meanwhile the Platte Grenadier Battalion Journal recorded activity in the garrison at New York. "2 June - We remained absolutely peaceful in winter quarters, as regards the enemy and other changes, and nothing new excited us. According to today's orders Lieutenant General Clinton has been named commander-in-chief of the army and Sir William Howe is returning to Europe.

"15 June - The troops in the region of Kingsbridge entered camp. The Hessian troops here are in the brigade of Colonel [Carl Wilhelm] von Hachenberg and consist of the Koehler Grenadier Battalion and the Hereditary Prince and Truembach Regiments.

"July - Early this month the army from Philadelphia arrived in this region, having come through lower Jersey. All the troops marched by land to Sandy Hook, then went aboard ships, and were brought over here. The heavy baggage arrived here by water. The enemy harassed our troops constantly. The arriving troops were landed on York, Staten, and Long Islands and entered camp there. Most, however, came to York Island, including the entire Hessian corps. The troops had barely landed when [Charles Hector,] Comte d'Estaing arrived at Sandy Hook with a French fleet of eleven ships-of-the-line, not counting frigates, and blockaded the harbor. Our local fleet, commanded by Admiral Howe, was in a bad situation, very weak, and could not attack the French, but had to adopt a defensive position. We remained in this situation fourteen days and anticipated an attack at any moment. Meantime all the old ships were repaired and, as much as possible, prepared for defense. It is said that Comte d'Estaing departed for Rhode Island without undertaking the least thing.

"August - We finally received reports that Comte d'Estaing intended to attack Rhode Island and actually had already entered the harbor. Part of the land forces on board [the French ships] had landed on that island and joined a considerable number of rebels who had crossed from the mainland onto Rhode Island and placed our forces under a full and very tight blockade. Admiral Howe strengthened his fleet with as many old ships as he could outfit and which had any resemblance to warships. General Clinton embarked an English corps consisting primarily of Light Infantry and Grenadiers in order to sail up the [Long Island] Sound to Rhode Island.

"A fortunate maneuver enabled Lord Howe to accomplish his task. Although he had no intention of engaging the French, which according to rumor his fleet was in no condition to do, his arrival, even at a distance, gave Admiral d'Estaing such a fright that he left the harbor at Rhode Island. A short time later, he again entered the harbor but did not stay long nor undertake anything of consequence. Instead he departed for the second time and sailed to Boston. The [American] army followed the admiral's example and withdrew to the mainland. Our troops attacked his rear guard during this retreat, losing many people in so doing, without, it is said, doing the enemy any material harm. Meantime we continued to occupy Rhode Island, although we had to burn the entire fleet of frigates and other ships that were there, to prevent them from falling into enemy hands.

"24 September - Until today the troops have remained quietly in their camps on York, Long, and Staten Islands. General Lord Cornwallis crossed the North River to New Jersey with a strong corps. Lieutenant General von Knyphausen marched over Kingsbridge to the heights near Philipse's house with another strong corps. All the troops bivouacked.

"11 and 12 October - The troops marched back into their previous camps, without being harassed by the enemy. As soon as the army returned, a strong corps of Englanders was embarked under the command of Major General Grant in order to go to the West Indies. The Seitz Regiment is to embark for Halifax.

"26 October - According to orders received yesterday, the grenadier battalion marched from Kingsbridge to New York today.....

"November - The end of this month the Truembach and Wissenbach Regiments, the 71st Regiment of Highlanders, a battalion of light infantry, and several provincial corps embarked, it is said, to undertake an expedition to the southern provinces."

The Hesse-Cassel Jaeger Corps Journal entries concerning duty in New York in the latter part of 1778 include the following. "9 July - Today the French fleet, consisting of twelve ships-of-the-line and three frigates, anchored at Sandy Hook. It had come from the Delaware, which our fleet had left only a few days before. We can expect nothing except an attack on New York, for which reason, we hope soon to see Admiral [John] Byron, who was to have followed the French from England, and is supposed to have a decisive naval force with him. We have taken all possible defensive measures.....

"18 July - The enemy fleet sailed out to sea, without having taken any action. Reportedly Washington has detached troops to Rhode Island.....

"26 July - The news that Rhode Island is under siege, and that the French fleet sailed there, seems to be factual. Meantime, Lord Howe has assembled all his warships, if not to attack the French under Comte d'Estaing, at least to annoy him until Admiral Byron arrives, which we anticipate will occur at any hour, as one of his ships has already arrived at Halifax. We are greatly concerned about Rhode Island, and doubt that the garrison there can withstand a siege.....

"10 August - Congress has found it necessary to detach a brigade against Colonel [John] Butler who commands the Indians, and all the inhabitants who live along the area bordering the Indians have had to flee to escape the depredations of the Indians.

"20 August - According to certain information, the French fleet entered the harbor at Rhode Island on 9 August, then saw Lord Howe's fleet on 10 August. They raised anchor to sail against Lord Howe. Also, General Sullivan has blockaded Newport, so General Clinton has detached 4,000 men from the army and has himself gone up the Sound to relieve Rhode Island.

"7 September - Today General Clinton returned from Rhode Island, after the French had withdrawn, and the garrison was secure. He arrived there with 4,000 men, unfortunately one day too late to engage General Sullivan on the island. As it could no longer be supported by the French fleet, Sullivan raised the siege on 29 August and was then closely pursued during his retreat. Lord Howe has kept the Comte d'Estaing occupied with his maneuvers, and both fleets have been scattered by a storm.....

"28 September - This night a detachment of Light Infantry attacked a regiment of enemy dragoons in the Jerseys and captured it. The unit was known as Lady Washington's Dragoons and consisted of about 100 men.....

"4 October - Reports are that the enemy headquarters is at Quakerhill, two brigades are at North Ferry, and General Scott with the Flying Corps and Cavalry is at Bedford. These dispositions make it clear that Washington does not intend to attack New York, although some had expected him to do so.....

"14 October - The English fleet made preparations to sail to the West Indies. Four thousand English under General Grant were embarked.

"6 November - Another expedition of about 2,500 men, consisting of Delancey's Corps, York Volunteers, and the [Hessian] Wissenbach and Woellwarth Regiments were embarked today, but the destination remains secret.

"13 November - We received news today that the enemy army has entered winter quarters, and that the headquarters is at Chatham in Jersey.....

"So ends the campaign in the year 1778. Both armies remained in their winter quarters, nothing being undertaken by either side, and we directed our attention and our hopes to the operations in the West Indies."

Lieutenant Piel noted transfers from the New York garrison, mentioning embarkations for Halifax and an unmentioned destination."23 September - The Garrison Regiment von Seitz boarded ships to strengthen the forces at Halifax in Nova Scotia.....

"30 October - The Woellwarth and Wissenbach Regiments today marched to the region of New York, where they are to embark aboard ship."

The von Mirbach Order Book also contains references to incidents of interest during 1778 within the New York garrison, and gives details on the organization of the chasseur company formed under the command of Captain George Hanger, Lord Coleraine. "21 July - General Schmidt's Brigade will supply the following men to a chasseur company which Captain Hanger of the Hessian Jaeger Corps is to command and which is to be formed from the Hessian infantry regiments at this place.

"Prince Charles Regiment will provide one non-commissioned officer, one drummer, and eleven privates. "Truembach Regiment will provide one non-commissioned officer and ten privates. Mirbach Regiment will provide one non-commissioned officer and ten privates. Seitz Regiment will provide one non-commissioned officer and ten privates.

"Healthy and robust men are to be taken for this duty and men who are sure not to desert; therefore dependable men must be assigned. They are to be prepared to march on the shortest notice

"The colonel orders that the soldiers chosen to fill the order are to be kept separate and assigned no duties outside of camp.....

"23 July - Those officers who are assigned to the chasseurs are to report at the Morris house at ten o'clock in the morning on the day after tomorrow, the 25th of this month, with their weapons, etc, where they will be inspected by His Excellence, General von Knyphausen. Each one assigned will have the specifications of the sizes for his uniforms and accessories with him. Pay will be advanced to the end of the month.....

"24 September - Ensigns [Georg] Albus and [Wilhelm von] Horn, who have been in Hessian service up to this time, have been assigned to the English army with the rank of ensign and are to have command over the non-commissioned officers and privates of the Brunswick troops who have been exchanged by or have fled from the enemy."

Feilitzsch also noted activities in New York during 1778 and expressed his dissatisfaction with service in America. "11 July - Please God, send us to Germany. The entire army is dissatisfied and does not wish to go to New England, as is expected. The French warships are reportedly outside the harbor.....

"16 July - We marched at seven o'clock, about six miles, to the redoubt on Spitting Devil.... This is the point where York province begins. All the heights have redoubts, forts, or blockhouses. We are very secure. The enemy can not attack us without suffering heavy losses. However, we are not here as defenders, but rather to attack, but the French fleet still lies near Sandy Hook. God grant that they will be defeated, otherwise we are lost....

"17 July - I will always hate this life. God grant me help soon.....

"29 July - The French fleet left our harbor and according to rumor an English fleet is just outside with many provisions. I wish with all my heart that this is not true.....

"3 August - A fire was set during the early morning in New York and seventy houses were burned down. Some disgruntled rebels were arrested.

"4 August - There was a violent thunderstorm such as on the previous days. A sloop near York was struck, blowing it up. One catastrophe after the other. The English fleet is not here, only a few provision ships, and desertion from the army is rampant.....

"18 August - I sincerely believe that we will leave America this year, which is what the army wishes and hopes for. Further, it is my belief that we will go to New England. About the fleet which necessarily dictates our fate, we have disturbing news. A long wished-for English fleet has not arrived. We do not know what has happened to it. Pride and courage are very low. Apparently the English have need of their fleet in Europe. Would to Heaven I could make this war only in the newspapers of Europe. Then I would gladly participate.....

"30 August - We hear very favorable reports from Rhode Island, but they have not been confirmed. This much is certain, the rebels launched an attack supported by the French.

"31 August - Today a patrol of 100 men went out to Philipsburg. The rebels fell on the rear and seven men are missing, including one man from our company, who was killed. All these people were in the rear guard. The patrol retreated quickly and they could not follow.

"Suddenly the reports have changed. At three-thirty this afternoon the Rangers and Emmerich's Corps fought an engagement with the rebels. We got revenge. Both corps broke off contact. The rebels appeared with 300 men and attacked a small patrol which at once retreated, leading the rebels into an ambush where they were immediately counter-attacked by the Cavalry and most of the Indians were cut down in the most gruesome manner. They probably lost sixty to seventy men, including several officers as well as the captain of the Indians. Our losses for the English amount to about twenty dead and wounded.

"1 September - Today I learned from ten deserters who came in that the jaeger whom I thought had been killed yesterday was wounded and captured.

## Enemy Views (1778)

"15 September - I heard about the situation in Rhode Island, including that the French fleet had departed. At the same time the rebels retreated. Therefore they were attacked by our forces but had made very good disposition [of their troops]. Our regiments participated and lost seven dead, and our total losses were possibly 260 men.....

"28 September - ... During the morning we heard a heavy small arms fire from Jersey. Cornwallis had gone foraging there with the main army and General Grey was ordered against a large magazine which a dragoon regiment, called Lady Washington's, protected. The English Light Infantry attacked it and only six men survived; fifty were killed.....

"18 October - Ten English and two Hessian regiments have orders to embark. Some say they are going to the West Indies; others say one place and another; and all their guessing can be wrong.....

"27 October - There is talk of an expedition. The English Captain [Patrick] Ferguson was on the east coast of Jersey at Egg harbor with 300 men and destroyed the ships, the harbor lumber facilities, and the stores there. When [Count Casimir] Pulaski heard this he advanced with 600 men, but the English went aboard ship. During the evening, however, a rebel officer by the name of Geliat [William Joseph Juliat], who had previously served with the Hessians, deserted and pointed out how Pulaski could be attacked. Ferguson, therefore, landed, killed one colonel, two captains, and one lieutenant and sixty men. I am not sure of the number of captives.....

"8 November - Our regiments are still embarked but no one knows for certain where they are to go. The army is becoming very weak. The enemy expresses no fear of us. We have many servants who are rebels and among ourselves I can not see what we can accomplish here with so few troops. To our proposed peace suggestions the rebels have given no acceptable answer. They are approved by many who wish to serve the King. The enemy says we will return to Europe this winter. God grant it is so, but personally I believe we will never again see my fatherland.....

"16 November - We left our corps at seven o'clock in the morning and arrived at Hellgate Ferry at noon. We were carried across and remained in quarters overnight. - Something comical, my landlady did not want to put me up. She did not believe me to be an officer. I was thus embarrassed before the girls in the house.....

273

# Enemy Views (1778)

"18 November - I could not sleep well last night. My host is an English-American who owns many pigs, which were camped outside my window. They made a terrible noise all night. When I went out the door I had to wade through manure up to my knees. We are no longer to receive forage. I must sell my horse. Everyone is annoyed just as I am. I have no wood, except for what I have stolen.

"29 November - Our duty is not strenuous. No officers go on picket duty, but the jaegers must work all the harder because they have received no quarters in houses. Therefore, they have to build huts. This makes a lot of work and the troops have many reasons to complain. Additionally, there is no wood nor building materials. It is rather cold and this is very hard on the men. If I were to enter all the rumors here, which are spread about, it would amount to only lies. Currently it is said that we will return to Europe in two months. Would to Heaven it were true. However, the English peace commissioners have left and the last favorable terms offered the rebels were not accepted. Therefore, we can certainly not assume it will happen. Instead we will have another difficult campaign.....

"18 December - Our huts are still not ready. It appears first that the hard rain and bad weather has begun and second that the rain has penetrated all our hard work. The water stood above our shoes in the huts, and the army had to move out of the huts because it rained harder inside than under the open sky. Now each one must be covered with reeds and straw. The troops are unhappy about that. I fear there is little chance of success in the coming year. The weather is good today but yesterday it rained hard. True, the weather is cold, but last year at Philadelphia we had snow and cold weather at this time.....

"25 December -A frightful storm and cold. Only with great difficulty could I get out of my quarters. It was very fortunate for the men that the huts were finished. Still the storm blew the snow in terribly so that in some huts the snow was two feet deep.

"26 December - Still the same weather. I can not remember having had such in Germany more than once. The cold increases and I recant what I wrote. It is colder than in Pennsylvania....

"28 December - Still just as pretty and just as cold as previously. In many places the snow lies twelve foot deep.

"30 December - The cold continues. I have never seen it like this in America. The Sound is almost completely frozen and we must make ourselves secure from an attack by the rebels. This is being done. However, it is rumored that our provisions are exhausted. That would be a great misfortune, but during the winter, time is passed with such stories. Such as now it is said for certain, and mentioned in the newspapers, that 25,000 Russians are coming. The transport ships have already gone to Riga from England to pick them up. If Heaven grants it, it will be a pleasant sight for me, certainly the most enjoyable in America."

The Waldeck diarists also reported on events occurring in the New York area in 1778. Chaplain Waldeck wrote, beginning on 28 June, "Another fleet arrived from Philadelphia. Now all our ships have been removed from Philadelphia and the Delaware, and the entire army is on the march to New York....

"29 June - The army is still in the Jerseys, where, during the night, we heard heavy firing....

"30 June - There was an alarm this evening. A heavy fire was heard in Jersey, both cannon and small arms. Our regiment was put under arms and remained on the alert all night long. The artillery drove past on the way to Elizabeth Point.....

"3 July - Now misery sets in. Our supply of meal and bread is exhausted. The fleet from England is eagerly awaited, and further, we have nothing except what comes from England. The army receives a small portion of rice instead of bread. The rebel army on the other hand has an over-abundance of all foodstuffs, while we have a shortage.

"4 July - Our army still stands in Jersey and the fleet of 200 ships lies off shore at Amboy.

"5 July - ... At noon another fleet arrived. At the present time we are still as much in doubt as to what will be undertaken during this campaign as we were in the previous year of 1777. Some even believe the army will be sent back to Europe. In short, things appear more confused than at any previous time.

"6 July - The entire army boarded the ships at South Amboy. I rode as quickly as possible to the Flagstaff in order to see such a spectacular fleet sail by.... There were over 300 ships, including the admiral's ship, the *Eagle*, of 64 guns, on which Lord Howe sailed, and which looked very good.

"7 July - An exceptionally active and disruptive day. Nine English regiments came to Staten Island and set up their camp as neighbors to us, both to the right and to the left, and thus vastly strengthened the army on Staten Island.

"8 July - I see the provisions ships with casks of flour arriving, and wish that the poor soldiers will once again receive bread.

"9 July - Admiral Howe again sailed out of port with a great number of warships, perhaps to engage the French fleet, which is generally reported to have already arrived on the coast of America.

"10 July - More warships departed and it is high time, as the French fleet is no longer only a dream, but has actually entered the Delaware. Lord Howe took all the volunteers from the merchant ships aboard the warships, and sailed out to sea.....

"12 July - At seven o'clock we held church in camp, to which many Germans came because of the so-called tailors' draft for the English regiments.[32] This afternoon Captain von Haacke returned from captivity.

"13 July - For a long time we have had our fun at the expense of the French fleet. But it is not funny any longer. Lieutenant Brumhard came from the Flagstaff as we were gathered around our horses and assured us that the large fleet which could be seen lying near Sandy Hook was really a French fleet of ten ships-of-the-line and as many frigates. Everyone who had a horse was curious and rode to the Flagstaff. From there we saw them lying in the most beautiful order and every ship showed the white French flag. The admiral's ship was called the *Languedoc* and the admiral was Comte d'Estaing. The *Languedoc* was a ship of ninety guns, and the others had 80, 70, 74, and 64 cannons. Our admiral, the experienced and famous Lord Howe, lay with his fleet in sight of the French, and we daily expected a naval battle between the two fleets, which we would be able to watch in comfort from our camp.

"Lord Howe sent a frigate to sea in sight of the French fleet. The frigate sailed with a full wind and full sails, directly past the enemy fleet. Never in my life have I seen a ship sail so that hardly a cannon could be fired at the frigate before it sailed past like the wind. It was sent to Rhode Island and along the coast to warn our ships that an unexpected guest had arrived on the coast. It was an exceptionally clever trick as well by Lord Howe, as also by General Clinton, that they had gotten the fleet and the army away from Philadelphia. It had apparently been the plan of the French to blockade the entire fleet which lay in the river before Philadelphia. Then Washington would have pressed forward with his entire force and encircled the army at Philadelphia. But even if Lord Howe had remained lying in the Delaware, it would have also been possible for d'Estaing to have entered the harbor at New York. In short, it was a terrible situation which had no sooner arisen than it was over. Both the army and the fleet were at Philadelphia when the plan proposed by d'Estaing had been drawn up. But England should not sink so low. It was already an unheard of insult that a French fleet should sit in the face of Lord Howe, admiral of the sea power whose flag floated in triumph over all the waters of the world, and whose fleets covered the oceans.

"I was at the height by the Flagstaff just when many Englanders were gathered, sputtering and cussing. I believe no bitterness between nations can be more deep-rooted than that of the English against the French. Every young seaman volunteered to serve on the warships to fight against the French. At this time, a merchant ship, which had no fear of encountering an enemy fleet here at New York, the most important port on the American continent, came from the ocean. A French frigate broke from the fleet and, to be sure of capturing the ship, raised an English flag instead of the French one. The ship drew nearer, the frigate fired a cannon, lowered the English flag, and raised the French one. And the ship was captured as were eleven others in a few days.

"14 July - At the present we are not in the best situation. It would have been much worse, however, if the French trick had succeeded. The harbor at New York is blockaded so that no ship can get in or out. A French ship-of-the-line lies in the East River and the entire fleet is at Sandy Hook. On the land side, we are so completely closed in that we can not possibly be pressed more closely together. General Washington has spread his army out so beautifully that from here on the height we can see some of his positions. From Elizabethtown to Newark, to Second River, Hackensack, Aquakenunk, etc. Only the water separates us from Washington's army.....

"20 July - We have been curious as to what would take place between the two fleets which lie undisturbed beside one another, watching each others every move. Lord Howe would have attacked if he had only a single ship which could challenge the *Languedoc*. We do not have a single ship on the coast with more than 64 guns. On the other hand, the French have many ships of 70, 80, 90, or 100 cannons. Nothing in the world is to be more wished for than that Admiral Byron, who is expected daily with his fleet, would arrive, as then we would have relief on the ocean. He has 80 and 90 gun ships in his fleet and will be able to engage the French. It appears Lord Howe is awaiting the arrival of this fleet.

"21 July - Washington is very busy transferring his army across the Hudson River near Kings Ferry, and his outposts are not far from Kingsbridge. It appears that his intention is to capture New York. If this transpires, he will lose many men, but for us, it will be the end. If the French fleet strikes the harbor at the same time that Washington attacks on land, it is to be feared that it will be a classic siege, and will starve us out. At present the rumor is that Byron's fleet has been scattered by a storm and several badly damaged ships have arrived at Halifax. It looks bad for our army just now.....

"25 July - At daybreak the French fleet was no longer to be seen.....

"3 August - During the night fire broke out in New York. The fire began in a storehouse where items were made for the ships. It is assumed the fire was set by someone sympathetic to the rebels. And this disgruntled person will not rest until all New York lies in rubble. We heard that 100 houses were already lying in ashes, and the fire still has not been extinguished. We were very concerned about our baggage house, because everyone who wanted to protect his belongings, had sent them there.

"4 August - One misfortune after the other seems to be piling up on New York. A terrible storm gathered over the city today and from here we saw the lightning flash. During the afternoon several ships arrived, by which we were informed that the lightning had struck a warship, a sloop laden with 248 tons of powder. Although many ships were in the area, the accident had primarily damaged the houses which were near the harbor. It did not leave a single window unbroken.

"The rebels will certainly consider these quickly following, one after the other, disasters to be comforting signs that Heaven and all the elements are opposed to the King's army.....

## Enemy Views (1778)

"19 August - A packet boat came in six weeks from Falmouth. The news which it brought caused everyone to be gloomy, and there is not an Englishman who did not exclaim his sincere 'God damn' about the present circumstances. We have been waiting for reinforcements for three months already, and our situation becomes more desperate with every passing day, as the army must be reinforced to maintain its present posts and before anything can be undertaken. It even appears nothing will be done during this campaign. The English navy can claim to rule all the oceans and her flag may wave over all the waters of the world, but the great naval hero, Lord Howe, must sit idly by and watch England's arch enemy sailing along the coast of America, and know that he can do nothing to prevent it, as the post at Sandy Hook is the key to the harbor of New York and must be protected. Admiral Byron with additional naval strength has been expected since early June and is to be followed by Admiral [Augustus] Keppel. The army awaits some sign of activity from the fleet. We openly spoke of the joy we anticipated when, under the roar of our cannons, the French fleet was engaged, captured, destroyed, or driven aground. O vanity of joy, the packet boat has brought news that Byron's fleet was scattered by a storm and unable to regroup.

"And that Admiral Keppel lies at anchor off St. Helens, while we fear the Brest fleet will also appear on the American coast.....

"29 August - ... Nineteen thousand rebels have landed on Rhode Island and begun building strong points in order to place it under siege. The generals commanding are Sullivan, Lafayette, and [John] Hancock. General Clinton embarked 2,000 men who have departed today with a favorable wind.....

"1 September - Admiral Byron has arrived. Three ships of 74 guns, of his fleet, came in.....

"3 September - The entire fleet is lying just behind our camp. The sick, of whom there are a great many, were brought on land and placed in hospital tents behind our camp. On many ships, 300 men were sick. During the previous war, England lost 80,000 sailors and the present war will cost as many more.....

"5 September - Now there is an impressive sea power in American waters. Lord Howe has 71 warships under his command, not counting the many armed merchant ships.....

"1 October - The 2nd Battalion of Light Infantry, the 72nd [Regiment], and the Queen's Rangers crossed the Hudson at Dobb's Ferry. This force met the 3rd Virginia Dragoon Regiment, which is known by the name of Washington's Guard and consists of men of good family, with beautiful horses. Our troops attacked with bayonets and slaughtered all of them so that only three were able to save themselves by flight. The number of dead is unknown, but must be great, as our men gave no quarter and took only fifty prisoners, who were for the most part wounded."

## A Southern Expedition

Reuber's diary contains an account, commencing 6 November 1778, of the transfer to the south of one of the detachments mentioned above. "We two Hessian regiments [Truembach and Wissenbach] were embarked at Brooklyn Ferry on the South Harbor together with seven English regiments. Most of these were composed of Americans, residents of that country, an English Scottish regiment, a light corps of cavalry, one battalion of English Grenadiers and Light Infantry. All of these regiments and corps were assembled together in a fleet and lay quietly all day, before the city, in the south Harbor.

"9 November - Early in the morning the agent gave the signal that we should sail to the lighthouse on Staten Island. We dropped anchor and remained there while we received provisions, water, wood, peas, grain, rum, beer, meat, bread, and everything else for which a ship's captain was responsible, so that nothing was missing. He also had to provide for the ship's crew.....

"12 November - The wind was still unchanged but toward evening a west wind came up and was so strong that the ship rolled violently. It became a storm and some of the Hessian soldiers became nauseous and vomited.

"13 November - The west wind became ever stronger and such a storm as to make a person think everything would be lost. It looked very bad and nothing remained but the threat of sinking. Some ships tore loose [from their anchors] and the anchors were lost and holes opened in the ships. We lost two anchors from our ship. A third one, called the emergency anchor and weighing 29 hundredweight, was lowered on a new anchor rope 150 fathoms long as thick as a chamber pot in the middle. It had never been used before. Now it was our salvation in the sea and secure against all dangers. Those which had torn loose and missed the exit passage were thrown on land by the storm and stuck fast. It was something to see how high the water rose when a wave came waltzing in and struck a ship which was stranded on the shore. It made such a noise that a person would think everything would be broken to pieces and this continued for 48 hours. Then the storm abated but many ships were stranded and presented a pitiful appearance until they could be refloated. The damage was repaired and everything was put back in order. We awaited a favorable wind.

"15 November - The ships which had broken loose returned again and repaired their damage. Those which suffered the most damage and which could not easily be repaired were replaced in our fleet with other ships while the damaged ships remained behind until they could be repaired.

"16 November - When we woke early in the morning and went on deck we had a northeast to east wind. Therefore our commodore fired a signal shot to raise anchor and sail into the sea. But our plans faded, we again dropped anchor, and remained lying at anchor during the day.

"17 November - Northwest to west wind, cold, raw weather. Ice formed on the ship. Toward noon the captain of the crown's ship fired a cannon followed by a signal to raise anchor and set sail. The captain said that after we sailed for only two days, we will no longer be cold....

"22 November - ... We made little headway and could use our time no better than to praise God for his protection to this point and to ask His continued presence. 'Above all, during the evening the soldiers sang God's hymns from he small books which we called half a man and because the storm had abated.' ....

"26 November - A good northwest wind for us to travel with and which returned us to the desired course. The sailors became increasingly well-acquainted and more trusting of our soldiers. They often received rum to drink from them [the soldiers] and traded bread in return, but secretly, because it was forbidden. The sailors were not allowed to drink except that which was served with the water and called grog.....

"5 December - I can not fail to mention here the special pleasure which the officers, as well as the soldiers, took from the Holy Word. 117 miles.

"6 December - A Dutch battle- or warship cut across our course en route to the East Indies. It lowered its flag to our command ship and the same honor was returned. We remained on deck, with pleasure, under a star-filled sky for a long time this evening....

"7 December - Early this morning it began to rain. Toward noon the sea became restless and some waves beat against the ship. One hit near the front of the ship, by the bowsprit, where there is no railing, and knocked a fine cabin boy into the ocean. We looked back at him in sorrow but could do nothing to help him.....

"13 December - A west wind and stormy so that the sea became restless with heavy rain and the ship rolled violently. A very unpleasant day. At night it was so dark that every ship had to display a lantern so as to avoid colliding with one another. Suddenly there was an alarm on our ship. 'The whirlwind was in our sails and the ship began to shake violently.' The captain was immediately alert, hurried out of his cabin, climbed into the rigging and shouted loudly, 'All hands on deck.' The sailors hurriedly came on deck. Meanwhile the captain grabbed a harpoon and threw it at the mainsail. As soon as there was a hole, which a man could put his finger through, a tear developed. The sail tore to pieces and fluttered in he air setting us free again. We had almost gone under because the whirlwind could not move out of the sail.....

"16 December - Still no hope of reaching land and we do not even know where we are going. If it will be [St.] Augustine, Charleston, or Savannah, we still do not know....

"17 December - With a south wind the sailors worked on the anchor ropes. Then we saw that it would soon end because all those things were set in motion and even the carpenter made oars....

"18 December - The commander raised a flag that some of the ship's captains should come to him. This gave us hope that w3e would soon arrive. The soldiers were also instructed to tend to thei8r weapons and equipment so that they would have everything prepared to go on land.....

20 December - The sailors told us early in the morning that land had been seen and a lighthouse at the harbor entrance. But which

harbor? That we did not hear and it was hidden from our eyes. Because we were quite near and believed we would land, we had raised white flags as if we were French, as the residents of Charleston might be able to see us and believe we would enter the harbor.....

"24 December - Early in the morning, at daybreak, there was suddenly an alarm. We saw land and during the excitement the command ship saw a strange ship which was not far from land. The agent [ship] at once gave a signal to be alert and our command ship sailed rapidly forward. Soon thereafter it returned to the fleet and brought the strange ship with it. Then we sailed directly toward the Savannah harbor. Suddenly we again saw land and a lighthouse on the left side of the harbor, dropped anchor, and lay there during the night. Our command ship remained lying before the harbor as a watch ship, near E. [Here, and later, the author uses letters which were apparently keyed to a map.] The other warship, called the *Violence*, had fourteen 26-pound cannons. A row galley had two 36-pound and eleven 26-pound cannons. [This seems unlikely.] These two warships entered the harbor posing as friends and sailed as far as H in the bend, which place is called 'the mud hole', and dropped anchor. Near the city there were no warships except a Spanish light frigate with a few cannons and a small privateer of twenty cannons. As Savannah was now lost, the Frenchman set fire to his ship [the privateer] and departed. An American row galley wished to sail up the harbor at D but grounded fast. The English could not reach it because it was in fresh water where there was no ebb or flood tide. This was most annoying and an obstacle to us because it blocked the water and it was not until after Christmas that our two ships, which had lain at H, flying white flags, as if French, raised an English flag one day before the attack. Then they were heavily fired upon from both sides and at the same time our fleet also sailed up to the city.

"27 December - We Hessian and English soldiers were landed near H and the city of Savannah was at once surrounded and stormed from three sides. The two Hessian regiments, Rall [now Truembach] and Wissenbach, made the first assault from the water side. Three regiments of English DeLancey's [Loyalists] and three regiments of Green Rangers and a regiment of Scots made the second and third assaults, one against [St.] Augustine, the third against Ebenezer toward Charleston. A small corps of light horse, one battalion of grenadiers and the light infantry completed the approximately 3,000 man total. We captured a great amount of booty in Savannah from the province of Georgia, and 1) captured a Spanish light frigate, 2) a French ship was blown up, and 3) an American row galley had run aground and stuck fast for a long time. The English made preparations and then built a ship at D on a small side stream near Ebenezer. They took it past the American ship at high tide and then equipped it with a 36-pound iron cannon. Next some English volunteers, as a crew, and the ship sailed against the American row galley. The American ship was aware of the English and wanted to raise its anchor but the English already had it in a tight situation and fired a 36-pound shot. This hit on the forward part of the ship where the cannon sat and killed thirty Americans. The battle was won and during the confusion the English boarded the ship in a rush. It was like a river the English moved so quickly and it was fortunately captured. The English volunteers came sailing up with their prize and a *feu de joie* was fired. There was a large amount of indigo, rice, and a supply of salt and a cannon, which was all paid for with prize money by the King of England. The two Hessian regiments entered the barracks on garrison duty. Now the old year has flown away and we began 1779."

## Another Expedition to the South

Another of the expeditons which h sailed from New York in 1778 contained the Waldeck Regiment, as noted by Steuernagel. "As the regiment was ordered by the commander-in-chief to go to Jamaica and from there to Florida, Pensacola to be exact, the men boarded ships in the harbor between New York and Staten Island on 19 October 1778. AS all the ships which were to sail together had not assembled, we had to be at anchor hor until the last of October. Finally, on 1 November, when the ships had met a few miles from the harbor at a place called Place land Hook, they sailed here and gathered with us to make a flotilla.

"Therefore, we raised anchor and departed the following morning, the second, with this fleet, and sailed into the ocean....

"On the ninth we parted from the fleet on the Atlantic Ocean. We experienced nothing to hinter our journey toward Jamaica and we continued on our way.

Enemy Views (1778)

"We had sailed only a few days, when we already noticed a remarkable difference, of drawing nearer to a warm climate and being en route to the West Indies. Soon the heat was unbearable, even though it was the end of the month of November, which caused us to remove our woolen clothing, and most wore only a shirt....

"We could have traveled in a much more direct route to Jamaica if we had not had to worry about the enemy....

"I have forgotten in my report to say that when we had calm and good weather, a Sunday divine service was held aboard ship. In this regard, when we arrived in Portsmouth in England, on 30 June 1776, we had received and divided a large number of song books which had been sent from Waldeck. - Initially these books were said to be gifts from our prince, later, however, we had to pay one-half pound sterling....

"The second of December 1778 was a joyous day for us, on which Jamaica showed itself to us. The same day we ran into the harbor of Port Royal and dropped our anchor before the city of Kingston."

Chaplain Waldeck provides additional information concerning the journey to Jamaica as his ship became separated from the fleet. "12 October - We received orders to be ready to go aboard ship.

"13 October - A detail was dispatched to bring all the regimental baggage from New York to the ships.

"14 October - Several Hessian regiments, which were known to be sailing to Halifax, were embarked.

"15 October - We were supposed to embark today, but there were no ships available.

"16 October - Our baggage was put aboard ship today. The army received orders to go aboard ship.

"17 October - We finished preparations for our departure and sold our horses. I received five guineas for mine.

"18 October - It was another nice day. We held church in camp at seven o'clock and this is probably the last time for it to be held on Staten Island. During the service, we saw our ships approaching from New York. I dined with the colonel, during which time the captain of the ship *Springfield*, on which the colonel will embark, entered.

"19 October - Regimental baggage was put aboard ship.

"20 October - Today is the second anniversary of our arrival, and nearly on the same spot we again board ship to leave this part of

America. By eleven o'clock the entire regiment was aboard ship. I knew that we would not sail today and therefore remained on land until toward evening.

"21 October - As we were hoping to depart, we took on provisions for another 25 days, as we had on board only enough for two months.....

"23 October - Our destination remains uncertain, although it is reported to be Pensacola. We had the pleasure of receiving letters sent out in June and we know it will be a long time before we get any more.

"25 October - Held church aboard the *Springfield*, where I remained all day.

"26 October - Several more transport ships arrived, which are to sail with our fleet.....

"31 October - The wind was favorable, the warships made the signal, and we set sail. One after another the entire fleet followed. Our negligent captain had not returned from New York. Nevertheless, we had to leave and immediately collided with another ship, so that we had to cut the ladder on the aftermast. While this was in progress, the captain arrived. The sea was so stormy and the movement of the ships so great that nearly everyone was seasick....

"1 November - Frightfully unpleasant, stormy weather. In the winter months when the storms and waves keep the sea in constant motion, a trip for me is unpleasant from the very beginning. The waves were as high as the ship and we feared we might break loose from our anchors, of which we had put three out. At night there was even less rest than during the day. No one could close his eyes because when he lay down in bed, he could hardly keep from falling out. Our bags, equipment, and everything that was breakable, broke during the night. These was such a clatter in the cupboards in the cabin that it seemed nothing could remain in one piece. Truly, I would rather participate in a land campaign in Germany during the winter, with all the resulting unpleasantness, than undertake a sea voyage in these winter months. No one can give a correct description of such an event. If I lie down under a tree, exhausted by wind and rain, the earth will at least remain steady under me and let me enjoy my rest, even though the wind howls and the rain beats down on me in torrents. But on the sea, the ship groans as if about to break in pieces. The waves throw it about from one side to the other, so that a man does not have enough hands with which to hold on. If a person, who has not learned patience, goes to sea, he will learn it, whether or not he wants to.....

"6 November - Everything upset me. I could not stand the smell of coffee and it was work just to pour it. It is easier to pour a cup of coffee and drink it while riding a horse at full gallop, than here. The ship's captain gave us a keg of the best port wine that can be found. I made my breakfast on a glass of this good wine and a piece of ship's bread. At noon, while the sea was stormy, I drank nothing else, and during the evening I would again drink two or three glasses. Young Mueller suggested this comforting practice to me. Above all the good man served me well in as much as he was in good health and I was sick. My man [Philipp Henrich] Volcke could not function because of the motion of the ship.

"7 November - During the previous night no one could sleep. I thought the ship would break apart. In the continual danger which surrounds us, we eventually become free of fear and so indifferent that we do not care if everything is lost. Heaven knows how one can endure it. A storm and one sees only mountains and valleys, great foamy waves build so high that it seems they will swamp the ship at any moment.

"9 November - The fleet separated and Commodore [William] Hotham went with General Grant and his troops toward Barbados.

"10 November - During this night it was pitch black. The wind, although not strong, changed direction frequently. All ships had to work the sails. Only our sailors were inattentive to the course of the fleet, and continued on the old course when the rest of the fleet turned. The warship noticed *Crawford* missing, went looking for us, and found us at one o'clock, to our peace of mind and inner consolation. Captain [Thomas] Symonds of the warship immediately ordered the course for our crew to follow, and the crew now was stimulated to be more alert, because the authority of the captain of a warship, which leads a fleet, over the captain of a transport, compares to that of a major over a corporal. A 'God damn' passed over from the warship set everything straight. Captain Symonds is a wonderful Englishman. - This was during the night of the eleventh to the twelfth.

"12 November - We expected to find the fleet again today. However, we had not the least sight of it, not even a glimpse of the sails or masts. The warship called over to our captain to take pains to stay near the warship as many American privateers sailed in these waters, and one had to fear falling into the hands of a French frigate as well, as Comte d'Estaing had left Boston and sailed for the West Indies.

"13 November - The wind was contrary and the frigate let go our tow. This afternoon we were in good spirits and the ship's crew only slightly less so. Suddenly we saw two strange ships. The frigate called for us to raise all possible sail and to do everything possible to follow it. Of course we could not follow it, because one must understand the difference in sailing between a warship and a merchant ship is comparable to an oxen wagon chasing a coach with six horses around the world. Our *Solebay* was two miles ahead of us when we noticed that one of the two ships was a frigate of about the same class as ours. We thought if it were a French ship, the English will defeat it, fight as it might. Then we noticed the other was a privateer of eighteen cannons. Our warship had to take that into account. We sailed poorly and had no cannons on board. Our frigate raised the English flag and fired a cannon. The other ship did the same which indicated to us that it was also English. Both sailed so that the other ship was caught between them, lowered its sails, and surrendered.

"It was an American, which we kept in our fleet. The other was the frigate *Venus*, cruising in this latitude. An American frigate of eighteen cannons had been seen by the warship, also, which without a doubt was to have accompanied the captured ship through these waters. This one used the opportunity to raise and English frigate sail and sail away. The guardian angel surely was watching over us - if our warship in the same night, day before yesterday, when we followed the wrong course, had not set out at once in search of us, we would have been captured today. The American ship certainly would have captured us and taken us as prisoners to Charleston or Boston. And the regiment would have been unaware of our fate. But as it was, we had the protection, and all American privateers fled as soon as they saw our frigate.....

"16 November - Again we had surprisingly miserable weather. The sea rolled over the ship. The wind and waves howled so violently it was impossible to carry on a conversation in the cabin. One had to lie in bed, as it was not possible to stand or even to sit. Even the sailors said that this was such a stormy sea voyage as is seldom made, and these sailors are for the most part tired of the war. On the other hand, those on the warships always want war, and hope Spain gets into the game so they get additional opportunity to seize prizes on the ocean and in all waters, and get rich therefrom. The transports are nothing but merchant ships which otherwise, at this time of year, would be engaged in sailing to the West Indies, or more likely, to America, and returning in the best possible time. Or they would be carrying trade to the Mediterranean Sea and their trips to Smyrna, Alexandria, Cairo, and all the parts of the world would not take longer than two months. During the stormy winter months they would be in a safe harbor and enjoy all the pleasures of a big city. On the present service, however, the seasons are ignored and wherever the demand for troops leads, that is where they are shipped, regardless of what season of the year it might be. All our altering the location of the army can only be conducted by water, and because of the great difficulty, I half wish the war would lead somewhere else, where a general could determine when his auxiliary troops should be at a certain place and position. But who will presume to determine when troops should be ordered to a certain place when instant help may be necessary. This is an advantage which the rebels have and will always keep. They march by land and always have enough to eat, and when we arrive, by water, we go on land emaciated, sick, weak, stiff, and without strength. The stoutest heart fails to accomplish its purpose when the body is so exhausted. I have almost come to believe it will be impossible to defeat them if they continue to use the advantage, just as they do, on land. Their trade is tied to the sea, and I hope England will give serious consideration to control of the sea, where she can survive the war, and eventually capture all the American ships....

"19 November - We saw two strange ships. The frigate cut us loose and chased after them. One was from Holland and the other was an American privateer. This one sailed away and the Hollander remained near us for 24 hours and then continued on its way. If the frigate had not protected us, here again we would have been taken.

"20 November - So hot that twice the ship had to be soaked down.....

"22 November - On the coasts of the West Indies, where we now are, the rainfall is very heavy. For several days the stormy weather and rough seas had kept us in our cabins. Today the skies cleared and the sea was no longer so frightful. We climbed up on deck like old women who leave their dank rooms after a snowy and fog-filled winter, and hobble on their canes into the new, shining spring sun, and there in the fresh invigorating air, cough up all the stove smoke they have swallowed. In this manner we wobbled up on deck, and I again felt so strong that I sent my servant below to light a pipe of tobacco for me, something I had not tried for some time. The sky was bright without a cloud. Suddenly the wind sprang up, which immediately blew up a rain cloud, and in a moment poured down a torrent of rain. In ten minutes the sky was again as bright and clear as previously.

"23 November - Strong winds which were still contrary. We still knew nothing of our other ships, and because we had the warship with us, we were worried about them.

"24 November - We were now in those helpful winds which please the seafarers. The English call them trade winds and they blow at certain times of the year always in one direction. At this time we can keep these winds until we arrive in the West Indies, and they will soon carry us there. They are the best winds that can be wished for. They blow softly and make few waves, as if one were traveling on an even meadow.....

"26 November - To this point, we still had extra provisions. Now all that was gone, however, and we had only ship's bread extra. So we also had to live like the sailors. We did, however, enjoy a good glass of wine. And when it was calm, Captain Pentzel and I would sit at the table until evening, drinking a bottle of French wine, talking about Waldeck, and counting the young men, mainly those capable of supporting a wife, as compared with the number of marriageable women, and thus we sought to alleviate the boring days aboard ship.....

"30 November - The warship was on alert here because Hispaniola belongs half to France and half to Spain, and from their harbors they had seen us come sailing past....

"1 December - We hoped to see Jamaica, our assembly point, where we are to take aboard water and provisions, and where we are to join our other ships again. We actually saw land again, but it was Cape Navasa, a small uninhabited island, which because it has no spring water, has no buildings. We went to sleep with the hope of seeing Jamaica in the morning. One sleeps so well when the trade winds support hope, much as the weary traveler, who, near his goal, lies down to rest in the shade of a tree, his last provisions exhausted, and then once again takes up his staff and continues on to the waiting city.

"2 December - Our hopes of yesterday did not deceive us. Filled with uncertainty contending with joy, we left our stale cabins before sunrise, hurried on deck, and saw Jamaica lying before our eyes. It was above all, the happiest moment; one which I can imagine but not describe, when a man after a long, miserable, stormy, and dangerous sea voyage sees land again for the first time.... My grandmother had a saying when she was annoyed. 'I wish you were where the pepper grows!' Now I am where the pepper grows.

"At eleven o'clock a flag was raised to request a pilot, who was all the more necessary as our captain had never been here, and a more dangerous coast had to be passed before we arrived at Port Royal....

"And how good and wise it is that the Creator put this ability in our souls, so that we so easily forget the unpleasantness of the past and enjoy the present good with a happy heart. O, it that were not the case, where could a poor soul find hope? And who is more lost than a man who has lost hope, who must remain forever on the ocean and never have the pleasure of being on land? God bless these dark-skinned beauties [who deliver fresh fruit to the ships], who brought us these refreshments. They have done for us what the Good Samaritan did for the neglected, wounded man and this gives them favor in our eyes, although their intent was only to sell us something which would refresh us.... I was shocked however, by their attire. They wore a green or white summer hat of silk with many feathers.... Their bare breasts and the most beautiful white skirts showed off so well with their dark skin. That is their attire....

"We also heard that our other ships, fortunately, had arrived several days ago, but had sailed on to where they could more easily take aboard water.

"3 December - Our ship had sprung a leak on the voyage and took so much water that it had to be pumped out every two hours. Additionally, we had the unfortunate situation, which could have had unpleasant results for us, that only one pump on this miserable Scottish ship functioned, and the other one was completely useless.

"Because the one pump was in constant use, it developed such a leak that it lost all suction. The ship's carpenter, who most clearly understood the danger of the situation, told the captain the pump must be raised and repaired. This was accomplished with much effort. In order to overhaul the ship and restore it to better condition, it was taken to the dockyard....

At Howard's Tavern "I had the pleasure to meet many of the gentlemen of our regiment. The other gentlemen departed and Lieutenant Wiegand, the regimental surgeon, and I refreshed ourselves and drank a good punch with M. Howard. Our mutual enjoyment was very great. Everyone thought we had been captured and each assumed this to be the case as no one had met us in Jamaica. The fleet had taken a completely different course, and sailed in part among the Bahamian Islands because the agent, in the absence of the frigate commodore, decided this route was the safest course. And we sailed with the frigate the straightest, although in the present circumstances, the least secure way, and arrived safely in port, also. We would not have been able to say this if the frigate had not provided protection for us. But then I would have written this in Charleston, Boston, of Philadelphia.

"If a person fortunately survives a sea voyage and at the end is still in good health, the joy is so much greater than when he manages to survive another peaceful year-long period on land. O, what a stirring joy, even to shake the hand of the private soldiers and to see the unconcealed joy in their faces. We had so often discussed aboard ship the possibility of the other ships arriving here safely, and now we met one another and for the most part all were in good health. Our friends had worried even more for us, as they did not know if the warship had found us or not. Against all expectations and despite having given up all hope, we saw one another again for the first time today in Kingston. The entire officer corps of the regiment ate in one hall.

"5 December - We sailed from Kingston farther up the harbor toward Rockford, where our other ships lay and where we could more easily take on water. The water springs out of a cliff about a quarter of an hour distance from the harbor. From here it flows through a narrow and paved, white-washed ditch which leads to the harbor, where the boats sail under a spout and fill their barrels with a minimum of effort.... I did not go ashore but went to the ship *Britannia*, where I baptized a child, and then to the *Christian*, where I remained until evening.... It became known that Comte d'Estaing had sailed out of

Boston harbor. Admiral Byron missed him in a storm and thick fog, and now everyone was worried that in a short time he would be here in the West Indies. Therefore, it was assumed also, that we would not sail for our designated Florida, but would remain in Jamaica as a defense force against the French fleet. We had often discussed this possibility during our voyages.....

"9 December - The ships had taken on their water by now, and we departed from Rockford and lay at anchor once again at Kingston.....

"24 December - A pilot came aboard and we raised sail, and shortly dropped anchor again at Greenwich. On such a hot Christmas Saturday, we gave our lives over to the stormy sea.

"25 December - Truly, I have never experienced such a hot Christmas Day. Instead of, like our countrymen, who can hardly protect themselves from the cold, we find ourselves in a part of the world where Christmas is warmer than in Europe during the dog days. I write this with open doors and windows and wearing only a shirt, which still makes me too warm. What a change, and how many reasons to think kindly of us in the West Indies, to drink our health in Rhine wine and we drink theirs in Madeira and glasses of punch, which we here in the island source of its creation, enjoy. I will always remember this Christmas Day sealed deep in my soul.

"We raised anchor but could go no farther than Muskite Fort.

"26 December - We again set sail, but the lack of wind prevented our passing through both sandbanks and we dropped anchor again. In the evening twilight, the packet boat from Pensacola came past. Our pilot asked about news of that place but only learned that sixteen merchant ships had been lost there during a storm.

"27 December - We departed early and came to anchor at nine o'clock at Port Royal, where our other ships already lay.

"28 December - Everything is now ready for our departure for West Florida, but we remained at anchor.....

"31 December - We headed out to sea with a fresh wind, and the same day the land was lost from view."

Enemy Views (1778)

## The Battle of Rhode Island

Asteroth recorded events in Rhode Island throughout 1778, including the following. "10 January - Lord Howe arrived in the harbor at Newport. He came from Philadelphia with all the transport ships because the harbor at Philadelphia freezes over so that during the winter no ship can remain there. Lord Howe is the senior naval commander on the water of all the ships in English service, whether men-of-war or cargo ships. His brother, [Sir William Howe], is the field marshal in America over all the troops in service in America.

"24 May - During the evening the 22nd Regiment, the English Light Infantry, and the Hessian Jaegers were embarked to go to Bristol. They had to cross a body of water half an hour wide, but did not commence their attack until the morning of

"25 May - when they landed on the enemy side and at once captured an enemy position. The rebels retreated as they did not have the spirit [to resist]. They, [The English], exploded a powder magazine near the defensive position. With the position destroyed and the cannons spiked, they proceeded to Bristol which they set on fire within half an hour. They then advanced to the pretty little city of Warren where they set fires at the four corner. They then retreated from the island and successfully returned to their boats. Two thousand men were on the way from Providence as a reinforcement [for the rebels]. Fifty-eight rebels were brought off as prisoners. The Hessian losses were two men wounded and the English had two killed and three wounded.....

"11 June - Six ships arrived from New York with a 500-man free corps of men who had deserted from the rebels.....

"16 July - A fleet with four regiments arrived from New York.

"17 July - They all debarked and set up camp near the city. They included two Ansbach and two English regiments. We had a continuous peace and quiet until

"29 July - During the morning we heard that ships had been seen and in the afternoon a fleet of sixteen sail appeared, all heavy men-of-war. These lay at anchor outside our harbor at Princeton Neck. Although they had arrived without warning, our engineers had taken the precaution to complete a new position on the harbor and two old

294

ones had been repaired and all were well-provided with heavy cannons. The rebels behind us were seen on the 29th. During the evening two men-of-war sailed to the other side of the island where an 18-gun frigate, the *King Fisher*, and two row galleys were on watch. As our three vessels noticed the two men-of-war approach, the ship's captain at once reported this to Commander Pigot and requested instructions. The general ordered him not to fight but to burn his vessel at once and for the crew to flee onto the island.

"2 August - Ten ships were sunk. Cargo ships with three masts were sunk before our batteries so that the French ships could not come too near to our batteries.

"Three French men-of-war sailed past Conanicut Island against our island where three frigates and a cargo ship were. Our ships were set on fire at once. However, a mate, in setting the ship on fire, made the fuse to the powder magazine too short and lit it too soon, before the crew had gotten off. Fourteen sailors blew up with the ship.

"18 August - At four o'clock in the afternoon the French admiral's ship and seven other men-of-war entered the harbor under full sail. We had three defensive positions near the city, all of which were heavily armed. The first position at once gave the signal and fired a 24-pound cannonball, to which the enemy at once responded. All the cannons were fired, which made a frightful cannonade from both sides. However, the French passed fortunately and lay at anchor by our island. Our positions were not damaged and incurred no losses. At evening General Pigot gave the order that the Landgraf and Ditfurth Regiments should pull back at once to the trenches before the city because the rebels had landed 25,000 troops near Bristol Ferry. That day we burned down nineteen houses which stood before our trenches and all the livestock on the island was driven to the city.

"10 August - Admiral Howe arrived with his fleet and lay at anchor at Princeton Neck.

"11 August - The French fleet passed back out of the harbor and the English also sailed. They met together on the ocean and in the resulting frightful cannonade it was easy to imagine what a terrible sound a ship with 70, 80, or 96 guns of 60 pounds creates when a barrage is fired. The inhabitants fearfully fled into their cellars. Our positions defended themselves gallantly. The rebels pressed us into a corner so that soon we did not know which way to turn as their shots fell into our camp. The cannonade from both sides was continuous throughout the day.

"20 August - The French fleet approached once more and lay before the harbor.

"22 August - This morning the fleet was gone again.....

"29 August - A report arrived that the rebels had retired. At once the order came for the English Light Infantry, the Jaeger Corps, and the von Huyn and the two Ansbach regiments to march and for the others to move out ahead of our trenches. The enemy retreated to the end of the island and halted where we had made two defensive positions. General von Lossberg had the command. The von Huyn Regiment was ordered to capture the Artillery Redoubt by storm and at once charged against it. However, as they got within shooting distance they were fired upon as if it came from the skies. The enemy advanced on both sides, surrounding our regiment so that it appeared no one could survive the situation. But God helped and we again retreated. Our regiment suffered 83 men dead and wounded. They remained there until the night of

"31 August - when all the rebels withdrew. The Ansbachers entered camp at the Artillery Redoubt where 8,000 rebels had been when the Huyn Regiment tried to capture it....

"1 September - Admiral Beuer [Byron ?] arrived with sixty ships and entered the harbor. General Clinton arrived in the harbor with 6,000 men but did not land. Instead on

"4 September - They left during the morning.

"9 September - They burned down a city named Bedford which is 32 miles from Rhode Island and captured an island opposite Bedford, from which they took 7,000 sheep aboard ship and transported them back to Rhode Island for the troops. Thereafter we received two pounds of fresh meat and five pounds of salted meat every seven days and because bread was scarce, we received five pounds of bread and two pounds of rice every seven days."

Stang's March Routes entries provide brief mention of the activities of the Ansbach-Bayreuth regiments, including the movement to Rhode Island in 1778 and the subsequent participation in the defense of that location. "9 July - We again broke camp and went aboard the ship named *Spring*.

"10 July - We then sailed and picked up the newly raised [provincial] regiments and again anchored. Five sailors deserted from this ship.....

"13 July - We anchored and during the evening were observed and fired on by a rebel row galley and a fort. Then our ships also returned the fire, following which the enemy withdrew.

"14 July - We again set sail and arrived at two rivers, neither of which would give in to the other, and at five o'clock again anchored.

"15 July - We sailed and at nine o'clock in the evening entered the harbor at Rhode Island and anchored at the city of Newport.

"16 July - We disembarked and marched through the city of Newport with music playing and set up camp a mile outside the city.

"20 July - We broke camp, marched through the city of Newport, and were shipped over to the island named Conanicut.

"29 July - At midday we again broke camp and were shipped across [the bay], marched beyond the city of Newport, and set up camp. This was because twelve French warships had arrived and entered [the bay] under an astonishing bombardment.

"8 August - An English fleet of 49 ships, namely warships, transports, and provisions ships arrived.

"10 August - The nine French ships again departed and sailed out into the sea with a frightful bombardment and cannonade. Then the English and French ships dueled one another. This evening our regiment moved out on picket with two guns.....

"18 August - About 2 1/2 miles ahead of us the rebels have made fortifications against which our positions fired.

"19 August - The rebels and French fired against us. Their first shots wounded three English soldiers in a tent and a horse in the chest, so that we had to break camp and move to another location. We fired without letup.

"20 August - The twelve French ships arrived again and anchored on the coast. Some had their masts shot away and were severely damaged.

"22 August - They sailed away again.....

"29 August - Early in the morning, at four o'clock, we returned to our camp and at five o'clock again broke camp and advanced against the rebels. This advance continued.

"30 August - Our regiment had eight dead and wounded.

"31 August - During the early morning the rebels shipped across to another island named Bristol. During this time the Commanding General Clinton arrived in the Rhode Island harbor with reinforcements. The fleet consisted of six warships, twelve frigates, and forty transport and provisions ships. We set up our camp at the advanced positions.....

"27 November - We entered winter quarters in the city of Newport.

"12 December - I played for a ball aboard Admiral Byron's ship."

Prechtel, who was commissioned during 1778 while at Rhode Island, wrote about the transfer to that place and the events which followed. "9 July - Both Ansbach regiments were embarked on the transport ships still lying at anchor in the East River at Blackwell's Ferry, and today remained lying at anchor.

"10 July - At three o'clock in the afternoon the fleet went under sail and during the evening anchored in the East River.....

"13 July - As soon as the anchor had been dropped, at five o'clock in the evening, the fleet, and especially the transport ship *John and Betty*, on which was Grenadier Captain von Seitz, of the von Seybothen Regiment, was attacked by two enemy row galleys. The frigate escorting the fleet and several transport ships immediately fired on them.

"The enemy row galleys retired toward land without having gained an advantage.

"15 July - Underway at four o'clock in the morning and on our right passed the small island of Block Island, where we then entered the ocean. At nine o'clock in the evening the fleet entered the seaport at Newport, on Rhode Island.

"16 July - At one o'clock in the afternoon we debarked at Newport. The regiments entered camp about one-half mile from the Pitch....

"When the Ansbach regiments arrived on Rhode Island, the following regiments were on the island, under the command of the English General Pigot namely: 1) the English Light Infantry, 2) the 22nd, 3) the 38th, and 4) 44th English Regiments, 5) the Brown, and 6) Fanning Provincial Corps, 7) the Landgraf, 8) Ditfurth, 9) Huyn, and 10) Buenau Hessian Regiments, and 11) the 54th English Regiment.

# Enemy Views (1778)

"On the water side of Newport are the following defenses: 1) the fort on Brenton's Point, which is continuously manned with one captain, one lieutenant, and 100 men, 2) Fort Goat Island, in the middle of the Newport harbor, on which the Stone Battery is manned by one lieutenant and thirty men, and 3) the North Battery, which also has one lieutenant and thirty men....

"20 July - Today the two Ansbach regiments were transferred to Conanicut Island and entered camp under the command of Colonel von Voit.....

"29 July - This morning in the region of the lighthouse we saw a French fleet which anchored not far from the lighthouse at eleven o'clock at midday.

"We received the order from headquarters at Newport, at the same time, for the regiments to leave the camp and return to Newport. The regiments entered the camp close to the city of Newport....

"30 July - The French war fleet consisting of about eighteen sail, spread out to the left and right of the Newport harbor and fired a cannonade against the outer defenses on Conanicut Island.....

"3 August - Six transport ships were sunk in the Newport harbor so that the French fleet could not sail into the harbor.....

"5 August - Two more ships were sunk in the harbor and some walls outside the city were destroyed.....

"8 August - Many houses behind our front were burned down today by the English.

"As the French war fleet had a good wind, this evening it sailed into the harbor with ten ships and anchored. Our three defensive positions on the water side, Brenton's Point, the Stone Battery, and the North Battery, gave a good account of themselves.

"The French ships fired a frightful cannonade against the defenses. it lasted two hours but no one was wounded.

"During the night the English set fire to a frigate in the harbor and four houses behind our front.

"9 August - ... An English fleet consisting of about 26 ships appeared near Block Island and because of the war fleet lying at anchor in the harbor, returned to New York.

"10 August - ... At nine o'clock this morning the French war fleet prepared to sail and with a very strong cannonade, which lasted one and one-half hours, sailed out of the harbor.

"The French war fleet therefore left the harbor because they thought that the fleet, which had been near Block Island yesterday, was a new English war fleet. However, it had been a provisions and convalescent fleet from New York.....

"14 August - The enemy army, under the command of the American General Sullivan, daily drew nearer to our army.

"15 August - ... Today the enemy set up camp about one mile from us and we could see it on a height laying opposite our front.....

"19 August - During the entire day our defenses cannonaded the newly constructed enemy forts.

"Today the enemy fired his cannons, 18-pounders, at our defenses and our camp for the first time.

"A soldier in the English camp had his foot shot off.

"A ball went through the tent of an English private and killed and wounded eight musketeers at one time.

"Therefore, no one was safe in our camp and during the evening it was moved behind the great defensive position of Tominy Hill....

"20 August - The French war fleet, now consisting of thirteen sail, arrived before the entrance to this seaport this evening and dropped anchor....

"21 August - The French war fleet, before daybreak, cut their anchor ropes and sailed into the ocean.

"22 August - In camp at Tominy Hill.

"The cannonade on this day, especially from the enemy, was not as strong. However, from the English side, bombs were thrown at the enemy workers.....

"27 August - At one o'clock tonight, 2nd Lieutenant Prechtel [the author of this diary entry], of the von Voit Regiment, at the forward post with 23 men, was attacked by the enemy, who had a strength of about 200 men.

"Private Riess, of Captain von Stain's Company of the von Voit Regiment, was wounded during this incident...

"28 August - At eleven o'clock at night, 2nd Lieutenant Cyriacy was attacked three times at the outpost.

"One man at his post was killed and two men were wounded in the feet while on patrol.

# Enemy Views (1778)

"29 August - As the enemy General Sullivan vacated his camp during the night, our army of 4,000 men immediately marched forward, in order to fall on the enemy's rear.

"Near Windmill Hill a battle took place. This lasted from seven o'clock in the morning until four o'clock in the afternoon.

"Further, the regiments withstood the cannonade from the enemy's defenses the entire day and spent the night on Fort Windmill Hill....

"The enemy army, consisting of 20,000 men, retreated behind the large defensive positions of Windmill Hill and the Artillery Post.

"30 August - Our army withstood the enemy's cannonade which was like yesterday's, but no one was wounded.

"31 August - During the past night the rebels shipped their troops across to New England at Bristol Ferry, and all their troops are posted there. Therefore, early this morning both evacuated forts, Windmill Hill and Artillery Post, were occupied by fifty men of the Ansbach and Hessian troops. This occupation, however, was replaced by the Hessian Landgraf and Ditfurth Regiments during the morning....

"General Pigot departed for England and therefore the command over the troops was assumed by the English General Prescott.

"1 September - General-in-Chief Sir Henry Clinton arrived in the harbor at Newport with a fleet of seventy sail, as a relief force. Because the enemy had already left Rhode Island, General-in-Chief Clinton and the fleet sailed back to New York.....

"26 November - We broke camp at Windmill Hill and marched into winter quarters at Newport, where the von Voit Regiment was quartered in Thames Street.....

"28 November - The von Seybothen Regiment entered winter quarters and received quarters in the district of the North Battery.....

"10 December - During the night there was such a terrible windstorm that the houses, which here are all made of wood, swayed like ships.....

"14 December - The eleven English men-of-war, which until now had spent the winter in this port, sailed for the West Indies today, under the command of Admiral Byron....

"26 December - Today there was such a wind and snow that the people in the streets of the city could hardly breathe. The snow reached the windows of the second story."

## 1778 in Canada

For the "Hessians" in Canada the year 1778 was a year away from home and a year of garrison duty in a foreign land. Captain [Friedrich Ludwig] Schoell, commanding the remnants of the Hesse-Hanau Infantry Regiment, reported the following incidents, among others, to his prince in letters throughout the year. In a letter of 23 June, he wrote, "All the troops of the detachment under my command are, thank Heavens, all healthy and well. They are adjusting to life at this place, and since being detached from the regiment, I have had no losses. Your Highness, I can most humbly assure you that all the men have conducted themselves as becomes proper and honorable soldiers. I can also report to Your Highness, that with the concurrence of Lieutenant Colonel von Creuzbourg, I have granted Musketeer [Peter] Bode of the Leib Company permission to marry the widow of a jaeger named [Johann] Eichel. I flatter myself also that Your Highness will graciously approve, as I now have only three wives with the detachment and the mentioned woman is a very industrious and good woman....

"After being relieved at Fort Chambly ... I received orders on 26 January to unite the detachment with the mentioned [Hesse-Hanau] Jaeger Corps, and to perform duty with it. We marched there together during very cold and bad weather, along the Chambly River to St. Antoine, where we halted and made camp. I finally camped in the parish of St. Denis, opposite St. Antoine. This march was the result of a movement by the rebels at Albany, who gave an indication of attacking us. However, because the route was so bad and the cold so severe, they could not carry it out.... We broke camp here on 30 March and marched into the parishes of Terre Bonne, La Chenaye, and Riviere du Chene, where the inhabitants had begun a rebellion, and so we were sent there to subdue them. At present I am in the parish of St. Eustache on the Riviere du Chene.

In a letter of 27 July, he wrote, "Your Highness, herewith I most humbly send a report of the detachment and report most humbly that I was delivered the recruits by Captain Hense. These were seven non-commissioned officers, three drummers, and 93 privates. I also received complete uniform items, 96 shirts, 96 pairs of shoes, and 204 pairs of stockings for the detachment from him.

"I am in the greatest embarrassment because the recruits brought no uniforms or weapons with them, nor any for the rest of my detachment. The troops really need such items. I had long white overalls made for the recruits at once, in order to improve their situation and wrote to General Haldimand requesting weapons from the English supply house, until such could be received from Germany.

"Your Highness, I most humbly report also that because I have so few officers and non-commissioned officers for the presently very strong detachment, I have made four additional vice-corporals whom I have put on the roster and also given warrants as corporals because the non-commissioned officers with the newly arrived recruits include many bad soldiers, have a very difficult duty, and because the troops are very widely dispersed.... I lie here now completely alone with 160 men, without having any officer with me, because Lieutenant [Ludwig] von Hohorst lies at Mascouche de Terre Bonne, which is more than fifteen miles from here, with fifty men, and Lieutenant Seiffert, together with Ensign [Friedrich Ludwig] Kempffer and 66 privates, has been detached to Trois Rivieres. That strong detachment and the considerable traveling which I must do, create large expenses....

"I repeat herewith most humbly to Your Highness that Surgeon Weiss requested of me, most humbly, to present the case for his release to Your Highness, as he is inclined to seek his fortune here in this land. Also, Grenadier Gruenewald requested that I most humbly ask Your Highness to allow him to remain here five or six years, when the troops leave Canada for Europe, so that he can work at his trade as an engraver, at which he can earn very much here. Musketeer [Adam] Schwab of Captain Scheel's Company, born at Gainbach in Darmstadt and married, has been unable to perform duty for a long time and limps on the left foot, which he claims was injured by a batteaux on Lake Champlain. I have had it examined and all the surgeons assure me that it is an old injury. He is of almost no further use as an invalid, and he has no great desire to remain here. Therefore I await Your Highness' gracious order....

"Thank Heaven, all of the men of the detachment are healthy, but many of the recruits have the itch, which is a natural consequence of bad water and the ships' provisions, and which, when it is cured, makes the men very healthy and protects them against serious illness, as we of the regiment have learned from experience....

"Here in Canada everything is peaceful and the Canadians wait impatiently for the arrival of the French, which they fully expect."

On 6 September Schoell wrote, 'Since the last most humbly transmitted report to Your Highness, two recruits have died. The others are beginning to get sick. It is nothing of importance, but only the result of the salted ships' rations and the change of climate.

"I must also most humbly report to Your Highness that I have had to detach Lieutenant Seiffert with six non-commissioned officers and sixty privates to Trois Rivieres. General Haldimand ordered that they were to perform duty there as artillerists. I ordered 29 recently arrived artillery recruits, as well as two artillerists whom I had here in the detachment, and 29 men from the old detachment to go there. The general made arrangements with the 29 musketeers for a pay increase so that they are to be paid the same as the artillerists from now on.

"Your Highness, I must most humbly report at the same time that Ensign Kempffer requested me to most humbly seek his release from Your Highness. He desires to seek his fortune in this country and asks that his humble request be graciously granted.... Captain Hense brought sixty weapons with him from Portsmouth, which now are made at the King's expense with a cylinder loading stock and are to be given to the recruits to use. Now I am short of cartridge pouches and swords, because only cartridges came with the sixty weapons. The uniforms of the recruits are beginning to show much wear, and I do not know how I can start the winter in that condition."

On 9 October 1779 Schoell reported on crimes committed by men of the unit during 1778. "On 27 November 1778 the Drummer Schroeder, Grenadier Dephner, Musketeers Bauer, Haemerle, and Mueller attacked a resident in Petite Riviere du Chene at night, vigorously beat him and his wife, and according to their statements, planned to rob them, but did not take anything. This incident was reported to me the next morning and I did all that I could, as the residents did not know the perpetrators, in order to find out who they were. I was fortunate enough to uncover the whole plot. The further consequences of the thing can be seen by Your Highness from the investigation and resulting court-martial, which Lieutenant Colonel von Creuzbourg will most humbly submit to you....

## Enemy Views (1778)

"On 23 December 1778 I marched with the entire detachment into winter quarters on the Island Jesus, and entered the parishes of St. Martin, St. Francis, and St. Rose. The island lies ten miles beyond Montreal and is not one of the best quarters areas."

# 1779

### Canada 1779

The year 1779 passed in Canada with only the routine of garrison life being reported by Captain Schoell in letters to his prince. He noted the ever prevalent desertions, punishment, and the misfortunes suffered by the invalids in a letter of 9 October 1779. "On 23 February 1779 the Recruit Caspar Weber, born at Ober Pimen, deserted. I caught him again on 23 June 1779 in Montreal and he was punished by running the gauntlet ten times. On 3 August 1779 Free Corporal Busch and Corporal Orbig, as well as four musketeers and three cannoneers, escaped from captivity here in the detachment. There was also a musketeer with them who had deserted at Halifax, but soon thereafter was again captured by the von Seitz Regiment, which is quartered there and with which he had served for a time. He was then sent here on the first departing ship and was confined here at the detachment on 22 September 1779.

"On 16 July 1779 Cannoneer [Joseph] Elzer, who had lain dangerously ill in the hospital at St. Jean, deserted therefrom and despite all efforts to find him, he could not be caught. On 23 June 1779 Corporal Spahn, who was serving with the Artillery, was ordered to Niagara with eight cannoneers. Grenadier Weitzel from the regiment, who had escaped from captivity, reported there and is still in Niagara where he is to perform duty with Corporal Spahn until that detail is relieved, which General Haldimand promised to do in the near future.

"On 14 August 1779 the Musketeers Bauer and Pulfer robbed a resident in St. Rose and as the resident reported it to Ensign Kempffer, commanding there, who then investigated the incident, Musketeer Pulfer deserted but the next day was again seen in the region of St. Rose, in the woods, and as Musketeer Bauer believed that when Pulfer was recaptured Pulfer would identify him, he made a plan with Musketeer Leonhardt, born in Alsace, and with Musketeer Port, born at Echenheim, and all three deserted. I tried everything, even sending out several patrols from the detachment, and also several Canadians, who know the woods better than we do. The Canadians brought Musketeer Pulfer back in arrest on 18 August 1779. Musketeer Port, because he regretted deserting, returned voluntarily on 23 August 1779.

Musketeer Bauer, who had planned to make his way to Albany, was captured by an English command lying at Yamaska, a parish about twelve and one-half miles below Sorel, and sent here in arrest. Musketeer Leonhardt, who was separated from Musketeer Bauer after deserting, was recaptured again in Montreal, from which place I had him returned in arrest. Following that, Musketeers Bauer, Pulfer, Leonhardt, and Port were sent to Lieutenant Colonel von Creuzbourg and tried. The four musketeers were punished on 23 September according to their sentence, as follows: Musketeer Bauer was punished by running the gauntlet, through the whole detachment, ten times, and as a result he was declared unfit to be taken into Hesse-Hanau military service again. Lieutenant Colonel von Creuzbourg asked the general to take Bauer on a ship, which he promised to do. Musketeer Pulfer was punished by running the gauntlet fives times. Musketeer Port, because he voluntarily returned, was punished with forty lashes and Musketeer Werling with fifty lashes. All the deserters were then administered the oath again and released from arrest. Musketeer Bauer, however, was not administered the oath and is still in arrest.

"I also most humbly report to Your Highness that Sergeant Heisterreich has been unfit for duty for nine months. He is quite lame on one side and the local doctors think nothing will cure him but a mineral bath, which however, is not available here. Musketeer Wolf is also very sick and as long as we have been in this country, he has had scurvy. He will have difficulty recovering therefrom. Musketeer [Johann] Wilhelm, who came with the recruits, has severe epilepsy and can perform no duty as he often has attacks when on sentry duty. Therefore I most humbly ask Your Highness if he may not enter a monastery here, where he will be well cared for as it is managed by the Catholic religion.

Cannoneer Merz froze his foot last winter and the toes were amputated so that he can no longer march....

"The entire detachment is, thank God, still healthy, except for those listed in the report, and the troops have become fully accustomed to the climate. As the enemy gives us nothing to do, I do not neglect to earnestly drill, and as often as possible, to conduct sham exercises at the exercise area. I have drilled the entire detachment twice weekly throughout the summer, but unfortunately, the entire detachment is not uniformly armed."

## West Florida and the Mississippi Region in 1779

Chaplain Waldeck continued his account of the voyage from Jamaica to Pensacola with the Waldeck Regiment in early 1779 and with the subsequent garrison life in West Florida. "1 January - Again a year is past and truly the first on the stormy, unfriendly sea. Captain Pentzel treated with good Madeira wine, which enabled us to toast the New Year properly. On this New Year's Day we were comfortable as one can be on the ocean. We conversed and discussed our distant homeland.....

"7 January - Our ship took a frightful amount of water. The captain blamed the strong sun under which the ship had to sit for an entire month in the West Indies. The heat eased considerably and a blanket was again needed at night....

"15 January - ... We cast the lead and found 43, then twenty, and at one o'clock, thirteen fathoms under us, which was the surest sign that we were close to land, which the fog prevented us from seeing. It is worth noting that in the Gulf of Mexico the depth can be measured long before land can be seen. The fog continued to thicken and it was necessary for safety for all ships to drop anchor. While I was writing this on my bunk, and was complaining about the miserable finish, I heard one of our soldiers call from the mast, 'There is land and the whole fleet.' Full of joy, I ran up on deck and saw through the thinning fog, but as in a dark distance, the peaks of the sand dunes of West Florida. God be eternally thanked! The blood again raced through the arteries, and joy was to be seen on everyone's face. In the evening we raised our anchor....

"17 January - The weather and the wind changed so that we were able to steer directly toward the harbor of Pensacola.

"At eleven o'clock the pilot came aboard. We met an outbound fleet here, part of which was bound for Jamaica, and part for England. And this fleet would inform the English newspapers that the reinforcements for Florida had arrived. And I hope that through this channel the people in our fatherland will also get the news.

## Enemy Views (1779)

"The wind died down and we could not proceed farther into the bay. It was a beautiful day, cold in the morning and warm during the day.

"18 January - .... At noon the wind improved and we were fortunate enough to enter the harbor at three o'clock. Anywhere else that one might enter a port, he would be curious to see the city. Here, however, one could already see from the ship that this must be a miserable place.

"19 January - After we had, according to the reckoning of the ship's captain, sailed 3,463 English miles between 20 October 1778 and 18 January 1779, we saw the end of our prolonged and stormy sea voyage. But instead of the hourly anticipated debarkation, the order came that we were to remain on board ship, and then later transfer to smaller ships on which we would sail to the Mississippi River. That was certainly a sorry damn situation. Here there were no ships that could carry us there, and there nothing to eat or drink.

"20 January - The order that we were to go to the Mississippi has been lifted. We are to debark. But that too is cancelled because first, houses have not been built in which the troops will be quartered. Truly the English are not employers worthy of hiring Germans into their service....

"21 - 29 January - We remained aboard ship, although we have already been bored with this for a long time. In the city absolutely no preparations have been made for quartering the troops. Also no kitchens set up where the troops can prepare their food, and only now the soldiers have been ordered to begin work on the cooking excavations.

"30 January - Troops debarked from the *Springfield, Crawford,* and *Christiana* [sic]. The day was as hot as by us in mid-summer. Our entire officer corps was assigned only six rooms. The parole today was Waldeck and the countersign Hanxleden. Our cooking facilities are still not set up. Therefore, we had to eat our meals at the coffee house or wherever we could get something, and all of it was bad and expensive.

"2 February - The two companies on the *Britannia* landed today. We began to take our meals with a German native, to whom we give two Spanish dollars in addition to our regular ration money, that is, four pounds per week, and we are fed quite well. A packet boat came from Jamaica and brought the news that Russia and Holland have joined England, and that both powers will declare war on France, if it does not cease supporting the rebels.....

"8 September - As we were dining Commissary Marc wrote a note that a three-masted ship was just opposite the harbor. We were full of curiosity and anticipation. Late in the evening it entered the harbor. It was a packet boat of eighteen cannons, which could sail indescribably swift. How we were deceived. It brought no good news, but just the opposite. Spain had declared war, and the battle between the fleets had not been to our hoped-for advantage. Byron and [Samuel] Barrington had fought like lions and their ninety gun ship had captured seven French ships. Barrington had dueled with the French admiral's ship *Languedoc*, but been seriously wounded. Immediately after the engagement, Barrington sailed for England in a frigate, and took seven French ship's captains as prisoners with him. Because they had not done their duty, the troubled situation in the West Indies will be put before the Admiralty. The French fleet is stronger than ours by twelve ships-of-the-line.....

11 September - We received orders to be prepared to march at a moment's notice.

"12 September - We did not hold church because the entire garrison is busy with preparations for battle and the Light Infantry has been chosen for a special assignment. There is nothing but war to be seen here and we are in such a fix, that I cannot see how we will work our way out of it. If only a warship would come to strengthen our harbor.

- - - - - - -

"P.S. -- Our Grenadiers left here on 20 June and the reports from them which we occasionally received are worse than one can imagine. Many troops have died and the rest are sick.

"2 August - The Major's Company left for the Mississippi. The 29th of August Captain Alberti, Sr., departed with a part of his company.

- - - - - - -

"13 September - The packet boat which brought the Spanish declaration of war will not depart, but will remain here for some time as a protective force for the harbor.

"14 September - As anticipated, we are to make an attack on New Orleans. With this in view, four Indian chiefs from the Choctaw tribe met with the general this morning, and 200 from that tribe will take part in the attack.

"15 September - One hears that 700 rebel light dragoons attacked the Creeks and handled them very roughly. The Spaniards have reportedly landed in Apalachee Bay and tried to seduce the Indians to their side with rich presents. That is bad news from both east and west. An express came through the wilderness from the Mississippi with letters for the general. The commandant, Colonel [Alexander] Dickson, who was not aware of the Spanish declaration of war, saw activity on the other side of the river, however. He sent an officer across to ask the Spanish governor what this meant. The governor only answered that he was too busy to answer at this time, but hoped this would not be taken in any way wrong.

"16 September - Colonel Dickson today sent another express by land, who rode through the wilderness in thirteen days. The Spanish have taken the field with 1,500 men. Captain von Haacke has already gone to Baton Rouge with our two companies, and most of the troops are sick. Colonel Dickson has pulled back from Manchac and burned everything that he could not take with him. Two ships which had taken our troops there have already been captured by the Spaniards and Colonel Dickson had sunk another himself. Captain Alberti's command had not yet arrived and still had to pass the Spanish batteries. As was expected, the good man, his command, and even his ship were captured. O what the Mississippi has cost us in good men. It has ruined our regiment. O Mississippi, spare our noble legions....

"19 September - Church was again postponed because of the rain and the large work commands which are taking the cannons from the ships. Now an expedition is to go against New Orleans. It is surely not an opportune time of year because during this month there are frequent storms. During war this can not be avoided, however.

"20 September - Still one more day survived without Spaniards. As soon as a person awakens, he looks out to sea to check if a Spanish fleet has arrived. What will become of us? Certainly nothing good. If the Spaniards do not get us, we will nevertheless die out in time. That is certain. Germany seems like such a good land where there are all sorts of good fruits to be had. If only wild plums and crab apples grew here. No, even these are too fine for this cursed land. Truly, we ask now for nothing better than wild plums and crab apples. But it is our burden, of all those which life holds, to be robbed of all pleasure. Spain held Pensacola as a penal colony, but even for criminals this is a hard punishment, if endured for very long.....

"23 September - The packet boat which arrived recently, sailed out in order to cruise at the mouth of the Mississippi, and gather intelligence on the condition of the Spanish batteries, and if armed ships are present there.....

"26 - 28 September - Nothing especially new. Many warlike preparations, a new battery placed near the storehouse and a floating battery built. News arrived that the Spanish have cut communications between Baton Rouge and Natchez. Lots of bad news and poor prospects for our unfortunate troops on the Mississippi.

"30 September - More Indians than usual, and from all tribes, have been gathering here to ask for presents. They clearly see that in the present situation, it is more necessary to flatter them so as to keep them friendly. And if it is not to our advantage, still we must give them presents so that they will not take up arms against us. On the other hand, the Spaniards do all they can to draw these savages away from us.

"Well, another month in this miserable land has passed. Hopefully it will be the last September that we must spend here.

"1 October - Cool, rainy weather. October has always been a month during our time in America which held something special for us. In '76, during this month, we were still aboard ship and arrived at the beloved New York. In the year '77, we went aboard ship again during this month and sailed up the Hudson, or North River. A miserable and very difficult passage. In the year '78, we again went aboard ship on the 20th of the month and traveled via the West Indies to this cursed West Florida. And in this year, we will undoubtedly undertake a sea voyage which is certain to be the most unpleasant of all.

"11 October. Again bad news. An express came from Georgia, and reported that 26 French ships-of-the-line had arrived at Savannah. Everything is going amiss and this affair will end as it did for Burgoyne's army.... Our situation becomes more dangerous every day.....

"18 October - We firmly believe the embarkation of troops is about to occur, because the baggage is already on board. But it remains undone.....

"20 October - This day has always held something special for us, and we anticipate, from all signs, that we will go aboard ship today.... Yes, the day held something special for us -- a courier came from Mobile. Colonel Dickson with his entire command have been taken prisoners -- and that includes most of our regiment. Mississippi, a loss for our regiment, which will be irreparable as long as the war lasts. Now the general's proposal to go to the Mississippi to rescue this corps will be even more difficult. The English, who are proud of their military strength, refuse to believe all of this, but it must be true. If there had been another bed in the cabin of the ship when Captain Alberti last left, then I too would have been captured. God knows how long or how short the time may be, how long we will remain free. Any night our fate may be determined, and it is strange that no fleet has arrived from Havana.

"21 October - The express, about which one spoke yesterday, did not arrive, and the English are willing to believe it all to be lies and that the newly arrived reports were fiction....

"22 October - Still no express, although he should have come already yesterday. It is really surprising, even though we know that the present strong winds have swollen the rivers which he must cross. Also, he does not have the best horse. And who knows what problems can arise for a courier who must travel through savage tribes before he finds the best way?

"23 October - The English continue to believe it to be only lies and tricks which the governor of New Orleans, [Don Bernardo de Galvez], has circulated to the effect that the English troops and positions on the Mississippi were in Spanish hands. Otherwise our general would carry out his plan of going to the Mississippi with the designated troops, and if the wind did not blow too strongly, the order to board ship would be given. Adjutant Stierlein came into our room at nine o'clock and brought the news which we had dreaded for two days, that the express from the Mississippi had arrived at headquarters. The news and letters which he brought in no way contradicted what one had surmised already yesterday, but placed the unfortunate, and until now doubtful, situation in a clear light which as near as we can determine this evening, puts us in the following position:

"Colonel Dickson, who could no longer hold out at Manchac, and whose full situation and unfortunate circumstances the general, already a week previously, had hindered by refusing reinforcements and cannons, saw himself forced to abandon Manchac. He sent the troops from our regiment, under the command of Captain von Haacke, to Baton Rouge and placed himself with the English troops between Baton Rouge and Manchac, and hoped here to await reinforcements from Pensacola. And that Heaven still had so much patience - here ships are built, armed with cannons, armored with stinking cowhides instead of leather siding - and that all proceeded so slowly, so lazily, as if there were no war. O that everything should be lost. No wonder that a person, who sees it all, curses the establishment.

"The Spaniards had sought to bring the savage Indian tribes, which are called the Choctaws, to their assistance through all kinds of gifts and especially with pearls and jewelry for their wives, and 200 of these sat themselves between our troops and Colonel Dickson, and prevented the retreat of the latter and the consolidation at Baton Rouge. The next day, the Spanish Governor Don Galvez came with a vastly superior force and launched an attack from all sides. Colonel Dickson saw no alternative but an honorable capitulation, which the clever and deceptive Don Galvez offered. All the troops at Baton Rouge and Natchez were included in the capitulation. Although the rashness of some Englishmen passed judgment on him concerning this point, at least we have such a good opinion of Colonel Dickson's character, that it would be impossible for us to form a premature judgment about him until we know all the details. According to the capitulation, all troops departed the Mississippi, were sent to an English port, and on their word of honor, were not to serve again for eighteen months. The inhabitants have eight months in which they have the freedom, either to become Spanish citizens, or to dispose of their belongings. Their stock and other produce will be purchased at a generous price by the Spanish governor. The corps at Natchez had been cut off by the Spaniards, and even if this had not occurred, Natchez would have been captured by the Americans who were already on their way down the Ohio. We will learn more exact details through a flag of truce which is expected here every hour from New Orleans.

Enemy Views (1779)

24 October - The wind was very strong and quite sharp. We held ·church at seven o'clock. When the weather is so windy, I always wish for at least a shed in which to hold services. It is now nearly four years during which we have held church services in the open air, and this during winter and summer. In other wars, there are winter quarters and in such, churches are also to be found. Here in this lousy war, there is only a wilderness, 500 miles long, and nothing more, to give pleasure. On all sides here, one has to put up with a lot of unpleasantness, and everything joins together to make this war even more so.

"25 October - Is it possible to think of something more stupid than that one would again doubt everything one heard yesterday from the courier as well as others? The general, who is still disturbed by the whole annoying situation wherein he finds himself with all his troops, and the whole province of West Florida, does not now know how to determine if he should go aboard ship, or how he should alone strive to defend Pensacola. Is that not a cursed land in which to conduct war, where most of the corps are captive for five weeks, and a 1,200 mile stretch of land can be captured, without the commanding general being sure it has happened? Yesterday the general unloaded his baggage from the ship. Today at seven o'clock the order was given to remove the provisions from the ship *Thomas* again. At eight o'clock another order to cease the operation and the general ordered that his baggage be loaded as quickly as possible. This afternoon, the troops are to embark. Nothing here is firmly decided, first one thing and then another. In this fashion the whole thing is finally accomplished in the most likely manner. To tear the general out of his vacillation and get a firm decision, the governor and his entire council sat down, studied the incoming reports and queried the couriers who had recently come in. They found after all this searching that a 1,200 mile stretch along the Mississippi had been captured by the Spaniards and all our troops had been taken captive. As a result, it was too late to send support and too far and too difficult a sea voyage to undertake. It seemed best to secure only this place. This was the decision of the governor, His Excellence, Peter Chester, with his councilors. The general was satisfied with that and gave orders for the baggage to be brought ashore again.....

"26 October - Today the express returned, which the general had sent to Colonel Dickson. Because the savage tribes during the present

315

war adhere more to Spain than to England, he had been unable to penetrate their territory, but had seen it as necessary to return with his letters. The Indians, in general, complain that they can not carry on further trade with the English traders because the prices are too high. Therefore, the express brought the letters back unopened. However, he told us many special circumstances concerning the incident on the Mississippi. Initially our troops forced the Spaniards back with severe losses, which on the Spanish side amounted to 400 dead to our 23 dead. The following day the Spaniards set up a battery, against which our troops made a sally, and after the Spaniards lost 150 men, they were dislodged. Finally, Colonel Dickson saw no other choice except surrender, as he could not save himself in any other way. Our situation is still unknown. The general gave the order that the baggage should be brought ashore again, and the contemplated expedition to the Mississippi has been canceled.

"29 October - ... One bit of bad news follows close on another just now. Today intelligence from Georgia that our army was completely surrounded, and the French fleet was close on the coast to assist in cutting off relief from New York. At the time when this express left, Savannah, the capital of Georgia, was already under siege so there was no hope that the troops could be saved in any way. The naval hero, who has captured so many ships and thereby created such an impressive fortune, Sir James Wallace, is reportedly captured with his ship *Experiment* during this incident. He surely sold his capture at a high price.

"30 October - The constant drumming and the drill of the many corps awakens one from sleep at an early hour. I get up early, go out on the gallery, and look toward the sea, but still neither Spanish nor French fleets are to be seen, and this provides one with the knowledge that one more day can be lived in peace, but that can be changed any morning.....

"15 November - The news came ... which suddenly raised the spirits of all the English. The French had landed 10,000 men from their fleet in Georgia, and an equal number of Americans came from the side toward the Carolinas in order to capture the capital city of Savannah, and all of Georgia, as quickly as possible. Relying on their superior numbers, they planned to capture our troops who numbered only 4,000. As earlier at Rossbach, however, they also came to such a sad end, as did the men there. The French as well as the Americans suffered heavy losses, and during the retreat, a serious breach developed between the Americans and the French, when the former accused the other of not fulfilling their responsibility. From our side, 300 cannons, taken from the ships aground by the English upon the approach of the French fleet, were turned on the enemy. This victory instilled in the people of Georgia a great confidence in our troops, and they now believe that Charleston will soon be captured.

"16 - 18 November - The capitulation articles concerning our captives on the Mississippi arrived here. The officers as well as the enlisted men have retained all their personal belongings, and marched out with flags flying and music playing. Along with this came another report. Our wives, during the siege, together with the children, left the fort and in order to find a place of refuge, apparently went into the forest, and there both women and children were slain by the savage Indians.[33]

"26 November - Nothing but a flag of truce from New Orleans, under which the Grenadier Company of the 16th Regiment returned. We also had the pleasure of receiving a few letters from our friends in captivity. In these letters we were informed, unfortunately, that our people are dying off like flies and many more have been struck down sick. Lieutenant Leonhardi died 26 September on the Mississippi on the journey from Baton Rouge to New Orleans, and Ensign Noelting was killed in the fighting aboard ship on the 22nd.....

"3 December - We had a rather sleepless night. About three o'clock the cry of fire was raised as the general's house was burning. There could have been serious consequences if the fire had spread. The storehouse stands close behind the general's house, and if it had caught fire, we would have had no choice but to starve to death or to surrender to the Spaniards, as this land does not produce any means of nourishing people. The same situation applies to the nearby laboratory in which much powder was stored. Only today I received my letter from Lieutenant Strubberg. He wrote that his life as a prisoner was quite satisfactory. He praised the hospitality of Governor Don Galvez. Privates as well as officers are given friendly treatment by the local inhabitants, and the captives are allowed complete freedom of movement. And, anyone who has been in Pensacola will never again in his lifetime be hard to please. The captured officers are frequently invited to dine with the governor.....

"12 December - Now the work on the fort at Gage Hill is being pushed twice as hard as before. The most stupid preparations which can be taken are undertaken here. Since the outbreak of the Spanish war, we have hastily begun to construct batteries. Previously, kitchens, bake ovens, and latrines were laid out and then built with the greatest care. The news arrived today that the Spaniards are marching on Mobile and that they will visit us, by land, from there. Now everything is in turmoil. The general ordered work on Gage Hill to be speeded up, but the carpenters from the city, who earn two and one-half dollars every day working on the fort, pay no heed to the general's orders, do not show up for work, and neither the governor nor the general can force them to work as it is against English independence. These carpenters consider themselves to be gentlemen equal to the governor and general.... Is it reasonable to assume that somehow one can get out of this situation, and above all, get away from this cursed and uninhabitable Florida? The Mississippi has always been praised. We too have praised it. Now none of our people return from the Mississippi. They die there like flies, currently as many as three a day. The Grenadier Company of the 16th British Regiment, which served near Natchez, has returned and the troops are so sickly, that they will never regain their health. They look like death and die daily. It is certainly no place for human beings, otherwise nature would have provided for them by allowing foodstuffs to be grown here. But there is nothing but 200, 300, or even 400 miles of white sand, and those who build here are called fools, as there are better regions to develop."

Waldeck closed his entries for 1779 with despair on 28 December. "There are 800 Americans not far from Mobile and reportedly, together with the Spaniards from New Orleans, they have plans for Pensacola."

Steuernagel also commented on activities in West Florida and on meeting a fellow countryman. "As we had obtained and loaded provisions and fresh water here [Jamaica], we set sail on 31 December [1778], on a New Year's Saturday, in the most terrible summer heat.... In this Gulf of Mexico we observed ... that at times the wind was so weak that ... the ship barely moved from where it sat and had to be soaked down with water daily so that it would not rot .. and on the

18th we were able to land at the designated debarkation point at Pensacola. As the necessary repairs to the barracks were not completed, only three companies were put ashore, initially, and the remainder on the 21st of February.....

"I must make a special note here, that we met an interpreter among this nation [of Indians], who was a German, and still more, if you will believe it, a fellow countryman, a Waldecker, born in Koenigshagen, who deserted in his youth and secretly fled from the Waldeck castle.

"There is much to remember here. However, for the sake of brevity, I will only note that this discovered Waldecker, supposedly named Brandenstein, was a chief of about 2,000 Indians. At least he had adopted the dress, customs, and manners of the savages. Only his white color and beard indicated that he was European by birth.[34]....

"As we now daily await the enemy, that is the Spaniards, and because Pensacola was an important place, and because of the nearness of Mexico, which provided the Spaniards with many advantages, therefore, most of the work now was strengthening the defenses and even more importantly, the harbor defenses and other fortifications, as quickly as possible, in order to resist an attack. To this end, by Pensacola and also at the Cliffs, which set at the mouth of the harbor, we turned to with a will to the work of building defenses, sometimes working at night to continue the improvements.....

"On the 19th the Grenadier Company was ordered aboard ship, to go to Baton Rouge, also in the region of the Mississippi.

"In the month of August, Major von Horn's Company and one corporal and fourteen privates of Colonel von Hanxleden's Company received orders to board ship and sail to the same region.

"On the 30th [of August] Captain Alberti, Sr., received orders to follow them."

Enemy Views (1779)

## The Southern Colonies in 1779

Reuber's diary entry for 1 January 1779 is a summary of the entire year's activity in the south, after the arrival of the Truembach Regiment in the closing days of 1778. "The New Year with God. The English marched 21 miles inland to the city of Ebenezer on the Savannah harbor. In the spring the Rall Grenadier Regiment [designated the Truembach Regiment at that time] also received orders to march inland to Ebenezer to relieve the English. It remained on duty there until the news came that the English General Clinton would come from the north with a fleet and besiege and capture Charleston. General [Augustine] Prevost of the 60th Regiment came with his command, on land, from Augustine to Savannah and took over the command of the province of Georgia. We made an attempt to land with our army, such as it was, at Charleston. But before we could cross the Savannah harbor near Ebenezer, we encountered great privation and danger before, with force, we could break through and fortunately advance.

"After we had crossed the harbor, the Americans pulled back into the Charleston defenses. We came to a small seaport over which there was a bridge. The Americans had cut the bridge timbers half through and when the British Light Infantry was in the middle of the bridge, there was a terrible noise. Immediately they lay in the water but no one was killed. The complete attack plan was frustrated. We Hessians could not advance but had to wait until the water was lower and we could all wade through. Meantime the Americans were on the opposite side and as we approached, they had cut loose all the rafts and boats. However, we had 200 wild Indians with us as an advance guard, and those wild, naked people immediately jumped angrily into the water and swam across because the boats had all been removed. As a protection from being shot while we crossed, the English Cavalry lined up beside us. In case someone fell they could quickly pick him up. Before anyone from our army had crossed a strong storm struck and night overtook us. We had to lie down close to the water. The Americans had half cut down all the trees in our path and as the storm now hit, one tree after the other fell, making a great crashing sound in the forest so that we believed that everything had fallen to the ground. There was thunder and lightning and it rained. The cartridge pouches and knapsacks were soaked by the water and we had to lie there. All the fires had been put out by the rain and we had to persevere until morning.

"With the coming of day we looked about uneasily and had to work and clean up for half a day before we could continue after the Americans. Then we had to march a full day before we caught up with them. When we were quite near Charleston, we arrived at a seaport which was called Ashley Harbor and which we crossed on the Ashley Ferry. After crossing we marched onward for four English miles and then encountered a 26-pounder and small arms fire. The English were extremely angry at the rebels, drove them back into their defenses, and set the outer part of the city on fire. The entire English force pulled back to the Ashley Ferry to wait for the English Field Marshal von [sic] Clinton to come to Charleston from New York in the north and to take the city by storm.

"Now, however, things were quite different. The English fleet turned out to be a French fleet, Comte d'Estaing with 6,000 Swiss and French [soldiers], sailing directly toward Savannah in order to put us under siege. We had to leave Charleston hastily and struggle through the wild and uninhabited islands. When we came to Stono Ferry, which was on a medium size bay extending from Charleston and running inland, the entire English army set up camp just across the bay and the Rall Grenadier Regiment had to remain on this side of Stono Ferry and an English row galley provided cover for the regiment. The Americans then attacked the Rall Grenadier Regiment with their full force and we had only the row galley close behind us during the crossing, but it could not provide much help. It had no maneuvering room, the bay was too narrow. It did fire a 36-pound cannon. There was a deep ravine by which the Americans sought to get behind us, but that one shot had taken out forty men. That frightened the Americans who directed their small arms fire against the row galley so that it could no longer protect or help us. The Americans had the high ground and our regiment had the low ground. When they charged against us they began firing and their bullets flew over us and into the water. But then the entire English army broke camp and the full force came on the run and at the same time gathered all the little boats and were carried across the water to our relief and charged against the Americans. Things turned bad for them but just then an American ship with sixteen cannons approached and was about to fall upon our rear. Before the ship arrived the Wissenbach Regiment which remained in camp challenged the ship with its regimental cannons and delivered some well-aimed shots. Next the Grenadiers of the 60th Regiment came and seized the ship which was called the *Rattlesnake*. Here the cannons and flags which the Rall Regiment had lost at Trenton on 25 December 1776 were recaptured at Stono Ferry and we received our cannons back.

"Then the French fleet entered Savannah harbor before all the English had assembled in the city. Comte d'Estaing with 6,000 French and Swiss and 7,000 Americans called on the city to surrender. The Comte having called for the surrender, the English Field Marshal Prevost requested 24 hours to consider the demand, and during the night the rest of the English army, which had not yet arrived at Savannah because of the French fleet, were able to pass the French outposts. When all the English army was in Savannah, General Prevost gave his answer to the Comte with a 26-pound cannon shot, which was the same as replying that if you want our surrender, you will have to win it with the sword.

"Thereupon the French and Americans began entrenching operations as did the English. We had our four cannons in the city and the warships lying before the city. From those we took all the cannons and placed them in our line in all the defenses and trenches, and all the defenses and batteries were occupied with sailors serving as artillerymen because we had no heavy artillery, except for the regimental guns. Then the activity began on both sides and continued for four weeks. As it did not create a break [in the lines], the French finally decided to attack our right wing which was not successful for the French, however. The citizens and the English Light Horse were there, and behind batteries E and F,[35] the English Light Infantry was held in reserve. When the attack was underway, they also struck against points A on the left wing and along the entire front at points D, E, F. Initially there was a frightful cannonade against the two Hessian regiments and then suddenly still. Then the action commenced again on our right wing. The French charged, wave upon wave, and broke through the abatis at point E in our line. They wanted to attack the defenses where the city's citizens were, at point E on the right wing. However, the Light Horse and the English Grenadiers and Light Infantry all surrounded the defenses and the French had to retreat, leaving 200 men lying dead before the defenses. As the French and Americans retreated, our entire line and especially our right wing, where the most commanding positions were at E and F, opened fire with cannons on the French and Americans. When this affair was over, there was an armistice while the dead were buried. It was considered possible that they would make another attempt but no one knew when or from where it would be made. They wanted to break through in the middle of the barracks, which was a long stretch with no cannons, as well as on both wings. As the enemy began siege operations toward the barracks area, the barracks were destroyed during the night and only the ground level was left standing. Cannons were placed in all the window openings and the middle was knocked down to make a round battery containing fifteen 26-pounders. Then the French changed their plan. Suddenly there was an alarm for us. General Clinton and a fleet were not far from the southern part of America and therefore the French raised the siege, and the 7,000 Americans and everything pertaining thereto was put aboard ship. We were free and the fleet sailed off into the ocean.

"A few days later General Clinton was before Savannah harbor with an English fleet with Hessians and Englanders. He proceeded to Charleston and put the city under siege. The Hessians and Englanders were successful and fortunately captured it, and all the Americans that were in the city, the forts, and defenses were made prisoners of war. After that had been accomplished, General Clinton and most of his troops went aboard ship and returned to New York. In Savannah we received a fleet with nothing but provisions and all sorts of food, merchandise, and everything which we found necessary and enough for an entire year. There was sufficient rice, but no potatoes in this southern climate. If we wanted to cook some we had to buy them by the pound and they did not taste good. 'They stuck in our throats.' In late summer 1779 the Rall Regiment received orders in Savannah that we were to sail to Charleston as an occupation force. The Knoblauch Regiment, formerly the Wissenbach Regiment, remained occupying Savannah with the English. Therefore we went aboard ship and sailed north for two days. On the third day we were outside the Charleston harbor and sailed right into the city and disembarked. We joined the Ditfurth and Benning Regiments as the occupation force in Charleston and remained in garrison there until 1780."

## The New York Area in 1779

The Feilitzsch diary entries in 1779 record events in the New York area and Feilitzsch's often repeated wish to return to Germany. "1 January - Praise Heaven another [year] has begun and the last one survived, despite many crises. Heaven protect me in this year also. Do not treat me according to my desserts, but allow me to return to my fatherland this year. Then I will praise and never forget you.

"There is no longer any bread or flour. Therefore the troops receive oatmeal which does not thrill them and with which they can make nothing. The provision fleet did not leave England until October. If everything goes well, it could still be a long time in arriving and we still long for bread.....

"9 January - Today the weather changed. It rained all day and has been nice since. The cost of living has increased sharply and for a lot of money, nothing is to be had. It is especially true with bread. The common soldier has it the worst. His pay is not sufficient to buy bread. Complaints are heard daily and it is necessary to feel sorry for the men. The frequent crimes which occur create problems for us officers. The jaegers steal and slaughter their landlords' cattle at night. Such complaints arise daily. We check them out every day but to no avail. Reportedly two provision ships arrived in New York yesterday and the fleet has anchored at Sandy Hook. Heaven grant that this is not just a rumor. We do not know how to appreciate our good fortune. Supposedly our regiments in Rhode Island have it even worse. Except for their provisions, they can buy nothing fresh. Furthermore, they do not even have a tree, nor a piece of firewood. How happy they will be when the weather improves and turns mild.....

"26 January - ... We hear from South Carolina that General Grant has made good progress. The Indians under the leadership of [John] Butler have created great fear among the rebels. Even the people of Philadelphia are starting to tremble.

"5 February - Lieutenant [Johann] Beck, who arrived about twelve days ago with our reinforcements, came to York on leave and did not report back at the end of his leave. Therefore he is being sought everywhere. Our first reports were that a boat had been damaged and sunk opposite York at Brooklyn Ferry, by the ice breaking up and that everyone had drowned. Therefore we believed +++ he had also drowned. However, today we had the unpleasant report from Lieutenant Colonel [Andreas] Emmerich that Beck had been with him, in disguise, passed himself off as a private person, and enlisted in Emmerich's Dragoons. The next day, however, Beck came to him and confessed that he was an officer in our service. However, this did not help him. He was released from our service and was to have sought his fortune as one of Colonel Emmerich's men. This individual at once transferred him back to us and as this no longer satisfied him, he was to have his discharge. He wished to return as an officer but we have no further reports. We can believe nothing other than that he has gone over to the rebels. We have the embarrassment that an officer has deserted, although we have lost nothing in the individual. However, would to Heaven that it had occurred somewhere else.....

"23 February - ... The Hessian Lieutenant [Louis de Foigny de] Montluisant received his discharge. However, he went to the outposts and planned to go over to the rebels. He was forcibly arrested and brought to the provost in York. What is happening now to the officers? It appears we are losing our honor and I almost believe it has already disappeared.....

"3 March - As I have recorded my most noteworthy daily activities here, I can not fail to note follies. Love has caught me in her net here in America, also.[36] The personality of my good friend has once again awakened my life. Although this individual is not especially beautiful, nevertheless her understanding, if I were not +++ bashful and also frivolous person caught in her net. I am in love with everything about her +++ think she is beautiful. However, I am also too weak to express my feelings. All the fruit which I hope to have from this harvest +++ will consist of only looking, and the father and mother who love their daughter more than I, from all appearances, will not be disappointed. A few minutes to be alone with her, the happier you are B +++ and it is just as good for me. I can make the following suggestion +++ and good +++ Germany you are forgotten. We have very beautiful, warm weather. Several English regiments went to Elizabethtown in Jersey under the command of Colonel [Thomas] Stirling. They burned several enemy magazines and houses and brought back 22 prisoners. Several gentlemen of the Congress, who were staying there, barely escaped. General Tryon went with English and Hessian troops to Horse Neck, destroyed some magazines, set fire to some ships, and captured three cannons and forty prisoners. However, as the rebels were much stronger than we were, the captured cannons had to be abandoned, but were spiked. A large amount of livestock was brought off, however.....

"18 May - Without warning, the order came to get wagon horses and to prepare the heavy baggage for moving in order to send it on its way on the shortest notice. Most of the troops have already moved out of their quarters and some have gone to York Island.

"19 May - As our army does not have the strength nor capability of taking the field, I can not understand where it can go. It is either to fool the enemy until the reinforcements come from England, or we will move up the North River, which we will surely do. Reportedly a strong fleet is coming from England. There are also reports of a successful battle in Georgia. Certainly 20,000 men would eliminate all our problems. Then we could leave America with honor. However, the rebels will surely not allow England to do this.

"28 May - ... We finally received the order to march tomorrow and therefore our peaceful winter quarters will come to an end. We can anticipate much fatigue and unrest. How happy I would be if this were our last campaign. However, I will have patience and give myself over to the higher will and to Him, who has protected me during two campaigns and other great perils. It is a small favor to protect me in a third one, and I can undertake it with more peace of mind if I do not disturb myself with too much nonsense and forget the things on which I tend to dwell. We are such wretched people; and me in particular +++."

## Clinton's Attack on the Hudson River Forts

The end of May Feilitzsch recorded Clinton's move up the Hudson River, against the American defenses on that river. "28 May - We left Flushing at three o'clock in the morning. We marched to Lawrence Neck and embarked in flatboats, together with the English Grenadiers. We crossed the Sound to York province, and as soon as we were on land, marched through Winchester to Cortlandt's house, beyond Philipse's and on to Philipse's Manor, sixteen miles, where we had camped last fall. Even today I can recall the great heat which I had forgotten in my peaceful quarters. Heaven protect me during this campaign, and I hope to recover during the coming winter, when I will certainly not again commit such folly as in Flushing....

"30 May - It rained a bit. Suddenly at one o'clock a patrol of 300 men, under the command of Major Prueschenck was sent out. Other officers included Captains Ewald, Lorey, and Waldenfels and Lieutenant Ebenauer, [Maximillian] Cornelius, and me. We embarked on transport ships at Philipse's Ferry. We found Hessians, who had just arrived from Virginia, already on board. We had 600 men on board. We lay there until three o'clock, when the anchor was raised, and we sailed up the North River.

"31 May - The fleet anchored at eleven o'clock at Tellar's Point and we debarked at twelve o'clock, under the command of General Vaughan. Unexpectedly, I saw many troops who were the elite of the army, about 2,000 men. N.B. -- They had just returned from an expedition to Virginia., the English Grenadiers, the Light Infantry, the 33rd Regiment, the Legion, Ferguson's, three battalions of Hessian Grenadiers, and Robertson and 200 jaegers. We marched three miles to the right with the 33rd Regiment and the Hessian Grenadiers, and occupied a high hill. The others cut off Verplanck's Neck. I went on picket duty. A corps of rebels was eight miles from us, but everything remained quiet. One hundred jaegers and the 17th, 63rd, and 64th Regiments were landed on the Jersey shore, opposite, and not far from us at Haberstraw, where the enemy had several batteries. Those which were on Stony Point were captured when the enemy abandoned them, after setting them on fire. We then set up a battery there, and with the help of some row galleys, opened fire on the rebel Fort Lafayette on Verplanck's Point. Next a frigate and a row galley passed the fort in order to cut communications to the north.

"1 June - The cannonade commenced at daybreak and at noon the fort capitulated. Four officers and 71 men were in the garrison. A battery was nearby. It was small but masterfully and well-fortified, but the entire armament was only three cannons. If they had 200 men and more courage and artillery, they could have made it very difficult for us. Shortly thereafter a very good uniform was found with a silk lining, and nearby the body. Both were found hidden. The prisoners disclaimed any knowledge. We were told that possibly it had been a high ranking Frenchman. About two o'clock we marched three miles farther and into camp at Herecland's Creek, two miles from Peekskill.

"3 June - At eight o'clock in the morning our army marched through Peekskill to a creek about three miles beyond. We met several dragoons and skirmished with them. We suffered no losses but the enemy did. We learned later that a colonel was killed. I have never seen such plundering as on this march. The troops had permission to do so and Heaven protect the house which a jaeger entered.....

"16 June - ... If Heaven could only get me out of America, but things do not go as I would wish. I must remember the real reason of our discontent. This fate is certainly very cruel for those who think as I do +++ Lord, how much I must put up with here!

"17 June - Rainy weather. The longer we remain here the more unpleasant this camp seems to me. I have no good friend to speak with, my health is not good, the region is completely wild, bare cliffs and unpleasant. I never remember such a miserable camp. How cruel fate has been, and does not seem to change.....

"26 June - There is talk of news which I am almost afraid to enter here. It is reported that General Pigot, who commands in South Carolina, was defeated, captured, and annihilated during the attack on Charleston, just like Burgoyne. God grant that this is not true, otherwise we dare not hope for peace. Work on the fortifications is continuing and everything is being done well.

"27 June - ... We received the order to march. At eight-thirty we moved out and at ten o'clock embarked on the ship *Caledonia* near Fort Lafayette. At two o'clock we sailed back down the North River with the ebb tide, but with a contrary wind. The troops from Jersey and the Jaegers were embarked with us. A garrison of 1,500 remained there.

"28 June - We sailed again at three-thirty in the morning with a contrary wind. It rained very hard. Yesterday we collided with another ship and I was nearly on no ship, if I had not been a fatalist. At ten o'clock we anchored. We sailed with a favorable wind at one-thirty and by three-thirty we were already near Philipse's house, where we anchored. An order which we received led us to think that we would continue down river. However, this changed everything +++ unfortunately and the gentlemen, from pride, came one after the other.

At nine o'clock we received the order to disembark and we entered camp at twelve o'clock.....

"8 July - On the third I forgot to note that three regiments arrived in the Sound from Rhode Island.....

"13 July - I received news of General Tryon's expedition. He landed at New Haven, burned enemy stores, sixteen ships, and several houses, and captured three cannons. In so doing we lost three men. A seventy-year old man was stoned to death by twenty English soldiers because he railed at and cursed us. The rebels carry their wickedness to such extremes. No one believes that such barbarity can be expected from them. Fairfield consisted of 300 houses and was burned down because the inhabitants killed an artillery guard. The troops then embarked again and the fleet continued up the Sound, but we do not know where it is going.....

"16 July - About two o'clock this morning we heard several can-non shots on the North River. At five o'clock they were quite near us. It was signaling between ships, but they signified nothing good. At first we thought the enemy was marching against us and therefore made preparations to meet them. During the afternoon, however, we received the sad news which made us especially downcast. During the night the rebels had attacked and captured the newly-established Fort Stony Point. We received orders to be ready to march.

"17 July - We hear so many falsehoods and rumors that it is discouraging me from making better entries here.

"18 July - ... Today we learned more about the surprise at Stony Point. The enemy planned to attack only the pickets and, because they heard that the pickets were always in a poor state of readiness, this happened and was successfully executed, without a shot being fired. The enemy took advantage of this opportunity and continued on, taking the fort without the least resistance and without loss. Colonel [Henry] Johnson was the commandant; the 17th Regiment, two companies of grenadiers, and 100 men of Robertson's Regiment made up the garrison. Of this number, thirty were killed with bayonets, fifty wounded, and 250 taken prisoner. The others fled into the coun-tryside. In their defense, the English say that the rebels made the attack from the water. Be that as it may, they were not alert. Today our four regiments went aboard ship in order to relieve the fort at Verplanck's Point and to recapture the other. Our march was for the same purpose, or at least to threaten the enemy.

"19 July - After the enemy had heavily cannonaded and bombarded our Fort Lafayette, they saw our troops arriving aboard ship. They were at once discouraged and called up a row galley. Forty cannons from the fort and four mortars, as well as their own cannons, were directed against us. As they say, Fort Lafayette was not such an easy conquest. The commander of the fort fired upon them in such a frightful manner and sank the rebel ship with all its cannons. The rebels abandoned the position. Our troops took possession [of the sunken ship] without any resistance and recovered the cannons from the water because the water is not deep there. The ship's masts are fully visible.

"N.B. - On 17 July General Tryon returned from his expedition, and this afternoon Lieutenant Bickel also returned. They had burned many stores in New Haven. Norwalk suffered the same fate, but the English took very few prisoners. They killed everyone. Many will call this terrible, but anyone who knows the rules and customs of war will say with me, this is the way to end the war.....

"26 July - ... Today one officer and fourteen privates, deserters from Colonel Armand's Corps, arrived. They were all Germans and part of them had been brought to Boston in ships and part had been captured with Burgoyne.....

"30 July - At three o'clock in the morning 150 Infantry and our Cavalry made a patrol as far as Tarrytown. Our Cavalry clashed with sixty dragoons who had already skirmished with Emmerich, from whom they had made six captives. Our Jaegers joined in, however, and recaptured the prisoners and one rebel, who due to misunderstanding, was severely wounded. Four rebels were killed on the spot. We lost one horse.....

"24 August - ... On the nineteenth of this month the rebels had attacked Paulus Hook. After many of the garrison had been withdrawn, the rebels approached during the night. They captured a redoubt and spiked a cannon but did not have time to accomplish anything more, because the fire from a small redoubt, in which there were Hessians, was so heavy against them. They did capture forty men, however, and lost one captain and six privates. One unfavorable incident after the other. It seems that our situation is not the best.....

30 August - I received good news in letters from Germany, but they also greatly embarrassed me. First, I received my promotion to captain and with it the question, did I wish to be recalled [to Germany]. Second, however, because of sickness and fear I could not ask so much, although I very much wished to do so.

"2 September - The rebel reports tell us much about [John] Butler, the commander of the Indians. They scalp and cause the rebels great fear, but it is believed, as a large corps has marched against them, that they will be brought under control.....

"29 September - At seven o'clock in the morning Captain von Wangenheim, Lieutenant [Wilhelm Friedrich Ernst] von Reitzenstein, and 100 men went on a command beyond Fort Knyphausen on the North River because the enemy was expected to land there. This would place the general, who is at Monizeb's house, in great danger. The Bose Regiment which was there had to move to York because it was too weak for duty. Everyone was sick and half of our army lay in the hospital."

The Hesse-Cassel Jaeger Corps Journal also noted events in the northern part of America in 1779, including Clinton's move up the North River. "1 May - The 42nd Regiment, the [Hessian] Prince Charles Regiment, [Francis] Lord Rawdon's Corps, and the Grenadier Company of the Guards were embarked under General Mathew to destroy enemy magazines and ships along the coast of Virginia and primarily in Chesapeake Bay.....

"30 May - At one o'clock this afternoon Brigadier General Mathew returned from Virginia with his detachment, and lay at anchor near Philipse's house. He left Portsmouth six days ago, having captured and burned many ships, and seized a large amount of booty.

"The following troops were ordered to embark at once near Philipse's house: The English and Hessian Grenadiers, the Legionaires - dismounted, Robinson's Corps, Light Infantry, 17th, 63rd, and 64th Regiments, and 300 jaegers under Major Prueschenck. The embarkation was completed about ten o'clock.

"31 May - At two o'clock this morning the troops aboard ship moved up the North River and at eleven o'clock anchored at Fertride Hook - also known as Tallerspoint [Tellar's Point]. One hundred jaegers, the 17th, 63rd, and 64th Regiments, as well as Robinson's Corps, at once debarked on the west bank at Stono Point, where a detachment of the enemy had begun, but not yet completed, some defensive work, which they left immediately. Major General [James] Pattison, who commanded this detachment, occupied these works and set up a battery at once, while Major General Vaughan landed the rest of the troops on the east bank at Verplanck's Point, where the enemy had built Fort Lafayette, and occupied it with a detachment. This was blockaded by General Vaughan. Major General Erskine, who commanded the rest of the army at Philipse's house, marched out toward ten o'clock in the morning to the heights at Dobb's Ferry, where he took post with the right wing protected by the heights of the Sawmill, and the left on the North River.

"1 June - Major General Pattison opened fire on Fort Lafayette from Stony Point at daybreak this morning with a battery containing one 12-pounder and a howitzer, with such good effect that the enemy captain commanding therein, plus four subalterns and seventy men, surrendered about ten o'clock. The fort was a regular rectangle with double palisade sides and a moat.

"General Erskine sent out a patrol to the other side of White Plains today to reconnoiter the enemy, and to observe the movements of General Gates who was at Providence, but Erskine was unable to obtain definite information nor to learn anything about the enemy.

"3 June - On reports, that the enemy had assembled a number of cattle on the Croton River in order to provision his army and to prevent our seizing them, General Erskine marched out at eleven o'clock with the Cavalry, Jaegers, Rangers, the 23rd Regiment, and 200 men of the Bose Regiment, leaving all baggage behind, to Sing Sing, where the 23rd Regiment and a detachment of the Bose Regiment were posted on the road to White Plains. The remaining troops marched off on the North Castle Road. The Cavalry and the Rangers seized the cattle and eighteen men watching them, and drove the cattle back to the camp at Dobb's Ferry for use by the royal hospital. The Jaegers served as a rear guard on the return march, which took place at night, but they were not followed.....

"5 June - The 42nd Regiment, Prince Charles Regiment, and Lord Rawdon's Corps returned from Stony Point today, and went into the army's former camp at Philipse's house. The corps of Major General Erskine also marched there from Dobb's Ferry.....

Enemy Views (1779)

"18 June - General Washington is encamped at Smith's Gloves, and reportedly has only a very weak army. General Gates is still in Providence with the New Englanders as a covering force for the borders of New England.....

"27 June - The construction at Stony Point and Verplanck's Point is completed and now consists of the following: Stony Point: Lieutenant Colonel Johnston [Johnson], forty cannons and 100 artillerymen, 17th and 33rd Regiment, and Ferguson's Corps. Verplanck's Point: Lieutenant Colonel [James] Webster, twenty cannons and forty artillerymen, 63rd Regiment, Robinson's Corps, and two companies of grenadiers.

"The positions cover King's Ferry, the main road from Boston and all of New England to Philadelphia and the southern provinces, which greatly handicaps the enemy. The rest of the troops embarked today in order to rejoin the army at Philipse's house.....

"3 July - During the preceding night the 7th and 23rd Regiments, as well as forty jaegers -- under Lieutenant [Alexander] Bickell -- went to Frog's Neck to unite there with the 54th Regiment, Landgraf Regiment, and Fanning's Corps, which arrived yesterday from Rhode Island, and are to undertake an expedition under Major General Tryon against the New England coast.....

"8 July - News reports are to the effect that the enemy Major General Sullivan with his subordinate brigadiers, [George] Clinton, Maxwell, [Enoch] Poor, [Edward] Hand, and [James] Potter, arrived at Wyoming on the Susquehanna on 23 June in order to drive off the Indian partisans, Butler and [Joseph] Brant.....

"14 July - Major General Tryon with the detachment under his command, which sailed from Frog's Neck on 4 July, issued a proclamation to the inhabitants of New England, to lay down their arms, and promised to protect them, if they would remain peacefully in their homes. Thereafter, on 5 July, he landed at New Haven in order to determine the attitude of the inhabitants. However, he found they had abandoned the city, and the militia had occupied a defensive position called Black Rock. He did not wish to attack this position, but drove part of the enemy out of the city, where they had taken a post, burned all the public buildings and magazines, and returned to his ships the next morning. On the sixth he sailed to Fanfield [Fairfield ?], burned the city, as the inhabitants had all taken up arms, embarked and sailed to Huntington Bay. He sailed from there on the eleventh, to Norwalk, laid that place in ashes also, and then returned to Whitestone on the twelfth. The forty jaegers, who were engaged with the militia most of the time, lost two killed, four wounded, and three made prisoners.

"16 July - During the past night, about two o'clock, we heard a short cannonade at Stony Point, which we believed meant an outpost there was being attacked. In that we were not mistaken, and heard to our amazement the next day, that the enemy had attacked and captured Stony Point.....

"1 August - An English captain from a transport ship, who with 38 sailors had deserted from prisoner of war status, arrived in New York in a sloop from Boston, and brought the news that the Bostonians had outfitted a fleet in order to go to Penobscot to capture the English post which had recently been established under Brigadier General [Francis] McLean, at that place, for the purpose of protecting the woodsmen cutting timbers for building ships. Therefore Commodore George Collier sailed with the *Raisonable* and the frigates *Greyhound, Blonde, Virginia, Galathea, Camilla,* and the sloop *Otter,* to disrupt the enemy's plan.....

"19 August - During the past night the enemy Major Lee, with 400 men, stormed Paulus Hook. He passed the moat in front of the abatis, the abatis itself, and entered the position before the Englanders were aware, and captured them. A Hessian non-commissioned officer and fifteen men, who had the picket in a blockhouse, ran out in order to see what was happening. He and ten men were captured. Captain [Henrich Sebastian von] Schallern however, with one officer and 25 men, threw themselves into a small redoubt, and began firing at the enemy. Although called upon to surrender, he held his post. The enemy, therefore, retreated with his prisoners -- 100 men -- after having set fire to several barracks.....

"2 September - By the July packet, which left Falmouth on 7 July, we learned that England had found it necessary to declare war against Spain, and this happened today in New York when Governor Tryon conducted the usual formalities.....

"9 September - Sir George Collier's expedition against the New England fleet has had rather good consequences. Sir George sailed on 2 August with his squadron from Sandy Hook, and reached the Penobscot River early on the fourteenth. The enemy squadron had already been blockading Brigadier General McLean for three weeks, and the last thing they expected to see was the English fleet. Initially it appeared as if they would defend themselves. Instead, however, they sailed up the river after taking on board the soldiers who had been conducting the blockade on land. On the approach of the English ships, they set fire to their ships, and the troops retreated into the woods. The sloops *Hunter*, of 18 guns, and the *Hampton*, of 20 guns, fell into English hands before they could be set on fire. The remaining ships which burned were fourteen ships armed with 32 to 16 cannons, as well as 24 transport ships, so that not a single ship escaped. Sir George had the good fortune to capture the brigs *Nancy*, of 16 cannons, and *Rover*, of 10 cannons, at sea, while they were cruising before their fleet, and therefore enabled the complete surprise of the squadron. The enemy had to make their return journey to Boston through the forest, which for the most part, is uninhabited and a wilderness."

The Journal briefly notes the misfortune suffered by units attempting to sail to Canada, and other activities in the New York area during the remainder of the year. "8 September - The 40th Regiment and Lossberg and Knyphausen Regiments embarked in order to sail to Canada.....

"4 October - Of the troops, which on 8 September had sailed to Canada, a single ship returned, with the sad news that they had been scattered by a storm and some of them had been destroyed, which no one knows for certain. Further reports indicate that the sunken ship had part of the Lossberg Regiment on board, and another, on which were Major von Stein, with part of the Knyphausen Regiment, was captured after having lost its mast and become a complete wreck, and that the troops had been saved.....

"17 September - Lord Cornwallis was embarked with the 7th, 23rd, 33rd, and 57th Regiments, Queen's Rangers, and the Irish Volunteers to go to Jamaica.....

"24 September - Lord Cornwallis went to sea today.

"28 September - A Spanish ship was captured by an English privateer, and in the log book it was found that the French fleet had been seen on 31 August on the Grand Bank, on a westerly course. This was the reason Lord Cornwallis had been called back, and preparations made for the defense of New York, because Jamaica was therefore out of danger, and apparently New York must be the destination of the fleet. Lord Cornwallis returned therefore on

"29 September - to Sandy Hook, whereupon the troops debarked and were placed for the protection of The Narrows and the landing places at Denyse's house.....

"26 October - The troops from Rhode Island arrived at New York and no troops are now stationed there.

"7 November - The army moved into designated winter quarters on York, Long, and Staten Island.....

"19 November - General Washington has quartered his army at Morristown.

"19 December - General Clinton now saw himself in a condition to continue the operations in the southern provinces, and to this end, the following troops were embarked today: the English Grenadiers, Light Infantry, 7th, 23rd, 33rd, 42nd, 63rd, and 64th Regiments, 250 jaegers under Major [Philipp] von Wurmb, the Hessian Grenadier Regiment Huyn, a detachment of chasseurs, one battalion of the 71st Regiment, Ferguson's Corps, the Legion, and the New York Volunteers.

"24 December - The above troops sailed to Sandy Hook in eighty ships under the cover of five ships-of-the-line and five frigates. Lieutenant General von Knyphausen now commands in New York."

The Mirbach Regimental Order Book also contains a number of orders indicating activities of the English and Hessian forces in America, including a general pardon issued on 31 March 1779 to all deserters returning to their units; 16 September 1779 orders for the embarkation of the Cornwallis command noted above; and the order for the formation of a corps of chasseurs issued at New York on 8 December 1779, the latter which reads as follows; "From the following listed regiments, a detachment of chasseurs is to be taken, consisting of three officers, eleven non-commissioned officers, two drummers, and 100 men. From 1) the Leib Regiment - one non-commissioned officer and nine privates, 2) the Landgraf Regiment - the same, 3) the Hereditary Prince Regiment - one officer, one non-commissioned officer, one drummer, and ten privates, 4) the Prince Charles Regi-ment - one officer, one non-commissioned officer, and ten privates, 5) the von Ditfurth Regiment - one non-commissioned officer and ten pri-vates, 6) the von Donop Regiment - one non-commissioned officer and eight privates, 7) the von Lossberg Regiment - one non-com-missioned officer and six privates, 8) the von Mirbach Regiment - one non-commissioned officer and eight privates, 9) the von Bose Regi-ment - one non-commissioned officer and nine privates, 10) the von Huyn Regiment - one officer, one non-commissioned officer, one drummer, and eleven privates, and 11) the von Buenau Regiment - one non-commissioned officer and eleven privates. Total - three officers, eleven non-commissioned officers, two drummers, and 100 privates.

"Second Lieutenant [Ernst Wilhelm] von Anderson of the Here-ditary Prince Regiment, whose date of rank is 26 February 1776 and who served previously with the chasseurs, is ordered to do so again. The other two officers, second lieutenants, one each from the Prince Charles and the von Huyn Regiments, have more recent dates of rank. For the soldiers dependable and robust men from Hesse are to be chosen and no foreigners, and as many as possible are to be taken who served in the chasseur corps previously. They are to remain with their regiments for the present but must be ready to assemble at the Common Place in New York on the shortest notice. If part of the Huyn Regiment is to be embarked, those chosen for this assignment are to be sent here. The von Ditfurth Regiment is to send its men here immediately, as should the von Lossberg Regiment."

Other significant comments on garrison life include the following entries. "11 December - All invalids and widows are to embark for Europe next Monday morning at ten o'clock in the following order:

"The 26th Regiment at Whitehall.

"British invalids at the Hay Wharf.

"Hessian and Ansbach invalids at the Wood Wharf.

"The women for England.

"The women going to Ireland at Roomingstep.....

"22 December - The general-in-chief is greatly displeased to learn that the captains of transport ships have been so poorly treated by the officers of the army. The general-in-chief hopes that this disgraceful conduct will be made known in published orders in order to prevent such practice in the future."

## Disaster at Sea

Piel noted Major Lee's attack on Paulus Hook and then recorded a detailed account of the unfortunate effort to send the Lossberg and Knyphausen Regiments to Canada - certainly one of the most frightful disasters of the war. "19 August 1779 - Paulus Hook, a fortified peninsula in Jersey, the city opposite New York, was occupied by our side with about 200 men of the loyalist provincial troops. The largest part of that command, under Lieutenant Colonel [Abraham Van] Buskirk marched inland in order to drive off a detachment of rebels. To replace this absent force of the garrison, Captain von Schallern of the Hereditary Prince Regiment and Ensign Kress of the Lossberg Regiment, with forty men of the Hachenberg Brigade, were shipped over to Paulus Hook yesterday evening. The rebels, who had news of the departure of Lieutenant Colonel Buskirk, attacked Paulus Hook this morning before daylight, immediately took two blockhouses, one of which was occupied by provincials and the other by a non-commissioned officer from the Hereditary Prince Regiment and fifteen men. The rebels went farther and took the main fortification with six metal cannons, in which a provincial non-commissioned officer commanded. Thereupon, the commandant, Major [William] Sutherland, threw himself with Captain von Schallern, Ensign Kress, and 25 Hessians into a small fortification. The rebels called upon them to surrender, but these few Hessians defended themselves so well that the rebels retreated and the position which was already in their hands, was vacated without the least damage or loss of equipment....

"8 September 1779 - Today the Lossberg and Knyphausen Regiments, under the command of Colonel von Loos, were embarked on the following transport ships: Lossberg - *King George, Adamant,* and *Badger;* Knyphausen - *Archer, Triton,* and *Molly.*

"These ships raised anchor this afternoon at three o'clock, sailed out of the harbor, and after half an hour, again lay at anchor between York and Staten Island. The Lossberg Regiment was assigned on the ships as follows: On *King George* - The entire company of the colonel and the largest part of the Lieutenant Colonel's Company, as well as the artillery detachment for the regiment. The officers on this ship were: Colonel von Loos, Captain [Friedrich Wilhelm] Krafft, Lieutenants Schwabe and Piel, Ensigns Graebe and Kress, and Regimental Quartermaster [Christian Leonhard] Heusser.

"On *Adamant* - The entire companies of the Leib Company and Major [Caspar Friedrich] von Hanstein, Captains Steding and [Constantin] von Wurmb, Lieutenant [Wilhelm Christian] Moeller, and Ensigns [Henrich Carl Friedrich] Zengen, [Johann Henrich] Rathmann, and Waldeck.

"On *Badger* - The entire company von Alten-Bockum, Lieutenant Zoll, and Ensigns [Friedrich Christoph] Henndorff, [Christian] von Wald-schmidt, and [Johann Ludwig von] Koven, and Regimental Surgeon [Friedrich Wilhelm] Oliva.

"N.B. - The diary for this sea voyage was kept on board *King George*.

"9 September - This morning at ten o'clock we went under sail and anchored again at two o'clock in the afternoon near Sandy Hook. At five o'clock the agent with the ships which had the English 44th Regiment on board joined us, whereupon the fleet, escorted by the warship *Renown*, of 50 guns, went under sail. Because the ships had not all assembled yet, and the commodore or the agent had not yet given the transport ships their orders, at eight o'clock this evening we again lay at anchor within sight of the lighthouse at Sandy Hook, although the wind was very favorable for us.

"10 September - This morning we missed four ships, among which were *Archer* and *Triton*, on the first of which was Colonel von Borck and on the latter Lieutenant Colonel Heymel of the Knyphausen Regiment. These ships were not aware yesterday evening that the fleet had dropped anchor, and therefore had sailed away. Today we remained lying at anchor. This afternoon all ship's captains were called to the agent through a signal and received orders concerning the order in which the fleet would sail, and that Quebec was their destination....

"11 September - This morning the missing ships were again present, except for the *Archer*, which was still missing. Meanwhile, at eight o'clock, the commodore gave the signal to raise anchor, and by nine o'clock the fleet was under sail. The weather was beautiful, the wind blew strongly from the southwest, the waves were rather high, and most of our people got seasick. At two o'clock in the afternoon we lost sight of land.

"12 September - A bright sky, wind from the southwest. The *Archer* still has not been seen. In the afternoon, calm. This morning we saw innumerable porpoise and if it is true that these indicate a storm nearby, then they have never more accurately prophesied than this time. Toward six o'clock a strong wind suddenly arose from the northeast. The storm grew steadily rougher. During the night, at ten o'clock, the *King George* was gone from the fleet. Therefore, we fired a cannon to see if the commodore would answer, but we heard nothing.

"13 September - Overcast and the same stormy wind. This morning we saw the fleet in the distance behind us. Toward evening we had sailed too far ahead. Thereupon our ship's captain lowered some sail and placed our ship behind that of the commodore.

"14 September - Yesterday's weather except that the storm was stronger and the sea more restless. The fleet was widely scattered but throughout the entire day we had most of them in sight.

"15 September - Today the storm was the strongest, so that even the ship's captain admitted he had never experienced such a strong, or long-lasting storm. It was as if one hurricane followed another. All sails ripped to pieces like paper and fluttered about the masts like rags. We tied the helm securely and the waves ran over us. At noon we met the ship *Molly*. It had lost its aftermast and a part of its mainmast. We believed now the storm was at its height, but from hour to hour it grew more frightening. The sky and water appeared as one and it was no longer possible to determine if it rained from the clouds or the ocean. The waves continuously rolled over the ship with a dreadful sound, breaking the cabin windows in pieces so that it was necessary to make everything water-tight, using solid materials, and to use a light to see during the day. We kept pumps going constantly to which we assigned soldiers because the sailors had their hands full. No one aboard ship could remain the least bit dry. All beds in the cabin were soaking wet. The chicken houses on deck were broken to pieces by the waves and all our poultry killed. We had to give our ship's captain, Kelly, credit that due to his attentiveness and devotion to duty, the ship came through the storm with a minimum of damage, and without losing its masts.

"16 September - The previous night was one of the most frightful that can be imagined. The storms and waves raged against the ship so that we expected to go under at any moment. This morning the storm and waves eased somewhat in their strength. The sun broke through the clouds and once again we could go on deck. We had again raised a sail. Nothing of the fleet was to be seen except a ship close behind us which had raised a distress flag. It still had all its masts but suddenly, as we watched, it lost the upper part of the middlemast. The sea was too high and the wind still too strong to permit us sailing near the other ship, and therefore, we gradually lost it from sight. There were many dolphins to be seen about our ship.

"17 September - A clear sky and northerly wind. The sea was again rather calm and we sailed at random throughout the morning because all the ship's crew were busy repairing the damage which the storm had done to the rigging. We glimpsed a ship in the distance ahead of us, which we assumed to be an enemy because it appeared to flee. We also discovered another ship off to our right which had lost its aftermast and a part of the mainmast. At noon according to the quadrant readings we were at $27^0$ [37 ?] north latitude. Therefore we had been driven three degrees south of New York. Toward evening the ship's captain, from the crow's nest, discovered a large ship which had lost its mainmast, and near that another ship, which had lost all its masts.

"18 September - Beautiful weather, but contrary northerly winds. At eight o'clock we discovered a large ship in the distance which had lost its mainmast and another which had no masts at all. The closer we came to these ships, the more clearly we saw that the first was the *Renown* and the other the agent ship *Springfield*. Shortly thereafter we noticed a third ship which also appeared to have no masts. Toward twelve o'clock the commodore raised his flag and fired a cannon from which we could see the smoke, but could not hear the sound. Thereupon we immediately raised our flag. We were at $36^0$ 13' [north latitude] at noon. Toward evening the wind steadily slackened.

"19 September - Weak easterly wind and pleasant weather. We noticed again the ships we had seen yesterday, but now they were much farther away. Therefore we raised more sail in order to overtake them. At noon we were at $36^0$ 06'. The wind swung to the northeast. All our maneuvering of yesterday and today was made in a vain attempt to approach the commodore, until finally, shortly before sunset this evening, when we were able to catch up to him. We raised our flag at the peak of our forward mast as a sign that we wished to speak to the commodore. Therefore he sent an officer in a boat, who brought our captain a written order that in case we became separated from the commodore, we were to sail directly to Halifax in Nova Scotia. From this officer we learned that the ship which the commodore had beside him was a rebel ship coming from the West Indies loaded with rum and sugar, and that it was armed with twelve cannons. It had lost its masts in the last storm. The *Renown* had chased this ship since yesterday and only overtaken and captured it this afternoon. The captain of this rebel ship had stated that since the storm, he had seen four ships without masts, which apparently belonged to our fleet.

"20 September - Variable wind, first from the east and then from the west. The ship *Springfield* joined us. It was in a pitiful condition having not only lost all three masts and the bowsprit, but also its three boats. The commodore sent a naval officer to us and informed Colonel von Loos that, after serious consideration, he considered it best to turn back to New York, where obviously all the other ships which had become separated from us, and had suffered damage from the storm, would consider it necessary to enter.

"25 September - A favorable southwesterly wind and very pleasant weather. Because the *Springfield* was unable to keep up, the commodore took it in tow. At noon we were at 37⁰ 46'. During the afternoon the commodore sent an officer to our ship's captain and requested that he take the captured rebel ship in tow because it greatly hampered our speed. About eight o'clock in the evening this ship came near us. We threw it a line which was fastened to our aftermast. It was bright moonlight and the most pleasant evening which we had experienced during our entire voyage.....

"28 September - ... At daybreak this morning, in the distance to our left, we saw a two-masted ship.... The strange ship remained with us, so that our fleet now consisted of five ships....

"29 September - ... An officer from the *Renown* visited us today. We learned from him that the ship which had joined us yesterday was a rebel ship coming from the West Indies, which had been captured by the English privateer *Tartar*. At the time when we had the violent storm, it had been ninety miles away and had felt nothing of the storm....

"30 September - ... Shortly before sunset the captain, from atop the mast, saw two ships to the north, which steered directly at us. He believed them to be enemy privateers....

"1 October - ... At daybreak we saw three small ships behind us and shortly thereafter, three more off to our right. At nine o'clock we saw Sandy Hook and at the same time a frigate and her tender, which appeared to be cruising at this area. As soon as these ships which were behind us saw the frigate steering toward them, they turned and were soon lost from sight....

"Here [at Sandy Hook] we learned that the *Archer*, the day after our departure, had again returned to the harbor here and several days later was sent after the fleet under convoy of the frigate *Camilla*. Furthermore, the two transport ships *Favourite* and *Crawford*, from our fleet, which had the 44th Regiment on board, had already entered the harbor at New York.

"3 October - Today at last, the ship *King George* came from Sandy Hook to New York. The troops were landed and entered camp near Greenwich, a mile from New York.

"12 October - Today we changed camp and set it up near the city. This evening the *Badger*, with Captain von Alten-Bockum's and the rest of the Lieutenant Colonel's Company arrived at the harbor here. Their ship was in a terrible condition. It had lost the middle and aftermasts and during the storm had collided with another ship -- *Clementine* -- which had severely damaged it. After the storm it was followed for two days by an enemy privateer and fired upon with cannons, but because Captain von Alten-Bockum would not surrender, the privateer had sailed away. On the ninth of the month it was attacked by another privateer with twelve cannons and because *Badger* had no cannons at all, it was necessary to surrender. The privateer took the ship's officers, as well as twenty privates, on board. However, because Captain von Alten-Bockum was sick, he was left on the *Badger*, with the regimental surgeon. The soldiers' weapons were taken on board the privateer. The English frigate *Solebay* rescued *Badger* from the hands of the rebels and fortunately, today brought it into the harbor at New York.

"13 October - Today the troops were landed from the *Badger* and joined us in camp. Concerning the ships *Molly* and *Triton*, we hear that the first was taken into Philadelphia and the latter into Egg

Harbor, by the rebels. The ships *Adamant* and *Empress*, in all probability, have sunk. The ship *Clementine* was in a sinking condition when, fortunately, two English privateers arrived, took the troops off, and brought them to New York.

"14 November - N.B. - when in the future the Lossberg Regiment is discussed, it will be understood that it consists of the companies of Colonel von Loos, Lieutenant Colonel Scheffer, and Captain von Alten-Bockum."

The Platte Grenadier Battalion Journal also noted the disastrous undertaking. "28 September - Two companies of the 44th Regiment were landed on the island [Staten Island]. This regiment embarked fourteen days ago with the Old Lossberg and Knyphausen Regiments and went to sea during the equinox [23 September] in order to go to Canada. A transport ship, on which were troops of this regiment, sank. A ship on which Colonel von Loos sailed, returned to port without a mast. During this time the ship commanded by Captain [Ernst Eberhard von] Alten-Bockum was captured by a privateer but retaken by the English warship *Solebay* and has now returned. A transport ship commanded by Major [Ludwig August] von Hanstein is still missing. Two transport ships of the Knyphausen Regiment were captured by the rebels and one of those taken to Philadelphia and the other to Little Egg Harbor, according to news brought to us by people from New Jersey. The third transport ship for that regiment is still missing at this time. It was the worst time of year for their departure, as the inevitable storms always appear at this season."

The ship taken into Little Egg Harbor was the *Triton* on which Lieutenant Wiederhold kept an account of the ill-fated expedition and provided the following description of the ship on 8 September. "The embarkation of the regiment began at eight o'clock in the morning and by noon everyone was aboard ship, as it was said that the anchor would be raised the same day. The ship *Triton* has two masts, what the English call a brig or brigantine. It has six cannons, namely four 6- and two 4-pounders, as well as two swivels, very small cannons which fire a half pound of iron, mounted on an iron fork which can be placed wherever one wishes. However, the ship was not in the best of repair for making a long sea voyage. No bedsteads were taken on board for the officers who therefore had to lie on the deck the entire time. For the soldiers there were only fifteen, and so poorly made that after a few days they collapsed. One-third of the men had to be on deck day and night. No toilet facilities were provided. Therefore the troops were in fear of falling in the sea and drowning whenever nature called, and neither broom nor any other instrument was available which is used for cleaning. There was not a drop of vinegar nor anything which a European considers necessary for a sea voyage, in order to maintain health. What was worse however, was that the ship was poorly provided with crew members, as we found only seven in number, namely the ship's captain, mate, steward, cook, the last two of which had enough to do with their regular duties and were unable to do much else on the ship, and three others, of whom two were boys, although the compliment called for eighteen.....

"10 September (Friday) - At daybreak however, we found ourselves completely separated from the fleet.... Lieutenant Colonel Heymel ordered the men to dress and take up their weapons. Meanwhile I inspected the cannons and found them full of dirt and filth and the rammer even stuck in the middle of the barrel. With much effort I pulled it out, cleaned and singed them out, and loaded them all with all sorts of scrap materials and such from the ship as grape shot."

A storm struck which by the fifteenth left the ship as a floating derelict without masts and in danger of sinking, Even the cannons broke loose and were "rolling about for a time on the deck, beating against the iron kitchen standing on the deck with its large kettle in which a meal could be cooked for all the men at one time. Then all four cannons rolled overboard into the sea, taking most of the ship's railings with them. The fifth cannon passed, due to the back and forth movement of the ship, through the so-called hatchway,...opening it and made a passageway directly downward in a perpendicular path, through the soldiers to the bilges of the ship, without disturbing or injuring a single soldier....

"The sixth cannon however, was directly above on the cabin, continued its back and forth marching, violently beating against the sides of the ship during every change in direction so that it would have eventually broken, as it had already broken the wheel which turned the rudder....

"Four of the sailors could or would not do any more work and had lain down in bed. No one else would go near the cannon for fear of losing an arm or a leg. All of our men lay still and waited, part sighing and weeping, part with prayers, and others from fear, as if in shock, awaited the last minute of life.... I explained to them that they knew that I had been sick with a fever for four weeks and had come aboard ship sick. Nevertheless, because of my love for them and the survival of all of us, I had made myself come forward to try to get some help, which was necessary for our survival as no one was willing to save us, but all declined.... So that I said to them, 'I will stay with you on deck, take hold with my own hands, and share the same fate with you, as I am hopeful that we wish to save the ship and ourselves.' Still no one came forward until I said, ' Is there no non-commissioned officer who is healthy, ambitious, and with a Hessian heart, who will follow me and help me?'... Finally, we succeeded but Fusileer Radna broke his right arm in two places and I suffered a smashed little finger on my left hand. Next, I led them to the pumps.... This continued until about three or four o'clock in the morning when the pump broke ... Therefore a tub was fastened on a line, lowered, filled with water, pulled up, and emptied....

While this was taking place, Wiederhold noticed the ship's captain making plans to abandon the Germans and prevented this, but *Triton* was finally captured by two American privateers and taken into Little Egg Harbor. Wiederhold who had been made a prisoner of war at Trenton on 26 December 1776, was once again a prisoner.

Feilitzsch reported the disaster in his diary also, commencing on 17 October 1779. He then summarized the English position at the end of 1779. "The 44th Regiment and the Knyphausen and Lossberg Regiments, which left here six weeks ago, encountered the most terrible storm ever. Two ships of their fleet fell into rebel hands, some returned here, and several are still missing, which either sank or are also in rebel hands. We have never had a period of such a time as this. God watch over the English at sea. This will place us in an even worse situation.....

"27 October - I went on picket duty. Everything was quiet, but the enemy approached and assembled at White Plains. The reason could be that the English have left Verplanck's Point and Stony Point and the rebels have free passage to act. These forts, which were of such importance to us, were abandoned without a fight. The garrison from Rhode Island has arrived at New York, leaving that island, also. We have conquered nothing but lost a lot this year. Our winter quarters are to be behind Fort Knyphausen. Conditions are improving for us but the news is worse every day.

## Lieutenant Feilitzsch's Return to Europe

Feilitzsch then goes on to describe his recall to Europe and the departure for Europe of the invalids and those no longer involved with the fighting. "30 October - I went to New York to visit our regimental headquarters. I was very satisfied because our colonel was determined that I was to return to Europe, having received my recall....

"7 November - At twelve o'clock today the corps received orders to march. I did not accompany it however, but left the company at ten o'clock and said goodbye to all of my duties. I moved to New York until the fleet for Europe is ready to sail. God grant that it sails soon. How happy I am not to be forced to spend this year in the beautiful winter quarters where the Jaegers will be. They are building huts for the winter, near Morris house, two miles beyond Fort Knyphausen.

"18 November - By means of an express ship from St. Augustine, the report has arrived that Admiral [Marriot] Arbuthnot has announced the following reliable news. The French with 4,000 men and the rebels with 7,000 men stormed Savannah on 9 October. They were defeated with a loss of 3,000 men. The French have gone back on board their ships, and the latter have retreated to the Carolinas. They quarreled after the attack and it almost came to a battle. As for myself, I am still here awaiting orders to embark. God, who has brought me this far and seen me safely through three campaigns, will surely see me across the sea in good time and safely back to my fatherland. From what I hear, the Jaegers are still forced to lie out under the open skies despite the very cold weather. They must carry all the wood needed to build their huts, on their backs, for three miles.

"1 December - My stay here is becoming a very long one, but I must admit that if I must go to sea, I do not look forward to it....

"2 December - ... The orders which arrived today were to embark [to return to Germany] on the sixth.

"5 December - There was a terrible snow storm all day and it turned very cold. I received a countermanding order concerning my embarkation. On the other hand an order was issued for 12,000 men to be ready to embark. Possibly we will sail part way with them.

Enemy Views (1779)

"8 December - I rode out to visit the Jaegers and my good friends and to take my departure from +++ - foolishness. It was quiet grievous to me. It is still very cold.

"11 December - The order came to go on board on the thirteenth. Today a ship arrived from the West Indies from which we heard that it knew nothing of the French fleet. A ship also arrived from Savannah which confirmed the victory over the French and rebels. The first lost 67 officers and 700 men, some say 1,000, and the latter 50 officers and 500 men.

"13 December - At ten o'clock in the morning we were ordered to embark. We waited on the Wood Wharf until eleven o'clock when a thick fog and rain forced a cancellation of the orders. It was so dark I could hardly find the city.

"15 December - We went aboard ship at ten o'clock in the morning. I went with the last boat and, because the wind was against us, had to travel until one o'clock. Our ship is the *Charming Nancy*. In my entire life I have never been so cold as at this time. We brought a half-dead jaeger aboard ship with us. My transport consisted of Lieutenant [Adolf Daniel] von Strahldendorf, Regimental Surgeon [Andreas Friedrich] Pflug, and 45 men, invalids and those recalled. Our ship is well-equipped. God be with us to England.

"16 December - It was reported early that the badly frozen Jaeger [Johann Adam] Liebermann died this morning at four o'clock. We still lay at anchor. There had been a heavy snow so that it was no longer so cold. Toward evening our dead companion, as usual, was sewn in blankets filled with stones and thrown overboard.

"17 December - During the morning the Medic Berger died and as usual, at sundown, was thrown overboard. We sailed from five to six o'clock and anchored near Staten Island.

"18, 19, and 20 December - We had an astonishing storm. We had to remain at anchor. Our ship rolled considerably and we wished to sail onward.

"21 December - At nine o'clock the anchor was raised. The wind was from the southwest and not especially good for our departure. We anchored at one o'clock near Sandy Hook. The storm was strong and our ship rolled violently. What would it be like on the ocean?

"22 December - I can not adequately describe our fleet; the appearance of 130 to 140 transport ships, including ten to twelve armed East Indiamen and a lone sloop with eighteen cannons. - Therefore our escort is weak. - The wind is very good, from the northwest, for our departure, but unfortunately we still lie at anchor. Toward evening our sailors brought four French seamen, captured on a warship, aboard and a German who had been an officer in Prussia and then for the rebels. He claimed to have deserted and come to New York. His name is Wolffen and he is treated as a prisoner by us.

"23 December - The wind was from the north, the sea was calm, and at twelve-thirty we sailed, beginning our voyage in the Lord's name. The wind increased toward evening so that we sailed six miles in an hour, and the sea remained calm. During the night we lost sight of the American coast.....

"25 December - The wind from the northeast and therefore not as good as we would wish. It is very much like a storm. Lord abide with us. Early this morning we saw a sad sight. A two-masted ship had developed a leak during the night so that the water entered very quickly. It approached our ship. A merchant on that ship bound for Madeira transferred with his baggage to our ship. The captain from that ship was already alongside our ship. The sailors complained bitterly when they had to return to their ship and turn back to New York. Heaven protect them. It will soon sink. At four o'clock the wind was from the north and it rained hard. At twelve o'clock the storm began and by four o'clock it raged terribly. Our provisions and baggage, which had been protected and securely tied, tore loose. Even the doors caved-in. No one was sure of his life in the cabin. During the night it was frightful. I would like to forget this Christmas Day.

"26 December - At three o'clock in the morning the wind which had blown so terribly, abated. However, the seas ran exceptionally high all day. Our ship was continuously thrown back and forth. The cracking noises were frightful. We still believed we were about to sink. Nothing could be cooked, and we could see only six ships from our fleet.

"27 December - We had a good wind from the northwest, but our ship was still very unsteady. We were all miserable. All my limbs ached from trying to hold on in bed. Toward evening the wind increased and during the night we had another storm. A servant who wished to make our baggage more secure fell and lay dying for half an hour."

## The Evacuation of Rhode Island

Meanwhile Asteroth recorded the withdrawal from Rhode Island and the unit's subsequent deployment to the south. "26 January 1779 - The English Light Infantry and General Bose of the Landgraf Regiment were embarked. They were ordered to return to the main army....

"9 June - The order came from General Clinton that the English 54th Regiment and Fanning's Corps, as well as the Hessian Landgraf Regiment, were to be ready to march....

"The beginning of October 1779 General Prescott provided the information that the French fleet was not far from Rhode Island and everyone expected that they would make an attack. At the same time all the regiments received orders to bring the heavy baggage to Newport. This requirement took until

"11 October - when, during the morning, an English fleet of seventy sail, which was believed to be carrying troops sent to reinforce us, arrived. However, the same day it was learned that horses and men amounting to a regiment had been designated to prepare the ships because there was an order for the entire garrison to evacuate the island.

"13 October - The baggage was loaded. The chaplain and the auditor went aboard the ship *Rising Sun* with Colonel [Lubert Franz] Kurtze; the second ship was the *Bali*; the third was the *Swan*. The regiment was on these ships. The King's troops all left Rhode Island with us. Nothing in the defenses was destroyed except for the barracks in some and the cannon foundations, some of which were burned. These changes took until

"25 October - In the morning the commander gave the signal to embark. The flat boats were all ready at the designated place on Princeton Neck, where the troops were to embark; the two Ansbach regiments first, Huyn, Ditfurth, and two English regiments being the sum total. By six o'clock in the evening everyone was embarked and we sailed at once in a fleet of 102 ships with the best wind.

"27 October - We anchored in the harbor at New York. After a quarter of an hour a ship came and dropped anchor. The anchor broke loose and was lost. It [the ship] came toward us and because our captain could do nothing to prevent it, the two ships crashed. Because we had felt ourselves to be so safe, we panicked. They remained hanging together for half an hour. Then another [ship] came from behind us and passed within a hand's width of us. Other boat crews came to our aid and helped separate the two ships. Our ship had lost two anchors and was badly damaged.....

"3 November - ... Note -- On the voyage from Rhode Island a three-masted ship was lost at the place known as Hellgate....

"The chaplain and the auditor remained with the regimental quartermaster.

"19 December - The order to march at seven o'clock came at two o'clock in the morning. The baggage could not be taken with us because the river was frozen over. Therefore an officer and twenty men, with sixteen wagons, were detached to care for it.

"20 December - At daybreak we marched seven miles. We received orders to enter cantonment quarters in Flatbush and did so. Even as we were setting up camp, the order came to move by water, but it was too late to embark and we returned to a barracks where British Grenadiers, who had come off ship that day, were quartered. It was extremely cold. Those who were sick [and being transported] in the wagons were nearly frozen to death. Many soldiers had frozen noses, hands, or ears. The next morning we continued our march on the water and were at once embarked on a ship of the fleet which numbered 100 to 200 sail. The troops named for this expedition were the following: all the British Grenadiers, Light Infantry, and three regiments; and secondly the Hessian Grenadiers and the von Huyn Regiment, a total of 10,000 men. General Clinton turned over command at New York to General von Knyphausen and went on this new expedition with us.....

"2nd Christmas Day, 26 December - We sailed with the best of winds and began our new journey. After four hours land was completely lost from view.

"28 December - The sky was dull and heavily overcast and a strong north wind arose which caused all of us to worry as to what would develop therefrom. By evening the wind was increasingly strong. The admiral signaled for the sails to be taken in and for the fleet to spread out. Our captain took in the sails at once and tied the rudder fast as the storm was upon us. The ship was given its head. It lay first to one side and then to the other; first the bow sank, then the stern; then a wave engulfed the ship. We all lay in our beds in the darkness holding on to whatever we could in order not to fall out and, as one, lamented our fate. We wished it were day as the night seemed never to end. First, someone called out that his bed was full of water; then another, 'Where can I go so that I can stand up or lie down?' Next, someone came crawling and said his bed was covered with water and he could not remain in it. Finally, the blessed daylight came. Now, I thought, I will see what my chaplain is doing in his cabin. I could hardly get there, even by crawling. I found everyone there to be sick and no one wanted coffee. It was almost impossible to keep a fire. I wished it [the storm] would soon abate in order to make preparation of the noon meal easier. I returned onto the deck and looked at the height of the waves. First the ship was in a valley and then on a high mountain. I could see no other ship due to the tumultuous seas. I did not remain long on deck, but returned to my bed in the ship. Someone had vomited, others stood by the ladder holding their hands over their mouth, not knowing how to get up on the deck, where they could vomit, quickly enough. Some picked up their shoes and vomited. One man ran about in his stockings, another was bounced about, and the third tied himself fast. This continued until

"29 December - At evening the storm abated.....

"31 December - During the evening a black cloud appeared. It soon began to lightning, but it was accompanied by the best wind, which filled all the sails. We lay down to rest with the greatest pleasure. But what a shout the mate used to wake us up, as he had the watch. He shouted, 'Captain and all my children, wake up at once or we will sink!' In a minute everyone was alert. It was a whirlwind which so strongly blew into our unfurled sails. The wind was a great force against the ship before all the sails could be taken in. It swung about at right angles. I ran up on deck to see what was happening because it seemed as if the masts and rudder would break. The most frightful aspect was that the fleet was so close together. The admiral fired sixteen cannon shots. The warships out to the sides answered with six shots. The admiral made a signal with five lanterns and most of the transport ships displayed a light at the bow of the ship so that one could see the other in the tumult, as it was very dark. This storm lasted for half an hour and the sky brightened."

As the year ended for Private Asteroth, he surely wished he were back home in Germany.

Prechtel recorded details of the Ansbach-Bayreuth regimental activities during 1779 in his diary. "8 April - Thirteen men, of Captain Stain's Company of the von Voit Regiment, cooked and ate root cicada, or schirling. Immediately after eating them, all became deathly sick. They were given milk and liquids to drink to cause vomiting, after which twelve of the men: 1) Medic Roessler, 2) Corporal [Georg] Fuerst, 3) Drummer [Georg Nikolaus] Reichart, 4) Privates [Thomas] Salamon, 5) Private [Johann Stephan] Goert, 6) Private [Georg Friedrich] Seehart, 7) Private Schneider, 8) Private [Heinrich] Scherz, 9) Private Hoepf, 10) Private [Bartholomai] Hiller, 11) Private [Christian] Wetschell, and 12) Private Bauer recovered. Private [Johann Christian] Auerheimer, who could not be made to vomit, died after three-quarters of an hour.....

"11 October - ... Fifty-four ships, escorted by three frigates, entered the local harbor. They are all empty transport ships on which the local army is to embark. Today the embarkation of the artillery was begun, during which an English artillery soldier was crushed by a howitzer.....

"15 October - The Ansbach regiments received the following transport ships for embarkation: The von Voit Regiment: 1) *Mertschery*, 2) *Shipwright*. The von Seybothen Regiment: 1) *Silver Eel*, 2) *Nestor*....

"25 October - The army at Rhode Island broke camp and retired to Brenton's Point, where the regiments were embarked in the following order: 1) The Hessian Buenau Regiment, 2) the von Voit Regiment, and 3) the von Seybothen Regiment of Ansbach, 4) the von Huyn Regiment, and 5) the von Ditfurth Regiment of Hessians, 6) the 43rd Regiment, 7) the 38th Regiment, and 8) the 22nd Regiment of Englanders, 9) the Hessian Jaegers and English Light Horse, and 10) Brown's Corps of provincial troops, which had been on Conanicut Island....

"After all the troops were on board, the fleet, consisting of 130 sail, went underway at seven o'clock in the evening. The frigate *Blonde* carried the commodore.

"We sailed the entire night with a very favorable wind and at twelve o'clock at night, the fleet had already entered the Sound at Block Island.

"26 October - We sailed all day with a good wind and at twelve o'clock at night, near Huntington, a small city lying on Long Island, we anchored.

"27 October - We sailed at seven o'clock in the morning and during the morning passed the numerous rocks in the water, the dangerous Hell's Gate, or in German, 'Hoellen Thuer'. At one o'clock in the afternoon the fleet entered the seaport of New York.

"From Newport to New York it is 175 miles and we sailed this in 36 hours.

"At Hell's Gate the transport ship, on which was General Prescott's baggage, ran onto a sandbank. The transport ship *Mertschery*, which sailed behind the ship, and had to follow the same path, raised all sails and sailed past this ship. In this manner no one was hurt and the ship was moved off the sandbank so that it could not sink, and the baggage was still saved....

"The von Seybothen Regiment was landed and entered the camp at the Farmers' Gardens at New York.

"19 November - Because of the conquest of the city of Savannah, Georgia, a *feu de joie* was fired. The regiments at the headquarters at New York, are the following: the 42nd Scottish Regiment, the two Ansbach regiments, and four Hessian grenadier battalions.

"At five o'clock in the evening these marched to the great parade ground, outside the city, on the North River. When it was completely dark, a 21-gun salute was fired from Fort George. Following this, a rotational firing [of small arms] was carried out from the right to the left wing. From the troops on command at Paulus Hook, the same type of firing was carried out. When the three volleys were finished, the regiments gave a very loud shout of hurrah. Those persons favoring the Crown, illuminated their houses. The Commanding General-in-Chief Clinton, with his entire suite, was present.....

"15 December - The invalids, who are to return to Europe, were embarked.

"Non-Commissioned Officers of the von Voit Regiment
and Invalids Returned to Europe

"1) Second Sergeant [Johann Heinrich] Wiederhold, of the Colonel's Company, 2) Quartermaster Sergeant [Johann Friedrich] Dorn, and 3) Corporal [Johann Adam] Weiss of the Lieutenant Colonel's Company, 4) First Sergeant [Johann] Raab and 5) Corporal [Leonhard] Schneider, of the Major's Company, and 6) First Sergeant [Paul] Schmid, of Captain von Stains's Company.

"First Lieutenant von Feilitzsch, of the Jaeger Corps, and Second Lieutenant von Strahlendorf, of the von Seybothen Regiment began their trip to Europe today.....

"19 December - The four Hessian grenadier battalions, the English 64th Regiment, and a detachment from the Jaeger Corps embarked.....

"21 December - The troops embarked on the nineteenth of this month sailed from here this morning for Charleston.....

"23 December - A transport ship, on which were fifty jaegers of the troops which left the harbor on the 21st of this month, and was lying at anchor at Sandy Hook, had the anchor rope broken by an ice flow. Therefore, it was driven through the entire harbor by the very strong storm and onto land near Brooklyn. This ship was stove in and taking water. The jaegers were saved and were landed at New York....

"24 December - Private Baender, of Colonel von Voit's Company, on the forward post of the Naval Stores watch, had challenged, four or five times, in English and German, a boatload of sailors that was approaching him. It was transferring baggage from the ship involved in yesterday's incident. As no one answered, he fired and killed a sailor."

Finally, Stang added a comment worth noting on 19 December. "A fleet of 59 war and transport ships departed, on which our invalids returning to Europe, also sailed."

## Clinton's Expedition Against Charleston

The Platte Grenadier Battalion Journal entries reflect the problems of seaborne movements using sail power, specifically the attempted transfer of the regiments to Canada and the movement of the force sent to the southern colonies during late 1779. "17 September - ... Today we received orders to be prepared to embark with the other Hessian Grenadier Battalions and to submit the required lists. In addition to our four grenadier battalions, 200 Hessian jaegers, two battalions of English Grenadiers, two battalions of Light Infantry, the 7th, 23rd, 33rd, 37th, 54tht, and 57th Regiments, the Queen's Rangers, Fanning's Corps, and the Volunteers of Ireland were ordered to embark.

"19 September - The order of the previous date was changed and the Hessian Grenadiers and Jaegers were not to embark.

"21 September - Six of the mentioned English regiments and the Queen's Rangers embarked today but remained lying off Staten Island. Lieutenant General Lord Cornwallis had command of these units.....

"30 September - The corps commanded by Lieutenant General Lord Cornwallis landed but was ordered to remain ready to embark again at any moment. The landing took place supposedly because Admiral Comte d'Estaing arrived in the southern provinces with a French fleet and army and made a descent upon Savannah, in Georgia. Savannah and the troops in that place are reported in great danger. General Prevost, who had advanced as far as Charleston, to which place the troops commanded by General Cornwallis had been ordered, and who had called upon the city to surrender, upon receipt of this news, pulled back to Savannah in the greatest haste. It is even reported that after capturing Savannah, the French plan to visit us here. With this in mind the old ships here are being repaired so that they can be sunk in The Narrows to prevent the French from entering should that fleet come here.

"11 October - The corps commanded by Lieutenant General Cornwallis was embarked again.

"12 October - They were again debarked because news came from the south that Savannah had actually been put under siege.....

"18 November - We were informed, in orders, that not only had the French and rebels formally placed Savannah under siege, but had actually stormed the defenses and been beaten back with severe losses. Our joy was all the greater as everyone had already given up that place, the entire province, and all the troops assigned there....

"December - At the beginning of this month the Grenadier Brigade received orders to be prepared to embark and the following assignments were made:

"Assignment of Transports
for the Brigade of Hessian Grenadiers

"Linsing [Battalion] on *Kingston* and *Polly* - Blue [Division] - to display one red ball on the fore [mast].

"Vacant [Battalion] on *Royal Briton* and *Amity's Providence* - Blue [Division] - to display two red balls on the main [mast].

"Lengercke [Battalion] on *Two Sisters* and *Munificence* - Blue [Division] - to display one red ball on the main [mast].

"Graf [Battalion] on *Caledonia, Corsica,* and *Eliza* - Blue [Division] - to display two red balls on the fore [mast].

"Generals [Heinrich Julian] von Kospoth and [Johann Christoph] von Huyn on the *Andrew*.

"Hospital [ship] *Sally* to display yellow at the foretop masthead.

"19 December - After all baggage was loaded the troops also went on board today. The Graf Grenadier Battalion embarked on the above designated ships in the following manner:

"The staff, artillery, and a part of Captain Hohenstein's Company on the *Caledonia*.

"Captain Bode's Company and a part of Captain Neumann's Company on *Eliza*.

"Captain Hessenmueller's Company and the remainder of Captain Neumann's and Captain Hohenstein's Companies on *Corsica*.

"The Grenadier Brigade was relieved at New York by the Landgraf, Donop, and Leib Regiments.

"22 December - About ten o'clock this morning the ships in the East River weighed anchor and set sail. Near Governor's Island our ship, *Caledonia*, was in danger of being run down by another, but the care and ability of our ship's captain, to our great joy, minimized this. Our nemesis suffered the loss of a stern corner from his ship and considerable rigging. At two o'clock in the afternoon we anchored near Sandy Hook, where a fleet of 108 ships lay.

"23 December - Today a fleet of more than 100 ships sailed for Europe from Sandy Hook. The Hessian invalids, commanded by Captain [Philipp Ludwig] Reichel, were in this fleet. A number of ships assigned to our fleet came from New York today and joined with us....

"Captain [Johann Adam] Bauer of the Angelelli Regiment with recruits for that regiment and the Wissenbach Regiment" also sailed with the fleet.

"We sailed out with a most favorable wind and before evening had lost sight of land.

"27 December - This was a pleasant spring day. According to our ship's captain we had already reached the Delaware Capes today, but because we are far out to sea, we could not see them. At nightfall a strong south-southeast wind arose which developed into a full blown storm by midnight.

"28 December - The storm continued and the night was sad for us. We began to receive the unpleasant effects of a winter voyage.

"29 December - Toward noon the wind let up and the storm abated. The fleet which was widely scattered was brought together again by the warships. A warship had taken the transport ship *Anna*, on which were Captain Hanger's Chasseurs, in tow and brought it back. This transport ship had lost its middle mast in the storm. The storm had driven us back a great distance.

"30 December - At noon our ship's captain took a sighting. According to his reckoning we were at $37^0$ 47' north latitude. It is obvious, however, that this observation is incorrect, considering that the last storm drove us backward.

"31 December - We had pleasant weather on a rather restless sea."

Lieutenant [Christian Friedrich von] Bartholomai not only noted the problems of the seaborne movement facing Clinton, but also recorded the other difficulties faced by Clinton in the closing days of 1779. "At the beginning I will make a suggestion as to why the expedition was not preferably made on land, or at least postponed, since I have already pointed out that the army never dared to penetrate deeply inland, [see comments in the Introduction to this volume] and with such a small corps, to undertake an 800 mile march in the dead of winter, through provinces occupied only by enemies, across great rivers, would be the height of insanity.

"Still, I am not able to clearly explain that the expedition was absolutely necessary and under no circumstances could it have been postponed.

"Therefore it is necessary to understand the situation in which our army found itself.

"At the start of the year 1779, the English, except for Canada and a small island, controlled only the city of New York and a district of about twenty miles in circumference, Long Island, Staten Island, Rhode Island, Paulus Hook, and Halifax in all of America, and only at the end of the year 1778 had General Prevost been able to capture the city of Savannah in Georgia.

"Our army in New York, due to the reinforcements sent to Savannah, Halifax, Pensacola, and St. Augustine, was seriously weakened and the local fleet was barely able to maintain its stations. Opposing us the rebels had a good standing army and a large French fleet to support it. Although the general-in-chief could not undertake the least decisive action, he cleverly decided, in part to prevent Washington from attacking our position and in part to cut communications with White Plains, to send some troops up the North River to capture the two forts at Stony and Verplanck's Points, and to give the enemy something to do in his own country. General Tryon with several thousand men was sent up the East River and made several attacks along the coast. In addition to these operations Cornwallis, with all the men who could be spared here, was ordered to Savannah to reinforce General Prevost, but due to the most unfortunate luck, had to turn back without accomplishing his objective due to contrary winds.

"We were in this situation when the French fleet appeared, whose operations on land and water could not be given the least impediment by our few ships.

"Now it was necessary for all of us to expect additional expeditions and to look to our own defense and safety.

"Therefore we abandoned the two conquered forts on the North River and, to secure the land side of York Island, a great defensive line was laid out above Fort Knyphausen. The smaller outlying works from Fort Independence to Number 8 were demolished. And, as experience had taught that Rhode Island could not be held without the protection of a good fleet, and that there was a serious risk that the defenders, who were Ansbachers for the most part, would be captured, this island was completely abandoned.

"These precautionary measures were also necessary because the French, by their return, had demonstrated their intention to undertake this easily accomplished conquest.

"Meanwhile the enemy plan was as follows: The French were to capture the only English occupied place in the southern part of North America, that is, Savannah, which was weakly garrisoned, and make themselves masters of Georgia. If this were successfully carried out, General Washington was to attack New York from two sides; from the side at Kingsbridge and across Staten Island, for which purpose a corps had been assembled near Fort Lee in New Jersey.

"In order to carry out this well-formed plan Comte d'Estaing landed several thousand troops near Savannah during the fall and joined a rebel corps under General [Benjamin] Lincoln. Fortunately, Comte d'Estaing conducted a long correspondence with the old General Prevost, giving him time to assemble his widely scattered troops and giving the engineer [James] Moncrief, with the help of several hundred driven-together Negroes, time to throw up some defenses, hurriedly, to protect the city. When Comte d'Estaing was convinced of General Prevost's intentions, his anger caused him to launch an all-out attack which resulted in his receiving a serious wound and many other losses, including the respected Pulaski, who had his own corps, to be beaten back. It was necessary for d'Estaing to return to his ships and the rebels quickly departed on land.

"This singularly fortunate incident suddenly changed the entire situation in America and gave the English time and opportunity to recover. As Comte d'Estaing had called upon Savannah to surrender in the name of the French king, it was also the French intention to take the city by storm. The importance of occupying the same, which had been realized too late and which, because of its weak defenses made it now appear open for conquest, was this.

"As Congress, or more correctly, all the rebel provinces, are short of money with which to buy materials of war such as weapons, munitions, uniforms, and above all medicine, from the French and Spanish, these items are paid for with the products of the land. Indigo, rice, cotton, tobacco, wood for ship-building, turpentine, and all these items are products of the southern provinces which are shipped out through the harbors of Savannah and Georgia.

"So now, not just to prevent another French attack, and not to protect Savannah from an attack by the rebels, it was necessary to send a reinforcement and to become master of Charleston, because this harbor controlled South Carolina just as Savannah controlled all of Georgia.

"However, after fully considering that the French would not lightly yield their presences there and knowing that in the coming spring another French fleet was to be expected, and that above all, an army could not tolerate camping in the field, undertaking siege operations, nor conducting long marches there during the heat, beginning in June, it was necessary to begin the expedition immediately and to have concluded it by the end of May.

"In this situation the commanding general-in-chief, Sir Henry Clinton, who had been granted unlimited authority by Congress [Parliament ?] to conduct the war as he thought best, knowing he would create enemies regardless of his actions, had no other option than to make a choice between two evils. He had to leave the English grasp in Georgia as it was and forget trying to enlarge it, which gave the enemy control of the treasury, or he must decide to undertake an expedition before the end of the year, despite the dangers involved, because of the greater advantage which could result to England. Therefore, he chose to undertake this important measure. I believe, after outlining all the opposing arguments in another place concerning the threatening misfortunes, that the expedition to Charleston in the winter was necessary and could not have been conducted in a better manner.

"With this in mind, completing the work on the line near Kingsbridge was pushed twice as hard, the warships lying there were made ready, and many transports were loaded with provisions. At the beginning of December Vice Admiral Arbuthnot sent several frigates out to determine if the ships returning to France from Come d'Estaing's fleet had actually departed.

"These preparations could not be carried out in such a secretive manner that Washington would not learn about them.

"Therefore, he not only sent an order alerting General Lincoln, the commander in the southern part of North America, but also detached some troops from his army to go there, which, however, on the long march in the middle of this cold weather, resulted in most of the men deserting.

"Also the troops in New England, as well as those in New Jersey, made various movements, but the commanding general did not react to them, but only drew the regiments and corps assigned to the expedition gradually closer together.

### December 1779

"The 15th - The frigate *Roebuck*, which had been sent out, returned and brought the news that Comte d'Estaing had returned to Europe with a part of his fleet and the ocean was now safe. Thereupon the transport ships received orders to obtain fresh water and then to anchor close to York Island.

"At the same time the ships returning to Europe for repairs were to be prepared to sail and to take on board the invalids and those being recalled from the English and German regiments.

"Because the army would be seriously weakened by these departures, the inhabitants of New York City volunteered to help with the duty in the city in an emergency.

"As a result, additional regiments and corps designated to accompany this expedition marched out of their assigned winter quarters and moved close to New York in order to be embarked.

"From the English: The 7th, 23rd, 33rd, 63rd, 64th, and 71st Regiments; two battalions of light infantry commanded by Colonel Abercromby; two battalions of grenadiers commanded by Colonel [John] York; the New York Volunteers commanded by [John] Althouse of the Sharp-Shooters Corps; Ferguson's Corps; [William Schaw], Lord Cathcart's Legion, both foot and mounted, under the command of Colonel [Banastre] Tarleton.

"From the German troops: Four battalions of Hessian Grenadiers commanded by General von Kospoth; the Huyn Infantry Regiment; 100 of the so-called Chasseurs which were formed with men from the British [German ?] infantry regiments and were commanded by the Hessian Jaeger Captain Hanger, who is an adjutant for General

Clinton; and a detachment of Hessian and Ansbach Jaegers. All these troops together, according to the best calculations, without engineers, but including artillerymen commanded by Major [Peter] Traille, 100 pioneers and guides, marines, and sailors, amount to 6,975 men.

"General Clinton, Lord Cornwallis, Major Generals Leslie, von Huyn, and von Kospoth, as well as Brigadier General [James] Paterson, also went with the expedition.

"The following warships sailed as the escort, under the command of Vice Admiral Arbuthnot, with the blue flag: 1) *Robust*, 74 guns 2) *Russell*, 74 guns 3) *Europe*, 64 guns, and the admiral's ship 4) *Raisonnable*, 64 guns 5) *Defiance*, 64 guns 6) *Renown*, 50 guns 7) *Roebuck*, 44 guns, carrying Lord Cornwallis 8) *Romulus*, 44 guns, carrying the commander-in-chief 9) *Defoe*, 32 guns, and 10) *Perseus*, 20 guns.

"The challenge was Number 59; the reply, Howe.

"Each ship's captain received a sealed envelope in which the place was written noting the fleet's destination. However, this was not to be opened, under the strictest punishment, until the ship had been completely separated from the fleet and had not seen it for several days.

"All the officers were ordered to sell their horses and to supply themselves with rations for several weeks.

"The 19th - The Jaeger Detachment, consisting of 195 Hessians and 55 Ansbachers, none of whom were recruits, marched out of their huts near Morris' house, above Fort Knyphausen, during a cold spell and marched along a hard-frozen road to New York. Eight officers were with them, namely, from the Hessians: Major von Wurmb, Captains Ewald, [Johann] Hinrichs, and [Franz Christian] von Bodungen, and Lieutenants [Johann Ernst] Winzingerode and [Johann] Scheffer; from the Ansbachers: Myself and Lieutenant [Jacob Ernst] Kling. Most went aboard the ship *Apollo* and Captain Ewald and Lieutenant Winzingerode with fifty jaegers went aboard the *Pan*.

"The ship *Apollo*, on which I sailed, was about five years old, had 44 guns, twelve of which were left behind, however, to make room for the jaegers. As a result the ship rolled more than usual. The ship's captain, John Adamson, was a stingy and, like most ship's masters, not an especially polite man. Instead of 25 sailors, he had only nineteen on board, including four or five very young lads. The mate was an old man; an incompetent and degenerate fellow, responsible for harmony, discipline, and cleanliness on the ship.

"The 20th and 21st - We remained at anchor near the wharf at New York while the remaining troops were embarked. The days were bright but the cold was penetrating. This region, which is called The Narrows, was opposite Long Island and already covered with thick ice. We heard that the general-in-chief had given command over the troops remaining behind to General von Knyphausen.

"The 22nd - Together with the many ships which had taken on cargo, we sailed to Sandy Hook, where the New York harbor begins, and lay at anchor near the lighthouse.

"The fleet for England with the invalids and returnees on board, consisting of nearly 100 ships, still lay at anchor here.

"The 23rd - Today we had to remain at anchor, although the wind was favorable, because the artillery and munitions had not yet arrived aboard ship. The fleet bound for England departed, however,....

"The 26th - All the remaining ships followed early this morning and at twelve-thirty in the afternoon we raised anchor. The weather was bright and the movement of the fleet, consisting of 96 sail, presented a pleasant view. Later the northwest wind was very favorable for us. However, while exiting the harbor, near Sandy Hook, the discipline which was customary during Lord Howe's command, was not seen.

"The 27th - Already today our favorable northwest wind began to fade and toward evening only a weak, dissimilar breeze was stirring. This caused our ship to develop an unpleasant roll and did not bode well for us. At evening a complete calm set in, indicative of an approaching storm. Unfortunately, it struck us early and about midnight a strong, contrary wind arose which in a few minutes became a storm. All the sails had to be lowered, the rudder was tied fast, and the ship was given over to the wind and waves. As the night was quite dark because there was no moonlight, and because the fleet had to remain close together, we were in great danger of ramming another ship or of sinking from some other cause.

"The 28th - All day today and during the night the storm continued with such fury that the entire fleet was scattered. Anyone who has traveled on the sea already knows the discomfort such a storm causes. He can also imagine all the unpleasantness which six persons closed in a small cabin experience, surrounded by a great amount of baggage, during the continuing storm, when a hundred small items tear loose and fly about. If it is also considered that this storm was in the winter, when we could not have a fire for heat, it will be easy to understand what a cold body and an empty stomach had to put up with, because, as is known, cooking is not allowed during a storm. However, all of this was of little consequence considering the deadly danger lurking in the midst of such a large fleet on a pitch black night with the frequent fearful shouting of the sailors.

"The 29th - At noon the storm abated somewhat and we noted a sad result of the storm. The ship *Anna*, on which there were 100 jaegers of Althouse's Company and, as we later learned, thirty of our jaegers, in the previous night had lost the middle and after masts, when rammed by the large hospital ship. Thereafter it drifted about among the ships of the fleet. As the ship carrying the horses was not to be seen, either, our sailors assumed it had foundered. This storm struck between Cape May and Cape Charles. During the afternoon the wind was tolerable but not favorable for us.

"The 30th - During the morning the wind eased from hour to hour until it became a complete calm during the afternoon. The air was as warm as it is in Germany in the summer. We were still fifteen sea miles from North Carolina. As pleasant as we found this change in the weather, so unpleasant was the whirlwind which struck us toward evening, accompanied by sharp flashes of lightning, and once again the ships of the fleet sailed in a confused manner. Our ship was also in no small danger as we were suddenly driven toward the admiral's ship. Fortunately, the admiral's ship made a slight turn and we backed our sails. In this manner we prevented the disaster. About midnight a contrary wind arose again and allowed us to go to sleep.

"The 31st - Because of the contrary wind and the persistent cold weather, the last day of the year was very unpleasant for us. We also had a continuous heavy rain which increased our displeasure."

# 1780

## The Winter Voyage to Charleston

The year 1780 opened with Clinton and a large part of the English and Hessian forces in North America still on the ocean with the intention of making the southern colonies the main arena of the war. Lieutenant Bartholomai, an Ansbach-Bayreuth jaeger attached to the combined Hessian-Ansbach Jaeger detachment sailing with Clinton, continued his account of the voyage from New York to South Carolina. "2 January - This day was even stormier and a bad day for us. The wind had changed to a storm yesterday and drove us directly toward the rocky and dangerous coast of Cape Hatteras. The mate had already told the crew that the water was shallower by the hour and there appeared to be no method of escaping disaster. Deathly fear was to be seen in every face and we expected at any moment to founder, but the storm then noticeably changed. The admiral used this situation to signal the ships to turn, and with the help of the current we were able to prevent being driven nearer to the coast....

"3 January - The storm appeared to have grown stronger. The movements which the endangered ship made were so violent that it appeared at any moment the masts would break and the pieces tear loose. In such deathly anxiety, during which the ship repeatedly fired emergency shots, we spent the night, completely exhausted in both body and spirit.

"4 January - ... Our sailors assured us that they had never seen a storm of equal strength and duration, which is easy to believe, because from the month of December until February, because of the usual storms, not a single ship, let alone a fleet, risks entering the ocean. However, the war makes half of the impossible, possible. As the water in the ship had risen without being suspected, and had risen to over twelve feet, an inspection was made and the leak discovered. It was under the cabin, above the steering rudder. Therefore, in a place where it could be repaired and was fixed as well as conditions allowed. It was also done just in time as nightfall was approaching when the storm again increased, and on ....

"6 January - raged with unbelievable fury. It is not possible to describe the misery and fear which we faced. Furthermore, the pro-

366

visions, which had been taken along to last three, or at most four, weeks ran out and what was left had to be used sparingly.

"This storm struck us between Cape Hatteras and the island of Bermuda.....

"10 January - ... Because of a shortage of zwieback the sailors came near mutiny against the captain, but this situation was resolved by the other officers.....

"12 January - The storm struck again with heavy rain and sleet and it became frightfully cold.....

"14 January - The wind continued just as strong so that while many ships fired distress shots, none was able to provide assistance.

"15 January - A stormy whirlwind replaced the former wind and caused the fleet a great amount of trouble. Nevertheless, on

"16 January - the sea was quite tolerable. The transport ship *George*, with Light Infantry on board, took advantage of this opportune time and raised an emergency flag. The fleet halted and, upon a signal from Captain [Thomas] Tonken, each ship in the fleet lowered a small boat into the water to be used to carry the men of the *George* to other ships. Those individuals were so distraught from experiencing the fear of death that everyone exerted great effort to insure that the men and their possessions were taken off in the boats sent to their rescue. They were very apathetic. The removal had barely been completed when the wind again increased. It was necessary to take in all the sails and make all provisions for giving the ship over to the wind and waves.....

"18 January - The wind was more favorable, but the current which had caught us, pushed us backward six miles every hour. This disrupted our voyage once again. All the troops were removed from the transport ship *Swan*, which had developed a serious leak....

"19 January - The wind became more contrary again, but not as strong. The crew of the ship *Juno*, which had sprung a leak, transferred to other ships. This too was accomplished just in time as at eleven o'clock, midday, a signal was given to prepare the sails and masts against another storm.....

"21 January - The weather was cold with rain and sleet, and very unpleasant for us poor creatures in the cabin as the wicked wind frequently blew the smoke from the coal fire into the cabin. Captain Ewald passed near us today and informed us that his ship and four others had collided in The Narrows at New York and that his men had been transferred to other ships.....

"27 January - Today I reached a conclusion concerning the extent that being accustomed to something controls us. During the first storm everyone was despondent, during the next, passive, and during the last one, we had become so accustomed that none of us took the least note of the violent movement of the ship nor the high waves. On the other hand, the salt provisions, with all their unpleasantness, were wolfed down without any qualms.

"28 January - Such an unusual cold set in that despite the unbearable smoke, we were compelled to have a fire in the cabin. We cast the lead and found bottom at 25 fathoms. Although this was a more than adequate depth of water, we had to take in most of the sails and proceed with great caution because this entire coast is full of sandbanks.

"28 and 29 January - During the afternoon the sailors discovered land ahead from the top of the mast. While daylight still lasted, we hurried onward. However, as we had only nine fathoms at nine o'clock, we had to tack.....

"31 January - Today the weather was very mild but so foggy that it was impossible to see the least speck of land. This is the rare fog which hindered Columbus so much upon his discovery of America. It is not like the usual fog on land, but stretches for thirty miles or more over the ocean and so thick that ships traveling very close together can not see one another. Therefore, it is necessary to signal their presence to one another by beating drums, shooting, and blowing horns.

"Toward noon a calm set in. We still had seven and one-half fathoms of depth. The warships returned, but because of the shallow water, anchored somewhat farther from land. The *Romulus* took over command and at three o'clock gave the signal to anchor. This occurred later at four-thirty in the Georgia roadstead between Tybee Island and the harbor at Port Royal. As the fog would not clear and the ships were still not close together, the admiral gave a signal every half hour from the ocean by means of a cannon shot, which was answered each time by the *Romulus*."

The Platte Grenadier Battalion Journal entries for 1780 also begin with a continuation of the recital of events during the voyage to South Carolina. "2 January - Yesterday's calm weather changed into a strong storm tonight. The wind and waves raged continuously in the most frightful manner. The waves often went over our ship and we always expected one to swamp us. A large iron pot, a large case, and a large piece of iron torn loose by the storm made the danger more imminent by rolling back and forth as no one dared enter where these items were. One of our sailors, who was sick, lost his life when the loose case rolled over him. As our ship was not very big, we were affected even more by the violence of the storm. Our situation was made worse because neither we nor the ship's captain was able to cook, which made all of us really sick. Including the ship's captain, we had only sixteen sailors, of whom one had already died. We also had to worry that if the storm continued for a long time, and the ship withstood it, and if the sailors became sick, then the duties would not be carried out as necessary and we would naturally be in grave danger, because no job in the world is more dangerous than that of a sailor in a storm. In this situation the English sailor is better than all others. The difference on our ship was that we had all come here from Europe with only German and Dutch sailors. While the latter showed their faint-heartedness at the least danger, the courage of the English seemed to increase as the danger increased. The fleet was so scattered today that only two or three ships could be seen at times. When the waves, high as mountains, crashed angrily over the ship, it seemed each time as if we were hurrying to our destruction.....

"6 January - We had weather like yesterday's. To our great surprise we had completely lost the fleet last night and saw not a single ship today. Therefore, we did not even know what course to steer. We had not only to fight the storm but had to expect at any moment to fall into the hands of a privateer as our ship did not have a single cannon on board with which to defend ourselves. The ship's captain and his entire crew seemed more concerned about this last danger than we were.

"7 January - The storm continued. To our great joy today we discovered the fleet, or at least some ships, and a warship. According to the noon observation we were at $30^0$ north latitude or already past Charleston. True, we were far out to sea because the storm had made it necessary, due to a contrary northwest wind, to sail far out to sea.....

"16 January - During the afternoon a ship loaded with supplies raised an emergency flag. Immediately all the boats, on a signal from the admiral, gathered around the vessel in distress. The people and part of the stores were moved to the frigate *Perseus*. The ship was leaking and at evening was given over to the wind and waves. It was the *Swan*.....

"19 January - This morning the admiral and agent Tomkins made the signal for all transport ship captains to transfer the troops from one transport ship to others, immediately. The ship was also called the *Swan* and had Light Infantry on board; most of whom were placed aboard the Hessian hospital ship *Sally*. The English hospital ship *Lion* had rammed the *Swan* during the night, making the latter unfit for use. A passing transport ship, *Lucretia*, gave us the wished-for report that the 51 missing ships of the fleet were again safe with a ship-of-the-line. The news was the more pleasant for us because we had worried about those ships and had been unable to learn anything of their fate until now....

"20 January - Last night was the worst we have had yet. The storm raged until noon today without letup. The ship received such strong jolts from the waves battering against it that everyone felt it could not stand this force much longer without sustaining damage. According to the reckoning of the crew we were driven backward a great distance last night and to our collective displeasure the contrary wind continued to blow.

"21 January - We had rainy weather but it was also warm and pleasant and the wind was favorable. Suddenly during the afternoon there was a whirlwind which tore the fore topsail of a ship traveling near us. The ship immediately raised the distress flag because we were far behind [the fleet]. No warship was nearby and the weather was foggy. Toward evening the ship in distress was far behind.....

"1 February - About ten o'clock this morning the *Romulus*, which was the only warship with us, weighed anchor and all the transport and store ships, of which there were 36, followed. We sailed back into the sea. According to the noon observation we were at $31^0$ 51' north latitude. As soon as we reached the open sea, we set our course straight for land. Toward four o'clock in the afternoon we saw seven of the warships belonging to our fleet at anchor. When we reached them, we discovered for the first time, to our great joy, that we could see land directly ahead of us, from the deck....

## Enemy Views (1780)

"2 February - Toward noon the warships *Romulus* and *Roebuck* weighed anchor. The transport ships lying nearby did likewise and steered toward the land lying ahead of us. At five o'clock in the afternoon we were lying at anchor in the mouth of the Savannah River, near the lighthouse on Tybee Island, seventeen English miles from Savannah. A large number of ships were already lying here. The transport ship *Polly*, with two grenadier companies of the Linsing Grenadier Battalion, had already arrived here three weeks previously. The two companies camped on Tybee Island as had Major Martini and his company of the Huyn Regiment.

"3 February - Last night, despite being at anchor, was very restless for us. We could not picture the danger, and we could not even have called it a danger. With the outgoing tide our ship grounded with such a heavy crash that everyone was alarmed and went on deck. No one wanted to remain below deck, fearing the ship would breakup, but because the entire fleet lay at anchor all about us, we thought about the boats and lost our fear. With the flood tide the ship floated free. We had to raise the anchor at once and tack until morning. We sailed three times toward land, before taking a pilot on board at seven o'clock in the morning. He took us to a safe place. We landed today on Tybee Island.....

"9 February - Although many ships were still missing and the fleet was not fully assembled here, which caused us to fear that they may have been scattered or sunk during the storm, we set sail today after provisions and water were provided for thirty days. Toward evening the warships *Europe* and *Russell*, which had been cruising in the meantime, joined us and we then lay at anchor. A part of the fleet remained lying at Tybee Island but no ships with troops on board.....

"11 February - The anchor was raised about eight o'clock this morning and the fleet, which now consisted of 47 transport ships and a row galley, because the warships could not approach so near to the land but had to remain in the ocean, entered the North Edisto River at noon and lay at anchor near the mouth of the river, between the islands. At four o'clock in the afternoon the Jaegers, Light Infantry, and the British and Hessian Grenadiers landed on Simon's Island and marched to Simon's house the same evening. It was believed that a bridge there led across a creek to John's Island.

"12 February - The rest of the troops, except for the artillery which had to remain on board the ships because of a shortage of horses, landed on the previously mentioned island and immediately marched to join the troops which landed yesterday. All the troops carried provisions from the ship for three days and marched to John's Island yet today. The transport ships remained lying in the North Edisto River and all their boats were landed with provisions today and sent to the army along the various creeks which create these islands."

Asteroth also sailing with the same fleet, recorded the following information about the voyage during the opening days of 1780. "16 January - A ship appeared which had been separated from the fleet and it at once made a signal. The commodore than made a signal that the captains were to travel to him in their boats and ordered a halt. We were all attentive to learn the meaning of this. We saw the boats going to the other which had displayed a red flag on the foremast. The English soldiers were very active, put their knapsacks on their backs, climbed into the boats, and were all taken from the ship because it already had taken in six feet of water. In the evening we sailed away and the ship sank.

"18 January - A signal shot was fired to inform us that tomorrow the ship *Swan* is to be unloaded.

"19 January - Soldiers and provisions were unloaded. Ships' crews and soldier volunteers helped man the pumps and bring the cargo safely to land.....

"31 January - We saw land and anchored at Savannah.....

"2 February - Toward noon we anchored at Tybee Island."

## The Siege of Charleston

The army under Clinton's command then moved ashore and captured Charleston as noted in the account by Lieutenant Bartholomai, commencing on 1 February 1780. "We again weighed anchor and sailed toward Tybee Island. The wind was very weak and therefore the fog was even thicker. We had to sail with the lead being cast constantly. As our ship's captain did not heed the sailors calling the depth from time to time, before we were aware, we were aground on a sandbank during the evening and the ship settled slightly on its right side.

"2 February - Before daybreak Captain Tonken sent several boats to transfer us onto land. As it was pitch black and because the ship was wet due to the heavy fog, making the coming and going very dangerous, everyone remained aboard ship and waited for the flood tide, which, with the help of some more sailors from the fleet, freed us at about four o'clock in the morning. However, as it was still not light enough to get underway, we immediately dropped anchor again. Finally we set sail again at nine o'clock, but as there was almost no wind, we traveled mostly by being towed by sailors in small boats, until we were able to rejoin the other transport ships near the lighthouse in Savannah Sound. Captain Ewald came aboard out ship today and told us about the circumstances of his shipwreck. His fifty jaegers were put aboard two other ships, including thirty on the ship *Anna*, which had encountered misfortune and not returned to us. During the end of May we learned that it had been driven to England.

"A perfect example of sea travel! When an individual who wanted to go from New York south to Charleston, which is 800 miles away, travels several thousand miles to the north and arrives in England.

"What the troops on this voyage experienced is beyond description, as can be understood from the following:

"Of the 46 days spent aboard ship from New York here, we traveled 36, including 25 days and nights of storms and thirteen days with contrary winds. Four or five ships had to be unloaded on the high seas and as of this date, ten transports and a warship are still missing. Also, there is almost no ship in the fleet which did not spring a leak. Of the horse ships, not a single one has yet arrived. Add to this the unpleasant and unhealthy coal smoke which every movement of the ship drives into the cabin....

"3 February - Today the ship *Spring*, with recruits for the Savannah garrison regiments of Wissenbach and D'Angelelli, sailed to Savannah. Captain Ewald and Lieutenant Winzingerode, who had gone aboard that vessel after their shipwreck, came aboard our ship. The commander-in-chief sailed to Savannah today, also, and the admiral sailed with the warships, except for the *Vigilante*, which was on station here, and several row galleys, to Port Royal to take a position there.

"We heard today that the Spaniards had captured the fort at Mobile in Florida and taken a company of Waldeck Grenadiers prisoner.

"Three hundred Cherokee Indians have arrived at Savannah, who, because of their barbarity, will not be used on this expedition.

"Several of the missing ships rejoined our fleet today.....

"6 February - Because of the frequent rain and thick fog, the weather today was very unpleasant. Several missing ships came in. During the afternoon an agent came to our ship and gave the order to our sailors that in case of a landing they were not to engage in plundering for fear of severe punishment.

"7 February - Some sleet accompanied by cold weather and we were assured by the oldest people that such an event had never occurred previously. The ship loaded provisions for forty days today. The general-in-chief and the admiral both returned from Savannah today. The *Roebuck raised* the admiral's flag and General Clinton went aboard the agent's ship.

"8 February - The fleet was ordered to be prepared to get underway. Meanwhile a recently arrived transport ship, which had a leak, was unloaded.

"Now everyone speculates as to how and where the general-in-chief will attack Charleston. Finally, having learned how the project would be executed, which we initially had to guess, I will now on 8 February, outline General Clinton's plan, in order to give the reader the opportunity to thoroughly evaluate this venture.

"Charleston can be attacked from three sides; from the sea by the army, from the land across the Cooper River from Savannah, and from the islands. However, the Cooper River route is not a possibility as we are not masters of North Carolina and the local region, nor from the sea, as the harbor is protected by Sullivan's Island. Therefore, the general-in-chief had to chose the side from the islands. To mask this intention from the enemy, the warships in the Port Royal River made various movements and General Paterson had to march with his corps from Savannah toward Charleston. This project, fortunately, went well. As a consequence, the fleet, consisting of about sixty sail, on

"9 February - weighed anchor at nine o'clock in the morning and entered the North Edisto River. The wind was very weak and we could not sail very far. We anchored at evening near Trench Island.....

"11 February - We saw several enemy ships in the distance which appeared to be observing us. They immediately withdrew. Toward twelve o'clock, noon, we were among islands, near the mainland, grouped like a half moon, which formed a harbor. The admiral, by means of a signal, ordered the flatboats lowered into the water and the ship's captains were to report to Captain Tonken to receive the secret orders concerning the debarkation. We immediately anchored.

"For our debarkation we received the following orders: The 1st debarkation - Light Infantry and British Grenadiers; the 2nd debarkation - Hessian Grenadiers, Jaeger Detachment, and 33rd Regiment; 3rd debarkation - 7th, 23rd, 63rd, 64th English and the Hessian Huyn Regiments.

"In further orders the army was divided into the following brigades: The Light Infantry and British Grenadiers commanded by Major General Leslie. The Hessian Grenadiers commanded by Major General von Kospoth. The 7th and 23rd Regiments commanded by Lieutenant Colonel [Alured] Clarke. The 33rd and 71st [?] Regiments commanded by Lieutenant Colonel Webster. The 63rd and 64th Regiments commanded by General von Huyn.

"The first debarkation began at five o'clock in the evening. The general-in-chief and Lord Cornwallis landed with it. The second debarkation was to begin, also, but because of darkness and a heavy rain, it was postponed.

"12 February - At eight o'clock the second division debarked. We were put ashore on Simon's Island, which is a point on John's Island, about six or seven miles from our ship. We took along provisions for three days. We remained here until the remaining troops were landed.

"As we were not familiar with this island and had no guide with us, we were mislead by a naval officer who had never previously been on this coast, knew very little about the land, and who led us around for several hours through the woods and water in a fog which settled in. Things were no better for the troops who had landed yesterday. Because they had no one to show them the way, they had spent the night in the woods. What losses this corps could have suffered during a pitch black, very rainy night, in an unfamiliar woods, if this island had been occupied by only a few hundred militiamen....

"13 February - We heard today that, as I have said previously, General Paterson is on his way here by way of Purrysburg and Two

Sisters with the Light Infantry Company of the 72nd Scots Regiment, the 2nd Battalion of the same regiment, Ferguson's Corps, the York Volunteers, the North and South Carolina Provincials, and the dismounted soldiers of the Legion and the 17th Dragoon Regiment, because all the cavalry horses were lost at sea.

"14 February - Colonel Webster received orders to occupy the posts at Stono Ferry with the Jaegers and the 33rd Regiment. Although he is not familiar with the land and because of a scarcity, had no guides with him who could speak English, he marched calmly onward with no side patrols and only an advance guard of ten or twelve men, thirty yards ahead of the column. As we emerged from the woods we entered a marshy stretch about 600 to 700 yards long covered by small round defensive points which extended to the Stono River. The colonel had ordered a young Negro to lead him to Stono Ferry. However, because the ferry house was on the other side of the river, the Negro thought he wished to cross over. Therefore the whole column marched in this manner without bothering to look around. Suddenly the colonel was aware the rebels occupied the houses on the elevated bank on the other side. These were a detachment of Pulaski's Corps, infantry and cavalry, and we were not more than 200 yards from them because the river is very narrow here. In part now there were no boats available to take us across, furthermore, in part the colonel had no orders to cross. Our rifles were quickly loaded, I think rather too late, and we made a right turn. Fortunately, the rebels had no cannons and were so shocked to suddenly see such an audacious column marching toward them that they forgot to fire as they must have thought that possibly a landing had been made at another place and we had arrived here to be transferred across. As we approached so close and had already passed the above described difficult stretch, and because the morasses could not be avoided, less than half of the Jaeger Detachment was present when the enemy fired on us with grape shot.

"This was the unfortunate route where in the previous year the good Colonel [John] Maitland, after so bravely defending the ferry house with 500 to 600 men and two cannons, against 5,000 rebels with six cannons, lost nearly half of his command during his retreat. We pulled back in great haste and remained for a time in the woods....

## Enemy Views (1780)

"15 February - The general staff and the engineer Major Moncrief, who had defended Savannah so well, came to reconnoiter the passage. They went more than half way along the swampy road and placed a double jaeger post ahead of them, which the rebels fired upon. Our Jaegers also fired a few shots into the enemy house. The engineer wanted to find a dominating height and for this purpose had two English field pieces with him. However, the region on this side of the river was entirely unsatisfactory. At the same time a patrol was sent along the bank to find a shallow crossing place through which to wade. However, because of the deep morass none was discovered. Toward evening, however, on the upper reaches some old boats were found which the enemy had failed to destroy and by which means, during the night, several companies of Light Infantry were transferred across near Waite's house, forcing the rebels to abandon their posts. A Negro who came across the swamp from Charleston brought the report that General Lincoln, with 6,000 to 7,000 men, had gone against General Paterson and that only during the last few days had work on the defenses been resumed, because the enemy had thought the storm had completely scattered us. Also, no relief force had arrived from General Washington....

"17 February - A patrol was sent out to get cattle for the corps and Negroes to work.....

"23 February - It began to snow today and ice formed on the surface of small bodies of water. These two occurrences had never happened previously in this province in the memory of the Negroes.....

"25 February - Two patrols, one from Webster's and one from Clarke's Brigades, were sent out again to seize cattle for the army. Captain Cornwallis commanded the first with 100 men, of which I had the honor to command thirty jaegers.

"Because I include myself in the description of the patrol's activity, it is necessary that I initially explain to the reader that I do not do this to show my knowledge and cleverness, because here in America similar patrols are the usual duty of every jaeger, but only to give an example of how little caution the English employ in their undertakings and how easily this duty, which after a time one becomes accustomed to, can lead to the loss of honor and reputation.....

"27 February - After Colonel Webster made a small patrol through the woods and nailed up placards encouraging Negroes to come into the English lines, the colonel received orders to pull back.....

"1 March - Yesterday evening many small boats arrived here, which departed again today under the escort of an armed boat. From these we learned that a ship with artillery and munitions had sunk and that the warship *Defiance*, 64 guns, had run aground on the coast near Tybee Island. During the afternoon a patrol of Pulaski's Cavalry came near our outposts, but as they saw the Jaegers run forward to engage them, they quickly withdrew. Tonight an English soldier of the 23rd Regiment deserted his post. This was very disadvantageous for us because thereby the enemy learned that we have no cannons in our positions.....

"30 March - Was a hot day for the Jaegers. I have already said that the Jaeger Detachment formed the army's advance guard and from these a captain with sixty men was sent ahead. We had just passed the Governor's house, about four miles outside Charleston, when several shots were fired by our advance guard at some enemy cavalry who had come too close and of whom one man was killed. Shortly thereafter the firing increased. Three hundred rebels, consisting of light infantry and Negroes, had lain an ambush along both sides of the road, in the woods, and had a small defensive position behind them to cover their retreat. Therefore they gave our advance guard a warm reception. The general staff, which was following close behind on horses, halted and the remainder of the Jaeger Detachment rushed forward to support the advance guard. This took place with such swiftness and ardor that in less than fifteen minutes, despite the morass before us, that was difficult to pass, and despite our being only 200 men, the enemy was driven into flight.

"We then halted on orders from the general because the region here was in the form of a defile and no one could tell whether or not the enemy had cannons supporting them. Also, the rebels had placed our mounted general staff, which had halted, in danger, and shot the Earl of Caithness in the upper body while he was halted beside the general-in-chief. As a company of Light Infantry then moved forward to cover our left flank and fired several shots from one of their field pieces at those in flight, the enemy abandoned the position which the advance guard immediately occupied. It had been the enemy commander's intention to draw us before his cannons, during the heat of battle. However, as they gave way, we also withdrew from the trap, so they reentered their position. They remained there only a few minutes and then made their retreat. We took this opportunity to fire a number of rifle shots after them, which hastened their evacuation. The general-in-chief personally expressed his thanks to the Jaegers for their demonstration of bravery during the skirmish. One jaeger had been lightly wounded and one was missing.

"During the affair we learned how important it is to be familiar with a region. If we had not had a thorough knowledge of this area, it would have been easy for the enemy to have cut off our detachment beyond the Black Creek dam during the skirmish. As it was, we were not hindered during our withdrawal....

"31 March - The Jaeger picket moved forward to the woods and morass near the Gibb's house, so that the general staff and the engineer Moncrief could be protected while the defensive works, which extended beyond the Black River dam, could be reconnoitered and the city and its defenses, from which we were about a mile and one-quarter, could be observed from an empty house.

"As can best be determined from here, the Charleston defenses are laid out in the form of a half moon and 57 gun embrasures can be counted along the front.

"I must note here, however, that the otherwise so clever Moncrief initially misjudged the distance by 400 yards, as we later determined, when laying out the batteries. This error was apparently caused by the city's defenses being somewhat elevated.

"According to people with knowledge of such things, the siege will take much time and effort, because: 1st - The defenses are considerable and in good repair. 2nd - The enemy has far more artillery than we have. 3rd - We must first make ourselves masters of Sullivan's Island, which has a strong fort protecting its troops. 4th - We must clear the French and American frigates out of our way, and 5th - We must bring all the cannons and munitions in boats, through the creeks, from James Island and because of a shortage of horses and equipment, move them into the trenches with the help of blacks and sailors.

"1 April - With difficulty the Ashley River was crossed from Linning's Creek to Gibb's Ferry, yesterday and today, and then onward to the park at Gibb's house. The Negroes moved the cannons, munitions, and provisions up, and the greenhouse was converted to a laboratory. All the wooden houses in this region were then torn down and made into a new sort of mantelet by Major Moncrief. They were made of timbers and boards, six feet high and twelve to fourteen feet long, and provided with three base supports to hold them upright. These were used to construct batteries and redoubts. The fascines and straw sides were quickly completed. As soon as the engineers had set them together, the shapes of the battery or redoubt were finished and the workers then threw dirt from the trenches upon them. This method is very practical but only possible in sandy and soft soil.

"Today the missing jaeger was found in the underbrush by the river. In examining him it was discovered that he had been killed by three bullets and his death posture indicated that he had prayed for forgiveness.....

"5 April - Today there was a heavy cannonade. This evening our battery near the distillery also began to fire toward the Cooper River to clear it of enemy ships. As the general-in-chief wished to show the rebels that our preparations were completed and we were ready to burn the city down, he allowed the two redoubts constructed by us across the Ashley River on James Island, at Fenwick's Point and near Linning's house, to fire into the city for two hours. At the same time our two row galleys lying at the mouth of the Wappoo Creek opened fire with heated-shot, setting some houses on fire. The rebels were so astounded by this compliment that during the entire time, they fired not a single shot.

"Two hundred sailors moved into the works to help handle the cannons. During the night a battery of nine 24-pounders was set up in the first parallel, on our right wing, between redoubts one and two. These guns were manned by the sailors.....

"7 April -The enemy again fired rather strongly. However, the sailors' battery, which greatly distinguished itself throughout the siege, did its duty and, when so ordered, fired many heated shots into the city. About one o'clock in the afternoon eleven sloops and schooners with troops passed down the Cooper River into the city. It was a reinforcement from Washington and consisted of 600 men. The rebels raised a great victory cry and throughout the night rang the bells amidst a continuous cannon fire.

"We were also no less joyful, because Captain [Robert] Collins arrived with eighty English artillerymen, who were much needed. He had been separated from the fleet during the storm and just when his ship was about to sink, he was saved by an English privateer. He was taken to Bermuda initially and then brought here.

"During the night the enemy fired a heavy cannonade; nevertheless, a redoubt for six large cannons was constructed in the form of a half moon, which the enemy failed to discover. This brought the enemy defenses 200 yards closer and four 24-pounders were immediately placed in Redoubt Number 6. The armed boat was placed in the water and the Light Infantry cleared an enemy double outpost from ahead of the abatis. By this means it was accidently learned that during the first skirmish with the Jaegers on 31 March, the enemy had suffered one captain, one lieutenant, one sergeant, and seven men killed, and General Lincoln's adjutant and twenty men were wounded. Those heavy losses were the reason that no mercy was shown to any stray jaeger.

"Before I continue, I will mention serious consequences can result from a small error during a war.

"If the engineer, as I have mentioned, had previously reconnoitered the swampy road to the redoubt and made the necessary repairs, Redoubt Number 6, which borders on the Cooper River, could have been provided with heavy cannons yesterday evening, or at least this morning, by which means the sloops carrying the enemy reinforcements could have been given a warm reception. As it was, we patiently watched the vessels sail past us in the rain.

"8 April - This was a memorable day. The navy had planned to come to the aid of the army by firing a cannonade from the water or possibly making a landing. Although the inhabitants of Sullivan's Island, who by means of Fort Moultrie had blockaded the harbor, appeared too annoying and too dangerous, it was decided nevertheless to pass this region of enemy fire and many sandbanks. Therefore this afternoon, Admiral Arbuthnot fortunately led a fleet consisting of fourteen sail, frigates and armed transport ships, past an exceptionally heavy cannonade from Fort Moultrie and dropped anchor between the fort and the city. His losses consisted of seven dead and twenty seriously wounded. The second ship, the frigate *Richmond*, lost its masts

381

and an armed transport ship, after its cargo was removed, was set on fire during the night because it had run firmly aground on a sandbank.

"As audacious and as fortunate as this undertaking was, so it was no less unnecessary. The admiral had forgotten to ask if the way from Sullivan's Island to the city was open and if it were possible to attack the defenses from the water side, successfully. However, he found the channel so well blockaded by nine sunken ships that it was impossible to approach closer to the city and the batteries were so placed that he could not attack them. Nevertheless, the rebels were so shaken by the audacious undertaking against their fortress that during the night and on

"9 April - their batteries were almost unheard. The inhabitants were so shocked that they took their finest belongings to the left bank of the Cooper River and retreated out of the city. During the night a battery of six cannons was laid out 300 yards ahead of the parallel between Numbers 4 and 5, and strenuous efforts made to place large cannons therein.

"In considering Gibb's house, where our artillery park, powder magazines, and laboratories were located, I found sufficient reason to moan about the English carelessness. At every camp site in the world, it is customary in those places where cannons and munitions are, to have a guard and especially to place a double guard on the laboratory to prevent all individuals who have no official business from entering, because an enemy plot or other carelessness can cause the powder to blow up or the cannons to be spiked, which could possibly destroy the entire camp. However, the English not only allow everyone to enter the park, but even the deserters, who as a rule are kept under close observation and at a distance from the camp, were to be seen at the magazine and in the trenches, even though we had reason because of our few cannons, to be careful and because of a shortage of munitions were often restricted during the day to firing only three shots an hour and the soldiers were given a reward of half an English shilling for every cannonball they recovered.

"To tell the truth, the English must credit the advantage achieved by their weapons, not to good conduct, or their precautions, but only to blind luck and the mistakes of the rebels.

"10 April - As the engineer Major Moncrief saw that it was not possible to silence the enemy cannons with his weapons, and had decided therefore to capture the city by digging only saps in sandy soil, it was necessary to have a well-directed and limited fire to cover the workers. Therefore today one captain, one lieutenant, and sixty jaegers were sent into the trenches to accomplish this purpose. The enemy cannonade was very lively today, but the frigates continued to lie at anchor near the city.

"At six o'clock in the evening the general-in-chief, through Major [Willliam] Crosbie, called upon the city to surrender, but received as an answer that sixty days had passed before he, General Lincoln, was aware that General Clinton intended to take hostile action against the city. As he no longer had any doubts, however, he would wait to see what would happen.

"The third armed boat was brought into the Cooper River. During the night work continued on the previously begun batteries and communications trenches, from the first parallel to this one and weapons were placed in the finished positions. The enemy interrupted this work frequently with cannon fire and bombs.....

"12 April - At four o'clock this afternoon a frigate and three armed brigantines, without firing a shot, passed Fort Moultrie under a heavy enemy fire and joined the fleet. Two deputations from North Carolina came to the army today with offers to raise 1,000 armed men if they were protected by English weapons.

"As the rebels still held the land on the other side of the Cooper River and the general-in-chief feared that General Lincoln would retreat from the city with the garrison at night, Lieutenant Colonel Webster was sent along the Dorchester Road on the right bank of the Ashley River with the 33rd Regiment, the Legion, and Ferguson's Corps, in order to cross the Cooper River to cut the rebel communications and force the abandonment of his defenses on Lempriere's Point.....

"15 April - ... Today we also received the welcome report that a few days ago, Colonel Tarleton, with his Cavalry, had attacked Colonel [William] Washington near Bacon's Bridge. About thirty dragoons, including Major [Pierre Francois] Vernier, the commandant of Pulaski's Corps, were killed and about sixty dragoons and 200 horses, as well as equipment, were captured. Colonel Washington, who was wounded and captured, escaped into the water. As a result of this affair, Pulaski's Corps ceased to exist. As small as this affair appears to have been, it is very important for us as it assures our occupation of Bacon's Bridge over the Cooper River, made Colonel Webster master of many provisions, and cleared the way to move closer to the Wando River, placing him in a position to cut all communications with the city by way of the Cooper River. As a further hindrance to all communications with the city on the river, several armed ships were posted in Servan Bay and others in Spencer's Inlet.....

"19 April - ... At the same time we received the most welcome news that after an eleven day voyage a fleet with a 2,600-man reinforcement, artillery, and munitions had arrived from New York. The troops on board consisted of the 42nd English and the Hessian Ditfurth Infantry Regiments, the Brunswick Corps, Volunteers of Ireland, the Queen's Rangers,. and some New York militia. With these reinforcements we are finally in a condition now to close off Charleston.

"The King of the Lower Creek Indians, who had been told that our army was in very poor condition in order to get his nation away from supporting the English, came to us. On orders of the general-in-chief he was shown about the camp and in the trenches.....

"21 April - During the afternoon General Lincoln sent a flag of truce to our general-in-chief, offering to capitulate, and suggested to this end that a six hour armistice, which last, with the agreement of Admiral Arbuthnot, was accepted. Later, however, after the rebels had requested, among other conditions, freedom to pull out of the city and that they not have to surrender as prisoners of war, the state of hostilities was resumed at ten o'clock.....

"24 April - Captain Hinrichs and Lieutenant Winzingerode moved out as usual and entered the trenches before daybreak.

"The rebels made an attack from their left wing against the work on our right, in which were Lieutenant Winzingerode with thirty jaegers, and an officer and fifty men of the Light Infantry.

"As the English, until daybreak, when they saw the Jaegers coming, occupied the post, in their usual manner, but without loaded weapons or fixed bayonets, and had not been especially alert, they were not aware of the rebels until they sprang over the breastwork. The Light Infantry, who were neither on guard nor able to fire against the enemy, ran away so that Lieutenant von Winzingerode was forced to retreat. At that time four jaegers, including one Ansbacher, were allowed to return. During this confusion it would have been easy for the rebels to ruin our bomb battery which was nearby, but as soon as our second parallel began to fire, they ran so quickly that their troops left thirteen muskets and two hats on the ground before our position....

"About twelve o'clock the rebels pulled back to their abatis and shouted, "Avances! Tires!' [Advance! Fire!] while still delivering a continuous fire by platoons.

"25 April - As our troops were still thinking about yesterday's rebel attack, they thought the rebels were attacking again. Therefore the workers ran from the trenches and the covering force fell back, some in good order, some not in good order. The second parallel occupants, who thought our retreating troops were enemies, fired upon them, killing one Scottish officer, four Scottish soldiers, and two Hessian grenadiers. Twelve English and two Hessians were wounded. About one o'clock the error was noticed. No rebels had come beyond the abatis, and furthermore, at daybreak, they pulled back from the first abatis. We fired a bomb after them in revenge. If the rebels had been smart and daring, what could they have accomplished in this situation!

"After the general-in-chief had been strengthened by the reinforcement from New York, and as Colonel Webster with his troops could not cover all the approaches, Lord Cornwallis crossed the Cooper River with the Volunteers from Ireland and the North and South Carolina militia in our armed boats and took over command. This opportunity enabled us to capture an enemy schooner with six cannons, loaded with rum and rice, which had grounded firmly on the shore on that side and was awaiting the flood tide....

"26 April - ... As obvious as it was that ships could not draw nearer the city, Admiral Arbuthnot planned, because a favorable wind blew today, to attack the city from the water side. We were also fully prepared to storm the city. With this end in view the Light Infantry moved into the trenches. However, the entrance [to the harbor] was so completely blocked with sunken ships, that nothing developed from the plan.....

"29 April - Today we received the most pleasant report that the rebels had vacated the defenses on Lempriere's Point and retreated into the city. Lord Cornwallis immediately occupied the position. We took four cannons, much ammunition, and a number of small ships. With the loss of this post, the rebels have lost all possibility of retreating overland.....

"6 May - Today the enemy fired very little. However, a smart Englishman was found during the bombing. Since we began work on the third parallel, many troops had been killed and wounded by fire from an empty house lying between the two enemy abatis, without anyone exerting the necessary effort to destroy it. Finally, today, the artillery officer was able to get close enough to set it on fire.

"During the night the enemy fire from cannons and small arms was continuous. In the defenses as well as in the city, everything was in motion. Apparently they had been advised to burn the old houses thinking we were about to storm the city. Toward this end, we had completed the necessary preparations for opening the second and third parallels. They were equipped with 23 guns, 2 howitzers, and 22 mortars, of which one was 13 inches. The rebels continued their firing during the night although we had disrupted it.

"7 May - ... The captain of a transport ship wished to visit the trenches as he desired learning from whence the cannonballs came. However, he had hardly raised his head above the parapet before a ball hit him dangerously in the head. When reproached for his curiosity, he said, ' I did not believe that it is so dangerous for a person to take only a quick glance.'

"We heard some significant signals on the Cooper River and learned that when Admiral Arbuthnot sought to correct his mistake, he had decided to capture Fort Moultrie. To this end he had made landings at two places, early in the evening and, according to reports, when few sailors were on the island. The occupants of a detached defensive position were attacked and captured. The fort was then called upon to surrender. As the commandant saw that the sailors and marines had landed on the eastern shore and were prepared to attack, he surrendered and with his 150 men was made a prisoner of war. We also captured twenty cannons in the fort. The sailors made fun of the poor defense as the rebels marched out and, instead of weapons, held oars in their hands.

"At the same time the best of news was received. Colonel Tarleton had attacked the enemy cavalry on the Santee River, cut down many, and captured forty men. This incident developed in the following manner. Lord Cornwallis sent Lieutenant Ash with a detachment of mounted Light Infantry on a reconnaissance to Lenud's Ferry. As that officer did not take the necessary precautions, he was cut off by the rebels and captured. Therefore, Lord Cornwallis sent Colonel Tarleton with the Legion in pursuit of the enemy, consisting of cavalry commanded by Colonels Washington and White. Tarleton overtook them near Lenud's Ferry, attacked with his usual spirit, routed the entire force, and captured 100 horses. The two colonels barely escaped, making a dangerous swim across the wide Santee River. Most of the remaining troops drowned, part in the river, and part remained stuck in the swampy banks of the river.

"Lieutenant Ash, who was already in a boat with his troops, waiting to be transferred across the river, seeing his rescuers on the bank, threw the guards into the water and joined with Tarleton....

"8 May - At daybreak, the commanding general sent Major Crosbie into the city once again, informed General Lincoln that Fort Sullivan was in our hands, his cavalry destroyed, our approaches were nearing his defenses, and there was no hope of his being reinforced; and ordered the fortress to surrender with the warning that if the obstinate defense continued, he would be responsible for the harsh treatment accorded his troops. Although General Lincoln admitted the truth of the situation and also knew his provisions were exhausted, he believed that his obstinacy would instill determination against our assault, which he hoped to defeat with the help of his numerous cannons, because our fleet could do nothing to assist. At that the French consul, who did not wish to be taken prisoner, emphasized that it would take time to change the embrasures and to strengthen the defenses. This was another factor in the surrender negotiations. Other objections to General Clinton's capitulation articles were pointed out, so that the writing of these went back and forth, until

"9 May - When everything fell apart at eight o'clock in the evening. Our batteries and those of the enemy cannonaded one another, mixed with platoon firing and the throwing of bombs throughout the night, with all their might. The sky was filled with fire and it seemed to us as if the earth shook. General von Kospoth, in his quarters at an hour's distance from the city, was injured by a cannonball which caused a pot hanging over his bed to fall on him.

"However, our firing was as nothing compared with that of the enemy. It is customary during every siege in the world, that the firing by the besieging force must be stronger than that of the force being besieged, in order for the first to protect the works undertaken against the fortress. With us the opposite was the case, in that the besieged had five embrasures against each one of ours. Despite this great difference, we proceeded with our efforts, which were greatly aided by the loose, sandy soil, so swiftly that we extended our third parallel to the right against the enemy's left wing, all the way to the canal and laid out a new battery. The duty of the Jaegers, who had to hold down the enemy's flanking batteries, was very difficult and dangerous.

"10 May - The heavy cannonade continued causing the death and wounding of twenty men, including one jaeger. During the night we built a covered passageway across the canal and passed the first enemy abatis. A lodgment was also begun within thirty yards of the enemy abatis, although the enemy fired heavily with cannons and muskets against it.

"11 May - During our entrance into the trenches today we took a different route through a covered-over swamp. Nevertheless, we had to tolerate the cannonballs. The lodgment begun during the night could not be occupied yet, but work on it was continued. The rebels continued their cannonade and doubled their small arms fire which later made it necessary for me, as I had to support this new project, to place my thirty jaegers within twenty paces of a detached enemy position. Consequently the parallel was almost completely exposed to the enemy musket fire. I asked the English colonel commanding in the trenches to issue us ammunition from the Light Infantry supply, which we then fired so continuously that in two hours, from 2,000 rounds, almost none remained.

"Meanwhile the general-in-chief gave the batteries the order at nine o'clock in the morning, as he was justifiably annoyed by the foolhardy resistance of the enemy commander, to fire on the city. Within a short time seven houses were set on fire. When they were in full flame, he halted the firing in order to give that hard-headed individual something else to think about. However, as the enemy continued to fire with cannons and muskets, our batteries began to fire shells into the city. Pressured by this fierce confrontation, at two o'clock in the afternoon, General Lincoln sent an adjutant, accompanied by a drummer, with a letter to the general-in-chief. Lincoln wished to give in to the suggested points but requested that the militia and citizens of Charleston not be treated as prisoners of war. The general-in-chief refused this request and Lincoln was forced to surrender the city according to the articles which the general-in-chief thought appropriate.

"Thereupon, it was ordered by both sides to halt all hostile action....

"12 May - At four o'clock in the afternoon, the garrison, consisting of between 4,000 and 5,000 men, moved out of the city, playing a Turkish march and, as prisoners of war, stacked their weapons between the two abatis. One company of English and one company of Hessian Grenadiers, with two cannons, occupied the defenses; the 7th, 42nd, and 63rd Regiments occupied the city; and the admiral occupied the works which covered the harbor.

"Upon entering, a large English flag was raised over the city gate which was saluted by 21 shots from the cannons in our positions.

"All the siege troops moved out and formed two lines.

"The rebels appeared thin, miserable, ragged, and very dirty. Their officers appeared to be primarily young people and poorly dressed, each in a different colored uniform and with different facings, which gave the officers of their army the appearance of comedians about to commence a show, which together with their troops, without shoes, made a very comical scene.

"Chagrin and anger, on the other hand, were to be seen in all their faces.

"Among them were 7 generals, 26 colonels, 42 lieutenant colonels, 105 captains, and including the militia and French, 6,000 men.

"The names of the generals were as follows: Major General Lincoln, Brigadier Generals [Charles] Scott, [Daniel] Huger, [William] Woodford, Moultrie, [Lachlan] McIntosh, and the French engineer [Louis le Begue de Presle] Duportail.

"The troops consisted of the following brigades: Colonel Beckman's Artillery Brigade - Continental Battalion, Independent Company, Charleston Battalion, Cannoneers, Smith's Carolina Continental Battalion.

"Colonel Symmonds' Charleston Brigade - Colonel Schmid's 1st Battalion, Colonel Ager's 2nd Battalion, Monsieur Brinting's Corps.

"Brigadier General Scott's Brigade - Colonel Marion's South Carolinians, Colonel Thompson's South Carolinians, Colonel Little's North Carolinians, Colonel Hopkin's Virginians, and Colonel Schmid's Virginians.

"Brigadier Huger's Brigade - Colonel Clark's North Carolinians, Colonel Patten's North Carolinians, Colonel Makband's North Carolinians.

"Brigadier General Woodford's Brigade - Colonel Russell's Virginians, Colonel Gist's Virginians, Colonel Nevil's Virginians, Lauren's Light Infantry.

"Brigadier General McIntosh's Militia Brigade - Colonel Maybank's, Colonel Garden's, Colonel Shiven's, Colonel McDougal's, Colonel Giles', Colonel Hicks', Colonel Richardson's, Colonel Kirshaus', Colonel Goodwyn's, Colonel Harlington's, and Colonel Tinnings's.

"General Lincoln's adjutant, who was dressed completely in a liver-colored summer suit, wore a wide green sash across his body, which indicated he was the adjutant general.

"We captured fifteen flags, 343 cannons, including 21 metal ones, and 2 mortars, as well as several howitzers and coehorns, and 5,416 rifles, mostly of French and Portuguese manufacture. The best rifles and flints, for the most part, had been thrown in the water.

"In addition to those items, we captured large magazines of rum, rice, and indigo, as well as a large amount of munitions.

"We took a total of 49 ships and 120 boats of various kinds. Among which were the frigate *Boston*, now the *Charleston*, of 36 guns; *Providence*, 32 guns; *Ranger*, now the *Halifax*, 24 guns, and *Avanturier*, 24 guns, as well as *Pulakko*, 18 guns, and five three-masted ships. Nine ships were sunk, including an old East Indiaman ship of 50 guns; the frigate *Queen of France*, 32 guns; and three three-masted ships. In the Wando River, thirteen vessels, including one with three masts, loaded with cargo, fell into the hands of Lord Cornwallis' Corps."

The Platte Grenadier Battalion Journal contains the following entries of interest concerning the capture of Charleston. "27 February - A number of transport ships arrived in the North Edisto River from

Tybee Island and lay to near the fleet already there. The two grenadier companies of the 63rd and 64th Regiments were on these ships which had become separated from our fleet and until now were believed to have been lost. There was also one battalion of the 71st Regiment of Highlanders, which came from Savannah, and two companies of Negroes. The others were store ships and horse ships, the latter from Savannah, with a number of wagons. These ships brought news that the warship *Defiance*, 64 guns, of our fleet had stranded in the Savannah River.

"28 February - After the troops and horses which arrived yesterday in the North Edisto River marched to the army, the cannons and artillery from the transport ships were taken in boats on the water to James' Island. Because the horses brought with them were insufficient to pull them, horses were taken from all the officers and all captured horses were used to pull the artillery and wagons.....

"7 April - Ten schooners came down the Cooper River with a 1,000-man reinforcement under the command on board of General Scott. They had marched from Stony Point on the North River in New Jersey last December and had been almost four months on this difficult march. As soon as they arrived at Charleston, which occurred at sundown, a loud cheer was heard in the city accompanied by a continuous ringing of all the bells.

"8 April - We had one of the most beautiful scenes. At four o'clock in the afternoon nine of our warships passed Fort Moultrie on the flood tide by dull weather and a strong south wind. The firing by both sides was exceptionally heavy. The tenth ship ran upon a sandbank near the mentioned fort. The ships had to pass very close under the enemy cannons which raked them constantly. *Roebuck* was the first ship and *Renown* the second ship. These had their foremasts shot away, otherwise there was no damage to the others. *Romulus* lay to opposite the fort and fired a continuous bombardment. Despite the strong wind, nothing could be seen of the ships but the flashes, due to the smoke. As soon as the ships had passed Fort Moultrie, the general excitement in the city could be felt, because all the cannons and mortars grew quiet. Nearly 6,000 men were on the wall, who wanted the pleasure of seeing the ships blown out of the water. As soon as the second [ship] cleared the fire from the fort, everyone left the wall and shortly thereafter, a great many small vessels were seen on the

Cooper River, heading inland. This and the road to Mount Pleasant were the only communications which the city had with the interior. The city was now completely cut off. We therefore had revenge for yesterday's cheering. The rebel and French ships retreated, part into the Cooper River, part under the city's defenses and made not the least effort to move. The enemy had sunk many ships so that ours could not approach too near the city and be in a position to fire against them. Our ships had seven dead and fifteen wounded. The large ships could not cross over the bar but had to remain in the ocean. *Renown*, 50 guns, was the largest that could cross.

"9 April - We received news that the tenth ship, which ran aground yesterday, was a transport ship and last night, because it could not be floated free, it was set on fire. Today four cannon boats and two flat boats equipped with cannons were brought here, overland, about two English miles, from the Ashley River to the Cooper River, on a locally built machine which had two wheels in the front and a skid behind. This machine was pulled by 134 Negroes. The enemy was very busy moving their belongings out of the city and into the country on the Cooper River.

"11 April - ... A ship with cannons and ammunition, such as had brought us from New York, had sunk. The artillerymen who had been on it were rescued and taken to Bermuda, which created a great problem for us. This situation was also the reason that the siege could not be started earlier. Of a necessity, also, cannons had to be taken out of the large warships, unloaded out at sea, brought to James' Island on other ships, and then brought here on land. The shortage of artillerymen was made good with sailors.

"30 April - Since the last date the work has gone forward every night as noted above. On our side we were now approaching so close to the enemy that it was possible to throw a stone into the enemy lines. A reinforcement arrived from New York, consisting of the Ditfurth Regiment, the 42nd Regiment of Scots, the Queen's Rangers, Lord Rawdon's Corps, and Colonel Brown's Corps.....

"4 May - During the night a three-masted ship lying near the city was silently boarded by our side and brought away. In the morning, when it was inspected, to our great surprise we found that the only men on board were those suffering from small-pox. With reference to small-pox, I must take note here that the people of this country, just as in Germany, fear it as much as the black plague. People who get it are immediately isolated.....

"7 May - The investment was continued as above. Our Jaegers have done great damage to the enemy in the city. Otherwise nothing has especially affected the siege since the last entry. The sailors in one of the batteries, despite orders to the contrary not to shoot at the houses in the city, have done so, causing the greatest damage. The fire from this battery can be distinguished by an unceasing persistence and these jacks [sailors] often fire a full broadside....

"8 May - We learned that Captain [Sir Andrew Snape] Hammond of the navy, with sailors and marines, had attacked and captured Fort Moultrie. A large part of the defenders had already withdrawn and only 184 men were captured. However, they had provisions for 500 men for six months. Forty-one large cannons and a 10-inch mortar were also found therein. The fort reportedly was oblong and very strong. It is built of palmetto logs and lies parallel with the ships' cannons. Of the enemy ships, all but five three-masted ships, near the city, have been sunk, although there are still a large number of very small ones. This morning the enemy was called upon to surrender and therefore there was a ceasefire....

"9 May - The ceasefire continued until nine o'clock this evening but because the city would not surrender according to the offered articles, the cannonade and bombardment was resumed in earnest by both sides. Our closest parallel extended to the canal connecting the Cooper and Ashley Rivers, and small arms fire could be directed into the enemy embrasures. Therefore kegs of musket cartridges were placed in the trenches so that the troops could fire at will.....

"11 May - The enemy sent a flag of truce from the city asking for a ceasefire, as they were ready to negotiate a surrender.

"12 May - Following an agreement yesterday to capitulate, the troops of the garrison marched out of Charleston, through the Hornwork, this morning at ten-thirty, with music playing and flags flying. As they were not allowed to play a British march, they chose a Turkish one. Near the Hornwork the prisoners stacked their arms. The number of Continentals and militia, including officers, amounts to about 6,000 men. Seven generals, 1 commodore, 10 regular regiments, and 3 battalions of artillery, not counting the French nor militiamen, were captured. General Leslie took possession of the city and the defensive works facing our lines with the grenadier companies of the 7th and Guards Regiments and four cannons. As soon as this had taken place and the enemy flag lowered and the British flag raised, the 7th and 63rd Regiments marched into the city. Meantime, all of our troops entered the lines. The militia was not allowed to march out with the others and their weapons were taken from them in the city. This applied to the French, also. Officers were permitted to keep their swords. After the captives had surrendered their weapons, they were returned to the city during the afternoon. The number of cannons in the defenses, including the metal ones, supposedly amounts to 400. The ammunition magazines are considerable, but provisions, except for a few items, had been nearly exhausted, which is said to be the primary reason the city had to surrender. During the entire siege our troops suffered 265 dead and wounded. The Graf Grenadier Battalion had two officers, Lieutenant [Johann Jacob] Fritsch and [Andreas] Oelhans, wounded, and two grenadiers killed and eight wounded.

### The Occupation of Charleston

Following the surrender of Charleston, Lieutenant Bartholomai continued his diary with a description of Charleston's defenses. "13 May - During the afternoon the captive officers, of whom there were a great many in the city, gathered improperly and loudly shouted, 'Congress lives!' As an uprising was feared, their sidearms were taken from those gentlemen....

"14 May - ... Annoyance and anger is seen in every face. Above all, they can not stand the sight of the Jaegers, which is natural, because they all served under arms and according to reports of their officers and all captured letters, the Jaegers and the bombs caused the majority of casualties, so we can not expect any special kindness.

"What Charleston's defenses consisted of, were as follows:

"On the land side - a regular hornwork with eighteen cannons, which is called the old royal defenses. The scarp is a wall of brick which is covered with oyster shells and a cement coating two feet thick, which therefore does excellent service because it can not be breached by the largest cannons, but only gives way, and also a swampy ditch spanned by a stone bridge.

"The gate which is in the middle of the revetment is protected by a lunette filled with earth, which has a double palisaded trench. Under the covering fire of small arms from that position is an entrenched position in the form of a half moon, opened toward the city, which has a trench six feet wide and equally as deep, between a double row of palisades, sheltered behind a strong abatis. The entrance to that position is also through a half moon, with a trench covered by a moveable chevaux de frise. On both flanks of those positions, two detached positions have already been laid out, protected by small arms fire, of which the one on the right rests against the Cooper River and the one on the left on the Ashley River. Both are covered to the rear by a swamp which has an ebb and flood tide from the two rivers. Through that flooded area there had been a twelve feet wide and six feet deep canal, running 100 yards in front of the trenches, to carry water, by means of dams, past the swamp to the trenches. It too was behind the abatis over which a portable bridge had been constructed and the entrance through the abatis had a well-guarded swinging gate. The detached defenses were connected with the main entrenchment by palisades and trenches and, during the siege, by a revetment. It was planned to have those on the left connected in the same manner, but they were too close and therefore the left wing was the weakest point. Therefore, if an enemy captured those detached works, the rest of the defenses could be attacked in the rear.

"The French engineer Duportail, who had been sent here fourteen days before the capitulation by General Washington, discovered the weakness of the detached positions and therefore included the hornwork in the system of trenches. If we had not completed our work so swiftly, he would have been able to put the defenses in a much better condition.

"On the water side - the defenses which covered the wharves and the harbor were laid out very well and provided with revetments, especially the so-called royal position, which was built of brick and oyster shells, also. The eighteen feet thick breastwork consisted of whole palmetto logs, through which, as previously noted, no cannonball can penetrate. They were filled with packed sand. At the point of the neck lay a fort which, with the point, formed a long triangle. It was built with traverses of the same material and had three tiers of cannons, consisting of 27 x 18- and 24-pounders, which completely covered the harbor. Therefore the only way that the city could be attacked from the water side was with floating batteries or bomb-galleys. The Cooper River was blocked with sunken ships, except for a narrow channel, which was covered by the small arms fire from the defenses. On the Ashley River side were all the wharves from which it could be anticipated that his batteries could not be adequately fired upon through the logs and furthermore, the defenses contained 100 or more cannons. For these reasons it was impossible to attack the city with ships from the water side. If a landing with flatboats were to be tried, the entrance to the channel leading to the city was so narrow that it would have been necessary to tolerate a dangerous cannonade. If even this were to be risked, the troops going ashore would still be sacrificed needlessly, because of the narrow defiles.

"15 May - During the afternoon a great misfortune struck Charleston due to the carelessness of the English. The artillerists were occupied taking weapons of the captives into a building, which had been an enemy magazine, when it blew up.

"Six buildings, including a poorhouse and a brothel were destroyed in the flames and, not counting the many residents and rebels, 200 or more of our men were lost, including the English Artillery Captain Collins, a Hessian artillery officer, Lieutenant McCloy of the 42nd Regiment, seventeen English and two Hessian artillerymen, a Hessian grenadier, and many English and Scottish soldiers. Without describing the sad sight of shattered, maimed, and half-dead people, who were struck down at the same time, or by the discharge of 5,000, mostly loaded weapons, many who were at a great distance were killed and wounded, and all the swords of the captured officers were melted. As great as this misfortune was, it could have been even worse as another magazine containing 400 barrels of powder was located only 200 yards away. If this had caught fire a quarter of the city would have been laid in ashes, as in the vicinity of the magazine there are only wooden houses.

"There are two reasons for the catastrophe. Either a loaded musket must have fired when it was thrown in and had ignited the stored powder, or a rebel had intentionally set it off in anger. Neither is an excuse for the English carelessness. What reasonable person would thoughtlessly throw loaded weapons into a powder magazine when a struck flint, resulting from a fall against another weapon, could cause the weapon to fire?

"And if it were set, why wasn't such a dangerous place better guarded and why was everyone allowed to enter? If this misfortune will instill greater vigilance remains doubtful, as there was another powder magazine on the Cooper River which was provided with a sentry who paid little heed to persons entering. This was very disturbing to a conscientious Hessian officer, until he was able to convince the English to keep a better guard on it in the future.

"If this unfortunate event had not occurred, this long, complicated, and difficult siege, which was conducted with few cannons against the enemy's numerous weapons, would have cost only a little over 200 men, because the rifle fire of the Jaegers, which must have seemed incredible to a European, was employed daily against the enemy cannons in order to silence them. Therefore, the enemy, behind his strongest defenses, lost more than 600 men. In order to maintain strict law and order in the city the Dirfurth and Huyn Regiments marched in to reinforce the garrison.....

"17 May - Work commenced on the preparation of the necessary passes so that the enemy militia could be sent home until their exchange.

"18 May - The cannons were taken aboard ship, the city defenses cleaned, and demolition of our trenches was continued as swiftly as possible.

"20 May - In order to reduce the threat of a secret uprising, the captive officers were sent to Haddrell's Point under escort, from which place their parole allows them to travel within a radius of six miles."

The Platte Grenadier Battalion Journal entries for this same period give the following account of the magazine explosion. "13, 14, and 15 May - The militia prisoners were released to their homes, inland, on parole. Today a large powder magazine, in which there was a great amount of munitions, blew up, without anyone knowing the cause initially. Although uncertain, it was said that the enemy weapons were taken there, one had fired [accidently], and this had caused the disaster. The number of victims can not be learned with certainty, but could amount to several hundred. Of the Hessians, an artilleryman, a cannoneer, and a carpenter, both of the Linsing Grenadier Battalion, were killed. This afternoon the Ditfurth and Huyn Regiments crossed the Ashley River from Wappoo Neck and entered quarters in the city. The 42nd Regiment also moved in.

"21 May - Nothing of consequence has happened since the last entry, except that the officers' sidearms were taken away because they created disorders in the city. Hoards of militia went past our camp and inland. Our transport ships exited the Stono River, crossed the bar, and entered the Charleston harbor. We received orders to be prepared to embark on designated ships which brought us from New York and on which our baggage was still being held. Meanwhile a number of Negroes, who had followed and taken employment with the army, part due to the shortage of foodstuffs, part to get away from their masters, began demolishing the defensive positions erected against the city. The corps designated for embarkation were the Jaegers, Light Infantry, British and Hessian Grenadiers, the 42nd Regiment, and the Queen's Rangers

## Clinton's Departure from Charleston

Bartholomai's account of activity following the conquest of Charleston continued on 21 May 1780. "As it was recalled, that the rebels had hidden many magazines inland, the Light Infantry and Queen's Rangers marched at daybreak today toward Dorchester and Strawberry to seize them.

"The army, except for the Charleston garrison, received orders to prepare for embarkation.

"News was received from Lord Cornwallis that as soon as his corps had arrived at Manigault, the rebels had abandoned Georgetown and retreated toward Camden. Many residence of South Carolina came to us with their horses and weapons in order to fight for the royal army.....

"29 May - The transport ships loaded provisions and fresh water and then lay at anchor at the wharf.

"30 May - The Jaegers went aboard transport ships *Apollo* and *Dispatch*.

"31 May - The Hessian and English Grenadiers went aboard ship. Our daily provisions were very difficult to obtain because despite the general-in-chief's order that all stores were to be opened on 1 June or he would forcibly open them, there was still nothing to buy from this stubborn nation.

"1 June - The following was published in orders for the army: Having learned that a troop of rebels was on the border of South Carolina, Colonel Tarleton was ordered to go there by Lord Cornwallis. At three o'clock in the afternoon of 29 May, after having traveled 105 miles in 54 hours with the Cavalry and the Infantry of the Legion, with the latter mounted behind the Cavalry soldiers, the detachment met the rebels, consisting of the 11th Virginia Regiment, several detachments from other Virginia regiments, and some artillery and cavalry, under the command of Colonel [Abraham] Buforth, near Vaxhaws, on the border of North and South Carolina. Tarleton called on them to surrender according to the same terms under which the Charleston garrison had surrendered. This was absolutely refused. Therefore the action began in a woods. Because of the necessity of leaving some horses behind and because he had to post a large number in reserve, the colonel could not attack with his full command. Therefore he took only 270 men, Cavalry and Infantry, but because he allowed the Cavalry to use sabers and the Infantry to charge with bayonets, he was able to rout the enemy. One lieutenant colonel, three captains, one adjutant, one quartermaster, and 97 privates were killed. Three captains, five lieutenants, and 42 men were wounded, and two captains, one lieutenant, and fifty men were captured. Only a few saved themselves by flight. Three standards, two 6-pounders, two royals, two wagons with ammunition, and 26 wagons with weapons and equipment were captured. Our losses consisted of two officers and eight privates killed, one officer and fourteen privates from the Infantry and three officers and thirty men from the Cavalry wounded.

"2 June - This morning the Queen's Rangers went aboard ship. The warships and frigates assigned to escort our fleet set sail, passed through the channel, and dropped anchor with the fleet near Sullivan's Island.

"As Charleston must be adequately occupied and in order to take the rest of South Carolina from the rebels, as well as to insure that this newly acquired province will not be attacked by the enemy, Lord Cornwallis remains as governor and general-in-chief in South Carolina with the following troops: General Prevost commanded the Wissenbach and D'Angelelli Regiments, as well as the militia, which constitute the occupation force for Savannah where a secure citadel was established so that the garrison could be reduced. However, as the general returned to England, General Clarke assumed command.

"At Charleston, where Brigadier Paterson commanded, the 7th, 63rd, and 64th Regiments and the Ditfurth and Huyn Hessian Regiments were the garrison.

"In addition to those forces, Lord Cornwallis retained: two light infantry companies from the 71st Regiment, one from the 16th Regiment, and one from the 60th Regiment.

"Two grenadier companies from the 71st Regiment, one from the 60th Regiment, and one from the 16th Regiment.

"The 23rd, 33rd, and 71st English Regiments, Brown's Corps, York Volunteers, North and South Carolina Volunteers, North and South Carolina militia, Ferguson's Corps, a detachment of York provincials, the mounted and foot members of the Legion, three troops of the 17th Dragoon Regiment, Savannah Light Horse, a corps of artillery and pioneers, and [Francis] Lord Rawdon's Corps.

"The engineer Moncrief took over the task of repairing and improving the Charleston defenses.

"3 and 4 June - The remaining troops went aboard their assigned transport ships, which then met a provisions fleet coming from New York.

"This was the end of an expedition, which drove the French commitment out of its defenses, completely removed its presence, and nearly eliminated all Congress' credit, which is most necessary for independence. And, if this seems to be an exaggeration, it can be shown that: 1) we suppressed the rebellion in South Carolina, 2) retained Georgia, 3) secured a firm foothold for the reconquest of North Carolina and other provinces, and 4) the rebels were forced to divide their forces, so that we were able to send reinforcements quickly, by sea, which because of the great distance offset the rebels' quick movement on land."

The Platte Grenadier Battalion Journal relates the difficulty of crossing the bar at Charleston and the voyage to New York. "30 May - The Jaegers embarked in their previously assigned ships in the Cooper River.

## Enemy Views (1780)

"31 May - The British and Hessian Grenadiers embarked. In compliance with today's general orders, each regiment was allowed to take ten Negroes, whose masters were in rebel service.

"4 June - The ships sailed away from the city. Today we passed Fort Moultrie, whose breastworks were made of palmetto logs, which were laid out in a square, one on top of the other, and filled with oyster shells. We could not cross the bar today. Many ships run aground here. The warships had crossed the bar already yesterday and lay at anchor outside. This difficult expedition, during which the Graf Grenadier Battalion, as noted, suffered one severely and one lightly wounded officer, two grenadiers killed and eight wounded, and one grenadier captured, therefore came to an end. The number of sick was tolerable, considering the difficult sea voyage, the subsequent duty, and the poor living conditions in an unhealthy climate where the troops continuously had to lie out under the open sky. Although the heat was very oppressive during the day, it changed as soon as the sun set to a cold, penetrating fog, which made everything damp and wet. It grew steadily colder as night set in and by early morning had turned to ice. The land itself is full of swamps and morasses. For the most part the water is bad and in the shallow wells and springs it is as warm as milk or even hotter, all day long. In the deeper wells it is colder but after standing a short time in a barrel, it is warm enough for a bath. Vegetables and garden produce are surprisingly rare. Therefore it would not have been surprising if we had more sickness than we actually had....

"Today we weighed anchor but due to contrary wind could not cross the bar, where the channels through the sandbanks are very narrow and it is impossible to pass without a favorable wind. Many of the transport ships ran aground today. The warships had crossed the bar yesterday and lay at anchor on the other side.

"8 June - We have had to lie on this side of the bar since the last date above due to contrary wind. Today the wind shifted in our favor and between eight and ten o'clock in the morning the transport ships passed fortunately over the bar. After the entire fleet had assembled around the admiral's ship, we sailed out to sea at about noon. About three o'clock in the afternoon we saw land for the last time. We steered southeast. The fleet, including the warships, consisted of about 100 ships.....

"15 June - ... One ship of our fleet had dropped far behind and was attacked by an enemy ship. The latter had to cease his attack when a warship of our fleet approached it....

"16 June - ... A war sloop ordered our captain to make as much sail as possible as a strange fleet had been seen in the distance. From the top of our mast our ship's captain saw eight ships together, following us with full sail. At the same time we received the report that a French fleet of warships was supposedly on this coast. Therefore, due to the discovery by our ship's captain, we were in a tight corner, because we had no other warships with us except for the two frigates and the war sloop mentioned above. The ship's captain said that if they were warships, they would certainly have caught up with us by tomorrow morning and it would be difficult for even one of the transport ships to escape.

"17 June - Early this morning, at daybreak, the ships assumed to be enemies yesterday, made a signal that they were friends. At the same time we saw the coast of New Jersey. According to the noon observation we were at 40⁰ 01' north latitude today. Toward four o'clock in the afternoon we saw the lighthouse at Sandy Hook and the lead ship entered New York harbor. Unexpectedly such a heavy fog developed that we could not see Sandy Hook nor a single ship. It was necessary for us to lay to before the wind. Suddenly a strong wind sprang up and stormy weather, which caused us, in fear of grounding, to sail out to sea again.

"18 June - As last night's fog continued, it was necessary to continue firing and beating the drums so that the ships would not run into one another. With a strong wind and a stormy sea we had to tack all night. In the morning we were close to Sandy Hook, surrounded by a large number of transport ships which belonged to our fleet. At nine o'clock in the morning we dropped anchor near Cole's Ferry on Staten Island and again met the warships on which were the admiral and General Clinton.

"20 June - All the troops landed on Staten Island."

## Enemy Views (1780)

### The Battle of Camden

The Huyn Regiment, and Private Asteroth, did not return to New York after the capture of Charleston, but remained in that city during the latter part of 1780. The following are some of the more interesting entries in Asteroth's diary during the period. "1 June - Clinton went aboard ship with the British Light Infantry and Grenadiers and the Hessian Grenadiers. Lord Cornwallis assumed command.....

"6 August - Lord Cornwallis joined his army which, since the capture of Charleston, had moved inland 120 English miles to the city of Camden.

"16 August - During the night General Gates with 9,000 men came to capture him [Cornwallis] and his 3,000 men. Cornwallis was aware of the plan and was well prepared. Fortunately he won and took 800 prisoners, artillery, and ammunition, 300 wagons, and all the baggage. Half of the enemy were killed or wounded. N.B. - *Feu de joie*.

"24 November - General [Carl Ernst Johann von] Bose landed here as brigadier over the garrison. General [Hans] von Knoblauch arrived with the same ship. He was a recent arrival from Hesse and received the regiment of the dead General [Carl Levin] von Truembach.

"28 November - The jaegers of the von Ditfurth and von Huyn Regiments, who had been on the ship *Anna,* on our trip from New York, arrived here.[37] In the first storm they had lost two masts. A man-of-war tied a line to them and helped them along. However, in the second storm the man-of-war had to turn them loose to save itself. The ship *Anna* was allowed to go with the wind. Still, God delivered them safely to England. Now, once again, all have arrived safely in America.

"10 December - A ship loaded with merchandise came from England but sank on the bar. The crew was saved, however."

### Activity in West Florida

Activities in West Florida during 1780 were noted in the diary of Chaplain Waldeck, commencing on New Year's Day. "Thank God, another year has passed and life takes a new direction. This is the fourth year which we have spent in an area of the world so far from our homeland. The first in America was celebrated in Elizabethtown and it was the most pleasant. The second was on Staten Island and still good, still filled with joy. The third was spent in the West Indies during our sea voyage here. Now the year 1780 here in Pensacola. When I write that word, I need write nothing more to refresh my mind, as it encompasses everything which fills by heart with sorrow. The entire officer corps gathered at Captain Pentzel's at seven-thirty and went to congratulate the colonel. At eleven o'clock everyone paraded over to the general's and from there to Governor Chester's.

"3 to 7 January - Our soldiers must work like the Israelites in Egypt, going from watch duty to fatigue duty, and this continues day after day. The soldier's life is really one of slavery.....

"3 February - The general has assigned Captain Pentzel the task of escorting the [Spanish] officers, here on parole, back to New Orleans. They left today with a flag of truce on the sloop *Christiana*. Commissary Marc was sent by the general, when this opportunity arose, to arrange the financial accounts of our prisoners.....

"6 February - Storm, thunder, and lightning, and an earthquake. Everything in the room shook, and clothing, hung on the wall, fell to the floor. This quake lasted about one minute, and truly, it could not have lasted much longer nor come again without causing the barracks to collapse. As soon as our door burst open, sparks from the neighboring room were blown over the gallery and into our room, so that the outbreak of fire as well as an earthquake was to be feared. Several chimneys were blown down by the wind. The quake itself, the crashing of collapsing houses, the shrieks of a family caught under the debris, the lightning flashes which followed quickly one after another, and the night made darker by the black thunderclouds, the roar of the stormy sea throwing its billowing waves upon the shore, and the rolling crash of thunderclaps, were startling. All this contributed to make the night so frightful that I could hardly believe such a storm could be survived on land. It is only in Pensacola that nature exerts all her fearfulness through the strength of the elements to destroy as she pleases. The wind eased about one o'clock in the night, but we did not lie down to sleep until near morning.....

"16 February - The laborers at Fort George leave their jobs, but the poor soldiers are so worn out that one is riled just to see how things are done. A little bread and unnourishing salted meat is his diet, and this is his only meal, from twelve to twelve-thirty; during the remaining time he gets nothing, not even a pipe of tobacco. The soldier from this small and bad nourishment becomes weakened, and this weakness becomes an illness because his blood and strength can not be renewed here with vegetables and other fresh foods. So he dies.

"17 November - We had a social get together this evening, and were speaking of the Spanish war when Lieutenant [Wilhelm] Keppel, who was in charge of the guard, entered and with excitement and elation said two Spanish deserters had just come in. They each had a weapon taken from our captive soldiers. The news, which they brought, was good news for us. It was definitely the plan of Governor Don Galvez to besiege and capture Mobile and Pensacola. All the armed ships and troops which he had been able to muster were with him. He even had 1,000 Negroes with him. His victory apparently certain, he was approaching the coast on the night of the fourteenth to the fifteenth, when a terrible storm arose which battered and scattered most of his fleet. Don Galvez was on board a brig of sixteen cannons which was driven so far this way that it had been seen here. Those who saved themselves from shipwreck, assembled at Mobile Point and off Dauphin Island, and fortified themselves as they anticipated we would take advantage of their misfortune and launch an attack. A single frigate and 200 men could have carried out this action.

"The deserters also told us that they suffered greatly from lack of provisions because the provision ships had been scattered and for each man the ration was half a biscuit and for four men, four pounds of salted meat. Don Galvez had reportedly sent an open boat to New Orleans with the order that all ships there should be sent to him with provisions and to take his men on board again. Six hundred men drowned in the storm, and seven ships were wrecked, so that Don Galvez is no longer in condition to undertake any action against us. That is how God alone has fought for us, and none of our strength has been used to help. He caused the storm to strike, which scattered our powerful enemy who was so near to us. This could have taken its toll from us, also, as we had outfitted ships to attack New Orleans, and chosen a stormy and inopportune time of the year for an attack. And this all powerful rescue by God could have come at no more opportune time, as it is during this month that we now await not only the packet boat, but also a frigate from Jamaica. And if our harbor is thus protected, I am of the belief, that we can withstand a number of attempts against Fort George. How fortunate we are, to win time by the Spaniards' misfortune, so that our fort can be placed in a defensible condition. In addition, however, I am glad that Don Galvez has come out of all this safe, as everyone must respect him for his intelligence and humanity. He chose the best time of year for his undertaking, he had no heavy defenses to fear in our harbor, our fort was not finished, and still he was not successful, because it was not God's will.....

"29 February - ... An express came overland from Georgia with the most pleasant news that we had not been forgotten, and that our post was not to be left unsupported. On the 25th of December of the past year, three regiments were embarked on twelve transport ships, the 57th, 42nd, and Lord Rathers [Rawdon's ?], plus three frigates and two sloops-of-war, for Pensacola. These ships are to be expected here soon and it is just in time as everything is now in disorder. The general at once sent a courier to Mobile, where this news will have a good effect and cause great joy, as Don Galvez and his are already at the city, and have cut communications between here and Mobile. If these frigates come in the next few days, Don Galvez can be trapped in Mobile Bay. That is the way of events during wartime. Changes occur making a situation look so dark that no way out can be seen, until suddenly there is hope where one thought no hope could have been expected. We had only hoped for help from Jamaica, from whence none came, but instead we will be strongly supported from New York. And if the Spaniards hear of this, it can only make us more peaceful and secure.....

"1 March - A restless night, caused by a thunderstorm which lasted all night. The news from yesterday, which I so happily recorded, is doubted today by everyone, and I assume it is a fantasy meant to frighten Don Galvez. And if this intent is obtained, it will have served its purpose. Above all, every bit of news which arrives tends to make us more mistrustful, as we have been deceived so often. The Light Infantry from the 60th Regiment moved out of the camp again and into the city. [Lieutenant] Governor [Captain Elias] Durnford reported to the general that the Spanish Governor Don Galvez has called upon the fort at Mobile to surrender, to which he returned the answer that because of his duty to king and country, he could not surrender until forced to do so by the most strenuous onslaught. Therefore, Don Galvez sent a galley farther into the bay and close up to the fort, but cannon fire from the fort forced it to retire. The Spaniards then took position on a height opposite the fort and set up a battery to fire on the fort. Therefore, the general began to prepare to march to Mobile with every soldier who was in any condition to undertake such a march.

"5 March - Early today the 60th Regiment marched out, although it rained the entire day. Our regiment is to follow tomorrow.

"6 March - Our regiment, or more correctly, the greatest and most useful part thereof, marched toward Mobile at six o'clock. Every soldier received a five day supply of rum and bread which he had to carry. Officers and men took only that which could be carried. The officers had their own rolled blankets fastened on their backs. This is a march which would be unheard of in German wars and if described by a participant, many would consider it impossible that troops and light artillery could travel 120 English miles through an area consisting only of wilderness. Immediately behind Fort George the wilderness begins and extends more than fifty miles before any developed place is encountered. The troops must spend every night under the open sky.

"16 March - A man came from the village which lies opposite Mobile. He had heard a heavy cannonade the previous Sunday and seen the Spanish flag flying on Tuesday. It seems Mobile fell before our relief troops arrived.

"18 March - It rained hard and the 16th and 60th Regiments returned this evening, and there are reports that our troops have recrossed the Perdido River. The general arrived earlier and all the inhabitants are displeased with him, as they are of the belief that he could have saved Mobile, which his vacillation lost. They wish that he had remained here and given the field command to Colonel von Hanxleden, which they believe would have made the expedition more successful.

"19 March - Toward four o'clock the artillery and our regiment, plus the Pennsylvanians arrived. All our men and officers returned here healthy and in good spirits. It is hard to imagine, after hearing the stories of the difficulties our troops encountered, that not a single one from our regiment was lost. They have waded water to their knees, and during the entire fourteen days, have not once had dry clothing. They have had to cross deep rivers on fallen trees, where a single misstep meant drowning without hope of rescue. Except for the rivers and a few plantations, there is nothing but wilderness as far as can be imagined. They have heard wolves howling in the distance and close by. They have had more than enough fresh meat, of which there is available all that one might wish, if he wants to shoot it.....

"27 March - The *Earl of Bathurst* at nine o'clock made a signal to indicate a fleet approaching from the east, and at eleven o'clock, fired twelve cannon shots. No one knew if the fleet were friend or foe, but we assumed it to be our fleet from Jamaica. Toward three o'clock we were able to see from here that there were a great many Spanish ships, and the entire fleet consisted of 21 ships. They are at anchor now on the other side of Rosa Island and will undoubtedly take control of the harbor tomorrow. This I write in comfort in my own peaceful room, but what the day will bring is already written in the book of omniscience, in which is recorded the fate of all provinces and all nations. We have had it in Pensacola, which has never had a lucky star shining on us.....

"30 March - Today the Spanish fleet could no longer be seen and we can not understand that, as they have the best wind today for entering the harbor, or at least to move closer to the Cliffs, and to take anchorage there. Work on our camp continues to be pushed. Everyone is waiting in anticipation and no one understands why the Spaniards have not launched an attack. The English flatter themselves with the hope that this means an English fleet from Jamaica has followed the Spaniards. However, we believe that the admiral is not concerned about our harbor, and since the greatest and best part of West Florida has been lost, retention of this post has insufficient value to justify sending reinforcements here. In a few days we will learn what the Don's intentions are.

"31 March - It was very warm. The Spanish fleet appeared again from the west, and the wind is so favorable that they can enter the harbor this evening, and then, if it is the Don's desire, they can hit us with a strong bombardment from their ships early in the morning....

"1 April - An officer, who came from Mobile on parole, solved the puzzle as to why the Spanish fleet had disappeared from view. The entire Spanish fleet, with 1,500 men, was at Mobile Point and was to join Don Galvez and then come here. We have received reinforcements, also, but on whose assistance little is to be relied, namely 300 Choctaw Indians, who are divided within their own nation, and 300 Creeks, of whom a great many are already here, and whole families pass our camp daily. We can trust the Creeks a bit more than the Choctaws, as the Creeks have had a more constant friendship with the English, while the Choctaws tend to favor the Spanish.

"... Colonel von Hanxleden has the overall command in the camp at Gage Hill. Lieutenant Heldring was presented his captaincy in the regiment.[38] The governor announced that in our present dangerous situation the inhabitants were not to sell or trade rum to the Indians, as the problem of dealing with drunk Indians is well-known. Colonel von Hanxleden, in appreciation for the hard work, gave the regiment an ox and decided to continue this practice every Sunday in the future, in order to bolster the spirits of the soldiers from the depressing work-load, and to encourage their eagerness to continue working for the King.....

"25 April - Our flag of truce to New Orleans returned. Major Pentzel returned in good health and we received letters from our acquaintances there. The major and Commissary Marc had to put up with a great deal as they were not allowed to enter New Orleans.....

"13 August - The frigate *Mentor*, which had sailed out on a cruise, sent in a Spanish sloop loaded with cannonballs destined for New Orleans.

"14 August - Aboard the captured Spanish ship were many letters from Mobile, some to friends in New Orleans, some sent to Havana, which held the most bitter complaints about the miserable conditions in Mobile. We have no complaints of this nature yet. We suffer short-ages of several things here. However, the Spaniards have a surplus of all miseries at Mobile. We are healthy and they are sick and have no medicine. And most of all, the complaints are about the Indians who take scalps so close to their sentries that no one dares to go half a mile into the woods.....

"25 August - ... The French are held responsible for inventing the scalping knife and supplying the savages with it, to be used against the

English, which as long as the French were in Canada and on the Great Lakes, they did. Now all these Indians are on the side of the English and hold a great hatred against the French and especially against the Spaniards.....

"19 November - ... We heard that Don Galvez had actually sailed with a fleet from Havana to conquer Pensacola and West Florida, but a severe storm near the Tortugas Island scattered this fleet, and nothing is known of his whereabouts.

"27 November - We hear that Don Galvez with most of his fleet has arrived at Mobile and will soon make his visit to us.

"December - The Indians, who have become our enemies now, planned to attack the camp and massacre everyone.....

"31 December - Another year is at an end and if it will be the last one in Florida, we need not know. It is all immaterial. All is in vain."

Unfortunately Chaplain Waldeck's diary covering the remaining years of the war was apparently lost and with it his account of the capture of Pensacola in 1781.

Steuernagel also recorded some of the events of 1780 concerning the activities of the Pensacola garrison and the forces in West Florida. "On 6 March 1780 an expedition was undertaken toward the Perdido River and Mobile, to go to the assistance of Durnford, the man commanding there, who was surrounded by the Spaniards. Our intent was frustrated, however, because as we crossed the Perdido River and arrived at the Tensaw River, we received he report that Lieutenant Governor Durnford and his men had been forced to surrender to the Spaniards.

"We had to return to Pensacola. How difficult the journey through such a wilderness, where one could not find his way nor still less encounter a human habitation. I can not describe it accurately, and therefore only briefly mention it, and then we learned that our people who had gone to the Mississippi the previous year had been taken, and that even Captain Alberti, Sr., and his command had been captured. I will just not add more detail here.

"On 28 March 1780 all the troops from Pensacola were moved to the camp at the nearby constructed Fort George, and Colonel von Hanxleden was given command of the fortification and the troops.

Enemy Views (1780)

"On 6 April Lieutenant Colonel von Horn, his two sons, Sergeant Stuckenbruck, and a transport of nineteen men arrived here, and were the third recruit transport."

## A Cold Winter in New York

In the opening days of 1780 General von Knyphausen was in command at New York and his worst enemy was the extreme cold weather. The cold and its effects were noted in the Hesse-Cassel Jaeger Corps Journal, commencing on 15 January. "The continuing cold since Christmas Day has so covered the rivers with ice, that one can walk and ride across them. Therefore, General Washington considered this as an ideal time to undertake some action against the troops remaining here, and to take advantage of all the opportunities which this occasion offered. His first thought turned on the garrison on Staten Island. This island had been robbed of its natural defensive strength by the rivers freezing. The garrison was not strong, and appeared to be in great danger, especially as it could not be supported from New York, because the ice was not yet solid, and there was no way to make a crossing. General Washington had noted all this and detached General Stirling with 3,500 men in sleds, which had been gathered at Morristown, and carried the men across the snow to Bergen, in order to attack the garrison. But the English General Stirling, who commanded on Staten Island, received reports of the enemy advance and was prepared to receive them. Not withstanding, the rebels crossed the ice during the night of

"16 January - near Decker's Ferry, and established outposts on Brusky Heights, cutting off the Queen's Rangers at Richmond, and the troops at the Flagstaff, from those in the headquarters' defenses at Cole's Ferry. General von Knyphausen ordered a number of flatboats to be gathered at The Narrows, where because of the strong current there was still some open water, and toward evening he ordered the 80th Regiment into the boats in order to try, if at all possible, to cross over during the next ebb tide. The enemy did not want to risk storming these defenses from which all the snow had been removed. The cold was too great to tolerate for an extended period, and the fear that the embarked troops might surprise them, caused the enemy to pull back across the ice on the night of the seventeenth. A troop of

English provincial dragoons attacked their rear guard, and many of the enemy suffered from frozen hands, feet, and ears.....

"21 January - The North and East Rivers are so completely covered with ice that cannons can be transported across them. It is now possible to cross to Staten Island - thirteen miles - with a wagon. New York therefore is like a part of the mainland and is open to enemy attack. Lieutenant General von Knyphausen has taken all possible precautions to prevent such an occurrence. The Jaeger Corps was dressed every night, and constantly sent patrols along the North River, even though a chain of occupied defensive positions was already in existence there."

Prechtel's diary also contains comments on the frozen rivers. "14 January - Today the East River is frozen so that many people have crossed from here to Brooklyn, on the ice. However, at eleven o'clock, midday, the tide came in and the river immediately opened again.

"15 January - ... The enemy crossed the Kills River, which is frozen over, from Amboy to Staten Island, with 9,000 men and attacked our troops. One thousand men of the regiments lying in garrison here were detached as a reinforcement. They were embarked at four o'clock in the afternoon, but because of much ice, were unable to sail and therefore had to be debarked again.

"16 January - ... The 1,000 men, who were to have sailed to Staten Island as a reinforcement, were embarked again this morning and because the ice still prevented them from being shipped over, at eleven o'clock, midday, they were again debarked.

"The enemy reportedly remains on Staten Island, but in the area toward Amboy.

"17 January - ... The enemy, under the command of the American General Stirling, withdrew from Staten Island.

"The British troops on Staten Island, commanded by the English General Stirling, during this attack, suffered four dead. On the enemy's side, twelve men were made prisoners of war.....

"20 January - At present the North River is frozen so that the detachment at Paulus Hook, about one mile off New Jersey, can cross back and forth on the ice.....

"25 January - During the night a strike force, consisting of 400 men from the regiments lying in garrison here, marched across the ice on the North River, to Paulus Hook, and from there to Bergen, in New Jersey. Beyond this enemy city, a rebel picket of thirty men was captured. These troops were brought here during the night, by our forces, as prisoners of war.

"22 February - The North River remained frozen over from 20 January until today. During this time all provisions were carried across the river to Staten Island with wagons."

## General Knyphausen's Move into New Jersey[39]

The Hesse-Cassel Jaeger Corps Journal reported an invasion led by General von Knyphausen into New Jersey in June 1780 with considerable detail, the most important entries which were as follows. "5 June - The army under Lieutenant General von Knyphausen was ordered to march tomorrow, leaving behind all equipment, wives, sick persons, etc. A detachment of 100 jaegers under Captain von Wangenheim was to remain at Morris Hill, also.

"6 June - At two o'clock in the morning the Jaeger Corps and the Guards were embarked in eight sloops at Turtle Bay on the East River and set sail at one o'clock, passing New York, where the rest of the army was also embarking, and dropped anchor near Cole's Ferry on Staten Island. Here, at four o'clock, the troops in 56 sloops and schooners had come together, lifted anchor, and sailed to Decker's Ferry. However, because the wind and tide were contrary, they reached the ferry only at seven o'clock in the evening....

"7 June - ... The Jaegers were to take position in the front [of General Mathew's Division at Connecticut Farms] on the Springfield Road, and had the task of driving the enemy from the terrain which he still held in that area. This occurred with the loss of some wounded, and the corps took post in a corner of woods which had thick growth on the right and left, which had to be occupied by the detachments, and to their front at about 600 yards, there were houses. The enemy took post behind these and had to be dislodged, which nevertheless, occurred with the loss of some wounded, and the corps established another post there, which was as disadvantageously located as the first one. The enemy continued to fire and pressed forward several times with the bayonet and new reinforcements, but was always repulsed until finally driven from the field in our front, where both sides left men dead. As often as he was beaten back, so often he returned with a fresh attack, and this continued until about one o'clock, when suddenly the Grenadier Company of the Light Infantry was detached to support the Jaegers and to drive the enemy back as far as Springfield.... [Following more contact with the enemy] we had one officer - Lieutenant Friedrich Ebenauer of the Ansbach jaeger Corps - two non-commissioned officers, and 44 jaegers wounded. Our people had been fully engaged and had exchanged fire the entire day with the enemy, whose losses could not be determined. However, we found several dead officers and many dead privates and made five prisoners....

"At eleven o'clock in the evening the army broke camp and marched back toward Elizabethtown. A strong thunderstorm made the march difficult. At daybreak the army repassed the city and camped at Elizabethtown Point, close to the water.

"8 June - The baggage was taken back to Staten Island, followed by the Jaegers since they had no more ammunition. The Cavalry was also shipped over to Staten Island. The remaining troops however, camped in such a position as to invite an enemy attack on the Point. Toward ten o'clock the enemy appeared in force, and attacked the 22nd Regiment which had to soften the initial enemy advantage. As, however, the Buenau and Ansbach Regiments moved up to support, the enemy pulled back with a loss of many men and was pursued as far as the city. It was not the entire enemy army, but a corps under General Stirling, which had been detached from the army in order to observe us.....

"13 June - Our mounted Jaegers, at seven o'clock in the evening, crossed the bridge to Newark to attack the enemy cavalry picket, which, however, was warned in time and departed. N.B. - It is nearly impossible to surprise the enemy at any time because the farmer or his son, also his wife and daughter, shoot a rocket up or run along the footpaths to report to the enemy.....

"16 June - Today we received news that General Clinton with a part of the troops from Charleston had returned.....

"19 June - At ten o'clock General Clinton arrived at the army and reconnoitered its dispositions as well as the enemy's outposts.....

"23 June - At three o'clock in the morning the following regiments marched toward Springfield.... The royal troops formed on the heights on this side of Springfield. General Mathew commanded the right wing and was to cross the river in order to seize a height lying on the enemy's left front, while General Tryon was to force the bridge, which led directly to Springfield and was defended by two columns. The 38th Regiment was given this task. The Jaegers divided themselves to the right and left of the bridge, waded through the water, which was rather deep, and drove the enemy from the opposite shore with a heavy fire. At this moment also, the regiment pressed forward onto the bridge and drove off the enemy posted there.... Thereafter the army marched back after setting fire to Springfield. The Jaegers composed the rear guard and could hardly make their way between the fires of the already collapsing houses.... After our arrival in camp we received orders to send our baggage to Staten Island at once and at twelve o'clock all the troops followed."

The Prechtel diary entries also cover the von Knyphausen move into Jersey and other events of interest during 1780. "6 June - Today an expedition consisting of 7,000 men, under the command of the Hessian Lieutenant General von Knyphausen, sailed over to Staten Island in flatboats and schooners and made night camp at Decker's Ferry.

"7 June - At four o'clock in the morning the army moved out and was carried across the Kills River in flatboats.

"As soon as the Field Jaegers, who constituted the advance guard, arrived at Elizabethtown, an uninterrupted small arms fire began. The army marched on to Connecticut Farms.

"There the enemy was attacked and in the fighting 2nd Lieutenant Ebenauer, of the Ansbach Jaeger Corps, was killed....

"At twelve o'clock at night the army retreated back to Elizabethtown and set up night camp close to the Kills River.

"8 June - The 17th Dragoons and the 22nd Regiment, both English regiments, moved forward toward Elizabethtown. The latter, however, marched to the right of the woods. Although these regiments exchanged shots with the enemy the entire morning, they were completely driven back into the lines by midday. As a result the Ansbach von Voit Regiment at once moved forward and fired on the enemy with cannons and small arms, charging three times, one after the other, and with such a terrible fire against the enemy from cannons and small arms that the enemy could no longer withstand the fire, but had to retreat all the way back to Elizabethtown....

"The enemy losses on the other hand, were one major, two subalterns, and seventy privates, a total of 73 persons.

"After half an hour, the enemy again opened fire on our outposts. Therefore, every outpost was reinforced with a field jaeger and by this means, the enemy was silenced.....

"15 June - ... During our stay here, three defensive positions have been built on the Kills River. Also, a floating bridge over the Kills River between Staten Island and Jersey had been constructed with 29 one and two-masted ships.....

"17 June - ... The floating bridge across the Kills River is 270 strides long....

"Washington's army retreated during the night to Chatham, but continued firing with cannons at the workers. However, it was very quiet at the outposts.....

"22 June - Lieutenant General von Knyphausen moved forward over Springfield this morning....

"The enemy was attacked near Springfield, but withstood the heavy fire very well.

"During the evening the [English] army retreated into the lines near Elizabethtown....

"During the evening the army received the order to immediately vacate the Jerseys. Therefore, at ten o'clock in the evening it withdrew, in the best order, across the floating bridge to Staten Island. The outlying pickets formed the rear guard."

## Arnold's Treason

Prechtel continued his diary entries, writing of activity in the New York area, including the execution of two members of the Ansbach-Bayreuth contingent for desertion, and of the treason of Benedict Arnold. "26 July - This morning the following sentence was pronounced against the recaptured deserter [Johann Heinrich] Rhau, who had deserted on the twelfth of this month. Because of his having committed disloyal desertion, he was to be punished by hanging. But, as this was an especially severe punishment, it was changed to death by a firing squad.

"28 July - The deserter Rhau, of the von Voit Regiment, was executed behind the front at seven o'clock this morning.....

"31 July - The deserter [Joseph] Glatz, of Captain von Eyb's Company, of the von Seybothen Regiment, who had been captured, was sentenced to be hanged by a court-martial, and he was immediately so notified.....

"2 August - Private Glatz, ... notified of the death sentence by hanging, had the sentence changed to death by a firing squad, and this morning at seven o'clock this was carried out behind the front.....

"15 August - People were pressed onto the warships. Therefore, from ten o'clock in the morning until one o'clock in the afternoon, a line moved out of the city stretching from the East River to the North River.

"16 August - ... Due to the press activity, the line was again employed from four until eight o'clock in the morning.....

"27 August - ... The American General Arnold defected to the English army and arrived at headquarters in New York yesterday with twenty deserters from the enemy.

"General Arnold was immediately taken on by the English army as a brigadier general.....

"9 October - ... The unhappy fate which the English Major [John] Andre, the adjutant general for the general-in-chief, Clinton, received from the enemy was reported here and made known to the army today.....

"11 October - ... An expedition under the command of the English Major General Leslie was embarked at Staten Island yesterday. It consisted of 3,000 men and is to sail to Virginia.....

"19 October - The von Seybothen Regiment entered winter quarters today in the brewery on the North River at New York.....

"28 October - The agreement for the exchange of prisoners by the English side, as well as by the American side, was agreed upon on the 25th of this month, and published for the army today.....

"22 November - The von Voit Regiment moved into winter quarters today in New York and entered the North Church on William Street."

Musician Stang also commented on Arnold's treason and desertion to the English. "26 September - General Arnold, a colonel and 700 men [!] deserted to us from the rebels."

The Hesse-Cassel Jaeger Corps Journal contains the following comments on activitites in the New York area during the latter half of

1780. "20 July - Most of the army was ordered to embark at Frog's Neck tomorrow in order to go to Rhode Island, as the war fleet had already sailed for that place today in order to attack the French.....

"23 July - Today the troops at Frog's Neck went on board. Only 300 jaegers under Captain Ewald went on the expedition because Lieutenant Colonel von Prueschenck was sick. The rest of the army marched to Kingsbridge and camped on the Heights of Hotham under the command of Major General Tryon.....

"31 July - Our fleet returned from Huntington and lay at anchor at Whitestone because the French had already fortified themselves on Rhode Island and Admiral Arbuthnot did not consider it advisable to attack them there.

"1 August - This evening the field equipment for the troops which lay at anchor at Whitestone was sent away as they are to go into camp on Long Island.....

"10 September - Today we received reports that on 16 August, near Camden, Lord Cornwallis had defeated General Gates. This affair occurred at daybreak. Both armies had broken camp, each to attack the other. They met during the night, while on the march, and after a brief skirmish between the advance troops, both armies halted and the action began at daybreak. The American army became confused and was defeated. Gates lost five cannons, nine flags, and all his baggage and ammunition, most of which was taken from him during the pursuit by the Cavalry. Also, the Cavalry and Light Infantry sent in pursuit of the enemy, by the general, captured 400 men. Gates' total losses amounted to 800 dead and wounded, including Major General [Johann] Kalb and Major General Rutherford, as well as 1,200 prisoners. General Gates, because of the misfortune and reportedly because of the confusion during the retreat, has been suspended from command and replaced by General [Nathanael] Greene. On the other hand, had General Gates been successful, the inhabitants who had made a sort of oath, would have taken up weapons and burned all the royal magazines. This however was prevented by his flight and several leaders of these desperate measures were arrested.....

"27 September - The enemy Major General Arnold arrived in New York today. He had found it necessary to take flight in the *Vulture* sloop-of-war, which lay at Stony Point, because Major Andre, with whom he had been discussing the handing over of the defenses of West

Point, which Arnold then commanded, had been exposed at Tarrytown during his return, and papers found on him which he had received from Arnold.

"3 October - Despite the strenuous efforts which General Clinton exerted to save Major Andre, his adjutant general, Andre was hanged yesterday at twelve o'clock in the enemy camp at Tappan. General Washington held a court-martial, in which all the rebel generals were present, concerning Andre. He had been three days with General Arnold, had seen the defenses himself, had developed and participated in the planning of the manner in which they were to be put into the King's hands, and had been captured in civilian clothing during his return to New York. His life was forfeit. The specific plan was: Arnold already had torn down the palisades in the outer wall in various defensive positions, which were to have been replaced with newer, better, and stronger materials. He would then take the troops out of the defenses and march against us, off to one side, where he could easily be cut off from the fort. The English Light Infantry therefore, had already marched from Long Island to the Jaeger camp in order to be able to march with us the moment Andre returned.

"7 October - Major General Arnold has been made a brigadier general and has received a new corps of foot and mounted personnel called the American Legion, to which, by public proclamation, he has invited all American officers and soldiers.

"Major General Leslie embarked today with the Guards and some other troops in order to sail to Virginia.

"10 October - A detachment of 100 jaegers under Captain von Roeder were sent to join Major General Leslie in order to sail with the expedition, also.....

"9 December - From Carolina we hear that Major Ferguson, who commanded 800 militiamen, was attacked on 7 October near King's Mountain by the enemy General [Otho H.] Williams with 2,500 men, and after a hard-fought battle in which Willliams, as well as Ferguson, was killed, Ferguson's troops surrendered after the action ended. The rebels held a field court-martial and hanged some officers and the colonel of the English militia.

"10 December - General Ewald [sic - Arnold ?]embarked today with the 80th Regiment, Rangers, Robinson's Corps, and about 100 jaegers under Captain Ewald in order to go to Virginia, because

General Leslie had departed from there and gone to Carolina to join Cornwallis."

The Platte Grenadier Battalion Journal record of events in the latter part of 1780 includes the following entries. "22 June - The battalion landed in New York [upon its return from Charleston] and joined the garrison there. There were no other troops in New York but Robinson's Provincial Corps. The citizens had to do duty in the city....

"24 July - At six o'clock in the morning the Graf Grenadier Battalion embarked in small vessels at New York and went through Hellgate to Whitestone where we embarked on the two transport ships, *Margaretha* and *Woodland.* The other troops embarked here were 250 Hessian Jaegers, two battalions of British Light Infantry, two battalions of British Grenadiers, the wing companies of the English Guards, and the 37th, 42nd, and 43rd Regiments, the other Hessian Grenadier Battalions, and the Landgraf and Leib Regiments. The fleet assembled at Whitestone. It appears the preparations are for going to Rhode Island, where the French fleet noted above in June of this year had not only captured the harbor, but had also landed the troops which it had on board.

"26 and 27 July - The rest of the fleet came up the East River. Travel through Hellgate with large ships is very dangerous and therefore proceeded very slowly until all the ships had passed through. As soon as all the ships had arrived here, the fleet set sail at six o'clock in the evening and traveled up the East River. The fleet consisted of three frigates, a war sloop, and 62 transport and store ships.

"28 July - This morning we lay at anchor in Huntington Bay on Long Island and the ships received orders to take on water. Two frigates from our fleet continued up the East River, supposedly following Admiral Arbuthnot, who had gone with the warships into the ocean near the east end of Long Island or the exit from the Sound or East River.

"30 July - The frigates which sailed ahead day before yesterday, returned. A signal to sail was made immediately and we returned to Whitestone. We dropped anchor there about eleven o'clock in the morning. The troops received orders, that as soon as the field equipment could be brought from New York, they were to land on

Long Island, but the ships were to maneuver. We heard that the two frigates mentioned above had been driven back.....

"9 November - From the start of this month on, the troops in camp began to enter winter quarters. Today the Hessian Grenadier Brigade moved into winter quarters, the Linsing and Lengercke Grenadier Battalions at Jamaica and the Loewenstein and Graf Battalions at New Flushing. The officers entered houses, the non-commissioned officers and privates, however, entered huts built at both places, after we had been in camp at Whitestone from early August until today. On 8 October a corps of troops at this place, under the command of General Leslie, embarked. Of the Hessians, only a detachment of Jaegers and the Bose Regiment were included. In addition to these, there were two battalions of English Guards, the 82nd Regiment, and Colonel Fanning's Corps, and the rest of the 17th Regiment, plus the light infantry companies of the provincial corps, under the command of Colonel [John] Watson. The corps landed at Portsmouth in Virginia, and later left that post and went to Charleston.....

"11, 12, and 13 December - One hundred Hessian jaegers, commanded by Captain Ewald, the 80th Regiment, Robinson's Corps, and the Queen's Rangers, all under the command of General Arnold, embarked on an expedition to Virginia. General Arnold came over to our army from the rebels in the past September. He was under suspicion of having joined the royal party as he had made a great many enemies among the rebels during the past year. It is said that during this time he had a secret correspondence with General Clinton and had sought a favorable opportunity to surrender a large number of the troops under his command. No more favorable opportunity had presented itself than the one of his being commandant of Fort Defiance [West Point] on the North River.

"The plan to surrender this fort and the troops therein was developed in the following manner. Our side was to attack and the commandant would immediately surrender. The adjutant general, Major Andre, secretly left the guard ship *Vulture* lying in the North River, during the night, and fortunately reached General Arnold in Fort Defiance. According to the agreement and the plan outlined to him, Major Andre, dressed as a local native, returned by land. He accidentally encountered some militiamen, who questioned him and finally held him as a spy, even though he had a pass from General

Arnold. Andre was taken before General Washington, who was in the area, and Arnold, who learned of Major Andre's arrest, quickly went in a boat to the above named guard ship lying in the North River, and eventually arrived safely in New York. He was made a brigadier general with the British troops and received the above command. Major Andre was court-martialed as a spy and, despite all of General Clinton's efforts, hanged. We received news from the troops embarked with General Arnold that they had landed in Virginia."

The Order Book of the von Mirbach Regiment contains a pair of interesting orders in 1780 concerning the women with the Hessian regiments. The first deals with removing temptations that face the men and the second with the necessity of obtaining consent for marriages. "11 February - The colonel has learned that often in the companies, and especially in the huts, where the soldiers' wives sell all types of liquors, non-commissioned officers and privates have been playing all sorts of card and dice games and even tempting passing soldiers from other regiments with drinks, even taking their money. Therefore the colonel with the strictest and most urgent orders, orders that it is forbidden for anyone to play, so the company officers and patrols are to inspect the huts frequently in order to prevent the resulting excesses. The colonel especially advises the company commanders that the inspection be exactly carried out and if a non-commissioned officer should be apprehended, he is to be placed in the stocks according to the regulations and a private is to be arrested at once and reported to the staff......

"21 February - ... It is the gracious order of His Serene Highness that no person belonging to the lower staff or commissaries is to be married in the future without the knowledge and consent of His Excellence Lieutenant General von Knyphausen, whose approval or refusal, after an investigation, is to be final.

## The 1780 Transfer of Troops to Canada

Although the von Lossberg Regiment had suffered severely in the 1779 attempt to have the regiment transferred to Canada, the men were again ordered to board ships for Canada in 1780 as related in the diary of Lieutenant Piel. "15 May - The regiment was embarked near Brooklyn on Long Island....

"23 May - At seven-thirty this morning we set sail. Our fleet now consisted of thirty ships, including the war sloops *Otter* and *Swift*, the armed ship *Recovery*, as well as various corps. The wind was northwesterly and we had to tack all day. At eleven o'clock in the morning we had passed the point of Sandy Hook and were in the ocean.....

"26 May - ... At three o'clock this afternoon the ships *Recovery*, *Blenheim*, and four others which were destined for England, left the fleet.....

"25 June - ... It was almost impossible to have a more beautiful view than that which we had this morning, in a not overly-wide river, with the island Orleans on the right and the mainland on the left, everywhere covered with houses, gardens, fields, and forests, and everything in the full bloom of spring, and in addition, the waterfall of Montmorency, which surpasses all art, and on the left, the city of Quebec, of which part lies on the summit and part at the foot of a high peninsula and projects the most beautiful view in the world. At eleven-thirty we entered the harbor and lay at anchor close to the city.....

"27 June - Today the regiment landed and was quartered in the township of Beaufort.....

"29 June - This morning the transport ship *Archer*, with Colonel von Borck as well as one and one half companies and the artillery detachment of the Knyphausen Regiment, which spent the past winter on the island of St. Johns, arrived here."

## Comments of Convention Prisoners

In a letter to his prince in January 1781, the then Major Pausch reported on conditions existing in 1780 for the Convention prisoners at Charlottesville. "Your Serene Highness I must report in full submissiveness how I have many times humbly requested of Major General Philipps, who assumed the position of commander-in-chief of this entire unfortunate army after the departure of Lieutenant General Burgoyne, to be exchanged along with a determined number of officers from all the other nations serving in this corps, including the prisoner of war Lieutenant Bach. I have the pleasant hope, after this spring, to find myself with the largest part of the artillery company entrusted to me, according to all appearances, once again actively engaged and performing duty in Canada.

"Our fate, by the end of this year, will have been hard for thirty months, and even that much harder, because we have had the most painful feelings due to the pitiful conditions and complaints of our good and upright men, especially during the period of a shortage of provisions during the previous winter and spring, accompanied by an excessive increase in costs, a very cold and long-lasting winter, which made it impractical for our providers to deliver through the extremely deep snow, so that finally the need became pervasive. Late in the spring a new American colonel and commander of our guards, by the name of [James] Woods, made such good preparations that flour and meat were again delivered into the magazine, and this misery was corrected. He also relaxed our restrictions, so that some of the troops could go out, and could again buy and sell. Despite all afflictions however, most of the men tolerated this with patience and resolution. They try their best to feed themselves, no matter how miserably, as circumstances allow.

"On 24 November of last year I received the news of my actual exchange, but I could obtain no wagon until 8 December, despite my best efforts. During that time therefore, I adjusted my accounts with Lieutenant Sartorius and gave Lieutenant Dufais his instructions to the most humbly accompanying, exactly named tables and lists, and the report resulting therefrom, of: 1st Lieutenant Dufais, four non-commissioned officers, one drummer, twelve cannoneers, Wagon-master Zicklamm, one journeyman wheelwright, and one artillery servant, a total of 21 men, for whose maintenance the still remaining supply of small clothes items were left behind, with which they will be able to help themselves for some time, and possibly even until an imminent general exchange, for which there is still great and high hopes, which we still hold...

"Before my departure from Virginia, all the English Convention troops had already marched off to Fort Frederick in three brigades. However, I found them all together in Fredericktown [MD], where I also learned positively that all the German troops belonging to the Convention, who were still lying in their barracks upon my departure from Albemarle, were to be sent to Lancaster in the near future, and were to be placed in the barracks in that town and county.

"If this is done in the very near future, then many of our men, without having to wait longer for a general exchange, will be assembled here and very well-provisioned. By then they will have crossed two rivers, the Potomac and the Susquehanna, the two most difficult obstructions, and be no more than 163 English miles from New York, where they will also find much help for carrying them over the remaining waters, as at the present, those in Pennsylvania, previously supportive of the Colonies, have changed and separated [from their allegiance]. Those who ransomed themselves have their freedom after withstanding much privation, need, and danger, day and night, in the woods and marshes where there were no roads and they had to wander in order not to be recaptured and thrown into jail by the Americans. Also, they must live without seeing or receiving anything to eat for three to five days at a time. A portion of them have fortunately come over [to English controlled areas]. However, a portion were also captured and thrown into the most terrible imprisonment in irons or severely mistreated. What they on occasion withstood and still must tolerate, they must attribute to a shortage of money due to the Convention. - This especially hurt the officers because the non-commissioned officers were paid every eight months, and the privates every ten months. When, at times, several months' pay was delivered, this could only be made in bills of exchange, which the troops could only exchange for sterling, and had to accept that at barely half the value.

"Everything else previously pertaining to this unfortunate part of the Royal Army in North America and the difficulties experienced, Colonel von Gall will be able to provide in detail to Your Serene Highness' most gracious knowledge, with far more circumstances and far more clearly."

A number of other letters from various members of the Hesse-Hanau contingent of troops provide a glimpse of the situation for the Hesse-Hanau troops during 1780. Captain von Germann, writing to his prince from Charlottesville in February 1780, wrote "May it please Your Highness to see in the most humble reports accompanying, that on 19 September of last year, that, except for Private [Wilhelm] Grimm, your company suffered no losses. That is all the more surprising to me as the men up to now, because of a scarcity of provisions, have had to put up with so much. Now everyone hopes once again for an exchange in the near future, of which there are supposedly definite reports. If this hope is again groundless, I fear that the desertions will be even more numerous next summer than ever before. The company has been supplied with small clothes items as best possible and all the troops are healthy, which is surprising in our present situation."

Captain von Buttlar, writing from captivity at Charlottesville on 4 July 1780, commented on the reason many of the Convention prisoners deserted from the camp. "Musketeer Grimm, who deserted on 4 April 1780, was made a prisoner of war again by an American patrol and brought here. Musketeer Weingarten met a similar fate, having deserted on 21 June 1780 from these barracks and been returned on 22 June. A few days earlier Musketeer Hinckel deserted, but despite all my efforts, I have not had the least information as to his fate nor where he might be. The false assumption that a prisoner of war has a better chance of being exchanged than a Convention prisoner, is the cause of these desertions, and it is difficult to convince young people, who are unaccustomed to misery, to have patience in this sad situation. Poor provisions and even a scarcity of food, together with high prices, are also contributing factors. Nevertheless, I spare no effort to console the men with the most convincing arguments and the best hope is always to remember the illustrious and gracious father of our country, who constantly strives to provide for the welfare of his subjects."

## Canada 1780

On 23 October 1780 Captain Schoell reported to his prince on events occurring in Canada within the Hesse-Hanau contingent under his command. "Surgeon [Wilhelm] Schuetten has requested his release and at the same time desired to send a letter to Your Highness. I could not convince him to do otherwise. Above all he is a young, ill-bred, and obstinate individual who understands very little about his profession, but is still defiant. He has done very little in the detachment except shave beards....

"On 2 March 1780 the Cannoneers Reif, [Johann] Jahn, and [Johann] Handel were arrested because they sought to be engaged by an English recruiting non-commissioned officer. An investigation was held and they were punished by running the gauntlet according to the sentence by Lieutenant Colonel von Creuzbourg.

"On 11 March it as reported to me by Corporal Kohlep that Musketeer Leick had told him that Corporal Buss tried to get him to desert when the mentioned Leick was about to lie down to sleep. I investigated the situation at once and after gathering further information, arrested Free Corporal Buss at once. After contacting the auditor of the Jaeger Corps and investigating further, I found that Corporals Orth and Becker, and Musketeers [Philipp] Menck and [Peter] Fix were also implicated. I sent Lieutenant Colonel von Creuzbourg the results of the investigation, from which Your Highness will be sent an extract, as all investigations conducted by the detachment have been most graciously sent to him. Lieutenant Colonel von Creuzbourg directed those arrested to receive the following sentences: Corporals Buss, Orth, and Becker were permanently reduced in grade and the first is to run the gauntlet on two days, twelve times each day; Corporal Orth is to run the gauntlet on two days, eight times on each day; and Becker is to run the gauntlet on two days, six times each day, through the entire detachment. Musketeers Menck and Fix however, to be punished by running the gauntlet on one day. This pronounced sentence was carried out against the five arrestees....

"On 26 June ships arrived from New York, bringing Free Corporal Hausmann and fourteen musketeers and one drummer, Bombardiers Moerschel and Hestermann and three cannoneers, and two drummers from the Artillery. All had ransomed themselves [from captivity]. Among the musketeers, two arrestees by the names of Schenot and Huffner were included because while in New York they had again deserted from Captain von Schlagenteufel of the Brunswick troops, who commanded all the troops assembled in New York, and tried to enlist in an English free corps. After an investigation, the two mentioned musketeers were punished according to the sentence by Lieutenant Colonel von Creuzbourg by running the gauntlet.

"Two companies of the Hesse-Cassel von Knyphausen Regiment and three companies of the von Lossberg Regiment came with the ships from New York. The other companies of the two regiments are partly in captivity, and partly lost in a storm on a previous voyage coming here. Colonel von Loos and Colonel von Borck arrived with them. The first received a brigade immediately after arriving here, in which I am assigned with the detachment and he formed a combined battalion from the five companies of the two regiments.

"On 2 July Grenadier [Johann] Weitzel arrived at the detachment. He had ransomed himself and arrived here after a long and difficult trip by way of Oswego.

"On 23 July Musketeers [Georg] Freyensoehner and [August] Velden, of Colonel von Gall's Company, arrived here. They deserted from the rebels at Fort Stanwix and arrived here after a difficult and tiring trip under constant pursuit by Indians serving the rebels, naked and bare with close cropped hair, because the Indians had cut off all their hair. On 26 July the Artillery moved about a mile out of the city and entered camp there. I gave them the presently surplus old tents and field items to take with them....

"As in many incidents the requirement of sending a provost from another corps has created very great expenses, therefore Lieutenant Colonel von Creuzbourg consented to the request that Drummer [Samuel] Otto, of the detachment, who had volunteered, should perform the duty of provost. This Drummer Otto is furthermore small, can not play, and even if he could, he has no drum,."

Johannes Moerschell, who had been praised for his conduct at Freeman's Farm by Captain Pausch, nevertheless sent a letter to his prince on 1 October 1780 concerning his abuse by the same Captain Pausch. The letter reads in part, "May it please Your Highness to allow me to present that I, Johannes Moerschell, entered Your Highness' service already in 1762 and during that time have sought to demonstrate loyalty and obedience toward my superiors and my service to the best of my ability.

"Now, in the time when we were not yet in captivity, I served with the greatest pleasure, also even after a long time in captivity, until we were transferred to Virginia, when I was not in a condition to do what was ordered of me and which did not seem important. Therefore on 8 April 1779 I was unexpectedly shouted at by a cannoneer from about 200 yards from my barracks, that I was to report to Captain Pausch. When I arrived two non-commissioned officers were ordered to hold me, and on his orders had to hold me and the captain himself performed the punishment, without asking or telling me my crime, or what I had done, other than to chastise me and strike me with the flat of his sword. I was so confounded that I, having received about twenty blows, sank to the ground and surrendered to the heavy hands. However, that was not enough, but according to what the men told the captain, I wanted to join the scoundrels, that I was no longer of any value in this life, and was of little consequence. So I received sixty or seventy blows without an investigation or my knowing what wrong I had committed, nor could I learn before the punishment, why I had to put up with such a cruel punishment.

"I therefore found it necessary, according to my poor condition in eight days, before I could walk again, as I had no other choice remaining, and if I wanted to preserve my life, than to commit perjury. This was unpleasant for an individual who had served eighteen years. [This seems to indicate that he broke his oath by deserting or by confessing to a crime he did not commit.]

"However, thereafter, since that time, I have had few healthy days and seldom find myself in a condition to perform Your Highness' service. Therefore I most humbly ask Your Highness for my discharge because I find myself unfit for service. There were reasons enough to maintain my perjury, which however, never crossed my mind, and I would rather suffer death, if I had not thought to redeem myself and to go to Canada, where we arrived on 16 June 1780 at Quebec in Canada, and because I reported with the troops to Captain von Schoell, he assigned me the command over the Artillery which was present there."

## Continuation of Feilitzsch's Return to Germany

"2 January 1780 - The wind from the north-northwest with a terrible storm. We could not cook. Rain and hail alternated and it was very cold. I am not ashamed to say that I prayed almost the entire day and wept. I am too weak to describe my misery during this time.

"3 January - Thank God! The storm has abated. The wind blew hard from the northwest to west. We call it good weather but can not cross the cabin without the risk of breaking our neck or leg. Also, we now have no other ship near us. We are alone. Lord have mercy upon us!....

"5 January - A strong southwest wind. The ship shook violently. We have sailed very rapidly on our entire voyage to this point, but still we have covered less than one-third of our journey, by my reckoning. God deliver us to England soon! Had I known all of this misery previously, who knows but what I could have been resolute enough to have taken my own life.....

"13 January - A strong southwest wind with much rain. It was nearly impossible to cook. The wind changed at three o'clock this afternoon and came from the northwest so that I hope to see the coast of England tomorrow. This wind is very good for us but I fear a storm. Please God make me wrong!

"16 January - A good west wind, a calm sea, but rain in the morning and cold in the afternoon. Otherwise I continue to hope from day to day to see land. According to the reckoning of our ship's captain, we have no hope of being there in less than eight days.....

"24 January - Again a strong, contrary southeast wind with high seas. A Frenchman died and many people are sick. We were all terribly hungry. A soup was cooked for three hours although the waves beat over the ship. By noon it was a bit better. [In English] 'I can't ashame to confess that I dropped Tears the whole day, and sent a great many prayers to our Lord. I felt a good deal considering the bad Fate of my Life time my berthday until now: but I deserve a good deale more, God strong the me' [End of English] +++. This morning a ship was quite near us. We put on all our sails to get away. Good Lord, what a quarrelsome society!....

"1 February - An east wind, rain, a storm with hail, and to tell the truth, it lay a foot deep on the deck. We could not cook, 'but what a bad compagne'....

"8 February - A sailor sighted land from the mast....

"9 February - ... We could not be sure, since the sun was not shining, where we were, but the captain was of the opinion, according to the depth, that we were near the Isle of Wight. God be praised for helping us this far! He will continue to watch over us.....

"11 February - ... Thank Heavens, for the first time we saw the English coast. What a pleasure. It can not be expressed. We are thirteen Stanges[40] opposite Portsmouth. Because the wind is unfavorable, we lost ground. At three-thirty we anchored in the harbor close to the Isle Of Wight. Toward evening a boat came from the warship and took off all of our sailors.

"12 February - Very cold with a strong wind. Four ships of our fleet entered. From them we heard that they saw seven ships of our fleet sink during the storm, and our frigate *Solebay* lost three masts and had to return to New York. Heaven only knows how many lives were lost, but God has brought us safely here. Pressing sailors continues very diligently and therefore all of them run away and hide.....

"16 February - Very cold weather. The ship, which at the start of our voyage from Sandy Hook had been reported as taking water, also sank. The sailors, after three days on the sea in a boat, reached a Dutch ship and have now arrived here.

"22 February - After the captain has again obtained a crew and we are ready to sail, the wind is again contrary. It is very strong from the north and for the first time since we left New York we must once again put up with the extreme cold. The salted provisions which I have eaten, unfortunately begin to show their effects. My scurvy swelling causes me much discomfort and at the same time the number of our sick increases daily. Lord let us soon be put ashore, otherwise much misery will result. At twelve o'clock we were beyond Spithead. Our fleet is more than fifty sail. I can not yet determine our escort. I recognize the frigate *Daphne* and it is my belief that still others must be with such a fleet.

"23 February - A north wind like yesterday and not very favorable. At twelve o'clock we passed Dover and then tacked back and forth. We anchored near the city at five o'clock. At midnight we entered The Downs and at four o'clock anchored near Deal.

"25 February - We anchored at four o'clock in the morning not far from Sheerness, a harbor in the Thames and at twelve o'clock we began tacking. However, because the wind was contrary from the west and a storm wind broke something on our middle mast, we had to anchor at two-thirty. At four o'clock the wind raged so terribly that one of the many single-masted sloops cruising near us sank. Although it was not far from us we could not provide any help because our boat was securely fastened on the deck. The crew of the ship all drowned. This misfortune disturbed me greatly. No event had such an effect on me as this. Many say death is inevitable, but I think this is more gruesome and can not be compared with any other.....

"1 March - At five o'clock in the morning we sailed again with the flood tide and a contrary wind, as far as Woolwich, where we anchored at ten o'clock. The wife of an invalid died. She could not be lowered into the water and therefore, I was sent to Woolwich to obtain permission to bury her. It was approved and she was buried at five o'clock on the best place.

"2 March - We sailed at seven o'clock in the morning and at ten o'clock finally arrived, after a short voyage, in Deptford, which is 24 miles from London. At noon I traveled in a small boat to the city and upon my arrival heard that our prince was there. I immediately went to pay my respects and I can say nothing else but that he received me graciously. I also had the great honor of dining with him during the evening.

"3 March - I completed my business, in so far as possible, with our agent, as this was of some importance and was of great concern to me. During the evening I again had the great honor of dining with the Margrave.

"4 March - I received money for our remaining journey. My accounts, which were not completed, greatly embarrassed me. I received the order today to deliver them and therefore I was unable to take in the sights of London. I took leave of the prince this evening, also. The running about has caused a great deal of pain in my scorbutic foot.

"5 March - At ten o'clock I traveled back to Deptford in the common coach and as I was about to change to another carriage at twelve o'clock, to my great displeasure, our baggage was held up by customs. Therefore we had to wait until it could all be inspected. Taxes had to be paid on everything because I insisted on remaining there until I could take everything with us.

"6 March - At noon our baggage was inspected. At three o'clock we boarded a single-masted sloop. At three-thirty we sailed and at six o'clock were again back in Gravesend, where we anchored. That evening I went into the city because there was very little room on our ship.

"7 March - At six o'clock in the morning those troops who could march were disembarked and at seven o'clock we began our march on land to Chatham. I rode in a post chaise and arrived there with the troops at ten o'clock. We were quartered in the barracks. At one o'clock the remaining men and the baggage arrived from the sloop. I had already encountered a part of the Hessian invalids here. Every place is full of English recruits intended for America.....

"13 March - An unpleasant time, one day after the other, spent there. Everything of note here, which can be seen in a short time, I have seen. No socializing and no conversation. Why shouldn't I wish soon and preferably to be in Germany, in my fatherland?

"27 March - Idleness is the root of all evil. A person goes walking to drive away boredom, then he enters the Post [inn] and gets drunk, sometimes remaining all night. Sometimes he goes to the Jew, 'because he has a very fine maid servant, and not of A Natur' +++ in this manner a person goes through the city and acts like a fool, passing himself off as a Frenchman, a Spaniard, or a Russian.....

"9 April - The weather is still terribly cold and it snows about noontime every day. Today we received the pleasant order that in a few days we are to embark. As I attended a comedy a few days ago, it is necessary for me to mention that, among others, an English officer spoke rather loudly and at once a laborer told him to be quiet. A beautiful lady sat beside me. 'I must confess that I fell in love with her. However, she paid me no heed and I found my feelings were in vain.' The ribbons of her coiffure nearly blinded me and the next day I could hardly see.

"13 April - After the Hessians were embarked on the twelfth, not only did the time pass very slowly, but I was also embarrassed feeling I might be forgotten. However, when we were embarked in a boat at nine o'clock this morning at Chatham Dock Yard, I was lifted over with care. At eleven o'clock we were not far from Sheerness and went at once on board the transport brig *Emerald*. It was a newly-built ship and this was its maiden voyage.

"16 April - We awaited the order to sail. The wind was northwesterly and terribly strong. The water was rather restless....

"22 April - West-southwest wind. We sailed out of the harbor at two o'clock in the afternoon and anchored where the Thames and Chatham Downs meet. Our escort, the frigate *Levine*, of 32 cannons, also lay there, awaiting the departure on our journey.....

# Enemy Views (1780)

"27 April - A southwest wind and rainy weather. We did not trust ourselves to enter without a pilot as we feared a strong wind gust might cause us to crash or to be thrown on the shore. A pilot came at eleven o'clock and we anchored at twelve o'clock. At two o'clock we entered the Soue River. When we reached Hellevoetsluis, we needed another pilot. Therefore, the fleet tacked. There was a terribly stormy wind. Some ships hit one another and were badly damaged. We ran aground but worked loose after three o'clock and then dropped anchor.....

"29 April - A very favorable southwest wind with good weather. At eight o'clock in the morning we sailed and at twelve o'clock, God be praised! we arrived at Dordrecht. Lord grant that this is the end of our sea voyage! I am sick of it. At four o'clock in the afternoon the recruits arrived from Nijmegen. Captain Cramon, who commanded them, took charge of my transport.

"30 April - At nine o'clock in the morning we embarked in a Dutch sloop but remained at anchor near the city during the day. It was a rainy day. The city looked pleasant to me because of its cleanliness. Nevertheless, I would not be caught dead in Holland.

"1 May - Very beautiful and warm weather. We sailed at five o'clock in the morning but there was almost no wind. We had to halt during the afternoon after having traveled about ten miles.....

"5 May - At four o'clock in the afternoon we arrived at Nijmegen. We at once transferred to German boats in which I was not especially pleased.

"6 May - During the afternoon the order was sent to me, in the presence of Captain von Cramon, by the commandant that I should continue our trip as soon as possible.

"7 May - We remained lying there, because first we had to send for horses which were to pull our ship.

"8 May - At four o'clock in the afternoon we moved out. We went a short distance. I was happy to get away from the impertinent Dutch.

"9 May - Not far from Cleve, which is Prussian, we visited the last Dutch customs station. We then entered the Rhine and sailed as far as Emmerich, which is Prussian, where we remained overnight.....

"16 May - Because we changed horses here [Cologne], we had to remain until afternoon. Therefore I had time to do some sight-seeing

434

in the city, which was not worth the effort. The Dome, however, from a religious, decorative, and size point of view is noteworthy.....

"22 May - We ... entered the Main River, and at seven o'clock arrived at Frankfurt. The crowd of people was terrible, and we were seen as some kind of monsters.

"23 May - We left at twelve o'clock and arrived at Hanau at six o'clock.....

"27 May - We arrived at Wertheim in the evening. The people there whom I had met on the previous march [to America] extended many courtesies to me.....

"31 May - A relative detained me in the city so that I only overtook our ship at Ochsenfurt. From there we continued to Marksteft, where we finally finished our trip on the water, and, as this place belongs to Ansbach, we entered quarters.

"1 June - At five o'clock in the morning we marched out and at nine o'clock arrived at our quarters in Oberrittelsheim.

"2 June - We moved out at five o'clock and arrived at Uffenheim at eight o'clock.

"3 June - We marched again at five o'clock and arrived at Marktbergel, where our quarters were, at nine o'clock.

# 1781

## Mutiny in the American Army

The year opened with mutiny in some units of the American army. The Hesse-Cassel Jaeger Corps Journal provides information on the event commencing on 4 January 1781. "The army received orders to be prepared to march. The Pennsylvania Brigade, which like the rest of the enemy's army had received neither pay nor good provisions until now, revolted on 1 January. Everyone, with the exception of the officers, was determined to go home. Major General Wayne, who commanded them, exerted himself strenuously in an effort to get the troops to return to duty and made them great promises, but to no avail. They chose officers from among their non-commissioned officers and a certain Sergeant Williams accepted the overall command. They seized four cannons and all the provisions and marched to Bordentown, having decided as one not to return to duty until they were given their pay, their discharges, and good provisions.

"5 January - At seven o'clock this morning an express brought orders for the Jaeger Corps to march at daybreak. We moved out at nine o'clock and marched to the far side of Jamaica, where we spent the night in barns. The Hessian Grenadiers had vacated Jamaica and marched to Gravesend.

"6 January - The Jaeger Corps marched at seven o'clock, through Flatbush, over Gravesend, to Denyse's Ferry. There they were embarked on schooners and at dusk landed at Decker's Ferry on Staten Island. We found the Hessian Grenadiers and the Light Infantry quartered there and we received two barns for our entire corps. General Clinton himself was there in order to see what the outcome of the revolt would be, and if there were not some advantage to be obtained. He had, to this end, also sent emissaries to make all possible offers to Williams.....

"10 January - Unfortunately two of our spies, who were to take Clinton's overtures to Mr. Williams, were discovered because of their carelessness, by the militia, and hanged on the spot.....

"15 January - Williams with his troops and the deputation from Congress have not come to a complete understanding. Meantime, however, it appears the event will have a favorable outcome because a subscription has been begun in Philadelphia to raise gold and silver with which to pay the soldiers.....

"20 January - A part of the Jersey Brigade has likewise revolted. The situation, however, was quickly resolved and two of the rebel leaders were hanged."

The Platte Grenadier Battalion Journal entries concerning the mutiny were: "January - At the start of this year a mutiny broke out in the rebel army. Between 2,000 and 3,000 men, under the command of General [Henry] Knox, left their winter quarters at Morristown in New Jersey. These malcontents moved from Morristown toward Elizabethtown, took a secure position on a height, and demanded their many months back pay, in hard cash, better uniform items, and better provisions. Therefore three Hessian and two British Grenadier Battalions, the Jaegers, and two British Light Infantry Battalions were transferred from Long Island to Staten Island today in order to be nearer these malcontents. General Clinton himself went to Staten Island and commenced a correspondence with them. Reportedly our side promised them all back pay if they came over to us. However, they refused this offer, as it was never their intent to come over to us, but they would remain neutral and return to their homes. These malcontents have been reconciled with Congress and General Washington, and rejoined the rebel army again as the result of promises, exhortations, and being given part of their pay.

"10 January - The above mentioned corps of our army returned to winter quarters on Long Island, having accomplished nothing."

Lieutenant Prechtel noted the mutiny as follows: 6 January - According to reports, 2,500 men of the Pennsylvania militia have quit Washington's army because they have not been paid for two years.

"Supposedly they have spiked the cannons at Morristown and burned the magazines there.

"They have built defenses with four cannons on the heights of Amboy, in the Jerseys.

"Some troops from the Light Infantry and the English Grenadiers have been sent there and it is believed that they will soon march here.....

"13 January - The affair noted on the sixth of this month, about some American troops quitting, is true. However, they received their pay in good hard cash from Lieutenant General Washington and have returned to their army."

## The Siege and Surrender of Pensacola

The final days of English control of West Florida were recorded as follows by Quartermaster Sergeant Steuernagel. "On 31 January Colonel von Hanxleden with 100 men, eleven provincial cavalry, and 300 Indians was ordered to proceed to a place called French Village, in the Mississippi region, to drive the Spaniards from a fortification at that place, and to destroy it. To this command the Waldeck Regiment provided Captain [Alexander] von Baumbach, Lieutenants [Josias Theodor Friedrich Ludwig] von Wilmowsky and Stierlein, Ensign [Wilhelm Theodor] Ursall, three non-commissioned officers, three corporals, one fifer, one drummer, and seven privates.

"On the eighth, toward evening, we heard the sad news of the fate of this expedition; how on the previous morning at six o'clock, during the attack, our worthy and steadfast Colonel von Hanxleden, Lieutenant Stierlein, and Lieutenant Gordon of the 60th Regiment were killed, and Captain von Baumbach and an officer from the provincials were wounded.

"The Spaniards suffered heavy losses in this affair, in that many were killed in the attack, being shot and wounded by bayonets, and their magazines were set on fire. From what I have heard, our gallant Colonel von Hanxleden lies buried in the wilderness and the Spaniards fired a rocket over his grave as a tribute to his honor.

"On the ninth the remnants of his command returned......

"On 9 March 1781, the Spaniards, whom we had expected for some time, finally appeared and showed that they were serious about Pensacola.

"An armed ship, *Mentor*, which was the only protection for our harbor, fired seven cannon shots outside the harbor, the signal that an enemy had been discovered nearby in the Gulf, and from which, early in the morning, we heard three cannon shots. About nine o'clock we saw 38 ships, which approached Ross [Santa Rosa] Island from the east and sailed about off our harbor on this day.

"In the evening they went to that island, where they landed their troops.

"This night the last ship which had arrived in port was sent to Jamaica to report the siege. On the tenth the Spanish fleet blockaded our harbor at Pensacola.....

"On the eighteenth His Excellency Don Galvez decided it was time to take a better look at the Pensacola defenses. He sailed into the harbor this afternoon at one o'clock with his brig and two row galleys, but at such a distance from our Fort Navu, which had ten cannons at the harbor entrance, that we could do no damage to him. This evening the houses near the waterfront were burned down to prevent the enemy using them as quarters or hiding places.

On the nineteenth we saw the Spanish fleet, from men-of-war to open boats, as they raised anchor and entered our harbor under full sail. The wind was so favorable for them that even our two hour cannonade could not hinder their operations.

"On the twentieth a troop of Indians arrived, which had taken some Spanish scalps. They also brought a Spanish sailor they had captured with them. Naked and bound, he was led about our camp on a rope by a very solemn-faced savage who let out a dreadful shriek. They had cut his hair and painted his face with many colors, as they do.

"They showed him to our governor and were then going to burn him alive, according to their custom. However, the governor and some others showed their compassion for this poor wretch and promised to do everything possible for the Indians if they would surrender their captive. This did not satisfy the savages who demanded their revenge with blood for blood. Finally, after the earnest pleading of General Campbell and Governor Chester, they allowed themselves to be talked out of their prisoner and gave their opponents the apparent gift, on the promise of the general that he pay with his life. He had wounds all over his body.

"On the 25th, sixteen more ships arrived, mostly French, to join the Spanish fleet. They came from Havana. Now we learned that the Spaniards had a total of 22,000 men who besieged us.

On 11 April the entire Spanish army was put ashore. Our Indians became somewhat excited and fired on them, but could not resist them. As soon as we saw that the Indians were retreating and being forced back, we rushed a detachment with two cannons to the Indians' assistance, whereupon the Spaniards again retreated to their ships.

Some were also drowned in the water and died. By this attack the Indians received a pronounced and miserable lesson from the Spaniards.

"On the 22nd the remaining Spaniards were landed and set up camp not far from Pensacola. Because our force was so weak and consisted of only 600 men, it was completely impossible to undertake a sortie or to attack the enemy. They remained in their camp until the third day. Then they were to have been attacked by us with a detachment with some cannons and howitzers, but the same day some deserters betrayed us, and our undertaking came to naught. Among the deserters was one of our free corporals, [Franz] Hintenberger, of the Catholic religion, which resulted in the enemy changing their camp.

On the 23rd the Spaniards in the second camp were attacked by one of our detachments and a party of Indians, driven out of their fortifications, several officers taken prisoner, some killed, and three wounded brought back to our camp. Additionally, in so far as time could be taken, their fortifications were burned and destroyed....

On the 27th we saw and understood that during the night the enemy had thrown up fortifications opposite ours, which were in a woods. We now tried to hinder them with all our strength of cannons and bombs. However, the recently arrived French had so strongly entrenched that night, that we could no longer hinder them and with our few troops could undertake nothing further, except to protect ourselves as individual soldiers and use a restraining bombardment and cannonade. Therefore, day and night, there was a cannonade to breach our defenses....

On 8 May, at nine o'clock in the morning, we had a misfortune when an enemy bomb ignited our powder magazine in the outermost battery, and blew 52 men into the air, wounded many, and completely ruined our fortifications, also.

"This very unfortunate accident made a very favorable opportunity for the Spaniards, in that now everything was in the greatest confusion. The enemy pressed us with such strength and determination that we had to raise the white flag, whereupon the Spanish adjutant general was sent over to discuss a capitulation. In the meantime, however, all of our still serviceable cannons were loaded with grape and canister. Despite this enemy pressure, which mounted in strength, our brave General Campbell did not lose courage, but let the enemy know that in case the proposed articles were not accepted, he, with his still few remaining troops, would resist to the last man.

"Finally the Spaniards understood that it would still cause many bloody heads. So they perceived it as advisable that they accept our proposed capitulation and concluded it. The adjutant returned a third time and presented the final articles signed by the Spanish general.

"Still, the enemy had more of which to be ashamed. Our weak force gained true honor, because the enemy, since 9 March, with 22,000 men besieged 600 men and still on 10 March [sic - May] we marched out of our fort with flags flying and with martial music, and Spain paid the costs when we were transported free to North America, specifically to New York...

"I would say a great deal at this point about our captivity, but for brevity, let me only say, that on 4 June 1781, which was also the King of England's birthday, we sailed with eleven ships from West Florida to the Island of Havana and Dominica....

"On the fifteenth, in the afternoon, we entered the harbor of the West Indian island Dominica, in Havana, and lay at anchor. After a few days we continued our journey onward toward North America, specifically Fort Reinfort, and upon our arrival there were disembarked near Brooklyn on Long Island, quartered in earthen huts, and thus sat out our period as prisoners of war. During this time, the following: Their Excellencies Captains Haacke and Alberti, Sr., and Their Excellencies Lieutenants Strubberg and Brumhard, returned after their captivity."

Pausch noted the arrival of the Pensacola garrison at New York in a letter to his prince, dated 16 June 1781. "Ten small Spanish vessels, flying white flags of truce, are said to be lying at anchor at Sandy Hook. They have the English and the Prince of Waldeck's troops, captured at the capitulation of Pensacola, on board."

The Hesse-Cassel Jaeger Corps Journal entry of 9 July 1781 also acknowledged the loss of Pensacola and the return of the garrison to New York. "Don Galvez has captured Pensacola. He besieged it with 20,000 men for nine weeks and the English garrison, consisting of 1,100 men, surrendered and are not to serve again against Spain or France.[41] No notice was taken of the rebels. A part of these troops arrived in New York, as well as their commander, Lieutenant General Campbell."

# Enemy Views (1781)

## Garrison Duty in Charleston

Private Asteroth reported on his life in the garrison at Charleston and on the events coming to his attention during 1781. "26 February - A fleet appeared in the morning which toward evening arrived in the harbor. We learned at once that there were Germans on board.

"27 February - The identity of those persons was discovered when 200 recruits landed; namely, seventy Hesse-Hanau Jaegers, two Brunswickers, three Anhalt-Zerbsters, and their assigned officers. The Zerbsters had white uniforms and white gaiters. Two chaplains were with them, the Reformed Chaplain Naumann and Catholic Chaplain Pather.

"Sunday, 26 March - At eight o'clock in the evening all the bells began to ring. There is a bell tower here with eight bells, which hang at our garrison church. It is customary when good news arrives, to indicate this with the bells. That happened this evening. There was a commotion in my quarters. The host, who claims loyalty to the King because it is necessary, shook his head and was mournful and complained that he was not well, but he was eager to hear this news before he went to bed. He asked me to be so good as to ask about as he believed it must be something very important. Curiosity had held me also and I decided to go to the church. Fortunately I met the choir master of the church. He greeted me with a joyful hurrah, which the English use as a word of exultation. I asked him what was new. He said a dispatch rider had just arrived from General Cornwallis [with news] that he had sharply defeated the rebels of General Greene's army. I visited briefly at the church and made my greetings to my colleagues. I then returned with the greatest pleasure in my heart to my host who hurriedly asked if I had heard anything. I told it as I had heard it and was conversed with about the news for more than an hour. Then he went to bed. Soon Chaplain Kuemmell came home and also told me all the news.

"27 March - The order arrived that the garrison was to fire a *feu de joie* at five o'clock in the evening. My excitement would not let me miss this so I went with several good friends to the place, namely, by the [city's defensive] lines and looked in amazement at the number of onlookers. The number of young women going to and fro was beyond count. Finally the cannons roared and three times the weapons were

442

fired, each time with a joyful shout, "Hurrah! God save King George!" This was wonderful to see. We returned to Widow Frebeln's, had a pleasant conversation, and drank a pair of bottles of wine to the good health of the King and Cornwallis. Finally, everyone was ready to go home, but someone said we did not need lanterns, so as a lark we accepted the suggestion. As we entered the street, everyone had lights in the windows, some five, some even nine, and before every pane. We counted sixty in two rooms of one. Where no lights were standing in the windows, rocks were thrown and the windows broken. Quickly lights were placed there, also. When I reached home, Chaplain [Georg Christian] Stern and Auditor [Friedrich Adolf] Steuber were with my chaplain. For our enjoyment I had to put five lights at each window in the room. I must say, a most pleasant evening.

"3 April - The previously mentioned recruits were embarked to go to their regiments in Canada.

"Easter, 15 April - Sixty men taken from the three regiments were assigned to the Light Dragoons.

"17 April - All the horses in the city were collected and from these the best were selected. They [the Light Dragoons] received short green jackets and marched to join Lord Rawdon's army. Lieutenant [Friedrich] Starckloff of our regiment was given command of them.

"2 June - A fleet of fifty sail was seen, which entered the harbor this same day with 4,000 Irelanders and provisions. The troops marched to join Lord Rawdon and a regiment remained in the city. N.B. - I had and took little part in these activities. For the most part I was involved with confirmations. I had taught a youth from the regiment while in Rhode Island and now a drummer, Jacob Voelcker, of the Benning Regiment. When they arrived at the garrison in Charleston, four boys had grown enough to go to school. I had a pleasant little room. My chaplain told me that I should conduct a school for the children. It began, fortunately, on the first of August, 1780, and was held every day from eight to ten or eleven o'clock in the morning. Meanwhile we changed quarters to where there was an adjoining Quaker church in which there were benches just as in a school. I went to the administrator and requested permission to conduct a school in the church. With the greatest respect he at once gave his consent and took me to the sexton, from whom I was to pick up the key every Monday. My students were Friedrich Fogt [or Vogt], Georg Reiss,

Joha Doers [or Doerr], Conrad Schnacke and two from the city of Charleston.

"23 September - I received the following students from the Benning Regiment: Carla Prensell, Martin Mann, Hartmann Mann, Johannes Naumann, Henneryetta Schnacke, and Conrad Dinges.

"6 July - Early in the morning we heard the news that the English General Wellesin had been captured by the Americans. An English patrol was sent after them. Fortunately, at noon on Saturday the rebels were encountered; a colonel, lieutenant colonel, captain, lieutenant, and ten men who were searching for watermelons. Thirteen were cut down without mercy, but the colonel was spared as he told where the general was being held in a house three miles from the spot. Sunday at twelve o'clock they returned General Wellesin and the American colonel, who was in irons, to Charleston.

"15 September - At two o'clock in the afternoon 150 American dragoons came to within six miles of the city of Charleston, at the first inn - the so-called Quarter House - where officers and people of the city ride every day for pleasure and to dine. These rebels encountered eight English officers and arrested six citizens at their noon lunch. A noteworthy incident occurred between an English captain and an American captain. The Englander did not wish to surrender, drew his pistol, and pointed it at his enemy's chest. Each shot the other dead on the spot. A citizen swung onto his horse in an effort to save himself. He was killed at once by the enemy. The others were taken as prisoners of war.

"4 August - Colonel [Isaac] Haynes, who was already noted when captured and his life spared, was hanged for his crime."

Enemy Views (1781)

## The War in the South

During 1781 several battles were fought in the southern colonies but Reuber's entries indicate the more typical activity in the area. "In the year 1781, in the middle of the summer, the Americans again approached and were seen by our outposts and it was necessary for us to provide large detachments and pickets at our lines.

"Finally, we pulled back completely to where the great defenses were and formed our line from one harbor across to the other to await them [the Americans]. However, they were not willing to risk it until finally on a Sunday. There was a large room at an inn, about two and one-half miles from another inn opposite Ebenezer Ferry, on the harbor, where many ladies and officers and gentlemen go walking for pleasure and where the owner had an understanding with the Americans. However, an English row galley lay in the harbor on duty, which was to search all the merchant ships approaching land. These ships had to visit the guard ship and allow the inspection. Only after this had taken place could they proceed to the city and sell their cargo. Well, the owner had organized a dance and told the Americans about the affair. Therefore a small ship approached land posing as a merchant ship with hay and straw. When it sailed to the guard ship to be inspected, fifty American soldiers who were under the straw stormed aboard the guard ship. Then they went to the owner of the inn, robbed all the guests, returned to their ship and departed. At once there was an alarm sounded in the city as the Americans advanced. We were quickly under arms but they never attacked as they only wanted to pick up the owner of the inn. He had already absconded with the rebels, leaving his possessions behind and dared not return as long as we were there."

## The Battle of Cowpens

The Hesse-Cassel Jaeger Corps Journal, on 17 February, reported on the battle of Cowpens. "From the *Halifax*, with the November [1780] packet by way of Charleston, we hear that Lieutenant Colonel Tarleton has been defeated in an action with General Morgan. Tarleton was detached from Lord Cornwallis to follow General

Morgan, who commands the enemy Light Infantry and a militia corps. Morgan retreated ahead of Tarleton until he took a firm post in the Cowpens. Tarleton, therefore, became excited and considered Morgan trapped. Tarleton camped the night of the seventeenth in a vacated camp of the enemy and attacked him the next morning with his usual rashness. Morgan had his militia in front and these, as he had expected, fled. Tarleton pursued eagerly, maybe not in the best order, and suddenly encountered the enemy Infantry aligned in order, which he met and turned the attack into a rout. A large part of the English Cavalry escaped. The Infantry however, for the most part were captured; likewise two cannons, 35 baggage wagons, 800 weapons, one field forge, etc. were lost. This unfortunate affair greatly upset Lord Cornwallis, who, nevertheless, marched against General Greene.

In New York the diaries and journals were recording the impressment of sailors for the fleet and the movement of reinforcements to the south. Prechtel noted, "22 February - As people were pressed for the English warships again today, the von Voit Regiment had to draw the line around the city.....

"4 March - The 76th Regiment of Scots and the Hessian Hereditary Prince Regiment were embarked...

"5 March - The expedition consisting of the two regiments [mentioned above] and the English Light Infantry, under the command of the English Major General Phillips, departed from here yesterday."

The Hesse-Cassel Jaeger Corps Journal also noted the embarkation on 6 March of "The Light Infantry, 87th and 76th Regiments, and the Hereditary Prince Regiment, under the command of Major General Phillips ... and as the reports from Carolina indicate that Lord Cornwallis has advanced into North Carolina and detached 400 men to occupy Wilmington, it is assumed, not without some basis, that General Phillips will sail to Virginia in order to made a diversion in support of Lord Cornwallis."

The Platte Grenadier Battalion Journal also recorded activity in the New York area. "4 March - The 76th Regiment of Highlanders, which had previously been in huts on Laurel Hill, marched to New York in order to embark for Virginia. The regiment joined a small corps of troops under the command of General Phillips, going to the previously noted province.....

"July - At that start of this month the French troops under the command of General Rochambeau joined the army of General Washington on the North River and gradually approached our outposts near Kingsbridge. Near Fort Independence our Jaegers had a skirmish with them. Captain von Rau of the British [sic] Jaegers had died during a patrol some days previous. The enemy bivouacked near our outposts, so close to Harlem Creek that the Jaegers this side of Harlem Creek had to vacate their camp below Fort Knyphausen at night. The army Refugees, who had built huts on the other side of Harlem Creek at Morrisania were plundered by the enemy and many taken captive, wounded, or killed. Everyone on the other side of Harlem Creek had to retreat to this side. We no longer occupied anything but Redoubt Number 8, which the enemy was very near. We remained still, rested, and did not exert ourselves, except for firing several cannon shots at the enemy. After a stay of several days, the enemy again marched away from Kingsbridge without having undertaken anything. They went farther up the North River. As soon as the enemy had departed, pontoons were brought from New York to Kingsbridge to demonstrate that our side was not completely idle and only on-lookers to the situation.....

"5 September - ... General Arnold, who had returned from Virginia on his own, went with a small corps of troops to New England and destroyed New London and its harbor and several forts. During the conquest of Fort Griswold, the 40th and 54th Regiments suffered severe losses. No one from Hesse accompanied this expedition except 100 jaegers under the command of Captain von Wangenheim."

### The Battle of Guilford Courthouse

Sergeant Koch, with the Bose Regiment, recorded a rather detailed account of the battle on 16 March at Guilford Courthouse, beginning shortly prior to the battle. "We rested during these two days. Our commanding general, Lord Cornwallis, sent General Greene a flag of truce, saying, if he were a real general, he would stand and make a fight.

"The flag of truce returned and brought the order back.

"Tomorrow there would be a battle. He would stand like a man.

447

"The enemy general was informed that the Hessians were on the left wing and would attack his right wing. Therefore, he reinforced his right wing.

"The enemy army had a strength of 10,000 men.

"On 16 March we were in battle formation.

"Lord Cornwallis' corps consisted of three battalions of Guards and one battalion of Guard Grenadiers, the 23rd, 33rd, and 71st Regiments, the von Bose Regiment, 200 Hessian and 100 Ansbach Jaegers, the 17th English Light Dragoon Regiment, and the North Carolina Regiment.

"Lord Tarleton, with the Cavalry, formed the advance guard, the North Carolina Regiment the rear guard, all told 5,000 men.

"Cornwallis learned from a spy that the enemy had reinforced his right wing because the Hessians would attack there. Therefore, each regiment had been given a barrel of cognac and told they should stand fast and would have nothing to fear because Cornwallis corps was weak...

"The battle began at nine o'clock in the morning.

"The von Bose Regiment deployed to the right and attacked the enemy's left wing, which consisted of riflemen or marksmen, armed with rifles.

"General Leslie commanded our right wing. We advanced against the enemy without a shot coming from the enemy against us.

"About 100 yards from the enemy line, they delivered a general fire and 180 men of our von Bose Regiment immediately fell.

"Colonel [Johann Christian] DuBuy at once ordered, 'Fix bayonets! March!' Before the enemy could reload we charged against them with our bayonets.

"Everyone was bayoneted.

"The enemy retreated back into the bushes which were behind them. The small arms fire from the enemy and us began in earnest. This firing ignited the foliage of the bushes and many of the wounded died in the fire.

"During this excitement the von Bose Regiment pulled out of the battle line and pursued the enemy, but before we knew it, the enemy attacked us again, in the rear. The regiment therefore, had to divide into two parts.

"The second, commanded by Major [Friedrich Heinrich] Scheer, had to attack toward the rear against the enemy who were behind us, and forced them once again to take flight.

"Lord Tarleton came with his Light Cavalry and pursued the enemy.

"During this time Colonel DuBuy advanced with the first part of the regiment and Major Scheer returned with the second part of the regiment and rejoined the first part.

"As we no longer saw any enemy before us, the small arms fire of the von Bose Regiment ceased and was no longer heard.

"We halted.

"Lord Cornwallis was still exchanging small arms fire with the enemy. According to the sound of the firing, Colonel DuBuy with the von Bose Regiment had already advanced about half a mile farther forward and had outflanked the enemy, which the enemy was not aware of, nor was General Cornwallis, because of the heat of the battle.

"Lord Cornwallis thought the von Bose Regiment had been captured because he no longer heard firing from us.

"Colonel DuBuy deployed the regiment to the left through the bushes at the double and arrived on the open field.

"There we encountered the enemy and attacked him in his rear. Our small arms firing began again.

"Lord Cornwallis ordered the English to charge against the enemy and completely defeated them.

"Lord Tarleton, who had already advanced about three miles with his Cavalry, destroyed the fleeing enemy.

"Thus ended the Battle of Guilford Courthouse today, 16 March.

"The battle began this morning at nine o'clock and ended at one o'clock in the afternoon.

"The enemy lost ten cannons which fell into our hands. On the battle field the enemy left 2,550 dead and 2,018 wounded.

"On our side the von Bose Regiment had thirty non-commissioned officers and privates killed and fifty officers and 200 non-commissioned officers and privates wounded. The Ansbach and Hessian Jaegers suffered twelve dead and twenty wounded. The English Infantry lost 73 officers killed and 855 non-commissioned officers and privates killed.

"The total of dead and wounded was 1,900 men.

"We had won the battle.

"We remained on the battlefield for three days, under the open skies without tents.

"Lord Cornwallis sent a flag of truce to the enemy General Greene requesting that he send his surgeons to tend the wounded, who had been placed in the six houses at Guilford Courthouse.

"We buried the dead.

"However, the situation was now very bad for us. We had won but we had no foodstuffs, no shoes on our feet, and no shirts on our bodies.

"During these three days each man, officers as well as privates, received four measures of corn instead of bread and for meat, such cattle as the enemy had left behind were brought in by the militia and slaughtered. We placed the corn on the fire to cook it. Then it was taken from the container and eaten. The meat was either boiled or roasted on sticks and eaten. Cognac and rum were no longer to be had.

"Here we stood. There was no hope of help from our army because we were 700 English miles distance from it, in the middle of North Carolina. Our army in New York could not know where we were. They considered us to be lost.

"Cornwallis saw the sorry situation. He held a secret council with the generals and Colonel DuBuy. It was decided to begin the return march to the sea, and to deliver the severely wounded as prisoners of war.

"On 20 March we began our withdrawal. The lightly wounded men were taken in wagons and on horses.

"No enemy followed us.

"We marched eighteen miles each day.

"At evening we camped and the royal militia brought us cattle and some flour. The cattle were slaughtered and the meat was cooked or roasted and the flour was made into cakes and cooked on a board in the fire. From the hides of the slaughtered cattle, each soldier cut a strip and tied it to his feet.

"It continued this way until 4 April. This was a march of 288 miles.

"On 5 April we went to Williamsburg in Virginia, a seaport.

## Enemy Views (1781)

"English warships and provisions ships lay at anchor at Williamsburg.

"We camped there for fourteen days.

"We received a double ration of rum each day at that place and our full provision of meat and ship's bread. Each soldier received two pairs of shoes, three shirts, and a pair of long trousers. Because our Hessian weapons had become useless, the von Bose Regiment received orders to turn in those weapons and to obtain new English weapons at the same time."

### A Naval Engagement

Even as Cornwallis was moving toward the Battle at Guilford Courthouse, in the north a naval engagement was shaping up, as reported in the Hesse-Cassel Jaeger Corps Journal, beginning on 12 March. "Yesterday the French fleet sailed from Rhode Island. It has 2,000 men on board and it is believed that they are meant for the Chesapeake, as the Marquis de Lafayette has been detached from Washington's army with 2,000 men in order to cooperate with them.....

"16 March - Today war was declared on Holland.....

"20 March - Yesterday General Phillips sailed.....

"27 March - Admiral Arbuthnot yesterday sent an express boat to inform General Clinton that he had fallen in with the French fleet under [Paul Francois Jean, Comte] de Barras off the Virginia Capes on 16 March and engaged it. He gave the following account thereof

"At daybreak on the sixteenth the frigate *Iris* made the signal for having discovered several ships in the distance to eastward, and was then ordered by a signal from the admiral to keep these ships in sight. The admiral at once gave the signal to form in line and made all sail. He overtook the French and the engagement began at twelve-thirty. It lasted two hours until the French retired. The English did not follow, but instead entered the Chesapeake.... The French fleet has returned to Rhode Island. Their loss on the sixteenth is not certain. That of the English is eighty dead and wounded.

"The French say that their undertaking in the Chesapeake Bay against General Arnold was betrayed and claim that although they retired, they were prepared at all times to renew the action, if Arbuthnot so desired. They would have done so anyway if several of

451

their ships had not been so heavily damaged, among which, especially, were *Conquerant* and *Ardent,* which had received fire from three English ships, and *Romulus,* which had opposed the English admiral's ship, would have been either sunk or captured if it had not been saved by special circumstances. Notation: The special circumstance to which the French refer is: Admiral [Samuel] Graves in the *London* wanted to break the enemy line. The *Romulus* opposed him. Therefore, he engaged it and certainly could have sunk it, but would have had to come out of the line. Therefore Admiral Arbuthnot signaled him to *remain* in line, and as he did not execute at once, Admiral Arbuthnot fired several shots into the *London.* This brought a quarrel between the two admirals and is said to be the reason why the enemy was not pursued. The admiral, however, was blamed for having wasted the best opportunity for completely destroying the French fleet."

Prechtel noted the engagement and damage to the fleet in diary entries beginning 30 March. "On the sixteenth of this month a naval battle occurred between Admiral Arbuthnot and the French fleet, in the vicinity of Chesapeake Bay. The English drove the French completely away, so that they again had to enter Rhode Island and three warships were taken in there without masts.....

"13 April - Yesterday Admiral Arbuthnot arrived at Sandy Hook with his war fleet. Five warships of this fleet, which on 16 March of this year were damaged in the battle in the Chesapeake, must be repaired here, including the admiral's ship, also, arrived in the harbor and lie at anchor in the North River."

### Activities in Virginia

On 4 May the Journal noted that, "The French fleet has made no movement from Rhode Island. A camp has been established at Peekskill for their troops and General Wayne has made preparations to strengthen the troops in Virginia with 1,200."

The Journal also noted that on 27 April, "General Arnold went with the rest of the troops [under his command in Virginia] to Osborn, where he arrived at noon. Four miles beyond Osborn lay a number of enemy ships, and as they would not surrender, he brought four cannons to bear on them. Although the ships laid down a heavy fire, nevertheless Arnold's pieces, and especially the rifle fire of the Jaegers, had such a good effect, that all the ships surrendered. Two ships, three brigs, five sloops, and two schooners were captured, while many others were set on fire prior to the enemy abandoning them. Arnold had no boats with which to take immediate possession of them. At five o'clock in the evening General Phillips joined Arnold and after the boats arrived on the 29th, all the troops went up the river to Warwick. On the 30th the troops marched to Manchester. The Marquis de Lafayette had arrived at Richmond the day before and had drawn the militia under [Friedrich Wilhelm von] Steuben and Muhlenberg to him. As Richmond lies just opposite Manchester and is only separated by the river, he was a witness to the smoke rising from the magazines set afire by the English. The same evening the troops returned to Warwick and there destroyed a flour storage center and several beautiful mills.

"From the first to the sixth [of May] troops returned to Hoyesland. On the seventh they again went up the river and landed at Brandon. On the ninth the Light Infantry and a part of the Rangers went to City Point in boats and the rest of the troops marched to Petersburg, where they arrived that night, after a long march. As the troops left Bermuda Hundred, Lafayette marched to Williamsburg by means of a forced march via Long Bridge over the Chickahominy River. Therefore the fleet returned to Brandon and by means of this maneuver forced the Marquis, as quickly as possible, once again to turn back. He arrived at Osborn on the eighth and planned to cross near Petersburg, but just then the English troops unexpectedly met him and made several officers, who were to have obtained boats for the army in Petersburg, prisoners.....

"19 May - General Phillips is reportedly deathly sick. Lieutenant General Robertson therefore went in a frigate to the Chesapeake today in order to assume command of the troops there.

"20 May - Through the chief quartermaster's orders we learned that Lord Rawdon had defeated General Greene with 1,400 Continentals and a corps of militia near Camden on 19 April. After the affair at Guilford, and as Lord Cornwallis had gone to the Cape Fear River, Greene took his best troops and cavalry in order once again to fall on South Carolina and arrived at Camden after a march of eighty miles. He planned to overrun the posts in that area but luck was not with him. Lord Rawdon marched with a far bigger force from Camden and attacked him in his camp on Hobkirk's Hill....

"28 May - Lieutenant Robertson ... returned today with the report that General Phillips had died on the fifteenth and that Lord Cornwallis with his troops had joined those at Petersburg and had taken over command....

"10 June - The American Legion and the Loyal Americans returned to New York from Virginia, with General Arnold."

Meanwhile the Ansbach-Bayreuth regiments and the 43rd Regiment were embarked on 30 April, according to Prechtel, with the following ship assignments:

"Ships for the von Voit Regiment

1) *Alicia*, staff ship

2) *Providence*, Lieutenant Colonel and Major

3) *Ocean*, Captain von Stain

"Ships for the von Seybothen Regiment

1) *Alexander*, staff ship

2) *Wisk*, Major

3) *Caladonia*, Captain [Friedrich Ludwig] von Eyb.

"The commodore is in the frigate *Charon*.....

"9 April - At nine-thirty both admirals, Arbuthnot and Graves sailed from Staten Island with the war fleet and the transport ships. They then dropped anchor at one o'clock in the afternoon near Sandy Hook.

"The war fleet consists of the following ships:

| Nr. | Name | Guns | Men | Captain |
|---|---|---|---|---|
| 1) | *London* | 98 | 750 | Admiral Graves |
| 2) | *Bedford* | 74 | 600 | Commodore |
| 3) | *Royal Oak* | 74 | 600 | Admiral Arbuthnot |
| 4) | *Robust* | 74 | 600 | Philip Cosby |
| 5) | *America* | 64 | 550 | Samuel Thomson |
| 6) | *Europe* | 64 | 550 | Schmidt Child |
| 7) | *Prudent* | 64 | 550 | Thomas Burnett |
| 8) | *Adamant* | 50 | 370 | Gideon Johnson |
| 9) | *Charon* | 44 | 280 | Thomas Symonds |
| 10) | *Media* | 28 | 180 | Henry Duncan |
| 11) | *Roebuck* | 44 | 280 | Andrew S. Duncan |

12) *Assurance*    50    300    W. Sweeney

"The transport fleet consisted of 23 sail.....

"13 May - At nine o'clock in the morning both fleets went under sail and were soon on the ocean.....

"20 May - At seven o'clock in the morning the Virginia coast was already seen. Toward midday we passed Cape Henry on our left and entered Chesapeake Bay, with Hampton lying on our right. At five o'clock this evening we anchored in Chesapeake Bay, near Hampton Roads, eight English miles from Portsmouth.

"Two English frigates, the *Thames* and the *Gaudalupe*, lie here at anchor.

"At seven o'clock in the evening all the transport ships set sail and entered the James River, where they anchored at nine-thirty at night.....

"At four o'clock in the morning we landed near Portsmouth. Both Ansbach regiments paraded through the city and entered the camp outside the line commanded by the English Major General Leslie.

"The Hessian Hereditary Prince Regiment was already here and was quartered in Portsmouth, because it had not been provided with tents.....

"31 May - General Arnold arrived at Portsmouth and departed for New York immediately.....

"10 June - During this night an expedition was made by the 160-man garrison of Fort Great Bridge and 240 English troops, a total of 400 men, under the command of Major Maxwell of the English 80th Regiment.

"These troops marched to Black Swamp to attack the headquarters there of the American General Gregory, sixteen miles from Fort Great Bridge, near Baendts on Warrent Swamp. They could not cross the river, which was twelve feet deep, and therefore had to return and reenter their former camps.....

"25 June - Today the English Major Maxwell again led an expedition against Black Swamp, with a force of 200 men from the English 76th and 80th Regiments and eighty men of the German command at Great Bridge. The enemy fort, containing eight cannons, was conquered. One colonel, two majors, three captains, eight lieutenants, and forty privates, a total of 54 persons, were made prisoners of war. The enemy cannons were dismounted and spiked. The remaining enemy baggage was burned and the fort demolished.

"Private Horn, of Major von Seitz' Company of the von Voit Regiment, was missing after this affair. According to other soldiers, he had gotten stuck in the swamp.....

"15 July - At six o'clock in the evening the two Ansbach regiments embarked....

"Four hundred Negroes with 347 wives and 223 children were brought here to Portsmouth today and transferred across the Elizabeth River. They were from North and South Carolina and Virginia.....

"29 July - At nine-thirty in the morning the fleet sailed and at a quarter to eleven, as the wind became contrary, again anchored opposite Hampton.

"At a quarter to eight in the evening it sailed again, but immediately dropped anchor.

"Lieutenant General Lord Cornwallis today went aboard the frigate *Richmond*, on which was the commodore.....

"1 August - Sailed at three o'clock in the afternoon and anchored at eight o'clock in the evening on the York River.

"2 August - Sailed at seven o'clock in the morning and at nine o'clock in the morning dropped anchor at Yorktown.

"The 80th Regiment debarked yesterday evening at Gloucester, which is a small place and lies on the right side of the York River.

"Yesterday evening two frigates sailed to Yorktown and lay at anchor there. When the enemy saw their approach, he retreated at once to Williamsburg.

"As a result, today the regiments debarked in the following order:

"The Jaeger detachment and the Queen's Rangers to Gloucester and

"The Light Infantry, the 43rd, 76th, von Voit, and von Seybothen Regiments to Yorktown.

"Lieutenant General Lord Cornwallis, who commanded the corps, went to Yorktown with his headquarters.

"The troops entered camp very close to the city in a line...

"Upon our arrival the inhabitants fled with their wives and children, leaving behind all their furniture and belongings."

## The Summer of 1781

Koch noted the movements of Cornwallis' command into and within Virginia during the summer of 1781. "We arrived at James Ferry where we lay for fourteen days, completely quiet and restoring ourselves, which was very necessary. Our transport ships arrived and brought the men who had been left behind in New York. They were again healthy. We also received uniform items and shoes of which we were in great need. We also received tents again, which we had not used during the past two years.

"At this place Lord Cornwallis' land movements came to an end after a seven months march covering 1481 English miles, or, if three English miles equal one German mile,[42] then it amounted to 494 German miles.

"Here General Lord Cornwallis received the order from the Commanding General Lord Clinton that Lord Cornwallis was to proceed to Yorktown in Virginia with his corps and secure his position there until he [Clinton] arrived with his main army.

"In compliance with this order we went aboard the transport ships and sailed with a good wind.

"We arrived at Yorktown in eight days and anchored. We landed on 3 May at Yorktown, marched to the other side of the city and set up our camp.

"Colonel DuBuy, of the von Bose Regiment, was ordered to New York and Major [Maximillian] von O'reilly assumed command of the regiment.

One hundred men from each regiment were ordered on work detail to make fortifications and trenches. We were on a small island, surrounded by water and had only a wooden bridge for crossing over.

"Lord Cornwallis had 6,000 men.

"We had such a secure camp that 20,000 would have been unable to overrun us.

"We lacked nothing in the way of foodstuffs. We received our bread, meat, and rum. Everyone received a York half-shilling and an extra pint of rum, and instead of coffee we had chocolate to drink.[43] A battery of 21 cannons was placed at the wooden bridge. We remained here for six weeks. We saw no enemies but neither did our main army come here.

"After six weeks we had finished our work and had strengthened our defenses."

The Hesse-Cassel Jaeger Corps Journal reported on activities in both the north and south during the summer as well as the eventual movement of Washington to the area of the Chesapeake. "7 July - The French troops under Rochambeau joined those of General Washington [in the New York area]. They consisted of the Bourbonnois, Soissonois, Santonga, and Royal Du Pont Regiments, the Legion of Lauzun, and Artillery, in all 4,000 men and 300 horses. The rebel army consists of about 9,000 men. The French are on the left wing, and according to all reports, the object of their operations is New York, but this must be held in abeyance until their fleet arrives from the West Indies.....

"17 July - Marquis de Lafayette attacked Lord Cornwallis near Portsmouth in Virginia on 6 July as he was crossing a river, but was defeated and had to leave three cannons and 300 dead and wounded behind. He had a strength of 3,000 men and believed most of the army had crossed the river and that he would engage only the rear guard. He found himself in error, however, as the Lord had heard of his approach and lain in wait for him.....

"24 July - ... In Carolina things are not going well. General Greene has occupied Camden and captured Augusta. Lord Rawdon has had to withdraw into all the English outer posts and Greene has now put Ninety-Six under siege.

"25 July - On the previous Sunday a party of Loyalists went from Lloyd's Neck to Middle Essex in New England and surprised the local population at church services. Fifty men and forty saddle horses were seized and brought back as prisoners. A partisan raid in a civil war.

"26 July - ... General Greene stormed Ninety-Six but was repulsed and found it necessary to raise the siege because reinforcements from Charleston, namely three regiments, recently arrived from England, under Lord Rawdon, were near the posts.....

"11 August - Today the fleet with the German recruits arrived [at New York]. They had sailed around Scotland and spent 93 days at sea. The men were exceedingly sickly.....

"18 August - The enemy army is moving and crossing the North River. Everyone believes that Washington plans to attack New York and will march toward Paulus Hook and Staten Island. *At least General Clinton is of this opinion,*[44] although Lieutenant Colonel von Wurmb, who has permission to engage spies, gave the general a report that New York will not be attacked, but that Washington is marching to Virginia. This is based on two reasons: first because the commissary has ordered forage and bread to be collected and ready as far as Trenton and along the Delaware River; second because an American woman, mistress of a distinguished French officer, was sent to Trenton, where she is to await the arrival of the army....

"29 August - ... The enemy army suddenly dropped the pretense and marched toward Trenton, crossing the Delaware there and thus clearly showing the intention of going to Virginia.

"30 August - Therefore the greatest part of our army, including 300 jaegers, was ordered to be prepared to embark.

"31 August - The 300 jaegers under Lieutenant Colonel von Wurmb marched at three o'clock this morning in order to embark from Kingsbridge. However, they were ordered back and the entire embarkation was cancelled.

"1 September - Admiral Graves sailed for the Chesapeake with the fleet as the French are said to have already arrived there.

"3 September - General Arnold with 100 jaegers under Captain von Wangenheim, the 40th, 54th, and 57th Regiments went by ship today to New England.

## The Siege and Surrender of Yorktown

Sergeant Koch wrote a rather lengthy and detailed account of the siege and surrender of Yorktown. "The enemy General Washington arrived with his army of 24,000 men and blockaded us on the island from the land side. Small arms fire was encountered at the outposts but the enemy did not risk approaching the bridge.

"Lord Cornwallis sought to lure the enemy onto the island where he could destroy the enemy with his battalions. Therefore he demolished the battery at the bridge and all the outposts were pulled back in hope of achieving a victorious battle the following day. This was

459

heartily endorsed by the entire corps, as Cornwallis could rely on his corps.

"Everyone awaited the day.

"At daybreak no enemies were to be seen and no shots were fired. The outposts were pushed forward again and the enemy remained completely inactive on this day.

"In the evening the outposts were pulled back again. During the night the French and Spanish fleet arrived off our harbor, blockading us on the seaside and in our rear. The French had landed 12,000 men, who joined with General Washington's army.

"At daybreak we saw 36,000 Americans and French ahead of us in the trenches which they had thrown up during the night. We had to fall back into our strong defenses.

"Our batteries were fully manned: behind the large battery, behind the trench line, behind every company and every secure camp. We had no warships except for two frigates from which the cannons were removed and placed in batteries on land.

"We began firing with cannons against the enemy in trenches. The enemy could not yet fire as they still had no batteries. Many enemy were killed while working. This lasted four days before the enemy began shooting at us.

"A forward battery in which Lieutenant [Nicolaus] Runck did duty was manned by the von Bose Regiment. The French had noticed that the men in that position were relieved half an hour after dusk in the evening. The French approached from the side where the entrance was. When challenged, 'Who's there?' They were unable to answer.

"The French charged the position firing against it heavily with small arms. Our new relief force arrived and charged against the French, driving them back.

"The French left many dead at the position.

"On the fifth day as the enemy had completed his batteries, he immediately began to fire at us very heavily.

"The English Artillery, of whom there were only 100 men with us, had mostly been killed and the gun carriages for our cannons were shot up so that we could only fire occasionally.

"On this night the French began a bombardment with 21 bombs. We were safe from the cannonballs, but not from the bombs. The first four days we of Major Scheer's Company were still safe from the bombs. The French could not direct the firing into our camp because they could not see over the high batteries and the high trenches behind them, nor over high fortifications, but behind the shattered houses where the company stood, we did our cooking.

"So the French noticed a camp was there and fired bombs at that place.

"The first one hit Major Scheer's tent, exploded, and blew the tent into the air, but the major was not injured. Everyone had to leave the tents. The second one sent my tent into the air as well as the knapsacks of the soldiers, and Lieutenant Bunte's portmanteau. The third one blew up Quartermaster Sergeant [Georg] Kleinschefer's tent. The fourth one sent the weapons' cover into the air and knocked the weapons about, but not a man was wounded. We noticed that only four bombs were fired at our company and we were aware that they had done us no harm.

"The English and the other troops were more heavily bombed and lost many men.

"This continued day and night. Our batteries were shot to pieces and demolished. We had to repair them during the night, which caused us to lose many troops engaged in the work.

"We hoped each day to see our main army but it did not come. During the night of the tenth day the French stormed our pickets' position on the left wing, occupied by the von Bose Regiment, and conquered it. Those not killed were captured. From that regiment, fifty were killed, captured, and wounded.

"During the night a bomb hit our powder magazine, blew it up, and some English artillerymen were killed. Our battery was shot up so badly that we could use only one cannon. We had cannons enough but no gun carriages for them, no powder, no cannonballs remained, and only a few English artillerymen were still alive."

Lieutenant Prechtel, making his entries in a diary rather than a memoir like Koch, provides much more accurate, and certainly less biased, information. He also noted the frequent desertions among the Ansbach-Bayreuth soldiers and the many men who were wounded by the steady bombardment. "10 October - At three o'clock in the afternoon the enemy opened fire with the cannons in his newly constructed fort opposite our left wing.

"Firing upon the frigate *Guadalupe* was so strong that it had to retreat into the harbor....

"The enemy fired bombs at the frigate *Charon* this evening which caused it and also a transport ship in the harbor to be burned completely.

"The English Major Gordon arrived as an express from New York and brought the news that an English war fleet was near the Chesapeake....

""11 October - The regiment entered the trenches in which our tents were also set up, and are thus protected from the cannonballs, at least....

"13 October - The enemy fired mostly 200 pound bombs and 42-, 36-, and 24-pound cannonballs into our camp.

"On the other hand, the English only had one 24-pounder set up in our line, and further, were provided with no heavy bombs.

"Wounded in the tents in the trenches, from the von Voit Regiment, were:

"1) Privates [Conrad] Koerner and

"2) [Caspar] Appold, of the Colonel's Company, by a bomb which landed in the tent; the first had a foot shot off, and the latter received a wound in his knee.

"3) Private Fuchs, of Captain von Stain's Company, was wounded in the chest by shrapnel from a bomb.

"4) Private Wagner, of the Lieutenant Colonel's company, was instantly killed when a 200 pound bomb landed in the tent of Corporal Gachstetter. Four others in the tent were not wounded.

"5) Corporal Schuster, of the Colonel's company, while on picket, had his right arm shot off.

"Wounded of the von Seybothen Regiment was: Grenadier Nuezel, whose foot was shot off by a bomb.

"14 October - ... About eight o'clock at night the enemy attacked our right wing, but was again driven back.

"Immediately after this attack, both of our outermost positions on the left wing were attacked and after a short engagement, conquered. The largest, with 100 men, was under the command of the English Lieutenant Colonel McPherson, and the smaller position was commanded by the English Major Kempel.

"After this conquest, the left wing of the line as far as the von Seybothen Regiment, was attacked. However, a terrible cannon and musket fire was delivered from the English lines so that the enemy had to pull back into his defenses....

"Both servants of Captain von Eyb and Captain [Christoph] von Metzsch were wounded by a spent bomb which they were trying to dig up.

"16 October - The English Grenadiers and Light Infantry made a sortie tonight into the enemy camp and in the greatest haste spiked eleven of the enemy's cannons. One captain and three privates of the French army were made prisoners of war. According to their comments, a French war fleet of 33 sails has arrived again in the Chesapeake from France and joined the other French fleet lying at anchor there.

"The French army reportedly amounts to 15,000 men....

"The English Light Infantry and the Guard Regiment were transferred across the York River to Gloucester this evening in order to attack the enemy there. However, as the enemy was as strong on the other side as on this side, this plan remained unfulfilled.

"During this time, the Hornwork, in which the Light Infantry had been, was occupied by a detachment from the von Voit Regiment, commanded by Lieutenant Colonel von Reitzenstein.

"17 October - ... A flag of truce was sent from the English side into the enemy camp this morning.

"Note! As soon as a flag of truce is sent out, a halt is immediately made to the firing. However, it continues only until the flag again arrives back in its camp.

"The Light Infantry and the Guard Regiment arrived back here again from Gloucester at noon and took over their former post.

"Private [Johann Simon] Kern, of Colonel von Voit's Company, had taken food to his comrades with the detachment in the Hornwork. As he was about to return, he was killed by a cannonball....

"A flag of truce from the enemy entered the outer lines.

"This evening a flag of truce was again sent to the enemy from the English side. After which, from five o'clock in the afternoon on, a cease fire resulted.

"At eight o'clock at night the powder magazine, due to carelessness of an English artilleryman, who took a light therein, blew up. As a result, twelve persons were killed, among whom was Private [Jacob] Gunckel, of the Major's Company of the von Voit Regiment, who just at that time, found himself there as he went on sentry duty....

"19 October - At three o'clock in the afternoon the entire English army marched out of Yorktown with music playing and cased flags, and after both defensive positions on the left wing had previously been occupied by American and French troops.

"From the enemy trenches onward, the American army stood on the left, before whose middle stood Lieutenant General Washington, and on the right, the French army, before which was Lieutenant General Rochambeau.

"Both armies paraded in the finest order and we marched in columns between them. Where they ended, the English army marched up in two lines and at a quarter to five in the evening lay down their weapons.

"After the ceremony the troops returned through both armies, which had their weapons grounded, to the city of York and reentered their former camp.

"From the 9th to the 17th of this month, more than 16,000 bombs were fired into our camp.

"The army which Lieutenant General Lord Cornwallis commanded had 5,000 men. The American and French armies, on the other hand, amounted to 40,000 men."

Koch's account of the siege continues, "As we now had given up hope of our main army, Lord Cornwallis began to negotiate surrender with the enemy. The capitulation was refused by the enemy on the eleventh day and again on the twelfth day.

"Therefore Cornwallis immediately resumed firing from the battery. The enemy also began firing heavily again. As night fell Lord Cornwallis ordered that all officers' horses be appraised. They were then taken to the water and killed.[45]

"Our sick and wounded and some baggage were taken across the river on the seaside where our army was to go.

"The thirteenth day there was again a ceasefire and again negotiations, but also again refused. As night fell Cornwallis would not yield on his terms. He ordered the entire corps, except for the Ansbach and Bayreuth Regiments, who were to remain in place and to occupy the posts in the trench line, to march to the river at once and to go aboard the ships.

"We marched at once and arrived at the river. Two English regiments had already entered the flatboats. Suddenly a storm wind arose, upset the boats, and dumped the soldiers into the water. The English swam back to shore.

"At that moment the Ansbach major approached and reported that all the Bayreuth outposts had deserted, taking the password with them. Lord Cornwallis immediately ordered, 'Left about! March into the trenches!'

"The deserters had disclosed that Cornwallis wanted to transfer the entire corps across the river and await the main army there. Therefore the French General Rochambeau wanted to storm the trench line at once.

"General Washington and Lafayette, as was told later, advised against that. It was a ruse by Cornwallis and after they committed their army, that could happen. They would not consent because they knew the English main army had not yet gone aboard ship and at best could not arrive in less than eight days. Cornwallis had provisions for only five or six days. He was also short of powder and therefore would have to surrender.

"Still General Rochambeau stuck to his objective. Our trench line contained sixteen regimental cannons and twelve small howitzers from the warships, which had continued to fire. During our return march, Captain Rall was killed at my side by a piece of a bomb.

"Everyone had barely reentered the line when the French shouted 'Vive le Roi!'

"But now our entire line fired at the enemy with small arms, cannons and cannisters, and howitzers with balls and cannisters, so that they no longer gave loud but only individual voices.

"Our firing continued for two hours, until almost no one had any more cartridges, and the enemy fled.

"It was very dark and we had to remain under arms throughout the night, even though the enemy cannonfire had ceased.

"During the night the French had gathered their wounded. At daybreak we saw that the enemy was again in his former positions and that many French dead lay before our lines.

"A truce was made. The enemy dead were buried.

"On the fifteenth the enemy sent a capitulation proposal to Cornwallis.

"Lord Cornwallis sent his counter-proposals back, which he refused to soften. The enemy refused these and Lord Cornwallis again opened fire from the lone battery which we still had.

"The day passed quietly without cannonfire. The following night Lord Cornwallis wanted to show the enemy that despite their great strength, he could still accomplish something with his corps. Early in the morning, two hours before daybreak, our entire corps had to charge the enemy trenches, force our way in, beating and stabbing to death the French and Americans who were in the trenches. And, after we had shown this, we hurried back to our lines before the enemy army arrived.

"On the sixteenth day we remained under arms in the trenches and the cannonfire continued.

"The enemy sent a flag of truce inviting our capitulation. Lord Cornwallis replied that they had his conditions and if they were not acceptable, the negotiations were ended.

"The cannonfire continued until one o'clock on the afternoon of the seventeenth day, when the enemy fired the last shot. It killed the regimental surgeon of the Hereditary Prince Regiment and the regimental drummer of the von Bose Regiment.

"The enemy sent Lord Cornwallis the terms he wished.

"Suddenly there was peace. It was 19 October 1781.

"Lord Cornwallis gave the order for peace. All the regiments marched back into their camps. The French troops relieved all the posts and occupied the batteries, but no Americans were to be allowed in our camp. We are prisoners but the regiments occupy their own camps with their own troops.

"The French officers from the German Regiments [serving with the French] came to us and visited our officers, but the French would not allow the Americans to pass to us.

"The terms were made known.

"Lord Cornwallis corps surrendered to the Americans. The officers and men are to keep their personal belongings, the officers their sidearms. Lord Cornwallis and half of the corps of officers and their belongings and the sick were taken aboard six ships. Only one staff officer remained with each regiment in captivity. Their destination is Frederick in Maryland. At nine o'clock on the twentieth Lord Cornwallis' corps marched out and stacked arms, not far from the fortifications. It marched out with flags flying and music playing, and after laying down the weapons, it marched back into camp.

"We marched out with flags flying and music playing. The French and Americans had formed two lines and came to present arms for our flags and played a march. However, we were dissatisfied and bitter toward the rebels. It was strictly forbidden for us to display any misconduct during our march through the lines, but many could not help but say, when the French were not present, that the Americans would not have been able to capture us.

"The French and Americans were surprised that our corps was only 4,000 men strong as they had always believed Cornwallis corps was 15,000 men strong.

"We had lost many men but there were also many sick who were left behind and did not go into captivity.

"After we had stacked arms, we marched back into our camp."

## Clinton's Indecision

While Yorktown was under siege, General Clinton took a number of uncertain steps to try to create a diversion or to send reinforcements to General Cornwallis. J.R. noted some of these measures, commencing on 6 September. "The regiment left its camp and marched to New York, where, near the Flea Market, it was embarked aboard three ships, *Kepel, Antelope,* and *Munificency,* as the regiment, with several other regiments, was to undertake an expedition. It soon departed on signal and sailed to Denyse's Ferry between Long and Staten Island, where the other transport ships lay with troops on board.

"21 September - All the troops were landed on Staten Island and entered camp.

"12 October - These troops again went aboard the same transport ships with orders to be prepared at the earliest news to go aboard the warships which were present.

"18 October - At Sandy Hook, where the fleet lay at anchor, these troops went aboard the warships which were there. Our regiment went aboard the *Royal Oak* and *Ajax,* both 74 gun ships.

"15 November - As the previously planned expedition failed to materialize, the regiment was landed on Long Island and entered cantonment quarters in the barns at Gowans, a few miles from Brooklyn Ferry.

"The Hesse Cassel Jaeger Corps Journal provides similar information, beginning on 4 September. "The following troops were ordered to embark on 6 September: 400 jaegers under Lieutenant Colonel von Wurmb, the 17th Dragoons, all the Grenadiers, the 42nd, and 57th Regiments, and Leib and Prince Charles Regiments.

"5 September - The French fleet with 26 ships-of-the-line lies in Chesapeake Bay and has blockaded Lord Cornwallis. Admiral Graves has only nineteen ships-of-the-line and two fifty gun ships. The frigate *Pegasus* also has sighted Mr. de Barras with eight ships-of-the-line, as he is sailing from Rhode Island to the Chesapeake to unite with de Grasse.

"6 September - The troops were embarked today aboard transport ships.....

"13 September - ... This night a frigate arrived from the Chesapeake with the news that on the fifth an action occurred between the two fleets, but without a decisive result. On the arrival of the English, the French slipped their anchors and sailed against the Englanders.

"15 September - The transport ships sailed to The Narrows today.

"19 September - This morning Admiral Graves returned with his fleet and we at once noticed that the action on the fifth had not been the most fortunate one. Only twelve of our ships-of-the-line had been engaged; the others had not fired a shot because our maneuvers had been so poorly directed. At least the admiral has been blamed for making a great mistake by letting the French ships sail out individually without attacking them at once. From the fifth to eleventh both fleets maneuvered off Cape Henry. On the eleventh the French returned to the Chesapeake where they lay joined together with M. de Barras, who had arrived there in the meantime and unfortunately had captured two of our frigates which had been sent in to cut off the French harbor buoys. Thereafter, Graves, with his nineteen ships-of-the-line could no longer attack the French and so decided to return to New York. Further, it became necessary on the thirteenth to burn the *Terrible*, of 74 guns, because it was very old and had been damaged greatly in the action.

"20 September - The embarked troops today went to Staten Island and were set on land. Our warship fleet went to New York in order to complete repairs there.

"25 September - ... An express boat came from Lord Cornwallis. He has still not come under siege. Washington however, has arrived at Head of Elk and is waiting for the French transport ships which will take him to Virginia.

"28 September - The warship fleet is too damaged to be repaired. The troops received orders to be prepared to go aboard the same. The army train has been assembled at Staten Island and many pontoons have been loaded on wagons, as if the army is to go into the Jerseys.

"2 October - The Grenadiers and Jaegers marched to the south part of Staten Island and camped at Richmond, the Jaegers at Old Blazing Star. This movement makes a diversion into the Jerseys appear likely.....

"10 October - Today the troops on Staten Island marched back to Cole's Ferry in order to go aboard warships. This allows the Jerseys to recover from the fear of a diversionary attack.....

"12 October - After the troops passed in review before Prince William Henry, they embarked on board the transport ships.

"13 October - A stormy southwest wind drove a warship against the *Shrewsbury*, losing its bowsprit. Several boats capsized in the fleet, causing some drownings....

"14 October - Most of the warships, except for the *Europa*, and the transport ships, sailed to Sandy Hook. The transports lay alongside the warships, enabling the troops to cross from one to the other across boards placed between the ships....

"After the embarkation, the warships crossed the bar; they set sail this afternoon at four o'clock with a weak southwest wind. There were 24 ships-of-the-line, three 50 gun ships, and two fireships.

"20 October - ... The fleet sailed in three divisions.

"25 October - We saw the Capes of Virginia.....

"28 October - Wind northeasterly. We saw Cape Henry and entered the bay. At four o'clock in the afternoon we saw the French fleet lying at anchor, ready to challenge our using the passage. Our fleet was in line and lay to. The admiral sent on land for news. This he obtained, but to the effect that Lord Cornwallis had been captured.

The wind was very favorable for the French to attack us whenever they wished.

"29 October - Our fleet still lay as before. The French were peacefully at anchor. The day was still and beautiful and at four o'clock in the afternoon the fleet set sail in a weak wind for New York. The French watched us from a distance from two frigates.....

"3 November - At noon today we went from the warships onto the transports and were landed this evening at Denyse's Ferry. As the wind began to blow exceptionally hard from the northwest however, we had to remain at anchor.

"4 to 12 November - ... Many ships exhausted the supply of provisions and water but nothing could be done to help them, because no boats could be lowered....

"13 November - Today the ships finally entered The Narrows as the wind had eased. The troops debarked....

"14 November - The French and Americans were very thorough in planning the works necessary for the siege of Lord Cornwallis. Initially they began on 30 September with the approaches and on 6 October their first parallel was completed at a distance of only 600 yards from the English defenses. During the evening of 9 October they opened batteries and soon silenced the English with their ceaseless bombardment. During the night of 11 October they began their second parallel and on the evening of the fourteenth, stormed and conquered two redoubts commanded by Major Campbell, which protected the English. These were absorbed into the second parallel, upon which the French worked untiringly, during the same night.

"Lord Cornwallis saw that when the cannons in the second parallel opened fire, he would not be able to withstand it, as his defenses were too weak. He made a sortie therefore, before daylight on 16 October with 320 men, commanded by Colonel Abercromby, and spiked eleven cannons. This did not help much however, because they were soon bored out and by evening the parallel was completed. Lord Cornwallis was convinced the post could no longer be defended and decided to cross over with most of the troops to Gloucester, where his light troops were being blockaded by a French corps, to try to proceed to New York by land from there, as he planned to overcome the French corps. He had already sent over part of his troops in sixteen boats when in the same night, a dreadful wind storm arose which prevented his continuing the operation. Next morning he brought them back across and the French opened fire with their batteries at daybreak, so destroying the English defenses that they could have been stormed when the French so desired. Lord Cornwallis therefore decided to capitulate. On 19 October the capitulations was signed by which he and the troops surrendered under the same terms as accorded at Charleston. Cornwallis says: York was meant to be only a fortified camp. He had only begun work there on 1 August and he had only 400 pieces of engineering equipment. He would never have chosen this position if he had not been ordered to do so. From the beginning, when Washington came to Williamsburg with his army, he would have sought either to engage the enemy on an open field, or to proceed to New York by land, if he had not received firm assurances from Sir Henry Clinton of a reinforcement which kept him from the choice of these desperate measures. Finally, he received a letter of 24 September assuring him that the fleet with reinforcements would sail on 5 October.....

"15 November - ... A part of the enemy army is on the move to Philadelphia to go into winter quarters. Another part however, has gone south to strengthen General Greene, who is sitting not far from Charleston. Wilmington has been abandoned and all the posts in South Carolina have been pulled back to within a few miles of Charleston. The rebel army is wintering at Morristown. This is one of the most peaceful winter quarters of the entire war. Neither army has undertaken any activity as if the surrender at Yorktown has already brought an end to everything."

Finally, the Platte Grenadier Battalion Journal also describes the uncertainty and eventual futility of Clinton's efforts to save Cornwallis' command. "5 September - The Hessian Grenadiers were embarked on the ships.... The wagon horses and artillery horses had been delivered previously to the quartermaster general department. The wagons and equipment and the artillery were taken aboard ship. Only a very little baggage was taken on board. The women had to remain in the huts at Denyse's Ferry, where a non-commissioned officer from each battalion commanded. Because here at Denyse's Ferry our camp was located on an old swamp, we suffered a great many sick. Even Lieutenant Colonel [Carl Wilhelm von] Graf had to remain behind sick with a fever at Denyse's Ferry. During this time, in which a corps of troops was involved in embarking, General Arnold, who had returned from Virginia on his own, went with a small corps of troops to New England and destroyed New London and its harbor and several forts. During the conquest of Fort Griswold, the 40th and 54th Regiments suffered severe losses. No one from Hesse accompanied this expedition except 100 jaegers under the command of Captain von Wangenheim.

"In addition to the Hessian Grenadier Brigade, two battalions of English Grenadiers, the 22nd, 37th, and 47th Regiments, a detachment of 400 jaegers under the command of Colonel von Wurmb, the Prince Charles and the Leib Regiments, and a number of recruits for the units in Virginia were embarked today at Denyse's Ferry and New York.

"16 September - It is said that Lord Cornwallis has been closely confined by the enemy at Yorktown in Virginia and these embarked troops are meant to be a relief force. Generals Washington and Rochambeau have marched there with the troops under their command and the French fleet supposedly is much stronger than ours. At present our fleet lies here in the harbor and repairs the damage inflicted by the French fleet at the start of this month in the engagement on the Virginia coast. In the engagement we lost the ship *Terrible*. Because it had not only developed leaks on the voyage coming from the West Indies, but had suffered greatly in the above engagement, it was set on fire during the night and burned so as not to fall into enemy hands.

"21 September - All the above troops disembarked at Cole's ferry on Staten Island and entered camp around the Watering Place, after having lain at anchor on the ships between Long and Staten Island from the fifth until today.....

"29 September - We received news that all of the troops camped here are to embark aboard warships.

"2 October - The Hessian Grenadier Brigade moved out from the Watering Place and marched to Richmond, the Jaegers to Blazing Star, and the two British Grenadier Battalions to Philipse's Point. The rest of the troops, which were to be embarked, remained in their former camps.

"9 October - We marched back from the above mentioned places into our former camps at the Watering Place.

"11 October - All the troops embarked in the previously designated transport ships which lay at Cole's Ferry on Staten Island.

"16 and 17 October - Until today the transport ships lay at anchor at the mentioned place. The warships, which had been repaired and supplied with provisions and water, came here during this time from New York and then went to Sandy Hook. During these two days all the transport ships, on which the troops were embarked, joined the warships at Sandy Hook.

"18 and 19 October - The troops on board the transport ships were embarked on the warships....

"Because the Grenadier Brigade had very many sick officers, nineteen Brunswick and Hanau officers were assigned to do duty on this expedition. No baggage was allowed to be taken except what a servant could carry in an emergency. The women, of whom not one was allowed to accompany the expedition, remained with the baggage on the transport ships, which returned to New York.... The ships were very full of people and the accommodations were greatly reduced. The officers were put up in the wardroom with the naval officers and during the night had to sleep on the floor. Non-commissioned officers and privates were put by the heavy cannons and had to find places to sleep between the cannons. The staff officers and senior captains, for the most part, were quartered with the [ships'] captains. On the evening of the nineteenth the fleet sailed out to sea as an even larger fleet from England entered near Sandy Hook.....

"25 October - ... Everything aboard ship was made ready for an action and we expected that such would occur today, although no enemy ships were to be seen. Therefore the ship's officers thought we would enter the bay today or this evening. Our ship's captain went aboard the admiral's ship *London* this afternoon and returned to us with the most astonishing, unpleasant news, that Lord Cornwallis and his army had surrendered already on the nineteenth of this month and been made prisoners of war.....

"28 and 29 October - We cruised continuously outside the bay and saw enemy frigates doing the same inside the bay. As soon as ours approached them, the French frigates withdrew. Despite the French fleet being much larger than ours, the French showed no signs of desiring to engage in battle with ours, but remained peacefully inside the bay. About two o'clock in the afternoon the admiral signaled for the ships to assemble and for all the frigates to join the fleet. After the signal was answered, all the ships set sail and steered toward the north. Apparently we will return to New York.

"2 November - ... This fruitless and too late undertaken expedition was now ended and we are again to go aboard the transport ships lying here for that purpose. If we had embarked on the warships fourteen days earlier, Lord Cornwallis probably would not have been captured and all our hopes for success in the southern area would not have been destroyed. The second Burgoyning will undoubtedly contribute to an unfortunate conclusion to the war. Before we leave the warship I can not fail to mention that we owe the navy the greatest appreciation for the courtesy extended to us. As long as we were on board the ship we were treated not only very splendidly with food and drink, but they sought to make it as pleasant for us as circumstances would allow. We brought no bedding with us and instead received sailcloth and flags. As blankets, all the navy and marine officers lent us their overcoats. Beside the ship's captain, Captain Knight., there were five naval officers and a volunteer from the warship *Terrible*, sunk in the last action, serving as lieutenants, and a captain and two lieutenants from the marines. We paid nothing for the accommodations provided by our comrades. The strictest organization, discipline, activity, and the exceptional cleanliness aboard the warships merited not only notice, but also wonderment. If these rules were rigorously enforced among the troops on the transport ships, we would not have had so much sickness. It is astonishing to see how many men, how many cannons, how much armament, munitions, provisions, how much ship building material and other items are to be found on a 74 gun ship, and yet everywhere there is comfort and space. All of this is the result of good and strict discipline. Nothing more could be wished for than that this good organization and system could be exactly observed in building houses. There would be no reason to complain about houses built in this manner failing to please the eye symmetrically from without and giving comfort within.

"3 November - We were transferred from the warships to the transports in rather stormy weather.

"8 November - We spent the time until today on the transport ships due to contrary wind, in a terrible situation, because we had no provisions, and to make matters worse, the weather was very cold.

"9 November - Part of the vacant Graf Grenadier Battalion was landed. Several of the ships were driven out into the sea and then returned to Denyse's Ferry on Long Island, where all the troops were landed and we entered our former camp....

"This ended the unfortunate campaign of 1781. If it will be the last, as many believe, only the future can tell."

## Captivity

Lieutenant Prechtel, who had been chosen by lot to accompany the enlisted Ansbach-Bayreuth soldiers into captivity, made the following diary entries, among others, pertaining to that period in 1781. "21 October - At twelve o'clock noon, the prisoners were escorted out of Yorktown by the American militia, consisting of 500 men with two cannons. Halfway to Williamsburg, night camp was made under the open sky.

"The captured officers had to give their blacks to the enemy.....

"30 October - The prisoners of war from Gloucester were taken on another route and joined us again at Fredericksburg. The prisoners of war were escorted two miles farther [beyond Winchester, Virginia] into a woods where already two barracks for captive troops had been built. These were truly very poorly put together and as they were not half adequate for quartering the troops, the men had to build new barracks later on, but already at this time it was very unpleasant and as cold as in winter.

"This place very quickly took on the appearance of a great city and was permanently occupied by a detachment of 200 American militia, commanded by a colonel.

"The officers had to obtain their quarters in the city of Winchester, or the surrounding area, and for their own money. These quarters cost from six to eight Spanish dollars per month, each dollar equals two florins and thirty groschen.

"The soldiers are visited by their officers two or three times per week and to prevent misconduct, a subaltern must daily maintain a watch in the barracks of the Ansbach regiments."

Prechtel noted the desertion of many men of the Ansbach-Bayreuth regiments and that many of the men enlisted in the American or French service.

"2 December - Grenadiers [Heinrich] Ockell, Wachler, and [Johann Wilhelm] Rossel, of the von Voit Regiment, deserted from [Gloucester] and were taken into French service.....

"24 December - Drummer Hopfer and Private [Conrad] Weiss, of the Major's Company of the von Voit Regiment, deserted from the barracks and then engaged in the American Light Horse at Newtown."

The hautboist Stang seems to have faired better than most of the other prisoners, however, as he noted in an entry of 6 November 1781, "We marched through Winchester and five miles beyond. Then we entered our barracks in the woods where we are to spend our captivity and be quartered....

"I spent my time there as a dance master."

Koch also recorded events of his march into captivity. "The third day [after the capitulation], when we were to march off, Lord Cornwallis came, said his farewell, and cried.

"He said, 'My true, good children be calm and remain patient. I have looked out for you. You will be well taken care of. You will receive provisions just as you received from the royal army and no one will insult you.'

"Moved and saddened, we marched away in three columns, escorted by the Americans....

"We heard heavy cannonfire on the ocean. We listened carefully, everyone was excited.

"The Americans took up their weapons. The American officers said, 'Good soldiers stay calm. Your fleet, even if it is there can no longer help you.'

"After being addressed by our non-commissioned officers the soldiers grew calm. We saw not one of our officers, who had been quartered in houses.

"During the entire march, no matter where we went, men, women, and children stood and, when they saw us, the von Bose Regiment, old and young called out, 'That is the regiment, the rascals who killed our husbands, our fathers!' That was because of the Battle of Guilford Courthouse. The riflemen, or marksmen, who participated in the Battle of Guilford Courthouse were Marylanders. Those who survived had falsely described our regiment, white flaps with turned up brims and red tassels on the hats. That was a sign that they would give no quarter.

"The people, young and old, picked up stones and threw them at us as we marched along. Our troops did not allow this to go unanswered, but picked up stones and scattered those assembled.

"To curtail these disturbances, the American officer marched his troops on both sides of us and wherever a group was assembled, peace and quiet existed.

"Therefore we arrived at the destination of our captivity in Frederick [Maryland].

"Our von Bose Regiment and the Hereditary Prince Regiment were quartered in the poorhouse. Each company received one room which was so small that no one could lie down.

"Most of the soldiers took their blankets and used them to make tents in front of the poorhouse, where they then lay down. There were a few houses there but the guards would not allow us to enter them.

"We had to put up with this for three days.

"On the fourth day six covered wagons arrived. They were stopped by the guards and asked what they wished. Their answer, 'We wish to sell potatoes to the prisoners.'

"Everyone who wanted potatoes gathered around. When they wished to pay for the potatoes, the people said, 'No, you need not pay for them. We are loyal to the King and if you wish to go with us, secretly sneak into the wagons so that the guards do not see you.'

"Suddenly the wagons were filled with soldiers. The guards saw this but did nothing because most of them were Loyalists who did not want to see anything.

"Now we had room enough. The English were in barracks on the other side of Frederick. We lay in the poorhouse for fourteen days.

"There was talk during this time which the Loyalists spread and which was told to us by the guards who also favored the King. An English fleet lay off Baltimore. It had troops on board and weapons. As soon as they were landed at Baltimore, the Loyalists would take up weapons, release the prisoners at Frederick, and then attack the rebels.

"The signal as to when this should begin was as follows:

"During the night the Loyalists were to assemble. In the woods and bushes on the right side of Frederick a fire would be set, which would flare up. This was to be the signal for the prisoners to overpower the rebel guards, seize their weapons, and then assemble where the fire was burning.

"The rebels reacted to this with fright. The third watch was strengthened and no one was allowed to leave his house.

"Our troops, von Bose and Hereditary Prince Regiments, also the Ansbach-Bayreuthers, had already for some time been with the Loyalists residents and working for them.

"However, the English were still together in the barracks.

"Suddenly during the night there was an alarm and cannon shots were fired. As soon as the English were aware of this they attacked the guards, beat them to death with sticks, took their weapons, and began shooting. They set the barracks on fire and fled toward the burning bushes.

"An additional 100 men were joined to our guard. We remained calm and quietly watched.

"An American colonel came and asked the guards if we had remained peaceful. When he learned that no one had ventured outside the houses, he withdrew 100 men again.

"By daybreak 3,000 Americans had gathered, who then marched toward the bushes where the fire still burned. When they arrived they found nothing but the burning fire, no Loyalists and no English, and so came back.

"The English had struggled through almost to Baltimore. However, because there was no English fleet, they once again had to surrender."

### Other Activities in 1781

In a letter dated 2 March 1781 to his prince from New York, Captain Pausch commented on how some of the convention prisoners were able to return to English control and of a rumored reinforcement. "The additional exchange of Lieutenant Colonel [Johann Christoph] Lentz and the remaining [Hesse-Hanau] officers, as well as a part of those from all the other nations of Burgoyne's army, supposedly has been decided and agreed upon. Their arrival here, however, is still uncertain....

"The list of those German and English officers of the Burgoyne Convention who were to be exchanged was only sent to the enemy headquarters of General Washington about seventeen days ago. In this particular case I am greatly embarrassed concerning what is surest and best to do with the packages, after our previous separation and the apparent meeting in the future.

"The report most humbly sent with Colonel von Gall remains unchanged except that Sergeant [Adam] Kohlep died four weeks ago in the jail in Philadelphia and a cannoneer by the name of [Johann Georg] Schwab, according to Captain von Bartling of the Brunswick Grenadiers, by claiming to be his [Bartling's] servant, was exchanged and is now here by me. This cannoneer was one of the captives from Bennington. He ransomed himself in 1778 and joined the company at Winterhill near Boston. Later, however, on the march to Virginia, having joined Major General Phillips' suite, he claimed to be sick and remained behind. Nevertheless, however, he was listed as a deserter together with the others who remained behind, because I knew nothing about and am still uncertain if his claim is valid....

"A new reinforcement, which supposedly consists of 6,000 Wuerttembergers and 4,000 English troops, is expected here from Europe daily."

In a letter of 16 April, Pausch mentions newspaper reports and the need for the Convention prisoners to vacate the barracks at Charlottesville when an English force approached too near to that place. "The accounts contained in the local newspapers are filled with embellishments, as required by necessity, not only to cheer up the army and navy, but also to increase the satisfaction of the inhabitants in our small local districts, and to keep them in higher hopes.

"The news has arrived here from Virginia that our troops held under the Convention were required to leave the barracks, which they built, with all other troops. When they moved back into them, all the woodwork had been disfigured and ruined. This had resulted due to Brigadier Arnold's approach to Williamsburg.

"The most humbly mentioned troops have all suffered a hard winter. Most, even the officers, as well as non-commissioned officers and privates, lived without houses, huts, or tents, in the woods and had to survive such misery, until Brigadier Arnold withdrew. Then all the Germans were returned to their ruined barracks in Albemarle County."

Pausch continued reporting events in America in a letter of 8 June 1781. "On 22 April of this year the German troops destined for Canada, who arrived from Charleston, South Carolina, lay at anchor here in the East River. On the 24th they debarked at the Brooklyn

Ferry on Long Island and were quartered in barns at Flatbush, five English miles from this place. The 25th was a day of rest for those troops. On the 26th I received a general order from Major General von Riedesel and had to provide weapons for the Jaegers and the seven recruits for your illustrious regiment, which consisted for each man of a musket, a bayonet with scabbard on a black leather strap, and similarly a black cartridge box. Even before all these items and cartridges had been sent over from New York, a battalion had already been formed for duty at Brooklyn Fort and its environs, consisting of the following:

"The exchanged dragoons and those of the dragoons who had ransomed themselves were a unit. Also the exchanged Brunswick Grenadiers and the same who had ransomed themselves, together with 120 of the newly arrived recruits, were formed into four companies under four captains, with a fifth company under my command, consisting of those exchanged and those who had ransomed themselves, and the newly arrived recruits of your illustrious regiment, including the recruits for the Jaeger Corps, amounting to a total strength as noted in the most humble report. The Anhalt-Zerbst recruits, of whom there were only one officer and 47 men, are commanded by their own officers, who must perform various duties with them. However, they conduct drill with Your Serene Highness' regiment here, in order to participate at parade, as otherwise they perform the Kaiser's style of drill.

"Fort Brooklyn and all its small outerworks, including the ferry and the magazine in the town proper, was formerly occupied by English recruits, destined for all the regiments, joined in one battalion. However, suddenly, and not voluntarily, toward evening they were silently and swiftly forced to become sailors, put in sloops, and taken on board ships, where they were much needed. That occurred on 29 April and the same evening a detachment of dragoons occupied the fort, its outerworks, and Brooklyn....

"The latest, and repeated information, from the newspapers is that all the non-commissioned officers and privates of the Convention prisoners are to be considered as prisoners of war and guarded as such with strict limits. All their officers, without exception, are to be taken from their regiments in Virginia and Maryland and sent to Connecticut, about 590 miles from Virginia. Likewise, in every situation, they are to be considered as prisoners of war. If carried out, this will create obvious adverse effects on good order and discipline, which can already be noted, although their officers are still with them. That this misfortune will effect our troops seriously, I doubt no less because the rebels had nearly completed working out the details in the presence of General Phillips, and wished to put it into effect. However, he was absolutely opposed to the implementation of this project which is in violation of the Convention.

"A few days ago the confirmed reports were received here that Major General Phillips was suddenly attacked by an extremely dangerous illness and died of it a few days later. The confirmation of his death has also appeared in the newspapers, and that he was to be buried at the church in Petersburg, [Virginia]....

"Concerning our departure for Canada, I can most humbly report nothing; if it will be undertaken soon, later, or not at all, because here there is much talk and much speculation about it, but always ambiguously. There are many reasons to believe the general wishes to keep it secret here, until possibly the order will suddenly be given, the embarkation will take place, and we will set sail....

"Lieutenant von Lindau of Your Serene Highness' illustrious regiment and Lieutenant Bach of your artillery serve with the Combined Battalion here. The Regimental Surgeon Heidelbach diligently tends the sick. I do my daily and other duties with two dragoon and four infantry captains of the Duke of Brunswick's troops, in a battalion here at this post."

In a letter of 6, or possibly 16 June, Pausch provided the prince with more information about the situation in America. "Almost all the Hesse-Cassel regiments and grenadier battalions have taken on Negroes as drummers, pipers, and pack servants, which the European recruiting creates. I have followed this practice and at little cost have engaged three drummers for the Artillery Company so graciously entrusted to me, as well as a hunting horn blower for the Jaeger Corps, and sent a commission to a good friend in Virginia for a pack servant and twelve artillery servants, each between fourteen and eighteen years of age and well-developed. I hope most humbly, if this local recruiting is not disapproved there, to have possibly fulfilled Your Serene Highness' most gracious intention, as these blacks passed muster as musicians and servants in all of the regiments and have served well. It is possible, if it meets Your Serene Highness' approval, to fill the whole regiment in time, with similar blacks. The artillery and pack servants would always be available to support the most humbly mentioned musicians and to replace their losses. If it were to please Your Serene Highness to approve this most humble project, I wish nothing more than the limits as to the recruiting costs, as well as having you most gracious order and limits set for me as to the age, marriage state, and children....

"The Brunswick Dragoon Regiment has filled its needs with black drummers, which were however, a present to Major General von Riedesel from Brigadier Arnold."

Pausch informed his prince of his pending departure for Canada in a letter of 24 July 1781, written on board ship at Staten Island. "Your Serene Highness, today I have the greatest pleasure to finally and most humbly report about our departure from here for Canada, which surprised us quite suddenly, from on board the transport ship *Montague*, on which I and the entire regiment and jaeger baggage was embarked on the 22nd, but on which the detachment was embarked on the 23rd of this month."

Finally, on 17 October 1781, Pausch was able to write of his arrival back in Canada. "Your Serene Highness, to lay this in most sincere submission most humbly at your feet, occurs for the first time again from Canada, where I, with those men of Your Serene Highness' illustrious regiment and artillery reassembled in New York, together with the recruit transport brought out by Lieutenant Thoma for Your Highness' Jaeger Corps and some of the men belonging to the regiment, arrived here before Quebec on 15 September of this year at six o'clock in the evening. The next morning, from whence I at once made the report of our arrival to Major General von Riedesel and His Excellency, Lieutenant General Haldimand. The same day I received the order from the major general to debark everyone the following morning, the seventeenth, and to have the troops march off at a convenient place near King's Wharf at about nine o'clock....

"We have given up hope of an early exchange of those who still find themselves in captivity, officers, non-commissioned officers, and privates....

"Our voyage from New York here to Quebec took a long time and at that time was made unpleasant by bad weather, and often seemed dangerous at perilous places in the Gulf and on the St. Lawrence River. Nevertheless, under the protection of the Almighty, from 23 July to and including the sixteenth of this month, amounting to 56 days that we were on board, we happily survived all misfortunes and have already forgotten. Not a single soul died except for a small child, whose mother also suddenly died at the start at Brooklyn. He then followed her, and was buried in the mentioned gulf....

"Here it is very quiet at present and even more peaceful than in Europe during an uninterrupted period of peace.... Because of the present time of the year, we have nothing more to anticipate in the Gulf and the enemy's operations on land appear impractical considering the astonishingly deep snow here, and, also because of the great distances and the uninhabited regions, which results in a shortage of provisions, and leaves nothing except possibly raids by small patrols to be expected. As the enemy no longer has any positions on a single lake, the lakes have even less use. Should they undertake warlike preparations during the winter at some distant places in the forests, by gathering the necessary wood for construction, it could be nothing more than batteaux, and without ships, which are essential for an undertaking, nothing is possible."

Letters from other Hesse-Hanau officers to the prince during 1781 primarily are concerned with the Convention prisoners. An undated letter from Captain [Christian] Eschwege refers to a move from Charlottesville to Winchester and the officers being separated from their men. "On 20 February we received orders from Colonel Wood to march at once to Winchester, and as there were not sufficient wagons available, most of our sick and our baggage had to be left behind. Privates [Conrad] Krieg and [Caspar] Kempf were detailed to guard it. The two hautboists [Adam] Mueller and Insdorf, Jr., who upon request to the commanding officer, Colonel [James] Wood, had leave [to work] on the land, remained behind at the barracks in Albemarle. Also Hautboist [Georg] Insdorf, Sr., and Private [Johannes] Hallatschka remained behind sick. The company had not a single man sick nor a deserter during the entire march from the barracks to Winchester, nor during the three weeks when the regiment lay at the warm springs. However, while there we received orders again to march to Lancaster in Pennsylvania. We had already reached the border of Maryland when we again received the unhappy order from Congress to return to Winchester. During this march, on 5 April, Privates Caspar Kohlep and Carl Lentz deserted from the camp near Martinsburg, and Privates Peter Stein and Philipp Mahr deserted from the bivouac near Winchester on 10 April.

"During the morning of 11 April the order from Congress was made known to us that our men were to be separated from us and we were to have no further command over them, and actually the same afternoon they were taken from us to a barracks four miles from Winchester by a detail. How disturbing and painful this moment was for all the officers, can be more easily understood than explained. To the present time no officer has been allowed to visit our troops in the barracks. However, I hope it will soon be permitted. Still, our men are not closely confined and we see some of them every day."

Captain von Buttlar wrote on 29 January 1781 about the necessity of moving out of the barracks at Albemarle when the English advanced into that area. "A short time ago however, an event occurred whereby an English fleet entered the harbor at Richmond, a port about ninety English miles from here, and as the troops, which were on board had landed, we received the hasty order, at that time, to march. The baggage and sick individuals were left behind and we were taken thirty miles from here, where we had to bivouac in the woods until after the English again had departed from Richmond. We then received the order to march back to the barracks in Albemarle County. During the opportunity, Musketeer Baecker deserted from Your Highness' Company. Previously he had leave to work in the country in order to earn something, and after receiving the order to return to the company, he remained away. However, I am certainly convinced that he has not been lost, but will submit a letter requesting pardon to the regiment."

On 23 August Buttlar wrote to the prince from East Windsor, Connecticut, where the Convention officers were then being detained. "Upon my arrival at the regiment in Winchester the officers of the Convention troops had already been separated from the soldiers. The German regiments marched into the barracks and the officers received orders to take quarters within a radius of about seven or eight miles of Winchester, with the special restriction that no one was to go to his regiment nor to have any connection with the soldiers.

"After we had been in this arrangement for seven weeks, both officers and men received orders, the first to go to East Windsor in the province of Connecticut, the latter to march to Reading in Pennsylvania. The regiment moved out one day ahead of the officers and the officers were given a special march route. We met our regiment again at Reading in Pennsylvania, about 45 miles from Philadelphia, but were allowed to remain in the city for only one night. We had to obtain information about the companies surreptitiously, and I have the pleasure, Your Highness, to submit my most humble report....

"Musketeer Bohlaender married near Lancaster in Pennsylvania, after requesting permission to marry from Lieutenant Colonel Lentz and me, and who might have deserted if refused. However, his marriage lasted only three weeks, and, as his wife has died, I did not consider it necessary to make my most humble report about it."

Having been exchanged, von Buttlar next wrote to the prince from New York on 15 October 1781. "Your Highness, I must most humbly report that to our absolute greatest joy, on the past 13 September, at East Windsor in the province of Connecticut, all the Convention officers of Burgoyne's army received our exchange. However, we did not leave East Windsor until 5 October and arrived on the eleventh, happily, in New York....

"I brought two drummers, two lance corporals, and three privates with me here to New York, who were all brought along under the designation of officers' servants. These were Drummers [Jacob] Gewald and [Wilhelm] Giese, Lance Corporals [Philipp] Heintzinger and Krieg, and Privates Hallatschka, Bohlaender, and Kaiser. All of us are presently in New York, but during the coming days are to go to Long Island, where we are to remain until the coming spring, when we are to be sent to Canada."

Lieutenant von Buenau reported on the recruit transport which he escorted from Germany in 1781. "Your Highness, I most humbly report how we sailed from Bremerlehe on 10 May and, without entering an English harbor, arrived here in New York on 11 August. We constantly had favorable winds and would have completed our voyage in nine weeks if our commodore had not chased prizes [French and American] ships. We passed New York and sailed so far to the south that we left Charleston behind us. The heat was unbearable, all the water foul, scurvy and putrid fever were rampant. The ship *Ester*, *on* which I was with my men, had eighteen dead. The misfortune was much greater than I present. I brought the men most graciously entrusted to me on the ship, fresh, healthy, and clean. But I think back on the embarkation of the Free Corps with horror. The ship on which I was, held 200 men, 150 of whom were men of the Free Corps. I required of all the companies, that each company cleanse itself, and here the real dregs of the entire corps came together, men who had already become half dead from vermin and rash. This was not enough. The ship was converted to a hospital and 22 dangerously ill individuals were brought on board. The ship was the largest in the entire fleet and had no ventilation, so that soon there was a full contagiousness. I had already complained about my needs to Captain Hense in Bremerlehe and I thought I would not be able to save a man therefrom . Aboard ship I did not lose a man, but on land, since 23 September, when the first one died, I have lost six men, namely:

"1) Christian Gottfried, from Eckartsberge in Saxony, 5' 5 and 1/2" tall

"2) Conrad Schreiber, from Cronau in Hesse, 5' 7 and 3/4"

"3) Johannes Voeller, from Angersbach in Riedesel, 5' 6 and 1/4"

"4) Johannes Schranckel, from Offenbach, 5' 5"

"5) Heinrich Boehher, from Cuxhaven in Hesse, 5' 3 and 1/2"

"6) Johann Georg Bick, from Nassau in Weilburg, 5' 1".

"The fleet to Canada has already sailed and all the recruits must remain here during the winter."

Captain Schoell, in Canada, reported events concerning Negroes and Indians to his Prince in Germany on 20 October 1781. "As several Negroes came with the fleet from New York, I have temporarily taken on two as drummers and await Your Highness' orders if more such can be used in the detachment....

"At least everything is undisturbed by the enemy and fortunately still as peaceful as in the previous year. However, there are rumors spreading that the French commanding general in America has won the Iroquios Indians over to his side with gifts and they are to attack here in Canada, over Niagara. But all of this needs confirmation and if it were to take place, they would be received warmly enough, as our army is once gain quite strong and in the best condition."

Lieutenant Piel, writing in his diary in Canada in 1781, noted the following special events. "25 September - Captain [Johann Henrich] Hegemann and Lieutenants von Waldschmidt and von Lueders came to Quebec from New York with 28 recruits for the Lossberg Regiment.  All vacancies created by the loss of officers when the ship *Adamant* sank in September 1779 have now been filled and the two lost companies are to be raised again in Hesse and sent here.  The regiment received the name 'Old Lossberg'.....

2 October - The greater part of the Knyphausen Regiment, which has been prisoners of war, was exchanged and performed duty in New York, so Colonel von Borck with the remainder of the regiment which was with him, was ordered to go there and this morning embarked on the ship *James and William*."

# 1782

## Activity in the Southern Colonies

War seems to have lost its appeal in 1782. Asteroth, in Charleston, recorded the following events in his diary, commencing on 3 July. "The news was spread in Charleston that the city was to be evacuated. This came from the rebel General Greene.

"20 July - We learned that Savannah had been evacuated.

"In August the cannons and munitions in Charleston were being loaded aboard ship.

"1 September - The commanding general in Charleston, Leslie, announced to the citizens and friends of the King, who had come from the countryside and retreated into the city with the English, that the city would soon be evacuated and that he could no longer protect them. Those who wished to remain here should go to General Greene and make their peace with him. Many who had done nothing against them [the Americans], went to him [General Greene]. They were not allowed to return to the city but had to take service with the Americans.

"28 September - In the morning 52 transport ships lay before the bar, as well as two men-of-war. They all entered the harbor during the day and the embarkation went swiftly. And among the Hessians, the desertions went even more quickly. Each morning there were four to ten who had gone.

"31 October - Two black dragoons arrived. They indicated that they had killed two deserters from the Benning Regiment with their sabers. An officer was sent out with them at once to determine the truth, which was established. The blacks received a reward of two guineas. The order was issued during the evening that parade would be held at precisely eight o'clock on 15 November. In the morning I went shopping at the market. I saw all the people running about and out of curiosity asked what was happening. The answer was that someone was being hanged. I ran in the direction to see what was happening, also, and saw at once the gallows built in the middle of the parade ground. I drew nearer. Soon a guard brought the poor sinner, a soldier of the 62nd Regiment. I watched during the questioning, while a major, lieutenant, ensign, and two sergeants of the same regiment were asked if so and so were true. They answered yes. The major said hang him. He was hanged!

"3 November - General Leslie announced that the residents who wished to go to East Florida or Halifax should flee. They should submit their names, then be embarked and sail away. The loading of cannons and munitions aboard ship went even more quickly.

"4 November - A general pardon was beaten on the drums at every [street] corner in Charleston.

"12 November - A hautboist of the 1st Grenadier Battalion D'Angelelli took the opportunity to return.

"18 November - Two men and a girl, who had taken English soldiers to the rebels, were discovered.

"19 November - They were sentenced before the entire command. The girl was put in prison until she paid [a fine of] fifty pound sterling. The two men were sentenced to 300 lashes and banished from the city. This was carried out during the afternoon. 1. A Hessian guard escorted them. 2. Two English drummers beat their drums. Their crime was written on the front and back of two half sheets of paper and fastened on their coats. They received their lashes during six tours [of the city]. In every street where there was the most traffic, they received fifty and at the city gate, it was finished off with a kick.....

"28 November - In the orders each regiment was assigned two ships. The heavy baggage was loaded the next day.

"11 December - At one o'clock at night the order arrived for all the regiments to assemble at the parade ground at seven-thirty in the morning on 13 December. The officers and non-commissioned officers of each company, at the same time, guarded the quarters until the regiments had marched to the parade ground. At nine o'clock it was announced with the beating of drums that at precisely ten o'clock the residents were to close all windows and doors of their houses. It took until one o'clock for the Ditfurth, D'Angelelli, and Benning Regiments to march, with music playing, to the water, where they were divided among the waiting boats and taken to the specified ships.....

"15 December - At midday the command from Fort Arbuthnot was embarked and the fort was set on fire.

"16 December - Most of the ships passed the bar, through which only one ship at a time can go because it is very dangerous. On one side are white markers, on the other black. They are made of wood and the sailors must use them as guides, otherwise no three-masted ship could travel through, even with a flood tide. At the middle of the bar we had only three fathoms, or eighteen feet of water. We anchored toward evening near the commodore and waited until the seventeenth, when all the ships had crossed the bar. During the afternoon the chaplain, and my insignificant self, was picked up to perform a baptism aboard the ship of His Excellency, von Bose. We hurried because the wind turned favorable for our ship. At one o'clock at night the commodore made a signal and set sail with the most favorable wind.....

"20 December - Our fleet divided. Seventy-two ships sailed for New York and thirty for England."

Reuber , while apparently writing to proclaim the superiority of the King's army, nevertheless had to accept the inability of that army to hold the southern colonies. "In the spring of 1782 many rebels pressed in around Charleston and we often had to send detachments out until finally the citizens of Charleston decided that if General Greene attacked the city from without, they would attack our rear from within the city, and it would soon be over. The citizens who wanted to do that had drawn up an agreement among themselves and signed it and sent this list with a Negro or black to the American General Greene. When he reached the city gate, however, there was a man who had to check everyone thoroughly, whether going in or out. The black was carefully examined and as he revealed it [the list], he was held. Therefore he confessed everything and surrendered the list. Everything remained quiet and peaceful in the city during the day but the next morning, before daybreak, the city commandant sounded an alarm instead of reveille for the English and Hessians. When we assembled at the alarm posts, all the squares and streets were occupied and at the main intersections a cannon was set up. Next the English city commandant took a detachment of Englanders and the list of citizens who had signed and took them from their houses. They were put aboard ship and were to be sent to Nova Scotia as punishment. When this had been done and all of them were aboard ship, the English commandant gave the order for all the wives and children of the men who had been rounded up to be out of the city in 24 hours. There was much alarm among the wives and children in the city. However, the situation was then given a thorough investigation and those who were found innocent were released. The guilty ones, however, were all sent to Nova Scotia as punishment. After this period the unrest which we had tolerated for a long time in and around Charleston was not as great. As the fall of 1782 approached the rumor was that we would once again vacate the south and return north to New York. The rumors grew steadily more persistent until they reached the point to the effect that all of South Carolina and Georgia were to be completely evacuated by the English and Hessians. [An announcement] was published and posted in Charleston that when all the English and Hessian troops were to embark to leave the city, no citizen was to open a door or window for three days; still less was anyone to be seen on the street for fear of severe punishment, until everything had ended. Above all, if anyone in the city undertook shooting or other crime during the evacuation by water, he was to be arrested and sent to Nova Scotia on a wild island where there was no wood.

"21 October - Suddenly there was an alarm and as we moved out and stood in the streets with our weapons, we were told that we were to march to the water even though every soldier had left something in the quarters. Therefore, everyone wished to return to the quarters; one had forgotten this, another that. At first that was allowed but many remained outside and had to forget everything. The non-commissioned officers had to collect everything that still had to be taken away and then we proceeded. When we reached the water the small ships were waiting and after we were on board the larger ships, they all sailed into the harbor and only some warships remained lying before the city to see if they [the Americans] entered. However, everything remained quiet and peaceful in and around the city.

"22 October - The entire fleet sailed from Charleston harbor and then again anchored to await the fleet from Georgia or Savannah and then continued onward.....

"25 October - A southwest wind, rather raw and variable, because we are no longer accustomed to being in the northern climate. After four years without seeing winter and then to suddenly encounter raw weather, one can easily understand why it takes a while to adapt to it again.....

"2 November - The wind still continued favorable and it is a great pleasure to stand in front of the forward mast and notice how the ship knifes through the water and waves. It throws up much foam when a wave strikes. Where the sun's rays bounce off the ocean one sees the reflected green color of the sea. Many of the soldiers are seasick. We have the same rations at sea as usual but the oatmeal does not taste good on Fridays because there is no butter or salt in it.

"3 November - An increasingly stormy northwest wind. We were awakened during the night by a signal shot. At the same time we received a repetitious shock. A case full of Stettin Zwieback began moving and fell into the interior of the ship creating a comical scene as we crawled out of our berths in the night and on our hands and knees gathered the zwieback.....

"7 November - A day of recovery and rest after surviving the rolling [of the ship]. A complete calm and warm, bright sky. We advanced only slightly but thanked God for His protection and asked for His continued support. Above all, here I noticed that the soldiers sang songs of praise morning and evening in the space below in the ship where we slept and when the weather permitted, on deck.....

"30 November - We had an east wind and the sailors assured us that we would soon see land. They took the anchor rope out of the ship and made everything ready. Our joy was boundless. Suddenly during the night there was a great alarm. The sailors shouted that we were very close to land and could see the lighthouse at Sandy Hook, outside New York.....

"2 December - Early in the morning we were disembarked on Long Island near Brooklyn Ferry and the former Rall Regiment marched to Schemoecke to the huts near the Buenau Regiment and were quartered in those huts.

"3 December - We broke camp at the huts early in the morning and marched to Gierge and were quartered there and provided with rum and butter-bread and later with peas, rice, and pork. During the night we had a warm place to sleep. When we awoke in the morning we received coffee and butter-bread and on the march our fellow Hessians from the Buenau Regiment also gave us rum and rice for our march. We had our winter quarters in Gierge and remained there peaceful and content until spring."

Enemy Views (1782)

Correspondence of Hesse-Hanau Officers

The officers of the Hesse-Hanau units wrote letters to their prince in 1782 primarily reporting on administrative actions. Captain Germann wrote on 7 May concerning the conduct of Major Scheel. "Lieutenant Colonel [Michael] von Janecke of the Hesse-Hanau Free Corps, on the fifth of this month, sent a letter to Colonel Lentz of the 1st Battalion, in which he reported that Captain Scheel, who was advanced to Major and transferred to the mentioned free corps, was very drunk upon his arrival there and openly declared to various officers of the Free Corps that supposedly I had said about the mentioned Major Scheel, that the officers of the 1st Battalion refused duty with him, and that he had supposedly been threatened with flogging if he did not request his release. However, both are groundless.

"Major Scheel was, while we were still in captivity in Virginia, given to drunkenness and the then commander of the 1st Battalion, Colonel von Gall, assigned the present Major Pausch, me, and Captain von Buttlar the task of remonstrating most emphatically to the mentioned Major Scheel about his conduct, and use every means to change his ways. This was done and we, because we saw it as the best means, offered him our friendship and association until he would find another way of life. However, he continued to perform the duty, which was miserable, during the time in the barracks."

Lieutenant Colonel Janecke, commander of the Free Corps, had written to Lieutenant Colonel Lentz on 5 May concerning this same problem. "His Serene Highness, our gracious prince, had the pleasure to name the previously Captain Scheel, of the corps under my command, major. Recently, after being assigned a short time by me, he became so drunk that he fell from his horse, lost his sword, and the watch had to carry him, nearly unconscious, into the hut of Lieutenant Schaeffer. Captains [Christian Ludwig] Count von Leiningen, [Christian Ludwig] von Schelm, and [Thylo] von Westerhagen, and Lieutenant [Jerome] Conradi publicly declared that Captain von Germann told them that the officers of the 1st Battalion refused duty with the present Major Scheel because of his disgraceful conduct and among other expressions, that if he did not obtain his release, they would drive him out of the battalion with sticks.

"Sir, as the senior staff officer of the Hesse-Hanau troops here, I see myself obligated to mention this unpleasant situation, and, in so far as possible, to prevent the evil consequences until it is reported to the highest level and orders are received from there."

Lentz replied on 6 May 1782. "I am truly sorry that Major Scheel had the honor of reporting to you in a drunken condition. I have fully informed His Serene Highness, my gracious prince and lord, and given the gracious commission as major in your corps to the mentioned Major Scheel, and in the report of 30 April he has been removed from the 1st Battalion and transferred to the Free Corps. The rest of what Count von Leiningen, von Schelm, and von Westerhagen, and Lieutenant Conradi of your corps said about the remarks of Captain von Germann of the 1st Battalion, I am not aware of, and the mentioned Captain von Germann apparently, upon questioning, must provide information about the subject, because the situation is completely unknown to me and it is incorrect to cause a staff, or any other officer, misfortune. Therefore, I can add nothing to His Highness as His Highness has never written to me about your corps, except regarding the promotion of Major Scheel."

Captain-at-arms Kirchoff, writing on board the ship *Little Deal* on 13 January 1783, reported to a 'High and Mighty Colonel' events which had transpired en route back to Europe with a detachment of invalids and other individuals. "On orders of Captain von Schoell, whose packet to you is attached most humbly, the listed troops are with me as lance corporals: Ewald, Kohlep, Diehl, Ruehl, Bickes, Weter, and Heyl. Also one invalid, by the name of Johann Mueller, has been ordered to embark with us on the first fleet sailing for Germany. We were embarked on the ship *Fare* on 19 October of last year, then transferred to the ship *Little Deal* after a few days, but the day before sailing, we were embarked on the ship *Dispatch*. At that time, Lieutenant Jung of the Hesse-Hanau Jaegers was assigned with us. We sailed on 16 November of last year from the island of Bic in Canada, and after tolerating many miseries and daily storms, we arrived on 12 December at Baltimore in Ireland, after the entire fleet had been scattered. Here we remained at anchor from the 12th to the 27th of the month because during the night, in the harbor, we experienced the most frightful storm. Both anchors broke loose, our ship ran aground upon the rocks, and we all saved only our lives from the greatest threat of death during the very dark night. The mainmast, which stuck out of the earth, crushed Philipp Jacob Heyl's skull and leg, and he died within a few minutes, and was thrown into the water by the waves which caused the ship to roll back and forth severely. Musketeer Bickes was seriously injured, Diehl and Kohlep injured on the head, Ruehl hurt on the arm, while I, in the greatest danger of losing my life at four o'clock at night, when all the people were already on land, thought of nothing but to save my lord's dispatches.

"The thieving inhabitants of Ireland tried to rob us of everything, even the things held in our hands. I lay myself down with my chest on the dispatches, in order to save them, and thank God, I was able to keep them. Even 11 guineas, 15 shillings, which had been given to me for the men, was taken from me in a thieving manner by the inhabitants. I recognized the man who had my money in his hand, but more than 300 residents, claiming the right of salvage, wounded me and Musketeer Wetter and we thank God that we could save our lives. Along the most wretched road, we then went 47 miles on foot to cove, to rejoin the fleet and were embarked on this ship.

"We were told we would sail to London in eight days, but how we will continue onward, we still do not know. Tomorrow a doctor is coming from Portsmouth to tend to my injury. Furthermore, I must most humbly report that the invalid Mueller died on 24 October on board the ship, and I had him buried on land the next day."

Captain Spangenberg, although suffering from a crippled arm, wrote to the prince on 8 November, from New York, concerning losses in his company. "Your Highness, I would have risked this most submissive written report earlier if I had not always had the hope, from one month to the next, that the sad situation of the company graciously entrusted to me would soon change, and I would have the pleasure of laying myself at Your Highness' feet with a somewhat more cheerful heart. My entire soul, from the past winter to the spring of this year, has been disturbed by the frightful losses, which among the entire corps were especially suffered by my company. All active care which I, as well as the company chief, as a loyal subject of Your Highness, have employed to check the increase, was fruitless, and unfortunate fate, moreover, at that time, was that my Captain von Schelm's Companies had their winter quarters on a height close to the North River, where a continuous storm wind beat against us, which caused the most healthy men, let alone the troops who were extremely fatigued from the recent sea voyage and various similarly endured fatigues on land, to suffer. To add to their misery, they were poorly dressed.

"To reduce this last inconvenience, I exhausted every bit of my energy and obtained the necessary clothing for my men and myself, in every possible way. My own situation during this miserable time was even sadder, because I alone had to care for the company because both junior officers had died, and my 1st Lieutenant [Carl Philipp] Eytelwein, during these most dangerous conditions, lay sick for three-fourths of a year. Praise God that we survived so long and that the terrible sickness let up and that during the present year I have prospects of hopefully better winter quarters in which to see the rest of my company in more permanent conditions, as the most humble duty requirement, with which I will never cease to sacrifice myself for Your Highness, should be contributed with complete loyalty."

Captain Eschwege submitted reports to his prince from New York and then later from Canada, during 1782. On 4 August he wrote from Long Island. "Since the last report of 7 May 1782, which I had the great pleasure to send to Your Highness, nothing else of consequence has occurred except that the Hautboist Insdorf, Sr., arrived here from Philadelphia on 8 May with a flag of truce, and once again joined Your Highness' Company. The Americans released him because of his age, without asking for anyone in exchange. It is especially disappointing to report that there is no hope of having our men, who are still in captivity, exchanged. According to the latest reports, which Colonel Lentz has received from Pennsylvania, the Musketeer Heinrich Koehler has rejoined the company.

"We have awaited the order to embark for four weeks, in order to sail to Canada. However, one week follows another and the best season for a fleet to go to Canada has arrived, so I do not know what that means. A few days ago the news arrived here that a French fleet of thirteen to sixteen ships-of-the-line is cruising outside the harbor at New York. This could certainly cause some hindrance and be the reason that we have had to remain here this month."

On 7 September Eschwege reported that he had been ordered to remain in New York while the rest of the exchanged men of the regiment sailed to Canada. "Your Highness, I have the pleasure most humbly to report that I have been ordered by my Colonel Lentz to remain here in New York to provide money, and when possible, uniform items, to the captives of the 1st Battalion who are still in Reading, and some in Philadelphia, in Pennsylvania, and after they are exchanged to take them to Canada. To accomplish this I have received an instruction from my colonel, which I, to the best of my ability, will strive to follow. My colonel has also ordered me, most humbly to report that as the passage between here and Canada is too difficult and slow, and as he therefore can not send orders to me from Canada, I should turn most humbly to Your Highness and await all further orders as long as I am here from Your Highness....

"A commission has again met in Jersey in order to work anew on a prisoner exchange. How far they have gone, I am unable to learn.

"Your Highness, I must also most humbly report that Hautboist Insdorf, Sr., who suddenly fell ill, died here in the hospital on 20 August. The colonel left Drummer Giese behind with me here. The fleet for Canada, on which the officers of the 1st Battalion are, sailed from here on the second, or third of this month. Your Highness, I must in truth admit that it made me very sad to be ordered to remain behind here in New York, as I had looked forward to Canada for a long time. Although I have the pleasure of commanding Your Highness' Company, I must be the only officer from the battalion who remains here. However, as that can not be changed, I only wish, from the bottom of my heart, that the prisoner exchange would take place soon so that I might be in condition to rejoin the regiment in the coming year."

Eschwege's next report was dated 1 October, at New York. "As, since I command here, no one from the 1st Battalion has ransomed himself, and as no flag of truce has sailed to Philadelphia, I have still not received the latest news about our captives. At the earliest opportunity I will write to the sergeant majors requesting that they send me a name list of all those men who are still in Reading.

"The recruit transport, which arrived some time ago in Halifax, is expected here daily. Concerning the fleet with which the 1st Battalion officers sailed from here, I have heard nothing since the time of their departure. I hope however, that they have had a good trip as the entire month of September was unusual, being without a severe storm, and the English fleet, consisting of 26 ships-of-the-line, is cruising along the coast and safeguarded their journey."

His report of 20 October provided information on the prisoner exchange situation. "Your Highness, I have the great pleasure most humbly to report that nothing developed again this year concerning the prisoner exchange, and it appears also likely that nothing will come of it in the next year.

"I have spoken with Lieutenant General Kempel, who is responsible for the exchange negotiations and was a member of the last commission. He told me that there could be no hope for an early exchange.

"First, the Americans want to negotiate as the Free United States, and second, they demand an exorbitant amount of money.... Still not a man from the 1st Battalion has ransomed himself out of captivity. A jaeger by the name of August Neuberger of Colonel von Creuzbourg's corps arrived here from Philadelphia on a cartel ship exchange. I will care for him here and send him to Canada at the first opportunity in the spring."

"On 15 December 1782, Captain Eschwege reported a number of men had ransomed themselves out of captivity and that a number of men had taken service with the Americans. "Your Highness, I have the great pleasure most humbly to report that on 5 December one surgeon, seven non-commissioned officers, and one private, and today, 15 December 1782, another seven privates of the 1st Battalion and the Artillery ransomed themselves out of captivity. The names of all these men may be seen by Your Highness in the list which I am sending to Your Highness, as well as those still in captivity and where they come from, which you may be pleased to see. [Not included with the manuscript from which this translation was made.]

"Your Highness will be surprised to see in the list that so many men have taken service with the Americans and still others have indentured themselves, but the Americans have applied cruel methods to force the men to do that. First Congress sent the captives written addresses in which they were informed that they had been completely forgotten by the King and by their princes, and that they had no hope of being exchanged. As a minimum compensation for their long confinement, Congress asks eighty Spanish dollars for each man and then he can have his freedom and settle in the country as a free citizen.

Those who can not pay the eighty dollars, should find a farmer, who will pay for them, and as a repayment, they are to work as servants for three years. The other choice is to become a soldier, as most are encouraged to do, and they have been promised many things. The sergeant majors brought two copies of the address which was read to them every day. I have had it copied word for word and send it to Your Highness herewith. [Not included.]

"Your Highness will be able to see the terrible lies the soldiers have been told. Those who refuse to take service and who do not sell themselves as servants, are thrown into jail and threatened to take service every day.

"I have reported this cruel treatment not only to Lieutenant General von Lossberg, but also to the Commander-in-Chief Lieutenant General Carleton. Lieutenant General Carleton immediately sent a protest concerning this to General Washington.

"The seven men who arrived today had taken service in a regiment which was called Congress' Regiment, but had taken service with the intent, at the earliest opportunity, to redeem themselves here in New York. They assured me that still other men of the 1st Battalion have taken service with this regiment and await the opportunity to come here. These men, and also the non-commissioned officers, who came from Reading, were brought through by well-intentioned farmers. I have myself spoken to these farmers and told them they should bring more of our men here. This they have promised me. Therefore I hope to receive more men soon.

"Some of the 1st Battalion took service on an American warship and planned to free themselves at the earliest opportunity. Only Corporal [Peter] Weber and Private Kohlep of Your Highness' Leib Company have taken such service. Most have sold themselves as servants and the others still sit in captivity. I fear that those who sold themselves as servants will have the least opportunity to get away because their masters will always keep a very close watch over them.

"The men who have come in here are all shabby. As I have only twelve uniforms available, I see the necessity of buying cloth in order to clothe the men. They have all had to tolerate a great deal on their marches, especially Sergeant-major Vaupel and Surgeon [Wilhelm] Gottschalk, neither of whom could walk well, but still had to make difficult marches. They could only travel at night, and had to avoid all main roads. Lieutenant General von Lossberg sent a regimental quartermaster to the captives, with whom I also sent to those members of the 1st Battalion and the Artillery, who are still in prison, money, blankets, and brown cloth for long breeches, which was a gift from the King. Furthermore, Lieutenant General von Lossberg has been very kind and has promised me help in every situation.

"I received a letter from my colonel in Quebec, in which I saw that all the officers of the 1st Battalion arrived safely on 6 October 1782. A packet of letter from Your Highness to my colonel also arrived here recently. I have them in safekeeping and as there are no ships to Canada at this time, I will not be able to forward them until next spring.

"Your Highness, I now request most humbly that as the orders given to me by my colonel were to remain here until a general exchange took place, and as there is no prospect of such an exchange, I most humbly ask Your Highness to grant me permission to travel to Canada next summer with the men who have ransomed themselves, or that I be relieved by another officer. My desire to return to the regiment and my long absence therefrom force me to this most submissive presentation."

In a 14 January 1783 letter, Eschwege reported the following events. "Your Highness, I had the great pleasure in my last report to mention that some of the men of the 1st Battalion, who had been in captivity, had taken service on an American warship. Now I have the pleasure to inform Your Highness that the frigate, on which the men took service and which had the name *South Carolina*, was captured by the English and brought safely into this place. After a thorough investigation, 29 men of the 1st Battalion and one man of the Artillery were found therein. I reported this at once to the Commander-in-Chief Sir Guy Carleton, who with the concurrence of Admiral Digby, had these men, who had already been taken to the guard ship with the other prisoners, brought here. All the men were individually questioned by a Hesse-Cassel auditor concerning their opinion of duty on the ship.

"However, their statements were all the same, that they had been taken captive and were forced either to pay eighty Spanish dollars or take service, and on the advice of many well-intentioned individuals who were loyal to the King, they took service on the ship because they had been told that this ship certainly would be captured immediately by the English as soon as it entered the ocean because there were reports that an English ship was cruising in the area, giving special attention to this ship. Or, if this failed, their contract on the ship was that they only had to serve six months and after that time they could go wherever they wished, and then they would try to return to their regiment. Therefore they were all released and given over to my responsibility.

"The month of December 1782 was also a very good month for the regiment and the Artillery because with the 22 men who had ransomed themselves, whom I already had the pleasure of mentioning in my last most humble report to your Highness, another 52 men returned this month. None of the men are performing any duty as I still have received no weapons for them. Their old uniforms have been patched as best possible and they have been issued small clothing items. Lieutenant General von Lossberg had promised to sent the men to Canada as soon as possible and I will direct all my efforts to insure that it takes place at the earliest time. Major General von Hachenberg, in whose brigade I have the honor to serve, is very kind and does everything possible to provide the best care for my men.

"The thirty men who were taken from the ship have been given nothing more than one Spanish dollar, each, against their pay credits, because I do not know if it would please my colonel if I paid out everything owed to them. But, since the day they came from the ship, they now receive their full pay.

"From Your Highness' Leib Company there was not a single man on this ship and I am sorry to mention to Your Highness that most of the men from the company have contracted with the farmers for two or three years, which time must be fulfilled, and I fear that it will be difficult even then to get them away. According to the information which I could get about the men, some of them have already married."

# Enemy Views (1782)

## Reports from Canada

From Canada, Captain Pausch's letters to his prince contained nothing of aggressive warfare. Writing on 16 July 1782, he provided the following information, including the reorganization of the Hesse-Hanau contingent, and the return of the regimental flags which had been kept hidden from the Americans after the capitulation at Saratoga. "I lay myself at Your Serene Highness' most gracious feet and with the most sensitive heart offer the most humble thanks for pleasing me by conferring the greatest favor on me of advancement to major, and most graciously entrusting me, for the time being, with the special command of Your Serene Highness' illustrious 1st Battalion, under the overall command of Lieutenant Colonel von Creuzbourg....

"I had the greatest pleasure during the afternoon of 3 July this year to receive ... the other most graciously inclosed orders, and both had arrived in a ship from London. In order to have your most gracious plans and orders most humbly fulfilled, the most favorable time for putting all the arrangements into effect here was missed, even though I also received the order from Lieutenant Colonel von Creuzbourg to do so at once. He arrived here on 8 July and personally arranged to have Your Serene Highness' most gracious orders carried out. The detachment previously here moved out of quarters early in the morning. Six companies of equal strength were created according to Your Highness' most gracious orders and the 1st Battalion was formed therewith, and so designated....

"The lieutenant colonel brought the flags from Major General von Riedesel with him from Sorel. The general had brought them here to Canada. They had already, as Your Highness ordered, been put on the flagstaffs on the eleventh, and now everything necessary, except the ornamental knots and painting the flagstaffs, has been done. In addition, on orders of the lieutenant colonel, I have put Your Serene Highness' worthy name, on the spur of the moment, at the top of the flag."

Pausch's letter of 15 August, also from Point Levi in Canada, mentions the lack of warlike activities. "As of this moment we have hoped in vain for the arrival of the officers of the 1st Battalion who are to arrive from New York....

"Otherwise everything is so quiet here that soon no one will be able to tell that there is a war, if it were not for the awareness caused by the local costs of daily necessities, which is caused by the seamen lying here in the harbor."

In the letter of 1 October Pausch mentioned the returning prisoners, rumored American activity, and the defensive preparations in Canada. "As of this moment we have given up hope for the arrival of the exchanged officers who belong here, or of mail from them, despite having had the welcome and joyful news spread more than ten times in Quebec that they and all the recruits, who are to come from Europe, would soon arrive in the Gulf and would soon be seen at Isle au Bic.

"Day before yesterday two small armed vessels arrived here, following one after the other.... These two vessels provided confirmation that a fleet of nine ships, with exchanged German troops from Burgoyne's army, recruits, and Hesse-Cassel troops was cruising in the Gulf of St. Lawrence, as the two vessels had just sailed through the fleet. Two store ships, which were still lying below Isle au Bic because of contrary winds, confirmed having seen five of the ships....

"The line of posts and winter quarters for the troops have not yet been determined as of this minute and not a single regiment knows where it will be assigned this winter. It is assumed here that as during the siege by Montgomery, the first turbulent winter in Canada, a strong corps of rebels and French are massing near Albany. Reportedly 25,000 men have assembled, who are to undertake an expedition against Upper Canada, in order to establish secure bases on Lake Champlain and Lake St. George for building ships and batteaux and magazines. Work is progressing quickly on the various fortifications at Isle aux Noix, St. Jean, Sorel, Quebec, etc., but unfortunately all the work is being done by soldiers."

Finally, the other Convention officers arrived in Quebec, as noted in Pausch's letter of 20 October 1782. "Your Serene Highness, I wish ... most humbly [to] report how Colonel Lentz, Major von Germann, Captains Buttlar, von Geyling, and von Trott, together with the rest of the exchanged subalterns, as well as the auditor and also Captain Dufais, Sergeant-major Mueller, two cannoneers, Wagonmaster Zicklamm, and the wagonmaster of the von Lossberg Regiment, the latter who was arrested for desertion, all happily arrived here on the sixth....

"On the ninth, upon the arrival of the colonel in camp, I had the 1st Battalion and the Artillery move to the front of the camp in order to give him honors, and at the same time to deliver the battalion and my previously held command."

Pausch's letter of 23 October from Point Levi informed his Prince of the location of winter quarters for the 1st Battalion and his dissatisfaction with them. "Your Serene Highness, I lay [before you], in most sincere submission, the general orders and directions concerning our winter quarters for this year and their line of posts, which arrived from headquarters yesterday. For Your Serene Highness' 1st Battalion and Artillery corps they are at St. Nickolaus, St. Antoine, St. Croix, and St. Lautbiniere, and according to one report, where all the Prince of Anhalt's troops made their quarters during the past winter. They are said to be the worst [quarters] in all of Canada, even worse than those of last winter at Kamouraska, Riviere Ouelle, and Ste. Anne, also on the south side [of the St. Lawrence River]. The two generals, His Excellency, Haldimand, and Major General von Riedesel, worked these out between them in a meeting at Quebec, and because we belong unfortunately to the brigade of Major General von Loos just now, we must remain in the district which he commands. His quarters and those of his regiment are the best, where, without him, the regiment was last year, namely, St. Thoma, L'Isle au Lau, and the adjoining parishes. Had we been Brunswickers this time, for which however I thank the omnipotent God that we are not, but with the greatest good fortune have the advantageously greatest pleasure to serve our most gracious and the most benevolent prince of Europe, we would possibly have been assigned also on the north side, between Trois Rivieres and Montreal, where the Brunswickers according to all appearances must settle, and where we and our soldiers would be better situated. However, such a lucky star does not favor us again this time with its glowing good fortune. The soldiers most graciously entrusted to us would be far better off spending the winter at Detroit, Michilimackinac, or Oswego, than here."

Finally, in another letter of the same date Pausch wrote as a father seeking the prince's approval of Pausch's son entering the military as an officer candidate. "My young and clever son, left behind in Hanau, wishes to serve in and to devote himself to the military, but in the service of Your Serene Highness, the best and one in which I have been happy. I lay myself with this, my, without Your Serene Highness' most gracious favor, poor but still hopeful son, at Your Highness' most gracious feet in most sincere submission, requesting that he be placed in the 2nd Battalion for a most gracious and wished for length of time, and in the greatest favor sheltered and employed, and then after he learns the service, to be assigned to me and my command, or to the 1st Battalion. I hope and am convinced most humbly and certainly that he will apply himself diligently at all times to strive, as much as it is within his present youth, to make himself entitled to this greatest favor. As he has no desire for any career except the military, it is better that he start early rather than late."

## Events in New York

J.R.'s diary reported the following events, among others, occurring in New York in 1782. "Note - 14 May - His Excellence, Lieutenant General von Knyphausen and Sir Henry Clinton sailed for England and Sir Guy Carleton took over command of the troops in America.

"10 August - The Knoblauch Regiment arrived in New York from Savannah in Georgia.

"15 August - The Waldeck Regiment entered the city."

Zinn also made a few entries of interest during 1782. "6 May - His Excellence, Lieutenant General von Knyphausen turned over his previously held command to His Excellence, Lieutenant General von Lossberg, and departed on

"13 May - with His Excellence, Lieutenant General Clinton who had been relieved by General Carleton, on board the frigate *Pearl*, and set sail at once for Europe.

"6 November - The regiment marched to New York again and entered winter quarters there with the non-commissioned officers and privates in the so-called 'red barracks'. The officers, however, were quartered with the residents in the city."

The Hesse-Cassel Jaeger Corps Journal recorded the following activities in 1782. "1 May - The army received orders to undertake no manner of movement without the express approval of the commanding general.

"The army exercises therefore, and since there is nothing else to do, exercises very diligently.

"5 May - General Carleton arrived in New York on the *Zeres* frigate, and brought the noteworthy news that the King has changed ministries and accepted the opposition party.....

"12 June - The army broke winter quarters and camped within the lines on York Island.

"The enemy is encamped at Verplanck's Point and absolutely quiet.

"3 July - The economy orders which have been in preparation for a considerable period of time appeared in orders today. All company wagons and horses, all surplus shipping, and all forage for captains [and all junior officers] has been cut off. Rations for staff officers have been reduced, and above all, many unnecessary commissaries and departments eliminated, and thereby there is really a great savings.....

"6 September - ... Charleston, just like Savannah which was vacated on 15 July, is to be abandoned according to the general discussion which is accepted as true by everyone. The troops in Savannah all went to St. Augustine, except for the 7th and Knoblauch Regiments, which arrived on 15 August at Sandy Hook.....

"13 October - As the German recruits who arrived in Halifax in August no longer will be coming to their regiments, it was decided today that their money and equipment should be sent to them. Also, officers and non-commissioned officers are to go there to drill them. Lieutenant [Franz Georg] Bauer of the Jaeger Corps is among those being sent.....

"17 December - The merchant fleet sailed for England, taking all the invalids and other people who otherwise are attached to the army, who either belong to destroyed corps, were incapable of performing duty, or who according to the new economic plan can no longer be employed, or were prisoners of war, so that throughout the army a large number of useless people have departed, and seen in retrospect, provide a savings on provision, wood, etc."

The Platte Grenadier Battalion Journal provided some additional information. "This year's winter quarters [1781-82] were occupied by the grenadiers and all the troops, undisturbed, in the places which had been assigned to them, without any changes. Nothing much was heard of war, except that since the arrival of Admiral Digby, who was assigned his station in New York and consequently the entire east coast of the rebel provinces, many more and more valuable prizes were taken from the enemy than had been taken by the previous admirals. The warships were no longer allowed to lie idle in the harbor for months at a time and a day never passed without the results of this aggressive policy being observed. The prizes were brought in daily and it had progressed so far that ships often had to lie for a long time in the enemy harbors before they could risk sailing out. In the public press complaints were read daily that the loaded ships dared not leave and the rebels therefore suffered great inconveniences. If all the admirals had been so aggressive from the beginning, they would not only have enjoyed the same advantages as Admiral Digby, but the rebels' commerce would have been greatly restricted and possibly their credit would have diminished.....

"7 May - Lieutenant General Sir Henry Clinton and Lieutenant General von Knyphausen returned to Europe. Lieutenant General von Lossberg assumed command over the Hessian troops in North America. During the departure of the two generals, the troops had to fall out and form lines, between which they marched from the headquarters to the ship on which they embarked, as the cannons at Fort George were fired.....

"13 August - The garrison from Savannah arrived in this region. With the evacuation of that place we also lost the occupation of Georgia, which had been held since the start of 1779 at such a great cost and the loss of so many men. The troops, which contained no Hessian units except the Knoblauch Regiment, were quartered in New York and on Long Island...

"We ended this undisturbed and in the middle of war, peaceful year, in which we undertook as little as our enemy. Nothing was missing except an open passage between the lines of each side through which everyone would be allowed to pass back and forth. Otherwise no one would have known whether there was peace or war."

Steuernagel's final entry of 1782 also ended his comments on the Waldeck employment in the American colonies because, "The further reports [written by Steuernagel] were lost at sea during a severe and disastrous storm.[46] So in conclusion, as the period of our prisoner of war status ended, the regiment was ordered to resume duty on 24 July

1782, and to this end we made our initial move to a camp not far from Brooklyn on Long Island."

Writing initially in 1782 from prisoner of war detention at Winchester, Virginia, Lieutenant Prechtel's diary includes entries on the following events. "27 January - As the order arrived from Congress at Philadelphia that the English prisoners of war should go from Frederick to Lancaster, and the German prisoners of war from Winchester to Frederick, both Ansbach regiments marched out of the Frederick Barracks at Winchester.....

"31 January - The regiments entered Frederick and entered the Frederick Barracks, under guard.

"The Frederick Barracks are about one-half mile from Frederick and consist of a barracks with two splendidly constructed wings.

"Four German regiments are here in captivity. The Ansbach von Voit and von Seybothen Regiments and the Hessian Hereditary Prince and von Bose Regiments.

"1 February - ... The English prisoners of war, who have been here in the Frederick Barracks, were led off today to Lancaster, in Pennsylvania.....

"29 March - Taken from the Baltimore newspaper: The Commanding General Sir Henry Clinton has been recalled back to England and General Carleton has been named commanding general of the English army.....

"2 June - ... The following legal American order was published for the local inhabitants: From the 4th instance on, no one in the future should support or provide quarters for a prisoner of war. In the event an inhabitant is caught doing this, he shall be punished with a fine of five hundred pounds local money, and if he is unable to pay, he shall serve three years as a sailor on an American ship. If, due to health, this can not be performed , he shall be punished with 39 lashes.....

"26 August - It is learned from the newspapers from Baltimore that a general exchange [of prisoners] is to take place and that the English Lieutenant General Cornwallis has already been exchanged."

During 1782 Prechtel reported more and more frequently on desertions among the Ansbach-Bayreuth regiments and that the men were being recruited and joining the American army. "26 August - Garrison Order - Frederick City, 24 August 1782 - Those prisoners of war who wish to remain in this country should immediately receive their freedom and receive a certificate from the war minister which will grant them every freedom of native born citizens, when a sum of eighty dollars is paid. John Wood, Colonel, Commissary...

"3 September - All prisoners of war who find themselves on the land, whether from Burgoyne's or Cornwallis' armies, must return to the barracks at once.....

"21 September - ... An American recruit transport, consisting of about 24 men, all from the four German regiments lying here in captivity, left here today.....

"22 October - Today the second recruit transport for the American army left here and consisted of about twenty men from the four German regiments lying here in captivity.

"23 October - ... The American recruiters, who had previously been here, departed, However, immediately other American troops from Armand's Corps took their place. Drummer [Johann Andreas] Wurzbach, formerly of the vacant Lieutenant Colonel von Reitzenstein's Company, who had deserted at Winchester, was with them.....

"1 November - ... The recruiters from Armand's Free Corps of Americans left here today for Winchester. All together they had enlisted five men from the four regiments lying here in captivity.....

"21 December - The American Armand's Free Corps came from Winchester and was quartered here. Within this corps there are at least fifty men from the two Ansbach regiments."

# 1783

## The Return to Hesse-Cassel

In 1783 England granted the American colonies the independence for which they had been fighting, and the Crown forces made a gradual withdrawal from the new United States of America. The German diarists noted these events in their writings and despite the perils of the ocean voyage many were glad to return home after the conflict, while others chose to remain in America.

Asteroth was en route to New York from Charleston when the year began but his diary entries for 1783 primarily cover his return to Germany. "1 to 4 January - During these days we saw land and anchored not far from Jersey. We continued to lie here from one tide to the next.....

"10 January - All the troops were landed and marched to Jamaica.....

"12 August - We embarked on the ship *Hind* [for the return voyage to Germany].....

"14 August - The entire fleet went under sail.....

"10 September - We anchored at Portsmouth, England.....

"5 October - We saw Germany.....

"10 October - We disembarked and marched by way of Gestendorf into quarters at Schiffdorf."

Asteroth and his regiment, the von Benning Regiment, formerly the von Huyn Regiment, then marched overland to Kassel by way of Bremen, Hoya, Stolzenau, Rinteln, and Hofgeismar.

"1 November - To Kassel in the Au and muster.....

"5 November - Granted leave.

"6 December - I was transferred to the Knyphausen Regiment"

Asteroth was discharged on 16 February 1784, later becoming a master stocking maker in Treysa and marrying Anna Catherina Foerster in 1785.

Reuber, of the D'Angelelli Regiment, formerly the Rall Regiment, made an initial entry in his diary in 1783, to the effect that, "We were drilled just as if in Germany. Suddenly orders came from the English headquarters that there was peace. Shortly thereafter this was also read to us and that we were no longer to treat the Americans in a hostile manner. Finally the day of joy arrived when we were told that all the foot regiments were to return to Hesse aboard ships and the remaining Hessians would sail in the second transport."

He then skipped to 18 August. "All the Hessian foot regiments at Brooklyn Ferry boarded the large transport ships in order to leave America and return to Germany, our fatherland, because now there was peace between England and 'The Free States of America'.....

"27 August - ... Still the wind did not turn favorable and we waited impatiently day and night for a good wind because we had turned our hopes and prayers on seeing our fatherland once again. But here we were and had to wait so long in this wild, unfamiliar land.....

"3 September - The wind shifted and came from the west and at once the signal was given to get underway. After we had wound in the anchor and sailed into the ocean the ship on which I found myself, the *Ballin*, which had been made two years ago, ran upon something as if it had hit a lost anchor or a rock. We thought it had broken apart. The ship's captain at once checked if the ship was taking water. Suddenly it slipped off. The captain ran about the ship, first below, then forward, then below again into the ship, but found nothing. However, everyone was frightened that we might have a problem at sea during the night if a storm arose and no one could help us. The ship's captain consoled us by saying that the ship had been built only two years ago, the crash had caused no damage, and no one need have further concern that water could enter the ship. Everything was fine. However, during the night, when everything was still and we lay in bed, as the ship rocked back and forth, water swished among the casks below in the ship.

"4 September - In the morning we told the sailors that there was water below in the ship. They laughed at us because it was a new ship and we soldiers were liars. And so the day passed. When it was again night, the water was even worse in the space below. It rose noticeably and we could not sleep because of the rushing of the water among the casks.

"5 September - In the morning the non-commissioned officers and privates once again told the sailors there certainly was water in the ship. They still laughed and said, 'That does not bother us, even if it is measurable.' The wind was favorable, the command ship signaled to put on more sail and to sail faster. Because our ship was excessively heavy and could not keep up, the command ship fired two sharp shots at us, which cost two carolin, and [the command ship] would not believe us. However, at night, we just could not sleep because of he water among the casks. The fleet had to tack all night because we could not keep up. When it was daylight we could barely see the fleet ahead of us.

"6 September - During the morning a vicious rumor spread among our men on the ship. Because we were so alarmed the sailors took the line with the iron weight and measured. We had seven feet of water in the ship. Immediately an emergency flag was raised on the aftermast and an emergency shot was fired. The entire fleet turned and at the same time the command ship gave a signal shot for the fleet to assist us. The command ship immediately sailed back through the fleet and came directly toward us. When opposite us he called to our ship's captain through a megaphone to ask what was wrong. The answer, we had seven feet of water in the ship, therefore we could not keep up. The commander at once put a boat in the water and a naval officer with some sailors came to visit our ship. Sixteen Hessians and four sailors immediately began working with two pumps. The naval officer remained until he saw whether more water was pumped out than came in or more water came in to make it worse. However, the water lowered. Therefore the naval officer returned to the warship and reported to his commander and then came back immediately to our ship. He told our ship's captain that if the pumps were not strong enough, the warship could give us bigger ones. However, our captain said his pumps were in good condition. Therefore the naval officer said he should pump diligently and seriously try to keep up with the fleet. He returned to the warship and sailed forward through the fleet to his position once again. Now it was night again and dark. The pumps were worked day and night without letup as long as we were at sea and we had to constantly relieve one another at the pumps. The commander apparently assumed we would follow and catch up with the fleet during the night. However, because it was now very dark and we had a mate, who was a Prussian, on the first watch and he allowed us to miss our course, we sailed past the fleet on our right and continued sailing on until daylight.....

"12 September - Because of the continuously strong winds and rain, many soldiers had to vomit but we did not lose our good spirits.

We kidded one another in our great distress as our ship took water and twenty men had to continue pumping. We were alone and did not know if we were ahead or behind [the fleet], and lived in constant fear and fright as to what could still happen to us before we reached England.....

"20 September - The wind from the north and strong and the weather raw. The ship staggered. A sailor was thrown overboard but he could swim well and was saved from the water.....

"8 October - ... We saw land, the coast of France, and it was not long until the entrance to Portsmouth harbor. Not long after that we also saw the city and Ryde [anchorage] opposite. We entered the harbor where many ships lay at anchor and where we thought the fleet to which we belonged would also be in the harbor already. As we arrived at the guard ship we were checked as to where we had come from and where we were bound. Our ship's captain answered that he had Hessians on board and came from New York with the fleet. His ship had taken water and he could not keep up, therefore he became separated from the fleet during the night and he believed it [the fleet] was in the harbor. As an answer we were told the ships had not yet arrived and we would not be permitted to anchor there but should continue through the Channel to Deal, anchor there, and wait until the fleet arrived. Then we would learn what was to happen next. So we sailed through the Channel, past a great seaport on our left, past Chatham [?], and then we saw Dover with the high hills which appeared as white as if covered with snow.... Then, after we sailed a little farther, on our left we saw the beautiful great city of Deal with its three castles and the coast. We anchored there with our ship awaiting the arrival of our fleet. We wished to be free of our distress and day and night pumping and expected to board another ship, but no one wanted us and we had to remain [on board] until we reached Bremerlehe.....

"12 October - At noon we suddenly saw a fleet approaching. As it came closer our command ship became aware that we already lay at anchor in the harbor. Therefore he sailed directly at us so that we thought he would sail right over us. However, he turned short and dropped his anchor. At once a naval officer came from the command ship in a small boat and took our ship's captain back to the warship, where he was possibly taken to answer why he had left the fleet.....

"17 October - We still lay quietly at anchor. The mate had no desire to sail again with our ship but nothing could change this. He had to make this voyage to Germany as captain. Our captain was in arrest on the command ship.

"18 October - Early in the morning the wind was favorable so the signal was given to raise anchor and depart and now we sailed into the North Sea toward Bremerlehe.....

"22 October - At daybreak a signal was given with a cannon shot to sail into the harbor in the region of Bremerlehe with the incoming tide. First is Helgoland and then the Danish or Holstein land and then up the Weser is Hannover land on the left. As we arrived in the region of Bremerlehe our entire fleet dropped anchor and the quartermaster guard was landed the same day in order to arrange for quarters for one night in Schiffdorf.

"23 October - All the Hessians who were in the fleet, including our regiment, were landed on the Hannoverian side.....

"24 November - We had our first day's march in Hesse and arrived in regular quarters near the fountain in Hofgeismar. General von Gohr of the Artillery came from Kassel and mustered the previously Rall and now D'Angelelli Grenadier Regiment in three sections. 1) Those designated A were discharged. 2) Those designated B had to remain and train another regiment. 3) Those designated C were granted leave and were to await their disposition, if and when they would be assigned to another regiment or would receive no further orders and could remain at home. After that had taken place we still remained at Hofgeismar for two days.

"27 November - We moved out of Hofgeismar early in the morning and marched to Kassel to be mustered before Landgrave Friedrich in the garden at the 'Bowling Green'. When we arrived at the Holland Gate we halted. Our commander [Marquis Luigi D]' Angelelli came out of the city, received his regiment, took the Leib [Body] Company and marched through the city with it. He then received five flags which we had lost at Trenton on 25 December 1776 but had retaken in the hard-fought battle near Charleston at Stono Ferry. At the same time we had retaken our cannons. Then we marched to the gardens of the Bowling Green and after Landgrave Friedrich had reviewed the regiment, we had to parade past him. We then marched back to Ober and Niedervellmar into quarters and had a day of rest.

## Enemy Views (1783)

"29 November - Our regiment was disbanded and we had to turn in all [of our equipment]. Those who had turned in equipment and had a letter A designation received their discharges and went home. Those who had a B, including the author of this book, had to remain and fifteen men per company were to train a new regiment but went home to await orders. Those who had a C after their names received leave orders and could go home to await their fate, after the other regiments had returned from America. This happened in the spring of 1784 and after all were back in their former garrisons, with God's help, this American campaign was finished. What will happen now we can only wait and see."

Reuber finally received his discharge in 1807.

J.R., of the former Leib Regiment, redesignated the Hereditary Prince Regiment in 1783, wrote in his diary entry of 11, 12, and 13 August, "Our regiments embarked for the voyage to Europe, namely, Hereditary Prince, Bose, Knyphausen, Ditfurth, Benning, Buenau, Knoblauch, and D'Angelelli.

"14 August - We sailed out of the harbor at Staten Island and then into the ocean. The provincial troops also received orders to be prepared to embark.....

"24 September - [J.R.'s brother] Philipp sailed for Nova Scotia and Port Rosaway, in the frigate *Libonetta*."

J.R. then jumped ahead to November and began an account of sailing for Europe as if it had been necessary to return to port after the August departure. "8 November - The Grenadier Battalions Linsing, Loewenstein, and Platte, plus the Leib Regiment, and Hereditary Prince and Prince Charles Regiments were embarked under the command of Major General von Wurmb. The Hereditary Prince Regiment boarded the following ships: 1) *Elizabeth*, 2) *William*, 3) *Grand Duchess of Russia*.....

"13 November - At eleven o'clock this morning the commodore gave the signal and we went underway. We entered the ocean but because many ships were behind us we had to lay to until three o'clock, waiting for them. During this time the fleet had assembled and we continued our voyage with a northwest wind. To get away from the coastline we took an east-southeast course and are now about 25 English miles from the lighthouse at Sandy Hook.....

"16 December - At daybreak we saw Cape Clear and the Irish coast off to our left. The *Ranger*, which had part of the Grenadier Battalion [?] on board, was the ship with the *Castor*, that we had seen yesterday....

"17 December - We saw the coast in the distance. From the sea it was quite majestic. A boat came from the land. We thought it had provisions to sell, however, there were three poor men in the boat. They offered to bring us into one of the Irish harbors. They told us that 1,400 English troops had arrived in Ireland...

"18 December - As the wind was still contrary and it was very difficult to enter the harbor, the ship's captain set his course toward Limerick, a trade city in Ireland. The ship's captain took a pilot on board. Because of the contrary wind, the captain decided to turn about and to sail to the harbor at Beerhaven.....

"24 December - Today the wind was very good for leaving the harbor and setting our course for the English Channel. We had loaded bread, fresh water, and peat. However, the wind became so strong at eleven o'clock that we had to anchor, but as it abated somewhat, the ship's captain decided to try to sail as we would have few provisions if we did not continue our voyage. We still had a long way to reach our destination in England. We pulled the ship around within the harbor so that toward two o'clock, after great effort, we were able to sail out of the harbor. The boat which was to take off the pilot was tied behind our ship and was nearly swamped.....

"30 December - ... In response to a signal, a pilot came aboard, who brought us safely into the Plymouth harbor, where we dropped anchor at two o'clock in the afternoon....

"31 December - The wind was especially strong. There must be a severe storm in the Channel at this time as in Plymouth harbor, which is a secure harbor, it is now impossible to travel in a boat. Therefore we can not be thankful enough for the harbor and that we were brought into the harbor at the right time."

Quartermaster Zinn, of the von Donop Regiment, recorded the following events in the regimental journal in 1783. "8 April - At twelve o'clock noon today the King's proclamation concerning the cession of hostilities was read from the city hall by the local commandant, Major Hewitsom, to a gathering of many thousands of people.

"3 June - Lieutenant Hausmann, of the regiment, received his release as a captain.

"27 September - Today the regiment received its first order to be prepared to embark for Europe.

"21 November - This morning the von Donop Regiment embarked on the assigned transport ships: *Spencer, Montague,* and *Everly,* which lay in the North River, in the following manner:

*"Montague* ... a total, including privates, wives, and children, 194 persons.

*"Spencer* ... in all, with non-commissioned officers and privates, 198 persons.

*"Everly* ... in all, 159 persons.

"26 November - During the afternoon, at two o'clock, we went under sail. By four-thirty we had passed Sandy Hook and entered the ocean.

"However, already on the second day, we separated from the fleet during a strong wind and sailed onward alone and without any special occurrences."

Although Recknagel can not be identified and therefore the authenticity of his diary may be in question, the author, possibly a member of the former Landgraf Regiment which at the time of the 1783 entries had been redesignated the Leib Regiment, recorded his unit's return to Europe. "3 November - The order was announced that three regiments and three grenadier battalions were to prepare to embark. From the fifth to the seventh the cannons and heavy baggage were taken to the ships.

"8 November - We were embarked. We went aboard the ship *Amphion* and there were 384 person aboard the ship, not counting the crew.....

"13 November - We had a cold northwest wind. At eleven o'clock more ships arrived, including the commander. At three o'clock in the afternoon we left the coast of America. The wind was favorable for us. The ship plunged through the waves like a horse. Our fleet numbered 26 ships.....

"16 November - Still the same wind and weather. The ship rolled constantly from side to side, and the waves beat over the ship. It is a pitiful situation when men have women with them in dangerous situations. When the weight of the water burst into the ship, a scream arose each time, for fear the ship would sink.

"17 November - ... When night came on the storm grew even more violent. The wind moaned, the sea groaned. The ship rolled constantly from one side to the other. Those men whose beds were lengthwise in the ship also rolled so that they lay first on one side and then on the other. Those who lay crosswise however, first stood on their feet and then on their heads.....

"2 December - The wind swung to the southwest but the storm continued. We could see a ship behind us which was flying two emergency flags. Therefore our ship's captain also raised a flag that he needed help. He then took in all the sails. The storm became even stronger. Evening approached. The waves beat against the ship so that the water stood a foot deep on the deck. At eight o'clock a corporal went to relieve himself. A stormy wave struck the ship, which was constantly rolling from one side to the other, so that a loose piece of wood struck him, breaking his leg. We lost [sight of] the other ship at eleven o'clock during the night....

"3 and 4 December - We had good weather, but still the storm of yesterday. The strong storm abated somewhat toward evening. At eleven o'clock we saw a lantern off to our left in the distance, followed by a flashing signal. This was the sign that there was a ship on fire, which needed help. In reply our captain signaled with a lantern as to what had occurred, and immediately took in all sails. At twelve -thirty the ship approached. The captain called to our ship that his ship was sinking. Five days ago he had suffered severe damage and there was seven feet of water in his ship. This was the ship with two emergency flags which we had seen on the second, but which, because of the severe storm, we could not follow. Now, however, all possible preparations were made to save the people.

"5 December - The first boat, carrying the ship's captain, and an English officer and his wife and son, arrived at two o'clock in the morning. From our ship the first mate and two carpenters were sent over to see what the situation was. Next, a boat was lowered from our ship to help with the rescue of 26 men, three women, and two children. It is easily understood how the people's spirits rose when they thought themselves to be safe once again. It was very troubling for us to consider what it would be like to be in the same situation and then not be as fortunate as these people. They were all rescued along with their most necessary baggage. The last boat returned to us at about eight o'clock. Then the wind increased again and was contrary. It became so stormy that all the sails, except the mainsail, had to be taken in again. At three-thirty in the afternoon the sail split, causing the captain to shout for help. Everything that could help was done. During the sail failure a second misfortune occurred. A piece of wood struck a two and one-half year old child, breaking its cheek and jawbone. The storm grew as strong as it had ever been before, so that between seven and eight o'clock the ship took on water several times.....

"7 and 8 December - ... Today the previously mentioned corporal died during the afternoon and was buried, or more accurately, buried in the sea, at four o'clock.....

"17 to 19 December - ... This morning we saw two ships to our right. They were on the same course with us. Toward one o'clock one approached us and set out a boat which came to our ship. Thus we learned the news. This ship belonged to our fleet and during the stormy weather had suffered severe damage. It had been loaded with cannons and ammunition, part of which had been thrown overboard in order to lighten the load. The other ship however, remained in the distance.....

"25 December - We had strong wind and at twelve o'clock dropped anchor in the Channel near Portsmouth. A ship from our fleet, with troops, already had entered the harbor ahead of us, and also two ships from the fleet which sailed from New York on 25 November..

"26 December - Today the third misfortune occurred. Colonel [Henrich Wolrab] von Keudel slipped on the deck, which was being washed and was still wet, and broke his leg.

"27 to 31 December - We lay at anchor."

The Platte Grenadier Battalion Journal also recorded the following events, among others, in 1783. "January - In this month, at the beginning, the garrison from Charleston arrived at New York. We thus lost all hold on the southern provinces of North America except for St. Augustine in Florida.

"March - At the end of this month we received the news that the thirteen rebel provinces had been declared free from England. This news spread a general consternation within the army and among the residents within our lines. For the Loyalists this was the most unpleasant news as they had never expected England to do this.

"August - Since the past spring nothing more has occurred except that there has been constant activity moving the Royalists from here to Nova Scotia, Canada, the West Indies, and Great Britain. The persons going to Nova Scotia and Canada received provisions for one year and a tract of unoccupied land. Although in fact these people, according to the preliminary peace articles, were to have their land and possessions, which they had abandoned, restored, the rebels would not agree to this and they were persecuted in the most cruel manner when they sought to see their belongings or even to inquire about them. The oppression to which these unfortunate people, even those who did not participate in the war, were subjected, passes all description. Nothing was left for them except to seek peace and security in the rough, wild, and undeveloped regions of Nova Scotia, Canada, and other places to which one transport after another was sent. Several Hessian officers and soldiers also took their discharges and went there in order to settle. A captain who went there received 3,000 acres of land; a subaltern 1,500 acres; a non-commissioned officer or private 150 acres, and each was given proportionate amounts of land. All officers and men of the newly raised English corps were placed on half-pay for life and received the above portions of land in Nova Scotia or Canada....

"Lieutenant [Joseph Henrich] Wiederhold, Ensign [Gottlieb] Grebe, and seventeen grenadiers of the Platte Grenadier Battalion took their discharges in order to settle in Nova Scotia.

"11 August - The first division of Hessians, under the command of Major General von Kospoth, consisting of the Ditfurth, Knyphausen, Bose, vacant Hereditary Prince, Angelelli, Knoblauch, Buenau, and Benning Regiments, embarked to return to Europe.

"September - During the month we were busy loading all war materials, ammunition, provisions, cannons, and similar items. A large amount of cavalry and infantry uniform items were sold by the British at auction. Wagons and horses and their equipment were in part publicly sold, and in part sent to Nova Scotia.....

"4 November - We received orders to be prepared to go aboard ship, which was firmly set to take place on the eighth of this month, in order to return to Europe.

"8 November - The Linsing, Loewenstein, and Platte Grenadier Battalions and the Leib, Hereditary Prince, and Prince Charles Regiments went aboard ship. All the troops were under the command of Major General von Wurmb, who embarked on the ninth. The Platte Grenadier Battalion went aboard the transport ships *Palliser* and *Range*. After having spent seven years and a half month in America, we departed. We embarked at the same place on the North River near New York where we had first dropped anchor in America in 1776. The only Hessian troops remaining in America are the Jaeger Corps, the Lengercke Grenadier Battalion, and the Young Lossberg and Donop Regiments, which have already been ordered to be prepared to embark aboard ship.....

"13 November - Toward eleven o'clock the commodore's ship *Dolphin*, 44 guns, approached from New York and at once gave the signal for the fleet to get underway. The anchor was raised and the fleet sailed out to sea. Including the commodore and several store ships, the fleet consisted of 25 sail. Our course was toward the southeast.

"3 December - ... Our ship's captain assured us that the sea had been higher at eleven o'clock last night than he had ever seen it in his lifetime. Three times he had feared that the water would come over the stern and onto the quarterdeck. Three times he had entered the cabin thinking the water had found its way through the window. He was glad that he had found all of us asleep.

"11 December - ... The ship's captain and everyone on the ship were in bad humor. At daybreak we saw a three-masted ship ahead of us, which we overtook at about twelve o'clock. The captain of that ship did not know where he was, either, because he had not been able to take a sighting of the sun since the eighth. The captain of that ship came aboard our ship and told us he had sailed from Virginia five weeks ago with a cargo of turpentine and tobacco for Cork, Ireland. In the storm noted on the sixth of this month, the captain found it necessary to throw the entire cargo, consisting of 400 barrels of tobacco and turpentine, overboard because the ship had been very close to sinking and he was able to save his ship only with the greatest effort.....

"13 December - At daybreak this morning we saw a large ship at a great distance from us. Our ship's captain recognized it as the transport ship *Duke of Richmond,* on which was the Linsing Grenadier Battalion. We immediately made a signal that our ship belonged to the fleet. Upon receiving an acknowledgment to our signal, we sailed toward that ship and overtook it.... It had become separated from the fleet and had seen no other ship of the fleet since [21 November].... Colonel [Otto Friedrich Wilhelm] von Linsing requested that an officer from our ship be sent over. Upon his return we heard that the *Duke of Richmond* had taken 160 men off an East India Company ship, which sank on the fifth of this month, and saved them. Our ship's captain told us that he had heard of this misfortune. The loss, including private belongings, amounted to 300,000 pounds sterling.....

"16 December - This morning we spoke to a Dutch brigantine, which had sailed six months ago from Demarara in the West Indies. It had absolutely no more provisions and was supplied with some by the *Duke of Richmond.* It sailed in company with us thereafter. Toward noon we spoke with a transport ship *Nancy.* It sailed from Halifax four weeks ago loaded with English troops bound for Portsmouth. Despite cruising in this northern latitude for ten days, it had not spoken to any ship from our fleet.....

"24 December - At daybreak this morning we passed quite near Point Portland, which lay some miles to the north of us. Toward ten o'clock in the morning we saw the Isle of Wight lying before us. By nightfall we had left it behind us and we steered directly for Dover.....

"26 December - After the wind swung to our favor again last night, we were able to pass Dover this morning. Because the weather was rather bright we could see the French coast. At twelve o'clock we dropped anchor at The Downs near Deal. Our commodore and agent and six other ships, on which there were some of our troops, including the *Duke of Richmond,* had arrived here on the 23rd of the month. The names of those ships were *Elizabeth, Two Sisters, Hannah, Apollo, William,* and *Commerce.* On one ship the Lengercke Grenadier Battalion had sailed from New York on 25 November and on one the Young Lossberg Regiment."

## More Hesse-Cassel Returnees

Activities in the New York area were noted in the Hesse-Cassel Jaeger Corps Journal as was the corps' return to Europe. "6 January - The fleet with the garrison from Charleston arrived in New York. They had a quick and good passage. The Jaeger Corps and the Hesse-Hanauers had to make a place for their quarters and therefore, on the seventh, are to march to Huntington and Oyster Bay, where they will be quartered.... The Ansbach Jaeger Corps was at Norwich and the Hesse-Hanau Corps at Oyster Bay. This district, as far as the east end of the island, was under the command of Colonel von Wurmb, and from which he allowed the collection of forage for the subsistence of the Cavalry, and at the same time, as all civil government had been superseded, he had to settle all arguments between the inhabitants.....

"7 April - Today the packet boat arrived in New York and brought the armistice and the Articles of Parliament. The armistice was then formally proclaimed in New York on the eighth.

"11 April - All the troops under Colonel von Wurmb were assembled today to formally hear the armistice. Broadsides were then sent to New England, and the inhabitants of Long Island likewise were made aware.

"29 May - At the request of Colonel von Wurmb, both the Jaeger Corps and the Hesse-Hanauers marched today to York Island and entered the barracks at McGowan's Pass, because since the declaration of peace, desertions had become so frequent and the situation in this place is such that despite all efforts, nothing could be done to prevent them.....

"2 June - Today embarkation lists for all the German troops were published and all possible preparations made for leaving America. The Loyalists embarked therefore, in hoards, for Nova Scotia, the designated place for refuge. The Americans have also already reduced their army which was very small before this action.

"9 July - A part of the Hesse-Hanau Free Corps was embarked today.

"15 July - The rest of this corps went on board today.

"25 July - The troops of Ansbach, Waldeck, and Zerbst were embarked.....

523

"4 August - The Ditfurth, Knyphausen, Hereditary Prince, Bose, D'Angelelli, Knoblauch, Benning, and Buenau Regiments received orders to be prepared to embark.

"12 and 13 August - The above regiments embarked.

"9 September - The provincial troops embarked for Nova Scotia.....

"21 November - Today the rest of the Hessian troops and the 80th Regiment embarked. The 80th Regiment had been at Kingsbridge and as an appointment had been made with General Washington to hand over that post and the one at McGowan's Pass, today, Colonel von Wurmb had been instructed to leave the post at eight o'clock in the morning, as soon as the Americans arrived. At seven o'clock the regiment was prepared to march out and as soon as the American corps of about 800 men was seen in the distance, marching here, the pickets and outposts were withdrawn and the regiment marched to McGowan's Pass, where the Jaegers remained under arms and thereafter marched to New York for embarkation. Nothing was given over to the enemy. Also nothing was done to let him in, but an under-barracksmaster was left on the barrier with the keys, which he was to deliver to the enemy commander with the following letter:

"To: Major General Head

Morris House, Nov. 21, 1783

Sir,

The present under-barracksmaster has orders to give you the keys to the defenses of the evacuated posts at Kingsbridge and McGowan's Pass.

I have the honor to be

the most obedient servant.

L.J.A. de Wurmb, Col.

"23 November - General Washington with the governor and the members of the assembly of the government of New York had already arrived at Kingsbridge yesterday and although New York should have been given over yesterday, this could not take place because too many things still had to be loaded and General Carleton therefore postponed the evacuation until the 25th.

"Everywhere in New York today people have begun to show the American flags, which however, are being torn down and this is causing various small disturbances....

"24 November - During the past night at about one o'clock, fire broke out in a brewery, resulting in several houses being burned down. This caused a general fear as the people for some time have feared the Loyalists would set fire to the city.

"25 November - Today New York was finally abandoned. The general-in-chief and the admiral went aboard their ship and the rest of the troops were brought to Staten Island.... By sunset we had passed Sandy Hook and as night fell, we lost sight of land.....

"27 November - Our mainsail tore and at six o'clock it became necessary to take in all sails.....

"1 December - ... At seven o'clock in the morning we lowered our sails and while lowering the middle topmost sail, the man at the rudder was knocked down by a heavy crash [of a wave] and the ship swung around, the sail fluttered, and lay against the mast which was in danger of crashing overboard at any moment. Nevertheless, the captain finally took the ship out of danger by cutting and lowering the sail."

The fleet sailed on during the remaining days of 1783.

## Departure from Canada

Lieutenant Piel, with the Old Lossberg Regiment in Canada, began his diary entries for 1783 on 30 May and then related the dangers of the sea voyage sailing back to Europe. "Although we have the dependable report that peace has been established between England and its enemies and we await the order daily, to be able to embark, nevertheless, today we had to send one captain, two officers, and 150 privates from the regiment to work [on the fortifications] in Quebec. We have confirmed reports that two new companies have been formed to replace those lost at sea in the year 1779.....

"2 August - The regiment was embarked at Point Levi aboard two ships, *Vernon* and *Friends Adventure*. On the first ship were ... in all, including women and children, 303 persons.

"On *Friends Adventure* were ... Major von Alten-Bockum's Company, the rest of Captain Krafft's Company, and the artillery detachment. All the other German troops had been embarked some days earlier.

"3 August - The Brunswick Major General von Riedesel, with the first division of the fleet, set sail.

"6 August - At twelve-thirty in the afternoon *Vernon*, as well as the remaining transport ships of the last division, sailed with a favorable wind.....

"11 August - ... Toward eight o'clock the wind died and therefore we dropped anchor. However, because we found that we had hardly two and one-half fathoms of water, the anchor was raised again. We actually touched bottom and it would not have been easy to have gotten off, if at the same time a small breeze had not come up and helped us to move off....

"12 August - ... This afternoon all ship's captains were called to the agent. The *Rising Sun*, on which was Lieutenant Colonel [Johann Georg Heinrich] von Rauschenplat with a part of the Anhalt-Zerbst Regiment, had developed a leak. Each ship therefore sent a boat in order to take the troops from that ship to the *Anne*.

"13 August - ... We remained at anchor and the day was spent transferring items from the *Rising Sun* to the *Anne*.

"16 August - ... At twelve o'clock the previous night the *Friend Adventure* called over to us that a soldier from the ship had deserted in a boat and was still in sight. We sent a boat after him and brought the deserter back....

"20 August - At nine o'clock [in the evening] we encountered such strong gusts of wind that we had to lower all sails, most of which were torn to pieces.....

"1 September - ... This morning a young sailor who was climbing the mast fell into the ocean. We lowered a boat in order to save him, but it was too late....

"4 September - Toward noon we became aware of a strange ship behind us.... It was the English *Hero*, on which were to be found Brunswickers and Zerbsters.....

"9 September - ... At noon the sky cleared and we saw the Eddy Lighthouse near Plymouth....

"10 September - Early this morning we were near the Isle of Wight and at noon lay at anchor at Spithead. Here we found several ships with Hessians and Ansbachers from New York.....

"13 September - ... At nine o'clock anchored at Deal. Here we met ships with troops from New York, Halifax, and Quebec.

"19 September - Toward noon our fleet of 22 ships got underway....

Enemy Views (1783)

"21 September - ... The Brunswickers left us here [at Wange-rooge] to go to Stade. At ten o'clock we were at the first buoy and the mouth of the Weser; at six o'clock in the evening we anchored near Lehe.

"25 September - An English major mustered the regiment aboard ship. It was then debarked and quartered in Gestendorf and Schiffdorf.

"27 September - The three companies started their march by way of Bremen, Barksburg, Ucht, to Minden, and arrived at Rinteln on 5 October, where a few days later the two companies from Halifax, the Leib and Krafft Companies, arrived by water."

## The Return of the Hesse-Hanau Troops

Writing at Long Island on 4 April 1783, Captain Eschwege noted his activities during the spring of that year. "The order which I received about four weeks ago that the Brunswick and Hesse-Hanau detachments were to be prepared to sail to Nova Scotia has not been canceled and I hear that the time of embarkation is to be about the fifteenth of this month. However, as there are now many rumors circulating about peace and the commanding general awaits confirmation by the next packet boat from England, this departure could be delayed and possibly even canceled. The final destination of both of these detachments is Port Roseway in Nova Scotia, to which place a large number of refugees are traveling in order to settle there, and these are to be accompanied by the two detachments. His Excellency, Lieutenant General Sir Guy Carleton has promised that both detachments are to remain there for only a few weeks and then to be sent to Canada....

"A few days ago I received a letter from Regimental Quartermaster [Ludwig] Flachshaar of the Hesse-Cassel troops, who went to Pennsylvania already in December 1782 to take money and uniform items to the captives. In the letter from Lancaster, dated 27 February, he wrote to me that he had encountered, from the 1st Battalion, one non-commissioned officer, five hautboists, and three privates in Philadelphia; one non-commissioned officer and 27 privates in Lancaster; one surgeon, three non-commissioned officers, and 28 privates in Reading; and seven privates in Frederick and Yorktown. He had also, now and then, met quite a number of men from the 1st Battalion with farmers in the countryside. However, he had not given them any money, but only consoled them about an exchange. These are men noted in the list, which I had the pleasure of sending to Your Highness last December, who have indentured themselves to the farmers. However, if an exchange should occur, I hope that many of the men will return."

On 27 April Captain von Eschwege wrote to his prince from Brooklyn. "Your Highness, I have the great pleasure most humbly to report that on 15 April I received the order, late in the evening, that the Hesse-Hanau and Brunswick detachments were to embark the next morning on 16 April. In the present situation the order was completely unexpected, as I firmly believed that I would keep these troops here until the captives, who were all awaited here in the very near future, had arrived, since the peace had been settled. They would then have completed a shipment, and I could have taken them to the regiment in Canada at the same time. However, both detachments were the first ones sent from here to Halifax. As a few Brunswick officers went along, they also had the Hesse-Hanau detachment under their command as far as Halifax. There officers of Your Highness' troops are available and they will take the detachment under their command, and, I assume, arrange for the voyage to Canada as soon as possible. With this fleet I sent seven non-commissioned officers, one surgeon, one drummer, and forty privates, and gave Sergeant-major Vaupel all the accounts concerning them. It is especially pleasant for me to send such good non-commissioned officers, on whom I can rely completely, with them.

"About eight weeks ago I received orders from headquarters that both detachments were first to go from here to Port Roseway, but the latest order was that they were to go directly to Halifax. I hope their stay at that place is not a long one, as the passage to Canada is now open.

"Since my last report to Your Highness, dated 4 April, six men of the 1st Battalion, who had taken service in the American Congress Regiment, have returned here. Three of them arrived here on 23 April and, as the fleet was already lying in the harbor, it was too late to send them with it.

"I have held back five non-commissioned officers and three privates of the 1st Battalion and one non-commissioned officer assigned to the Artillery. As only a few non-commissioned officers remain with the other captives, I considered it best to keep one from each company here, except for the Grenadier Company, none of which were here.

"All the prisoners from the army are to be assembled at a designated place in Pennsylvania or New Jersey, and yesterday I received the order from headquarters to be prepared to march to that place in a few days to receive the captives from the 1st Battalion and the Artillery."

From on board the transport ship *Joseph*, at New York, on 23 May, Captain von Eschwege continued reporting to his prince. "Your Highness, I had the greatest pleasure in my last report, dated 27 April, most humbly to mention that I had received the order from the Commanding General Sir Guy Carleton to send the Hesse-Hanau detachment and also that of the Duke of Brunswick, under my command, to Halifax at once, and for me to be prepared, personally, to travel inland to receive the remaining 1st Battalion and Artillery captives, and to bring them here to New York to be exchanged. I began my journey on 1 May and together with other officers of the army, under the command of Brigadier General Clarke, went from here to Philadelphia to await the resolution of Congress about the exchange. Upon our arrival it became obvious that all the difficulties had been resolved and the prisoners who were in Philadelphia received the order to march to New York at once. I found one non-commissioned officer and four hautboists of the 1st Battalion and three privates of the Artillery there, whom I sent with the first shipment. I then obtained permission to go to Lancaster and Reading to assemble our prisoners at those places. However, it turned out that they had already been ordered to march to New York several days previously. I met them already underway, and discovered that the Hesse-Hanau and Brunswick troops had marched in a division from Lancaster and Reading.

"In the division were a surgeon, three non-commissioned officers, and fifty privates of the 1st Battalion and four privates of the Artillery. I escorted all of these men safely over to Staten Island, where they lay a few days and then were loaded directly onto a transport ship. I received the order to immediately embark the other troops lying on Staten Island and, according to my orders, I was then to take all of these men to Canada.

## Enemy Views (1783)

"Since 13 May I lie on the ship and during this time more of the men of the regiment have returned. I hope at least that still other men who are scattered about in the countryside will return. It will surely be difficult for those who have indentured themselves to farmers for a fixed number of years to get away. However, I hear that Congress has sent an order to the farmers that all such men are to be released. It may possibly be another fourteen days before I leave from here, and during that time I hope that more will return.

"Of Your Highness' Leib company, I have sixteen privates here. I have reports of five or six who will surely return, if it is possible, since they have indentured themselves. However, the others have told their comrades, who have returned, that they have no desire to return to Germany and that they wish to seek their fortune in America. Among this number, the most definite are: Musketeers Koehler, Ort, Wald, and Stein, who have told their comrades they wish to remain in this country. Concerning Rueffer, Wiskemann, Traut, and Maul, and several others, I still have the hope that if they can get away from their farmers, they will return to the company.

"Shortly before my arrival in Philadelphia, Hautboist Mueller died of an apoplectic stroke. The other hautboists are all here. I have purchased a few new uniforms here at a very cheap price and given them to a few of those who no longer had any. All of them have received such small clothes items as were needed. I have received money enough here to pay out all amounts for which the men have credits. However, as I have no company books here, and do not know exactly what is owed each man, I have paid each one something on account and will return the remaining money to the regiment. If, after my departure, some men of the regiment arrive here, Lieutenant General von Lossberg has been so kind as to promise to take care of those men and to send them to Canada at the earliest opportunity. Furthermore, Lieutenant General von Lossberg has shown much good-will toward me and my men during my stay at this place."

Having transferred to the transport ship *Mary* prior to sailing from New York, Captain von Eschwege wrote to his prince from The Downs, England, on 31 July 1783. "Your Highness, I have the great pleasure most humbly to report that I received the order on 21 June 1783 from headquarters to sail immediately with the detachment under my command to England and to halt there at The Downs, where I was to await further instructional orders from Lord North, First Secretary of State of His Majesty, after my having sent a report to him.

"After a voyage of forty days I arrived here at The Downs on 31 July, without having lost a man during the crossing, and wrote to Lord North immediately, according to my orders, and requested further instructions from him. I await his answer hourly. Except for the ship named *John and Bella*, only two others, with Brunswick troops, sailed together from New York, and fortunately have also arrived here. Otherwise I have not encountered any Hesse-Cassel nor Hesse-Hanau troops here.

"About five days before my departure from New York, I received confirmed information from headquarters that the detachment under my command no longer was to go to Canada, but directly to England. As this detachment still was without weapons and I did not know if I could obtain weapons in England or anywhere else during my voyage to Hanau, I asked His Excellence Lieutenant General von Lossberg to help me with such. His Excellence had not the least difficulty in delivering the necessary weapons for my detachment from the Hesse-Cassel magazine, and ordered me to report it most humbly to Your Highness immediately upon my arrival here. Since my last report to Your Highness, dated 3 June, six more men of the 1st Battalion have returned to duty. Four of them arrived at the last moment prior to the ship sailing and therefore could not be provided with weapons. A Grenadier Schlingellof deserted from the ship at New York on 5 June 1783 and went inland again.

"As to what will now happen to the indentured men of the 1st Battalion and the Artillery, I am sorry to report to Your Highness that the efforts of Brigadier General Clarke have not gone as well as was expected, because very few men have come back. In an effort by Hesse-Cassel to do as much as possible, Major [Carl Leopold] von [sic] Baurmeister of the Young Lossberg Regiment was sent to Philadelphia also to do as much as possible to obtain their release. It is true that many of those indentured men have no desire to rejoin the regiment, but there are some among them who have a strong desire to return to their fatherland. Lieutenant General von Lossberg has had the kindness to insure me that if men of the 1st Battalion or the Artillery return to New York, he will care for them just as well as for the Hesse-Cassel troops."

531

Captain von Eschwege then wrote a series of letters concerning the detachment's return to Hanau. On 24 August he wrote from Bremerlehe. "On 2 August I received an answer from Lord North, who informed me that I was to proceed to Bremerlehe at once and then travel onward to the place of my final destination. However, as a few days later, three companies of the Hesse-Hanau Free Corps arrived at this place from New York, I was therefore detained not only a few days longer, but was sent aboard ship with those three companies, making the troops very cramped. However, we had a fortunate trip and arrived at Bremerlehe on 22 August without having lost a man.

"On the 23rd I and the detachment under my command landed and entered quite good quarters at once. The 24th and 25th were rest days and on the 26th we continued onward with our trip. The local official, who traveled as march commissary with us to Witzenhausen, laid out the march route that far for us, which I had the great pleasure to send herewith to Your Highness. [Not included here.] Upon my arrival here I was offered money for expenses and to pay the detachment under my command by a local merchant, on orders of the Hesse-Cassel agent who lives in Bremen. However, as I had been supplied with sufficient funds to pay the detachment until we reached Hanau, I did not take any. In addition to this money, I still have 500 pounds sterling in banknotes in the military chest. The three companies of the Hesse-Hanau Free Corps have received no pay for August and have no opportunity of getting money here. Captain von Franck is therefore very embarrassed and requested that I help him financially. Therefore I have already advanced him something for the August pay.

"With the payment for the non-commissioned officers and privates of the detachment I have managed until now according to the pay instructions of the 1st Battalion and the Artillery as it was done in America, and will continue to do so, without making any changes until I receive Your Highness' most gracious orders about it....

"March Route - for the Hesse-Hanau detachment, consisting of one officer, thirteen non-commissioned officers, nine drummers, and 76 soldiers, a total of 99 men, and the other three companies from Bremerlehe to Witzenhausen" [Not included here.]

Writing on 14 September, von Eschwege noted the detachment's progress. "Your Highness, I have the great pleasure most humbly to report that, according to my march route, I arrived at Witzenhausen on the Werra on 14 September with the detachment under my command.

"During the entire march through Electoral Hannover, there was not the lest complaint about a single man of my command. Also, on the other hand, my men were very much pleased by the hospitality of the inhabitants. However, I am sorry to have to mention to Your Highness that in the last night's quarters at Friedland, Musketeers Fischer and Mahr, Sr., quarreled and each wounded the other. Musketeer Mahr is dangerously wounded, having received two cuts in the head. Because of this danger, I have allowed him to be questioned by a Hesse-Cassel official here in Witzenhausen. Musketeer Fischer is only lightly wounded and I have placed him in arrest. As far as it is in my power, I will provide the best care for the dangerously wounded Mahr and have the surgeon apply all his skill for a recovery. Further, I will spare no effort toward maintaining the best discipline in my command while passing through Hesse-Cassel, and try to prevent all excesses."

Writing again at Nauheim on 24 September, he reported, "On the entire march through the territory of Hesse-Cassel not the least disorder occurred and not a single complaint was lodged with me at any of our night quarters. The wounded musketeer Mahr is progressing quite well and I have not failed to have the surgeon give him the best care. I still have Musketeer Fischer under arrest.

"I will march away from here tomorrow morning at seven o'clock and, according to my march route prescribed by Your Highness, will arrive in Hanau tomorrow."

Lieutenant von Lindau's letters concerning the Leib Company of the Hesse-Hanau Regiment during 1783 commence with one written while in winter quarters at Latbiniere in Canada on 15 June. "Sergeant-major Vaupel, Quartermaster Sergeant Lenz, and Musketeer Remy ransomed themselves at New York, as Your Highness will graciously see in the accompanying report. [Not included here.] In a letter which I received a few days ago from Ensign von Gall, from Halifax, I received the news that they and the other men of the 1st Battalion, who had ransomed themselves, reported there on 5 May. Your Highness, I most humbly must report that Musketeer Georg Tempell, born at Altheim, 5'11 1/4" tall, returned here to the Leib Company on 28 May. The mentioned Musketeer Tempell was left behind because of illness when the Burgoyne army retreated on 8 October 1777, and he fell into enemy hands. Thereafter he sat for a long time in the jail at Albany, but was finally released. From there he made his way to the Indians and fortunately arrived at Niagara, where he had to take service with Butler's Rangers, a royal provincial corps. After surviving two years, he finally received his discharge and permission to return to the 1st Battalion.

"I must also report most humbly that Surgeon Gottschalk left the Leib Company on 14 March 1782 and went to Your Highness Jaeger Corps as regimental surgeon."

Lieutenant von Lindau wrote from on board the ship *Hero* on 3 August. "Your Highness, I have the pleasure herewith, before our departure from Canada, most humbly to submit a report about Your Highness' Leib Company of the Hereditary Prince 1st Battalion and to report those changes which have occurred since my last most humble report from the cantonment quarters at Point Levi, dated 1 July, such as that Musketeer Caspar Zeh deserted from our cantonment quarters at Point Levi on 13 July 1783, but returned to the company on the twentieth of the same month. Corporals Bellinger and Tack, as well as 23 privates left the fortifications at Quebec on 13 July 1783 and returned to the company. The same occurred on 29 July, when four privates, previously in Quebec on work detail, by the names of Nicolaus Schmidt, Daefner, Bruchausen, and Friedrich Hassler, returned. I must also most humbly report to Your Highness that the following six musketeers of the Leib Company were given their discharges on 21 July 1783, and departed: Jacob Flueckmann, Christoph Hessler, Theodor Kling, Henrich David, Jacob Schmidt, and Georg Deshmer. We were all embarked here on 1 August and supposedly are to set sail from here tomorrow."

Writing from on board the *Hero* on 16 September, von Lindau noted, "Your Highness, I have the pleasure herewith to report our arrival at The Downs on the tenth of this month and most humbly to submit a report about Your Highness' Leib Company.... We arrived here safely on the tenth of this month after leaving Quebec 24 days ago, and I have the pleasure herewith most humbly to mention the changes which have occurred since my last report. I have met Sergeant Vaupel, Drummer Giese, and Private Remy here. They were ordered to depart from Halifax to return to Your Highness' Company.

Captain von Eschwege, as I have heard here, sailed for Stade with his troops five days prior to our arrival here. We are to sail from here with the first favorable wind."

The lieutenant reported the desertion of one of his men in a letter from Rinteln on 13 October. "Your Highness, I have the pleasure herewith most humbly to send a report on Your Highness' Leib Company of the Hereditary Prince 1st Battalion and to report that despite all precautions, Drummer Seebach of the Leib Company deserted during the night of 30 September, in the previous month, from the small ship at Bremen. I exerted all my efforts to get him back but failed to accomplish my purpose because, as I later learned, the Prussian recruiters had him. Your Highness can rest assured that I will not neglect to use all means and precautions to prevent further desertions."

Nevertheless, other desertions were reported from Hannover Muenden in a letter dated 24 October 1783. "With the packet now departing I have the pleasure most humbly to send a report about Your Highness' Leib Company of the 1st Battalion to Your Highness, and to mention that since my last most humbly submitted report, dated 13 October at Rinteln, the following changes have occurred. Musketeer Kuehn deserted on the thirteenth of this month and Musketeers Schauer and Spanier on the 21st of this month. With the first Your Highness lost nothing, as he was completely worthless as a soldier and he could have received his discharge from Colonel Lentz. I am especially sorry about the latter two however, as they were two fine fellows. Colonel Lentz can vouch for me to Your Highness that this was not my fault. I also must report to Your Highness that Musketeer Herrmann was released with his discharge on the fourteenth of this month."

Letters from other Hesse-Hanau officers include the following written in 1783 to the prince. Lieutenant Zincke reported his arrival in Germany, but without giving a place or date. "Your Highness, I have the great pleasure, by this means, most humbly to report that we received the last ship's provisions on the transport ship *Free Briton* on 12 October at Cuxhaven. On the thirteenth, at two-thirty, we were landed and at four o'clock we marched out of Ritzebuettel, and at ten o'clock in the evening arrived at quarters in Dorum in Hannover, having been escorted there by Lieutenant von Succow. The following men deserted during the night:

1) Grenadier Schlegel
2) Grenadier Schneider, II
3) Grenadier Fritz, and
4) Grenadier Binmueller.

"At six o'clock in the morning of the fourteenth, general march was beaten, at six-thirty assembly, and at seven o'clock march, whereupon we at once moved out and marched to Bremerlehe, where we were embarked on four small Weser ships. Tattoo was beaten at eight-thirty in the evening. Reveille was at six o'clock on the morning of the fifteenth, and we left the ships at nine o'clock in order to be mustered, passing before the Hannover Dragoon Major Niemayer. At twelve o'clock tonight we are to sail from here toward Bremen.

"In the absence of other orders, I have paid all the men according to the roster, as Captain Schunck had paid them on the march on land.

"I have had to keep Captain Wiederhold, because of his behavior and his continued drunkenness, even while under arrest, in arrest to this time, as I have no resolution to my first most humble report."

Captain von Buttlar also wrote a letter from Muenden on 18 October 1783 concerning events during the return to Hanau of troops under his command. "It pleased Your Highness to order Lieutenant Colonel Janecke to leave 200 weapons behind at Muenden for the 1st Battalion, which order he found here upon his arrival.

"In accordance with Your Highness' order Lieutenant Colonel von Janecke told me that I could receive these 200 weapons on Monday, 13 October, but I would be required to give him a receipt that I had received the weapons in the best condition. However, because the weapons were in especially poor condition and rusted, in short, in a condition that they could not be repaired in less than fourteen days and at a great cost, I refused to accept the weapons in exchange for the requested receipt. I agreed with Adjutant Schweinebraten to leave the weapons, protected in cases, in the house of the merchant Eckhardt, until the arrival of Colonel Lentz. If he would accept them, then the merchant Eckhardt would be given a receipt that 200 weapons had been taken from the cases. I thought, most illustrious Hereditary Prince, that this was the situation - as the captain of the Free Corps would not deliver good weapons, it was all that I could do.

## Enemy Views (1783)

"Day before yesterday, being 16 October, I sent to the merchant Eckhardt's house to ask if the weapons were in a place where they would not be further ruined, and received to my surprise the information in writing, that after the agreement made between Adjutant Schweinebraten and me at the merchant Eckhardt's house, the adjutant had delivered another order, namely to deliver the weapons and all the other arms to Hanau - and they were gone. As my proof, I can produce this letter. I must not neglect most humbly to report this incident to Your Highness, and leave it most humbly to Your Highness' discretion to dispose of as you please.

"I was here on 12 October and now wait impatiently on the battalion. First it is said they can be here in six days, then in ten days. As soon as I have confirmed reports as to where the battalion is, I will not fail to sail a day's trip toward it, in order to obtain my orders. Ansbach troops have been here since yesterday, waiting for a transport. The Weser is surprisingly low. Because of this situation, the troops often travel barely two and one-half miles per day."

Major Pausch's letters to his prince in 1783 informed the Prince of the Hesse-Hanau Artillery preparations for and return to Europe. In a letter written at St. Nicholaus on 16 June, Pausch noted, "An order from the general staff headquarters of Major General von Loos, dated 13 June of this year - The regiments of his brigade, including ours, should be prepared to be able to march at once to the place of their embarkation upon the approach of the next arriving fleet, because the German troops are to be returned to Europe as soon as possible.

"This is one of the most enjoyable orders which we have ever received or could ever receive here, and we now write with the most comforting and most hopeful joy, that we may again see the most gracious face of our most gracious and best prince, and be permitted to kiss the hem of Your Highness' robes in the most humble obedience. This is reinforced by a new order, which Colonel Lentz sent to me at Quebec, that the work detachment building fortifications was not to be continued, as possibly in one of the next few days, in order to be able to be closer to the place of our embarkation, our winter quarters would be changed and we would enter cantonments. The provisions ships which have arrived from England and Ireland are to be our assigned transports and have already been converted for that purpose....

"We still remain in winter quarters, impatiently waiting and hoping at any moment to leave them and to take our first, and also most pleasant step of our return to our most loved and above all other lands, the best fatherland, with the greatest possible pleasure.

Neither storms nor the most unpleasant weather can minimize our longed-for pleasure in the least, but I and everyone else, with the most steadfast heart, would face the most disagreeable travel conditions because we finally see our wish of again being in the most gracious, most favorable presence of our most gracious prince, being granted and fulfilled."

On 1 July Pausch wrote from Point Levi concerning items of unit administration. "The demoted and present Cannoneer Moerschell, despite previous implications and applied pressure, has still not confessed. However, because everyone said he knew about the entire plot, doubt remained, a trial was held, and he was punished at the 1st Battalion, in Colonel Lentz' presence, by running a gauntlet of 200 men, sixteen times in one day, following which he was released from arrest....

"Your Serene Highness, also to let you most graciously know the reason why the promotions for the regiment of His Highness the Prince of Anhalt-Zerbst, which received its commissions already in 1779, were not announced to the army earlier than my major's patent, most graciously granted to me by Your Serene Highness, which I had the greatest pleasure to receive here only on 3 July 1782 with a duplicate thereof at the same time. The primary reason can probably be that something in the drawing up of the subsidy treaty with Anhalt-Zerbst was somehow overlooked, because the regiment had only one colonel, who became a brigadier general, and with one major, namely Rauschenplat's brother, who took over the regiment. By this promotion the regiment found itself with one colonel, one lieutenant colonel, and a Major Wittersheim, and an additional captain, so that it was augmented with one lieutenant colonel and one captain. For that reason and for the sake of economy at the royal treasury, they were not recognized by the governor, His Excellence, Haldimand, and even less so announced to the army, but each one remained in his former rank, duty, and pay, which however, their prince made good, except for the pay.

"In 1781 the colonel and brigadier (one man) returned home, but nothing changed because he was still considered as colonel and commandant of the regiment. As finally, with my advancement, which the governor, after thinking it over, also granted and congratulated me, these were suddenly announced all together about ten days later in an order from the army headquarters. About eight days after the announcement, Lieutenant Colonel von Rauschenplat however, ordered his brother the colonel and brigadier, to be completely removed from future and pending orders on all appointment lists, and for himself to be listed as commander. That is all that I have been able to learn off hand, and can report most humbly to Your Serene Highness. Also, the Regimental Surgeon Heidelbach, at the same time as the arrival of Colonel Lentz, received Your Serene Highness' most gracious order granting him permission to marry already in October of last year.

"Finally however, I lay myself in most sincere submission at Your Serene Highness' most gracious feet, most humbly requesting that the format of my most humbly submitted letter of 15 August 1782 be most graciously pardoned and the reason therefore most humbly in the most devoted obedience to be explained. On about the thirteenth I went to the government [house] and saw a packet of folio and large quarto size had been delivered to the secretary of His Excellence and asked if letters and packets were being sent to Europe. I received the answer, 'Yes!' however, only packets as small as possible, because only a single-masted, small, very light, armed vessel with few dispatches was sailing. Even if I were to put together one as small as possible, it would have to be delivered by five o'clock on the evening of the fourteenth, without fail. The captain of the ship had been ordered to pack everything together in a small chest, into which he was to place a cannonball or lead, so that everything, should he see an enemy sail which he believed about to capture him, could be sunk instantly in this chest. The Anhalt-Zerbsters had to take back their large packets and were advised to wait for another, more certain opportunity. However, they also were granted time to prepare another very small packet, if it were absolutely necessary. This time all personal letters were forbidden, in order to reduce the size of the packet. However, within the next few weeks an armed packet boat or frigate would depart, but His Excellence could not yet mention a specific date.

"Lieutenant Colonel von Rauschenplat also had to prepare a similar small packet, which was also lined with flattened musket balls. Because of this singular and reasonable situation, and so as not to waste this small opportunity of being able to lay reports and news most humbly at Your Highness' feet, I was forced to grasp this format, and again beg on bended knees, most gracious forgiveness for a blunder made in guiltless manner."

Pausch wrote to his prince on 29 October 1783 from Melsungen in Germany. "On the 25th of this month, from noon until evening, I completed the embarkation of the Artillery aboard two Minden river boats at the Cassel Inlet in Minden, from which I departed at daybreak on the 26th, but allowed the troops to sail. These latter arrived in one boat the same evening at Wolfsanger, where I, still without letters of authorization, had the troops quartered. The second boat however, remained about two miles the other side of Spickershausen and only arrived here at about twelve o'clock noon on the 27th. I was allowed to sail through the locks at Kassel at once, and entered the inlet there in the most confident hope of finding the necessary boats ready and a march commissary there. However, neither was there, but I did receive the most humbly enclosed copy of the most gracious letters of authorization from the commissary of His Serene Highness, the reigning Landgrave, and orders from His Excellence Lieutenant General [Friedrich Christian Arnold, Baron] von Jungkenn to bargain for the boats as best I could and to pay for them, and also for horses and wagons for marching overland, with hard cash. Here I stood, without a march commissary and without money, in the greatest embarrassment. I arranged, still without having any money, for three large boats with three smaller boats to be pulled behind, at the cheapest and best price, to sail to Hersfeld for 23 old Louis d'or, embarked at once in these boats, and they were loaded and departed at one o'clock on the 28th. The ships tied up near Guxhaven during the night and the troops entered quarters there. About twelve o'clock noon on the 29th the boats arrived at Melsungen, but could not continue onward. Departure from Melsungen for Rothenburg will be early on the 30th, before daybreak, and I hope, if nothing unexpectedly intervenes, to arrive at Hersfeld tomorrow evening on the 31st, which the ships' crews have given much hope of accomplishing. As I had not the least money available with which to pay this completely unexpected expense of mine, I found it necessary to obtain fifty Louis d'or, amounting to 250 Reichsthalers in Hessen currency at the local conversion rate at Kassel, from War Councilor Hainier against a receipt.

"Sergeant List, who recently purchased his release from captivity and thereby ransomed himself, and the interim non-commissioned officer, Cannoneer Schwab, took their release on the 26th of this month and remained in Hannover Muenden, and according to all indications, they have taken duty there."

Pausch seems to have finished his written reports to the Prince with a letter of 6 November from Steinau. "Your Serene Highness, I wish to lay at your most gracious feet, in the most humble report, how I arrived this afternoon at precisely one-thirty with my command of Artillery most graciously entrusted to me, and plan to continue the march onward to Autenhasseln early tomorrow morning. From there, however, I await Your Serene Highness' most gracious orders, if I should press on the march without a day of rest, or if I have the most gracious permission to halt for a day of rest as is customary."

## The Return of the Ansbach-Bayreuth Troops

Hautboist Stang, who made more entries in his 'March Routes' in 1783 than in any previous year, continued to record information with minimal entries covering the march out of captivity, the voyage back to Europe, and the return march from the port to Bayreuth. "26 March - We received news of peace from this war between America and the King of England.....

"22 April - The Americans had a fireworks [display] and illuminated [the city] with lights, all because of peace.....

"1 May - The American guards were withdrawn from us.

"13 May - We took our departure from captivity and marched through Frederick.....

"19 May - We crossed another river named Brandywine Kill. My colleague deserted here.....

"28 May - We embarked again and sailed across New York harbor to Long Island.....

"6 August - The regiment was embarked on a frigate [captured] from the French with the name *Sibylle* and armed with twenty cannons.

"9 August - We sailed out of New York harbor into the ocean, for England, with another frigate with the name *Quebec*.

11 August - The frigate *Quebec* left us as our ship developed a leak.....

"24 August - At one o'clock in the morning, a Sunday, St. Bartholomew's Day, we received a frightful scare. We lost our middle mast due to the great storm.....

"1 September - At eight o'clock in the morning Major von Seitz died.....

"5 September - Major von Seitz was lowered into the sea and during the evening, with God's help, we saw the first land.....

"7 September - We sailed past Plymouth on a Sunday and anchored at twelve o'clock noon.....

"13 September - We were transferred onto a ship with the name *Eolus*.

"19 September - We set sail at five o'clock in the evening....

"27 September - We sailed in a channel. Denmark was on the right and Holland on the left. About one o'clock in the afternoon we arrived at Bremerlehe, which belongs to Hannover, and anchored there.

"28 September - We were mustered by an English commissary and transferred to small single-masted ships.

"29 September - We sailed at one o'clock in the morning with sixteen small ships, on the river named the Weser. It was St. Michael's Day. We sailed to Vegesack and anchored there.....

"2 October - It was necessary for horses to pull us to Bremen....

"3 October - We were transferred again to Hannoverian boats which were pulled by eight horses.....

"12 October - Through Prussian Minden where thirty soldiers were needed to pull us under a stone bridge with seven rounded arches. The masts also had to be lowered.

"13 October - Our soldiers had to pull us. To Vlotho where the Prussian [domain] ends.....

"30 October - We disembarked and marched through Hannover Minden, Hedeminden, Gertenbach, which belongs to Hesse, Bischoftshausen, Witzhausen, and Wendershausen.....

"5 November - We marched through Saalamess where we separated from the Ansbachers. Then through Dittellohr, Ohrelzell, which belongs to Fulda, to Ober and Niederufhausen, to Ritter and into quarters.....

"20 November - We marched to Bayreuth and were again quartered in the barracks. Finis."

Prechtel traced the progress of the Ansbach Regiment out of captivity and back to Ansbach in Germany in his diary. "2 to 6 January - ... An American detachment to reinforce the prison guards came here from Baltimore. Among them were both musicians, Fifer [Johann Jacob] Messerer and Drummer [Johann Burckhardt] Koehlner, of the Grenadier Company of the von Voit Regiment.....

"25 January - ... His Serene Highness has made a regiment of the former Jaeger Battalion and therefore three new jaeger companies have been sent to America, which, however, now lie at Halifax.....

"29 January - ... Order from the American Major Bailey - All prisoners of war who are in this state shall report into the barracks here by 10 February, and those here in the city and surrounding area, likewise.....

"27 March - ... The French cutter *Triumph* sailed from Cadiz to Philadelphia, as an express, in 36 days and brought the news that peace had been agreed upon on 20 January 1783.

"At three-thirty in the afternoon, to the ringing of all the bells by the oldest citizen, a parade was held throughout all the streets of the city, with Major Bailey participating. They had a white flag with them, and this procession was held because of the general peace....

"30 March - ... The American General Goetsch [Gates ?] arrived here and brought the news that New York was to be turned over to the Americans and as soon as possible, the prisoners of war were to go to Staten Island, or Long Island, in order to be embarked there for Europe.....

"13 April - ... Staff Captain [Joachim] Kimm of the Hessian Hereditary Prince Regiment cut his throat this morning at four o'clock, in his quarters. This evening he was carried out by six private soldiers and buried behind the barracks.....

"22 April - ... At eight o'clock this evening, because of the arrival of the Articles of Peace, a fireworks display prepared by the Ansbach Artillery Captain Hofmann, was held at the Great Place at the courthouse. Afterward, the bells were rung at both churches and the entire city was illuminated. Further, the Continental troops fired volleys by platoons, in all the streets of the city.....

"29 April - ... 'Order - The previously prisoners of war shall all have their freedom, but must always be back in the barracks by nine o'clock in the evening'.....

"9 May - ... The American Colonel Wood arrived here from Winchester and brought the order from General Lincoln from Philadelphia,

"1) The prisoners of war should be turned loose, and

"2) Their march away from here should take place as soon as possible.

"10 May - ... After the officers of the four German regiments lying here had assembled this morning in the barracks, the American Colonel Wood sent an officer to the barracks with the order from General Lincoln, which stated:

"That the previously prisoners of war were completely released from their captivity. The American guard therefore, also immediately departed.

"On the march, which is to start Monday, an American guard consisting of two subalterns and thirty privates will go with the regiments for protection.....

"21 May - The eighth march. We entered Philadelphia and the regiments were quartered in the New Jail.....

"25 May - The twelfth march. We passed Bannontown, Woodbridge, and Elizabethtown, and were carried across the Kills River to Staten Island. We entered night camp at Decker's Ferry.

"Lieutenant Pendergast was the commanding officer of the American guard which remained behind at Elizabethtown.....

"2 June - ... Regimental Surgeon Rapp, of the von Voit Regiment, actually accompanied us from captivity at Frederick to Philadelphia, but there, with his two servants, Private [Michael] Gerlinger, of the von Voit Regiment, and a private of the von Seybothen Regiment, he remained.....

"18 July - Chaplain Wagner, of the von Voit Regiment, received his requested release and wants to go to Nova Scotia with those favoring England.....

"6 August - The three Ansbach Regiments[47] were embarked on warships near Denyse's Ferry, on Long Island, in order to be shipped back to Europe.

"1)   On the frigate *South Carolina*, the entire Jaeger Regiment, under the command of Colonel von Voit.

"2)  On the frigate *Sibylle*, a part of the von Voit and a part of the von Seybothen Regiments, under the command of Colonel von Seybothen.

"3)  On the frigate *Quebec*, the entire company of Captain von Metzsch of the von Voit Regiment, under the command of Captain von Metzsch.

"4)  On the frigate [*Emerald*], the entire company of Captain von Quesnoy, of the von Seybothen Regiment, under the command of Captain von Quesnoy.....

"9 August - We sailed away from Sandy Hook and had a good wind the entire day.....

"11 August - ... Shortly before our departure from America, Grenadier Captain von Molitor, of the von Seybothen Regiment, on request, received his separation.[48] ....

"13 August - Our ships had actually received the order from the admiral at New York to remain two by two together and to sail with one another to Portsmouth in England. Alone! This did not happen and each ship's captain, as soon as he was on the open sea, sailed according to his own pleasure....

"23 August - The fifteenth day of our sea voyage, with very strong and stormy winds, but we sailed well.

"The middle mast of the frigate *Sibylle* was newly installed before our departure from New York. But it was one which was not meant for a frigate, but for a large warship. Because of the great height and weight, the mast began to sway, causing the rigging, which several times had to be restrung and tightened with great effort, to work loose.

"The rolling of the ship today, because of the strong winds which were very severe, necessitated lowering the mast onto the quarterdeck for fear that otherwise it would break off and place the ship in complete jeopardy.

"Therefore, at twelve o'clock at night, on the orders of the ship's captain, Fischerall, it was chopped down and thrown overboard with all the rigging and two large sails which were attached. During this activity, not only was the top of the aftermast broken, but also the railings on the ship were severely damaged.

"The rigging of this mast, due to the violent storm, hung behind on the steering rudder, so that for half an hour the mast was dragged by the ship, until finally, through the knowledge and advice of the naval officers, it was chopped loose from the steering rudder by the sailors.

"The ship *Sibylle* was formerly a French frigate which had been captured by the English during the war. It is covered with a copper bottom and has 28 guns and 200 sailors, plus 500 troops on board on this voyage.

"Twenty-six officers are living in the cabins and each has had spacious accommodations.

"However, this frigate leaked very badly, so that four times a day, and for two hours each time, sixty men had to work at the pumps.....

"1 September - ... Major von Seitz, of the von Voit Regiment, after tolerating a fourteen day nerve sickness, died at eight o'clock this morning on the frigate *Sibylle*, in the 43rd year of his life. Because land would soon be reached, the body was placed in a coffin, which was made on the ship....

"2 September - ... This evening the ship ran aground and was held fast. The water was frightfully restless and due to the rolling of the ship, the top of the aftermast broke off.....

"4 September - ... As the body of the dead Major von Seitz could no longer be retained, at nine o'clock this morning, attended by all the officers and private soldiers, he was buried. Although several heavy iron balls were tied to the coffin, he did not sink, but was seen as far as the eye could see, floating away on the water. Later Staff Captain Seidel, of the von Seybothen Regiment, gave a short eulogy.

"On the frigate *Sibylle*, the upper part of the aftermast was again repaired. On the other hand, the middlemast broke, which injured a sailor in the chest.....

"7 September - The 30th day of the sea voyage. At four o'clock in the morning we saw the area near Portsmouth, where we entered the harbor at twelve o'clock noon, and anchored at Spithead.....

"10 September - ... A fleet arrived here in the harbor [at Portsmouth] from Quebec, which had Hessians, Brunswickers, and Anhalt-Zerbsters on board. It had been twenty days en route.....

"12 September - ... In place of the frigate *Sibylle* we received two other transport ships, namely, *Eolas* and *Polly*. Colonel von Seybothen is to board the first and Major von Beust the latter.....

"14 September - Major von Beust, of the von Seybothen Regiment, and the remaining troops from the frigate *Sibylle* embarked on the *Polly* today.....

"19 September - At six o'clock in the evening we sailed from Portsmouth to Spithead and were at once struck by very stormy weather and rain, but we still had good wind.....

"21 September - ... This morning the ship *Eolas* and the two ships with Anhalt-Zerbst troops sailed for Bremerlehe.

"The ship *Polly* remained here because the ship's captain, Boyd, and the mate, Patterson, are not familiar with the North Sea and no pilot was to be had at Deal for less than sixty guineas. Therefore, one will be brought here from London, who will work for thirty guineas.....

"24 September - At four o'clock this afternoon the pilot named Stewart arrived here from London and at five-thirty we set sail with fresh wind.

"Therefore, the [lack of a] pilot is to blame that we were unable to follow our troops and had to travel alone, under the command of Major von Beust, to Ansbach, even though they had lain at anchor at Hannover Muenden for fourteen days.....

"7 October - The thirteenth day of our voyage. We sailed at seven o'clock in the morning and at eight o'clock dropped anchor at Bremerlehe....

"8 October - ... This morning the English Major Gunn held muster on our ship *Polly* and at eleven o'clock, midday, the troops began to transfer onto five single-masted Bremen sloops. In the evening the ships went underway and sailed throughout the night, with a contrary wind.....

"10 October - We sailed at nine o'clock in the morning and had to have the ships pulled, in part by horses, and in part by soldiers on the land.

"N.B. - In this region [near Bremen] boats were to be seen being rowed by women....

"11 October - During the afternoon the Ansbach troops were embarked on three Weser ships, which are called Boecke and anchored on the Werder.....

"19 October - We shoved off at seven o'clock in the morning.

"Our fleet on the Weser River consisted of eight ships; four of which had one mast and each, from Bremen onward, were pulled on land by seven horses pulling two ships connected together.

"The Prussian citizen and owner of the ships of the fleet, Casselmann, brings these troops from Bremen to Hannover Muenden for pay from the English Crown and at the same time, commands the fleet as admiral.....

"22 October - On the place where our ships had anchored the previous night [near Hoya], the Waldeck Major Pentzel was shot on his ship.[49]....

"31 October - Underway at seven 'clock in the morning and we passed Velpen, Eisbergen, the last Prussian village, and Dankers, Hesse, on the left; and on the right Huenerhaus, the first Hessen village, and Rinteln, which we entered at noon and where we spent the night.

"The Old Lossberg Regiment, which returned from America already one month ago, lies here in garrison and Lieutenant General von Lossberg is the governor.....

"8 November - ... At nine-thirty this morning our boat ran upon a rocky shoal. This caused the helmsman to be thrown overboard by the rudder. He righted himself again in the water, but stood up to his shoulders in the Weser River. He was picked up later by a boat and brought back to the ship in an angry mood....

"9 November - ... Private Saltmann, of Colonel von Voit's Company, fell into the Weser River this morning and was recovered again uninjured.....

"13 November - ... A Hessian brigade, which likewise is returning from America, under the command of General von Kospoth, is in quarters here and tomorrow will resume its march to Kassel, which lies about ten miles from here....

"The rest of the Hesse-Hanau Field Jaegers arrived here....

"17 November - We debarked in the morning. Today we began our first march on land and passed the Hannoverian village of Hedemuenden, where we were carried over the Werra River and next arrived in the Hessen village of Blickershausen and Ermschwerd, and entered quarters.....

"24 November - The sixth march.... We crossed over the Fulda Bridge at Breitenbach.

"About two and one-half miles from Unterhauen lies the Hessen city of Hersfeld. The garrison is from the Prince Charles Regiment.

"25 November - The seventh march. Major von Beust's Company had to march on to Bayreuth today, apart from us, and entered quarters at Hausdorf in Fulda. It was commanded by 1st Lieutenant von Altenstein.

"The troops of the von Voit Regiment were quartered in the small Fulda city of Huenfeld. Major von Beust received the order to go with [the von Voit Regiment] to Ansbach.....

"9 December - The seventeenth march through Ober Dachstetten, Graefenbuch, Unter Hessbach, Lehrberg, Neusses, to Ansbach, and then we marched into the barracks at Ansbach with music playing."

And with this final entry the Prechtel diary comes to an end.

Doehla wrote a much more enthusiastic account of the arrival back in his home area on 20 November 1783. "We marched from Kulmbach at eight o'clock in the morning, in a steady rain, with joyful and exulted cries of joy from many people who came to meet us.

"We marched, with dressed ranks, smartly shouldered weapons, and music playing an English march, into the city by the Kulmbacher Gate, through the city, out by the Upper Gate, past the former mint, over the main River bridge, to the Jaeger Street, and into the barracks, where everything struck us as very strange and would remain so for some time.

"I must remark that upon our entrance into the barracks, my father was present. We embraced and kissed and thanked God for His mercy in allowing us to be reunited in health and happiness and we shed many heartfelt tears of joy.....

"4 December - I left Bayreuth, returned home, and completely ended my military career."[50]

Not all of the Hessians, who survived the war, returned to Germany. As noted, many remained in the New World. Of those men, some returned to Europe later, some wanted to return, but could not, and surely most must have spent many hours wondering if they had made the right decision in remaining in America.

Johann Heinrich Henkelmann [or Henckelmann] served with the Hesse-Cassel Seitz Regiment in the colonies and in Nova Scotia during the Revolutionary War. He took his discharge in Nova Scotia, having married an American, or more likely a resident of Nova Scotia. As one of the Hessians who remained in the New World, Henkelmann's letter of 10 November 1783 from Halifax to a former comrade in Germany is of interest.

"I hope that by now you have shot a dozen rabbits in your own forest, enjoyed eating them, and while doing so have drunk our health. My darling, who sends her best wishes, has gone out again for the first time yesterday, after four weeks, during which time she has been indisposed with a dangerous illness - a sore throat. A treacherous illness. I have had a deathly fear, but now she is completely recovered. This is important enough for me to make you aware of it. Therefore I know she will continue to share my future....

"Now for what little is new since your departure. Last month our regiment was reduced. We are on half pay which makes my pay 300 guilder a year. I have been granted 750 acres of land on the Bear River near Annapolis, complete wardrobes for me, my wife, two male servants, and a maid, for one year, and shovels, axes, saws, etc., for the two servants. These are the reasons why I can not leave here this fall. I plan to give the servants the tools, let them work for me for three years, from which they will profit, and after that, to give each of them fifty acres of his own. The land is reportedly so good that Captain Molitor, who with about 100 soldiers and families from New York already lives there, has assured me that he would pay five dollars an acre to have it cleared....

"I hope, for heaven's sake, to depart from here for Carlshafen in June. I can live here, but better there, because I will not see a preacher going into the church in a leather apron. This is what disgusts me about America. My wife, an American by birth, also feels how much this item of apparel detracts from the holiness. In short, I will not remain here!

"Now my friend, I would like to receive a letter from you before I leave this province, and ask, what did you carry on the trip home and in what condition did you arrive? How are things with my Weyland Regiment, etc. One thing more, in addition to our half pay we also receive the rank we held in America. That is an unfortunate point which possibly, should war break out, might make it necessary for me to return to Halifax....

"One thing more, on the fifth of last month His Excellency, John Parr, Captain General, etc., appointed me the government agent in Nova Scotia and the Island of St. John over all the necessities for the soldiers who stayed behind and the Loyalists. I was not so foolish as to refuse this important position as it provides half pay for a lieutenant with retention of all military honors and allowances without requiring military service.

"The 70th Regiment went aboard ship today to sail to England. New York has still not been turned over [to the Americans]. Lieutenant General Campbell is coming here as commander-in-chief and Brigadier Fox is going home [to England]."

# 1784

## The Late Returnees

By the year 1784 many of the Hessian units were already back in Germany. Others, however, were still on the ocean or in barracks in England and months passed before they were home again. One of the units still actually in English service was the Hesse-Cassel Platte Grenadier Battalion, as noted in that unit's journal entries. "3 January - After lying still, here at The Downs, since the 26th of last month, and after tolerating stormy weather during much of the time, we weighed anchor about noon and sailed for the Thames River.... At eight o'clock in the evening we dropped anchor near Margate.....

"6 January - At nightfall we weighed anchor and sailed up the Medway River to Chatham, where we anchored between nine and ten o'clock in the evening.....

"8 January - We landed and entered the barracks. All our troops, from Major General von Wurmb, who commanded, on, were quartered in the barracks.... In these barracks lie all the officers of the Linsing and Platte Grenadier Battalions, the Leib, Hereditary Prince, Prince Charles, and Young Lossberg Regiments, a detachment of the von Donop Regiment, a part of the Artillery, and the Hospital, and several English officers.....

"1 April - As a result of the election of a new member of Parliament, which according to the English constitution forbids any soldier being present at the voting place, all the English troops stationed here in the city and lying in the barracks had already marched to Maidstone, eight miles from here day before yesterday and we had to embark today. Upon our arrival we were not only welcomed here by the inhabitants in a polite manner, but also during our entire stay we were treated in the most friendly way, although the English soldiers had to vacate the barracks upon our arrival and were then quartered in the inns of the city. The inhabitants would have gladly kept us with them longer if they had anything to say in the matter, even considering the inconvenience which they had been put to on our account. As a proof of our good discipline, I will note here an extract from the newspaper.

## Enemy Views (1784)

[In English] "Extract from St. James Chronicle from April 1th to April 3d 1784

"The Hessian troops are to embark on the 1th of April. Their Behavior during the Time they have been quartered here, has been sober and orderly. At public Worship they have shown a commendable Degree of Devotion and Attention. Too much cannot be said in Praise of the Civility and Politeness of the Officers, in short, they may, with justice, be proposed as Examples worthy the imitation of our Soldiery.

[Returning to German] "The Platte Grenadier Battalion received two transport ships, the ship *Palliser*, on which were a part of those who came from America, and *Castor*. In addition to these two, the following ships belonged to the fleet: *Mary, Hannah, Betsy, Amphion, Everly, Saucy Ben, Myrtle, Charming Nancy,* and *Admiral Parker*, on which were Major General von Wurmb and the agent, Lieutenant Schaffcoth, of the navy, *Macheral, Fame,* and *Miriam*.

"12 April - As the wind was almost constantly contrary until today, we only sailed from Chatham today. The ship *Betsy*, due to a strong flood tide and a strong wind, ran against a warship and broke off the *Betsy*'s aftermost mast, close to the deck, but caused no other damage. We anchored near Sheerness, where the ship *Neptune* joined us. Colonel von Wurmb was on board that ship with a detachment of Jaegers, who had been quartered in the barracks here.

"14 April - At daybreak, the fleet, now numbering fifteen ships, departed in pleasant, beautiful weather.....

"16 April - We had good, but very weak wind. At seven o'clock in the morning we weighed anchor and set sail.... Toward evening we lost sight of the coast of England, which this evening caused our ship's company a certain amount of melancholy. 'Who knows if we will see it again?' is often heard repeated.....

"20 April - Early this morning the wind veered to the west. It became very strong and drove us into the Weser. About one o'clock we anchored near Bremerhaven. We encountered the ships which brought the Hessians from Portsmouth to Dover, here. The troops, however, had already disembarked and gone on the river to Bremen. After a short, happy, and pleasant voyage from England, we finally arrived , happily, back in Germany, after eight years. It must be conceded by everyone, that we arrived here completely changed.

"22 April - After being mustered, the Jaeger detachment, the Linsing Grenadier Battalion, and the detachment from the Donop Regiment, all of which arrived with us, were embarked on Bremen boats and sailed for Bremen. A strong and contrary wind, however, made it necessary for this division to anchor near us.

"26 April - Although the debarkation of the Platte Grenadier Battalion and the Leib Regiment had been firmly set for the 24th of this month, because of a severe storm, which caused much damage in the area and during which we saw three men from a Bremen boat drown near us, the landing was postponed until today. After being mustered we left the English transport ship for the last time at noon today and entered Bremen boats, which immediately set sail for Bremen on the rising flood tide.....

"29 April - This morning we reached Bremen. We left the boats and embarked on Bremen barges. In Bremen, for the first time, the troops received bread which was made from crushed grain only and very black. Upon receiving it they made a very sour face and appeared much displeased with it. This was the first black, and furthermore crushed grain bread which they had in eight years. Now, for the first time, they clearly understood that they were no longer in America or England. We had five deserters here; the sixth was caught.

"30 April - We departed Bremen and lay to for the night about a mile away. During the departure two men of the Leib Regiment drowned close to the river bank.

"10 May - In the Prussian territories no non-commissioned officer or private was allowed ashore. The Prussians, however, worked to recruit our people. We met several good men from the Hessian regiments which preceded us and who had been recruited at Minden.....

"12 May - We reached Rinteln. Twenty-three foreigners were given their discharges here and they received a half month's pay upon their departure.....

"22 May - At six o'clock in the morning we left the barges and began our march to Kassel on land. The baggage and artillery, which had been brought here yesterday on other ships, was sent forward on the Fulda River. At eleven o'clock the Platte Grenadier Battalion and the Leib Regiment marched onto the parade ground in Kassel. The latter remained in Kassel and the first marched through the Castle Aue

Gate, across the pontoon bridge to Sandershausen, where it was disbanded on the 23rd by Lieutenant General von Gohrs.

"24 May - The grenadier battalion disbanded and ceased to exist, and so this journal ends."

The Hesse-Cassel Jaeger Corps Journal entries also contain a continued record of the corps' travels and experiences during the return to Germany in 1784. "8 January - Pleasant weather. By evening we were opposite Plymouth.....

"14 January - ... All night the wind was strong and on the following morning we found ourselves near the French coast.

"15 January - We passed Dover at one o'clock and dropped anchor at Deal in The Downs at two-thirty in the afternoon...

"16 January - We were ordered to return to Portsmouth where the rest of the Jaegers were to be found. The ship's captain however, explained the situation of his ship, declaring it unseaworthy. We were therefore to sail to Chatham. From today until the 26th, we had continuous northwesterly wind which was so strong that no ship could sail and we were therefore landed despite the very many dangers. Some of our ships tore loose from their anchors and were seriously damaged. Also, we lost one ship near Margate Road at eight o'clock in the evening of the 22nd. However, we had no further misfortunes and were able finally to sail up the Thames River until

"27 January - when we arrived at Sheerness, where we debarked and were given quarters because there was no more room in Chatham. The barracks were very good, but the officers' quarters were bad.

"4 April - The Hessian troops at Chatham and Sheerness went aboard their transport ships and sailed on

"14 April - to Germany, where they arrived after a pleasant voyage on

"20 April - near Bremerhaven, and from which place they were transported aboard Weser boats on the Weser to Kassel.

"17 May - The Jaeger Corps arrived in Kassel, passed in review along with the Linsing Grenadier Battalion and a portion of the Donop Regiment at His Serene Highness' riding school and were then mustered during the afternoon.

"All native Hessians were given leave and those non-Hessians no longer desiring to serve were given their release from service, as well as three months' pay. The entire Jaeger Corps however, was assigned, part in regiments, and those who wished to return to their profession as hunters, received half pay until they could obtain employment as such."

Recknagel and his unit began 1784 lying off Portsmouth, England, and his diary continues from that time. "7 January - Early in the morning the anchor was raised and we sailed into the harbor where we anchored between Portsmouth and Gosport. The captain at once had all the sails taken off in order to enter winter quarters. However, during the evening he received orders to sail out of the harbor at the earliest opportunity, and to sail to our destination according to orders.....

"17 January - The anchor was raised again and we left the harbor during the afternoon....

"23 January - We sailed until opposite Deal, and anchored again on the Thames.....

"27 January - We departed again at seven o'clock. At nine o'clock we ran upon a sandbank. Toward eleven o'clock the wind drove us off again. This evening we anchored near Sheerness....

"28 January - Toward four o'clock we arrived at Chatham, which supposedly is our destination...

"29 January - We were landed and entered the barracks or barracks quarters. Our arrival was accompanied by snow and cold weather, and we remained here during the months of February and March. These barracks are built of two or three story buildings, with alleyways.....

"1 April - We were again embarked on an armed ship. The number of our men was 86, which added to the others already on board, totaled 470 men, not counting the sailors.....

"10 April - The wind was favorable for us and we departed from here at twelve o'clock.....

"14 April - The fleet of fourteen ships set sail. The wind shifted however and during the afternoon we had to sail toward land, the reason being that we could not sail over the sandbanks today. We anchored again about three o'clock near Harwich.....

"16 April - The wind swung to the southwest and although it was weak, the anchor was raised at seven o'clock and we departed from here. During the afternoon the wind grew stronger and we made better headway. Toward evening we entered the sea and lost sight of the English coast.....

Enemy Views (1784)

"20 April We approached ever nearer to land and toward four o'clock in the afternoon happily arrived near Bremerlehe, except that during the entrance a ship rammed us again and that ship broke off its aftermast. Our ship suffered no damage from the incident.....

"24 April - The storm became so strong that almost none of the sailors could remember such. Three anchors had to be put out. Many of the small merchant ships suffered extensive damage. We saw one sink, on which two people were found dead. Reportedly 3,600 thalers were on the ship. This ship was brought to land by the crew of another ship.....

"26 April - We were landed and placed in small boats which were to take us to Bremen....

"30 April - We were transferred into the [Bremen] Boecke [boats] and departed from there today.....

"22 May - We arrived back at Kassel, having completed this voyage from America in six weeks, as we had to waste six months on the way."

Regimental Quartermaster Zinn of the Donop Regiment recorded that unit's return to Germany during 1784. "7 January - At about six o'clock our sailors saw the first land, namely the points in the Channel called Lands End and the Lizard.

"11 January - A cutter came from Portsmouth harbor and gave us an order from the admiral that we were to enter the harbor at Portsmouth, although our first order was to make a rendezvous in The Downs, not far from Deal. Therefore we anchored this afternoon at three o'clock, near Spithead.

"14 January - At nine o'clock this morning we debarked from our ship, as we were the first of our three ships which entered here, by the so-called Point, near Portsmouth, and marched through the city. Three miles distance along the London Road we entered the barracks at Hilsa.

"26 January - Those of the von Donop Regiment on the ship *Montague*, with Major General von Gose, debarked, and all the rest of the men who arrived here on the 23rd of the month arrived here in the above mentioned barracks. The reason this ship arrived later was that it had sailed directly toward Deal, as the designated rendezvous, and had then been ordered to come here. From this ship we learned that the ship *Everly*, with Major von Wurmb, had also arrived at Deal and

557

been ordered to go to Chatham, where they were quartered in the barracks.....

"2 April - At nine o'clock in the morning we were embarked near the Point at Portsmouth, together with some grenadiers from the von Lengercke Battalion, on board the ships *Admiral Barrington* and *Young William*, as follows:

"*Admiral Barrington* - Major General von Gose, Colonel Hinte, Captain Venator, Captain Murhard, Captain von Donop, Lieutenant von Nagel, Lieutenant von Bardeleben, Lieutenant von Westphal (Adjutant General), Lutheran Staff Chaplain Becker, and Regimental Quartermaster Zinn,

"*Young William* - From the von Donop Regiment, Colonel Heymel, Captain [Friedrich Wilhelm] Geisler, Lieutenant von Lepel, Auditor Heymel, Regimental Surgeon Stieglitz; From the Young von Lossberg Regiment, Captain [Louis Marie] von Mallet, Lieutenant [Johann Georg] Wiessenmueller, Lieutenant [Rudolf Wilhelm] Duncker, and Lieutenant [Georg Bernhard] Kersting; From the Platte Grenadier Battalion, Lieutenant [Johannes] Koerber.....

"11 April - About eight o'clock the signal was made to set sail. The agent came out of the harbor and the entire fleet went underway. After we had sailed four days with reasonably favorable wind, we came on

"15 April - at seven-thirty in the evening to anchor in the mouth of the Weser.

"16 April - About four o'clock in the morning we raised anchor and sailed close to Gestendorf near Bremerlehe, where our two ships met those of the von Loewenstein Grenadier Battalion, which had arrived from Dover Castle. After the rest of our entire fleet had arrived and assembled together, all the ships were mustered one after the other, by the muster master in Bremerlehe. After the muster however, we were immediately debarked in small boats from the transport ships and went on

"17 April - at three o'clock in the afternoon, up the Weser to Bremen.....

"22 April - All the troops embarked in the so-called 'Bremer Boecke', from the small boats, downstream from the bridge. The regimental officers were assigned as follows, in Boecke:

Enemy Views (1784)

"Numbers 19 and 20 - Colonel Heymel, Lieutenant von Lepel, Regimental Quartermaster Zinn, and Regimental Surgeon Stieglitz.

"Numbers 21 and 22 - Captain Geisler, Captain Murhard, and Lieutenant Bardeleben.

"Numbers 23 and 24 - Captain Venator, Captain von Donop, and Lieutenant von Nagel, Jr.

"After each Boecke had been assigned the appropriate number of men, they departed....

"23 April - from Bremen, at three o'clock in the afternoon, and most of them traveled as far as wind and weather would allow [each day].

"12 May - We arrived at Hannover-Muenden, where we lay until

"14 May - when we landed, and in accordance with orders received, marched to Kauffungen, Holtze, etc.

"15 May - That part of the regiment that was here was mustered and on

"17 May - after having had that part of the regiment which had remained behind at Chatham until 1784 rejoin us, we marched to Kassel, and into the designated barracks, where the regiment, as it is to be the garrison, is to remain."

J.R. began his 1784 diary entries while lying at anchor at Plymouth on 10 January. "The *Sovereign* arrived in Plymouth harbor with the last division of Hessian troops. It had 200 jaegers on board and had become separated from the fleet during a storm. Lieutenant General Sir Guy Carleton also arrived here.

"14 January - During the afternoon the wind improved. We took a pilot on board and at three o'clock, in company with the *Sovereign*, sailed out of the harbor.....

"16 January - As it is dangerous at night to approach too near to Dover, where the Channel is only seven leagues wide, we took in several sails during the past night and sought to remain in the middle of the Channel by tacking. Toward morning we put on all possible sail so as to profit from the wind and arrived at The Downs before night-fall. About eleven o'clock the wind was so strong that the upper portion of the boltsprit broke off and fell on deck. We sailed eight miles an hour and traveled so rapidly that we arrived at The Downs at three o'clock in the afternoon. We anchored opposite Deal, where we met many ships from all nations. We learned that our first fleet had been here twelve days ago and had gone into quarters at Chatham. The third division has also arrived safely in England. Half an hour after our arrival, the *Ranger* also arrived at The Downs. The ship's captain received orders to sail to the Medway River which lies not far from Chatham.....

"18 January - At five o'clock in the morning we raised the anchor. We passed Ramsgate and Broadstairs, two small country cities. At ten o'clock we dropped anchor not far from the lighthouse at North Foreland. We sailed again at five o'clock and at eight o'clock in the evening anchored near Marketroad. We lay there because of contrary winds and calm until

"23 January - We then ran upon a large sandbank called Bar Sands, on which a large pillar stands. We dropped anchor at three o'clock. Today we traveled within two miles of Sheerness, where a ship with jaegers had arrived and where they were quartered.

"24 January - ... After eleven o'clock we arrived at Chatham, where the other regiments had lain fourteen days in the barracks. It gave them great pleasure to see us. They thought we had been lost because they had heard nothing from us for two months....

"The following regiments were quartered there: The Leib Regiment, Hereditary Prince, Prince Charles, Young von Lossberg, and a company of the Donop Regiment, and the Linsing and Platte Grenadier Battalions.....

"30 January - Our commander received orders to go to London to get money to pay the troops. Therefore we traveled there in the post coach. I found the city quite pleasant. We remained there until 4 February, when we returned with the money to Chatham in a coach escorted by English Cavalry....

"We lay in the barracks during the winter.

"15 April - We marched aboard the ship *Roman Emperor* and sailed immediately to Bremerlehe. Near Bremerlehe we encountered a severe storm during which we expected at any moment to suffer misfortune within sight of our fatherland, because the sailors told us that due to the shoals here we were in great danger. The wind drove some sloops on shore and some grounded. The regiments were taken in river boats from the ocean to Hannover Muenden, from which point each marched to its quarters' city. Our regiment went to Marburg."

Only limited information on the lives of the individual soldiers after the Revolution is recorded in the diaries. Asteroth continued to make a few diary entries for 1784 and 1785, as follows: "16 February 1784 - I received my discharge from Major Biesenrodt. I then worked for a time as a journeyman for my brother Philipp.

"1785 - I became a citizen in the city of Treysa and a master stocking maker.

"22 June [1785] - In the name of God, I announced my intent to marry Anna Catherina Foerster, as I saw that it was not good for a person to live alone, and on

"Tuesday, 26 September - In the presence and with the consent of her parents, we were married."

# Miscellaneous

## Hessian Church Books

The reader could not form the best possible understanding of the former Hessian foes if a few selected entries were not included herewith from the church books maintained by the regimental chaplains. These entries disclose the human side of the soldiers and the joys, sorrows, and hardships of military life during the period of the Revolution. The following entries, only a few as samples, are presented to indicate the religious laws, customs, and attitudes of the Hessians and to provide additional interesting information on the character of the men involved.

Of the church books I have translated, that of Chaplain Coester of the Hesse-Cassel von Donop Regiment contains the most detailed comments when recording his religious activities. Some sample entries concerning marriages performed by Coester include the following:

"Adam Schuchard, sergeant in Lieutenant Colonel Heymel's Company, with Anna Martha Jacob from Homberg, 14 February 1776. N.B. - This Sergeant Schuchard cut his throat in the hospital at New York in 1782.

"Henrich Kehl, corporal in the Leib Company, with Maria Sabina Fuchs, daughter of Pastor Fuchs from Remsfeld. Homberg, 29 February 1776.

"Johannes [Adam] Sustmann, musketeer in Colonel von Gose's Company, with Maria Elisabeth Wiederhold, daughter of the deceased resident Reinhard Wiederhold, born in Udenborn, District of Borken. Married in America on New York Island, in the camp at Blumenthal, on 20 November 1776. N.B. - Due to insufficient funds the groom could not pay the usual eight Reichsthalers. Colonel [David Ephraim] von Gose promised that it would be paid later.

"At this point is Jarock, runner for Colonel von Donop. He married a girl from Brunswick, in America, with the consent of his chief, at Kreton in the spring of 1777. The wife died at Brunswick on Long Island in December 1779. N.B. - This woman died at Bushwick in the fall of 1779.

"On 31 August [1777], in the camp at Head of Elk, I married Johann Letzerich, non-commissioned officer of Captain [Henrich Friedrich] Wachs' 1st Company of the Hereditary Prince Regiment, and Martha Wacker, former wife of Corporal [Georg] Wacker, killed in action.[51]

"On 15 September 1777 I married the Hessian Jaeger Conrad Sackert of Major von Prueschenck's Company and Carolina Wetzler of Sebbeterode. This took place in the camp not far from Dilworth in Pennsylvania. N.B. - Major Prueschenck promised to collect the consent money and give it to me. N.B. - Six days later the woman was chased out of camp for being a prostitute.

"On 19 December 1777, at Philadelphia, I married Grenadier Abraham Loehler of the von Lengercke Grenadier Battalion and the young girl Elisabeth Well from Hesse-Hanau. The first marriage which I performed as a result of my duty with the von Lossberg Regiment in the winter huts at Marsten's Wharf, 1778-1779.

"After requesting permission of Colonel von Loos and the approval of auditor Heymel, I married the following persons in the winter huts at Hellgate on 17 January 1779:

"Fusilier Friedrich Busch of the von Lossberg Regiment, born in Schermbach in Bueckeburg, 24 years old, and Wilhelmina Catherina, nee Ohm, widow of the dead Fusilier Ludwig Clausing of the mentioned von Lossberg Regiment. The groom was a foreigner and therefore did not have to pay the eight thaler fee. N.B. - The bride lost her husband only 21 weeks previously, therefore I could not marry here because of possible pregnancy, as cited in the law covering a year's mourning, but Captain Hanstein and several other officers convinced me that the mentioned Wilhelmina Catherina, following the death of her previous husband two weeks thereafter - had given birth, so because of the unavoidable circumstances of the war, I made no objection to the marriage.

At "Flushing on Long Island, 1 January 1781, after Carl Ludolph, Grenadier of the von Lossberg Fusilier Regiment, born at Oldenburg, District of Schaumburg, received permission of his commander, Lieutenant Colonel [Wilhelm] von Loewenstein, to marry the widow Rosina Charlotta Leytmeier, also born in Oldenburg, and after paying the eight Reichsthalers and swearing an oath about his single status, the mentioned grenadier, after complying with the above requirements, was married on the above date to his bride without further objections. N.B. - The widow, whose former husband had been killed during the siege of Charleston in April 1780, had not yet completed her year of mourning, but because she had not accompanied him [to South Carolina], there was no possibility of her being pregnant from her former husband.

"New York, 13 January 1783, von Donop Regiment,... after Henrich Merten, soldier serving in Major von Kutzleben's Company received permission to marry, paid the eight Reichsthalers in cash for the maintenance of the Carlshaven Hospital for his first marriage, been approved by the auditor, and also been warned about swearing a false oath, and sworn that he was single, I married him to his betrothed bride Anna Gerdruth Villgraff, nee Schick, born in Abteroda, District of Witzenhausen, widow of the dead Grenadier Erhard Villgraff of the von Linsing Grenadier Battalion, after being shown the death certificate. N.B. - I gave each of them a marriage certificate at New York on 14 January 1783, as proof of the marriage.

"Upon having received permission, as well as having taken an oath that he was single, and because there was no other objection, the soldier Michael Bernhard of the Leib Company of the von Donop Regiment, a foreigner born at Schwicks in Lotheringen, was married by a priest to his betrothed bride, Charlotte de la Lime, daughter of Mr. Jean Baptiste La Lime, a resident of Quebec. This took place at New York on 2 February 1783. N.B. - Both were Catholic.

"On 26 July 1783 I married, upon presentation of permission to marry from His Excellency Commanding Lieutenant General von Lossberg, Casimir Theodor Goerke, lieutenant of artillery, with the young lady, Elisabeth Roosewel, born at New York."

Although no church book has been found for the Waldeck Regiment, Chaplain Philipp Waldeck commented in a diary entry of 14 December 1777 on one wedding, which he performed. "This man [an English commissary by the name of Osstin, had previously asked me to perform the marriage ceremony, but his bride was too anxious and in the meantime had gotten herself a bit pregnant. This necessitated a slight delay of the ceremony until today, when both the baptism of the child and the marriage ceremony took place. It is customary among the English, and therefore among the Americans, also, for the minister to kiss the bride at the conclusion of the ceremony. Then she kisses the groom and the rest of the guests."

Coester also recorded births and baptisms in his church book, including: "Hamilton Carl Henrich Haemer - Johannes Haemer's musketeer in the Lieutenant Colonel's Company, legitimate son, was born to Maria Elisabeth Haemer, nee Lohr, on 23 March 1776 at three o'clock in the morning on our trip to America, on the Atlantic Ocean, aboard the English transport ship *Jenny*. The ship's captain, William Hamilton, Lieutenant Colonel Heymel, and Lieutenant von Bardeleben were asked to be sponsors. The ship's captain was the first but because he was a Scotsman and a Presbyterian, he did not wish to hold the child to be baptized. His excuse was that it was not customary in his country, and second, as he was always at sea, he could not fill the duty which a sponsor has. This excuse seemed valid to us. Lieutenant Colonel Heymel therefore held the child to be baptized and gave the child the name Hamilton Carl Henrich. The name Hamilton it received from the ship's captain, over his objection, because he said if he should get to Hesse, or if the child came to England, I will recognize his name and then I will take care of him. This festive occasion was conducted while the sea was rather calm on the following day, the 24th of March. He was the first child that I baptized and possibly the first Hessian to be baptized aboard a transport ship on the Atlantic Ocean. N.B. - The child and his mother died in the autumn of 1777.

"Catherina Elisabeth - illegitimate daughter of Musketeer Adam Sustmann, of Colonel von Gose's Company, born at Wabern, and Maria Elisabeth Wiederhold, born at Gudenborn, District of Borken on 6 November 1776, at seven o'clock in the evening in the camp on the island of New York, and baptized on the ninth of the month. The sponsor was Catherina Elisabeth, wife of Corporal Johann Hassenpflug of Colonel von Gose's Company. N.B. - The woman, left behind, I do not know why, by her intended husband, who had promised marriage, had followed. She arrived with our second fleet, sought out her husband-to-be, and, as she set her first foot in his tent, gave birth to a young daughter. N.B. - Died at Philadelphia.

"Johann Friedrich - legitimate son of Peter Paul Wirth, field jaeger of the Hessian Field Jaeger Corps, and his wife Gertruth, born at Nastaetten, District of Rewinfels, was born to the world at Philadelphia on 30 December 1777 at three o'clock in the afternoon. I baptized him on 5 January 1778. Sponsors were Johann Ewald, captain of the Jaeger Company, and Lieutenant Friedrich Adam Julius von Wangenheim, Hessian officer of the Jaeger Corps.

"Bertold - born on 25 October 1778; baptized 1 January 1779. Father Christian Scheele, musketeer in Colonel von Muenchhausen's Company [of the von Truembach Regiment]; mother Elisabeth Bolt, from Hofgeismar; sponsor Berthold Koch of Captain Scheer's Company.

"Miss Sarah Patterson - a lawful daughter of Mr. Stephan Patterson, assistant in the General Commissary Department in North America, and of his wedded wife Mrs. Sarah Patterson, was born on the 5th day of June 1782 and christened by my ministry on the 28th of June 1782. Mr. Tuck, lieutenant of the British Legion and Mrs. Falkener, both performing the duty of Goships. The place where Miss Sarah Patterson is born and baptized is called Harlem Valley, ten miles north of New York. I gave the certificate on 22 September 1782. Mortua est. [This entry is in English in the original. Gossip, not goship, is a no longer used form meaning godparent. The 'Mortua est' is lined out in the original.]

"Baptismal certificate issued 15 May 1785. Bernhard Vogt - legitimate son, was born during the night of 9 to 10 July 1782 in the camp near Fort Knyphausen, and baptized by me on the twelfth day of the same month and year. Jacob Vogt, a Catholic, born at Fritzlar and presently a soldier in the Leib Company of the von Donop Regiment, was the father and Christiana Sophia, born at Hannover Minden, was the mother. Bernhard Naumann, soldier of the same company and born at Allmuthshausen, District of Homberg, in Hesse, was the baptismal witness. N.B. - Jacob Vogt, a very bad individual, much given to gambling and drinking, deserted from our service at New York in the year 1783.

"Henriette Goerke - the legitimate daughter of Field Artillery Lieutenant Casimir Theordor Goerke, and his lawful wife, Mrs. Elisabeth Goerke, born at New York, was born near Fort Knyphausen, according to the father's statement, on 16 September 1783, and baptized at the same place by me on 16 October 1783. Mrs. Margaretha Cosine, wife of Mr. Cosine, a lawyer at New York, and the gentleman Lieutenant Colonel Hans Henrich Eitel, commander of the Hessian

Artillery in North America, were the solicited sponsors. N.B. - Seven weeks and four days [later she died ?].

"Anna Catherina - legitimate daughter of Drummer Adam Schmeck, of Colonel Heymel's Company [of the von Donop Regiment], and his wife, Anna Martha, was born at New York on 15 October 1783, and baptized on the nineteenth of the same month. Sponsor: Reitze Amthauer, soldier of the same company, held the child for baptism in the name of his sister Anna Catherina, from Waltersbrueck. Died on the 21st of the same month, [and in Latin - may the ground rest lightly over her.]

"Andreas Maerthen - a legitimate son, was born to wedded parents at Chatham, England, on 15 February 1784. The father was a private soldier in the von Kutzleben Company of the von Donop Regiment by the name of Henrich Maerthen, from Zwesten, District of Borken, and the mother's name was Anna Gertruth, born at Ederode [Epterode ueber Witzenhausen], District of Witzenhausen. On 17 February 1784 the child was presented for baptism in the name of Jesus by the honorable member of the von Donop Regiment, von Kutzleben Company, by the name of Andreas Carteuser, born at Wernswig, District of Homberg.

"Elisabeth - a legitimate daughter of the corporal by the name of Johannes Zertz of Major General von Gose's Company of the Prince Charles Regiment, and his wife, nee Pflueger, born at Wickerode in the District of Kauffungen, was born in the Lisboner Brewery on the North River at New York on 3 March 1783 and baptized by me on the fifth of the same month and year. The godmother was the wife of Jost Eichlers, musketeer in Colonel von Lengercke's Company of the same regiment, Elisabeth Eichlers, born at Kreuzberg, District of Vacha [Philippsthal].

"Friedrich Henrich - illegitimate child, born to Sally Thomson, daughter of Mr. Thomson, a resident of Philadelphia. The father supposedly is Captain Christoph Friedrich von Waldenfels, commander of the princely Ansbach Jaeger Corps. The infant was born to the world on 9 June 1779, not far from Kingsbridge in America, and baptized 5 July 1779. Sponsor was Captain Johann Friedrich Henrich Lorey, chief of a company of the illustrious Hessian Field Jaeger Corps. Baptismal witnesses were Captain Venator of the von Donop Regiment and Lieutenant Ebenauer of the Ansbach Field Jaeger Corps.

N.B. - The baptismal certificate was issued by the von Linsing Grenadier Battalion 25 August 1781.

"Conrad - legitimate son, was born on 23 September [1779 ?] on New York Island, and baptized on the 26th of the same month and year. The father was a private soldier in Colonel Hinte's Company of the von Donop Regiment by the name of Henrich Bierhenne. The mother was Anna Martha, nee Wiegandt, from Falkenberg, District of Homberg. Conrad Scheffer, non-commissioned officer of the same company was the sponsor. Baptismal certificate issued 28 October 1783. The mother went with her second husband, Doenstaedt, a non-commissioned officer discharged by the von Donop Regiment, to Nova Scotia.

"Catherina Charlotta - an illegitimate child, was born at New York on 7 September 1779, and at the request of Lieutenant [Carl Friedrich] Fuehrer, baptized by me on 13 January 1780. The mother, a pleasant young girl, whose fate touched me, was named Cornelia, daughter of Mr. Bayeix, a citizen of New York. She claimed the father was Lieutenant [Louis] Descourdes of the Hereditary Prince Regiment. He had caused her downfall with a promise of marriage - nothing new in America, unfortunately. - In 1783 the father took his discharge, married the girl, and went to Nova Scotia.

"Andreas - an illegitimate son, was born at New York on 17 April 1780 to Barbara Rheider, born at Rhode Island and the daughter of an Anabaptist by the name of Rheider. The mentioned Barbara said Lieutenant Dietzel of the Hessian Artillery was the father and added that she had a child by him previously which was still living. N.B. - She calls herself Mrs. Dietzel, because she says, her marriage was made in Heaven. A soldier of the Leib Company of the von Donop Regiment named Andreas Zuelch was the sponsor on 20 April 1780 at New York. Therefore another pair of wretched boys and girls more in the world!

"Therefore, take care and do not be fooled by a man who promises to marry you! N.B. - Father and child died at New York in 1781.

"Maria Elisabeth - daughter of the Hessian provisions administrator by the name of Johannes Ebert, born at Wabern in the District of Homberg, and his wife, Maria Elisabeth, nee Pelotrow, from New York, in America, was born at New York on 2 October

1780, and baptized by me at the request of both parents on the thirteenth of the same month and year. The mother herself acted as sponsor and the baptismal witness was a good friend of theirs by the name of Samuel Comphiel, a citizen and resident of New York. N.B. - This Maria Elisabeth, wife of the provisions administrator Ebert, was confirmed at New York on 25 September 1780, after being instructed by me for a period of eight weeks in the Reformed religion.

"Philipp Adam - legitimate son of Christian Conrad Rummel, field jaeger in Ansbach service, born in Ansbach, and in Captain von Roeder's Company, and his wife, Margaretha Barbara Rincks, also born in Ansbach, was born at Flushing on Long Island on 18 January 1781, and baptized by me on the twentieth of the same month and year. The sponsor was Philipp Adam Wenig, private jaeger in Captain von Waldenfels' Company, also in Ansbach service.

"Maria Amalia - legitimate daughter of Hautboist Johann Ludwig Schmidt of the von Donop Regiment, born at Fuhlen in the District of Oldenburg, and his wife Maria Catherina, nee Brandenburg, from Hausbergen, not far from Prussian-Muenden, was born on York Island during the afternoon of 13 April [1781], and baptized on the fifteenth of the same month and year. Otto Friedrich Krueschel, sergeant-major of Major von Wurmb's Company, was the sponsor in his wife, Maria Amalia's name. N.B. - The mother died on [blank] September 1781 of [Slux]. The child was placed in a nursery at our cost because his father had nothing. - The child died 2 October 1781.

"Johann Georg Frey - legitimate son of Georg Adolph Frey, born at Groszenkeder in the Schwarzburg, presently servant of Major General Baron von Gose. The mother of the newly born was Margaretha, nee Rosenthal, from Vacha. According to the statement, the child was born on 6 October 1781, at four p.m., on York Island at the so-called Reed house. Upon request, I baptized it on 17 October 1781, with Johann Georg Wagner, servant of His Excellency, Lieutenant General von Knyphausen, as sponsor.

"On 9 September 1776 I was asked by a friend to baptize the five day old child of an inhabitant on Long Island, because the pastor had joined the rebels. I made some objections because I had not acquired sufficient proficiency in the English language to make myself understood to the people. However, the persistent entreaties of the parents overcame my objections. I went there and baptized the child according to our practice, with the regimental surgeon in attendance. The child was a girl. The sponsor was named Elisabeth Plaumens and named it Merry [Mary ?].

"The father was a poor shoemaker named Thomas Pauer; the mother Isabella Pauer. The place where they lived was a pleasant and lively little village directly opposite New York by the name of Brooklyn Ferry. Father and mother wept for joy over their good fortune that now their beloved child had been taken into the Christian fold by the bond of baptism. They spoke continual praises for me. And, as they had nothing else with which to show their appreciation, I had to drink a half glass of wine with the woman who had just had the delivery."

Chaplain Coester also performed confirmations, including the following. "On 20 October 1782, I confirmed Elisabeth Lentz, from Volmarshausen, a legitimate daughter of Johannes Lentz, private soldier in the D'Angelelli Regiment. According to the testimony, this Elisabeth was fifteen years old. She received a half year of instruction in the Christian religion from me. I conducted this holy instruction in the Morris house on the island of York [Manhattan], in North America, in the presence of Major General von Gose and various officers of the Prince Charles Regiment. - Two dollars, certificate 21 January 1786.

"Friderica Rosina Jacobi - daughter of the dead Corporal Friedrich Ludwig Jacobi, who had been in Prussian service, was born on 17 May 1770 at Koenigsberg. Her mother, Catherina Friderica, born at Ulm, was married to the soldier Christoph Stange, from Lochten, District of Finenberg, in the Hildesheim Monastery, of the von Donop Regiment. [Friderica Rosina] was confirmed by me, in the Christian religion, on 18 March 1784 at Chatham in England.

"On Easter, 31 March 1777, I confirmed two lads, who had already been taken on by the von Minnegerode Battalion as fifers. Both were children with good spirits and healthy intellects. I had instructed them in religion for nine weeks and never worked with greater pleasure than with these children. I easily gave them the basis for our religion, allowed them to memorize some, and how supple the human heart can be when a person has found the right way! They learned the words of consolation from the Bible and also the five articles without being forced to do so by me. 'It is good for you', I often said, 'My children. It will give you courage in danger and consolation in death, if you also keep it in mind.' That is what I said and those few words were enough to impress their tender souls. They gave me great pleasure here. How great it will be in the hereafter. May my future students give me the joy which these first ones gave me! The older was Johannes Krueck, born at Rinteln in 1763. His father was a grenadier in Captain von Wilmowsky's Company, named Henrich Krueck. The other [Nothing more follows.]

"On 19 May 1779 I confirmed a youth of Captain von Alten-Bockum's Company of the von Lossberg Fusilier Regiment, at New York. His name was Friedrich Heidenreich. He was born at Rinteln and was fourteen years old.

"On 10 May 1780 I confirmed a young girl, thirteen years old, at New York, in the presence of her parents. Her name was Anna Elisabeth Gleim, born at Melsungen on the Fulda. The father was Johannes Gleim, born at Hersfeld and a fifer in Captain von Mallet's Company of the von Mirbach Regiment. The mother, Elisabeth, nee Pflueger, was born at Rotenburg. N.B. - This girl gave me much pleasure, not only because of her eagerness to learn, but also because of her outward decorum, not a little joy.

"Martha Elisabeth Schaeffer - from Harle, District of Flensberg, who was confirmed by Chaplain Kuemmell at Rhode Island in 1778, because she could show no confirmation testimonial, was privately examined, and based on the remarks of her then master, the master baker Ostwald, of New York, she was admitted to the sacrament. Certificate issued 12 May 1780. N.B. - The parents are: Father: Henrich Schaeffer, sergeant in the von Huyn Regiment - Mother: Anna Elisabeth, nee Ditmar, from Singlis, District of Borken. Comment - Chaplain Kuemmel was at Charleston with the von Huyn Regiment at that time.

"On the second Easter Day, that is 1 April 1782, I confirmed Friedrich Almeroth, born at Homberg in Hesse in March 1768, after he gained the proper knowledge of the Christian religion, following his having reached his fourteenth year, in an open assembly at Marsten's Wharf on the island of New York. The father was the captain-at-arms of the Leib Company of the von Donop Regiment by the name of Georg Almeroth. The mother was Egidia Almeroth, born at Hersfeld."

Penance requirements were also noted by Coester. "Johann Adam Sustmann and his bride Marie Elisabeth Wiederhold stated their repentance to me on 20 November 1776, when I married them in America.

"At Philadelphia, on 28 February 1778, Musketeer Johannes Schneider, of Colonel Hinte's Company of the von Donop Regiment, born at Felsberg, came to me and said that he had committed an act of fornication with Elisabeth Assesmann from Felsberg. He was sorry for having committed the sin and promised to marry the unfortunate girl upon his return. As he then took communion, I dismissed payment of the penance.

"On 30 October 1780, the Artillery Sergeant Johann Henrich Brethauer, of the Leib Company, born at Klein Almerode, came to me and said that he had made an American girl, Polly Tiezen, from New York, pregnant, and his child was still living. If he could be given permission, he would marry the woman, but in any case, would always support the child and its mother.

"Grenadier Burghard Zehr of the von Knyphausen Regiment, born at Roelshausen, District of Neukirchen, declared that he had made a girl from New York pregnant, that he was truly sorry for his sin, and that to clear his conscience would like to have communion. As he swore on his oath to be more careful in the future and especially promised to conduct himself as a proper soldier, I allowed him to take communion with a clear conscience."

Deaths were also recorded in the church book, as follows. "On 5 January 1782 Conrad Giese from Hundshausen in the Judicial District of Jesberg, died. During his final years, he was the cook for Colonel von Heymel, the commander of the von Donop Regiment. I was not told his age. His end was the easy death of a Christian, who trusted his Redeemer to take him to a better world. He took communion twelve hours before his death."

## The Anhalt-Zerbst Church Book

Chaplain Braunsdorf of the Anhalt-Zerbst contingent maintained a less detailed, but more extensive church book. The church book, which is apparently the only known document written by an Anhalt-Zerbst participant in the American Revolution, provides the reader with an understanding of the rigors of eighteenth century military life, as may be noted from the following sampling of entries. "Koch, Andreas - Corporal, Green Grenadier Company, from Anhalt-Zerbst, married Sophia Schmidt, from Zerbst, on 21 February 1778 on the march at the first night's quarters at Roslau."

"Heyderich, Christoph - Private, Rauschenplat's Company, from Berghel, married Dorothea Maria Nohr, from Sondershausen, on 27 February 1778 on the march at Boherna in Saxony."

"Ludewig, Anthon - Carpenter, Green Grenadier Company, married Anna Magdalena Nohr, from Sondershausen [sister of the above ?], on 8 March 1778 at Klein-Bruechter in Schwarzburg."

"Steineck, Johann Georg Christoph - Private, Piquet's Company, from Frankenhausen, married Anna Catherina Crass, widow, on 4 June 1778 on the transport ship *Sally* in the English harbor at Torbay."

"Scheck, Bernhard - Sergeant-major, Piquet's Company, from Jever, ... married the widow Christiana Sophia Rosensteil on 30 December 1778 in the barracks at Quebec."

"Ruff, Michael - Private, Rauschenplat's Company, from Petersen in the Palatinate, married the widow Juliana Dorothea Preiss, Catholic, on 20 April 1779 in the barracks at Quebec after receiving special permission."

"Piquet, [Carl Friedrich] - Grenadier Captain, from Muempelgard in Switzerland, was married to a [Miss] Skeene, daughter of the English Colonel Skeene[52] by the English Chaplain Montmolin, on 26 April 1779 at Quebec."

"Nuppenau, Johann August Zacharias - Captain-lieutenant, from Zerbst, married Marie Riverin, Catholic, daughter of the deceased merchant Riverin from Quebec, on 12 December 1780 at Mon Loretto/Quebec."

"Winter, Martin - Private, Rauschenplat's Company, from Wisbaden [Wiesbaden ?], married the widow Sophia Buhlmann, from

Stade, on 4 January 1783 at Riviere Quelle/Quebec."

The following are a sampling of the sixty births and baptisms recorded by Braunsdorf between the time of marching out of Anhalt-Zerbst and the unit's return to Germany. "Matthaes, Johann August - 23 February 1778 at Brunis in Saxony. Father: Private Matthaes of Schwarzburg's Company."

"Wenzel, Johann Christian Heinrich - 13 June 1778 on board the transport ship *Present Succession* on the high seas. Father: Private Wenzel of Schwarzburg's Company."

"Family name unknown, Philipp Georg - 20 September 1778 at Quebec. Father: A butcher's servant for a butcher by the name of Huebsch, who is the sponsor. [The underlining of Georg in the original, in an unknown hand, as if it were the family name, is false, according to the German editors of the manuscript as Braunsdorf left an obvious space in the entry.]"

Wille, Johann Julius Georg - 21/23 September 1778 at Quebec.[53] Father: Private Wille of the Brunswick troops."

"Mast, Johann Martin Alexander - 3/7 December 1779 at St. Thomas by the parish priest Msr. Mesonbash. Father: Private Mast of Wietersheim's Company."

"Schoell, Carl Friederich von - 12/14 February 1780 at Quebec, from concubinage. Father: Captain von Schoell, of the Hesse-Hanau Regiment; Mother: 'A soldier's woman from the Brunswick troops, who lived with him as his mistress'."

"Paul, Christiana Elisabeth - 16 May 1780 at Quebec by the English city clergyman de Montmolin. Father: Private Paul of Wietersheim's Company."

"Rogge, Carl Michael Philipp, and "Rogge, Johanna Lena [Magdalena] Dorothea, [twins] - 17 May 1780 on board ship on the voyage from New York to Quebec, during the transport of Brunswick prisoners. [Baptized] 16 July 1780 in camp at Quebec. Father: Private Carl Rogge of the Brunswick troops."

"Piquet, Maria Elisabeth - 9/14 June 1780 in Quebec. Father; brigade major and Captain Piquet. [See marriage above.]"

"Nuppenau, Friederica Augusta, and "Nuppenau, Marie Charles [twins], 28 June/3 July 1781 at Nicolet. Father: Captain-lieutenant Nuppenau. [See marriage above.]"

"Piquet, Philipp Friedrich Carl - 13/17 September 1781 at Becancour/Trois Rivieres. Father: brigade maajor and Captain Piquet.

"Dogles, Robert - 3 December1781/25 February 1782 at Point aix Trembles. Father: Private Robert Dogles [probably Douglas] of the English 53rd Regiment."

"Nuppenau, Augusta - 24/26 October 1782 at Quebec. Father: Captain Nuppenau."

"Wolff, Friederich Benjamin Carl Hero - 20/23 August 1783 on board the ship *Hero* on the return voyage from America to Germany."

"Nuppenau, Timon Friedrich August - 21/25 February 1784 at Jever. Father: Captain Nuppenau." [Born after the return to Germany."

Chaplain Braunsdorf also recorded the deaths of 130 men, 7 wives, and 23 children and this unit was never in combat. Deaths resulted not only from natural causes, but also from child-birth, suicide, and even murder. Sample entries include, "Johannes Berges died on 16 March [1778] on the march to Lamspringe in Hildesheim. He was the provost for the Anhalt-Zerbst contingent, and of the Evangelical faith. His age was unknown."

"Johann Crass died on 26 April [1778] aboard the ship *Sally* and was buried near Glueckstadt in Denmark. [Now in Germany.] He belonged to Colonel von Rauschenplat's Company. Born in Mainz, he was of the Catholic faith and a wigmaker by trade. He had served two years and eight months in the military and was 42 years old. [See widow's marriage above.]"

"Anna Catharina Coje, nee List, died 26 August [1778] on the *Antelope* and was buried on land the next day. She was the wife of the Grenadier Adam Coje of Captain von Wietersheim's Company and had been born in Dessau at the Red Estate. Her father, a day laborer by the name of Christoph List, is still living. She was 25 years old."

"Carolina Sophia Margaretha Andress died on 31 August [1778] after being baptized in an emergency ceremony on *The Rising Sun* and was buried on land. She was the one day old daughter of Grenadier Christian Andress of Captain Piquet's Company."

"Frau Brandt, wife of Private Andreas Brandt of Captain Cogel's Company, died 8 September [1778] as she was about to debark from *The Rising sun* and was buried at Quebec. She had been born at Grathin, was of the Evangelical faith, and 35 years old."

## Enemy Views (Miscellaneous)

"Barbara Henkelmann, daughter of Private Veit Henkelmann of Major von Rauschenplat's Company, died on the *Wisk* on 29 August [1778]. She was one year and six months old.

"Johann Preiss, from the Tyrol, died on 11 September [1778] in the hospital Hotel de Dieu at Quebec. He was a member of Captain Piquet's Grenadier Company and had previously served the King of France for nine years. He was of the Catholic faith, a mason by trade, and had served in the Anhalt-Zerbst military since 5 September 1775. He was forty years old." [See marriage of his widow above.]

"Heinrich Fischer, born at Seiferode in Darmstadt, died on 13 September [1778] in the general hospital at Quebec and was buried in the Protestant portion of the cemetery at that place. He belonged to Colonel von Rauschenplat's Company, was of the Evangelical faith, and a tailor by trade. He was nineteen years and eight months old."

"Gottfried Grachelitz, of he Jaeger Corps, fell to his death from the window of the uppermost floor of the barracks on 16 September [1778]. Born in Basen in Schweidnitz, he was of the Evangelical faith, and a trained hunter. He was thirty years old."

"Johann Gottlieb Brandt, the small son of Private And. Brandt of Captain Gogel's Company, died 20 September [1778] in the barracks at Quebec. He had been born on 28 December 1777 at Zerbst." [See mother's death above.]

"Johann Georg Wilhelm von Zawadsky, corporal in the Anhalt-Zerbst Jaeger Corps, died 1 October [1778] in the hospital Hotel de Dieu at Quebec. Born at Zahne in Wittenberg, he was a trained hunter and had entered the military service on 30 October 1777. He was 27 years old."

"Christian Wenzel, the small son of Private Daniel Wenzel ... died 3 October [1778]. He had been born 4 February 1776 at Armstadt in Schwarzburg-Sondershausen."

"Friedrich Wenzel, son of Private Daniel Wenzel of Captain Prince of Schwarzburg's Company, died 12 October [1778] in the general hospital at Quebec. He was four months old." [See birth of Johann Christian Friedrich Wenzel above.]

"Margaretha Wenzel, wife of Private Daniel Wenzel of Captain Prince of Schwarzburg's Company, died 16 October [1778] in the general hospital at Quebec. Born in Nuernberg, she was 38 years old." [See death of two sons above.]

"Barbara Henkelmann, wife of Private Veit Henkelmann of Major von Rauschenplat's Company, died 25 October [1778] in the hospital at Quebec. Born at Germershausen in Wuerzburg, she was of the Catholic faith and 26 years old." [See death of daughter above.]

"Maria Christiana Coje, the only daughter of Private Coje of Captain von Wietersheim's Grenadier Company, died 30 October [1778] in the barracks at Quebec. She was one year and nine months old." [See death of mother above.]

"Ludewich Rosenstiehl, 1st sergeant of Captain von Wietersheim's Grenadier Company, died 3 November [1778] in the barracks at Quebec. Born in Holtzhalleben in Schwurzburg-Sondershausen, he was of the Evangelical faith and a tailor by trade. He left a wife without children behind and was 28 years old." [See marriage of his widow above.]

"Johann Adam was murdered at his post on the ship wharf at Quebec on the night of 5 November [1778] and thrown into the St. Lawrence River. His murderers have not been caught, although some sailors were arrested. From all indications it must have been sailors because his post had the task of preventing sailors from going to or coming from the ships after ten o'clock at night, which had been a daily source of friction. His head wound was apparently the result of being hit with a bottle as glass was found in his skull. He was a member of Major von Rauschenplat's Company. Born in Copenhagen, he was of the Evangelical faith and 21 years old."

"Michael Vollrath, drowned on the afternoon of 4 July [1779] after saying that he was going to bathe in the St. Charles River near Quebec. It is not clear whether he drowned with intent or by accident, but the first seems the case as the river in the area where he was found is not deep enough for someone to easily drown therein. He was buried without ceremony by the regiment in the English cemetery. He was a member of Captain Gogel's Company, of the Evangelical faith, and a linen weaver by trade. Born in Rodleben in Schwarzburg, he was 24 years old."

"Gottfried Wegener, of Captain Gogel's Company, hanged himself on the grounds of the barracks at Quebec on 5 July [1779]. Born at Potsdam, he was of the Evangelical faith and a rope-maker by trade. He was 22 years old. He was buried quietly outside the churchyard by the regimental servants."

"Christian Grashoff, of the brigadier general, Colonel von Rauschenplat's Company, died 9 October [1779] while working on the defenses near Quebec. He was suddenly struck by a stone during the blasting, in which he was engaged, and killed. He was buried in the English cemetery at Quebec with full military honors. Born at Quedlinburg, he was of the Evangelical faith and nineteen years old."

"Oldmann Frerichs died aboard ship on the St. Lawrence River 5 October [1779], and was buried on land. The ship was carrying the first recruit transport [for the Anhalt-Zerbst troops] from Germany. He was born at Sillenstaedt in Jever, of the Evangelical faith, and twenty years old."

"Johann Lein, a member of Captain Prince von Schwarzburg's Company, froze to death during the night of 23 January [1780] in the parish of St. Francois in the district of Quebec. He had been at the canteen, had something to drink, but according to his comrades was not drunk. During suddenly occurring bad weather he could not find his house and froze to death on the street. Born in the village of Wetzhausen in Greater Darmstadt, he was of the Evangelical faith, and a tailor by trade. He was 28 years old."

"Friederich Wendt, committed suicide with his own weapon in the garden of his host in the parish of St. Pierre in the district of Quebec on 17 February [1780]. He had previously attempted suicide in the garden but been prevented from doing so. For that he had been punished with a demotion which caused him severe depression and made him very sick. He was given his former rank and restored to duty and conducted himself in a proper manner, except that at times he complained about his sorry fate, because he had been a student in the orphan's home in Halle. He wished to spend this time studying but was prevented from doing so. His depression returned suddenly while in the country, so that he silently loaded his weapon and upon leaving the room of his host, said that he was going bird shooting, but then shot himself in the garden. He was a corporal in Captain Gogel's Company, born at Erlangen in Bayreuth. He was 25 years old."

"Christoph Lindauer drowned on 30 April [1780] in the South River in the parish of St. Thomas in the district of Quebec. This parish is divided lengthwise by the said river and settled on both sides so that one-half of the people, each time when they wish to go to church, must cross the river. Such was the case for this unfortunate individual.

He wished to cross the river to where his quarters lay, but the river was swollen by the heavy thawing and by nature was exceptionally rapid. The wind was extra strong and the soldiers were afraid, but because the inhabitants, who knew the nature of the river best, traveled with them, they entered the canoe, a rather frightful vessel cut from a tree and, if one can picture it, very much like a trough. When they reached the middle of the river, which was about 500 yards wide, the raging current tipped the canoe over and all the occupants were thrown into the water. Two farmers and two soldiers saved themselves, but this unfortunate individual and one of the local residents gave up their lives. He was a member of brigade major Captain Piquet's Grenadier Company, born in Erfurth, He was of the Catholic faith, married, and had left his wife behind in Jever. He was buried in a festive military style in the parish cemetery at the specific written request of one of the Catholic inhabitants of the parish by the name of Mesonbash to the commander, because Lindauer was of the Catholic faith."

"Note [written by Chaplain Braunsdorf] - I should note here that as long as we were in this land, and even while in the barracks, no one not of the Catholic religion could be buried in a cemetery, as the inhabitants were too scrupulous to allow that. Therefore a satisfactory place had to be located each time, where the body could be interred. Usually the selected spot was where a crucifix had been erected and where, in most cases, an encircling fence had been placed. Although this was not allowed, either, as we never asked, there was never a complaint and no refusal...."

"Maria Elisabeth Piquet, the only daughter of the brigade major, Captain Piquet, died 19 June [1780] at Quebec. She was ten days old." [See birth above.]

"Ferdinand Fritz, a member of Major von Rauschenplat's Company, drowned in the South River in St. Thomas on 25 June [1780]. He was drunk and waded several times through the mentioned river, where it was shallow, and each time crossed successfully. Despite the frequent warnings of his comrades he continued to do so until he missed the shallow portion, fell into a hole, which had a whirlpool, of which there were many in the river, was torn from the firm footing, and drowned therein, without hope of rescue. After several days his body was found some miles downstream at St.

Pierre and quietly buried. Born at Adelberg in Wuerttenberg, he was of the Evangelical faith, and a miller by trade. He was 26 years old."

"Friederich Krause, after ten o'clock on the evening of 5 September [1780], shot himself with the rifle of Captain Runkel, whose servant he was, in Runkel's tent in the camp at Point Levi. At that time he had an attack of melancholy because when he had been the servant of a man in Paris, that man had been stabbed to death, for which Krause was partially responsible. After the tent was taken down, he was buried the same night by the regimental servants at the spot where he had shot himself. Born in Breslau, he was of the Evangelical faith and 28 years old."

"Johann August Heyne, servant of Chaplain Braunsdorf [who made this original entry], hanged himself in the chaplain's quarters in Becancour Parish. He became melancholy during the three week absence of his master and while in this mood, hanged himself. He was a member of the brigade major, Captain Piquet's Grenadier Company, born in Zerbst, of the Evangelical faith, and 22 years old."

"Christian Hoffmann committed suicide by shooting himself with his own weapon in the living room of his quarters in Becancour Parish in the district of Trois Rivieres on 17 April [1780]. The reason, as he was never melancholy, may never be determined. He was a corporal in brigade major, Captain Piquet's Grenadier Company. Born at Eulenberg in Saxony, he was of the Evangelical faith, a shoemaker by trade, and 26 years old. He was buried the same day by the regimental servants."

"Christian Thiele drowned in an unknown and unfortunate manner in the Gentilly River in Gentilly Parish in the district of Trois Rivieres. A jaeger private in the Anhalt-Zerbst Jaeger Corps, he was born in Koenigslutter in Brunswick, of the Evangelical faith, a tanner by trade, and 26 years old."

"Anthon Ludewig, the small son of the carpenter Ludewig of Captain Gogel's Company, died in an unfortunate and unexpected manner on 15 May [1781]. The child fell into a kettle of boiling water, and although pulled out immediately, it was too late and he gave up the ghost. He was buried in Nicolet Parish where the accident occurred. He was one year, 9 months, and 2 weeks old." [See marriage of parents above.]

"Georg Nohre, private in brigade major Captain Piquet's Grenadier Company, died on 20 August [1781] in the service of the King in an unfortunate manner while cutting wood in St. Jean Parish in the district of Montreal. While cutting down trees, one fell on him, and he was buried there. Born at Sondershausen in Schwarzburg, he was of he Evangelical faith, a miller by trade, and 31 years old."

"Philipp Kalb committed suicide on 19 September [1781] in the quarters of Lieutenant von Heringen in Becancour Parish in the district of Trois Rivieres. He shot himself with a small hunting rifle during the absence of his master, the lieutenant, and was buried there by the regimental servants. Born at Tylle in Schwarzburg, he was of the Evangelical faith, a saltpeter refiner by trade, and 26 years old."

"Heinrich Matern drowned in the Becancour River in Becancour Parish in the district of Trois Rivieres on 9 October [1781] while transporting the royal provisions. The boat was heavily laden and the wind was very strong. The boat capsized in the middle of the river. The other occupants were able to save themselves, but Matern, who was an excellent swimmer and could handle this type of vessel very well, drowned. His body was found nine days later and he was buried with full military honors. He was a corporal in brigade major Captain Piquet's Grenadier Company, born at Speyer and 26 years old. He was of the Evangelical faith and a baker by trade."

"Carl Friederich Meyne died in an unknown manner on 28 October [1781] in St. Pierre Parish in he district of Trois Rivieres. On that day he had been with Captain von Wietersheim at that place and planned to return to his quarters at Becancour. There were many deep valleys lying between and he apparently fell down one of the hillsides, because he was fond of drinking, rolled into the St. Lawrence River, and drowned, because it was reported that his body was found in the river at Quebec. He was the regimental assistant surgeon, born in Schoennebeck, of the Evangelical faith, and his age was unknown."

"Georg Christian Harms drowned in the St. Lawrence River on 3 November [1781] while the regiment was moving into winter quarters. He was traveling with the baggage on the water when a storm arose which caused the boat to start to pitch. When this happened, because he was sitting on a case, he was thrown from the batteau, a rather large vessel, similar to a sloop, and fell into the water. Because there were numerous vessels of this type traveling close together, it was impossible to rescue him, and unfortunately he drowned. He was the regimental assistant surgeon, born at Hamburg, of the Evangelical faith, and 22 years old."

"Adam Apfel died 28 November [1781] in the St. Croix Parish hospital in the district of Quebec, after running the gauntlet. As a corporal he had led a group of privates into stealing. Once they had broken into a merchant's business at night and stolen bolts of all sorts of silk, cotton, and linen, as much as they could carry, which was first discovered after nearly a half year as the result of the theft of a small amount of sugar. As the gang leader, because he at the same time had misled his comrades, he was sentenced to hang, which sentence was then reduced to running a gauntlet of 200 men 36 times on three successive days, twelve times each day. This was carried out, and as a result he gave up the ghost three days later. After being demoted, he was a member of Captain Gogel's Company. Born at Muehlhausen, he was of the Evangelical faith, a cooper by trade, and 24 years old."

"Heinrich Harms froze to death on 4 March [1783] in St. Roi Parish in the district of Quebec. He was drunk and in the evening was returning to his quarters which sat high on a cliff. He apparently injured himself in a fall and lay unconscious until he froze to death. A private in Captain Nuppenau's Company and born in Hoelldorff in East Friesland, he was of the Evangelical faith and 28 years old."

"Heinrich Schiede froze to death on 12 March [1783] in River ouelle Parish in the district of Quebec. From all indications he chose this death for himself because he had wandered into a field in which a haystack stood, stripped off his winter clothing, sat down on the haystack, and awaited his death. He was a private in the brigade Major Captain Piquet's Grenadier Company. Born in Lauterbach in Hesse-Darmstadt, he was of the Reformed faith, and 35 years old."

"August Nuppenau, the only son of Captain Nuppenau, died 20 April [1783] in St. Roi Parish in the district of Quebec. He was six months old." [See birth above.]

"Matthias Michaleck died in the woods in Ste. Anne Parish in the lower district of Quebec on 3 June [1783]. It is not possible to determine whether or not he chose this manner of death. Previously he had committed numerous excesses for which he was demoted from corporal to private. This had made him very melancholy and later he and several comrades beat a farmer, resulting in his having to run the gauntlet. On the same day that he returned to the company from the hospital, he put some bread in his breadsack and walked for more than an hour into the woods, to where no one was to be expected. However, a farmer out hunting came across the body lying by a tree. The head had been beaten or hit against the tree until it bled. He was a private in brigade major Captain Piquet's Grenadier Company. Born in Steckenau in Bohemia, he had been a Catholic converted to the Lutheran faith in Zerbst. He had trained as a hunter and was 28 years old."

"Johann Hoffmann died 12 September [1783] on board the English transport ship *Ann* on the trip from America to Germany and was buried at sea in the channel between England and France the same day. He was a member of Lieutenant Colonel von Rauschenplat's Company, born in Rabitzka in Poland, of the Evengelical faith, and 40 years old."

"Johann Luding drowned at Hochsiel in the Hochsiel Deep in an unfortunate manner on 29 September [1783]. The ships, on which the regiment had arrived there, were lying so close together that it was possible to jump from one to the other. He tried to do this, but the ships parted and he fell into the gap between the ships, where, although he was immediately pulled up, he died. He was buried at the Hochsiel also. A member of captain Prince of Schwarzburg's Company, he had been born in Hameln in Hannover. He was of the Evangelical faith, a tailor by trade, and 32 years old."

## The Ansbach-Bayreuth Church Book

Pastor Georgius Michael Stroelein prepared a list of the births and baptisms made in the Ansbach-Bayreuth contingent serving in America during the American Revolutionary War. The following are extracted from his compilation. "1782 - At two o'clock in the afternoon of 3 October, there was legitimately born and thereafter baptized Ernst Friederich - The father is Georg Chateau of Meissenheim in Saarbruecken, a corporal in the jaeger Regiment. The mother is Anna Maria, nee Buettner, of Ansbach. Sponsor- Captain Ernst Friederich Wilhelm von Wurmb, of that regiment, who died of a wound received during action at Penobscot."

"1782 - Michael Peter - The father is Georg Arnold, a field jaeger from Ansbach; the mother Margaretha, nee Wunderlich, of Bayreuth. Sponsors - Vice-corporal Michael Peter Krueger and his wife Elisabeth."

"1783 - On 29 January, at Norwich on Long Island, there was legitimately born and due to an absence of clergy, only on 12 May 1783 baptized: Miss Ester Harriette Catherina. The father is Captain von Waldenfels of this regiment; mother Mistress Sarah Waldenfels, nee Forgon. Sponsors - Mistress Hedwig von der Heyde, wife of Captain [Moritz Wilhelm] von der Heyde, nee Hopson, and Frau Anna Catherina Bach, wife of Lieutenant [Joseph] Bach, nee Stiegler."

"1783 - On 24 July at Harlem Creek on York Island, there was legitimately born and thereafter baptized: Johann Martin. The father Tobias Wolff, field jaeger, the mother Anna Regina, nee Weyh. Sponsors - Corporal Johann Nikolaus Stoehr and Corporal Joh. Martin."

"On the return voyage from America, on board the ship *South Carolina*, 1783, there was legitimately born and on 11 August baptized: Carl Lorenz. The father is Conrad Hager, field jaeger, the mother Nancy, nee McDonald, of County Edinburg in Scotland. Sponsor - Corporal Carl Lorenz Hering. The child was named Carl as a reminder of the ship's name."

"1783 - At ten o'clock in the morning on 2 September aboard the same ship, there was legitimately born and thereafter baptized: Johanna Maria Carolina and Johann Carl Friederich. The father is Johann Lindner, field jaeger sergeant, the mother Johanna Catherina, nee Seiss, of Dorflas. Sponsors - Carl Friederich Neuss, surgeon of the same regiment and Johanna Maria Sabina Pausch, nee Engelhardt, of Ansbach, wife of the Jaeger Sergeant [Johann Michael] Pausch."

'N.B. - The boy was named after the ship's captain, John Brown; the girl after the frigate *Carolina*."

"1783 - At three o'clock in the afternoon of 15 July at Penobscot, during the absence of the chaplain, there was born, and after the Ansbach troops had returned at The Downs [England] baptized aboard the ship *The Brothers*, on 8 September: Anna Susanna: The legitimate daughter of Field Jaeger Joh. Conrad Hasster and his wife Cathar. Margaretha, nee Trips. Sponsor - Anna Susanna, from Rastal, wife of Hunting Horn Player Schramm."

"1783 - On 15 May, in the absence of Chaplain Erb, there was born at Penobscot, and on 8 September baptized: Johann Friederich. The legitimate son of Field Jaeger Georg Adam Benz and his wife Marian, nee Winter, of Fuerth. Sponsor - Field Jaeger Friederich Neues from Schwabach."

"1783 - On 27 September on the return march, at Bremen, there was born and on 2 October baptized: Johann Friederich. The legitimate son of Joseph Carl Wildscheck, hunting horn player, from Jucay in Hungary, and his wife Helene Herika, nee Koenig. Sponsor - Johann Heinrich Lachs, hunting horn player."

"1783 - At eleven o'clock at night on 23 September, there was born at Bremen, in the absence of a military chaplain, and on 29 October at Hannover Muenden baptized: Johann Ludwig. The legitimate son of Artillerist Johann Georg Weber of the von Voit Regiment, and his wife Regina, nee Ahold, from Frederick, [Maryland], in North America. Sponsor - Private Joh. Ludwig Heckert of that regiment."

"1783 - On 19 October on board the frigate *Auerbach*, on the North Sea, there was born and on 29 October baptized, by Superintendent Stoeckenesel, at Hannover Muenden: Maria Margaretha. The legitimate daughter of Musketeer Mathias Walther of the von Voit Infantry Regiment and his wife Regina Barbara, nee Schwenohl. Sponsor - Corporal Weinberger's wife Maria Margaretha."

"According to the enclosed statement from the father in New York, in America, there was born on 21 August 1782: Maria Carolina. The father is Johann Andreas Carl von Stein zu Altenstein; the mother is Maria Elisabeth, nee Grimm, both Evangelical. On 4 September this child was baptized at New York with David Grimm, merchant in New York, the father of the dear mother in attendance. Sponsors - Carl Heinrich von Stein zu Altenstein, the grandfather on the paternal side, Ansbach colonel and commandant at Erlangen, and his wife Sophia Charlotta von Altenstein, nee von Roth...."

[Enclosure] "My daughter Maria Carolina was born on 21 August 1782 and baptized fourteen days later. Sponsors - Sophia Carolina Charlotta von Stein zum Altenstein, nee von Roth; and my father-in-law, David Grimm, Merchant in New York in America.

/s/ v. Altenstein"

## Autograph Books

Another source of information for understanding the Hessians is to be found in their autograph books. Excerpts here are primarily to indicate who was asked to make entries and what they wrote. Peggy Grimm of New York, daughter of David Grimm and sister of Maria Elisabeth who married Johann Andreas Carl von Stein zu Altenstein, wrote, in English, in the book belonging to Captain Christian von Urff of the Hesse-Cassel Leib Regiment on 28 August 1780,

"The Friendship
Alas how little of ourselves we know,
How small a part of what we owe,
We promise friendship and perhaps intend,
But soon forget the promise and the friend!
Reflect a moment, ask your conscious breast
To whom the words were wrote, to whom addressed,
And 't will inform you for you see --
They were to you designed and wrote by me."

C. von Donop, captain [later major] in the von Donop Regiment, under the dateline of 4 March 1781 in Philadelphia, wrote this advice,

"Wait with joyful anticipation
The arrival of a better situation."

[This rhyming couplet in German uses time instead of situation as the last word.]

C.J.C. von Schueler, lieutenant in the Guard Regiment at the time of signing, but later in the Landgraf Regiment, on 15 October 1775 quoted Hagedorn's verse,

"To appreciate water, one needs a doctor or a reason."

Carl Simon Ludwig Wilhelm, Count von der Lippe, of the Leib Regiment, made an entry at Ochsenfurt on 28 February 1776. According to an entry by von Urff beside the count's comment, he was killed in a duel on board the *Unanimity* during the crossing to America.

On the same day a von Kutzleben, then a Hessian ensign in the Gotha Regiment, wrote the following lines. He died aboard ship near

Deal, on the English coast, during his return from America in December 1783, according to a note by von Urff.

> "A good book, a true friend,
> Are things I hold dear,
> And anyone who does not wish
> To associate with me
> Can do whatever he may wish."

Friedrich Wilhelm von Urff, major in the Leib Dragoon Regiment, son of the well-known [to the editors of the article containing this autograph book] cavalry general, the "Hessian" Seidlitz in the Seven Years' War, Georg Ludwig von Urff, who died on 20 January 1791 at Niederurf due to a fall from a horse, at the time of his death colonel and a knight of the Hessian Military Order, brother of the owner of the autograph book, wrote at Hofgeismar on 14 April 1774,

> "In the best possible world
> The friend, the philosopher, and the hero exist,
> And because we are all tender-hearted,
> A beautiful child is also to be found."

Ludwig von Gluer, lieutenant in the von Lossberg Regiment, wrote, at Philadelphia on 3 April 1778,

> "There is an old man, who never forgets
> That he was once young."

He shot himself, according to the comment added later by von Urff, at New York on 7 May 1779.

Johann Henrich Hegemann, lieutenant in the Leib Regiment, later captain in the Old Lossberg Regiment, wrote, at Newport on 19 February 1777 [in French],

> "A heart without love is like a regiment without a drummer!"

W. Wilhelm Johann Ernst Freienhagen, lieutenant in the von Donop Regiment, who died in America after having taken his release from service, wrote, on 31 January 1778 at Philadelphia,

> "Virtue and joy are forever joined,
> They are held together by a heavenly connection."

Emanuel Rosinus Hausmann, lieutenant in the von Donop Regiment, who later took his release in order to remain in America, dedicated a sketch showing a farm on a river with virginal juniper bushes in the background, at Philadelphia on 21 February 1778, and added,

"As beautiful as a rose may be, it still withers on the vine.
But a true friend remains true to the end of time!'

Another von Donop, lieutenant in the von Donop Regiment, who later took his release, became a court official in Eutin, and died at Ziegenhain, wrote, at Philadelphia on 15 May 1778, a retrospective comment.

"Adam lay sleeping in Paradise,
And a woman was made from his breast,
So you poor Adam paid full price,
Your first sleep, was your last rest."

Justus von Diemar, lieutenant in Ansbach service, wrote, at New York on 1 October 1780,

"Pretty girls are made for soldiers, not for clergy!"

Carl August Freienhagen, lieutenant in the von Donop Regiment, wrote, at Philadelphia on 15 May 1778,

"It is possible to earn a great reputation, Only one step at a time, along a narrow pathway!"

Another autograph book has survived, that carried by Philipp Marc, auditor of the Waldeck Regiment. A sampling of the entries in his book, include the following.

"Heritage at birth is not the reason for the heart being large or small,
A king may enslave a people, a slave may become king!'

"As often as you read these lines remember your sincere friend and servant  -- F. von Wilmowsky, Lieut." [Written at Pensacola, 1 January 1780].

And Chaplain Waldeck wrote on the same day at Pensacola,

"Love God, love yourself, love your fellow Creatures.
These are all your obligations. The first produces piety,
the second wisdom, the third social virtues.
My dear Sir! In reading these few lines you may remember
your sincere and most affectionate friend  -- Ph. Waldeck,
Minister of the 3rd Regt of Waldeck"

- - - - - - -

Just as I began this history, as written by the Hessian participants in the American Revolutionary War, with Doehla's comments about entering upon his adventures in 'God's holy name', I close it with his truly passionate prayer of thanks for God's protection throughout his years in America.

"Prayer of Thanks, completed by me, after a happy return to my homeland, in my birthplace of Zell; who visited the temple of the Lord with His sought-for assistance, and gave God, the almighty Protector and Keeper of my life, the praise and thanks offering by my lips; also gave the local house of God a red taffeta, and with silver lace trimmed, pulpit cloth, which cost three Guldens, as well as two guldens in cash, or one Spanish dollar, or all together, five Franconian gulden, not from pomp and pride, but to honor God; and after the sermon, issued the following written out prayer and my thanks, by Herr Thiermann, without mentioning my name, allowed to be read, as follows:

"Great and exalted God! You Powerful Lord of Heaven and Earth and the Boundless Seas!

"I thank you that you were my protection and help, and kept my body from the decay and the captivity, and from the snare a false tongue has released, and has helped me also against the enemy and has saved me, with your great and well-known compassion, from the bellowers who want to devour me, from a people in a far distant land, and with an unfamiliar language; out of the hands of those who sought to take my life; out of the many afflictions which I encountered; out of the sea. I was often near death, I was surrounded by the enemy and no one helped me; I sought help from the people and found none. Then I thought, God, on your compassion, how you have ever helped, because you save everyone who believes in you, and release them from captivity of the heathens.

"I prayed to God against their fury, and implored release from their hands, and called to the Lord, my Father, that He could not forsake me in my need, and when my enemies threatened, and I had no help, O God! I praise and thank you for having heard my prayer. You saved me from all danger.

"We had to go along rough pathways, and were carried off as a herd being stolen by the enemy, but now see Zion; your children, who were carried off with weeping and bitter, burning tears, return. Yes - They all return from the north and from the south, through the word of the holy and praiseworthy graciousness of God. The Lord has blessed us greatly so that we are happy. Therefore, I will thank you, Lord, in public, and praise you and your name for evermore. Amen.

"And now follows the song.

"Verse 1 - Praise God, I am home from America. The captivity is over. I pledge to praise, thank, and honor Jesus Christ, because you have led me through distant places with your hand.

"Verse 2 - I give credit to you, that I was not wounded and arrived safely home, that no enemy has harmed me. In short, Jesus, you alone are to be thanked that I am here.

"Verse 3 - Jesus, you have watched over me, and provided protection, by the angels, while on the sea, both day and night. Therefore, my heart is full of joy. I must praise you. Jesus, you, up in Heaven, who has done so much for me.

"Verse 4 - Now I ask, continue to show me your favor, and finally, allow me to reach my goals here on earth. May I always be blessed. Lead me from this difficulty and into eternal joy. Amen."[54]

# Footnotes

1. (p. 2) From *A Hessian Diary of the American Revolution*, by Johann Conrad Doehla. Translated, edited, and with an Introduction by Bruce E. Burgoyne. Copyright 1990 by the University of Oklahoma Press, p. 3

2. (p. 10) Bardeleben used two codes within his diary. Fortunately, I was able to solve one of the codes, but I have not been able to decipher the second code. The first code is a simple substitution code, but the second one seems more complex and seems to have been devised in order to prevent his comrades and superiors from reading remarks derogatory to them and the war effort.

3. (p. 14) The Devil's Mill, still in existence today, is mentioned in almost every diary by the men who traveled along the Weser.

4. (p. 18) Colonel Charles Rainsford.

5. (p. 18) This was the 1777 recruit transport containing replacements for members of the Hesse-Cassel contingent who had died or deserted during the previous year. The list of men is contained in the British Museum Additional Manuscript 23651, f. 139 and f. 145. The Hessian recruits were mustered at Nijmegen on 28 March 1777.

6. (p. 40) Fortunately, Pausch was not aware that about ninety percent of an iceberg is underwater.

7. (p. 48) Colonel Albrecht von Scheiter (or Scheither) contracted with the English government to recruit Germans to fill the ranks of English regiments. Rodney Atwood, *The Hessians, Mercenaries from Hessen-Kassel in the American Revolution, Cambridge University Press, 1980, p. 10.* The men so recruited were true mercenaries as opposed to the "Hessians" who were auxiliaries sold into the English service by their rulers.

8. (p. 54) Chaplain Waldeck's comment concerning witches can be more easily understood when it is known that the last witch burning in Hesse occurred in 1777! Evelyn Lehmann and Ingo Doering, *Friedrich II, 1760-1785*, Verein fuer Publikation der Stadt Kassel, Germany, 1981, p. 34.

9. (p. 68) As the designation of the Lossberg Regiment was not changed to "Old Lossberg Regiment" until 1782, it is obvious that this, as most of the Hessian diaries, was edited and material altered after the original entries were made.

10. (p. 70) Italics added by the translator.

11. (p. 79) As the first division sailed in two sections, this was actually the second division containing the remainder of the troops initially supplied by Hesse-Cassel and the Waldeck Regiment.

12. (p. 81) These probably were men recruited by von Scheiter and the diary entry Schreiber may have been an error in copying from the original document.

13. (p. 97) An exact translation of the diary entry would be 'I'll show you Kassel.'

14. (p. 100) While Colonel von Borck was reportedly killed at Fort Washington, he, or possibly a second Colonel von Borck, traveled to Canada in 1780 with the Knyphausen Regiment.

15. (p. 110) Europeans celebrate both 25 and 26 December as Christmas and refer to them as the first and second holidays.

16. (p. 114) It should be noted that many of Reuber's dates are in error.

17. (p. 130) The capture of General Prescott enabled the warring parties to exchange Prescott for Charles Lee and solved a serious dilemma for both supreme commanders. Howe considered Lee an English traitor and Washington had said if Lee were executed, an English officer, chosen by lot, would be executed, also.

18. (p. 137) In a later, more polished version of the diary, Waldeck changed the odds against the Waldeckers to ten to one. Marion Dexter Learned (trans.), *Philipp Waldeck's Diary of the American Revolution*, Americana Germanica Press, Philadelphia, 1907, p.26.

19. (p. 138) Pentzel was murdered or committed suicide while en route home on the Weser River in 1783.

20. (p. 139) Recruits were sent out each year to replace men who were killed, deserted, or rotated back to Germany.

21. (p. 143) The men who escaped from Trenton were assigned in a 'Combined Battalion' until after those who were captured were exchanged and returned to duty.

22. (p. 145) Because many of the men were still 'growing boys', it was necessary to periodically realign them by size.

23. (p. 158) A German hour is equal to the distance marched in one hour, or four kilometers, or two and one-half miles.

24. (p. 161) Due to illness while en route to the Dutch embarkation port, Captain Rheyer had remained in Europe.

25. (p. 170) The officer was Captain Johann Ewald, who noted in his diary how he lost out on the prize money. Johann Ewald, *Diary of the American War; A Hessian Journal*, trans. and ed. by Joseph P. Tustin, Yale University Press, New Haven, 1979, p. 76.

26. (p. 185) It seems strange that "Toward evening [on the previous day] we could already see large groups and complete regiments."

27. (p. 215) Captain Friedrich von Muenchhausen, aide-de-camp to General William Howe, noted that the Ansbach-Bayreuth soldiers were "Exceedingly tall and handsome fellows. Without doubt ... the tallest and best looking regiments of all those here." Friedrich Muenchhausen, *At General Howe's Side*, trans. by Ernst Kipping and anno. by Samuel Steele Smith, p. xvii.

28. (p. 217) The two infantry regiments from Ansbach-Bayreuth were initially the 1st or Ansbach Regiment, also referred to as the von Eyb Regiment, and the 2nd or Bayreuth Regiment, also referred to as the von Voit Regiment. When Colonel Friedrich Ludwig Albrecht von Eyb returned to Germany in 1778, Colonel August Valentin von Voit von Salzburg became commander of the 1st Regiment, which thereafter was also known as the von Voit Regiment. The 2nd Regiment became the von Seybothen Regiment as Major Johann Heinrich Christian Franz von Seybothen was promoted to colonel and given the regiment.

29. (p. 252) The English had vacated Philadelphia prior to this time and the city and the jail were under American control.

30. (p. 258) Supposedly Sichart also kept a diary of his wartime experiences but it has apparently been lost or destroyed.

31. (p. 258) I have inserted the three plus signs (+++) in place of coded entries which I could not translate.

32. (p. 276) I do not know the meaning of the term 'Tailor's draft' but assume it may refer to the impressment of young apprentice or journeyman workers in the city of New York.

33. (p. 317) As there is no further mention of the massacre by Waldeck or Steuernagel, it would appear that Waldeck recorded a rumor which later proved false.

34. (p. 319) This was the basis for a book by the German author Hans Lehr, *Der Herr der Wildnis [The Lord of the Wilderness]*. published many years ago in Germany.

35. (p. 322) The letters are obviously keyed to a map which I have not found.

36. (p. 325) Lieutenant Wiederhold also fell in love during his period of captivity in Virginia and, as will be noted in the Miscellaneous Chapter at the end of this volume, many officers married in America. Many enlisted men also married in America.

37. (p. 403) As will be noted later in this volume, the *Anna* drifted to England, apparently without the loss of any of the jaegers, and the men were then sent back to America.

38. (p. 409) Heldring served as the assistant engineer at Pensacola and may have even transferred to the English army for a time. England also offered him a captaincy. He spoke German, Dutch, and French, and probably some English. Several maps which he drew while at Pensacola are in the Clements Library at the University of Michigan.

39. (p. 413) I have found no explanation of why Knyphausen undertook this expedition, apparently on his own initiative, and it appears that when Clinton returned from the south, he ordered the men back to New York.

40. (p. 430) A 'stang' is a Swedish measure equal to about ten feet.

41. (p. 441) There was no provision in the capitulation terms about the garrison fighting against the Americans.

42. (p. 457) Generally a German mile is considered equal to six English miles.

43. (p. 457) Doehla also reported that a Dutch merchant ship loaded with chocolate had been captured by the English and the chocolate was divided among the regiments at Yorktown. From *A Hessian Diary of the American Revolution*, by Johann Conrad Doehla. Translated, edited, and with an Introduction by Bruce E. Burgoyne. Copyright 1990 by the University of Oklahoma Press, p. 173.

44. (p. 459) Italics added by the translator.

45. (p. 464) The slaughter of the horses is also mentioned in Edward M. Riley's "St. George Tucker's Journal of the Siege of

Yorktown, 1781", *William and Mary Quarterly* (Williamsburg) Series 3, Vol. 3 (1948).

46. (p. 507) This may account for the missing years of the Waldeck diary.

47. (p. 545) At this time the Ansbach-Bayreuth forces consisted of two infantry regiments and a jaeger regiment.

48. (p. 545) Captain Molitor had married an American, without permission, and although he served until the end of the war, he then took his separation and settled in Nova Scotia.

49. (p. 548) The diaries do not clarify how Major Pentzel met his death.

50. (p. 550) Doehla later married and became a master brickmaker like his father. He may have taught school for a time, also. He died a widower, at Zell, on 14 January 1820. *Tagebuch eines Bayreuth Soldaten des Johann Conrad Doehla aus der Nordamerikanischen Freiheitskrieg von 1777 bis 1783*, edited by W. Baron von Waldenfels, (Bayreuth, 1913), p. xxi.

51. (p. 563) Widows were required to remarry or lose their military benefits.

52. (p. 573) While more exact information is missing, it is my belief that this is the Colonel Philip Skene who was the commander of the provincial troops which accompanied General Burgoyne in 1777.

53. (p. 574) The double dates indicate dates of birth and baptism.

54. (p. 590) This prayer and song of praise by Doehla is taken from *Tagebuch eines Bayreuth Soldaten*.

# INDEX

597

ERSKINE, Gen 111 145-146 178
332 Maj Gen 332 William 86
ESCHWEGE, 497 500 Capt 496 498
527 Christian 483
EWALD, 160 Capt 154 159 170
173-174 260 327 363 367 373
418-419 421 Cpl 213 494 Gen
419 Johann 86 566 593
EYTELWEIN, Carl Philipp 496
FALKENER, Mrs 566
FANNING, 350 356 Col 421
FARMER, Capt 128
FAUCITT, William 24
FEILITZSCH, 43 163 172 179 184
233 239 256 261 266 271 324
326 346-347 429 Lt 159 170 230
FENWICK, 380
FERGUSON, 327 333 336 362 376
383 400 Maj 419 Patrick 273
FINTZELL, 212 Philipp 211
FISCHER, Heinrich 576 Musketeer
533
FISCHERALL, Capt 546
FIX, Peter 427
FLACHSHAAR, Ludwig 527
FLUECKMANN, Jacob 534
FOCHT, Johann Peter? 212
FOERSTER, Anna Catherina 510
561
FOGT, Friedrich 443
FORGON, Sarah 584
FOX, Brigadier 551
FRASER, Brigadier Gen 206 Gen
203 212 Simon 191
FREBELN, Widow 443
FREEMAN, 196 199 201 203 213-
214 428
FREIENHAGEN, Carl August 588
W Wilhelm Johann Ernst 587
FRERICHS, Oldmann 578
FREY, Georg Adolph 569 Johann
Georg 569 Margaretha 569
FREYENHAGEN, Carl August 20
Wilhelm Johann Ernst 20

FREYENSOEHNER, Georg 428
FRIEDRICH, Ernst 583 Landgrave 2
514
FRITSCH, Johann Jacob 394
FRITZ, Ferdinand 579 Grenadier
536
FUCHS, Maria Sabina 562 Pastor
562 Pvt 462
FUEHRER, Carl Friedrich 568
FUERST, Georg 353
GACHSTETTER, Cpl 462
GALL, Capt 144
GALVEZ, Don 314 405-407 409-
410 439 441 Don Bernardo De
313 Governor Don 317
GARDEN, Col 390
GATES, Gen 213 225 333 403 418
543 Horatio 205
GECHTER, Johann Conrad 229
Surgeon 245
GEISLER, Capt 559 Friedrich
Wilhelm 558
GELIAT, 273
GEORGE, Iii (king Of England) 1
GERLACH, Capt 205 208
GERLINGER, Michael 544
GERMANN, Capt 58 213 493
GERMER, Johann Anton 45
GEWALD, Jacob 485
GIBB, 379-380 382
GIESE, Conrad 572 Drummer 497
534 Wilhelm 485
GILES, Col 390
GINSBERG, 23
GISSOT, Capt 32 Johann Matthias
31
GIST, Col 390
GLATZ, Joseph 417
GLEIM, Anna Elizabeth 571
Elisabeth 571 Johannes 571
GOERKE, Casimir Theodor 564 566
Elisabeth 564 Elizabeth 566
Henriette 566
GOERT, Johann Stephan 353

GOETSCH, Gen 543
GOGEL, Capt 576-578 580 582
GOODWYN, Col 390
GORDON, Lt 438 Maj 462
GOTTFRIED, Christian 486
GOTTSCHALK, Surgeon 534
    Wilhelm 499
GRACHELITZ, Gottfried 576
GRAEBE, Ensign 339
GRANT, Gen 77 112 270 287 324
    James 75 Maj Gen 173 268
GRASHOFF, Christian 578
GRAVES, Adm 454 459 468
    Samuel 452
GRAY, Maj 153
GREBE, Gottlieb 520
GREEN, Christoph 228 Col 230
GREENE, Gen 237 442 446-447 450
    453 458 471 488 490 Nathanael
    124 418
GREGORY, Gen 455
GREY, Charles 153 Gen 179 181
    240 273
GRIMM, 147 245 David 146 585-
    586 Maria Elizabeth 585-586
    Musketeer 426 Peggy 586
    Wilhelm 425
GRUENEWALD, Grenadier 303
GUIN, Gen 124
GUNCKEL, Jacob 464
GUNN, Maj 547
HAACKE, Capt 441
HADDRELL, 397
HAEMER, Hamilton Carl Henrich
    565 Johannes 565 Maria
    Elisabeth 565
HAEMERLE, Musketeer 304
HAGEDORN, ---- 586
HAGER, Carl Lorenz 584 Conrad
    584 Nancy 584
HAINER, War Councilor 541
HALDIMAND, 538 Gen 303-304
    306 504 Lt Gen 482
HALE, Nathan 78-79

HALLATSCHKA, Johannes 483 Pvt
    485
HALLER, Col 229
HAMILTON, William 565
HAMMOND, Andrew Snape 393
HANCOCK, John 279
HAND, Edward 333
HANDEL, Johann 427
HANGER, Capt 358 362 George 270
HANSELMANN, Adam 212
HANSTEIN, Capt 563
HARCOURT, Lt Col 127 William
    126
HARLINGTON, Col 390
HARMS, Georg Christian 581
    Heinrich 582
HARNICKEL, Lt 122
HARTMANN, Paul 212
HASSENPFLUG, Catherina
    Elisabeth 565 Johann 565
HASSLER, Friedrich 534
HASSTER, Anna Susanna 584
    Cathar Margaretha 584 Joh
    Conrad 584
HAUSMANN, 212 Bombardier 212
    Carl Ludwig 200 Cpl 427
    Emanuel Rosinus 82 587 Lt 517
    Sgt 210
HAYNES, Isaac 444
HAZELWOOD, Adm 236
HEAD, Maj Gen 524
HECKERT, Joh Ludwig 585
HEERINGEN, 69 Col 81
HEGEMANN, Johann Henrich 486
    587
HEIDELBACH, Jeremias 194
    Regimental Surgeon 195 201
    Surgeon 481 539
HEIDENREICH, Friedrich 571
HEINEMANN, Jacob Conrad 136
    Johannes 245
HEINMULLER, 212
HEINRICH, Johannes 78
HEINTZINGER, Philipp 485

HEISTERREICH, Sgt 307
HELDRING, 594 Gerhard Henrich
 136 Lt 137 252-253 409
HELLER, Georg Friedrich 47
HENCKELMANN, Johann Heinrich
 550
HENKELMANN, Barbara 576-577
 Johann Heinrich 550 Veit 576-
 577
HENNDORFF, Friedrich Christoph
 339
HENSE, Capt 302 304 486
HEPPE, Georg Hermann 238
HERBER, Michael 214
HERECLAND, 328
HERING, Carl Lorenz 584
HERRMANN, Musketeer 535
HESS, Dr 192
HESSENMUELLER, Capt 357
 Henrich Christian 111
HESSLER, Christoph 534
HESTERMANN, Bombardier 427
HEUSSER, Christian Leonhard 339
HEWITSOM, Maj 516
HEYDERICH, Christoph 573
 Dorothea Maria 573
HEYL, Cpl 494 Philipp Jacob 495
HEYMEL, Auditor 558 563 Carl
 Philipp 11 Col 558-559 562 567
 Lt 229 Lt Col 34 47 88 339 345
 565 Philipp Wilhelm 228
HEYNE, Johann August 580
HICKS, Col 390
HILL, John 191
HILLE, Henrich Reinhard 126
HILLER, Bartholomai 353
HINCKEL, Musketeer 426
HINRICHS, Capt 384 Johann 363
HINTE, Col 558 572 Erasmus Ernst
 38 Maj 47 88 110
HINTENBERGER, Franz 440
HOBKIRK, 454
HOENE, Ludwig 213
HOEPF, Pvt 353

HOEPFNER, Christoph Georg 19
HOFFMANN, Christian 580 Johann
 583
HOFMANN, Capt 544
HOHENSTEIN, Capt 357 Georg 111
HOLZENDORF, Gen 171
HOPFER, Drummer 476
HOPKIN, Col 390
HOPSON, Hedwig 584
HORN, Pvt 456
HOTHAM, Lt 233 William 224
HOTHAN, William 287
HOWARD, M 292
HOWE, 95 158 180 223 238 363
 592 Adm 226 267-268 276 295
 Gen 55 84 92 98-99 101 111 116
 145 148-149 156 160-162 164
 178-179 183 185 204 206 215
 225-227 232 243 249-250 Lord
 268-269 275-279 294 364 Lt Gen
 80-81 90 142 Richard 55 112
 William 55 91 151 173 225 255
 267 294 593
HUEBSCH, 574
HUFFNER, 427
HUGER, Brigadier 390 Daniel 389
HUTHMANN, Christian 136
HUYN, 107
INSDORF, Georg Sr 483 Jr 483 Sr
 496-497
JACOB, Anna Martha 562
JACOBI, Catherina Friderica 570
 Friderica Rosina 570 Friedrich
 Ludwig 570
JAHN, Johann 427
JAMES, 391
JANECKE, Lt Col 536
JAROCK, 562
JOHN, 213 217 371-372 375
JOHNS, Capt 199
JOHNSON, 124 Gen 111 Gideon
 454 Henry 329 Lt Col 333
JOHNSTON, Lt Col 333
JONES, Thomas? 199

LEONHARDI, Johann Wilhelm 97
Lt 317
LEONHARDT, Musketeer 306-307
LEPNER, Mr 146
LESLIE, Alexander 153 Gen 118
154 244 393 420-421 448 488-
489 Maj Gen 264 363 375 417
419 455
LETZERICH, Johann 563 Martha
563
LEYTMEIER, Rosina Charlotta 563
LIEBERMANN, Johann Adam 348
LINCOLN, 389 Benjamin 360 Gen
362 377 381 383-384 387-388
390 544 Maj Gen 389
LINDAUER, 579 Christoph 578
LINDENBERGER, Lt 129
LINDNER, Johann 584 Johann Carl
Friederich 584 Johanna
Catherina 584 Johanna Maria
Carolina 584
LINNING, 379-380
LIST, Anna Catharina 575
Christoph 575 Sgt 541
LITTLE, Col 390
LOCHMANN, Sr 212
LOEHLER, Abraham 563 Elisabeth
563
LOEWENFELD, Lt 100
LOHMANN, Grenadier 44
LOHR, Maria Elisabeth 565
LOOS, Col 150 177
LOREY, Capt 267 327 Friedrich
Henrich 101 Johann Friedrich
Henrich 567
LOSSBERG, Col 106
LOWE, 249
LUDEWIG, 580 Anna Magdalena
573 Anthon 573 580
LUDING, Johann 583
LUDOLPH,
Carl 563
Rosina Charlotta 563
LUTZ, 242

MAERTHEN, Andreas 567 Anna
Gertruth 567 Henrich 567
MAHR, Musketeer Sr 533 Philipp
484
MAITLAND, John 376
MAKBAND, Col 390
MANN, Hartmann 444 Martin 444
MARC, Commissary 222 310 404
409 Philipp 6 588
MARION, Col 390
MARQUARD, Carl Levin 72
MARSTEN, 262 571
MARTIN, 261 Joh 584
MARTINI, Maj 371 Melchior 105
MAST, Johann Martin Alexander
574 Pvt 574
MATERN, Heinrich 581
MATHEW, Edward 151 Gen 154
331 413-414
MATTERN, Christian 220
MATTHAES, Johann August 574
Pvt 574
MATTHAEUS, Johann Justus 2
MAUL, 530
MAURER, Johannes 19
MAWHOOD, Charles 139
MAXWELL, 333 Maj 455 William
264
MAYBANK, Col 390
MCCLOY, Lt 396
MCDONALD, Nancy 584
MCDOUGAL, Col 390
MCGOWAN, 523-524
MCINTOSH, Brigadier Gen 390
Lachlan 389
MCLEAN, Brigadier Gen 335
Francis 334
MCPHERSON, Col 462
MEDERN, Capt 100 Friedrich
Moritz 98
MENCK, Philipp 427
MERCER, Hugh 124
MERTEN, Anna Gerdruth 564
Henrich 564

PAULI, Georg Heinrich 68
PAUSCH, 60 62 188 206 441 479
481-482 503-504 538 540-541
591 Capt 14-15 25 27 36 40 48
58 61 64 186 193 196 253 428
478 502 Georg 5 Johann Michael
584 Johanna Maria Sabina 584
Maj 423 493 537 Regimental
Surgeon 229
PELIUS, Pastor 8
PELOTROW, Maria Elisabeth 568
PENDERGAST, Lt 544
PENTZEL, 592 Capt 290 308 404
Christian Friedrich 138 Maj 409
548 595
PERCY, Hugh 79 99 Lord 100 112
246
PERTOT, Lt 228-229
PFISTER, Carl Friedrich 37
PFLUEGER, Elisabeth 571 Miss 567
PFLUG, Andreas Friedrich 348
Johann 212
PHILIPP, 90
PHILIPPS, Gen 186 188 192 196
198-199 Maj Gen 187 423
PHILIPSE, 268 326-328 331-333
472 Frederick 221
PHILLIPS, Gen 451 453-454 481
Maj Gen 446 479 William 64
PIEL, 21 115 262 338 Lt 37 69 73
123-124 128 249 255 270 339
422 486 525
PIGOT, Commander 295 Gen 248
295 298 301 328 Robert 247
PIQUET, 573
Capt 574-576 579-583
Carl Friedrich 573
Maria Elisabeth 574 579
Mrs 573 Philipp Friedrich Carl
575
PLAUMENS, Elisabeth 570
POOR, Enoch 333
PORT, Musketeer 306-307
POTTER, James 333

PRECHTEL, 29 43 56 162 217 232
238-239 255 260 298 353 412
415-416 446 452 454 543 549
Johann Ernst 16 Lt 300 437 461
475 508 Sgt 27 40
PREISS, Johann 576 Juliana
Dorothea 573
PRELL, 53
PRENSELL, Carla 444
PRESCOTT, Gen 247 301 350 354
592 Richard 130 246
PREVOST, Augustine 320 Field
Marshal 322 Gen 322 356 359-
360 399
PRIEUR, 220 222 Claude 219
PRINCE, Of Anhalt 504 Of Anhalt-
zerbst 538 Of Schwarzburg 576
Of Schwarzburg Capt 583 Of
Waldeck 441 Of Wuerzburg 18
PRUESCHENCK, 170 Maj 327 331
PULASKI, 360 376 378 383 Casimir
273
PULFER, Musketeer 306-307
PUTNAM, Israel 128
QUEEN, Of England 142
R----, J---- 4 19 34 40 45 49 89 102
108 151 162-163 177 233 467
505 515 559
RAAB, Johann 355
RADNA, Fusileer 346
RAINSFORD, Charles 18 591 Col
25
RALL, 125 142 Capt 465 Col 68-69
89 98 104 111 113-117 121 125-
126 136 252 Gen 116 Johann 2
Lt 100
RAPP, Surgeon 544
RATHERS, Lord 406
RATHMANN, Johann Henrich 339
RAU, Lt 86 90
RAUSCHENPLAT, 538 573
RAWDON, Francis 331 400 Lord
332 392 443 453-454 458 Lord?
406

RECKNAGEL, 517 556
REICHART, Georg Nikolaus 353
REICHEL, Philipp Ludwig 358
REIF, Cannoneer 427
REINECKIEN, Lt 197
REISMANN, Philipp 136
REISS, Georg 443
REITZENSTEIN, Christoph Ludwig 232
REMY, Musketeer 533 Pvt 534
REUBER, 5 7 24 36 40 43 48 50 66 68 82 89 104 280 320 445 490 510 515 592 Johannes 2 Private 22 Pvt 32 112 131 251
REUFFER, 46 Lt 38
RHAU, Johann Heinrich 416
RHEIDER, 568 Andreas 568 Barbara 568
RHEYER, Andreas Friedrich 161 Capt 593
RICHARDSON, Col 390
RIEDESEL, Gen 196 202 217
RIES, Johann Caspar 122
RIESS, Johann Caspar 116 Pvt 300
RINCKS, Margaretha Barbara 569
RIVERIN, 573 Marie 573
ROBERTSON, 327 329 Gen 255 James 111 Lt 454 Lt Gen 453
ROBINSON, 331 333 419-421 Gen 54
ROCHAMBEAU, 458 Gen 447 465 472 Lt Gen 464
RODNEY, Caesar? 177
ROESSLER, Medic 353
ROGGE, Carl 574 Carl Michael Philipp 574 Johanna Magdalena Dorothea 574
ROOSEWEL, Elisabeth 564
ROSENBERGER, Johann 214
ROSENSTEIL, Christiana Sophia 573
ROSENSTIEHL, Ludewich 577
ROSENTHAL, Margaretha 569
ROSSEL, Johann Wilhelm 476

ROSSMER, Johann 64
ROTH, Johann Thomas 212
ROTLEY, Gen 177
RUEFFER, 21 47-48 66 77-78 90 111 126 149-150 175 184 226 235 237 245 530 Carl Friedrich 29 171 Lt 72 86 88 100 126 148 167 244
RUEHL, 495 Cpl 494
RUFF, Juliana Dorothea 573 Michael 573
RUMMEL, Christian Conrad 569 Margaretha Barbara Rincks 569 Philipp Adam 569
RUNCK, Nicolaus 460
RUNKEL, Capt 580
RUSSEL, Col 390
RUTHERFORD, Maj Gen 418
SACKERT, Carolina 563 Conrad 563
SAHE, Mr 47
SAINTLEGER, Barry 204 Col 213
SALAMON, Thomas 353
SALTMANN, Pvt 548
SARTORIUS, Carl August 39 Lt 424
SCHAEFFER, Anna Elisabeth 571 Auditor 14 57 Henrich 571 Lt 163 493 Martha Elisabeth 571 Wilhelm Paul 5
SCHAFFCOTH, Lt 553
SCHAUER, Musketeer 535
SCHECK, Bernhard 573 Christiana Sophia 573
SCHEEL, Capt 211 303 493 Carl August 206 Maj 493-494
SCHEELE, Bertold 566 Christian 566
SCHEER, Capt 566 Friedrich Heinrich 449 Maj 460-461
SCHEFFER, Conrad 568 Johann 363 Lt Col 344 Peter Sr 212
SCHEIDE, Heinrich 582
SCHEITER, 48

VAUPEL, Johann Nicolaus 126 Sgt
534 Sgt Maj 499 528 533
VELDEN, August 428
VENATOR, Capt 47 50 74 144 558-
559 567 Julius Friedrich 20
VERNIER, Pierre Francois 383
VERPLANCK, 224 327 329 332-
333 346 359 506
VILLGRAFF, Anna Gerdruth 564
Erhard 564
VOELCKER, Jacob 443
VOELLER, Johannes 486
VOGT, 212 Bernhard 566
Christiana Sophia 566
Friedrich 443
Jacob 566
VOLCKE, Philipp Henrich 43 287
VOLLRATH, Michael 577
VONALTEN-BOCKUM, Capt 571
Ernst Eberhard 344
VONALTENBOCKUM, Ernst
Eberhard 116 122
VONALTENSTEIN, Lt 549 Sophia
Charlotta 585
VONANDERSON, Ernst Wilhelm
337
VONBARDELEBEN, Johann
Heinrich 4 Lt 49 67 149 558 565
VONBARNER, Maj 192
VONBARTHOLOMAI, Christian
Friedrich 358
VONBARTLING, Capt 479
VONBAUMBACH, Alexander 438
Lt 177
VONBAURMEISTER, Carl Leopold
531
VONBENNING, Capt 116 Friedrich
Wilhelm 91 122
VONBEUST, Friedrich Ernst 161
Maj 547 549
VONBIESENRODT, Georg
Wilhelm 124
VONBISCHHAUSEN, Carl Ernst 19
VONBOCK, Col 229

VONBOCKUM, Capt 343-344 Maj
525
VONBODUNGEN, Franz Christian
363
VONBORBE, Col 92
VONBORBECK, Col 93
VONBORCK, Col 339 423 428 487
592 Henrich 100
VONBOSE, 490 Carl Ernst Johann
403
VONBREYMANN, Lt Col 201
VONBUENAU, Lt 485
VONBUTTLAR, 485 Capt 254 426
484 493 536 Maurice 189
VONCOCHENHAUSEN, Johann
Friedrich 148
VONCRAMON, Capt 164 231
Christoph August 160
VONCREUZBOURG, Col 498 Lt
Col 302 304 307 427-428 502
VONDECHOW, Karl Friedrich 98
Maj 100 118-119 122
VONDERHEYDE, Hedwig 584
Moritz Wilhelm 584
VONDERLIPPE, Simon Ludwig 45
Simon Ludwig Wilhelm 586
VONDERMALSBURG, Wilhelm
248
VONDIEMAR, Justus 43 588
VONDONOP, 558 ---- 588 C 586
Capt 88 559 Carl Emil Ulrich 68
Col 68 75 89 125 169 227-232
562 Lt 68 Wilhelm Carl 11 47
VONDRACH, Wilhelm 123
VONECKERT, Grenadier Capt 217
VONELLRODT, Capt 217
VONENDE, Franz Hartmann 100
VONESCHWEGE, Capt 528-530
532 535 Friedrich 78
VONEYB,
Capt 417 463
Col 161 232 257-258
Friedrich Ludwig 454
Friedrich Ludwig Albrecht 593